JOHN HOLMES

A Life Measured In Inches

by Jennifer Sugar and Jill C. Nelson

Published in the USA by:
BearManor Media
PO Box 1129
Duncan, Oklahoma 73534-1129
www.bearmanormedia.com

ISBN 978-1-59393-674-7

Printed in the United States of America.
Cover Design by Kenji.
Book design by Brian Pearce | Red Jacket Press.

TABLE OF CONTENTS

CONCEPTION
by Jennifer Sugar

"How did you get the idea to write your book?" — It's one of the first questions that people ask me when they find out that I began the task of interviewing and writing *Inches* as a 21-year-old undergraduate student, studying math and science.

Anyone who knows me knows that I can be a little bit scatterbrained, so it is fitting that this book got its start by accident. I skipped class to go to the movies (to see *School of Rock),* but got there too late. My boyfriend (who is now my husband) and I asked the girl at the ticket counter what would be playing next.

"Wonderland. It's about John Holmes and his involvement with gangs, drugs and unsolved multiple homicides..." she said, reading off a card by the cash register.

Instantly, I recognized his name from the promos on my favorite, classic rock radio station, "Our sets are longer than John Holmes!" Although I had yet to see any of Holmes' numerous films, I understood the intimation and that piqued my curiosity enough to slap down my five bucks and student I.D. card.

About two hours later, I walked out of the movie theater in such shock and disgust at this portrayal of John, that I told my partner that I would never see a Holmes film! But within about a week, my interest in the unsolved Wonderland murders grew. It seems silly now, but at first, I wanted to solve the crimes. I looked for everything that I could find in print, on recordings and online about the Wonderland murders and John Holmes. Within a week of declaring I'd never see one of his movies, I'd seen two (*Dickman and Throbbin'* and *California Gigolo*)!

Not long after that, I began to wonder about the story of a boy from Ohio, who moved to California in the late 1960s to become the biggest, male porn star, ever, when the adult entertainment industry was brand new, illegal and underground. John went on to become famous for what was in his pants, and infamous for the dark days of his drug addiction, his subsequent involvement with the crimes leading up to the Wonderland murders, and his death at a young age from AIDS, which was still a relatively new disease to North America in the 1980s. I was amazed that there wasn't already a definitive biography about John Holmes — like him or not, he is a part of American pop culture history, with an amazing story — how could I not want to learn more and write about him?

Fortunately for me, there was a celebration in recognition of what would have been Holmes' 60th birthday (on August 8, 2004), and I found out about it just in time to be able to attend! "Fit for a King" was held at the Erotic Museum in Hollywood (that closed in 2006). The special event was emceed by Bill Margold, who graciously chauffeured me about town in his VW "Bearmobile" van and treated me to several meals, while I read questions off my list and listened to his fond recollections of the Golden Era of pornography and the man who he had dubbed, The King of Porn.

Bill Margold was my first interview, ever, and he was the perfect host to prepare me for the adventures that awaited me in meeting and interviewing people for the book! Ever the gentleman in opening doors and picking up the tab, Bill shocked me by talking loudly in a restaurant about a time when he was told by another adult performer that his "dick tasted like a football," and then he asked to finish my leftovers when I'd stopped eating my lunch. Although Bill is truly a one-of-a-kind (aren't we all?!), it may surprise anyone with preconceived notions about the adult entertainment industry that he never made me feel uncomfortable with any sort of sexual suggestions. I would like to thank Bill for his help in guiding me through the process of writing this book — both by providing helpful advice and connections for contact information — as well as capturing my vision for the book with his suggestion for its title.

In addition to Margold, I also had the privilege of meeting Rhonda Jo Petty, Bill Amerson, Kenji, and Cass Paley at the birthday event held in Holmes' honor. These initial introductions at Fit for a King were brief, but led to interviews and helped me to network with more of Holmes' colleagues and associates, who provided me with all of the resources necessary to complete this massive project. With his multiple connections from having directed the *Wadd* documentary, Cass Paley was also instrumental in furnishing me with contact information, newspaper articles and boxes of movies for review. I appreciate what Cass shared with me that made this book possible!

While still in college, I saved the bulk of interviewing and work on this book for summer vacation, when I could travel from Michigan to California. Over the next couple of summers, I conducted several other memorable interviews. There was the time that I interviewed Bill Amerson over breakfast at Denny's, after which he gave me a cryptic message to "say hello" to someone, knowing that I was leaving to interview her that afternoon. He then claimed that he could have been, anatomically-speaking, the only possible stand-in for John Holmes, while extending our handshake by holding my hand against his belly. (Possibly to his disappointment, I didn't ask to confirm his claim!)

There was also the time that I interviewed Paul Thomas on the set while he was directing one of his money-makers. I was lucky to have this glimpse behind the curtain to see what it is like on the set of an adult movie. Paul answered my questions in a quiet voice, while his cast and crew finished filming a scene by the pool. When needed, he would politely excuse himself from the interview to attend to directing the scene. When the scene was completed (everyone on set had agreed the best place for the money shot would be the actress' "tits"), and the camera was turned off, the spunky blonde held out her hands, splaying her manicured fingers.

"I need a paper towel!" she said. I'll always remember that; it was so real-world and unlike the image she had been of herself for the camera, only seconds prior to that.

I could go on about the memorable experiences that I had in beginning this project, and I wish I had the space to share more stories about the interviews and give all of the specific acknowledgments that everyone who was interviewed for this book deserves. But that would be another book! Of course, that (hypothetical) book would have to include the story of meeting my friend and co-author, Jill, who lives in Canada. We met at a John Holmes message board online and I invited her to join me as a co-author, after sharing my work with her and reading the reviews that she had written of the *Johnny Wadd* series. Luckily for both of us, neither of us turned out to be (too) weird and ended up being excellent partners in co-authoring this book, detailing every good, bad and ugly aspect of Holmes' life, while abstaining from criticism or judgment.

Without further ado, enjoy the read!
J.S.
6/16/13

ACKNOWLEDGEMENTS

A Life Measured in Inches would not have been possible without the help of those people who knew, worked with and/or loved John Holmes.

For sharing with us in interviews, thank you: Buck Adams, Bill Amerson, Sean Amerson, Juliet Anderson, Marilyn Chambers, Bob Chinn, Alan Colberg, James Cox, Don Fernando, Jamie Gillis, Michael Glaser, Jim Holliday, Laurie Holmes, Ron Jeremy, Kenji, Tom Lange, Amber Lynn, Bill Margold, Captain Mauzner, Sharon Mitchell, Mark Novick, Richard Olson, Cass Paley, Rhonda Jo Petty, Candida Royalle, Jared Rutter, Seka, Serena, Julia St. Vincent, Joel Sussman, Helene Terrie, Paul Thomas, Frank Tomlinson, Raven Touchstone, and Kenneth Turan. Special thanks to Bill Margold for this book's title and foreword, and to Kenji for its cover design.

We also appreciate the generosity of the people who have allowed us to use their photos and other resources in this book: Bill Amerson, the Associated Press, bluevanities.com, Richard Freeman at *Batteries Not Included*, Antony Ginnane (cover photo from *Fantasm* © TLN Film Productions, 1976; and *Fantasm* commentary © Antony Ginnane, 2004), Jason Green at Paradise Visuals, johnholmes.com, Kenji, Laurie Holmes, Lindsay Little at *Hustler* magazine, *Hustler* Magazine photography by Ladi von Jansky, original dialogue and script text from the motion picture *WADD: The Life & Times of John C. Holmes* provided by Hustler Video, Ian Jane at dvdmaniacs.com, Ron Jeremy, Kenji, Bill Margold, Mark Novick, Richard Olson, Dimitrios Otis at *realboogienights.com*, Cass Paley, *seka.com*, Julia St. Vincent, Joel Sussman, Jeff Thill at *Hustler* video, Kenneth Turan, and David Sutton at *VCX.com*.

Last, but not least, our dedications; to Jeffrey for his support and love, my family and friends for their encouragement! – J.S. Jill would like to personally thank Jennifer for the invitation to assist her with this extraordinary project, and also her family, friends, Hud, Corey, and Andrea for their devotion and love.

May you rest in peace, John.

HARDCORE MARTYR
A Foreword by William Margold

Every sociological movement has had its poster person.

But rather than belabor this foreword with lots of names and notions… allow me to offer you the image that the letter X is simply a twisted cross… and leave the rest up to your imagination.

So it's like this…John C. Holmes came into the flickering picture in the late 1960s — just as the hardcore film industry was starting to rear its pink pulsating head — and undulated gloriously through the 1970s and then smoldered into the 1980s.

Until his death in 1988, he was without question the most important personality in X. The fact is and it's made commandingly clear by Jennifer Sugar and Jill Nelson in their book *A Life Measured in Inches* — that although he has been gone for 20 years — his name is still synonymous with the word "pornography."

He was the first X-rated superstar and truly a living legend — envied by most men because of his prodigious penis and desired by any woman who wanted to try him on "for size." His was a mesmerizing wand of wantonness, aimed directly at the fevered minds of all those who dared to admit that they had sexual fantasies.

Charmingly content that he was known to all but in fact known to none, John played out his life like an overage juvenile delinquent, accepting little or no responsibilities for his actions — or his activities — in a masturbatory microcosm of society that I call "The Playpen of the Damned."

And for one who basked in the glaring limelight of fame, it came as no surprise that he would eventually sink into the darkness of infamy. Someone had to be sacrificed and John C. Holmes was there for the staking.

You've got to wonder, however, as you read through Jennifer and Jill's thoroughly and, at times, very painfully researched work if Johnny would have wanted it any other way.

"CAST" LIST AND BIOGRAPHIES
in alphabetical order

Buck Adams: Starred in several Penguin film ventures after meeting John in 1984 and the two became friends. Adams passed away in October 2008.

Linda Adrain: Partner and production manager to Bob Chinn during the initial years of the *Johnny Wadd* series.

Bill Amerson: First met John in 1969 at the Crossroads of the World, where Amerson worked as an adult talent agent and producer. Amerson shared a life-long friendship with Holmes.

Denise Amerson: Denise is the daughter of Bill Amerson and the goddaughter of John Holmes.

Sean Amerson: Sean is the son of Bill Amerson and the godson of John Holmes.

Juliet Anderson: Began her adult film career in the late-'70s and acquired the nickname "Aunt Peg" after an infamous threesome scene with John Holmes and Sharon Kane in a *Swedish Erotica* loop that appeared in the 1981 film, *Aunt Peg's Fulfillment*. Anderson was cremated, according to her wishes, following her death in January 2010.

Tom Blake: A former L.A.P.D. vice cop who met John when he was busted for pimping and pandering in the mid-'70s. Rather than facing a potential prison sentence, Holmes opted to provide Blake with information regarding porn film shoots during his three-year probation period.

Bunny Bleu: Started her adult film career in 1983 and met John when she was cast opposite him in the 1986 Penguin Production, *Lottery Lust*.

Paul Cambria: Cambria is a First Amendment attorney who gained notoriety by representing various films and individuals associated with the pornographic movie industry, including Larry Flynt.

Marilyn Chambers: A household name in adult entertainment, Chambers made her hardcore film debut in Artie and Jim Mitchell's 1972 hit, *Behind the Green Door*. Chambers and Holmes first teamed up together in 1980 to perform in *Insatiable*. Ms. Chambers passed away just ten days before her 57th birthday, in April 2009.

Bob Chinn: Met John in 1970 when Holmes approached him looking for work as a grip. A ten-year professional relationship developed when Chinn cast Holmes as the lusty, private detective, Johnny Wadd in the first adult film series. The *Johnny Wadd* series by Bob Chinn includes nine features.

Ronald S. Coen: Now a Los Angeles Superior Court Judge, Coen prosecuted John in his 1982 Laurel Canyon murder trial, in which Holmes was acquitted.

David Clark: First met John when he worked as a makeup artist on the set of *Swedish Erotica*.

Alan Colberg: Established an amicable work relationship with John in 1975 when he directed Holmes and Ric Lutze in *All Night Long*. Colberg went on to direct John in notable films such as *Tapestry of Passion* and *Superstar*.

James Cox: Directed the 2003 feature film, *Wonderland* that depicts the events of the 1981 Laurel Canyon murders, through a few viewpoints (although not including Holmes').

Eric Edwards: Began his film career as a mainstream actor. Edwards first met John in 1973 when they appeared together in *Exotic French Fantasies*.

Mitchell Egers: Represented John along with his partner, lead attorney Earl Hanson, during Holmes' 1982 murder trial.

Don Fernando: Currently directing Asian porn, Fernando began working as an adult performer in the late-'70s. Fernando met John on the set of *California Gigolo* where he was impressed with Holmes' acting abilities and gentle manner.

Sasha Gabor: Met John the same year he began his adult film career, in 1983, at age 38.

Jamie Gillis: Credited for conceiving "gonzo" porn with his *On the Prowl* series in the late '80s. Considered to be a first-rate actor, Gillis met John in the early 1970s. The two appeared together in *Swedish Erotica* loops and features into the '80s. A few months after a melanoma diagnosis, Gillis passed away in February 2010.

Antony I. Ginnane: Producer of the 1976 softcore film, *Fantasm* and its sequel, *Fantasm Comes Again*.

Michael Glaser: As one of the first to work in the area of video duplication, Glaser became acquainted with John through John's partnership with Bill Amerson and Penguin Productions. Glaser is the National Sales Manager for *Hustler* Video.

Al Goldstein: Founder of *Screw* magazine, Goldstein interviewed John several times throughout his career and wrote what he considers to be one of his finest pieces, "The Harder They Fall," where he covered Holmes' murder trial. Throughout his career, Goldstein has appeared before the courts defending the right to exercise sexual freedoms through freedom of speech.

Annette Haven: Probably the most beautiful brunette actress to have performed during the Golden Age. Haven met John on the set of *Tapestry of Passion*. She also played Johnny Wadd's main squeeze in *Tell Them Johnny Wadd is Here*, in addition to making other appearances with John.

Bobby Hollander: As a porn director, the late Hollander shot over 50 adult films and was one of the originators of video pornographic movies. Hollander first met John at his home in Los Angeles in 1981.

Jim Holliday: As the adult film industry's first historian and cofounder of the XRCO along with Bill Margold, the late Holliday's credits expand into directing and writing credits. Holliday became friendly with John after the two met backstage at an adult trade show.

John Holmes: The King of Erotic Cinema had a penis that could legendarily achieve up to 14 inches in length when erect. As the industry's first star, John Holmes was known for his gentle touch beneath the sheets. The King reigned supreme during his 20-year career.

Laurie Holmes: Former adult film star, "Misty Dawn," was John's second wife and widow. Laurie and John met on the set of *Marathon* in 1982 when she was 19 years old. Laurie oversees and protects John's legacy through John Holmes Enterprises.

Sharon Holmes: John's first wife of almost 19 years, in a marriage that they both kept private. She and Holmes were married at her parents' home in Fort Ord, California, in August 1965 after a five-month courtship. Sharon is a retired registered nurse, presently residing in an assisted living facility, due to complications associated with Alzheimer's disease.

Mike Horner: Met John on a *Swedish Erotica* set while shooting a spoof of *Superman*. With his classic dark looks, Horner is considered to be the Clark Gable of hardcore.

Ron Jeremy: Deemed as the world's most recognizable Ambassador to Porn by AVN in 2003, Ron and John shared a friendly but competitive camaraderie after Jeremy entered the adult industry in the late 1970s. The two top male performers appeared in several features together in the '80s. Jeremy is one of the first porn performers to have crossed over into and appeared in the most mainstream projects.

Kenji: As a still photographer, Kenji met John in the early-'80s and later worked for Penguin Productions. Kenji and John connected as friends because they could relate, having both grown up in Midwest America.

Tom Lange: The first L.A.P.D. homicide officer to arrive at the scene of the Wonderland Avenue crime scene on July 1st, 1981. Along with partner, Bob Souza, Lange was a lead detective during the unsolved, multiple murder investigation. Lange was also one of the homicide detectives in the infamous O.J. Simpson case.

Susan Launius: The only survivor of the brutal 1981 murders at 8763 Wonderland Avenue.

Gloria Leonard: After working as a Wall Street stock broker, Leonard entered adult movies in her late 30s. She first met John when they traveled to France in 1979 to perform together in three features.

John Leslie: Next to John, Leslie was one of the first adult performers to be inducted into the XRCO Hall of Fame on February 14th, 1985. He and John worked together in many popular feature films, in addition to *Swedish Erotica*. Leslie passed away in December 2010.

David Lind: Also known as "Killer Karl," Lind was not at the residence of 8763 Wonderland when the murders occurred, although he had been a part of the robbery at Ed Nash's on June 29, 1981.

Tony Lovett: Lovett first met Holmes at his induction into the XRCO Hall of Fame in 1985 and later wrote the piece, "Legends, Lies and Last Lays" that appeared in the August 1988 edition of *Hustler* magazine. Lovett eventually took over as head of VCA pictures that produced *Wadd: The Life and Times of John C. Holmes*.

Amber Lynn: One of the most prolific adult actresses, her career began in the 1980s when she was cast in films with Holmes.

Ginger Lynn: One of the most popular adult actresses of the video age who worked with John in at least three major feature films, including *Girls on Fire*. Lynn was one of Holmes' favorite costars.

Bill Margold: With a degree in journalism, Margold is considered to be the world's foremost adult film historian who crowned John with the title, The King, in 1973. Margold worked with Holmes throughout the '70s and '80s and is the founder of Protecting Adult Welfare (PAW).

Jon Martin: A comrade of Holmes, Martin first appeared in several feature films with the late actor in 1976.

Tracy Ray McCourt: McCourt drove the car with the Wonderland gang on June 29, 1981, when they robbed Ed Nash.

Dr. Sharon Mitchell: "Mitch" met John on a film set in 1980, where they ingested drugs before performing together. After retiring from the industry as a sex performer, Dr. Mitchell acquired her Ph.D. from the Institute for Advanced Study of Human Sexuality in San Francisco and opened A.I.M. in 1998, a medical facility that conducted regular HIV testing in Los Angeles until its closure in 2011.

Kitten Natividad: Began her career as a big-breasted cutie in Russ Meyer's cult films before enjoying her work as a soft core performer. Kitten first made John's acquaintance on the set of *John Holmes and The All-Star Sex Queens* in 1980.

Mark Novick: Met John in 1971 while he was employed as a cameraman in his father's company. John worked for Novick in over 40 loops and shorts known as *The Playmate Series* until the mid-'70s.

Richard Olson: Worked as a salesman for John and Bill Amerson's company, Penguin Productions, in the 1980s.

Richard Pacheco: Met John on the set of *Hot 'n' Saucy Pizza Girls, We Deliver* in 1979.

Dr. Vonda Pelto: Was the resident psychologist who observed and assessed John while he was held at L.A. County Jail during his trial.

Ann Perry: As one of the first female directors of adult movies and later the first female president of the Adult Film Association of America, Perry directed John several times when shooting loops during the late-'60s and early-'70s.

Rhonda Jo Petty: Met John when they costarred in *Little Orphan Dusty* in 1978.

Ernie Roebuck: Met John while working as a lighting technician on adult film sets in the '70s.

Candida Royalle: Founded Femme Productions in the 1980s, which produces pornography meant for couples and women. Candida first met John while working as an adult performer in *Hard Soap, Hard Soap* in 1977.

Jared Rutter: The original chairman of the XRCO, Rutter was present at the organization's first official event on Valentine's Day in 1985, where John was the first adult performer to be inducted into the Hall of Fame. Rutter is currently the Honorary Chairman of the XRCO.

Mike Sager: Although he never met John, Sager wrote an acclaimed piece about Holmes' turbulent life in a 1989 article titled, "The Devil in John Holmes," for *Rolling Stone* magazine.

Reb Sawitz: Former adult talent agent who served the adult movie business for over 30 years. Sawitz met John in the late-'60s and provided him with several work prospects and contacts.

Dawn Schiller: Became John's teenage mistress six months after meeting him, in the summer of 1976. Dawn lived at the Glendale apartment complex that John managed along with his wife, Sharon. Until December of 1981, when Dawn was 20, she was involved in a relationship with John.

Seka: Known as the Platinum Princess of Porn, Seka met John on the set of *Lust at First Bite*, released in 1979. The same year, she played a Wadd girl in *Blonde Fire*.

Serena: Mia Farrow look-alike/hippie girl, Serena, entered adult movies in the '70s. She met John on the set of *Swedish Erotica*, although they would appear together in several soft- and hardcore ventures.

Sheri St. Claire: After entering the porn biz during the onset of the video age, St. Claire met John on the set of *Lust in America* in 1985. In 1986, they costarred in *The Return of Johnny Wadd*, one of John's final American film appearances.

Julia St. Vincent: First met John during the filming of *Tell Them Johnny Wadd Is Here*. The film, which was the fifth *Johnny Wadd* installment, was produced by St. Vincent's uncle, Armand Atamian. Julia worked for his production company, Freeway Films, in the office and eventually became romantically involved with John. Julia did office work for his production company, Freeway Films, before becoming romantically involved with John. In 1981, she directed Holmes in *Exhausted: John C. Holmes, The Real Story*, the first documentary about a porn legend.

Joel Sussman: Still photographer who met John during the late-'60s and worked with him on the *Johnny Wadd* film series, plus other projects. They developed a trusting friendship that lasted through 1980.

Helene Terrie: Along with her husband, Kirdy Stevens, Terrie was introduced to John by his girlfriend, Sandy in 1964, when John was hired to appear in one of their nudist films. Terrie and Stevens are famous for the successful *Taboo* series.

Paul Thomas: As a formally trained actor, Thomas began his career in the mainstream market and played the Apostle Peter in the musical motion picture, *Jesus Christ Superstar* (1971). After meeting on the set of *Swedish Erotica*, Thomas and John costarred in several features during the '70s and '80s.

Frank Tomlinson: The former L.A.P.D. homicide detective met John in December 1981, when he and Tom Lange arrested John in Florida for his connection to the Laurel Canyon murders.

Raven Touchstone: Met John at her home in 1984, when she was a scriptwriter for VCX and John was employed as a line producer and performer for the same company. Touchstone wrote the script for Holmes' swan song, *The Return of Johnny Wadd*, which was released in 1986.

Kenneth Turan: Former *Washington Post* film critic, Turan met John while interviewing him for a book he co-authored with Stephen F. Zito in 1974, titled, *Sinema: American Pornographic Films and The People Who Make Them*. Turan is currently a movie critic for the *Los Angeles Times*.

Bob Vosse: The late Vosse directed John when he was the first contract player to appear in Caballero's *Swedish Erotica* series. Holmes' loops were hugely profitable and outsold any other adult performer signed on by Caballero — including the female leads.

THIRD-PARTY QUOTE KEY

The small superscript letter following some names in the text of chapters indicates that particular quote came from a source other than our own interviews.

a. *Sinema: American Pornographic Films and the People who Make Them* by Kenneth Turan (1974)

b. *Eros* magazine (1977)

c. *Exhausted: John C. Holmes, The Real Story* by director Julia St. Vincent (1981)

d. **Preliminary Court Hearing** transcript

e. **Contempt of Court** documents

f. *Hustler* magazine interview (1983)

g. **XRCO Awards** (1985)

h. *WADD: The Life and Times of John C. Holmes* by director Cass Paley (1998)

i. *Porn King* by John C. Holmes and Laurie Holmes (1998)

j. *The Man, The Myth, The Legend* by director Mark Novick (2004)

k. "**Wonderlanded**" by Bill Margold (2003)

l. "**Fit for a King**" at the **Erotic Museum** on Hollywood Boulevard (August 8, 2004)

m. "**An Interview with Bill Margold**" *www.dvdmaniacs.net*

n. *The Hardest (Working) Man in Showbiz* by Ron Jeremy (2007)

o. *Devil in Mr. Holmes* by producer Paradise Visuals. DVD special feature (2006)

p. *Batteries not Included* by Richard Freeman

q. *www.johnholmes.com*

> *"I think if he could have done anything he would have liked to have gone into furniture."*
>
> SHARON HOLMES

1.

Before Johnny Wadd

Ohio, Nuremburg and Los Angeles

Lengthy Credentials

John C. Holmes was born well-endowed, apparently; he would often joke that on the day he was born, the midwife exclaimed that he had "three legs and two feet."

As the first star of erotic films, John Holmes garnered international fame for his penis, but his legend was immortalized with a stamp of infamy due to his involvement in one of the bloodiest multiple murders in California history. Yet 20 years after his death, people still ask, "So, just how long was it?" It is a difficult question to answer; throughout the height of his fame, the reports of his length while erect ranged from ten to 14 inches, depending on the day and his level of sexual excitement.

Like any spin doctor worth his salt, he promoted his asset by unabashedly claiming, "I have a cock 14 inches long and as round as my forearm, six inches above the wrist." In a 1983 interview with *Hustler* magazine, he boasted that he could maintain an erection for up to five hours, "dripping sweat under Klieg lights hot enough to drive the temperature on a set up to 104 degrees. I can also keep an erection straddling a girl at the edge of a cliff looking down at 300 feet of nothing, with my knees bleeding from the sandstone surface. I come on cue."

Although many men might envy Holmes' manhood and fantasize about the sexual territories he explored with thousands of women on- and off-screen, John knew that many women were intimidated by his size. He claimed that he was a "sexual professional," and he developed a gentle, tender touch that fully aroused his partners and prepared them for his deep penetration.

Indisputably, John Holmes was and always will be the King of Porn, and like many Hollywood icons, his private life contained complexities, contradictions and fables. His ability as a convincing storyteller matched his level of sexual prowess, as he often blurred the line between reality and fantasy.

> *John Holmes*[f]: Usually, I can't even rent an apartment. I'll have a girlfriend rent it in her name and I'll go in at midnight after the lease is signed. I had to change my phone number seven times in one month because of a gay guy who kept calling in the middle of the night to tell me what he wanted me to do to him. When the telephone company traced him, he turned out to be one of its operators. Sometimes it's funny; more often it isn't. Maybe that's the price of fame.

Puppy Love

Before the fame, John Holmes was an energetic young man, not unlike any other 20-year-old, who had fallen in love with a bright, attractive brunette, nee Sharon Gebenini.

Sharon Holmes[h]: I first met John just after Christmas of 1964. He was involved with a fellow nursing student of mine and they came over to have dinner. That's when I met him. He broke up with Vera about two months after that — so it would have been the end of February, first part of March of '65 — and he started coming to the door, bringing flowers and asking me to go out with him. One thing led to another, and he had no place to live, so he moved in to my two-bedroom apartment. He was very young, very immature, but very sweet. Things just gradually evolved into a real tight relationship. We were married five months later.

Surely, as she had joked that she must have been the last virgin in California, Sharon probably was intimidated when she had her first glimpse of John's size. However, she said that he was very gentle and careful not to hurt her. He was also attentive to her needs.

John was guarded with people and made few close friends, but trusted Sharon, who agreed to keep their relationship secret during much of their nearly 19-year marriage. Following John's death on March 13, 1988, she participated in an interview with Mike Sager for the *Rolling Stone* article, "The Devil and John Holmes." Until Sager's interview, Sharon had very little contact with the media.

Mike Sager[h]: John was married to a very straight woman, a nurse. He was an ambulance driver when he met her, and he courted her in a very sweet way, picking flowers out of the house next door before coming to her house. He was kind of goofy through their marriage.

Sharon's relationship with him was very normal. He was her first. She sort of was marked with that her whole life; she never married again. She always had a fondness for him.

Ohio Boy

John's mother, Mary Holmes, gave birth to John Curtis Estes on the kitchen table of her parents' country home in Pickaway County, Ohio, on Tuesday, August 8th, 1944. Mary and her husband, Edward Holmes, were separated on numerous occasions throughout their marriage and John never knew his biological father, Carl Estes, a railroad worker. Edward, a carpenter, was the father of John's older siblings, Dale, Eddie and Anne. In order to help smooth over her indiscretion while the couple tried to reconcile following John's birth, Mary changed John's surname to Holmes.

Besides John's first wife, Sharon, John also revealed secrets about his childhood to his widow, Laurie Holmes, with whom he shared the last five years of his life.

Laurie Holmes: John was to porn what Elvis was to rock and roll. He was also a novelty. I've heard Ron Jeremy claim that he's the Porn King and I used to work with Ron Jeremy a whole lot, before I even met John. Ron couldn't hold a candle to John.

John was a star without ever being an actor. He was a star from the time that he was a little, tiny baby. He grew up after the time of the Depression and he had a manic-depressive father. He was abused, but even through the toughest times, he could make that family laugh at the dinner table with just a smile or just a look.

John was a very mysterious person. He was a very private person and drugs were his downfall, and yet, he did recover, but he spun his life around sex and relationships. It was like he was in the middle of this big sex web, that could span 1,000,000 different directions and he could be a different person. Because he did have the stardom — people were fascinated with him — they thought they knew him. There were different factors to John, but at heart, he was really a very private person.

John wasn't really a Holmes, but it was a secret that he didn't know until a couple of years before he would die. The father, Edward Holmes, from whom Mary was estranged, used that over her and threatened to tell John. It's kind of complicated, but he actually didn't know that he wasn't a Holmes until a couple of years before he died, when he went to Italy and had to get a new birth certificate. They sent him the original and he was like, "Whoa, what's this?"

He tried to make his mom feel good. He brought it up to her. He was like, "Mom, I've known for years." He really didn't, but he wanted to make her feel good. It was very sweet.

Sharon Holmes[h]: John was the fourth child. He grew up in rural farm country in Ohio. [Edward Holmes] was an alcoholic and John could only tell me he remembered arguments and yelling, his father falling across beds and vomiting all over the kids. I think John looked upon him as being the cause of all the things that happened to the family. John wouldn't touch alcohol until he was well into the porn business, because of thoughts of his father.

In *Porn King*, John's posthumously published autobiography, he made references to Edward as "an unshaven, sloppy and slobbery man with a horrible stench on his breath, leaning over and kissing me." Although his time with John was limited before his parents' final separation, Edward seemed to have left a lasting impression. During John's early years as an adult performer, costars recalled that he took vitamins and was a self-described "health-nut." In interviews with John during that era, he would often say that he did not take aspirin or drink anything stronger than coffee. According to the associates from the dawn of his career, it was true — to the extent that he drank in moderation and never smoked marijuana, which was ubiquitous throughout late-'60s and early-'70s.

Sharon Holmes[h]: John had two older brothers and an older sister. Probably about the time that John was three-and-a-half or four, his mother separated from her husband. They went onto welfare; Mary had not worked; she was a housewife up until that time. They moved into a project in Columbus, Ohio. She moved in with another woman in the same predicament, who had two children, both boys. That must have been an interesting household, with six children and two women who were working as waitresses or clerking in a store!

The one story I always loved from John's childhood was — he had told me this and then his mom verified it on a visit out here — John had an early introduction to pornography between four-and-a-half and five. John was home with the chicken pox, his mom was coming home from working a night shift, and there was this little collection of boys and girls underneath the living room window in the project apartment. They were on a first floor. When she finally got closer, she realized that John was in the window and had a nudie magazine that belonged to the other woman that his mother was not aware of and he was showing the centerfolds and the other pictures that he thought would be interesting to four- and five-year-olds. I guess they were all laughing and hamming it up until Momma got into the house, got the magazine and paddled his fanny with it. Maybe that was the start of the whole process for him.

John's mother and roommate had their hands full with the six children and budgeting to make the ends meet, but Mary found time to date. When John was six or seven years old, Mary mentioned a man named Harold in front of her children. Just the same, John was surprised when his mother said that she would marry Harold Bowman and that Edward was not going to be back.

Sharon Holmes[h]: I believe John was maybe eight or nine when his mom remarried. Harold worked for the phone company as a lineman and they moved from Columbus to a rural area, called Pataskala, in Ohio. Harold bought the house.

John was the youngest and probably the most insecure of the four of them. He was a bed-wetter as a young child; actually, he was still wetting the bed when he was seven. The three boys were sleeping together in the same bed in the projects, and all of a sudden, everybody had a room of their own and they thought it was wonderful. John discovered the woods, the stream, fishing, and frogging.

For John, living in the country was a welcome reminder of the times the Holmes children would visit Mary's parents at their home in Pickaway County. As a child, John had enjoyed helping out on the farm and the stories that his grandfather (who was also named John) would tell him while John sat on his lap.

In John's eyes, Harold initially seemed to be an improvement over Edward because he did not drink, but he had financial difficulties in supporting his new, large family. Mary frequently let her children know that they would have to work to earn money for their necessities, such as school clothes. To earn money, John and his brothers became adept at trapping animals, though as an adult, he was against hunting for sport. At that time, however, the meat helped feed his family and John did any work he could find to earn more money for the family.

The emotional stresses of managing a family were also too much for Harold, who began taking his anger out on the children, and nothing improved between John and his stepfather when Mary became pregnant with Harold's son, David. John was nine when David was born.

Sharon Holmes[h]: He was really happy there, until David came along, and then Harold turned on all four of the kids. "These are your kids and I'll tolerate them, but David is mine."

Because John was the youngest, he took the brunt of Harold's anger. He was the one that was always getting beat up because he wasn't smart enough to get out of the house when he saw him coming. I think his older brother was eight years older than John; [John's siblings] were in junior high and high school, and John was still in elementary school. When David was born, David was then center of Mom's and Dad's attention. Mom was good to all of their children, but in order to have an infant in the family it required a lot more of Mom's attention.

Laurie Holmes: [Harold] was a severe manic-depressive and he was very abusive. He was the family shame, but it's the truth. He ended up sticking his hand through a grinder so he could get social security.

Sharon Holmes[h]: The others kept away from home; they were smart enough to get out as much as they could. It wasn't a tremendously happy household. Mary and the kids, when they were on their own, dinner time was always a big event; everybody talked about what their day had been like. This ceased. At Harold's table, you kept your mouth shut. Mom and Dad could talk, but nobody put their two cents' worth in.

John had this ungodly habit of washing his spaghetti in his milk. John is probably one of the few adults who I've met who is addicted to milk. At the very least, he went though a gallon of milk a day, and sometimes as many as two and three in a day. ([John was] also addicted to caffeine; coffee. He went through eight coffees a day — I mean eight pots of eight cups, 64 cups of coffee a day!) He had a way, I guess, anything that had a sauce on it had to be washed in his milk, which I thought was a little bit strange. He played with his food and I think this was a means of getting attention at the table, where he had to keep his mouth shut. I think it's true, of all children: negative attention is attention.

When I met John, John was classic meat and potatoes. He ate three vegetables: carrots, corn and potatoes. I grew up around the world; I was interested in broccoli and spinach, and all these things he said he'd never eat. Italian food to him was Franco-American spaghetti or tomato sauce tossed over pasta and I'm sorry, I didn't grow up that way. So, I introduced him to Mexican food and all this other stuff, and turned him into a normal-eating human being. Well, California-style.

David was the snitch. Daddy would come home and David said, "John did this. John did this." Guess who got beat. Mary was not at home; I think she had begun working at Western Electric to bring more money into the family, and for her, to get out of what was not a happy situation. She loved her kids and I guess [she felt] guilty about turning their lives to something that wasn't as palatable as [she] had hoped it would be.

The beatings that John endured at the hands of his stepfather were, at times, unspeakably violent and it is unfortunate that John was too young to understand Harold's inability to appropriately deal with his emotions. Mary did her best to guide John with prayer and faith; she took her five children to a Baptist church every Sunday, where John had perfect Sunday school attendance and believed in God. At church, John found solace from his difficult family life, especially on those instances when he had lingered hours after Sunday school ended. Besides the church, John would also hide under the dining room table or at the public library, where he learned to enjoy books.

When John was a child, sex was taboo, especially in places such as rural Pataskala. The 1950s were a paradoxical era, in which Americans tried to confine sex to marriage and would not discuss sex, but in private, people did explore their boundaries and children were still curious about sex. Children on the farm had seen animals fornicating and John participated in a game with local children that he called "stinky finger," but no one would answer his questions about sex, so he explored them on his own.

Before David was born, John's siblings were old enough to go out at night, and on a couple of occasions, Harold and Mary hired a babysitter for John while they went on dates. John said that the girl was a high school sophomore with a thick body and an ample bosom. To John, it seemed that she was aware that she turned him on. In *Porn King*, John claimed that she gave him his first orgasm in the bath and made him promise to tell no one, at the risk of never having her baby-sit for him again.

When he was nine, just a few months after the babysitter had further aroused his sexual curiosity, John had sex with his first childhood girlfriend. According to John, she had taught him how to French kiss. He spoke about her fondly in *Porn King* and enjoyed the warmth and affection that they had shared, since he felt that was lacking within his family, who dealt with John's exploits poorly.

John admitted in *Porn King* that he believed his need for affection contributed toward his career choice as an adult film star; a career choice that has been a sore spot for members of the Holmes family, who have consistently declined the opportunities to share their memories of John.

Laurie Holmes: They're good people, but set in their ways. They just want to remember John, the little boy that made them all smile and they don't want to remember who he became. They like the John that they knew. They want everybody just to leave him alone — he's dead now.

John's Niche

Sharon Holmes[h]: Things escalated when John reached his teenage years. Harold had backhanded him off a chair, across the room. John went into the army at the age of 16 after, probably, the first time he had ever physically hit back at Harold. In this particular incident, he had been thrown down the stairs and had gotten up. I think John, at 16, weighed maybe 110 pounds, though he was six-feet tall. When I met him he was six-foot-one and 145 pounds.

So we're talking [a] skinny, big-jointed child, got up off that floor, decked Harold and told him straight out, as his mom was in the door, "You touch me again and I'll kill you."

Harold must have taken him at his word because he never touched him after that. John escaped out the back door with his mom running after, calling to him.

I think he probably spent two days away from home, roaming the woods as well as sleeping over at a friend's house. He went to his mother when he knew she was home alone. Harold always went to his mother's in Columbus on Sundays, [while] the kids and Mary went to church.

[John] waited until Harold had gone. "I'm going into the Army. I need you to sign me in. I'm not going to stay in this house, or I will kill him."

Mary felt that was the lesser of two evils; get him into the army — maybe that would help him. Two weeks later, he was in boot camp. He did boot camp, and from there he was sent right to Germany. He was in the signal corps. Most of the time he was in Nuremberg — almost three years.

Little is known about the time that John spent in Germany. John claimed to have frequented bordellos and made friends with a man from New York City, who taught him how to seduce women.

Just a couple of weeks after his twentieth birthday, John and his friend were released from the service, on August 24th, 1964. John said that he and his friend went to New York City. There, his friend taught John the skills needed to be a gigolo. Life in the Big Apple was very different from what John had known in Ohio and he was amazed at the number of beautiful women. Encouraged by the sexual revolution, John decided to visit his family on his way to California to start a new life for himself.

> *Sharon Holmes*[h]: When he came back from the service, I believe he spent about ten days in Ohio, and that was enough. Harold was civil to him because when John came back, he was bigger.
>
> That was all John needed, to see Mom and he said, "I'm going to California."

At 20 years old, he found a place to live, with a Garden Grove family who had moved from Ohio (they had been the Holmes' next-door neighbors in Pataskala). According to Sharon, the family had some involvement with pornographic magazines and she speculated that the family (whom John had not seen since they had moved away when he was 14), could have been one of his initial connections to the adult entertainment business.

When Sharon met John late in December of 1964, he was working as an ambulance driver and she was in nursing school. Sharon worked on a team that pioneered open-heart surgery at U.S.C. County General.

> *John Holmes*[a]: I delivered 13 babies, two sets of twins. And I had three or four hundred people die on me — freeway accidents and shit. It blows you up the first few times you have somebody die in the back of your ambulance.
>
> A lot of people get into this weird thing about trusting you with their children. I mean, kids are beautiful, like the essence of innocence, beauty, happiness and well-adjustedness. You've got a moral obligation to do what you've said you're gonna do. Don't hurt anybody physically or mentally in your whole entire lifetime and you've had a damn good life; you're cool. Don't fuck with children.
>
> One little Mexican kid — the father was grinding cigarettes out on him. All over his chest and back, cigarette butts ground out. So the guy shows up at the hospital and says, "Bullshit, I never laid a fucking finger on him."
>
> I can't remember what happened for about five minutes. I just blacked out for a minute. I went insane. Finally, they got me off the guy. I mean you should have seen the kid laying there. He was past crying and past hysterics. He was just laying there trembling with his

eyes as big as saucers and those fucking burns, so I just beat the fuck out of the guy. I didn't kill him. I regret that; I did not kill him.

Sharon Holmes[h]: He had quit the ambulance service in June of [1965]. That's when he asked, would I marry him?

And I said, "Yeah."

We were married in August of that year. John was still underage so his mother had to sign the papers that allowed him to get married.

We were married at my parents' home in Fort Ord and came back to Los Angeles. We were there for six weeks and started looking for a place. At that time, he had been working for Nips, the candy people in Glendale. He said he really liked Glendale [and asked,] would I like to get a place there?

I said, "Sure that would be fine."

He said, "If we move, I would like you to stop working."

I said, "Okay."

We ended up finding a place in Glendale, near Riverside Drive, so we were close to Griffith Park. It was a one-bedroom triplex. We had our own yard there. It was probably about five months after that he got the job with Market Distributors, which was the frozen food distributor where he worked for two years. He worked an evening shift from seven until three in the morning.

He was very possessive of me from day one. He wanted limited contact with people he worked with. I never met them, but I knew them all by name. Our leisure time was spent mostly at the old L.A. Zoo or the Riverside Park where the bridle trails were. We did a lot of window shopping because, at that time, there was one salary.

I'm an only child and that's a limited family, so to speak, but I needed to see them. He really learned to enjoy my grandmother, in particular. My mother was a little more reserved with John. I'm not exactly sure why, but they got along okay. We probably spent three out of every four weekends in Wilmington, which is where they had moved. I pretty much was happy with that, but I think he was pretty dependent on me to satisfy all his needs. That was okay with me.

John didn't have a lot of interests at that time. I like "people watching" and he started to appreciate that also. We could sit for hours and watch people, anywhere. We were happy together. He was very, very sweet; always had an arm around me, holding hands, that type of thing. I think he would have done anything for me.

It was a mutual, two-way street, but he had outside contact and I didn't, and I was slowly going mad. There's only so much you can do in a house. After we'd been married 11 months, I said I needed to go back to work. We discussed that and he decided that would be okay, but he preferred that I work in a limited environment.

I found a job in Glendale, working medical nursing in an office. I went into pediatrics, which I had hated in nursing school, and I loved it, so I was happy and he was happy. He still was very, very possessive. It was hard to get him to agree to go to a Christmas party or that kind of thing. He wasn't comfortable in large groups, particularly with people that he wouldn't have anything in common with. He was very aware of the fact that he was not as educated as he wished he could be. I think that made him a little self-conscious with the group of people that were a part of my working life.

After two years of working for Market Distributors, John began to have work-related health problems from late-'67 to '68.

Sharon Holmes[h]: He had three pneumothoraces, which are complete lung collapses within a space of seven to nine months. The first, he wasn't hospitalized. The second two, he was hospitalized for; they had to re-inflate the lung with a chest tube. The doctor tied it in with the extreme cold and felt that John should look for something else if he wasn't able to limit the amount of time that he was in the warehouse. He spent, out of eight hours of the day, probably six hours in these sub-zero temperatures. For some reason, his lungs were not able to take it. It was not a common problem, I guess. There probably was something genetically that was a problem for him.

The company really liked him and the owner said, "Would you mind driving a truck?"

John said, "That would be great!"

He started looking into that after getting out of the hospital after the last lung collapse. He went to the union and asked about it. The owner had told him how to go about becoming certified as a truck driver. Of course, John had been in the Army, so driving big trucks wasn't a problem.

He could have qualified for the license and the whole thing, but the union said, "Absolutely not, we have hundreds of truck drivers who need jobs. We're not going to certify somebody new," so that ended that job.

He was kind of at his wit's end, not feeling well and not willing to stop smoking, which put some stress on his lungs. He started looking for other things to do. We had moved from Western [Avenue]. At that point, we were living on Irving [Avenue] in Glendale, and we were in a house. He really didn't really know what he wanted to do, so he thought, I'm pretty charming, I'll go ahead and look for something in sales, so he did Fuller Brush for a good five or six months.

I'm the one who packed those bags up. He could keep the numbers straight because it was a printed invoice. When the material came in, I had to organize that for him. He enjoyed doing the door-to-door kind of thing and meeting all the different people, then he decided that wasn't for him.

There was a furniture store. He had gone in and talked with the man who owned it, so he worked there for a while. He had an absolute love of wood and he enjoyed working there. There were repairs that needed to be made on some of the things that would come from the factory, but it obviously wasn't going to support us well.

From that job, he then went to shoe sales and then I believe after that, he went to an early security company called Wilmart and they were training him for department stores and groceries, for picking up shoplifters. He was interested in it and he really got in to it, until the first time he had to go out of town to San Bernardino.

He called up and said, "It's too far away from home. I'm going to come home."

What was I going to say? — "You can't. You need to do this." So, he came home.

He knew antiques. His mother was into Depression glass and that sort of thing when he was growing up. He always liked end tables and trunks and could restore anything like that. Cedar chests, dinettes, end tables, book cases — he could work anything in wood and was pretty much self-taught.

Mike Sager[h]: One of my favorite things she told me was, he was quite a carpenter and he had built sort of an outhouse motif in the bathroom with the half moon on the door, the shingles over the commode. The commode was like a throne.

He had a fondness for boiling skulls; he had a human skull. They had a name for it ["Louise"]. [He had a collection of] all kinds of steer skulls, cow skulls — for a while, he worked at a meat-packing plant in Cudahy, which was the origin of how he became a porn star.

Sharon Holmes[h]: He could have built a house from the foundation-up. He knew plumbing, he knew electrical work — he was in the signal corps in the army and learned that skill there. Great house painter, wallpapering — he had an eye for that kind of thing. I honestly think he might have liked going making exclusive items for people.

Probably while he was at the height of porno, if he had done this as a sideline, he would have made a fortune out of people in the business. Like, "Wow, I have a chair that John Holmes made."

There was so much potential there, but who knows why he decided that this was the path he had to take.

> *"Nothing is obscene — providing it is done in bad taste."*
>
> RUSS MEYER

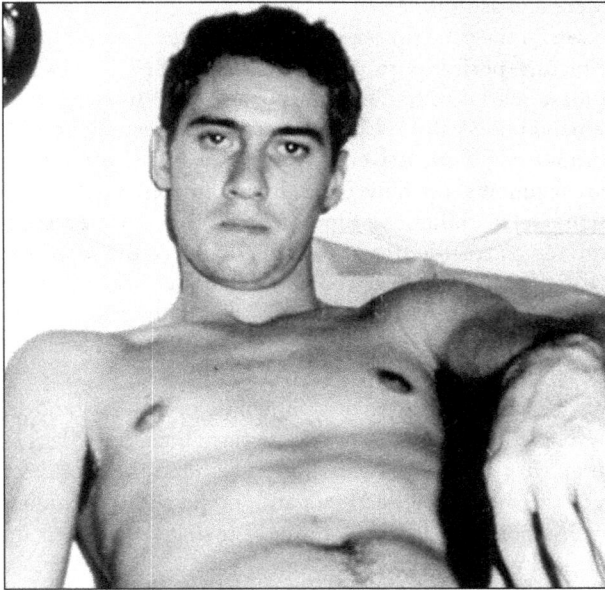

2.

Getting It Up

John and the Early Days of Pornography

Nudes in Cinema

Since the creation of the "Venus von Willendorf," (believed to have been made in 23,000 B.C.E.), artists have been interested in capturing nudity in every available medium. The advent of cinematography provided creative people a new outlet to explore the blurred boundaries of pornography and obscenity. "Pornography" has generally been defined as anything intended to arouse sexual desire, although because the stimuli for arousal vary from person to person, pornography is a subjective term whose meaning depends on contemporary cultural beliefs, practices and attitudes.

Working within the prudent era of 1950s America, Hugh Hefner presented his vision of picture-perfect porn via the first issue of *Playboy* in 1953. *Playboy* was the first mass-marketed nudie magazine and from its start, it featured stunning nude female models and celebrities in strategic, tasteful poses.

Some pornography fans, however, were eager to see something decidedly raunchier and acquired short films on eight-millimeter. Collectively known as "loops," the eight- or 16-millimeter films included one or more scenes that added up to, at most, ten to 15 minutes of footage. Most of the loops from the '50s were softcore, but they sometimes contained hardcore scenes. (For those readers who have been too shy to ask, hardcore pornography refers to films showing real sex and penetration, as opposed to softcore, which does everything outside of that umbrella.)

Loops were traded at stag parties, shown at peepshows and in small theaters; there were plenty of varieties to choose from including: "legs and lingerie," nude wrestling, "strip 'n' cheese" (which often featured the professional stripper, Candy Barr, or the model, Bettie Page), and "nudie cuties." Nudie cuties were the staple of '50s porno and were equivalent to *Playboy* stills in that they featured a lone naked woman.

Kirdy Stevens and Helene Terrie, a husband-and-wife team, began their flourishing careers in the nudie cutie market. Terrie wrote every single movie she and Kirdy directed together and will never forget how daring they were when making loops was illegal, yet enjoyed an exclusive fan base.

> *Helene Terrie*: It was 1960 and [the police] had a lot of power in those days. They said it was obscene [to film nude women]. Who knows what they thought. The girls were partially nude, [but] they weren't with anybody! Anyway, needless to say, they closed the entire street down.
>
> Kirdy went into the business where you would shoot a nude girl and then send the film [to be developed]. He would advertise in *Modern Photography* and *Popular Photography* and send them the 35- or the 16-millimeter, exposed, undeveloped film. Then they would go in their dark room and they'd develop these pictures. They weren't very long. Ten minutes sounds too long, but I don't remember. They

were shot in 16 [millimeter] and then he narrowed it down to eight, but they were all silent and they were black and white. Kirdy would say — he was so funny — that, his goal in life was to shoot something in color, with sound!

I don't even want to call it softcore because there was no simulated sex. These were even before softcore. They were for mail order. The Supreme Court ruled that there was nothing illegal about nudists. We figured that they could be at home; they didn't have to be in a nudist colony, so let's just shoot the nudists! We called it *Nudists at Home*.

Like Helene Terrie, Ann Perry's career as a writer and director of adult films began while she was wrote for '60s porno-director, Bob Cresse. Making pornography was definitely a man's world, but Perry worked her way up to the top, later becoming the first female president of the Adult Film Association of America.

Ann Perry[h]: In the early sixties, the X-rated films were really nudie cuties. It was a time with Russ Myers, who [directed the 1959 nude film, *The Immoral Mr. Teas* and] shot a lot of big-breasted ladies when I started in the film business. I worked for Bob Cresse a lot and various other guys that were shooting. There were certain rules that you had to follow. Often times you'd be jumping on trampolines, or in a swimming pool, and most of it was bare breasts. You couldn't show pubic hair. That was forbidden!

Around that time, I had a mail order company and I actually got arrested by the F.B.I. for selling film and shipping it across state lines. What it was, was a brochure showing a man and a woman sitting on a bed, holding hands and underneath the picture it said, "What do two people do when they fall in love?" Nowadays, it would be on TV — probably on the Disney channel.

As cases were won in court and as people got more artistic with what they were doing, it sort of segued from nudie cuties into a story line. The sex wasn't too serious because you couldn't expose the lower part of the body. Men always wore their jockey shorts because God forbid that the frame of the camera would show that he didn't have his shorts on; they could always prove in court that he was nude! Again, they didn't show pubic hair, but they could show women from the rear, so if they did a sex scene, for example, the camera was usually behind the woman, who was sitting on top of the guy — and he had his shorts on.

Male Nude Model for Hire

Between the time that John moved to California and met Sharon Gebenini, he had already taken his first steps on the road to becoming the first and most substantial icon of adult entertainment. Terrie and Stevens had just purchased a building in Hollywood for their business in 1964, and employed a girl who was responsible for introducing them to John that same year.

According to Kirdy Stevens, John's girlfriend's name was Sandy. John Holmes was involved in a romantic relationship that spanned from the '60s into the early-'70s with the XXX film siren, Sandy Dempsey. Therefore, it is quite feasible that the "Sandy" to whom Stevens and Terrie referred was none other than Sandy Dempsey, the cute, auburn-haired starlet with a slight overbite and a small butterfly tattoo on her left thigh. Dempsey later became one of the most popular actresses from the early years of hardcore erotica. The two were in several loops and films together.

> *Helene Terrie:* Sandy came in and said, "Can I bring my boyfriend?" and she brought John.
>
> [John was] very shy and sweet, retiring, and just kind of a nice person.
>
> Kirdy said, "Okay, I'll shoot him," but then he had more trouble shooting him because he didn't want to show anything. It was so hard to hide! Kirdy was shooting John with Sandy and two other girls, John's penis was so large that we were trying to push the girls in front so that you couldn't see it, because you could never show anything like that.

> *John Holmes*[b]: I was an ambulance driver. I washed cars, washed dishes. Let me tell you, I did all this shit, man, and I had a next-door neighbor who was a topless dancer — really cute — and one day she said, "How would you like to make $100?"
>
> I said, "Who do I have to kill? Of course!"
>
> She said, "Well, it's a stag movie."
>
> I thought, well, what if I want to run for government some day? — The chances are so nil, that I said, "Forget it, okay, I'd love to," and we got it together. They had to talk me into it for a while, but I did do one and they liked it.

Throughout the countless occasions in which he was asked to share about his introduction to pornography, John changed some details of the story, but it has always remained about the same. It aligns closely with Terrie's recollection of meeting John in 1964, although John was probably paid less than the $100 he had claimed to receive, according to Bob Vosse. Vosse was another pioneer in the X-rated film industry who cut his teeth by directing softcore loops before making hardcore features.

> *Bob Vosse*[h]: My first experience in the adult industry was with the 35-millimeter, Pussycat [Theater]-type films. In those days, they were black and white and that was basically the only source. The other

source, of course, was the not-so-legal, under-the-counter, eight-millimeter black and white that people showed at home. That was the start of it, of course; it grew from there.

In that very early time, strangely enough, girls were always paid a little more than the boys. It's true, more or less, today; basically, a good-looking girl is what makes you the money. In the early days, the guys were getting $35 for a loop and the girls would get $40. Whatever the price was, the girls would get a little more.

Johnny Does Hardcore

Helene Terrie: There was a bookmaker in Georgia who was arrested. The police found this porno film at his house and the Supreme Court ruled that there was no law against owning it, so Kirdy decided, "Gee, if you can own it, then you've got to be able to sell it."

We went to our very famous lawyer, Stanley Fleischman, and Stanley, who was a very, very big believer in the First Amendment rights, said, "Kirdy, I'll tell you what. I'll charge you $50,000 to take it from every state that they prosecute you in, up to the United States Supreme Court."

Kirdy said, "Okay." That sounded right and he really wanted to do it. He felt that the court had no right to tell you that you couldn't.

Kirdy made some hardcore loops and John was in the first one. It had to be before '69; I know [because Kirdy] got busted in '69. He shot it in '67, evidently, because the court looked pretty good.

I have a photograph of John [from the hardcore loop] and actually, we sent it out. The brochure was in color and John was in one of them with one girl. There were eight different loops. We sent a letter to all our mail order people that said, "Would you like to get it? Send two dollars and we'll send you a brochure." You had to say your age and so on and so forth.

During his 20-year tenure in adult films, Holmes appeared in over 1,000 scenes in loops and feature-length movies, but film stock from the '60s was not made to withstand the test of time, so some evidence of his earliest appearances have disintegrated or been misplaced throughout the decades. Fortunately, an astonishing amount of material is currently available for purveyors today on websites and compilation DVDs.

Some of John's original loops were crowned with such amusing titles as *The Virgin Next Door*, *Pleasure Pole*, or simply, *Big John*. In the years since his death, previously untitled loops have upheld that tradition, with ironic titles such as *Super Stud* and *Here Comes Johnny*. Early pornographers took great risks in making and distributing the films, so most of them did not maintain records of the loops, which could have potentially served to further incriminate them. The lack of bookkeeping also makes it difficult to know the precise production dates, however, observations of John's appearance, hairstyle, and assortment of jewelry (including mood rings, thin gold or silver bands on his pinky fingers, various watches, and an array of necklace pendants such as a bear and a prism) offer clues as to the general time frame in which each film was made.

> *Helene Terrie*: Kirdy was the first person that mailed hardcore in this country. Everybody said, "He's doing it, so we'll do it," but they weren't sending out letters saying, "We won't send you anything unless you say you want to get it." We'd send a brochure and then they would choose off of the brochure.

> *Bob Vosse*[h]: It was about that time, in 1968, when John came in with a group of people. No one knew him of course; didn't know he was overly-endowed; he was just another guy. Frankly, I never thought much about it. He got $35 dollars a loop like everybody else. His didn't sell any better than anyone else's, so why would you pay him more? That changed over the years, needless to say. It was quite a bit different toward the end — John's pay — because he could make you a lot of money. In all fairness, he deserved more than the other guys were getting and he made good money.
> In 1969, in the middle of the summer, they showed the first hardcore film down at the Cameo Theater on Santa Monica Boulevard. I was shocked out of my life to see real sex on the screen!
> From that point on, it was hardcore. Softcore, no longer so; except in certain parts of the country, where they couldn't get away with it: the south, the Bible belt, you know the point. And it grew from there. The Pussycat [Theater], of course, became hardcore. Then they started a whole chain of 16-millimeter features. I was shooting a lot of one-hour, 16-[millimeter] features that went into these mini-theaters all around the country. They just started sprouting up. You'd pay five dollars, go through the turnstile and see hardcore. This was the revolution.

In the era of "free love," many people enjoyed profiting from their sexual romps and deceiving authorities to appear in the films. The first pornographers and sexual performers were a group of unparalleled rebels and free spirits, who reveled in their right to put sex on film and made no apologies, for they believed their work promoted ideals of freedom of expression and liberation.

> *Bob Vosse*[h]: A lot of it was pretty sleazy stuff, quick back-room stuff, because it was all illegal to shoot. They were busting the theaters a little bit. They would take a film, but they could only take one, so you had another one out in the trunk of your car, you threw it in the theater and you kept going. They couldn't get to the theaters, so they started looking for the producers. The vice squad in Hollywood — they were

pretty organized. Lloyd 'Bad Ass' Martin — as we used to call him — was the head honcho. He led all the raids in Hollywood and would come crashing in your doors, confiscating everything. It was a legal battle all that time.

John Holmes[b]: We'd fight court battles. Every third month was a different type court battle. We'd [show] the girl — frontal nude, but the guy had to keep his back to the camera with his jeans on. Then they took the pants off the guy, but kept his underwear on and they got busted on it immediately. Morals charge and then they'd fight it in court and it was found not obscene, so they'd go back and shoot it. One person would fight it and then everybody would shoot it. Then they got to the point where they took the guy's underwear off and kept his back to the camera. Well, they got busted again, and another three month court battle. It was found not obscene, so they went one step further. All of this happened. It's hard to believe, but every time they would go one step further, they'd get busted on it.

Bob Vosse[h]: It was an amazing thing how the producers, the directors and the actors stuck together. They helped each other; the cops were the bad guys. We would meet at various places, get in the car, go some place where we'd have another car stashed, get in that car, go to a place, and no one knew where the location was going to be. They would try to follow us; they would try to catch us.

Helene Terrie: [Kirdy] got busted. The People of the United States of America versus Kirdy Stevens, but he was willing to go. Then, when Nixon was elected [in 1968] and he appointed three Justices of the Supreme Court, Kirdy said, "I can't fight this."

After Kirdy's three years of probation was up, *Deep Throat* was very popular, so Kirdy said, "I'm going back." We shot John in a feature [in 1974]. It was called *Lollipop Palace*. After he shot the movie, *Lollipop Palace*, [John would] come around afterwards to see if anybody wanted to have sex.

Interestingly enough, we shot another movie called *Little Me & Marla Strangelove* [in 1979], and in the movie the couples are watching John in the loop, that was his first [hardcore] loop. They put it on a projector like anybody would and they go, "Oh, my God, look at this guy!" and it was the loop of John.

The Anatomical Factor

Sharon Holmes[h]: At first, I think John was probably a bit embarrassed by his size because he knew he was different. I can't imagine why because he was in the service, he was familiar with whorehouses in Europe and had sex with married women. He had lots of sexual experience, but I don't think John realized how terribly unique he was until he got into porno.

Ann Perry[h]: John was a pleasure to work with. Occasionally an actress would come to me and say they didn't want to work with him. They were afraid of his incredible size.

Then, on the other side of the coin, there were a few actresses that said, "Please, I want to work with him. I love him."

I don't know how to put this delicately, but because of his unusual size, the women really got off on that. This one particular actress was a psychologist and she just begged to be with John. I think that she would have worked for nothing! She was in several of my films with John, and just loved working with him.

When I was using John Holmes in my films, he could get a full erection, which is why I called my film, *Getting it Up*. We shot stop-motion film of him getting it up. It was gorgeous and he had no problems.

John Holmes[b]: I've never even given it much thought. I suppose a big cock is 90 percent of it. Things happened, I suppose, because of the big cock.

Mike Sager[h]: For some reason, John Holmes captured the imagination. I never quite figured out why, except when you saw his penis it was like someone had done photo-retouching and blown up a normal, perfectly-proportioned penis into extra-large size.

"Big John"

Holmes appeared in more loops than anyone else and he had an opportunity to do a little acting as the genre progressed enough to include storylines that framed the sex. For whatever reason, John sometimes used pseudonyms such as Hal, Fred, Frank, and Larry, but with his head of curly hair and his all-natural, uncircumcised member dangling low between his long, slim legs, stage names did little to conceal Holmes' identity.

The set-up for many of these early loops would have Holmes appear as a guest in the home of one, or often two oversexed women, which allowed for John to showcase his arsenal to the max. In one of the clips, John spies on a voluptuous neighbor undressing through a hole in the wall of his apartment. Minutes after she catches him, the young woman invites him over for a little impromptu sex.

In a loop known as *The Queen of Sex* that originally appeared in a film called *Personal Services*, Holmes plays a sex-starved sailor named B.C. "Big Cock"

Buzzard. B.C. spends a few days in port where he hopes to get laid. Donning a black knitted cap, John is very cool and cocky as he stretches out his legs at a small table in a seaside bar. He proceeds to wager a bet with another patron as he intermittently chews gum, drinks beer and smokes cigarettes, while "Cute Ass," a 30-something barmaid, goes down on him. Holmes customarily smoked and chewed gum throughout many movie appearances. Later, sex-deprived B.C. meets his match in the beautiful "Queen of Sex" herself, auburn-haired Cyndee Summers, who shows him a good time in bed — twice. One of the funny lines in this flick occurs when B.C. laughs about his under-used penis to the Queen of Sex: "It's not much good to me out at sea, but it sure comes in handy when I'm in port!"

Although he did use pseudonyms, most of the time Holmes used his own name or a slight variation thereof. In a scene from the loop series known as *Here Comes Johnny*, John bursts into a young woman's apartment, gun in hand, before quickly disengaging the pistol and revealing the bigger sharp-shooter in his pants. This gun-toting performance was likely made shortly before John stepped into the role of his most legendary character, making it all the more significant as it foreshadowed the insatiable detective he would soon portray.

Big John is one of the better early loops, with a respectable plot and setting, which became fundamental as new audiences demanded more substance. The steamy two-part loop is about 20 minutes long and costars Barbara Barton, a sweet, very pretty, diminutive brunette who entices the pool boy. John plays the pool boy, his large package bulging in a tight, red Speedo. She lures him into her swimming pool on a hot, sunny afternoon, and seduces him. John achieves a full erection when they do it on a lounge chair and on the pool deck before climaxing in rapid succession. His first pool scene began a pattern in his career as an adult performer. During his tenure, John made love to more than a few women in swimming pools including Becky Savage, Maria Welton and Seka.

John was fully hard while working with the brown-haired Barton, which is noteworthy, as he was known to have had a genuine attraction to petite brunettes both on- and off-screen. Throughout his career, he worked with women who fit this description in over 75 percent of his movie appearances and a great number of the women in his personal relationships, including both of his wives. John explained his interest in brown-haired women with a generalization that brunettes must work harder than blondes to please men and get noticed because more men are immediately attracted to blondes.

Catering to Fans' Fantasies

It did not take long after pornographers dared to show Holmes penetrating women, that some pushed the boundaries into increasingly experimental, more forbidden realms. A famous group of loops that include titles — *Playmate of the Year*, *Super Cock* and *Wild Beauty* — show John with the sexy and enthusiastic Linda McDowell (a.k.a. Claudia Grayson), in the very early 1970s. In the most obscure of the three, John and porno-jock Rick Cassidy join pregnant Linda in bed for a slightly precarious bout of oral, anal and vaginal sex. In another, John answers an ad and arrives at Linda's home ready for action, wearing a worn leather jacket and sporting a goatee. Holmes is youthful and handsome, with his slicked-back, longish, wavy hair. Immediately, he sizes up Linda, with her dark, luxurious curls and an hourglass figure that caused one critic to declare that she was far too gorgeous for hardcore! The two of them immediately connect and are playful as they tease one another before getting down to pleasure, including an unforgettable anal scene in which John appears attentive and careful not to hurt McDowell. McDowell and John appeared in a handful of loops together in the early years of hardcore.

But the pregnant woman fantasy was not the last of John's early work that catered to a variety of tastes. According to Cass Paley, some of John's loops featured "golden showers," in which John would urinate on consenting costars.

Although few of the loops exist today, John also posed for magazines oriented toward a mostly gay and bisexual male audience before doing a number of loops oriented toward his gay fans.

> *John Holmes*[f]: Because nearly 50 percent of my audience is gay, I
> made one eight-millimeter, 15-minute loop specifically directed at the
> gay market. The film found its audience.

Holmes may have tried to downplay the number of loops that he appeared in for his homosexual male fan base, but in actuality, he appeared in about six gay, hardcore loops in the late-'70s. Certainly, John Holmes may have been in a few more gay scenes in the '60s, considering the fate of some of the earliest loops, but there is no evidence to support that John did a lot more for the homosexual market than what is available now, including *Just Good Friends*, *Black Velvet*, *Pool Party*, and the '70s masturbation loop shown in the 1984 compilation video release, *Singlehanded*.

Just Good Friends is a short, black-and-white film from the late-'60s, in which John and another fresh-faced fellow, Dave Harris, drink a beer together in a small kitchen before hitting the sack for some fun and frolic. John does not appear to be uncomfortable in the scene, but apart from full-frontal nudity and bare legs as he and Harris make out in bed, most of the segment is left up to the imagination of the beholder.

Singlehanded depicts baby-faced and bushy afro'd John masturbating just short of orgasm in a chair. In the clip, he is dressed in light blue pants and a matching, button-down, floral design shirt and indulges viewers in the fantasy of what John Holmes does during his private time.

In *Black Velvet*, another of John's '70s masturbation loops, he becomes aroused while cleaning a black motorcycle and he climaxes onto the surface of the engine.

The early-'70s loop known as *Pool Party* is a rarity, given that it contains a hardcore scene between John and another male. As was the case with some of

John's other early appearances (including *Pool Party*) he used the pseudonym, "Mike Spaulding."

During the Golden Age, it was not considered unusual for many sex performers to work on both sides of the fence during the preliminary stages and throughout their careers. John appeared to have respected and supported his gay and bisexual fan base throughout his career. His best-known feature that was intended for the homosexual market was made in 1983, *The Private Pleasures of John Holmes*.

First Amendment Rights

Bill Amerson[h]: They say the 1968, 1969 and '70 years — the business was not really technical. Most of the stuff, we had gotten away from. We had gotten away from the guys with the masks and the black socks. We had gotten pretty much away from the eight-millimeter, smoker-type of film. We started making 16-millimeter films. We were using 16-millimeter exclusively and we were making the features about 60, 65-minutes.

At the time, the stuff that we shot were simulated-sex films. They were called "spread beaver" films. I watched some of these and decided that I wanted to be a little more explicit. So I took a crew and we spent the weekend making five hardcore films. I made the very first hardcore films in the United States. I immediately went to jail.

Amerson's previous work experience included acting in B-movies during the 1960s. Amerson was indeed a significant player in the early days of hardcore film production.

[Former Pornographer/Associate of Bill Amerson]: I started in the mainstream business, but I had some friends who were in the adult business. On the weekends, I would be doing softcore, simulated adult [films] — I'd be doing production, sound, shooting, editing, and everything. I was involved in the whole production of those movies.

[Bill Amerson] has a major background in this business back to the very beginning. I went to school with his partner, so I was closer to the partner than I was to Bill, but [Amerson] was one of the first people in the business when this all started. This all came from high school — that's how I knew his partner and that's when I would do work on the weekend. During the week, I'd work on a "Bing Crosby/Henry Mancini" special put on by Monsanto, believe it or not.

Bill Amerson[h]: We were subject to go to jail [for] a lot for different things. The thing that saved us was a young attorney who took up the First Amendment right to free speech and started working with pornography cases, actors, crew members and producers.

Paul Cambria is a First Amendment attorney who has helped to protect the rights of pornographers including Larry Flynt, the producer of *Hustler* magazine.

Paul Cambria[h]: The First Amendment was designed to protect the ability of the new Americans to criticize the government without being punished for doing so. It was part of our Bill of Rights, [which] consists of a number of different things. Free speech was just part of being able to say what you wanted about the government and not have a reprisal.

One of the most frequently asked questions is, "Do you think Thomas Jefferson thought that the First Amendment would be applied to a John Holmes film?"

What the founding fathers tried to do was ensure that there would be free speech, whatever its form and they made it clear, "Congress shall make no law which abridges..." That means what it says. Obviously, in the olden days, they had bawdy speech, etchings and drawings — it isn't like the concept of human sexuality was foreign to the founding fathers. When they drafted this document, they didn't envision all the nuances of search and seizure; they didn't know we would have listening devices and tape recorders, but the Constitution clearly applies to illegal eavesdropping by the government, and nobody seems to have a problem thinking that the Fourth Amendment doesn't apply to that.

The same thing with speech; everyone knows that speech has always included the sexual element from time immemorial. We saw it in the Greek tragedies that we are able to read now, that are hundreds of years old, so sex wasn't foreign to them. That is the beauty of the First Amendment. It is so simple: we need to be free, we need to be able to express ourselves in all ways and government shouldn't step in and take that away from us. It covers everything.

A lot of individuals confuse the term *obscenity* and *pornography*. *Pornography* is a general term for anything that deals with sexuality, whereas obscenity is a legal test. The Supreme Court told us [in the 1957 case of Roth versus The United States], if this test is met and something is obscene, it is no longer covered by the First Amendment. It's like my right to swing my arm stops at your nose. There is a point, where the law has drawn a line, and obscenity is the legal point where the Supreme Court has drawn the line on erotica.

The "Roth Test" for obscenity is: if the material is taken as a whole, does it appeal to the prurient interest in sex and does it lack serious literary artistic, political, or scientific value? Those are floating concepts. Over the years, we've had a lot of litigation about what does "serious literary artistic value" consist of? What is prurient interest?

The court has said, *prurient* means a morbid, or shameful, interest in sex, as opposed to a healthy, normal curiosity in sex, so we've argued, what does that mean?

In a nutshell, the obscenity test measures something that appeals to a shameful interest rather than a healthy, robust interest in sex and it can fail both of those tests, for example, it can be beyond prurience and it can be unacceptable, but nevertheless, if it still has serious literary artistic, political or scientific value, it cannot be found obscene. The Supreme Court says all three tests must be there at one time. It's such a nebulous concept; it's like nailing fog to a tree.

The Money Trail

Bill Amerson[h]: There was a lot of big money and people couldn't believe that we actually had shown insertion and oral copulation. People couldn't get their money up fast enough to see these. Theaters all over the United States that had been showing the simulated features started showing the hardcore and they immediately got busted and they got shut down. That's when all the police activity started, and they started looking for manufacturers, the producer and the actors.

We got a lot of money for them, but we didn't sell the prints to the theaters; we rented the prints for maybe $2,000 a week, so you could take a $4,000 investment to make a hardcore film, and make a $60,000 profit. Those were the numbers in those days because it was all underground.

We used a variety of ways to ship stuff. We would pay 18-wheeler drivers to take our stuff to different places and we would pack the film in dry ice and ship them by train. And we would use Greyhound buses. We did a number of different things, because they were looking for us to ship regular freight, and we didn't do that. We would ship phony packages, and they would trace that package and think that they had us nailed and we would ship another one. There were so many different ways; you had to be creative to keep from getting busted on a Federal beef.

Theater owners were not the only entrepreneurs who smelled money after seeing hardcore. By the 1970s, one reason why pornographers were frequently accosted by police was because the F.B.I. was searching for the money trail of the organized crime syndicates.

Bill Amerson[h]: We paid people a lot of money in those days. A girl would get $75 and a guy would get $35. It's not like it is today, where a girl makes $2,000 a day or more. There was a select group of people that did the hardcore, so most of the people that you would see in the 16-millimeter hardcore films were pretty much the same. Then we started recruiting people from topless dance bars and we recruited a number of prostitutes that got involved. They found the money could be a lot better and they didn't have to do as much; out of an eight-hour day, they had maybe one sex scene.

The L.A.P.D. formed a special vice squad for pornography that we nicknamed the Pussy Posse. They didn't get really crazy about that! We sent them 15 T-shirts that we had made up, which, looking back on it, wasn't the prudent thing to do. It really pissed them off and I don't think they ever wore the shirts.

Things were a lot freer then as far as people and their attitudes. There wasn't as much uptightness as there is now. We didn't have Big Brother government, like we do now. People made a lot more money. There wasn't as much unemployment. As far as myself, I had just gotten into the adult film business in the early-'70s. We made a lot of money; we spent a lot of money. We thought that was a bottomless pit, all of us that were in the adult film business thought that there was never going to be an end to the things that we could do. I just remember a lot of years with a lot of money — more money than I knew what to do with. Money had really no value. A friend of mine said to me one time, "Money is only important if you don't have it," and that's pretty true.

Talent Agents

Naturally, with big money involved, the adult actors required agents, just like those in mainstream. Reb Sawitz was among the first to address the need for the talent to have representation, including John Holmes.

Reb Sawitz[h]: I was running [an apartment] building over on Normandy and Sunset with 42 units. It had a lot of females in there. I would see them go off to work everyday and when they would come back, I would ask them for the rent. They wouldn't have it because they hadn't been paid. Well, I was a big, bad biker at the time. I jumped on my Harley, got a couple of my club brothers and took the girls down to the photographer's place. I asked him why they hadn't been paid.

He said, "What for?"

We had a little bit of a talk, then he paid the girls and the girls paid the rent. Later in the week, they went to their agent, which was Anton Stone and Associates. Tony Anton asked me if I'd like a job.

I said, "Doing what?"

He said, "Agenting."

I told him I didn't know a thing about it.

He said, "Look, you went out and you collected this money. I don't think it would be hard to learn the rest of it."

I went to work for him for six months; I brought his company out of the red. We were doing very well. About a year went by and he quit paying me. Well, I knew enough about the business, being as I had to run it for myself while he was out playing games, so I moved a block away, took all my files into the Red Wine building with Bob Rhodes, who was a photographer. In one week I had enough money to move across the street with Kurt Richter, who was a cameraman.

I opened up what was Sunset International.

We ran ads in the paper. At one time, I had heard about John Holmes and Rick Cassidy — hot items. Rick was a good-looking guy; very well-built. John was a gangly, tall, very well-endowed male who came into my office and asked for work. And that's how I had met both of them.

I was in it almost 32 years. I was the oldest agent in the business, next to Hal Guthu, who prides himself on not doing any X work, so I guess I'm the oldest X agent in the business. I've been to court a number of times for blue laws that have been on the books for years and years. I spent more time in court than I did in my office.

Some of Holmes' fans and contemporaries believe that Reb was John's first manager, although many people profess that John managed himself. It is known that he paid an answering service on Santa Monica Boulevard during the entirety of his career. John never committed to an exclusive contract that would have limited his work to a single production company. He regularly stopped by the answering service to collect and organize messages pertaining to prospective film work, so essentially he did manage himself.

Matters regarding John's manager (or lack thereof) and his entrance into pornography are further confused by John's relationship with Bill Amerson, which lasted throughout the duration of John's career.

Bill Amerson[h]: I first met John in 1969, while casting for some still work, magazine stuff at the Crossroads of the World on Sunset Boulevard. We had an open casting call. It was the end of the day and in walked this really skinny kid with somewhat of an Afro haircut. He didn't look like the type we could use.

My partner said, "Go ahead and take a Polaroid of him, anyway. Have him go in the back room, take off his clothes, take a Polaroid and say 'Thank you, very much.'"

We went in the back room, he undressed and turned around. I had a Polaroid and I said, "You are going to be a star." That's how I met John.

I called my partner and I said, "Come in here. You are never going to believe this." And, I was right. He had read in the paper that we were having an open casting call and that's what launched his career, that very day.

My first impressions of John were that he wasn't too bright; he wouldn't stay in the business too long. He was very nervous and he just didn't seem to fit. He was an awkward kid, like a fish out of water. John never really became a good actor.

Some of John's former employers and associates have commented that Amerson was intimidating on some occasions; however, it seemed that as an agent, he understood that buzz is everything in creating a lucrative career in entertainment and helped to devise the legend that made Holmes the first porn star. Amerson said that one of the first stories he came up with was about John's entry into the pornography business, involving a girl next door who got him into it, but the truth, as Amerson claimed, was that they met while John was on disability while working for Market Distributors.

Bill Amerson[h]: John drove a forklift truck at a meat-packing place in Cudahy. He would drive in and out of a freezer and John got pneumonia. He decided that, while he was on disability, he would do something else to make some extra money, and that's how he finally came to us. He read in the paper that we were having an open casting call. That's what launched John's career — [after] that particular day, [he] never went back to driving a forklift truck.

Sharon Holmes[h]: About 1967 or '68, probably, is when he had his first contact with someone he met at a poker parlor in Gardena. He loved poker, which he had learned how to play very, very well in Germany. Occasionally, he'd go for an evening and he met someone in a bathroom there who talked him into doing stills. He said that he was interested in doing this because it would make money at that time. I don't know about the photographs, but John smoked Camels, and they would do comparison shots — him with an erection and a pack of cigarettes.

Sager's version of Sharon's poker parlor story suggests that the man who ogled John at the urinal could have been still-photographer, Joel Sussman, although to date, no one has taken claim to being the man in the bathroom.

Bill Amerson: We were shooting a movie in San Francisco. John became somewhat of a prima donna, and did pretty much what he wanted to, when he wanted to, and I didn't like that.
We were shooting a scene, and I said — I was playing poker with him for a couple of nights — I said, "John you're up in ten minutes."
He said, "Yeah, sure."
Well, 25-minutes later, he still hadn't gotten up.

He said, "I'll be there in…," and I walked over — he had a poker hand, he could have won — I took his cards out of his hand, and I threw them on the table.

I said, "He's out."

He jumped up and he said, "I'm gonna kill you!"

I said, "Give it your best shot."

And he just started laughing. He said, "No one's ever treated me like that before. I like you." Everyone always kissed his ass, but I never did.

John used to come to me and bring contracts for me to read for him. He didn't understand what they were about, so I'd tell him if they were good or bad. Then one day, he said, "I want you to be my manager and I will give you 20 percent of everything that I make."

I said, "I don't want 20 percent of everything you make, but I'll be your manager." The money didn't make any difference.

One Wife's Reaction

John had mentioned his interest in doing stills to Sharon when he told her the story about a photographer he met at a poker club in Gardena in 1967 or '68, however, he did not tell her of his intentions to work in other forms of pornography until late 1968 or '69. By that time, he had already appeared in magazine layouts and several loops and films, including hardcore, which Sharon apparently did not find out about until about until she was interviewed for the 1998 documentary, *WADD: The Life & Times of John C. Holmes.*

> *Sharon Holmes*[h]: I've found out since, that's when he first started doing films as well as magazine layouts and that sort of thing. I actually don't think he talked to me about entering porno until probably late '68. I was doing my own thing and he was doing his own thing. I don't think we were talking about it.
>
> I found him in the bathroom measuring himself one evening when I came home from work. I worked a day shift in an office. I came home probably about 5:30 at night and he was in the bathroom with a tape measure. I thought this was a little strange, but okay.

Sharon joked with John, "Are you afraid it's withering and dying?"

John said he was just curious, but 20 minutes later, he walked out with an erection. "It's incredible," John exclaimed. "It goes from five inches all the way to ten. Ten inches long! Four inches around!"

> *Sharon Holmes*[h]: I'd gone ahead and gotten undressed and was going to start dinner, when he came in and said, "I think I've found what I want to do. I want to do porno."

And I said, "Magazines, movies?"

He said, "Both; wherever it will take me."

I'm sorry, I was appalled. It didn't sound like something that one would want to make one's life work, but what do you say? I told him I wasn't particularly happy about it. Is this one step up or one step below prostitution?

I said, "Are you asking for permission?"

"No, I'm going to do this."

I said, "I'm not your mother, so you don't need to ask my permission; you're going to do what you want to anyway, aren't you?"

He said, "Yes."

It kind of leaves you speechless and it takes you a while to react because you don't believe you're hearing this — at least, I didn't! I thought, maybe passing fantasy, who knows?

"You can't be uptight about this," John told her.

It was a phrase that she grew accustomed to hearing during marriage.

Bill Amerson: The reason he got into the business was to make money. His name was John C. Holmes. He'd tell everybody that the middle initial, C, stood for "Cash," which it didn't, but he'd tell everybody that. He had no aspirations of being a star. He was very sexual and he found out he could make a lot of money doing it, so that is what he did. That was all he did; that was all he cared about.

Sharon Holmes[h]: He felt way back when this all started, that this was what was going to make him famous and make his fortune. He had the talent; I didn't think it was a talent, but he wanted to be filthy rich and if this was the way to do it — this was the way he was going to do it. He truly believed it had no effect on him whatsoever, and it really didn't mean anything to him. He would say, "Let's hop into bed, nothing wrong with this, babe." He had a voracious appetite.

John Holmes[c]: This fulfills one capacity in my life. It does one thing. This helps me create and it helps me vent emotions. It helps me vent things I want to be and do. I can express it — anger, hostility, sexuality, happiness, sadness. You can demonstrate anything you want to in front of the camera.

Sharon Holmes[h]: John had an extremely low sense of self-esteem. That never changed. He loved the adulation. He needed that. It didn't matter what kind of people felt he was famous or what he was famous for. In a way, we are all molded by our lives and experiences and because of his unique attributes, he felt that this was something that he could excel in.

I've never seen a porno film in my life, except for when John took me to Glendale once to see *I am Curious Yellow*. I think we were in the theater maybe ten minutes and I said, "This is not for me, I'm out of here!"

That was my full exposure, so I've never seen any of his films. I've seen very few in the way of layouts or anything like that, unless he thought it was especially interesting. Occasionally, he showed me these things.

He had so many other things he could do, but at that point, and he out-and-out told me, "This is probably my only shot at being famous for something. I want to do this. I really want to do this."

If he was away, it wasn't affecting us. That was fine as long as he was away, but when he was back and saying, "Well, I'm going to go to work for three days, I'll be gone," the thought in my mind was, "Where are you going, and what are you going to be doing?" It slowly but surely, kind of eroded my feeling for him. I still loved him, I still cared enormously for him, but I did feel that this was still a passing fancy. I always thought it might change. I hoped that it would change.

No one in the business knew about me; this was both his desire and mine.

Helene Terrie: I ran into him at Magic Mountain. He was with his girlfriend, or maybe it was his wife. They didn't have any kids with them. It was just the two of them.

Sharon Holmes[h]: When he had first started in the business, unbeknownst to him, I used birth control. I had three miscarriages in 17 months when we were first married and I thought God's telling me something, "the bad seed," so I made sure that I was not going to be pregnant. I'm thankful that I did because, could you imagine going through this with children? I think it would have been okay if we'd had children, but once he got into the business, he'd have worried how he could protect them.

In fact, John loved children and wanted to be a father, but he was sterile. There are many potential causes of male sterility and today it is known that up to 20 percent of men with a low or no detectable sperm count could be missing genes in the Y chromosome. This means that pregnancy is not only difficult, but this could account for Sharon's miscarriages because of the genetic defect in any male offspring.

On one occasion when John's mother visited John and Sharon's home in Southern California, Mary Holmes pressured Sharon with questions over John's profession and asked why she did not do something to stop him. Actually, Sharon had tried, but her efforts were fruitless.

Sharon Holmes[h]: I had tried when I said, "John, go to school. Get your G.E.D."

He had never graduated from high school. He went into the army when he was 16. He had never bothered when in the Army to complete his education. I said, "Do you want to go to school? Do you want to go to a trade tech, do you want to get your G.E.D. and go to [a] university?"

He really would have liked to do it, but he didn't want to spend the time.

I don't think he ever felt comfortable with who he was and his background. I think it gave him a false sense of security, like, "Well, I must be good if all these people think I am," and yet, he knew it wasn't. It wasn't really what he wanted to do, but what he felt he had to do. He felt there was nothing else he could do because it would involve too much time to educate him to do something else. This was fast fame and fortune, as far as he was concerned.

John Holmes[a]: I mean there it is, right now. You don't have to wait, go to acting school; you learn as you go and you get paid for it, too.

> *"You know, for many years people didn't know his name. They thought he was Johnny Wadd."*

BOB CHINN

3.

John Holmes, Johnny Wadd

The *Johnny Wadd* Series: 1970-1978

From Loops to Features

Bill Amerson[h]: The *Johnny Wadd* series was the start of the star system in the adult film industry. It became famous throughout the world. I would like to take credit for the *Johnny Wadd* name, but I can't.

In regard to the way that *Johnny Wadd* came about, it was the doing of another producer/director that John had worked with a number of times. They were shooting the film in MacArthur Park and they decided that they wanted to come up with a name for the detective character, and John wanted to be called Big Dick, along the lines of *Dick Tracy* and those different things.

The director said, "Let's use the name, 'Johnny Wadd.'"

John didn't really care about that, but the more he thought about it, the more he decided he wanted to do it. We'd run into people at, maybe, a hockey game and people would refer to him as Johnny Wadd. They didn't think about John Holmes and he became Johnny Wadd in his own mind.

John Holmes[i]: Feature movies were definitely a step above loop life. Scripts weren't necessary to churn out a loop; besides, scripts were evidence if found in a raid. Now we were given actual pages with story and dialogue to memorize, and we had shooting schedules that lasted days instead of hours.

Johnny Wadd was my first, real, screen characterization. *Johnny Wadd, Detective*, my first film with Bob Chinn, was a great working experience for me. It had a plot with substance, a large cast and crew. For the first time, I had a chance to work away from sheltered walls.

When Chinn created the character, he did not intend on making a series, however, theaters wanted more *Johnny Wadd* films, so Chinn gladly wrote more scripts to fill their demands. This became Chinn's most prominent contribution to the adult film market, as it was the first time that theater-goers were treated to a recurring blue-screen personality. Together Chinn and Holmes kicked the door open for "porno chic" classics such as *Deep Throat* (1971), *Behind the Green Door* (1972) and *The Devil in Miss Jones* (1973). The adult movie industry has not experienced anything close to the odd-couple tandem of Chinn and Holmes since.

Bob Chinn: I went to U.C.L.A. and studied film. When I finished at U.C.L.A., I couldn't get a job in the industry, except building sets and starting at the bottom. I wanted to go into mainstream, but back in the '60s, it was really difficult to get a job unless you knew somebody.

They weren't doing that much independent production. There was a lot of low-budget production, so rather than just build sets and work as a gofer, I started working on low-budget productions, where I could at least get work as a cameraman.

I worked as a cameraman on some X-rated movies, but they didn't call them that back then because this was before pornography. Everything was softcore, simulated. I started making my own productions.

Joel Sussman[h]: A lot of people got a chance to be creative in a business that you couldn't get into. The major studios wouldn't hire you. The unions would not let you do anything, so you learned a craft. A huge amount of people who do big films now started in this business.

Bob Chinn: In those days, some of these small theaters — they weren't even theaters, a lot of them were storefronts — showed loops, which were just a single girl playing with herself. They were easy; took 30 minutes to shoot and the model would be paid $35. You bought the film stock and that was about it, so I could afford to make those on my own.

In those days, you could not even show pubic hair. That's when I started. Gradually, we figured out that I could sell more if I would give a little flash of pubic hair here and there, so we started doing that. I was one of the first ones to go all the way and show everything. People were interested in seeing that. The next progression was to string loops together into a feature and do a story, which was wilder than the regular, softcore stuff.

I was always anti-censorship. I wanted to read all the banned books before they could even be published here. I had to get them in Europe. I thought since those could be published, I couldn't see why it couldn't be the same way with film and a bunch of other people started doing it the same way, either because they wanted to do it because it was exciting, or because they wanted the money. It was very dangerous because the police did come after you back then and if they could catch you shooting, they would arrest you, so it was a really exciting time of being rebels; hiding out and shooting and being one step ahead of the law.

Bill Margold[h]: I used to work at juvenile hall as a probation officer. I would go down to work in 1969 and 1970, and I would hear them talking about this man named Johnny Wadd on the radio. He was already legendary before I had gotten in the business in 1972.

Why was he called Johnny Wadd?

One day, I met him and I noticed why he was called Johnny Wadd, or "The King," or any other name; because he was proof that all men are not created equal; I'm talking about dick from my elbow, down.

Bob Chinn: They used to call him Long John in the early days. The first film was *Johnny Wadd*. Just about all of the release dates given [in sources such as imdb.com] are inaccurate because I made that film — it was actually released in 1970. I made it in 1970.

Jim Holliday critiqued adult films and worked with Bill Margold as historians of the industry. Holmes was somewhat close to Holliday, in part because both Holmes and Holliday shared the experience of growing up as Midwest farm boys, however, both Margold and the late-Holliday both honored John as "The King" of the adult entertainment industry.

Jim Holliday[h]: Thanks to the creator, Bob Chinn, John became instantly identifiable through one of his characters, the infamous detective, Johnny Wadd.

Chinn was writing, directing, schlepping the camera on his back while holding a light. I never cease to be amazed that people that can't separate time-dated material. If you can look at *The Maltese Falcon* and realize that this was done in Hollywood past, then you can overlook the fact that a lot of the movies in the 1970s have bell bottoms and those ridiculous hair styles, moustaches, beards, and sideburns that may seem anachronistic by the 1980s or '90s standards. They stand the test of time quite well.

There are *Johnny Wadd* films made in 1972 and 1977 that are better than 90 percent of the current videos being made today. These are the people that pioneered stuff. Some of the first movies didn't even have a wet shot. Why? Because these people didn't know they were supposed to put a wet shot in! What the hell?! They were the originators!

Most of the projects John was in had a couple of things they don't have today — namely a plot, and usually with a Sandy Dempsey, a Sandi Carey, a Linda Wong. The female supporting casts were the best-looking babes at the time, and gave the likes of Savannah, Janine or any of the '90s people a run for their money. They were certainly hotter, sexually.

Bob Chinn: All the early stuff I wrote myself under pseudonyms. I wrote the first four *Johnny Wadds*, the *White Gold* thing, *Tell Them Johnny Wadd is Here*, *The Jade Pussycat*, and *Blonde Fire*. I had a guy that wrote for me, too; Jeff Niel, who was my editor. If I didn't feel like writing it, I'd sit down and I'd tell him the whole story, including the dialogue, sometimes. Then, he'd write it out, and expand it into a good script. He was very good at that.

The Original, *Johnny Wadd*

Bob Chinn[h]: When John first came up looking for work, he came looking for work as a crew member, but since I already had all my crew — myself and two other people — I didn't need any crew members. He told me he was also an actor. Then he told me who he was and I realized I'd heard of him; an actress had told me about this man.

I said, "Well, I've heard about you, but show me your credentials." And he showed me his credentials. I said, "This is my Johnny Wadd."

That afternoon, I wrote the script on the back of an envelope and two days later, on Saturday afternoon, we filmed it.

For some reason, the theaters decided they wanted feature-length films. We started by editing five or six loops into a feature. Then, they decided they wanted sound — talking and so forth. We had to go out and buy a tape recorder and lip-sync them in. The early ones were like that. We probably shot *Johnny Wadd* mostly without sound and looped in later. We shot them in one day. Our budgets were $750 and we ended up with a 60-minute feature.

Linda Adrain was Bob Chinn's business partner and co-produced the first four films of the *Johnny Wadd* series.

Linda Adrain[h]: How we started — I went to a bank and we financed our first camera, just like a car. For three years, we made payments on it. I used my credit card to start getting credit at the lab. We had $300 credit and we just kept adding on and they weren't paying attention; we paid everything.

It was a time different from now. It was slower; it was easier. In a certain sense, it was simpler. It was fun in those days; we worked really hard. Bob would write the film, he directed it; he'd edit it on our dining room table. I would produce it and write the checks. I was the person that said no.

Bob Chinn: There wasn't much of a plot: somebody's missing and Johnny Wadd has to find her. A lot of them were shot in the same apartment — the cameraman's in Venice Beach.

It was just a one-day shoot. It cost $750 to shoot. I paid John $75; everybody else got $50 for the day. I edited it in two days and it was in theaters by the end of the week.

Linda Adrain[h]: I remember the first film was *Johnny Wadd*. We did a song under the titles, so if anyone has an original print, they would know the song. It was sort of like John's theme song. I know Bob always used Sergio Leone music, of *The Good, the Bad, and the Ugly*. The music fit perfectly for a skin film.

When I first met John, he was just starting out and he was really a gentleman. I have to admit he was very helpful, he was a nice guy, he was polite, and he was kind.

At 25 or 26 years old, John looked very young in *Johnny Wadd*, which starred his real-life mistress, Sandy Dempsey. Suddenly, the porno genre had an identifiable anti-hero in Johnny Wadd — a lanky, lounge lizard, with curly hair (sometimes slicked back), a thin moustache and a three-piece suit — who fought crime as a sideline to seducing the countless women who crossed his path. Having no formal acting training, Holmes as Wadd exuded a friendly, natural presence, with a gentle brand of finesse.

> *Joel Sussman*: What set him apart from other people was he actually could act a little bit, and he was someone you could kind of like. He does some funny stuff in the films.

> *Bob Chinn*: First of all, in those days there was nobody who could act and nobody could carry it off like that. Even with John it would be a stretch to carry it off. We did it as sort of a spoof-type thing. I figured if I could pull it off, I'd pull it off with him.
>
> You could put a script in front of him — you could write something on the set and put it in front of him. He'd look at it; he'd read it and take it in. Have it memorized.
>
> He'd try [to adlib]. If he tried it and it wasn't grammatically correct, sometimes I left it. I thought, well, it sort of works; it works better than what I wrote. If it works better than what I wrote, I kept it. Certainly, if an actor thinks that they have an idea, I always let them do it. I say, "Do it my way and I'll do it your way, and we'll see what works."

In spite of his average, unassuming looks, Holmes as Wadd believably lured one lady after another into falling under his persuasive powers. In a blink of one of his bright blue eyes, he was transformed from a man on the street into The King of Enticement. Part of the appeal of his Johnny Wadd character was the fact that he was not a cardboard cut-out.

> *Bob Chinn*: You look at people like Clint Eastwood, you look at people like John Wayne and you look at people that can just sort of come across. I think John [Holmes] was a couple of things. Men didn't see him as a threat. Even though he had a huge cock, they didn't see him as a threat because he seemed like a goofy, ordinary guy. He wasn't that good-looking, for one thing. He was skinny. For some reason, men just didn't see him as a threat, so he was popular. He became a star. I don't know how women see him — how *do* women see him?

It was good that once I could get his attention and tell him what we had to do, he could do it right away. I think that he would do it so that he could do something else later. He'd usually get it done right in the first take, but if I required other takes because somebody else was not good, he would do it and he wouldn't get pissed off like some of these prima donnas do now.

If I told him to jump from building to building, he'd do it, just to prove he could.

Flesh of the Lotus and Blonde in Black Lace

Bob Chinn: A couple months down the way, my biggest markets, New York and Honolulu — these people in the sub-distributor started asking, "Give me another one of these *Johnny Wadd* films."

I said, "Okay." I got a hold of John and made another one, *Flesh of the Lotus*. They were just moneymakers. I thought — I can't lose if I make these things. I saw the potential there and decided to try and capitalize on it, but I didn't think it would be this monster that it created.

Flesh of the Lotus is considered to be the most lackluster of the *Wadd* series. In the 1971 film, Johnny Wadd tries to solve the mystery of who killed his lover and he discovers the involvement of The Lotus Gang, a group of Chinatown thugs. Besides highlighting John's 12 inches, the film introduced his stunt work and was the first of Holmes' legendary fight scenes with Bob Chinn. In several of his films, Chinn made non-sex appearances (often using the pseudonym "Daniel Hussong"), since it was cheaper than hiring other actors, although he was more comfortable behind the camera.

Linda Adrain[h]: I did artwork, so I liked doing the posters, the one-sheets and I used to take all the stills. I was the cheapest person I could hire. I got to pay the bills, sort of handle egos — not that any of the actors would have egos! Between shots, I would dash in and take stills. We would use them for the one-sheets, press books, or we'd sell them to some of the magazines.

One of the A.F.A. [Adult Film Association of America] conventions was held at the Ambassador Hotel in Los Angeles. It was great. I had this long black cape, and I carried 16-millimeter prints underneath my cape through the lobby because we thought the FBI or other people were watching.

John Holmes[a]: I'm nervous every time I do it. It's not something you get accustomed to. It never gets like driving a taxi or working in a Sears lawnmower assembly line. It's nothing like that. There's always that kind of excitement, you know. That chance of danger.

Linda Adrain[h]: I think the big talent of John's was not his size or his dexterity; it was that he could cum on cue. There was one sequence at the end of a film, and we hadn't finished the point of the film itself. So, what we did, we counted John down from ten to one, and on one, he came. It was an amazing feat. That was his claim to glory.

Bob Chinn: The third one, though, he said, "I want more than $75 a day. I want $100 for *Blonde in Black Lace*."

I said, "Come on, this is going to be the last one!"

Blonde in Black Lace was the third *Johnny Wadd* movie. I thought, "Boy, these theater owners still want more of this?" I haven't thought about *Blonde in Black Lace* in a long time. I don't know if I like that movie or not.

John Holmes[a]: When you make a fuck flick, if it's done well, people go home and fuck. It's a deep thing. Two years from now, a guy will think back to that dirty movie he went to and it's something to jack-off to. It's a lasting thing. It's one of the strongest emotions there is.

You can go to a theater and if it's done half well with terrific actors and actresses, then you'll cry. Half the audience will break down and cry, and then for six months you'll look back and think, "Gee, that was pretty good," whenever someone discusses it, but if you go to see a hardcore flick, you'll remember everything about that goddamn movie. Everything.

The third installment, *Blonde in Black Lace*, was also made in 1971 for an impressively low $1000 budget. In this film, Wadd is hired by a woman who hopes to catch her husband in the act of an extramarital affair in order to have a case to divorce him.

Johnny encounters many women throughout the series of films who apparently are already more than a little familiar with his reputation. The female characters are often the sexual instigators and many of these trysts are cleverly executed — ranging from classy, sensual interludes following dinner and drinks, to down and dirty couplings on hotel sofas, in showers or on desktops. Even the simulated-rape scenes of the series, although rare, are provocative because the women appear to be perpetrators out to get Mr. Wadd.

Hawaii, the *Tropic of Passion*

Bob Chinn: In those days, we sold our films to storefront theaters. These weren't real theaters; they were just stores that ran 16-millimeter films. One of them was in Hawaii, called the Risqué Theater, which was owned by Chris Vicari and managed by Mavis Oda.

We went to Hawaii because they were really busting in Los Angeles. I couldn't shoot here. I told John, "I'm going to take a vacation to Hawaii, with my cameraman. I think we're going to take a camera just to shoot some scenery, and if you happen to be there..." So we didn't qualify under transporting him interstate for immoral purposes, "we'll shoot a movie with you," so, he showed up. We shot *Tropic of Passion* and we had a great vacation.

Tropic of Passion, shot on-location in 1972, depicts Johnny Wadd in his attempt to retrieve the only print of a sex film that stands in the way of an heiress from receiving her fortune.

Chinn recollected that John was quite a gentleman while in Hawaii: he made breakfast for everyone in the morning and collected the dirty laundry in the evening. According to Chinn, John was still drug-free during the time they were in Hawaii.

> *Bob Chinn*: He was a hard worker and he liked to play. He used to be very considerate.
>
> When we were in Hawaii shooting *Tropic of Passion*, the cameraman, a French guy named Alain [Patrick] — good-looking guy — met a Japanese tourist at the hotel. Sparks sort of flew, so John arranged a dinner for them. They went to the dinner and John had bought a whole bunch of gifts and given them to Alain.
>
> He said, "Tell her you bought these."
>
> He was that kind of guy. Little things like that, he used to do. Wake up in the morning, and he'd have breakfast made. Made a huge mess, he never cleaned up the mess!

> *Joel Sussman*[h]: He wanted to create moments, and step back and watch them happen. He'd pay for it to happen. He liked being in control. I think it was because he probably felt very inadequate most of the time, so he'd do this. He was a baby. You know, a big baby. He was like a little kid that never grew up. He had that kind of wonderfulness about him, that kind of a rich 15-year old, who had a Ferrari.

> *Bob Chinn*: I had booked the Risqué Theater on Hotel Street. We shot a scene there for *Tropic of Passion* and we used two of their dancers for one of the sex scenes.

Zelda Bergesson was one of the performers from the Risqué Theater who made an uncredited appearance in *Tropic of Passion*.

> *Bob Chinn*: After that, he got to know the owners — and he came back to make a personal appearance, but that was only a couple of

months. I don't think it was a year. He did stay a couple of months in Hawaii after *Tropic of Passion*.

Sharon Holmes[h]: There was a period of time when John was gone for almost five months working in Hawaii, doing nude dancing. He may have been doing photo layouts; I have no idea what he was doing. He did say he was going to a club there and he would be doing nude dancing. I'm pretty naïve about this stuff. God knows what else he was doing! This was as much as he was willing to tell me at that point.

John Holmes[i]: While in Hawaii, I signed a contract to work nights at a dingy downtown Honolulu club, performing simulated sex on stage with an attractive young partner. We never did anything, but we were nude and the act was choreographed to such a point that it was highly erotic! The girl and I created such a sensation that the club owner kept renewing our options.

Bob Chinn: We came back here and released it. It never did cool off here. It just got harder and harder to shoot, so I started shooting up in San Francisco.

Despite the fact that the films were still illegal to make, by 1973, the series was hugely popular — so much so that the films were re-released on 35-millimeter for a *Johnny Wadd* film festival.

Bob Chinn: *Johnny Wadd*, *Flesh of the Lotus*, *Blonde and Black Lace*, and *Tropic of Passion* were blown up to 35-millimeter and released in 1973. They were given 1973 release dates, when they were originally released years earlier.

Stretching the Truth

Joel Sussman[h]: People would stop him on the street and say, "You know Johnny?"

He'd go, "Oh, no, I drive a truck."

He did all these little games, but if somebody really knew who he was, he'd take a picture with them and he'd give them an autograph. He understood really well where his money came from. He knew by being a good guy to people out there, he would have a good reputation and people would buy his product, which is what any good actor with a brain does. He definitely had that really well under control.

Bob Chinn[h]: He was a pretty nice guy, if you could put up with his tendency to exaggerate everything. He loved to tell stories that weren't always the truth, but he actually believed them.

Despite John's propensity to lie, he was a hard worker and a gracious, budding celebrity. By 1974 Holmes had drawn a lot of attention to himself through his role in the *Johnny Wadd* films. That same year, Kenneth Turan, then a movie critic with the *Washington Post*, conducted one of the first interviews with John. Turan took a sabbatical in order to co-write his book, *Sinema: American Pornographic Films and the People who Make Them.*

Ken Turan [h]: In retrospect, I could see that he was self-mythologizing himself. What did seem sincere about him was his energy level. He said that everyone thought that he was on drugs — and I don't know if he was or was not at that point — but he claimed at that point in his life he was not taking drugs; he didn't even take Rolaids, he said he took nothing. He was very energetic, very high energy.

When he came into the hotel room he literally went into the bedroom and looked in the closet. He said he was fearful that there might be a bust — that I might be some kind of undercover operative, but he did tell a lot of mythological stories about himself. He talked a lot about being hired for stud services by various people and again they were great stories. They were fascinating. It was impossible then and it is impossible now for me to know how much of that was true, but he clearly liked talking about himself. He was an actor, he liked playing this part. I don't know — maybe he believed it.

Bob Chinn: After *Tropic of Passion*, we worked on *Evil Come, Evil Go* and a couple others. He was just a crew guy, in *Evil Come, Evil Go*, essentially. He appears in one scene in that, and he did the special effects for it. He loved doing that. *Evil Come, Evil Go* is a slasher film about two evangelical women who pick up men, take them home and kill them. It is a slasher film. There's one scene where a guy is laying there with his guts all hanging out and John would get such a big kick out of going to the market and picking up all this tripe and liver. It smelled terrible!

If I needed somebody in the early days to crew, he would crew; he would grip, he would carry equipment out. If I needed somebody to help with special effects makeup, with bullets going off and things like that, he would do that.

Well, he said he could. He said, "I've got a license."

He didn't have a license.

Joel Sussman: With John, everything he'd do, he'd always do with Bob. It was almost like, "I learned a new one, Bob, watch this."

It was awful. They were awful together. Bob felt that because he made *Johnny Wadd* that he made John famous and John never really liked the character. It wasn't the really important part as far as he was concerned.

Bob Chinn: I always had somebody that knew what they were doing. He would assist them, except for the special effects makeup in the horror film, and he did that all by himself. He did a good job.

He drank scotch and I drank a lot too, so we got along. Then he started getting a pretty big head as he got more successful. He wanted more than the $75 a day I was paying him, but we got along. I never socialized with anybody in the business. I guess the closest I ever came, was John and me would go to Las Vegas once in a while and have some fun, but I didn't know him that well, personally and he didn't know me that well, personally.

The Freeway *White Gold* Package Deal: *Tell Them Johnny Wadd is Here* and *Liquid Lips*

Bob Chinn: I just finished a softcore film called *The Devil's Garden* that I shot in Jamaica. I was at Pacific Film waiting for my friends one day and this blond-haired guy, tall blond guy, came up to me. He knew who I was and he said his name was Dick Aldrich.

He said he was the head of production for Freeway Films, and he wanted to talk to me. Freeway wanted me to make a couple of *Johnny Wadd* films. They wanted to revive that character. We went across the street to the bar, at the bowling alley, had a few drinks and agreed to do a project.

I was freelance. I had a contract more-or-less with Freeway Films, but it was an un-exclusive contract. So I made the *Johnny Wadds* for Freeway and a comedy here and there.

You know, it was fun in the beginning and I became sort of successful doing it. I was enjoying it when it moved from 16-millimeter to 35-millimeter. We were shooting in Panavision and that was fun. I could start making some real films then, well, almost real films because I never had complete budgets to work with. Everybody knew that I could make films very cheaply, so they'd give me a big budget, but they wanted me to make two films on it. So that's what I did: I made two films at a time, essentially — and on time.

Chinn's new arrangement with Freeway Films also introduced Holmes to Julia St. Vincent, a teenager who was working part-time in the Freeway office under the guidance and supervision of her uncle, Armand Atamian.

Julia St. Vincent: Armand was my uncle, the guy with all the money, and he owned the company. He worked with Richard Aldrich, who was also known as Damon Christian. Damon was the frontline director or producer; my uncle was the executive producer. Armand put up the money and went gambling. Richard was the one that took care of the money and appropriated it and talked to people when they got over budget, and Chinn was the director.

Bob Chinn: Armand owned Freeway Films, but every time he made a film, he went to the Bank of America and got a loan on his house. He made the film, and then he paid off the loan.

I had this script called *White Gold*. I'd never done it as a *Johnny Wadd* script, which is more elaborate. It was a long script, and it would have cost probably $13,000 to shoot.

He said, "Oh, that's a lot of money for a 16-millimeter shoot."

I said, "I can tell you what, we'll split it in half, and then you can have two films because it's a long script," so that's what we did.

The funny thing is, *Tell Them Johnny Wadd is Here* is the first of the two, but *Liquid Lips* was finished first, so *Liquid Lips* got released first. The second one got released before the first one!

Julia St. Vincent[c]: I remember when they were filming *Tell Them Johnny Wadd Is Here* and John was pacing around outside, cool as he could be, then they started into this scene that was supposed to be a softcore scene. The woman they hired was paid to do a softcore scene, but when he got her going, she went into it. John's gentleness coaxed her into a hardcore scene. The way he touched her, it was extraordinary, [for me] as a young, naive girl to have seen him do this.

Bob Chinn: We had a scene where Dick Aldrich played a part in it and he and John are supposed to be walking outside of the Ensenada jail, so we set up for the shot outside the Ensenada jail, like idiots. Of course, the police came out because we're not supposed to be shooting there and they hauled us into the office. What they didn't know was, we'd shot something, taken out the film and reloaded.

They were getting ready to write us up for everything, but John, being the quick-thinker he was, grabbed the camera, opened the camera and took out the film, saying, "Here, you can have the film. We don't have anything." That was sort of funny.

Then we just left, but we were worried about smuggling the film back across the border. We thought for sure we'd get busted because we'd done a lot of shooting down there and you're supposed to have a permit to shoot. We didn't - we just went down there and shot. That's what I always did; I'd just shoot, without a permit.

In John's classic fashion, he inflated the story in *Porn King* to make it more interesting.

John Holmes[i]: Filming on location had its drawbacks, as we soon discovered. While in Ensenada shooting prison conditions and squalid streets scenes for background shots, we were threatened with arrest for working without a permit. Facing a possible five-year jail sentence, we escaped only because our newer, revved-up engines could outrun those of the posse.

Joel Sussman: I don't even think he liked it with women, particularly. I just think he did it because it was what he could do real well. I really do. I think he really liked people and if he could please somebody, he would do it, and it seemed to please people when he could do that. He lived it; he lived the big life.

Bob Chinn: He started becoming sort of a prima donna. He knew he was the star. And he tried to exercise control in one way or another. Fortunately, I could work with him, but it irritated people like Dick Aldrich, the producer. He was responsible for the money and things like that. It irritated Dick a lot that he would act like a prima donna. I knew I could get whatever I needed from him without a problem, but when the friction arose, Dick would let his displeasure be known to John.

John didn't like people not being pleased by him. He needed to be liked; that's why he was always on. He was Leo, a triple Leo. His ego was so big that if somebody with a big ego (like Dick) would come down on him, he would become worse.

Up to this point, John had proven to fit many of the positive Leo characteristics; he was described as generous, warmhearted, creative, enthusiastic, broad-minded, and loving. For what it's worth, people born under John's birth sign, have also been described as pompous, bossy, interfering, and intolerant. Occasionally, John's behavior that hinted toward his negative persona began to show by the mid-'70s.

Annette Haven[h]: There was the shoot with Damon Christian and Bob Chinn called *Tell Them Johnny Wadd is Here*. This is when I first became aware John could have a negative component to his personality. He liked taking risks, I think.

I must have been in the bathroom doing my makeup and when I came out, everybody on the set is kind of like frozen and there's this banging on the door. Well, it turns out that John has locked out Damon Christian [a.k.a. Richard Aldrich], the producer of the film. Has locked him outside of the house and won't let him back in. And he's outside banging on the door saying, "Let me in, let me in!"

This is not good security. This is real obvious; this can be heard. As far as I'm concerned, this is very bad; we're not going to do this.

Bob Chinn, the director, wasn't doing anything. Everybody was intimidated by John; they didn't want to cross him. I'm sure they had good reason for that, but I just don't care. You do not endanger me; you do not do stupid crap.

I just said, "Let him in; you do it now," and one of the crew members went over and let him in because I think everybody realized it would be far better to cross John than to cross me. So we let Mr. Christian in and that was the end of that. John did very well in that scene.

Bob Chinn: Richard Aldrich once asked me, on the set of one of the films, "How can you put up with all his bullshit?"

To which I replied, "I put up with it because you can't and we need to get this film done." I didn't add that I was also amused watching John keep needling him. Richard and John really didn't get along. There was a huge clash in personalities there. John found that he could irritate Richard, so he took great delight in continuing to do so and this really didn't help matters much in the six films we worked on together.

The 1976 addition to the *Johnny Wadd* series shows the Private Dick in his attempts to rescue a friend from a Mexican drug-smuggling ring. *Tell Them Johnny Wadd is Here* was the first of the series to have access to a larger budget and it was an extreme success at the box office, in addition to two nominations at the 1976 AFAA Awards Show. The feature took one award at the 1976 show for Best Supporting-Actor, Carlos Tobalina. It became a source of frustration for John, as he did not earn awards from adult associations, which unfairly judged that John's popularity was mostly because of his incredibly large penis and disregarded his other talents and contributions to the adult film genre.

Bill Margold[h]: It's interesting that the first Erotica Awards honored a *Johnny Wadd* movie. Carlos Tobalina won a supporting actor award for doing absolutely nothing in the film.

He won the award and when Carlos got up there, he said, "I have no idea why I won this award." The King didn't get an award that night, but the movie that he was in got an award and it was very nice.

Liquid Lips, the intended sequel to *Tell Them Johnny Wadd is Here*, was even more popular with audiences, with over the top villains and a lighter, more humorous tone. *Liquid Lips* depicted Johnny Wadd in another attempt to put the kibosh on a drug-smuggling ring.

Bob Chinn: The girl in [the opening] scene was a model. She didn't do hardcore films. There was an agent in West Hollywood, named Hal Guthu, and he met a strange end. There was a big controversy about the way he died in his office. I needed a title sequence for that movie.

So, we went to Hal and hired a girl that had done softcore — well, she really wasn't into softcore, but she was a model, who did not do hardcore, of course. And I shot that title sequence with John, in Hal's studio, in the backroom.

I guess I was one of the few people who really got along well with John because I could accept him at face value, for what he was. You see in spite of everything, I kind of liked the guy and I believe he liked me, so we got on very well. One thing that helped is that he knew my limits and wouldn't push beyond them.

It's pretty well-known that John considered himself an expert on anything, even on subjects about which he knew nothing. I think it was his personality to simply fabricate the most outrageous stories about things in order to challenge people to believe what he was saying. If he was confronted by his inaccuracies, lack of knowledge or downright lies, rather than back down, he would simply expand his explanation into new realms in an effort to wear the detractor down.

The fact that I got along with John and we occasionally hung out with each other and took some trips together aside from our working relationship, did not make us close personal friends, however. We were, I suppose, friends after a fashion and we did share some great times together, but I have always kept my home life private. John was never invited to my house, nor was I to his. In fact, he never told me that he was married and I only met Dawn [a girlfriend of John's] once, when we were shooting some exteriors for *Liquid Lips*. At that time, he introduced her to me as his sister, so there is something to be said about John not letting people get too close in his personal life.

Household Name — *The Jade Pussycat* and *China Cat*

In 1977, Freeway Films asked Chinn to make a new *Johnny Wadd* movie. Wanting to return to the Chinatown theme of *Flesh of the Lotus* — with more cash to back him — Chinn wrote the script in homage to the 1941 film-noir/mystery *The Maltese Falcon*, with outstanding results.

In fact, *The Jade Pussycat*, an outstanding porno-noir, is on the list of director Paul Thomas Anderson's top ten favorite films. Anderson admitted that he borrowed scenes from the adult film and its sequel, but it has been said that imitation is the sincerest form of flattery. *Pussycat* also marked the only pairing of John Holmes with the dancer and former Broadway thespian-turned-adult actress, Georgina Spelvin, who had made a name for herself in hardcore playing the title role in *The Devil in Miss Jones*.

Bob Chinn: He never once asked for anybody specific to work with. He would just come and do his job with whoever was there. Just one actress, Georgina Spelvin [refused to work with John]. She didn't want to work with him.

I said, "Hey, do it for me, Chele."

He didn't want to work with her; they just didn't get along.

John Holmes[a]: She'll come in and get naked under those lights, and if she doesn't look right or smell good, I say, "Whoa, I'm not gonna work with this one," because if a chick smells, they don't take care of themselves. I've never had V.D. — never had the crabs, no syphilis, clap, gonorrhea, nothing. It's because some people I'll work with and some people I won't.

By the time of filming for *The Jade Pussycat*, Holmes was well aware that he and his alter-ego were quickly becoming hot property. Although this may have provided him with the leeway to put up an argument about working with certain people, John was still not above schlepping gear on film sets. One of John's co-performers, Jon Martin, appeared with John in several adult film ventures, including *The Jade Pussycat*.

Jon Martin[h]: One thing that always struck me was how cooperative he was. Nowadays, you would never find a person like John. He would help carry equipment in from the truck and help set it up. He was almost an extension of the crew. You'd never see that today. At that time there were other people because they saw John do it, so they thought, well, I should do this too. John was always a helpful; a very nice person to be around.

Chinn took a short break from both Holmes and Aldrich to work for Pacific Films before Aldrich and Chinn teamed up again for their production company they called Tenaha Timpson Releasing.

Chinn and Aldrich's company was formed to make a western-themed porno in 1978, called *Lipps and McCain*, which starred Paul Thomas. Admittedly, Bob Chinn would have liked to consider Holmes for the lead role, but because of the tension between Aldrich and Holmes, Thomas was chosen instead.

Following the huge success of *The Jade Pussycat*, Chinn and Freeway Films were ready to do a sequel once Tenaha Timpson's production of *Lipps and McCain* was completed. After the serious tone of *Jade Pussycat*, Chinn wanted to have more fun with *China Cat*, which parodied the hit television show, *Charlie's Angels* — with his own version of the Angels, called "Charlie's Devils": Barbi, Sandi, Sinthia, and Shari. In order to have a connection with *Jade Pussycat*, Chinn wrote the script as a seamless, two-part story that revolves around an abundance of shady characters and a very valuable jade cat.

Holmes was at the top of his game in the movies and his character was also doing well; established as a serious detective with an office of his own, a secretary and complimentary coffee for his clients. The series was incredibly lucrative and gave new adult talent the chance to become known among an established — and growing — audience.

> *Bob Chinn*: On the day I shot the Jennifer Richards scene I had some time, so I could work on it, which was good because she was very apprehensive about her performance and doing it right.

Jennifer Richards' made her adult film debut in *China Cat* as Shari, one of Charlie's Devils. Although Chinn took extra care with Richards because it was her porno debut, she made no other appearances in the genre.

Making "The Platinum Princess of Porn," in *Blonde Fire*

> *Bob Chinn*: Around the time of *Blonde Fire*, I was trying to do more with films because I had a bigger budget. I didn't have to shoot it back-to-back with any other film, so I could focus. I was able to do a little bit of something, although not much because I think our total budget for that film was about $12,000. It's a lot of money, but not much really. Other films were getting $25,000. That film was shot on 16-millimeter and you've got to take into consideration the cost of the film stock, the processing and everything else.
> John said, "Everybody else is paying me $1000 or more."
> I said, "I'll give you $750," because we didn't have that big of a budget, and he said, "Okay."

Seka was one of the most celebrated adult actresses of the Golden Age of Porn. Easily recognizable for her beautiful, platinum blonde locks, Seka made her debut earlier that year on the blue-screen in the 1979 film, *Lust at First Bite* (a.k.a. *Dracula Sucks*), which featured big name adult performers including John Holmes, Jamie Gillis, John Leslie, Annette Haven, Serena and Paul Thomas. Bill Margold also had a small part in this sexed-up Dracula movie. Margold recalled that John was so enamored by Seka, that when they had completed their scene together, Holmes informed Margold that he would "make her a star."

> *John Holmes*[c]: She falls in the top ten favorite people I've worked with. She isn't what you think she would be — she is overly beautiful; she's stacked like a brick shithouse. She is gentle, intelligent — she's not pushy, she's easy to work with, she's not headstrong. She is easily pleased, which makes her easy to work with, but she's got an insatiable appetite.

Seka's fame grew and she became known as "The Platinum Princess of Porn," after working with Holmes in several loops and films, including the classy, final installment of the *Johnny Wadd* series, *Blonde Fire*. In *Blonde Fire*, the stunning Seka makes an appearance in the opening as Wadd's lover in San Francisco. She re-emerges at the film's conclusion, wherein she and John engage in a tastefully shot sex scene on plush, blue velvet.

> **Bob Chinn**: Seka was naturally a little bit nervous. When people like Seka are nervous, they cover it up by being aloof, but [she and John] got along. There were no big sparks flying like we had said in the ad.

> **Seka**: I was scared to death because I'd seen him in films before and he was a big star. I thought, I've never met anyone of that status before. I don't know what I'd expected, but he was very nice. When we met, he was very polite and easygoing. He wasn't anything like I'd thought he would be. When we had to do a scene together, we sat down and talked before the scene.
> He said, "If there's anything you don't want to do, don't do it. Let's go over it," and we did. He was very gentle and very nice.
> It made me very comfortable. I always looked forward to working with John. He was one of my favorites. He was always very sweet, he was gentle and he was giving in a sexual way. He came in, did what he was asked to do, added ideas, asked questions, and said, "What about this or that?"
> Sometimes [his suggestions were] incorporated, sometimes they weren't, and if not he didn't throw a big, hissy fit. From what I saw and what I can remember, I never saw him get ugly with anyone. I didn't know Bob all that well, but it seemed that Bob and John were pretty tight. They seemed to be good friends.

Blonde Fire also had the distinction of being the final film that Chinn would direct for Freeway Films, at the request of Freeway's owner, Armand Atamian. Richard Aldrich, who had become Chinn's friend and drinking buddy, left the production company and Chinn found it too difficult to work with Atamian without Aldrich's presence.

The "Other" *Johnny Wadds*

John was often billed as Johnny Wadd (or some variation of the name), although there were only three films that used the name with permission from Bob Chinn. *The Danish Connection*, made by Manuel "Manny" Conde in 1974, was the first.

Bob Chinn: I had a lot of location footage left over [from *Tropic of Passion*] and the guy that did the sound mix on and sometimes edited my films, Manny Conde, said, "What are you going to do with that footage, Bob?"

I said, "I was going to throw it away, but I'll sell it to you, I guess, Manny, if you want to do something."

I sold it to him, and he made *The Danish Connection*.

Conde had felt that he could make a lot of money with a softcore *Johnny Wadd* film in 1974, so he asked director, Walt Davis, to write and direct additional footage to help frame leftover footage to complete the story. As part of his agreement with Conde, Chinn made a cameo appearance for continuity purposes.

In effect, Chinn had a hand in making *The Danish Connection* beyond his cameo. While he worked with Davis to make *Evil Come, Evil Go*, Davis was simultaneously creating a plot for *Danish Connection*, therefore the two films share a lot of the same actors, scenery, and costumes.

The second time that Bob Chinn permitted a friend to use the name "Johnny Wadd" was for the 1976 film, *Tapestry of Passion*. Alan Colberg had previous experience directing Holmes in X-rated films.

Alan Colberg: By the early 1970s, I had moved on to Hollywood. I had got a job with Allan Silliphant, who had made *The Stewardess*, which was a big 3-D hit. I ended up in L.A. in 1974. [John and I] had a mutual friend, Hal Guthu, who had a small stage on Santa Monica Boulevard, and that's where I met John.

I thought he was a total ass the first time I met him because he was a big shot, and I was the little guy. I guess we got along okay. He gave me his telephone number and we'd just see each other on and off sets. We kind of struck up a relationship.

I got hired to work for another company in 1975 and we made *All Night Long*. That was the first John Holmes movie that I made. It was starring Ric Lutze and John Holmes in a competition to see how many different women they could make love to under different situations in an evening. That's why we called it *All Night Long*. It was a 35-millimeter film.

Bob Chinn: When I was busy at Freeway, Joe Steinman and Essex Films always wanted me to come direct a film for them, but I never had the time. I was working for Freeway and Pacific Coast Films and all these other guys, so I always put it off. He wanted a *Johnny Wadd* film.

I said, "I just don't have time to do it."

Apparently, John was available and Alan Colberg is a friend of mine, so Alan said, "You mind if I direct a *Johnny Wadd* film?"

I said, "No, because I know you'll make a good one, Alan."

Chris Warfield was the producer on that one. I gave them permission to use my character, and they gave me a credit. Alan appeared as an actor for me in a couple of films to make up for it.

Alan Colberg: When John and I were working together, it was a good relationship, and we put scenes together. He was always the lead man. Nobody was like John. At that time, John was the only star, and he was treated with a lot of deference.

Another person that I worked with — and actually, he worked for me doing about anything he could — was Ronnie Hyatt. He doesn't go by the name Ron Hyatt anymore; he goes by Ron Jeremy. He was also pleasant to work with, but he was working his way up. At that time he was not the superstar of porn that he is now.

They all basically kowtowed to John. Everybody kowtowed to John in the mid and late 1970s.

Annette Haven was one of several feminists to work as an adult actress during the 1970s and she was John's "type" — a gorgeous brunette. Her earliest memory of working with John was on the set of *Tapestry of Passion*.

Annette Haven[h]: I ended up doing my first film with John Holmes, but he wasn't a name to me. He was just the star of the film, or really, his dick was. That's basically what sold John, but I was impressed with him because he had the wit and the extremely good mind to set up the arrangements so that Lesllie Bovee and I were sharing a bedroom that adjoined his suite.

I ended up exploring John's little suite area, and it was really interesting. His entire bathroom was one big line of vitamin bottles — about 45 bottles — because he was into health food. Then, he showed Lesllie and me our room and he gave me some really excellent head. I'm a serious jawbreaker, particularly at that time. You give me head for three or four hours - so what? But John got me off, in 15 or 20 minutes.

After John got me off, he didn't want to fuck me, which was even better. He went and fucked Lesllie Bovee, which was perfect, so John made a very big hit with me. And when he got on the set, he did his thing and didn't try to make a romance out of it. He was a professional; got it up, got it off and got the hell out of your hair.

Surprisingly, *Tapestry of Passion* was not an overwhelming hit in theaters and proved that the essential element to a *Johnny Wadd* film was the pairing of Holmes and Chinn.

Despite Chinn's generosity in allowing his friends to profit off of the Johnny Wadd name, many people would bill Holmes as such without asking the originator of the series. This was annoying to both Chinn and Holmes, so shortly after making *Tapestry of Passion* in 1975, John presented the creator of his most famous persona with a notarized affidavit that recognized Chinn's creation and sole ownership of the character.

Finally, in 1986, five years after the two had been together on a set and nearly seven years since making *Blonde Fire*, John telephoned Chinn to request permission to use the Johnny Wadd name one final time. At that time, Chinn resided in Hawaii with his wife and children. While on what would be a 13-year hiatus from making adult films, Chinn had no intentions of making another *Johnny Wadd* film, so he kindly gave John his blessing to use the name.

Only two short years before Holmes' death, John resurrected the infamous investigator in *The Return of Johnny Wadd*, which was the final appearance of the Private Detective. *The Return of Johnny Wadd* was produced by Penguin Productions, Bill Amerson's and Holmes' joint company.

> *Bob Chinn*: In retrospect, I sometimes wish that I had not been so generous, but if I had it all to do over again, I probably would have done the same.

"Every woman wanted him, every man wanted to be him."

BILL MARGOLD

4.

The King

Legend of Wadd

"The King" of Porn

Bill Amerson: He made pornography. He took it worldwide. He shot films over in Europe. He did all of that. He had the biggest dick ever in a movie.

Bill Margold: As soon as I met him, I instantly recognized what he was: an over-aged juvenile delinquent with a pot of gold at the end of his zipper.

Bill Amerson: Bill Margold called him "The King."

*Bill Margold*ᵐ: I first met John when I was running Sunset International, 6912 Hollywood Boulevard and he came up to the office. He looked like a little boy.

I said, "You're The King." He smiled at me. "You're the most famous person in the history of our business," and the history of our business was like four years old.

And he went, "Ohh…" and he started blushing.

I said, "And you will be The King until the day you die." Which I guess was somewhat prophetic. I have been accused of idolizing the man when in fact; I simply pay homage to the man who is the most important person and the legend of this industry.

Joel Sussman: He helped bring it from an eight-millimeter, back-room-business to full-on, Hollywood-lights and stars-signing-autographs business. He was the most important aspect of that of all people. It's really interesting that it was a guy, and not a girl.

Alan Colberg: He was a super man when I first knew him. He would do things that were amazing. He was definitely the star that he thought he was.

I remember we were shooting on the beach, and we were in an area that had a cliff that was maybe 60-feet tall. To get up to the parking lot, you had to walk a quarter of a mile to where the parking area was.

We didn't have something — it was up in the cars and I said, "Okay, well it's going to take a little while to go and get it. So-and-so, go walk down the beach, and go get it."

John says, "No, I'll get it," and he just ran straight up that cliff.

I was like, "Wow! That's pretty amazing."

He did a good job, he worked very hard, and he took direction as well as he could. There were no problems. I think that's why John did have a good reputation in the beginning because he did work hard. He tried his best and that's how I remember John in those days.

Today, Ron Jeremy's name may be the most recognized among male porn stars, although he began his work in pornographic films in 1978, more than a decade after Holmes' first X-rated appearances. It has been a somewhat sensitive area for Ron Jeremy; in fact, it has been a topic of conversation between him and Bill Margold, who has continued to recognize Holmes as the definitive King. Margold worked together with the late Jim Holliday to produce a deck of cards that shows the Legends of the Golden Age. In this deck, Holmes is one of four Kings, but Ron Jeremy is a Jack.

> *Ron Jeremy*: [Margold] put other people in front of me. Everyone laughed at him. I was so insulted, in his deck of cards, that he put me down on the list. I'm like, "Bill, let me introduce you to the world. If you look at A.V.N. [*Adult Video News*], the top 50 porn stars of all time — I was number one, Jenna Jameson was number two, and John was three — so we were two ahead of him." I don't mind being behind John Holmes, but don't put me two or three after that!
>
> I like to brag that because of mainstream, my name and face might be more recognizable around the world, but in the world of porn, I was never the box-office draw that he was and I'll be the first to admit that. I absolutely was not. In the world of porn, in the world of marketing and box-office persona, he smoked me. He beat me, by far, so that's why the word "King," is a fair title. Bill Margold never wants to take "The King" away from him and I'll accept that.

Affectionately dubbed "The Last Flower Child" by Margold, Serena began her adult film career in 1970 and first worked with John in the mid-'70s.

> *Serena*: Bill calls John "The King," and to anybody who is really in the business, there will only be one King, like Elvis.

Working Stiff

At 16 years old, Mark Novick, the producer of the 2004 documentary *John Holmes: The Man, The Myth, The Legend*, began his employment in the adult business behind the camera for his father's company, Pretty Girl Modeling Agency, which hired John repeatedly.

> *Mark Novick* [j]: I first got into the adult film business in 1970. I was the producer, director and cameraman. In 1971, I met John Holmes and over the course of the next four or five years, I shot over 40 films with him. John was not a great actor. He once said to me he'll shoot a 60-minute film for me, providing it was 57 minutes of sex and less than three minutes of acting.

We owned the Pretty Girl Modeling Agency. It had nothing to do with pretty girls. It had nothing to do with modeling. It was all about pimping and pandering. Girls would come in if they wanted to dance or to do nude modeling; if they were pretty enough or if they were into it enough, we'd talk them into a doing a movie.

One of the biggest assets to John's quick rise to fame was that he was free-lance and not exclusively contracted to a single company during the years he became famous as Johnny Wadd. Instead, he had a lot of employment options from several different production companies and John did seem to thoroughly enjoy his work at that time.

John Holmes [a]: [The director] knows he can shoot all of his fucking film and leave the cum shot to the last thing. He says, "I'll tell you when I've got a minute and ten seconds left, and I'll want it when I have a minute of film left." And he'll say, "Okay," and I'll cum. It's a mechanical thing; an on, off thing. I think, *cum*, I think *hard*, I think *soft*.

Bob Vosse [h]: The male is always the big problem. He's under a lot of pressure; he not only has to act and maintain a hard-on, there's 20 people all around watching him, lights all over him and this guy's expected to perform on cue. That's rough. Very few guys could do it, very few.

Bill Margold [h]: He explained to me that he would go across the street on Las Palmas, knock off a cum shot, come back to Reb's and wait until he reloaded, basically, run back, knock out another pop shot in the Red Wine building, come back — sometimes up to four a day at the horrendously low rate of $25 a pop shot. I wonder how many of the prima donnas of today would aspire to that situation!

According to Novick, Holmes had a remarkable ability to perform up to five scenes a day when they worked together, but a consistent challenge in working with John was his need to work with new females. On the rare occasion when John met a girl who was eager to perform with him spontaneously, he would contact Mark and arrange for them to get together. In return, Mark would drop what he was doing, meet with John and the young woman and immediately get down to business. According to Novick, two hours later, the film would be in the can.

Mark Novick [j]: We did a scene called *It Takes a Thief*. It was with Gilda and maybe it was method acting on his part. What he had to do was, sneak into the house and seduce the girl who was sleeping in bed and he was very good, maybe he was able to do it on instinct.

It Takes a Thief was one of only two short films which showed Gilda Grant (a.k.a. Barbara Barton) and John together. Grant appeared in only two hardcore films, although it is known that she was involved with John romantically for about five years throughout the late-'60s and early-'70s. John started living with Gilda in 1974. Around that same time, John also had a bedroom at a swingers' house where he kept many of his belongings, including clothes and jewelry. Interestingly, the loop *It Takes a Thief* was shot at this residence.

> *Bill Amerson*: Gilda was a waitress who worked at a bar on Santa Monica Boulevard. She was really a sweetheart, but she wasn't real bright. She and John had a relationship for years and she never had his phone number. Now, what kind of relationship is that if you can't get a hold of your boyfriend? She would have to call his answering service. He stayed with Sharon, on and off, during the period with Gilda. Gilda finally found out that he was married and shit-canned him. He was broken-hearted for a long time. If he ever loved anybody, it was Gilda.

The second loop that John and Gilda appeared in together was called *Big John and the Girl Scouts*, which featured Gilda and a young blonde as Girl Guides who offer cookies to John. However, it was not made available in adult bookstores because of the suggestive title and the unusual nature of the sex scene.

> *Mark Novick* [j]: They were young looking. The brunette was Gilda. I shot them in two scenes together and I never shot the same girl more than once. We did something I had never seen in a movie. John came in the blonde's mouth and she spit it into Gilda's mouth. It's something that at the time was not done. We got a lot of flack for that.

Eventually, John's employment as a sex performer and his affinity for working with new girls in every scene would land him in trouble with the law.

Sexual Professional

> *John Holmes* [c]: I show larger on the right so if I'm in a nasty mood and I'm going out I wear it on the right. Otherwise I wear it left. And also, things like getting turned on when you are at a bus stop or something and it rips the elastic on your shorts. I quit wearing shorts because of that.

Eric Edwards appeared in several films with John; the first of them was *Exotic French Fantasies* (1973), which also starred Linda Lovelace and Andrea True (who recorded the disco hit, "More, More, More," with the Andrea True Connection).

Eric Edwards[h]: The first time I met John was on some remote sound stage. I wandered around the corner of one of the flats of the set, and there he was. Since I had some dialogue to do with him, I introduced myself to him. Unfortunately, the guy was naked at the time — or fortunately, whatever you want to say — he was naked. Without hesitation, he came over and shook my hand. It's almost like a joke where you talk to a girl with big boobs and you're just always staring at her boobs instead of her face. I could not help myself when I talked to him.

Jamie Gillis, a 1970 graduate of Columbia University, worked with Holmes in several films during the acclaimed Golden Age and has been credited for developing "gonzo porn." In 1973, Gillis met John for the first time, for the film *Over Sexposure* when John picked him up for the shoot.

Jamie Gillis: You know John was off in a field by himself. He was John Holmes; he was "the dick." When I was next to John, I was very aware of what a lot of other guys probably go [through] throughout their lives. I never had that feeling before. I knew that I didn't have a small penis, but relatively speaking, it was certainly a lot smaller. So this is what it felt like to be, not inadequate — but just this is what regular guys feel all the time, is that they are inadequate.

Annette Haven[h]: Holmes had an interesting personality. I think he needed to compensate for a lack of self esteem, so he ran around telling everybody what a genius he was. He did have a high I.Q. I don't know whether he was a genius or not, but he was very, very smart. He was an intelligent person and then of course, he did choose to be in the adult film industry. He did choose to run around showing everybody his cock so that other men would feel inferior to him; so one has to assume that he initially felt a lack of self esteem. I thought that was why there was so much compensation.

He performed very well, always. There was one occasion, and I don't remember exactly what film it was, except that we were definitely in a residential bathroom. I had been using a sponge for the sex scene. John and I had done it and I went inside to the bathroom to clean up, and I couldn't find the sponge! I thought, oh, this is just fine. John and his big cock and obviously I'd lost the sponge up inside of me. And my hands aren't long enough.

I thought, John's hands match his cock! So I ran on the set and grabbed him.

He said, "What do you want?"

I said, "Come with me."

I got in the bathroom and I said, "You put it up there, and I want you to fish it out."

He said, "What?" He was a little bit taken aback.

But I said, "John, you've got to. I can't reach it, okay? I really can't. I've tried. I need you to get the sponge out. Otherwise it's just bad health for me, it's really bad." And so he did, he was very sweet, and he worked with me until we got the bloody thing out. He was able to reach it. He had long hands.

Al Goldstein, founder of *Screw* magazine, has appeared in several porn documentaries, including *WADD*, wherein he has acknowledged the reason why, as Margold has aptly put it, "Every woman wanted him, every man wanted to be him."

Al Goldstein [h]: I was always fascinated with John because he had everything I didn't have. He was hung like a horse; I'm hung like a squirrel. He had what all the guys dream about.

Would I trade my little, meager, Jewish cock for his cock?

Yeah, fucking-A, I would, and I'd throw in my kid, too.

Serena: He was a real legend before I met him; he's always been a legend. I thought I'd never meet him. I was looking forward to it, but he was kind of out of my league when I first started. I started out doing magazines, so finally I did movies and somehow, we got put together.

John Holmes [c]: A happy gardener is one with dirty fingernails and a happy cook is a fat cook. I never get tired of what I do because I'm a sex fiend. I'm very lusty.

Undeniably, the poor boy from Ohio with low self-esteem had come a long way in the new world of adult entertainment, and he relished the attention showered upon him by his admiring costars and adoring fans. According to the numerous female costars that he satisfied, John was attentive to their needs — he talked with them before shooting the scene, gave the actresses backrubs, and remained gentle throughout the scene.

Bill Margold: Sharon Thorpe, who'd worked with Holmes many times, basically accused me of being too big, too clumsy and too awkward a lover. This was a woman who had inhaled The King — vaginally, orally, and maybe even anally, but accused me of being way too painful and way too big for her, when in fact, I don't begin to measure up to The King.

Jamie Gillis: I remember Serena specifically saying telling me — I think she said that she liked John and he was very gentle and you know basically, any woman who ever mentions him, mentions him in a kind of approving way. John seemed to be a very gentle type. I guess the women were really happy to have that really excessive cock without being battered.

Bill Margold[m]: John prepared women for sex like a loaf of bread. He kneaded them before the onset of their scenes together.

John Holmes[c]: I treat them very different. One is very professional with a personal touch, and the other is personal with a professional touch. I treat each one with respect. Gentle, kindness, whips and chains. Bondage, domination and kisses.

Serena: He was very nice as a person, but he was very, very professional. We would just get thrown into a scene and do it. The thing about John was he really knew the industry and he knew the filming. He knew all the angles in more ways than one. He directed scenes that he was in because he was so good. He kind of took over and the best part of him was that he would always show the female's good side. He would do what the director of the film wanted before they even asked. He would show the penetration, he would show all the things that they wanted by moving you around. He would just physically move you.

Joel Sussman: He was smart. I mean, I say that in all the kindest ways. He had this way with the women on set — it was, "Oh, put your hair back over here, so we can favor her."

John Holmes[c]: Perhaps only 15 percent of the women I meet or run into, I care to have a personal relationship with. But the people I work with on screen, I'm most usually put into a situation of having to represent a personal relationship — in acting. She may not care to go to bed with me; she may not even care to speak to me, but because we are hired as actors to perform, we have to find a rapport.

Bob Vosse[h]: I'll give him credit; he was the easiest to work with, from the girl's point of view. He was extremely gentle. He was extremely well-manicured. He was nice to the girl; he gave her presents that he stole the day before off someone else, but she loved him. After a while, the girl was quite at ease. I never had one girl complain, or that wasn't willing to work with John again. In fact, most of them requested, "Can I work with John Holmes again?"

Alan Colberg: We would be in places — we would meet people and John would be so charming. He could charm anyone, especially women. I think his favorite game was meeting a new gal and seeing how long it would take to get her into a sexual situation. If he put his eyes on you and you were a chick — fugheddaboudit — you were his, unless he found something else to do and he walked away.

But John had a great personality. He could always command a situation — any situation that he was in, so that he would be the center of attention, and he did it very well. He was a very sweet guy.

Serena: We had behind-the-scenes sex on the movie set. We'd never meet somewhere in a hotel or something, but we'd go behind the camera and sneak off in a corner — or not sneak off, depending on how we were feeling. I would get him ready for the next woman. I was his personal fluffer on a lot of movies.

I would say he was charming, but he wouldn't paw like one person I can mention that's still working, [who] just comes up to a woman and grabs her by the hair and sticks his dick in her mouth. John wouldn't do that, but he might go up against the woman, and put his arms around her, or feel her breasts even, but he wasn't really overt. He really saved himself for the set. He would flirt with the girls, but he would never be obnoxious.

John Holmes[a]: It's a natural thing. It's a turn-on thing. I'm only sorry I'm not two people who can enjoy it. While you're here, man, you're here to fuck, to dig life. Enjoy it. Do your thing. Work. Become somebody or not become somebody. Do your thing in life.

Real-life Johnny Wadd

Bob Chinn: When I was working at a camera store in Torrance, about eight years ago or something like that, someone said, "You're Bob Chinn."

And I said, "Yeah."

And he said, "Well, you don't know me, but I know you." He introduced himself. He was with the Los Angeles Vice Squad — he's retired now. He said, "We tried to get you so many times, but where you were supposed to be, you were never there."

Sometimes we just left, right before [the police] came and I'd be working with John at the time. I think he probably saved my ass a few times, yes. They probably pressured him to get information. He always seemed to get out of it. Maybe he was my guardian angel.

John Holmes[a]: Everybody takes a bust, you know and this might be mine. It's a constant thing. It's a pain in the ass because when you're on a set, it's hard to get your mind into giving a good performance when in the back of your mind you know there might be cops pulling up in the driveway at any second, right?

On several occasions, John personally sought out young women to work with in films and paid them. A 1973 incident where he was caught doing just that put John face to face with law enforcement that was kept busy actively pursuing pornographers and adult talent. Following that incident, Tom Blake, a retired detective of the Los Angeles Police Department's Administrative Vice Division, grew to know Holmes quite well.

Tom Blake[h]: John was very famous. He was probably the biggest male porno star in the United States through the '70s and '80s. He was very well known for his tool, if you want to call it that.

He traveled all over the world; he serviced ladies all over the world. He probably had more sex with more women than you and I, ever, in a lifetime. At this time in the 1970s, he was getting $500 to $1000 for servicing these women and he bragged about it.

In Los Angeles and Hollywood, we had several film labs process eight-millimeter films. Most of those film labs would talk to us because they were like informants, also — because they were arrested for the production of the porno. You could arrest them for manufacturing these films and developing these films; they could be charged with these crimes, too.

A lot of them said, "Hey, it's just a livelihood for us. We make money for developing the movies."

I had three of four major films labs up in Hollywood — they would call me up and say, "Hey, we have some film in here that you should look at," or, "We have film that 'John Smith' brought over, and here is John Smith's phone number and address." And we knew who John Smith was. We knew he was a manufacturer and distributor of porno films.

We had an informant that advised us that John Holmes was going to be involved in a film with some other people and we were told that they would be meeting at a certain location in Hollywood. What they did in the production of films, is that they told the actors and actresses to go to a restaurant at a certain time and wait. They never told them where the film is actually being shot.

We were able to find out what restaurant they were going to be waiting at and we observed several women there, plus some males there, plus John at this location. We ran license numbers of the vehicles that they were in, found out where they were living and found out the names of these people.

At that time we followed them from Hollywood out to Moorpark — observed them going to a residence and doing the filming in this location.

We'd seen him at several locations and several shoots, but never were able to make a case on him. And John, most of the time, did not procure people to be involved in films. John was basically working through an agent and actually, being a star in the films, he was not the person who procured the females or other people to be in that film.

But on this particular film, he was actually the one that did the procurement of these two girls who lived in Calabasas, I believe, and at that time, they were only 18 or 19 years old. They were young girls and he actually obtained these two girls.

After we made the search warrants on the house where they shot the film, we obtained the film from the laboratory, and after we viewed the film, and ran the D.M.V., [we] found out who these two girls were and interviewed these two girls. They are actually the ones that turned the case against John Holmes. Even though the girls were — well, I don't know if they were willing participants, but it didn't matter if they were willing or unwilling.

They said, "Yes, John procured us to act in this film. He wanted to do various sex acts with us. He paid us money for this and we did it," and this is where your pimping and pandering came into violation.

We obtained the warrant through the Ventura County district attorney's office. Then Detective Joe Gandley and I, and a couple of other people, went to John Holmes's house in Glendale. John answered and let us in. We met his wife, Sharon — very nice lady. We sat down and talked a bit. We advised him that we were arresting him for pimping and pandering for that film shoot in Moorpark.

I mean, he was really nice. He said, "I'm an athlete. I don't smoke. I don't drink. I run every day."

He had a cupboard in his kitchen that probably had 25 or 30 vitamins he took every day. He was a health fanatic. Anyway, we ended up arresting him and booking him and I did not see him until we went to court in Ventura.

Some of John's work associates have had a difficult time reconciling what Blake claimed happened next. After John was arrested for pimping and pandering, to avoid felony charges which could put him in prison for up to three years, John agreed to work with Detective Blake as an informant against Holmes' own industry.

Ron Jeremy: While I'd always liked John Holmes — he was always very, very nice to me — I acknowledged a few things that I thought were very, very bad; that he was a paid informant for the police, which may explain why his shoots were never busted.

Mine were. Ours were busted, twice. We don't know if he actually ratted out my name, specifically, but when dealing with the police, they're not going to want to bust you, they're going to want to keep you working.

Personally, I don't think he did my two shoots, because I don't think he had any real knowledge of where I was shooting or when, but I think that he was never busted because he was working for the police. I was not and because I wasn't a paid informant, I'm open game.

Mark Novick[j]: John was a snitch, but that's not the same thing as being an informant. Even if you don't give the cops straight answers, what you are giving them is more information than they had before.

Tom Blake [h]: He took the choice of helping me out. We did a lot of cases. He was very cooperative and he enjoyed being Dick Tracy or the cop; he liked the role of investigating and getting information and passing it on.

I believe John wanted to be a police officer. Probably the closest he ever got to being a police officer was working with this and he really enjoyed it. We would tell John to do this and do that, and he'd go out and do it, and dig up all the information that he possibly could. He liked the intrigue — he felt like a cop.

I'm probably the only person in John's life that had the telephone number to his house. I could call him up, day or night, talk to him at his house, and talk to Sharon. We worked as a team for a number of years, until I left the porno industry and went into another field of vice work.

We'd go out to dinner together. When we went out to dinner, he'd drink milk, water and coffee; no booze. We cops — we'd have a couple of cocktails, or whatever.

John was shooting at the L.A. Police Academy Range. It was open to the public. He loved guns, and he was up there shooting probably once, twice a month. When he got involved with us, he and I were like — I hate to say, like brothers, but we clicked. We liked each other.

I smoked cigars at the time. He got me a box of Romeo and Juliet Churchills from Cuba. Probably the best cigar you could ever have. It was a box of 25 and he gave it to me for Christmas. I can remember that we were at the Police Academy, having lunch, and he gave me this box, all wrapped up.

He said, "This is your Christmas gift."

I said, "You know I can't accept this," but I opened the box and said, "I won't tell if you won't tell."

"Hey, Tom, it's yours. I know that you enjoy your cigars. Have them." They were the only Cuban cigars that I ever had in my life. He was a great person, he really was.

Laurie Holmes: No, he was not an informant. He would give them false information, and they knew that. Did that make somebody a snitch? No. What makes somebody a snitch is when you give them real information. Cops really don't like snitches — they don't have any respect for them, so why would Tom Blake like John? I'm sure the whole time John was playing with his head. I think [Blake] thought that [John] was interesting. He was star-struck by him, more than anything. Hey, it was cool, and he was having lunch with John Holmes.

What I really hated in *Wonderland* is that they portrayed him as this giddy, suck-up snitch. John was nothing like that. He was sophisticated, he was wise, he had a lot of honor, and he didn't believe in ratting people out. Yes, he would toy with the cops. He would actually give them wrong information just to confuse them. He said there are three people you can't trust: don't ever trust cops, don't ever trust reporters and don't ever trust lawyers.

Although Blake came out of retirement to contribute his recollections for *WADD*, a few more of Holmes' former associates within the porn industry have expressed doubts that John actually would have fed the L.A.P.D. vice squad much concrete information that led to arrests. Although Blake has never cited any names of films for which sets were busted, he has been adamant about his working relationship with Holmes.

> **Tom Blake**[h]: He was involved in a lot of the actual films that we made arrests on. There was one incident, up in the Hollywood Hills off of Hollywood Boulevard. They were doing a shoot at a house — there was a big, apartment house — and we were able to get up on the roof of this house.
>
> John said, "Hey, we'll be filming at that house. When the film gets done, I'll come out on the balcony and give you a violation."
>
> We wanted to go right into the actual shoot location and seize everything there. They filmed for about three to four hours at night. It was about midnight and there was a patio balcony up there, with floodlights. John came out there, naked as a jaybird. You know that it was John, because John was tall, skinny, and he had a big tool!

Swedish Erotica

> **Ron Jeremy**: I was a fan of John because of his gigantic *schmeckle*. He was definitely a box-office draw. People wanted to see this gigantic penis in some cute, little blonde. Harry [Reems] had become famous for *Deep Throat* and *The Devil in Miss Jones* — Harry had done those — he and John were the two best known. John Holmes' worst film would outsell Harry's best. Yeah, he outsold everything. John was huge. Caballero put John and Seka under contract.
>
> According to Paul Carrera and Caballero, they said that his worst film outsold Harry Reems' best film. That goes for Seka as well. In the world of porn, women are the draw; they put women on the box. John Holmes was a true box-office draw. The producer, director and owner

of Caballero, who put him under contract (before Vivid put people under contract) — according to these guys, Seka's best film could not outsell John's worst film. That's amazing!

> *Bob Vosse*[h]: I did the *Aunt Peg* series and *Seka* and all. I don't care who else it was, John would outsell. The worst John Holmes loop would outsell anything — the best of anything else at least ten to one. Because I saw all the figures, I saw all the books — it was unbelievable.

The most famous and most prolific loop series, *Swedish Erotica*, began around 1974 by Bernie Bloom. Originally, these loops were called Cinema Classics. Around the same time that *Swedish Erotica* had larger budgets to work with, Cinema Classics changed their name to Caballero and in 1976, Bob Vosse began directing for Caballero's *Swedish Erotica*. Generally, this series contained multiple silent scenes, with musical accompaniments added later; however, these loops had evolved quite a bit from those of John's early days in pornography. Most importantly, the women were aesthetically more pleasing as the adult industry matured.

> *Bob Vosse*[h]: When I started with Swedish Erotica about 1976, they had just started and they had signed John Holmes up. He was about the only one steady and he was doing well. They were shooting color, but they were still silent. When I came in, I talked them into sound and shooting on Eastman color negative; it improved the technical quality quite a bit.
>
> I talked them into, "Could we have a makeup artist?" They'd never heard of using a makeup artist on a loop. All of these little steps, including the boxes, to me that was a transition from the sleaze way of films under the counter. It began to sell in stores, and tapes and things. The quality would just jump out at you. We used the little colored scarf on the side. It was kind of a trademark. We put [panty] hose on the girls, dressed them up, had a full makeup artist on each one to do the loops, and we had good locations.

David Clark was one of the series' trusted makeup artists and saw Holmes on the set several times.

> *David Clark*[h]: Being a makeup artist, I would know this. He had the most incredible blue eyes. He wasn't averse to mascara, but he would always fight with me in the chair, and kind of say, "I hate makeup, I don't want to deal with this at all," and what was he was going to do to terrorize the producers that day, but somehow, he would always come through.

Back when my daughter was just five or six years old, when we had little money and long, long hours, she sent potato salad, and John used to appreciate that. John sent a lovely note.

He could be very charming and very difficult at the same time, but quite an experience.

Bob Vosse[h]: I was doing all the shooting in San Francisco, locations all over Sausalito. My job was to go find the locations, cast all the people and then shoot at least ten days out of the month. We had contracts with various people, including John's contract, which was for ten films a month.

One thing, as a personal thing that used to make me very unhappy about John, is if he was fresh and slept that night, he would do a good job and sometimes, he would do two groups in a day. But he wouldn't do that. He'd pick one of the little girls he hadn't worked with yet, he would talk them into coming up to his room that night, he'd sleep with them, then they'd go to the set to shoot and he'd have no interest in them. So I had to practically keep a guard on the door.

John worked with a few girls a number of times. But for the most part, he really didn't like to work with a girl but one time. I'm telling you he was the best I'd ever seen at convincing the girl and putting her at ease. Most were very apprehensive—they'd heard about John. When I interviewed them, I always thought my job with *Swedish Erotica* — my main job — was to find new girls to feed the monster. Day after day, I would interview and find these girls. He particularly liked short, dark-haired girls. These girls — most of them had heard of John Holmes and were very apprehensive about working with him because he was very large and they would be nervous.

Annette Haven[h]: John turned me on to *Swedish Erotica*. They needed somebody to set them up here in the Bay area and I had all the contacts in the Bay area because I kept files on everybody. So, I did all the production management. John referred me that particular account, which really did see me through the couple of years it took to get my career going well enough before I could demand enough money to make ends meet appropriately.

The line producer, Ilo, is a great guy. I had to hire women to work with John in what were sometimes anal scenes. I don't do anal sex; I had never done it with John anally, or anyone else in film. It's uncomfortable for me.

So when Ilo said that to me, it's like, "You want me to do what?! How can I ask somebody to do that? How do you expect me to ask some woman to do this?"

Ilo said, "It's really very simple. John's cock collapses. It really doesn't hurt anybody because it just kind of collapses down."

I thought, "What the hell, I'll try it," and that's what I explained to the women that John worked with when they asked me about it. I know that his dick does collapse down. His penis was kind of squishy when erect, so actually it wasn't that uncomfortable for them. At least no one ever complained. I think John must have been very good at it, too. That is true. Vaginally, he was able to be that large inside of you without injuring you, hurting you or causing any discomfort.

It was actually said that if John ever got fully erect, he'd lose consciousness due to lack of blood to the brain because his dick was that big. And it's true that his cock was never hard. It was like doing it with a big, soft, loofah; you had to kind of stuff it in.

Serena: He wasn't hard like other guys were hard because we always teased him that all the blood would rush to his dick. We really razzed him, but it was his tool to make a living. It was his money-maker. It was also such a fluke, as far as physical property — women who were not into porn would watch it because it was so bizarre. Their husbands would actually enjoy that and it would turn them more onto porn, because they wouldn't mind watching John.

Annette Haven[h]: I don't know about other women, but for me personally, I would prefer something in a smaller size that was actually rigid, that functions really well. Being stuffed full of Loofah is kind of interesting I guess, but not exactly sexual kicks. John isn't somebody I would fuck in real life, although I would let him give head to me — anytime. He did a good job there!

Bob Vosse[h]: The girls, some of them, would fall in love with John, and they wanted to work with him. "When is he coming back?"

I'd tell John, "Do you remember that cute little girl you worked with?"

"I didn't like her."

I said, "She's out here, she keeps calling. She wants to see you."

"No, I don't want to see her." He really had no interest in them after one time and that was it.

Mike Horner, an adult film actor, first met Holmes in the late-'70s. Having worked on the sets of *Swedish Erotica*, he attested to what a lot of people said about making the series; that it was a lot of fun.

Mike Horner[h]: The first time we worked together was a *Swedish Erotica* piece. It was a take-off on *Superman*. I think they ran into some problems later on with rights on the whole issue, but basically, I looked fairly close to Clark Kent and the *Superman* look — much closer than most people. But John Holmes fit the role more from the waist down.

So he wasn't even seen in the movie, except from the waist down; they used him for penis size. They used me just from the waist up. Basically what I'm doing was a softcore version of what John was going to do in a couple of minutes with the same women; so I end up doing, pretty much, fake scenes with Seka and Kandi Barbour. Then after we did our certain amount of footage they felt they needed with me, they have John come in and do hardcore with him.

We hung around the set, made jokes about each other. I wasn't going to get laid — he was going to get laid. He was happy about that. I was quite sad because they were both beautiful women. Now, they could be great-grandmothers!

Seka: It was fun most of the time. It was really cramped, small spaces. There was a fellow that shot most of the *Swedish Erotica* films, Bob Vosse, and he was a funny man. He was funny-looking. He swept his hair over to one side to cover a bald spot. I remember working with Mike Ranger once and the guys always gave the cameraman a three-second warning when the money shot, so to speak, was going to be delivered. This was a close-up shot and Mike Ranger gave the three-second warning when he came, and it went right into the camera lens, right over the cameraman, and right on top of Bob's head.

I thought Bob was gonna die. He went "EEEWW!"

I said, "Now *you* get the facial shot." It was amazingly funny.

Bill Margold[m]: I spent days in sound studios hyperventilating for orgasms and making voices for a lot of the silent loops that were made for *Swedish Erotica*. The interesting thing about it is that I was the voice for John Holmes in a lot of those because nobody else wanted to be his voice. I'm not sure why. But his getting off, his orgasms, his grunts — because Holmes had this scrunched up orgasm face, as if he was ejaculating cement out of his dick — I had to go through that, and if you do it long enough you want to pass out at the end of the damn orgasm!

Bob Vosse[h]: John had many assets and good points, but he came off like a used car salesman. I don't care what part you gave him — he was a guy who'd be bad as far as acting is concerned. He developed better (or somewhat better) as years went on as far as acting was concerned, but his popularity grew and when I started shooting him for *Swedish Erotica*. John was getting $1000 a loop at that time, which was quite a bit more than anyone else in the industry was getting. In all fairness, he deserved more.

Ron Jeremy: I came in more for the acting point of view. I know it sounds corny — who thinks of porn and things of acting? — But keep in mind, back when there was film and there was no video, no DVD, no internet — it was all just film, Panavision. We're talking the same cameras that are even being used today in feature films. These films had storylines, and plots. A lot of the same directors who were doing porn were doing mainstream. I don't want to mention names, but there were some very big-name directors of today, who started out doing porn then.

Just by being in so many movies, John Holmes got a certain screen presence, charisma and ability in acting. He probably became more of an actor from sheer experience, which will happen. Anything you do in life, if you keep doing it over and over again, you're going to get better at it. If you look at some of John's later films, his acting wasn't that bad. He got more, as they say, "screen savvy."

Seka: I don't think any of us had a great acting ability — certainly not me, and not John Holmes.

In particular, one adult performer has been given a lot of credit for his acting skills: Paul Thomas. He began his acting career in legitimate theater prior to switching gears in 1974 and immersing himself in hardcore movies. Thomas worked with Holmes in several features, including *Swedish Erotica*. Like Holmes, he believed that the adult market was a quick way to success and fortune.

Paul Thomas: As I entered the films, same time as John Leslie, Richard Pacheco, we were sort of taking over the leading roles. [John Holmes] was only in as a character, sort of a supporting role. But he wouldn't be as often the main part of the film, because we were better actors.

I liked John. He was a friendly person to be involved with. I'm sure he got in because of the size of his dick. When I was a fan of his, he was *Johnny Wadd*; he was the leading man in the movies. I had been a fan of his before I entered the industry. I'd admired him on the screen. He was nice and personable, friendly, but kept his distance. He wouldn't have been good in mainstream.

He never exhibited a lot of depth, either as an actor or as a person. You'd never see him really down. He was always fairly up. He certainly was careful never to be mean. But there was nothing particularly palpable to engage.

Bob Vosse[h]: He could change his whole demeanor; his whole attitude could change. Part of that was he was under pressure. When you worked a lot and you're expected to perform, and you'd reached the top, it's very hard to maintain and hold that edge all the time. When you're under the pressure to perform as often and as much as he was, quite often, if he didn't feel up to it, he would blame other people. It was the girl's fault, it was this, something was wrong, this kind of thing.

Just to give you a couple of examples. Once he got unhappy or mad on the set — he didn't like what was happening, but he had worked a long time and he was tired, so he just quit on Friday, said, "I'm catching a plane, I'm going back to L.A."

He wanted to come back to the office of *Swedish Erotica* and they would always have his money ready for him — never had an argument over money. Toward the end, at this time, he was getting $1500 per scene, per loop. This meant he was working ten days a month, so he was making pretty good money.

When he got back to L.A., it was late Friday afternoon and he ran into the office. There's no one left there except the telephone operator, someone at the desk. Everyone else, the boss had gone. John exploded; he wanted his money. And she said, "I can't give it to you, they're gone, it's closing time. You'll have to come back Monday."

John ran through the offices, all of the offices, jerked out every phone in the building, threw them over his shoulder, he could hardly run out of the place with them and he turned at the door and said, "Well, when you bring me my money, I'll give you your phones back." This was a typical John explosion, which made no sense. He was no angel.

The Good Little Boy

Joel Sussman: He never was a man; he was a little boy and everywhere I look, that's the John I like. That's what he and I shared together — not the bad little boy; we shared the good little boy.

The good little boy would do some amazing thing like go to the hospital and bring a kid some fucking big game, and he wouldn't even know that John was there. He'd just leave it and say, "Bye." The man did some amazing stuff. He didn't talk about it, but he did neat things that were just not necessary. Yeah — he'd take Christmas toys to kids. He was like Santa Claus.

Bill Amerson[h]: We went camping. We went fishing a lot. John loved to fish. He would go out almost every weekend, if he wasn't working, on a boat off San Pedro or Oxnard. We went to different lakes together.

We went to a lot of hockey games together. He loved baseball. He and Tommy Lasorda were friends. In only the style that John could befriend someone, he said, "Hey, I'm John Holmes."

He would have to put on a costume to go to work. Not only the clothes, but the face, the mind; everything had to change for him to be Johnny Wadd. Basically, he was a country boy. He just wanted to be liked, just wanted to be loved by everybody.

Bob Chinn: If he wanted something, he'd try and buy it from you.

One time I had something that he wanted, and he said, "I'll buy it from you. I'll buy it from you." Then he pulled out this watch he'd bought in Russia, and said, "I'll trade you for this."

"Okay, John. You know, just take it, if you want it".

And he said, "Take the watch, take the watch."

I said, "I don't want the watch." When I got home, the watch was in my coat pocket.

Bob Vosse[h]: I've got to give John a lot of credit; at the high point of our relation, I had real admiration for John's fast thinking.

Even though they had said there were no pornography laws in Oregon, on one particular shoot, we were going to shoot on Sunday, but I had a strange feeling about it, just the whole thing. We were trying to be very careful, using some of the old L.A. tricks by putting names on the film cans; phony, dummy rolls of film in there so if the police were going to come in they would get all the wrong films. You learn all those tricks how to survive in the old days. After a year-and-a-half of shooting there, openly advertising in the University of Oregon paper, casting, doing everything openly, one day I felt strange — that it's going to happen.

And by golly, it happened. Here they come in, the whole group, but they immediately go for me. They grab all the films on the floor, with all the labels on the property, which they immediately send to Kodak under guard, and they get back their *Donald Duck* cartoons. All of this with an $800 bill for processing. I thought that's pretty funny.

But John was cool. John hadn't actually started working that day. He was sitting over in the other room. He saw them. One of the laws that I remembered, hide the script because that shows intent to break the law — if you've got a script, it's all in writing. John hid the script between the old 33 records that were in the bookcase there. They looked for the script and they couldn't find the script.

They took me to jail. They booked me. They didn't even put me in a cell because I said, "I'm ready to bail out." I had a pocket full of money, so we bailed out, but it took a while.

Here's a point for John: John was fast-thinking. John got the bright idea that they might come over and raid the apartment and get all my films, and it could be worse. This is where I loved John, he was really thinking. He and my girlfriend (she had a key), they loaded all of my films — everything into a station wagon, took it out in the country and hid the station wagon.

Sure enough, when I got out of jail back to the apartment, they just showed up with a search warrant. They came rushing in. I didn't know John had emptied my apartment. I was worried silly — they are going to go in and take all of my films! We went in the door, right behind them. The place is empty. John had emptied this — he saved my life — I would still be in jail if he hadn't done that.

He was excited. We were having fun. Since we had taken them on both the films they had sent to the lab, we beat them on all of these points. I said, "Okay, John, we're not going to be able to do any more shooting right now. We'll have to settle this thing; you might as well go back to L.A."

He said, "No, I want to stay and help you," so, the next day John stayed over.

We took the station wagon load of films out into a friend's farm outside of Eugene and he had a big trash barrel where he burned his trash. We started unwinding the films, dropping them down. I said, "I don't think they'll burn; this is safety film and it's not going to burn."

We had a bonfire of about 25 feet, going up so high that I thought it was going to burn the barn down next to it. We had a great laugh out of all of it.

When I had to go to court a couple of days later when they got the films back, and found they only had Donald Duck cartoons for evidence, they offered to make a compromise and said, "If you'll just leave the state, we'll drop the whole thing, but don't come back to Oregon."

I can't go back to Oregon, but we had a good time while we were there.

During the same year that John began his work for *Swedish Erotica*, the soft-core feature, *Fantasm* opened at the Cannes Film Festival. The movie boasts a classic cast of top pornographic stars, including John Holmes, Serena, Candy Samples, Bill Margold, Rene Bond and Uschi Digard. *Fantasm* showcases a series of female fantasies, which range from a lesbian scene in a sauna to an imaginary adulterous poolside romp involving a bored housewife, Maria Welton. In Welton's scene, she conjures up her own interpretation of Romeo (played by Holmes) in a short titled, "Fruit Salad."

Australian producer, Antony I. Ginnane provided commentary for the re-release of the movie in 2004. He spoke about the segment, *"Fruit Salad."*

Antony I. Ginnane, **Fantasm DVD commentary**: The idea was that John would get out of the pool, sort of like Neptune. I can honestly say that you could time it when Holmes gets up out of the pool. The audience, particularly the female audience, actually sees his cock for the first time and there's an audible inflow of breath in the auditorium, coupled by a variety of comments among the girlfriends. It was a funny moment. It was certainly a talking point with regard to the film in Australia.

The underwater sequence was very, very heavily cut. In early versions that were around, I think it runs one to three seconds less. The close up of John's penis sold the movie, which had a good six months run. We were a little ambivalent about the pool scene because the actors were concerned about going into the pool if it wasn't a particular temperature, and that could have been an issue. It required getting specific camera housing for the underwater scene.

It was in *Fantasm Comes Again* where we had our falling out with John. The pool temperature wasn't to his liking and I think he was concerned that there might have been a diminution in the size of his appendage if the pool wasn't the right temperature, so he did a little prima donna on us and would not go in the water. We had him standing by the pool and Bill Margold wound up being the lifeguard who blows the poolside cuties' whistles.

In all actuality, John was not concerned about shrinkage because his scene was slated to be softcore. According to Margold, John was worried about getting sick with pneumonia while working in the cold pool, which was located high on a hill without any shelter. To John's credit, he may have not been such a prima donna after all, especially considering his problems with pneumothoraces in the past. Even the cameraman wore a wetsuit while working in the pool, but Margold and the women were not afforded that luxury.

> **Bill Margold**[m]: John Holmes was cast in the second one [*Fantasm Comes Again*] as a lifeguard. It was a Friday in February of 1977, when he called me up and said, "I can't go in that pool, they haven't heated it."
>
> I said "Hmmm…" and thought very quickly because, *A)* I'd already paid him and would be out all that money, and *B)* I figured what the hell, I'll try to get in the film twice. I said "Walk around on the deck, have them shoot you, and then go away."
>
> He said "Really?"
>
> I said, "Yeah, I'll take care of it." and I told the producer, "I'll see you on Saturday." He trusted me, so they shot some material of the girls looking at Holmes saying, "Hey, that's a great-looking life guard," and that was all Johnny needed to do and he left.
>
> I'd played football that morning in a league game at a park in Hawthorne and I'd gotten a concussion. I didn't have any feeling in my body and to this day, I don't know how cold it was. I came out of the pool after I shot whatever was needed to be shot — and it was simulated, so at least I didn't have to worry about getting a hard-on — but

I don't remember anything to this day, and I've watched the scene and don't remember anything.

The kicker to the whole thing though and something that I'm very proud of, is that a week later I received a letter from John C. Holmes, The King, and he returned the money and said "Thank you and live long and prosper."

He said that I was an honorable man and those were my sympathies towards him. He was honorable because he could have kept the money but he gave it back. That's always been something that warms me.

Making a Legend

Bob Chinn: He was the type of guy who knew something about everything, so no matter what you talked about, he was an expert. Untruths. A lot of it was so innocent. He would just build on a story, and build on it.

Among the circulating gossip during John's career, was the story that John Holmes was actually Ken Osmond, who had played Eddie Haskell on the television series, *Leave it to Beaver*. Mark Novick printed up over 10,000 box covers that promoted that rumor because John had told him that it was a fact. Holmes and Osmond, indeed, shared a likeness, but Osmond was at that time, an officer for the L.A.P.D. and he did not find the fable to be humorous; Osmond threatened to sue until the record was finally set straight.

Mark Novick[1]: One time John was dropped off at our secret rendezvous in a Mercedes. There was a pretty blonde driving. He got out of the car and I said, "John, who is that?"

He said, "That was Rona Barrett."

I looked at him disbelievingly and said, "You know Rona Barrett?"

He said, "Hell, she pays my rent."

I said, "John, you're just a gigolo."

He looked at me and said, "No, I'm just a John."

Ron Jeremy: He convinced people that he was an international pimp, and then people would believe it because he had been to Europe. We've all been told that. I never witnessed him given any money for sex, but he did have a ridiculously huge penis. It was the largest, white penis I think the business has ever had. John Holmes is and probably always will be the largest, natural, non-surgical white penis in the business. He had me beat by about an inch — inch and a half. I hate to admit that.

Al Goldstein[h]: I'd always heard the story that John had worked as a gigolo; that he worked the Hollywood circuit. And there's even the famous story that he would have a try with hors d'oeuvres and his cock would be among the hors d'oeuvres. Whether it's true or not, I want to believe it's true because it's neat, compact and it's a hell of a story.

Jim Holliday[h]: John was one of the master bullshitters and liars of all time. He had the ability to remember what he had told different people and carry it on. I think it was one of the first couple of times I talked to him — he had authored 23 books, and he owned 29 industries, and at the time he really didn't know that I'm allegedly highly educated and put two and two together and realized this was impossible stuff he was spieling to me.

Al Goldstein[h]: He was the man I think towered over the business. Not just with the girth of his cock, but he was the most interesting story in the world. He should almost be a Kennedy because his life is filled with such hubris.

He was confused about whom he was, where he came from, so he created a whole scenario: he was a fiction writer, his rich family, and the nannies raising him — it was wonderful.

And of course, since John Holmes was only a commodity, a product, an object, why should he tell me the truth?! But it was good bullshit. It was good razzle-dazzle.

Goldstein was frustrated after Holmes shared lies instead of his life story for when he conducted a two-part interview with Holmes during the mid-'70s for *Screw*, but most people had learned to accept John's storytelling as an integral part of his personality. Tony Lovett wrote a piece in 1988 for *Hustler*, five months after Holmes' death, called "Lies and Last Lays." At the conclusion of his research, Lovett surmised as to why John may have had a tendency to fictionalize his life.

Tony Lovett[h]: Here was an enigmatic character who portrayed himself as, I believe he said, he'd lost his virginity to a Swiss or a French maid; [he] portrayed himself in a very exotic light, in terms of his background, when actually the truth of it was the antithesis of all that. He seemed to have sold himself on this story as much as he did everybody else — if he did sell anybody else on it. But that was the line that everybody took on John Holmes and I think that was something he created to make up for the fact that his past wasn't that exciting or eventful, until he dropped his pants for someone and they said, "You're a star."

About his childhood, John was very guarded. He would tell people that he was born in New York and lived with a rich aunt who sent him to school for fencing, dancing and etiquette. According to John, his aunt had been married 15 times and took him to live with her in London, Paris, Michigan, and Florida. John also told people that he had lost his virginity at age six to a Swiss nurse-maid named Frieda. It was said in Mike Sager's 1989 article that John lost his virginity at age 12 to a 36-year old friend of his mother.

John claimed to have bedded all but three girls in his high school class, but he actually never graduated. It seemed to be a sore spot for John that he was undereducated, as he claimed to hold several degrees from U.C.L.A. (in physical therapy, medicine and political sciences).

> *Bill Amerson*[h]: John had so many stories about who he had been, who he was and what he was doing. All the stories were designed to cover up his pain, in my opinion. John had a very painful childhood. He always needed to be someone else. That way he got out of the pain that he was experiencing.

> *Jim Holliday*[h]: I'm sure a psychologist or psychiatrist could say the embellishments were stemming from some need for acceptance. Well, if bullshitting was a psychological compensation, he was still a compelling guy and whether it was a need for acceptance or not, I can't begin to speculate. He was still a charming, good guy. Rather than be a leader, because he was certainly looked up to — rather than be a follower, because he was his own man — John was just kind of John: going along with the flow.

> *John Holmes*[c]: We did a game one night at the mansion. We sat around and played, "How many girls have you gone to bed with?"
>
> I think it was slightly over 14,000. I did the orgy trip for two to three years, almost every weekend. Between tricks, freebies and girls in films — keeping track of the films and averaging out how many girls you go to bed with in each film helped a lot. It's slightly over 14,000.
>
> Embarrassing, isn't it?

When John discussed his own status within the industry, his lies had a tendency to involve numbers: the number of women that he'd slept with, the number of films he had been in (2,274), the amount of money he earned ($3,000 a day), the length and circumference of his penis (anywhere from 11 to 15 inches and "as wide as your forearm.").

> *Al Goldstein*[h]: The people who think that John Holmes slept with 14,000 women are into numbers. John wasn't a basketball player, so I don't' think he had sex with more than maybe 7,000 or 8,000.

The idea that John made over 2,000 films — we love numbers; it simplifies things. We live in a world of nebulousness and ambiguity. So any time you can make something finite, it simplifies things.

Joel Sussman [h]: I think he would make six [films] a day sometimes. If you could, in one day, be in six films, then I'm sure he made 2,000 films because he'd do like 20-minute loops. He did lots of that for a long time in the beginning.

Bill Amerson: With all the loops and ten-minute short things, he probably did. I never thought much about it. The point that he made love with over 11,000,000 women — or whatever it is — is mathematically impossible. You have to understand, a lot of that was my promo.

John Holmes [c]: Everything in life is an act; it's the performance that counts.

Bill Amerson [h]: John had the ability to talk to people, pick up what they were talking about and immerse himself into their personalities. He had a talent for talking to people and telling them what they needed to hear. John was a hell of a showman. John could have been one of the best salesmen in the world. He just knew where to go with whatever conversation was happening at the time, and he would do a 180 in a minute. He could be in this tremendous situation on one hand, talk to another group of people, and do a complete 180. It was amazing to see him dance and that's what he did.

Together, Amerson and Holmes created stories that John would share during interviews. Amerson's ability to make up stories about up-and-coming talent, he explained, boosted their box-office appeal. During our 2005 interview, Amerson admitted that he had continued to embellish stories after John's death because the legend is often more interesting than the truth.

"I really don't give a shit," he asserted, "…but if you didn't believe me, you wouldn't be here," regarding his own truthfulness in interviews. Then he reminisced about the legendary tales they would spin together.

Bill Amerson: John didn't finish high school. The story is that he went to U.C.L.A. to become a physical therapist. The only time John went to U.C.L.A. was to rob the cars in the parking lot! Now would that sell him? No.

John did have a job as an E.M.T. He worked on a paramedic truck. He did all the first aid, so we said he was a physical therapist. It was a wonderful thing. John was none of the things that he was built up to be. He was supposedly an officer in the Army, but he wasn't. No, John was in the Army, he was in the artillery.

As far as being a carpenter, if you gave John an hour with a hammer, he would break his thumbs. He would start building something, and he'd get halfway done, then he'd get bored and leave it. At my house, I had a fence; it was like, half-built. He'd get frustrated; he couldn't stay with anything.

He was a mystery to everybody. He was an enigma. We'd go to a hockey game; I'd have front row seats. He would start laughing and he'd jump up and somebody from the crowd would scream, "John, sit down you asshole!"

He'd turn to them and wave. He loved the publicity. We would get up to leave because the game was boring, and guys and their wives would come up and say, "John will you come to our house tonight? I want to watch you fuck my wife."

He was very gracious. Every time someone would say, "John Holmes?" he would say, "No, I just look like him."

When we had the gas wars out here, where every other day you could buy gasoline because of your license plate — some days odd, some even — we could buy gas anytime, anywhere. We didn't have to pay for it. I had a motor home, and we were on a trip. Wherever we went, we would pull into a station, and the station attendant would hold traffic back so we could pull up to the pump. John would go in, and they'd give us 100 gallons of gas, free, if John would sign, "I was here."

We never had to wait to get on an airplane. We could go to the airport and there would be people in line, and John would walk up to the attendant, and we were allowed on the airplane before they even called anyone.

We were at the Riviera Hotel — this is a cute story. We were gambling; John was a big gambler. We decided to take a break and go up to the roof. So we were on the elevator, and this little old lady, about 85 or 90 years old — a blue-haired person, got on the elevator with us. She had nickels from playing the slot machine, like five or six cups of nickels, and when she saw us, she started screaming, "You're John Holmes!" and she threw her nickels up in the air and grabbed at the railings. She thought she was going to be raped, or something.

John was picking up her nickels, saying, "No it's not really me!"

Scared the hell out of her!

John and I were fishing. This is a big story about John. He had a dragon ring and every year, he'd have one diamond added to it, and the story. The promo on it was that once a year a woman in England would send him a ticket and $10,000. He would go over and spend the weekend with her, come back, and she would have this ring, and she would put a diamond in it, then she would mail it back to him.

John and I were fishing one day, on a little rowboat, out on a lake — we were reminiscing one time, and John said, "Man, remember the old days? Remember when that girl used to send me a ticket to England?"

I looked at him, and I said, "What are you talking about?"

"I went to England, got $10,000."

I said, "John, you never went to England. That was a thing that I made up.

He said, "Oh yeah." He believed his own bullshit. He believed my bullshit.

John's custom-designed dragonfly ring, which had nine carats of diamonds, was very noticeable in his films, beginning with its first appearance in *The Jade Pussycat*.

Helene Terrie: We'd run into him at a party and he showed me his diamond ring. I said, "Whoa, that's a rock!"

And he said, "Yeah." He said this lady flew him from L.A. to Florida, and gave him a diamond ring to screw her. Well, he showed me the ring and we were at a swing party. Yes, he was there looking for action.

John Holmes[q]: Rene [Bond] and I used to go to the same orgy house. I'd never done it with her, but she was always my type. She had this thing that I liked, but the opportunity never came up. She was living with this one certain X-rated actor and it just never came up that I would work with her and then she married a guy who wanted to become her manager.

He had this thing about, "You're never going to work with John Holmes."

So, since we were going to the same orgy house... They had the world's biggest water bed there and they'd had it custom made. I mean you could make a wave at the end of it and ten minutes later it would come back to you; it was monstrous. Well, everybody got on the water bed at once. There must have been about 20 people on this water bed. Nobody even knew who was doing what.

It was kind of dark and twilight in there, and Rich came out and said, "John, come here."

I said, "What?"

He said, "I want you to…"

I said, "I don't want to do it."

He said, "Come on — it's Rene Bond!"

Rich set the whole thing up.

Tony, her husband was on the other end of the bed and I came around. Rene was giving somebody head and her ass was sticking up in the air so I just went at it and I started doing it. She was really getting into it. She was really getting off on it.

She'd orgasmed once and then Tony came around the other end of the bed to see what Rene was doing and he said, "Rene! Do you know that John Holmes is fucking you?!"

She said, "Oh! No, I didn't!" She didn't stop to look up to see. Didn't know it was me, so to keep out of trouble she said, "Oh, I didn't know that. John! Stop doing that! Tony doesn't like you." It was after that they finally had a falling out.

John may have lusted after Rene Bond because of her unavailability. When Bond, who was involved with Ric Lutze (another one of John's adult comrades), became available for John's personal fantasy at the orgy house, he was thrilled.

John fell in love with the German-born *Penthouse* fold-out Brigitte Maier after working with her in a pair of films, one being *Fulfillment*. The feature XXX film was directed by Chris Warfield, for Essex. She also starred in European loops and John was enamored of her for a few months after their first meeting in 1974.

Jamie Gillis: John seemed like a wholesome guy; a good guy; a gentle man. There was some kind of All-American sweetness about John. He had that Jimmy Stewart kind of thing. He was always very laid back — always sort of comfortable in his pre-drug time; always casual. He was a nice guy who got dragged into it because of his cock and I think he just got lost there. He should have been working at a gas station or something. I felt sorry for John. He was there, but I had a sense that the time was sort of passing him by.

John Holmes[a]: How long do I want to do this type of thing? Until I'm dead.

> *"I knew John before he ever smoked cigarettes, before he ever took drugs. He was like John Wayne. He would walk proud. He was a wonderful guy, and drugs really killed him."*

JOEL SUSSMAN

5.

Shooting Star

Drugs, Women and Hard Work

Remember Sharon?

John had kept his work in the industry secret from his wife for as long as he could. After Sharon had caught John measuring himself in the bathroom and he declared his interest in working in all types of pornography, she tried to deal with his decision, but was unable to separate his career in her mind from a life of prostitution and adultery.

Sharon Holmes[h]: It wasn't until 1973 that I found out how really deep John was into pornography. He had been lying quite a bit, saying, "No, I'm not doing a film. I'm doing the lights," or the sound. I found out because he left a still photograph out for a promo of one of the films he'd starred in. It was hardcore — showing penetration with women. Up until then, I hadn't seen any of that and it chewed at me, and it chewed at me.

John Holmes[i]: I should have been honest with her because when I did admit to what I was doing, her reaction was exactly as I'd feared it would be. "You mean you're having sex with other women?"

I told her they meant nothing to me. I had absolutely no feeling for those women; I was simply doing my job. That was the way I made money. It would take a special person to understand what I was saying. Sharon was special in many ways. She was bright, attractive, level-headed, and stable. But she could not accept my work.

Sharon Holmes[h]: I said, "I want to know exactly what you are doing and how often." John had never lied to me. If I confronted him, he could not lie to me. He'd try to gloss it over and I'd know he was doing it. It ate at me for about two months and then I thought, I'm married to a whore. I mean, that's the only thing I could equate it to. I felt it was a betrayal.

It probably would sound very strange to people that John and I were friends; we were no longer lovers. In 1973, his younger brother was living with us. Mary and Harold were having problems; Mary was pretty sure they were going to divorce. They were fighting day and night. She called John and asked if we would take David while they got this straightened out. I think he came to us in the fall [or] the end of summer of 1972, so by 1973 he'd been with us for at least four or five months. This was okay at that time.

We were on Irving [Avenue in Glendale, CA] at that time. We only had a one-bedroom house, but there was a room in the garage, which John set up for David — refinished the floors and the whole bit. David had a room of his own and we still had privacy; yet David was there and being supervised. At that time, I was much more aware.

John was telling me more of what he was doing, where it was taking him, and making more money at that time. I had reached the point where I couldn't handle it and a physical relationship.

I was hospitalized in February of '73 with pancreatitis. I was literally eating my own guts alive because of the emotional upheaval of my trying to deal with the situation. I couldn't handle it any more. This was somebody I hardly knew any more, except when he was home and not talking about the business. That was the old John; the John I knew.

A doctor sat down and talked with me, "You know, if this keeps up you're going to lose your pancreas. We're talking about you being a diabetic for the rest of your life. You're going to have digestive problems for the rest of your life. There's something you have to do about this. Do you know what is bothering you?"

Surely, you jest! [I thought] Of course I knew what was bothering me.

I came home and I scared John to death because I didn't look anything like myself. I had spent 24 hours of intense vomiting and diarrhea and I was losing blood. I think I probably dropped 15 pounds in four days. I was a sick cookie and I didn't feel so hot.

When I came home, David was still there. I told John, "John, we have to talk about something. What you're doing is ruining my health. I want you to call Mary; David has got to go back home. You and I have to work this out."

We kind of met a parting of the ways at that point. I said, "I have no problem with you living with me, but I don't want anything to do with you, physically. I don't want to hear about what you're doing. You tell me you're going to be gone for five days — that's fine with me. I'll do your laundry. I'll be your mother; I'll be your confessor; I'll be your sister; I'll be your friend, but I don't want to be physically associated with this."

He begged and pleaded, "This means absolutely nothing to me."

I said, "John, it doesn't mean anything to you, but it means a lot to me. I'm married to a hooker. I'm not comfortable with that."

By 1975, we slept in the same bed, we hugged, we kissed, we felt intimate with each other — but not sexually intimate.

It hurt him; I know it hurt him, because he was a very sexual person. It hurt me too, but I couldn't deal with it any other way, and he respected that. John had an extreme respect for me because I was an absolutely monogamous person. He never had to worry about me looking for someone else to meet needs that he felt I should have.

The doctor I worked for knew what John did and only the two I worked with in my pediatric unit knew. My best friend, Nancy, knew John way back when he was a normal person. Nancy is the one that kept me sane from 1981 until 1988. She really liked John and her husband, Joe, liked John as well. Teresa, the other girl, had said something once when she had learned from another source who my husband was. She had never met him — by 1970, John never came into the office. He called the office, he sent flowers to the office and this was his way, if he couldn't get through to call me. A florist would show up with a dozen, two dozen — depends on how guilty he was — five dozen roses at a time. It's not something I talked about to a coworker. This wasn't me and I was divorced from that issue at that point. The people I worked with were very protective of me. Maybe that's particular to medical people. You don't make an issue; private life is private.

Teresa learned from a person outside the office. I think maybe her husband might have had a porno movie and maybe John had come by. Maybe three or four days after she had seen him, she asked me if I was married to, "John Holmes, the porno star," and I looked at her and I exited to the bathroom very quickly, because you don't confront people in medical offices about their private life. Nancy and Doctor took her into his office and discussed the whole thing with her, and said, "This is not something we talk about, so forget you know anything and keep your mouth shut." There was never a discussion about it before.

I was comfortable with, "Well, John's out of town," and let it go at that. I never elaborated with anyone in the office. As I say, they were very protective of me and John was very protective of me. John was always concerned that I would be hurt by this. I was hurt enough as it was, by how it had changed our lives together. It couldn't spill into my professional life. That was mine. That was my life; he had nothing to do with it. I wanted him to be separated from it and he wanted to be separated from it, also, because he was embarrassed.

Just like Sharon kept John's work separate from her life at work, none of John's work associates knew that he was married. In fact, John adapted very well to keeping his work and private life disconnected.

Serena: I didn't know at the time that he was married. I guess he was as long as we'd known each other, but I had no idea whatsoever, and I had no idea that he did any drugs.

Joel Sussman: He didn't tell anybody about his real life. He compartmentalized life. He had these people he'd do this with and those people, and he never would mix people. It would be amazing to have a John Holmes party where all these people he knew would come at the same time. It would be unbelievable because I'm sure that he had really wealthy people he would service.

Serena: Every time I would see John, every time we had a scene together, he would always ask me to marry him. It always blew my mind. I was married at that time to my childhood sweetheart, but we only got married because of a film that we did with Bill Margold. We got busted and I got married to this guy so that we wouldn't have to testify against each other. We were married, but John would always ask me to marry him. I had no idea if he was serious or not, but he would ask me in a very serious way. I would always laugh it off, saying, "Oh no, I'm already married!"

I remember this one time, on a movie that was a really big production, he knew the photographer. Most movies didn't even have a still photographer, but this guy was a still photographer who was covering the whole thing. The photographer's name was Joel Sussman. I was staying with Joel because my husband and I weren't getting along. I was taking a shower, and I had cold cream all over my face. My hair was up in a towel and I came out into the living room. I was sobbing about my marriage because my husband and I didn't get along, and I was really upset.

John came over to visit Joel and we all sat down at a card table. I was playing Led Zeppelin, which was my favorite band at the time. It was this song that made me sadder and sadder. I was just getting blue. Then John started telling me the words of the song, but putting a different slant on it, as if he was saying it and it was a happy song.

He said, "Oh yeah, there's a girl with a towel on her head, and she's really, really sad," and I didn't even pick up on what he was saying at first because I was listening to the song. He was going, "She's got all this cream all over her face, but I love her anyway," and he kept going on and on.

I realized what he was saying when he got on his knees. I went, "Oh, my God! What is he doing?!" I said, "John! You idiot, I'm crying over my husband!"

I thought that was a very sweet thing he did.

John Holmes[b]: [Marriage is] antiquated. It's old fashioned. Eight out of ten marriages end up in divorce. Now, that's astounding. By 1980, eight and three-quarters of marriages will end up in divorce.

I think what it basically comes down to, is we're in a Barbie Doll syndrome. From the time a little girl is born, all she has on her mind is wedding dresses, dollies and babies and, "Let's get married." Mommy and Daddy are married. It's a constant strife on their minds. I mean, their parents had sex before they were married and they only got married because Mommy got pregnant. They thought, "Let's be socially acceptable," — and because they'd get a break on taxes. There are many reasons to get married, but if you really love somebody — if you're really hung up on them — then live with them. If it doesn't work out, if you find out you want to break up, you don't have to go through two or three months in a divorce court and be absolutely miserable.

Bob Chinn: He mentioned something about his wife once and I just thought he was bullshitting.

We went to Vegas to do a little gambling, and mess around. At that time, people didn't seem to recognize him. In Hawaii, a couple of times, he got recognized.

Sharon Holmes[h]: The places we went to were probably — I don't want to say not-upscale, but they were more family-oriented, very small, hole-in-the-wall places where we had found extremely good food.

The only time I ever remember being anywhere where he was a little concerned about [being recognized] was Benihana, in Hollywood, the first time he had ever gone to a cook table there, you know, where they prepare everything in front of you. He was so impressed with that. He insisted that we had to go. There was a method to his madness; we went very early, because the in-crowd, if you want to call them that, were all late eaters. So he was very furtive with that one — making sure he was seated where he could see everybody. I expected to be told any time to run to the bathroom.

We got through that meal and I said, "I don't want to live this way. If we're going to eat somewhere, let's not do it where you feel it's dangerous," so we didn't.

John could change looks very effectively by putting on a hat. His hair was his giveaway. He wore normal-people clothes. This was when Levis came out, so he dressed like a normal human being. He put on a sports shirt that he wouldn't be caught dead in anywhere else. He did not look like everyone expected him to look.

I don't think I really reaped the benefits until about 1975 when we had moved from a one-bedroom unit in the court that I managed for my employer. There was this three-bedroom house that had become available and the doctor asked if we wanted it. I said, "Well, I'd have to look at it." Even though I managed the court, I'd never been in the house. I said, "Well, let us look at it and I'll let you know."

We went down together; John opened the door and said, "I want it. I want it," because this would allow him to do something that he shone at, by restoring everything. He literally was down on his hands and knees, sanding after the electric sanding, staining the oak floors and coating them with urethane.

He put up maple shelving around the living room, one of the bedrooms, actually into the kitchen and the living room as well, for collection. We had a collection of all sorts of things. I remember there was an old-fashioned bookcase with drawers that he redid completely so that he could display some of his collection and mine. He did a marvelous job on that. He put in new windows or restored the old one, stripping the paint off of them on the inside so they were showing the actual wood. That type of thing.

When he was down from jobs or whatever this is what he was doing — normal things at home, doing repairs, going to swap meets, picking up items and refinishing them, and in turn selling them at garage sales. He was very good at it. He was also very good at sculpting; he could re-create things out of nothing. I don't have an eye for that. I'm not artistic, but he was.

About a week and a half before he thought the house was done he said, "What do you want to do with it?" I said, "Obviously we're going to need new furniture," because moving from a one-bedroom place to a three-bedroom, there's a lot of things.

Sharon told Sager that Holmes began working as a courier for the Mob around this time. "He'd come home from one of his movie premieres, take off his boots, peel down his socks and take out a wad of large bills. He'd say, 'Count this.' We're talking $56,000 in two boots."

Sharon Holmes[h]: So he came home the following day and plunked $25,000 in my lap and said, "Do what you want."

First thing I did was buy the washer and dryer because I never wanted to go to a Laundromat again, as long as I lived. I bought a new stove, new refrigerator, furniture and that sort of thing. We had kept things he had refinished or built himself.

I love my kitchen; I'm a good cook, and the kitchen was my favorite place in the house. I loved the house, but the kitchen was my territory only. John couldn't boil water. He was capable of opening up a milk carton and that was about it.

Oddly enough, several people that worked with John, including Bob Chinn, have commented that John would occasionally cook for the crew, such as during their visit to Hawaii, for the filming of the Johnny Wadd film, *Tropic of Passion*. Although Bob had also commented that John made a huge mess in doing so, which may indicate that cooking was not his forte and that this may have been a very rare occurrence.

Sharon Holmes[h]: I went wild in the kitchen. That was one area John knew, if he was going to bring me anything, bring me something for the kitchen and it gave him a new thing to look for at garage sales and swap meets. Old kitchen items like cast-iron pieces, match holders and that sort of thing. He was always able to buy me something for the kitchen and knew I'd be thrilled, as well as anything I collected.

I was in the house until August of 1981. John was last in the house probably up until maybe the second week of July when he fled L.A., so we were there for six years.

John's Girl, Dawn

Sharon was pleased that John agreed to conceal their marriage from the people with whom he worked and she would grow to accept his affairs. John had several lurid affairs, including his long-term relationship with Gilda Grant. However, John's most well-known affair was with Dawn Schiller.

Dawn Schiller[h]: My father had just divorced my mother in Florida; and I chose to go with my father and he chose to move to California.

On our way from Florida to California, through Colorado, we picked up a hitchhiker. We got to talking about if he knew anywhere to stay when we got to California. He knew of a place in Glendale. He had a girlfriend, who would probably allow us to stay, like, camp in the living room for a couple of days until we got settled. We arrived in California and she said yes, but that she would have to ask the manager first.

In walked John. He was the manager of the apartment complex. He didn't talk a lot; he was very shy.

Sharon Holmes[h]: Dawn came into our life in about 1976. She had come from Florida with her father, a sister and a brother.

Dawn was a 15-year old, who had a rotten home life. Her dad was retired from the military. He was one of those expatriates who settled in Thailand after Vietnam because of the drug connection. This was the first time he had been home since the Vietnam War. He picked up the kids and he told the wife — they were divorced — that he wanted to take them to California, to Disneyland.

They moved in — that was an interesting thing — with those five people and with the tenant in a one-bedroom court apartment. She was 15; skinny, skinny 15; big-boned, but a very nice-looking girl.

Dawn Schiller[h]: I can remember the first time he saw me, when he was approving our stay there. He looked me up and down and asked me how old I was.

I said 15 and he went, "Mmm mmm mmm, too bad." He started laughing, turned on his heel and walked out. It pissed me off to no end, which I don't like to admit, but that was the very first time that I met him.

John Holmes[c]: Each person is like a new hunk of clay: something new to work with, formulate, find out about, and create.

Bill Amerson: John had a thing for girls. Yeah, Dawn was 15. I know he liked her because she was young. She was 15 or 16 and he liked young girls. I don't ever remember him saying he loved her, but

I don't ever remember him saying he loved anybody. If he ever loved anybody, it was Gilda.

Joel Sussman: John had problems with being alone. He never would be alone; he had to be with somebody all the time.

Dawn Schiller[h]: After I met him, I thought, what an arrogant… , you know! What made him even think that? I was appalled and I had no idea [who he was].

When he left and we were settled in that night — the fellow that we hitched a ride with — his girlfriend said, "Do you know who that is?"

I said, "No. Why?"

"Well, that's John Holmes.

I said, "Who's that?"

And she said, "Come here." She opened her closet and she had a collection of marquees.

I guess that she was obsessed with him privately, as her manager, but I still didn't know who he was; just saw a bunch of pictures of the guy. I'd never seen a porno, you know.

Sharon Holmes[h]: John started his seduction scene probably about six months after that. He would hire Terry, who was Dawn's younger sister; they'd do gardening for their own money.

Dawn Schiller[h]: He did things, like he would hire my sister —

he never approached me alone. He would always approach me and my sister, to do gardening work and things like that. Then, he'd come in the middle, pay us — a 14 and 15 year old — we'd have some extra spending money.

Sharon Holmes[h]: I think he loved and respected me. We only had one confrontation, actually two confrontations, in all the time we were married. The one, I don't even know what started it. He looked like he was going to hit me and what he did, was put his hand through a wall.

I looked at him and I said, "Never, ever, ever think about doing it again, because sometime you'll sleep and you'll have your skull fractured with a frying pan." I said, "*Vendetta* is an Italian word I never forget. Don't you ever."

Bob Vosse[h]: John couldn't stand a dominating woman that would dominate his life or anything.

Sharon Holmes[h]: The second time was probably a little after Dawn had started working in the apartments, when she was still 15 and before they really had a relationship. The people they were living with, she came over and said, "You know, he's paying a little too much attention to these two girls and I think you should do something about it."

I said something to him, just off-hand that somebody had complained. I said, "I don't know what they perceive or whatever."

He got extremely defensive because I think he was plotting and planning, but at that point he'd done nothing. At that point, everything was innocent. He got very defensive and began to yell at me. We weren't having a knock-down-drag-out fight, but he'd never done this; he'd never raised his voice to me before.

My temper got the better of me. I control it very, very well. I took a 200-pound bookcase — books and all — that was between the front door and the kitchen door, and I picked it up and threw it five feet across the room and broke everything on his desk. I blackened his eye and cut the top of his head with it. I calmly picked up my purse and my keys and walked out the door. All I know was what the neighbors told me; he was frantic to know where I was.

That was the last confrontation we ever had of that nature, whatsoever. Nobody treats me that way, I'm sorry. He was completely flabbergasted; the look on his face was priceless. It was like your dog had suddenly turned killer on you.

He hunted all of Glendale for me. I went to the Eagle Rock Plaza and walked the stores there. Then I went to the Glendale Galleria. He finally caught up with me. He approached me with our next-door neighbor, Lori.

She was the only one who heard it, because my back kitchen door was open and she came over and said, "What has happened?" She hadn't seen me leave. "Where's Sharon?"

John said, "I don't know, she did this and she left and I don't know where she is."

They were out looking for me and they caught up with me about four hours later. Lori told me the next day, "I couldn't believe it. I expected you to be wild-eyed when we saw you."

I just calmly walked up to him and said, "Oh, you're okay now."

He asked, "Where have you been?"

And I said, "Where I've been is none of your business, but I'm ready to go home now."

Dawn Schiller [h]: [My sister] was a year younger than me, but she lived with her boyfriend who was 18. John used her to not scare me. Every move he made was to not make me run away in fear of him. Dad and I lived with the girlfriend [of the hitchhiker from Colorado]. Dad didn't like him, but as long as we were handling our own lives, he was fine. He was not an authoritative figure. When he divorced my mother, he was gone seven years prior to that, so basically, he came back as a friend.

Then, gradually, [John] would come over and he knew we liked to smoke pot. He always came home with the best stuff. "Here, try this," and he would flick it onto the couch, and he would leave — always a dramatic air.

We thought, "He's cool." My sister thought he was weird, because he was too old to be hanging around us and she figured that out, but I liked him and we had this attraction thing going.

He was doing that in order to be charming and I was enjoying it. I'd never had anybody care that way in my background. He would do things, like come back from San Francisco or wherever he'd been filming, and bring stuffed animals and gifts. When he came back, he never discussed any of his films or anything like that. It was considered work and he never brought it home.

John Holmes[b]: I don't even think of myself as a sex symbol. Really, I'm two different people. When I'm shooting, when I'm working, when I'm on a set or opening a night club — I'm John C. Holmes. And when I'm just me, I'm just John. It doesn't occur to me what I do for a living. So when I get old and it doesn't work anymore, I'll start functioning in another capacity.

I'm very adaptable. I do what I do best. When I am no longer able to do what I do best, then it's time to do something else.

Dawn Schiller[h]: I didn't know that was his job. I realized it after the marquees and all that stuff. It just didn't impress me. Apparently he was famous, but not in my circles — my tenth-grade circle in Glendale High School — so it didn't register; it wasn't reality. It was his other work that he kept separate from mowing the lawn, fixing the roofs and fixing the sinks.

Eventually, he courted me. This was a courting and it lasted a good six months. Always with my sister, I mean, she was like a chaperone. It got to the point where he had to pay her a Snicker[s] bar. Arm loads of frozen candy bars, he'd dump there, so she wouldn't bitch about having her apartment used to come over and share some pot.

One day after school, I went to visit my sister, not knowing that he was around and she said something very strange. She said, "I have to ask you something. What do you think of that John guy, the manager?"

I liked him and I was trying to hide it. He was also. I said, "Well, he's married, you know. What am I supposed to think?"

She said, "You like him, don't you?"

"Well, maybe."

She looked up — not at me, but behind me and he was in the kitchen. He just started laughing. He had a very voracious laugh and a smile that was deep.

He came out, I turned around and he gave me a hug and kissed me on the lips. He kept on laughing and walked out the door. I stood there and I looked at my sister, and realized that she had a new pile of Snicker[s] bars next to her.

She said, "He made me do it."

Then we started taking camping trips together to the beach, in a van. He had a Chevy van with a WADD license on there. I guess that was a series that he did. We started rock hunting and he'd invite us to go to a garage sale, but always with my sister. The camping turned into overnight camping and she had to be there, and her boyfriend had to be there. He always made it fun. He built a big bonfire on the beach and we'd have a great big spread, with cheeses and meats and all kinds of desserts. We'd do things, like get stoned and create peanut butter-brown sugarchocolate chip cookies, which was the ultimate when-you're-stoned fix.

He was quite a romantic. He set it up at the beach, that it just so happened that my sister wasn't there and he asked me to go camping by myself. It was like we both knew that it was the night.

We went to Malibu, Zuma Beach and went to Leo Carrillo, a campsite there. It was a full moon, low in the sky. It was perfect and he was very quiet. I can remember just watching him as I walked on the beach, sat on the rocks and watched the moon. It was very magical. Without saying anything, he got down from that rock, took my hand and walked to the van. That was the night. He was extremely gentle and just awesome. I felt as if I was his newborn child or something — that's how precious he treated me.

He took me to my very first porno, which was *Autobiography of a Flea*. I was just so shy. It was my first encounter with his reputation — his name and what it meant to people. People couldn't stop passing our seat. I didn't know what to expect.

I was with him, and it was fun. The very first time he spoke, I started laughing. I didn't mean it to hurt his feelings but it just wasn't him that I knew. He got mad and jabbed me in the ribs because we were in a group of people in the audience. That was for just a split second and then, he started laughing. We both started to laugh and we couldn't watch but the first ten minutes of the movie. We had to leave because we were just cracking up.

Bob Chinn: We were doing the fight scene for *Liquid Lips* or something like that — he brought a girl down, who he introduced as his sister. I think that was maybe Dawn. She looked like a real young girl, but we were just shooting a fight scene. If we had been shooting any sex, I wouldn't have let her near the place.

Bill Amerson: John loved women; absolutely very nice, to all of them.

Alan Colberg: I never double-dated with John. I do believe I met the young lady, the gal that he was hanging with — the gal that he left the state with when all of his problems started. He came over to our house. He was riding his bike and he left the young lady outside.

I said, "Why don't you invite her in?"

He said, "No, she's my maid, she can stay out there. I'm just giving her a ride." That would give you an idea of how John personally treated women. His private life, I never knew anything about; I never knew his wife; I never met his girlfriend.

Sharon Holmes[h]: Dawn was his sexual outlet from what he couldn't get in our marriage. He had everything else from me, but that. In other words, he could have it anywhere else, but that would be associated with the business.

Dawn Schiller[h]: I was a rotten kid. I didn't go to school before my dad came and divorced my mother, and I think that I made all of 15 days in tenth grade at Glendale High School. I was drawn to being around and making myself available to hanging. I was there in case he needed somebody. I'd look out the window to see if he was coming home. I found myself checking. It was intense.

It eventually became that I couldn't do without him. It was like I had to be with the person and the feeling was returned, as much as he could, aside from his work and aside from his wife. He loved me and he proved it in the time that we did have. He was a god to me.

First love? Yeah. Oh boy, yeah! And hard, with a master, you know, just somebody that had more charm in an old shoe than most people do in their whole life. I have to say, to this day, that I was in love with him, although towards the end of this relationship, I've done more than hate him. I can't deny the fact that, out of everybody up to this point in my life, this was somebody I was really in love with.

Family Life

Bill Amerson: John put David through school and loaned him a lot of money that he never paid back.

Sharon Holmes[h]: His brother David, when he was in high school with us in '73, introduced him to marijuana and it escalated.

According to Sharon, David introduced John to smoking pot, however, in the DVD commentary for *Wadd*, Cass Paley said that David claimed it was the other way around; David told Paley that John introduced him to marijuana. Whichever brother introduced the other, the fact remained that Holmes, who had prided himself on a healthy lifestyle and had abstained from using any type of illicit substance, liked it. Over the next few years, John maintained a professional attitude toward his work, but this act of self-indulgence led him to explore addictive and debilitating behaviors that would become a significant crux in his life.

Sharon Holmes[h]: Seventy-six is the year David came back to California from Ohio. He finished high school in Ohio, came back out here and he had married by that time. David had learned a lot about drugs, more in California, I think.

He started, "John, can you get some pot?" From pot, we went to magic mushrooms. "Let's try some pills. Let's do some reds, let's do some blacks. Wow, Quaaludes, wonderful."

It was fine with John; it was not fine with me. In my house, you didn't do drugs. This was not allowed. You want to screw yourself up, fine, but you don't do it in my presence, so David moved into the court where we lived. There was a unit left there. That's where all their drugs were done.

Things just went from bad to worse.

Dawn Schiller[h]: His brother and sister-in-law also rented a place there, so that was another place where we doubled our time.

He always had pot. The pot was just there and I smoked it. Sharon didn't.

Sharon was the manager's wife. She was very friendly with all the tenants and she didn't treat me any different than any of the other tenants. Everybody loved her and I was just — I was tormented. It was something that John never wanted her to know — would never tell her — had to be a secret. She did a lot of nursing, off-duty nursing for everybody in the unit. She is very caring and very nurturing, and you just don't want to do anything like that to her.

Eventually, Sharon and I — this was John's doing — he eventually brought us together. "Hey, Sharon and I are going to a swap meet. Want to go?"

I didn't realize the real relationship that they had, but John didn't want me to. He didn't want me to know that, because he loved her too and he was protecting his idea of their relationship, regardless of what the reality of it was. He would describe how she handled his job working in porn and that didn't phase their relationship, so I could understand how that didn't have to phase our relationship, either. He used her as an example to be understanding of everything. He was a very clever man.

I got to know her better and it was just an immediate liking. I had a great respect for her and I wanted to be in medicine. She was a guide for me, whereas John never spoke of his work at all and he never wanted us to get involved in it ever, ever, although we maintained his files. That was another job he gave me. I got to work as the office. I updated all the telephone numbers and addresses. He entrusted me with certain chores, like writing down people's names and, "Never repeat these to anybody."

My father left. My sister left and I was like, "Oh no, what do I do?"

Sharon Holmes[h]: Their father was connecting with some drug person from Thailand to here at that time, so he had money, but he didn't spend it on his kids and they wanted some independence of their own. When they decided to leave, he brought a Thai wife over to Parris, California, and Dawn stayed in the court.

At that point, David offered her a home with them for babysitting, because they had a four-year-old by a previous marriage. I felt sorry for Dawn because once she moved in with David and Karen, when David and Karen wanted some privacy they would throw Dawn out of the house, so she'd be sitting on the front porch with her fingers in her ears, avoiding the moans and groans. I have to admit, Karen wasn't a good cook, so this child weighed 80 pounds, wringing wet.

I used to pick her up from the front porch, "Come on, have dinner with me."

Dawn Schiller[h]: She knew that I didn't have anything to eat and she would cook extra. It would be at my front door. She saw me walking to work every day — I got a job at a convalescent hospital, because I wanted the medicine thing, although I never told her that. But I really, really admired her. She saw that I was walking everyday and she told John to go and buy me a bicycle, so I'd have transportation. In other words, she made sure that he took care of me in ways that I didn't realize.

I wanted to stay in the back, by the garages, where was 1010E. It was a little hallway with a shower and a hallway — an L-shape — with a kitchen and a toilet, which was like $50 a month. I dropped out of school, got a job as a nurse's aid in a convalescent hospital, and I was able to afford that unit on my own.

Sharon Holmes[h]: Dawn left the court in about the middle of 1979. She had gotten her G.E.D. and was still helping John doing the gardening. Her brother and sister had gone back to their mom in Oregon; their father was in Thailand. She wanted to stay in California. There was a garage apartment in the units, which was basically two rooms, with a living room, kitchen, shower and a bedroom. She moved in there, and was working in a nursing home as an attendant and doing work for John.

Dawn Schiller [h]: Eventually, I was invited over to dinners and stayed to watch TV, which stayed into falling asleep on the couch, while he went to bed. I'd wake up on the couch and I'd have all their dogs piled on me, and you know, eventually became part of the family then. Your dirty socks get piled up with everybody else's and you're helping with the dishes because you've eaten there. She taught me how to cook, "If you are going to eat tonight, you'd better learn how to chop an onion"—the essential things.

I had a moment there when I had my own apartment and eventually, that got let go and I moved into their spare bedroom. John and Sharon had the master bedroom and I had the spare bedroom. It had that little annex back there, which is where he kept all his files, his photos and things like that.

Sharon Holmes [h]: We became really good friends. I was trying to show her that John wasn't God Almighty, and I guess to a 15-year old, when you were showering her with gifts, telling her how wonderful she was, and how she learned fast — she would have done anything he wanted, and eventually did do anything he wanted.

Dawn Schiller [h]: We went all over the place, but we never went anywhere that involved any kind of porno industry. We went to the Saugus swap meet almost every Sunday. We went to Malibu, to the beach, together. After our first night together, he started taking me to the nude beach. Sharon never went with us there. That was somewhere where he was just like my knight in shining armor. He just loved to pick me up, walk out into the water with me. It was a fatherly thing, in a way, but like I said, he treated me very precious, like a newborn child. It was intense. Few people get that experience, ever.

John was very, very fun. We got into challenges and games and things like that. He loved to challenge. "Who won the best actress in 1974?" and we had the same interests in art and decorating, animals and plants, nature and food. I would sum up John as incredible, absolutely incredible. He was amazing. He was intense on every level. He took things to the limit. He did things to their utmost. He never did anything that was boring or half-assed, whether it be a small thing, like looking for rocks, he would find something amazing. He taught me a lot; he was a teacher in a way, to me, on many levels — not just about my self, but about things.

Sharon and John were becoming a family unit for me, which I didn't have. My father had, by this time, departed to go off and find another girlfriend and travel around the world. The holidays would come and Sharon, she was just really thoughtful and observant of you. She liked to give little gifts that made you reflect who you were, so a part of developing my teen years, she was the one to help me. You know, either floundering on the streets or smoking pot and making cookies with John.

Sharon Holmes[h]: They became intimate. It was interesting because I really liked Dawn. Dawn was like a daughter to me. We had a separate relationship and I wasn't aware of the complete involvement probably until 1978 that I became aware of it because John would tell her, "You don't want to embarrass Sharon, so this is private." This was a way to keep the blinders on me so to speak.

"Sharon, teach Dawn how to do the accounting for me. Teach her what the code means in little black book," which was a big black book. "Teach her how to write a business letter," because up until that, he'd bring me something and say, "How do I respond to this?" I would write them — I'm no typist, so he would take it to a professional typist and have it typed up and away it went. Basically, he was grooming her to take my place.

Dawn Schiller[h]: Sharon and John were collectors. John got me into collecting cobalt glass, which I still do, to this day. He was a wonderful sculptor. I can't even tell you how incredible. He would do a fisherman — fisherman's wrinkled faces — in clay, within a matter of days. Incredible bulldogs. He destroyed that after a while. He never did them in hard clay; he did them in soft clay, that gray stuff, and then he would put a glass dome over some of them and they managed to stay for a while. Poetry — he was into poetry. The skulls — we collected skulls, yeah.

Bob Chinn also recalled that whenever they were on location, John would search the gift shops high and low for penguins, because Dawn had been fond of collecting them.

John and Sharon shared a love for nature and animals. In the mid-'70s, Sharon said that she and John sold "Save the Whales" bumper stickers door-to-door and John would wear a custom-made, gold belt buckle that depicted a mother whale nursing her baby in the ocean.

Dawn Schiller[h]: We used to create a lot of pieces. You know the dragonfly ring? That's one of those rings. Well, that was one of those things that he had created by a guy. And his belt buckle — those were things that we put together and then they were gone; they were sold eventually.

John Holmes[q]: It was a dragonfly, whose wings formed the ring and I had 100 stones which totaled nine carats. I had rose-cuts, marquees and peridots; I had coffin baguettes all down the spine. It was real. After a shooting, I would have another stone set in. The ring represented the 100 films I was in. I saved one big place on the center of the dragonfly's back and I put a one-carat diamond in there, but even the bottom of the band was covered in diamonds, solid. The antennas had diamonds in the tips. It was nice and it was two inches long.

The gold dragonfly ring has quite a history of its own, due to its noticeable size and the fact that he had designed the ring himself. Some people believe that *Playboy* mogul, Hugh Hefner, is in possession of the ring. According to Laurie Holmes, Hugh Hefner and other friends in Hollywood financially supported John during the late-'70s, "John told me, 'Hugh is bisexual. When I needed money, I would call Hef and he would help me out for sexual favors.'"

Through *Playboy* publicist Bill Farley, Hefner told *The National Enquirer* in 2006, "I've never met John Holmes. I spoke to him on the telephone once shortly before he passed away. He told me he needed money and wanted to sell me a ring he felt was worth quite a bit of money. I told him I wasn't interested."

John was also known for designing jewelry that he would present as unique gifts to his friends. For example, John made Joel Sussman such a gift, when the photographer divorced from his wife. Sussman affirmed that the ring was beautiful and he was thankful for the alterations that John had made to his wedding ring. Unfortunately, his daughter lost the piece while visiting Africa.

> *Sharon Holmes*[h]: I was into mice and dragons. John was into bells — anything that caught his eye. He liked metal and he liked wood. It didn't matter where it came from; it could have been modern Mexican, it could have been old English, or whatever. If he could restore it, if he looked at it and thought he had an idea for it, it was his. He set up his own woodworking shop and repair shop so he could do this. When he wasn't working, he was coming home and doing what he wanted to do with that off time. That was fine with me because he was home, so I had somebody to mother.

> *Dawn Schiller*[h]: We always went out to eat after the swap meets or a long day and people would walk by. Sharon never acknowledged any of it. People would walk by and I'd notice that he would get really proud.
>
> Because Sharon was there he'd say, "I have to make a phone call."
>
> I saw him, once or twice, do an autograph, but he would walk them away from the table and he would get us up to leave almost immediately afterwards, so that they wouldn't pry. He had to make up a lie for the next time he saw them, I'm sure because they couldn't know who we were or where we lived.

> *Sharon Holmes*[h]: People marveled when they finally realized that I could go through this and not become a total wreck. "How did you live through this?" One day at a time, one hour at a time, one minute

at a time. John always admired that about me. Black was black, and white was white, and if he wanted an honest answer to anything, guess who he came to? He had a healthy respect for that.

I had a healthy respect for his loving nature. Those people he loved, he loved 100 percent, even if he was hurting them. He would do anything to spare that hurt, if he could. Whether it was keeping it secret, or there were things he just couldn't talk about. Obviously not with his family to any great degree because they were about the same way I was and were thankful they were back in Ohio and didn't have to deal with it.

I guess rural Ohio is not a big pornographic pool of interest, so they didn't have to worry about that. It was a little harder when Mary was out here. We did the usual: Disneyland, Sea World, and basically spent a lot of time at home. Mary and I got on very well. She knew that I really, really cared for John. I know she had always been dying to ask me how I could deal with this when she found out about it, but Mary was a little afraid of me because I was so self-contained. I don't show my feelings readily.

She was having a hard time resolving, "This is what my son does for a living. How can you stand it? You're his wife!"

She didn't understand what was going on and I wasn't going to bring it up. If you want to know, if you ask me, I will tell you, but I'm not going to volunteer it. If you want to ask me a question, I'll give you a straight answer or I will downright refuse to answer it.

I blasted her in Christmas of 1979 when she had a scene in my house with Dawn. Dawn was someone who was very well known to John and me. Mary looked her straight in the eye, in my house, and called her a devil — how dare she drag John into all this filth and how dare she walk into my house. John was not there. Dawn had come over to help me with some package-wrapping, and that kind of thing. Mary had been at David's house and walked in, saw her, and lit into her.

Dawn Schiller[h]: The few friendships that I did try to strike up with one of the girls after work, he threw fits over. I realized that he was jealous and I took it as a form of caring. He wasn't cruel then, at that point. He would be quiet, walk away and I knew that I hurt his feelings. When you hurt his feelings, he let you know. He was very, very sensitive and he and I had a relationship that was extremely sensitive. We felt each other's feelings, all the time and were very attentive to them. I wouldn't want to hurt his feelings, so I just came home instead of striking up a friendship with anyone.

When John was not there, he was secure in knowing that I was with her. He would find out from her or his brother. I could go up there [to David's house], which I didn't like to, because he tended to be very competitive with John and made me a toy in his eyes: "Well, if you can make her do that, then I bet I can make her do that."

There wasn't any emotional attachment for his brother. John, I would do for, because I loved him and his brother, David, I had no feelings for. As a matter of fact, I had harsh feelings for somebody who was jealous of his brother's girlfriend — or mistress, or whatever you want to call it. He tried to throw rocks into the relationship and he caused a lot of John's jealous fits intentionally — a few times. He didn't like the fact that I was so doting and was so involved. He was jealous.

Sharon Holmes [h]: I stood in front of her, and said, "Mary, sit down and shut up." She'd never seen me angry, ever; didn't know I talked like that.

I told Dawn to do whatever she needed to, but I said, "Mary, you and I are going to have a talk. I'm going to tell you what goes on in this household, so you'll understand and you'll learn to blame who is responsible for what."

I basically told her, the way things had been, how long it had been that way, and how very degraded her son was at that point. "I'm sorry, I don't care what David is telling you about who is dragging whom down with drugs. Let me tell you: David is the one who started this. John is the connection. Don't blame anyone but John or David. Your youngest son David is probably one of the biggest liars I have ever met and the most self-serving son of a bitch."

I thought she was going to fall off the chair with that one because she'd never heard me swear. "Don't ever confront anyone in my house again. When you know what is and when you have the courage to ask someone about it — don't condemn them without knowing."

"I'm sorry, are you going to condemn me? Did I contribute to this? Is this what you're seeing?" — I don't need that. I don't need that garbage. I was carrying around garbage I would never in my life share with her, that she wouldn't want to know. It's always better to keep the image you have of your children, I guess. You never want to think that your children can do evil or harm.

That was the last time I ever saw Mary. She went home to Ohio and she wrote a couple of letters thanking us for Christmas. By that time, I looked after John's sister's daughter for almost eight months. Julie went home with Mary to Ohio at that time as well.

I didn't have any contact with Mary again. Once after John had been arrested and during the trial, I called her, and I wrote her after John's death, about three or four months after his death. My contact with her stopped at that point, because I couldn't support her and support what she believed.

Julia, Another of John's Girlfriends

Sharon and Dawn knew about one another, but John also had other concurrent relationships that he worked hard to keep secret from Sharon and Dawn. While making the Freeway Films' installments to the *Johnny Wadd* series, he met a teenager named Julia St. Vincent.

Julia's relationship with John exploded towards the end of the '70s, but began with a few brief meetings during the summers when she would work for her Uncle Armand at Freeway. In fact, both Julia and her older sister worked for Freeway Films over the summers. Their mother felt that this would be a good office-work experience for her daughters and believed that their uncle would make sure to keep them out of trouble.

Joel Sussman: Her uncle was a big distributor of all the films. So I knew Armand; Armand was one of my employers. She was just this little 16-year old girl and Armand said to her, "Just stay away from John."

That's the dumbest thing he could have done! You don't tell some 16-year old girl to stay away from somebody, because then who are you going to go to at that point?

Julia St. Vincent: Armand owned a film company called Phoenix that made early bondage films, and stuff like that. Lee [Frost] didn't own it, but he was directing. Then Richard and [Armand] made *High Profanity* and *Peanut Butter Freaks*, which has John in it. Then they started Freeway Films to make some other movies. I was gone, then I'd come back for a summer. That's how I met John.

John was articulate, intelligent and sentimental.

Richard [Aldrich] was kind of like my uncle. I was 17, maybe younger, when I first hung around with those guys. I was a file clerk and at one point, Richard put me into a gore scene on *Tell Them Johnny Wadd is Here*. Armand went ballistic because he didn't want me in a movie because I wasn't of age.

I'm very gullible, even to this day. My family might do things, like at dinner, make a comment, and I'll go, "Really?" and they'll say, "No, we were kidding." They know I'll kind of fall for it.

I never knew why you shouldn't partake in bad things in your life. Now I know it can ruin you, but back then, I didn't know that. No one ever explained that to me and I never could connect the dots — that this behavior leads to that and then this leads to you hating yourself, and then you have a terrible life.

Back then, we didn't talk about sexual abuse. Drug abuse wasn't known, either. I mean, they literally did not have a drug abuse center. I went to a shrink for years, when I was 24 and she smoked pot in session. Her husband was a psychologist, he was on *Time* magazine and stuff like that. This was how I got to her. His wife did these therapy sessions twice a week and I went to another therapist, who did these holistic body therapies, to try to break me of all that.

They say, "Why did you get involved in that? You should have known better!"

Well, we didn't know better. No one educated people. It would have been nice, had I been in a better family environment, if I'd have grown up.

There was no such thing as drug rehab; they never once said, "We can't get through to you, because you're on drugs." I knew not to go there all fucked up, but nobody ever said, "You need drug rehab, that's your biggest problem. That's the reason you're willing to put up with so much shit is because you're on drugs! It's warping your sense of reality."

No one ever said that. It was like, "Oh you're on drugs? Well, let's work on your self."

You have to look at me, even at 25, as if I was 17. I never grew up, so I really couldn't put two and two together.

Here's a young girl, pretty attractive, heiress of a bunch of money, drives a Cadillac — I had money, in cash, if I needed it. There were no bounds on it. I could virtually spend whatever I felt like spending. So from his perspective, here's a pretty vulnerable person, let's go in there; let's go full-force.

Contrary to popular belief, John didn't have a fucking nickel to his name. He used to drive a shitty-fucking car and I used to wonder why. I decided it was because he didn't want people to know who he was. It was because he was famous, and he didn't want people to know. This wasn't the case at all.

One day in 1977, Dawn dropped John off at the set of *The Jade Pussycat* and stayed just long enough for Julia to be introduced to her. It was the first time that Julia met her and she did not bother to give it a second thought. Julia had welcomed the challenge of gaining John Holmes' affections after Armand had said to her, "John doesn't just drop his burrito for anyone," but she wanted it on her terms.

> *Julia St. Vincent*: As far as I could ascertain, John was empty at that time because when we went to that shoot, John was picking up on me. If he was so happy then he would have just come in, done his job and gotten the fuck out, right? But he was trying to get me to sleep with him and he got mad at me because I wouldn't fall for it.

> *Bob Chinn*: As much as John could love somebody, well, they were very close, but John was not a domestic-type of guy. He wanted to keep his options open.

Julia St. Vincent: Bob and his wife, Debbie, were my friends and whenever I talked to them, Bob used to say that John had these affairs with Ann-Margaret or somebody. Bob would tell me these stupid things, which were completely false.

John made a comment to me like, "I have two people at home who will do anything for me." He was mad at me and made that comment to get back at me. He stayed overnight at my house and got up every morning at three or four in the morning and left.

I don't know if Bob knew they were, but when John used to call me every day, I'd hear this screen door in the background. I presumed, based on everything I knew, that the reason was because he was at Ann-Margaret's house and there was this huge lawn, and he was in the servant's quarter. Little did I realize, he was in an apartment in Glendale and they had a crappy screen door! It's fucked up.

[John] spent a hell of a lot of time with me. I believe he knew how naïve I was, but he really didn't get through it. He never shook me up and said "stop it."

He did it one time, when we were on acid, which was a stupid choice, from his perspective — why would you try to convince someone of reality when you're fucked up? He broke my entire consciousness by doing it. He put extra acid in my food. We were at dinner and he took some acid. I knew he did it, but I had to deduce later that he put more in mine than he even took, if he took any at all. I was blazing, fucking ripped—I mean, I was seeing trails and weird shit. He was feeding me.

He used to love to feed people, well, me anyway. I would be like a bird, and he would say, "Open, open, open," and he'd put food in my mouth, and I would eat it. He fed me escargot, and stuff I'd never tried, so he could make me eat it. I was a kid; he was toying with me. He was a lot older than me, so I looked up to him as a "Dad" figure to me. Think about the pathology of why I was there to begin with.

When we came onto [the LSD] we drove from our house and we stopped at a 7-Eleven. I remember watching in the window and thinking, "Wow, that guy's doing everything he says." It was weird. From my perspective, it was like people just do everything he says. Anyhow, we went back to my house. He might have given me more than three or four hits.

I was fucking blazing; dead brain cells were happening. Then he concocts all this bizarre, spiritually-bordering conversation, about God and the stars, and it was just weird shit. On acid, you take things literally. You believe whatever; it's like being on a hypnotic spell. Then he got up and got mad. He said, "Don't you know who I am?"

I took that to mean that he's, like God, or something. I think he was trying to tell me, "I'm just a guy." He was trying to tell me this, but it was bad timing. So it ended up fucking with my head. Then he did some weird shit, we're talking psychopathic. He told me that I wouldn't remember a thing about what I'd just heard and he told me that if I did, he wouldn't believe me. He also made a comment about how people knew something and they got hit by a semi-truck.

The Godfather

Evidently, John kept very busy with his affairs with women and his work in movies, and while at home with Sharon, he did the work of an apartment manager — mowing the lawn, fixing windows, unclogging toilets and repairing holes in the roof — but he always was there for his godchildren. John, who had experienced the neglect and abuse at the hands of his stepfather, was often the only one who cared for and loved the Amerson children.

Sean Amerson: The John Holmes I knew was not the monster often summoned up in people's imaginations. He made sure I had new clothes, money for lunch. When I played ball in high school, it was John in the stands, not my dad. John drove me to karate, picked me up from football practice and always took a general interest in me and my life when no one else did.

Denise Amerson[h]: My dad and he, in a lot of ways, were partners in raising us. He was always there and he enjoyed that. He wanted to have a family and we were the closest thing. My dad wasn't always able to take care of everything all the time, so the only person that he ever trusted to take care of us was John.

It used to embarrass me sometimes and other times, it didn't phase me because it had been that way all my life, but I remember that one Christmas, it got to the point that we went to the market that we had been going to for years and we couldn't shop there anymore. We just wanted to be a regular family, so my brother and my sister and I got John a shirt for Christmas. On the front of it, it said, "No, I'm not him," and on the back it said, "I don't even look like him." If we went anywhere with him, we made him wear that shirt. He got a kick out of that. It's a family joke — he used to tell people that I was his girlfriend [to] embarrass me.

John was a big kid. He would always make sure that he took care of the fun stuff. He was always planning pranks and practical jokes, but there was a real serious side to John; a real fatherly instinct. He was protective of us and made sure for my father that we were always taken care of.

Bill Amerson: He really loved them and they adored him, too. He was there a lot when I wasn't there. If the school called and my son was in trouble, he would go and talk to the principal. He really took good care of them.

Sean Amerson[h]: My dad was extremely larger than life. He was running one of the larger adult businesses at the time. Everybody, it seemed, would line up to sit down and have a meeting with my dad. In order to have a conversation with him, I had to do one of two things. I had to do something really, really bad that required his attention, or set up a meeting — that inevitably he would not partake in.

One of the things that I think was really unique about my relationship with him was that, while they got into doing feature films, I would wake up in the morning, go to school and I'd come home, and they would be filming in the living room. I was in high school, maybe 14 or 15 years old. If you are a 15 year old kid, you're just hitting puberty and you walk into the living room and there's two girls doing each other, it's difficult to have any normalcy in your life.

There was actually a time when my dad was away filming something, or he was in Vegas doing one of the theaters and I had gotten in trouble. John was on my emergency card at school. In some odd thought, my dad put John down. So here I am in the dean's office, in high school and they're either going to arrest me and take me away, or my parents were going to come down and have a conversation with the police and the principal. They called up and said, "We'd like to speak with Mr. John Holmes, please." I'm sitting there and they hung up the phone.

"Mr. Holmes will be here shortly."

This was the late-'70s, so John was really coming on as a popular person back then. He was a media figure and just about everybody knew who he was at that point. The principal looked at me. "That's not *The* John Holmes, is it?"

I went, "It's *The* John Holmes."

In walks John, larger than life, into the principal's office, with a detective from the Van Nuys division. The principal and the secretaries all had eyes like saucers. John conducted himself in the most professional manner. It was amazing. You would never had thought he had that in him if you didn't really know him, but he actually took the time, sat down, discussed with them what I'd done, came up with some sort of solution on how to deal with it, discussed what my payment was going to be for the situation, and they worked it out. They negotiated some sort of settlement and we walked out of there.

Incidentally, I was famous in high school from that day on. We walked out of there and John was like, "I'm not going to tell your dad about this one. I don't think it's a good idea." I think, inevitably, he told my dad because he thought it might come up, but I skated on that way.

John, I think, noticed I was having a lot of problems in school and in a lot of areas, with drugs and things like that. My dad would scream at me for one reason or another. I'd go out by the pool and sit on the diving board. Twenty minutes later, John would come out, with a cigarette, sit down, and say, "Listen, your dad's really busy. He's got a lot of problems. A lot of people depend on your dad," and try and smooth things out between the two of us.

There was a period of my upbringing where I was really dependent on him as a primary caretaker. It's so odd to say, "I got a lot of my morals and the way I look at things from John," because a lot of people would look at me and say, "You must be nuts."

He was the one who would sit me down and talk to me about a relationship I was in with a girl. His perspective on it had absolutely nothing to do with the adult business. My dad would have nothing to do with me about it; he'd say, "Deal with it."

Denise Amerson [h]: We had such a loving family. My dad and John were involved in a lot of things — you know, it wasn't the typical childhood.

I remember one time when my sister broke my friend's arm and I called John because he was the closest to where I was living, and he immediately came over. My friend was so impressed with who John was that she forgot that she was in a lot of pain and needed to go to the hospital. We got her in the car and to the hospital, and just like everywhere else we went, the nurses were interested in talking to him. To get faster service, he told them that she was his daughter. They just flocked on her and they wanted to know everything. It took about two hours to set her arm.

He and I were in the waiting room and he was throwing gum, seeing how many times it would hit the screen on the wall in the waiting rooms. He was causing havoc all over the hospital, while everyone was trying to talk with him because he was John Holmes.

Sean Amerson [h]: He was just a guy who made me laugh all the time, always had a really good story. He was also the guy that picked me up when I was in a really bad spot in my life and sort of kept pushing me along to go forward and making sure I was going to be OK. I don't know what I would have done without him. I'd probably be dead of a drug overdose or in jail someplace because I was so busy trying to get my dad's attention. I could have done something really stupid, if it hadn't been for John.

When I was 15-and-a-half I got my learner's permit. My dad handed me a set of car keys and said, "Drive to the tunnel and back, and if you can make it, you can have a car when you're 16."

I'd never driven a day in my life, so there I was in the driveway in a car, with no experience, whatsoever. I got about halfway down the block and here comes John in his van. [He] pulls over and says, "Come on." He took me out, drove me around and came back, and goes, "I won't tell your dad."

There was a lot of, "I won't tell your dad." I never really knew if he did or not, but I never felt the wrath of my dad afterwards, so I was okay with that. I really appreciated that about him.

Denise Amerson [h]: He wasn't always honest, but he definitely had a heart as big as the world. With his personal life and his family, he was very rarely angry, cold, unloving or uncaring. He was just a good person. He liked everybody.

Sean Amerson [h]: I was constantly saying, "John, why doesn't my dad like me? He doesn't even want to talk to me." John would put his arm around me, tell me things were going to be OK and that my dad didn't hate me.

I had a lot of problems in that time period of my life, in finding an identity. A lot of my identity was so busy, screaming, "Hi, I'm here! Acknowledge me." [John was] the only person that I looked to, because he was the only person that cared at the time, who even paid any attention to me.

Keeping Up

Tom Blake [h]: When I got through with working that portion of Vice, I left and John was about through with his probation. He went his way and I went my way. I think after that he started going down hill. I left the work and heard that he got involved in narcotics.

I talked to him very little after that because what happens — they don't want you to be involved in a field that you are no longer working. I was not working pornography anymore. After I left, I was going to try to pass John off on somebody else to talk to in the porno field and John kind of slid away and said, "Hey, I don't want to talk to you." He didn't have to because he already did his three years. Since I wasn't there, he never talked to them again.

He knew that if he stepped beyond his bounds during the probation time he had the possibility of going to jail. After the probation, I don't know. He went on his way. It's kind of a way of life, you go this way and I go that way. He just ended up going the wrong way.

Bob Chinn: At the time of the first film I did with him, he didn't even smoke grass and told me that he rarely drank alcohol. By the time we were shooting *China Cat*, he was carrying around a flask of scotch and smoking grass.

Bill Amerson [h]: John always drank scotch. John always had scotch available either in his car or in his briefcase. John never carried less than a quart of J & B Scotch in his briefcase. Never wanted to be without, John always had a spare somewhere. John always drank.

It has been said that John referred to scotch as "the urine of the gods."

John Holmes [i]: I had done nothing but have sex for years and I was getting tired. Tired of never getting any sleep, that is. But more than sleep, I needed an energy boost. I found I was able to stay awake longer and think better, and be more stimulated sexually.

Sharon Holmes [h]: He was having trouble sleeping, having trouble maintaining an energy level. He was an enormously energetic person, almost hyperactive, when we first met. Over a period of time you could see the slowing down. It was harder to get up in the morning, it was harder to go to bed and fall asleep.

> *I burn my candle at both ends;*
> *It will not last the night;*
> *But ah, my foes, and oh, my friends —*
> *It gives a lovely light!*
> "First Fig," by Edna St. Vincent Millay, 1920.

John's drug use quickly escalated beyond smoking marijuana with his little brother. According to Bill Amerson, John began using cocaine in 1975 or '76 and began his longest, most committed relationship. He felt that cocaine gave him extra energy and at least initially, it increased his libido. Cocaine was prevalent, although forbidden on many sets, so performers seeking a boost in their sexual energy always could find ways to imbibe.

John claimed in *Porn King* that a female producer first introduced him to cocaine, although there has been much conjecture as to who had actually turned John onto the highly destructive vice. Amidst the finger-pointing, no one would ever admit to having given John his first line; however, John was a grown man, responsible for all his life's decisions.

Bill Amerson: [At first] John wouldn't do anything except smoke marijuana. One night, he came home from work and had cocaine. I said, "What are you doing with it?"

He said, "I really like it."

I said, "I don't want you to do that." I was pissed that he said he was going to do it anyway, but I said, "Well, if you're going to, let me show you how to do it." I thought that if he was going to do it, he wasn't going to do it in the streets where it could kill him.

John was naturally hyper. John was a doer. John was never one to lie around and do nothing, or lie around and watch television. John was always active. His metabolism would make him do these things. For a few years, John snorted cocaine on a daily basis. We could never go anywhere without John taking a serious amount of cocaine. If we went to San Diego for something, he would calculate that he needed three or four grams for the time.

Paul Thomas shared a story about using cocaine with John that traced John's use of the stimulant back to 1976, when they used copious amounts of cocaine together during the filming of *Swedish Erotica* and the Mitchell Brothers' production, *Autobiography of a Flea*. *Autobiography of a Flea* is an adaptation of a 19th century, anonymously-written piece of French erotica that deals with such taboos, including incest.

> *Paul Thomas*: I don't remember anything about any of the films that I did with Holmes, except *Autobiography of a Flea*. I can remember being in scenes with Holmes and I did cocaine with him in the bathroom to get excited.
>
> In hindsight, he was probably on cocaine most of the time. I did lines with John a lot. We used cocaine before every film. He always had it; I had it, too, but I knew he had it, so we used his.

In the mid-to-late-'70s, when John was first using cocaine, it did allow him to keep up with the pace of his personal life and movie career. His star power was fully intact at this juncture in his career and his work associates ignored his drug use because it had not yet become problematic. In fact, some of his best films were made during the period from 1977-'79, while Holmes was suppressing his vices.

> *Annette Haven*[h]: I think John was quite talented in his sexuality and how he utilized it, and he did a pretty good job of acting, too. He really did. He really was intelligent. He had a brain in his head. He did a good job of it. Nobody gave a damn about acting; nobody tried to encourage anybody to act. If you did that, you did it on your own, and John did. That was great.

> *Jim Holliday*[h]: He really didn't hit the stride with the big movies until about the mid 1970s. I think *Eruption*, from [1978], is probably the one that stands out from that decade.

> *Bill Margold*[h]: I was with him the night that he cried when he lost the award for his performance in *Eruption*, which was considered to

be his greatest role. It was the one movie where he had a chance to act. It was the one movie where he had a dimensional character, other than just being a dick. It also featured Lesllie Bovee, one of the hottest in the history of the business.

The Adult Film Association of America — the Erotica Awards were totally corrupt, and they decided to give it to somebody else, a Hollywood actor, if nothing else. It's rumored that Johnny didn't want to come to rehearsal, but they were so crooked, who knows if that's the reason or not.

I was going to congratulate him and they didn't read his name. He started to cry. He said, "I really wanted that, Billy. I really wanted it." It was so sad. He should have gotten something from them, and he never got anything from the A.F.A.A.

Sharon Holmes [h]: He wasn't getting what he felt he needed from the industry, and thought that he should be getting more awards, adulation and money. At the same time, he couldn't see that the drugs were keeping him from being able to perform at the level that had made him what he was. He couldn't handle this.

Jamie Gillis: The industry was trying to remove itself from John in a way. John was now just a "big dick." He was not a "serious artist." He wasn't a "great filmmaker." This was a time when people were thinking that they were doing great art, and didn't want to acknowledge John.

We never discussed it. We never talked about it, but it was a feeling I got. You know, considering his reputation and who he was, he should have been given a lot more attention. He never got any awards, he never got any attention because people were getting past the idea that we were underground and just big dicks. I felt sad about that because he seemed like a good guy. There was just something creepy about the way people dealt with John.

Comedies and Co-Direction

Bob Chinn: I didn't think I could write comedy well, so for the comedies, Dick Aldridge had a friend, who was a milkman [John Chapman], who wrote. I got the idea for *Hard Soap* and *Pizza Girls*, and then he wrote the scripts. With him, I just got the ideas. I didn't tell him how the whole story went. He figured that out and when he came up with *Hard Soap*, I said, "This thing is so ridiculously off the wall, it's surrealistic." I loved it.

During this era of prolific filmmaking successes, the feminist adult actress, Candida Royalle, first met John on the set of porn's version of the television soap opera spoof *Mary Hartman, Mary Hartman*.

> *Candida Royalle*: *Hard Soap, Hard Soap* was actually one of the first big features that I was in. My costar was Laurien Dominique. Laurien played the Mary Hartman character, and I played her best friend. We were best friends in real life and we did theater together. They really liked our chemistry, so they cast us together in it.
>
> I didn't even have a scene with John. I'd never met him before and he kept flirting with me and making eyes at me. Finally, we stopped for a break and he stood up, took me by the hand into this little room and he made love to me. He was very sensual and tender. Intercourse was not John's main deal. He loved going down on women; he loved pleasing women. People would say, "Oh, my gosh! Did it hurt?" It didn't, because he was very sensual, and really seduced me. He got me very turned on.
>
> He was just really sweet. I remember feeling embarrassed when I came out of there, but I think they were used to it. He called the shots, and if he wanted to go off and do something, everyone had to wait.
>
> I know that Laurien Dominique had a bit of a thing with him. I know she really liked John and they had a very sweet, tender thing going on for a little while. I don't think she ever felt hurt or done wrong by him.

John and Laurien first worked together in *Hard Soap, Hard Soap*, as well as Candida. Laurien and John later costarred under the direction of Alan Colberg in the 1979 film *Superstar*, a "mockumentary" that showcases Holmes. During the same time, it is believed that John also may have had a "thing" for sex kitten, Lesllie Bovee. After meeting Holmes on the set of *Tapestry of Passion* in 1976, Bovee appeared as John's leading lady in two of the most successful films of his repertoire: *Eruption* (1978) and *The Senator's Daughter* (1979). *Eruption* (a porn adaptation of the 1944 film noir classic, *Double Indemnity*) was shot on location in Hawaii and features a sunburned Holmes and Bovee as lovers. Holmes did all of his own stunt work for the film. It is reputed that Holmes' role in the film earned him a nomination for best actor at the Erotica Awards. John was discouraged when he lost.

With high incidence, John romanced his leading ladies throughout his best years in adult films. Perhaps it was of no coincidence that besides coherent plots, these quality films featured many of John's fiery hot sex scenes because he spent time doting on each of them to establish a bond.

> *Candida Royalle*: On the other side, he was a lot harder on the people he worked for. I always got the sense that John did feel strange about the fact that he made a living based on his sexual performance — on

the size of his penis. I think he had to compensate for that by kind of throwing his weight around.

I think that John was a completely unique person. I don't think he fit any stereotype, whatsoever. You know for all the negative things that may have come out about him later, there were, I think, as many positive things. There were many endearing and sweet things about him.

After Freeway Films' success of *Hard Soap, Hard Soap*, Chinn shared his girlfriend's suggestion for *Pizza Girls* with Richard Aldrich during a night of debauchery and pizza. Aldrich thought the idea was a great one, but Armand Atamian, having just completed the production of Chinn's latest *Johnny Wadd* film, *China Cat*, passed on Chinn's script. Like *Hard Soap*, the script for *Pizza Girls* was written by the talented milkman. Atamian missed out on some excitement during the making of film, not to mention a truly funny, campy romp.

Candida Royalle: People will often ask me, "What were some of your favorite times when you were in movies?" *Pizza Girls* does pop into my mind because it was just such a fun time. Again, it was Richard Aldrich, Bob Chinn — who were very nice to work with — and Laurien was in the movie with me. It was just this silly movie.

Bob Chinn: *Pizza Girls* is funny. I couldn't figure out whether Desiree Cousteau could act or not, but she was fun. I liked the way she was delivering her lines and everything. Then later, in the editing room, I saw it worked.

Richard Pacheco[h]: The first time I met John was on my third or fourth movie, called *Pizza Girls*. It was probably John's 1,700th or 2,000th movie and it was quite exciting to see him.

I had an emergency call in the afternoon. They said, "Please come to the set. We've had an accident. We mostly need your van, but please come."

I came to the set. They had set fire to Shakey's Pizza Parlor, and they have to leave quick. John, when I pulled up, was schlepping equipment like a grip. I thought, "That's pretty impressive, a big star doing that."

Bob Chinn: Apparently, there was a towel too close to the oven, and it caught on fire, and it was spreading quickly. John put it out. The owner wasn't there, fortunately. It wasn't that big a deal. It looked worse than it was; it just caused a delay of 30 minutes.

Richard Pacheco[h]: Later that day, I had a sex scene with Candida Royalle, and John stayed on the set. It's a funny story. I was new and very shaky about arousal on-camera. Seeing John there didn't exactly help. It's sort of like playing piano in front of Beethoven.

The sex scene started with Candida dropping to her knees, getting me hard and it was real quiet on the set. Everybody's talking in whispers.

The director says, "Roll sound."

"Sound rolling."

"Roll camera."

"Camera rolling."

And then the assistant director goes, "Quiet on the set!" Everybody just starts laughing. Well, I never got it back. The director gave up after a while.

John Holmes came up to me and said, "Good try, kid." I couldn't find a rock to crawl under.

Later in the day, John says, "Hey, how would you like a picture taken with the big fella?"

I wouldn't have even dared to ask. I had my own camera. He put his arm around me and we took the picture. He later signed it, "To Richard Pacheco, who taught me everything I know." This was real sweet. I reveled in that picture for years and sent it to many old high school buddies.

What I liked about being on shoots with John — when you saw a woman that was working with John for the first time — her excitement, her fear, her anxiety, was palpable and unbelievable. This was the moment in a woman's life when she found out if bigger was better, or not. We all live with this myth.

I really liked watching them before the scene and then when the scene happened, it was a magical moment that first time. Depending on the sensitivity of Holmes at the moment, or that of the director, the scenes were stopped and you never saw them, or they went on and they were rather brutal. Pornography is famous for that. But they were magical to watch, no matter what happened. Holmes leaves us this legacy. John Leslie once referred to Holmes as the "Babe Ruth of Porn," and that he was.

Carol Connors had made appearances on *The Gong Show*, an amateur talent show adjudicated by a panel of three celebrities. In 1978, Carol starred as her most famous X-rated character, "Candy," in *The Erotic Adventures of Candy*. Although *Erotic Adventures* was allegedly directed by Gail Palmer, Bob Chinn did most of the work without being credited. Palmer was the girlfriend of a producer, so she was occasionally given credit for directing films. In *Erotic Adventures*, she makes a non-sex appearance, wherein she introduces herself and offers narrative throughout the film about how a young girl named Candy loses her virginity and finds spirituality.

Bob Chinn: I've done fake co-direction and real co-direction. Fake direction is people who want to put their name on it. The real co-direction was with a guy named Jaacov Jaacovi.

Jaacov was the cameraman on this one or he was the editor, something like that. He wanted me to direct and he wanted John to star in *Little Orphan Dusty* with Rhonda Jo Petty. He'd just finished editing his last film. He's a director, too, but he didn't want to do the sex scenes.

I said, "Jaacov, if you only want to pay me half of my director's fee, you're going to have to direct half of the film."

So we split up the script. He did some scenes and I did some scenes, which worked pretty well because we were shooting around the same time. He would go out and shoot the stuff without the sound and I'd shoot the sound. Sometimes he would shoot the sound and I'd shoot the stuff without the sound.

But what was funny was he wanted to bill poor little Rhonda Jo as a Farrah Fawcett-look-a-like. She doesn't look anything like Farrah Fawcett, except the hair!

It was fun, and it was a real small budget. Jaacov didn't have much money but we managed to make the film.

Rhonda Jo Petty[1]: If I recall it was the first fist film I'd ever done. I was done on a motorcycle. I was done by myself and I was done by John Holmes.

Rhonda Jo Petty, a cult favorite among some motorcyclists, possessed a girl-next-door quality about her that delighted and excited her fans. For *Little Orphan Dusty*, Chinn directed her fisting scenes, which have been cut from many older versions of the film for being too graphic.

Bob Chinn: Jaacov couldn't do a fisting scene; he couldn't figure out how to tell them how to do it. I'd already done it in *Candystripers*.

Rhonda Jo Petty[1]: I was a nervous wreck. When I first met John, I was scared that John thought I was a little stuck-up bitch because I was so shy and scared. I was scared to death because I'd looked at this guy — I didn't really know him and he thought I was being quiet because I was a stuck-up bitch.

Once we got to know one another and he found out I was just scared to death, he was really so gentle and kind and loving, and so good with me. We ended up having a wonderful relationship for quite a few years after that. He was a wonderful person.

In 1978, Holmes was freebasing cocaine daily, but he was able to manage friendly relationships and professional work habits for the most part.

The Real *California Gigolo*

California Gigolo is a take on the television series, *Fantasy Island*, in which Don Fernando played the porn version of Tattoo. *California Gigolo* was not the first film in which Holmes and Fernando worked together, but this film gave them a chance to get to know one another better. It was summer of 1979 in San Francisco and John was habitually late for filming.

Don Fernando: Because he was my idol, I was scared to death. I was awestruck at meeting my idol, but he was extremely affable and very loquacious. Later, with Bob having hidden his problem with the cocaine, he was sometimes less talkative, but other than that he was a very friendly guy. He was clever like a fox, too.

Bob Chinn: I had so many problems with that shoot that, when I was in the editing room looking at the cut on *California Gigolo*, I said, "This film sucks. We've got to do something to pick it up!"

And the only thing I could come up with since I only had a half an hour to come up with it, was to go down to Venice Beach and shoot some stuff with pretty girls roller skating, put a song behind it, and maybe if people watch that they can forgive the rest of the film!

Don Fernando: He was an extremely gifted actor. When Bob gave him a script, he would do a "James Dean" on it.

I remember, Bob would tell him, "John you know what to do."

Bob would say, "Just improvise."

I learned a lot about acting from John, actually. He was a naturally gifted actor. He would take me off-camera, we would do one take. I was very young; I was around 31 years old then. I was young in the sense that I hadn't really acted that much and I didn't know about it.

He would take me aside and say, "Don, you should play it like this. Play your character this way."

I remember when Bob would ask if we were ready to start, he would say, "Can you give us about ten minutes?" Then he would direct the scene.

John would let Bob think he was directing. He was as sly as a fox. People can say what they want about John, but he never wanted to hurt anybody's feelings. He was very sensitive that way.

Alan Colberg: John had a huge amount of respect for [Bob Chinn]. He trusted Bob to do it right. John respected me too, but sometimes he would disagree with something I was doing and one time, he walked off the set.

John would have made a great director on any level. John would take over the set. If John were alive today, he would definitely be directing.

Joel Sussman and Serena have also commented on how John would take responsibility for his scenes in subtle ways to control the directing. In many of his films, John appears to angle his and the women's bodies for the best shot and oftentimes, he brushes aside their hair to afford the cameraman a clear shot of their expressions of ecstasy. Sussman believes that John's onscreen sexual performances were, "sensuous, erotic and never vulgar."

Don Fernando: The only side of John Holmes that he ever showed me was that he was always respectful of me, always. He was definitely a porn diva, especially if there was a star on the set, like Seka. He would puff his chest out. If there wasn't a famous star on the set, he would be so casual, almost meek, but if there was a real star on the set, he wanted their attention. He wanted to impress them. He'd put on the macho act, puff his chest out. He had no muscles, you know, but he would just stick his chest out. He'd grow two inches and I'm not talking about his cock; he didn't always have good posture.

I can remember we'd be sitting around on the set, having lunch and he would always sit at the head of the table. Nobody would say anything because he would command them. He told some incredible stories. Some of them were such bullshit, I just dismissed them. As an aside, he was a little bit of a walking encyclopedia with facts and trivia. He did know a lot about a lot of things. He would start telling his stories and then people at the table — especially Bob — would question the validity of what he was saying.

Then he would blush and say, "Yeah, but I almost had you guys, though, didn't I?"

He was an incredible storyteller. I think some of his stories were true — he said he was a Hollywood gigolo. We did a whole thing about that; *California Gigolo* was based on him. It was a story by Bob Chinn.

In a case of life imitating art, Holmes' reputation as a gigolo preceded him, and rumors swirled that he serviced rich women for money — or diamonds, as in the case of his dragonfly ring. At that time, mainstream celebrities rubbed elbows with the porn stars at parties. Like everyone flocking to adult theaters, celebrities were also fascinated with the sex performers and sometimes visited adult film sets to meet their X-rated counterparts. John claimed to have mingled with many famous personalities and he continued to demonstrate his machismo and virility on and off camera.

Don Fernando: As far as I knew, he was a swinging single. Cuckolds would pay him to fuck their wives in front of them. Rich guys and some Hollywood celebrities would contact him through Bob Chinn, and they would sometimes pay him thousands of dollars to fuck someone's wife.

I believe that because I know that in those days, at places like the Playboy Mansion, they had some crazy sex parties. Not just at the Playboy mansion, but also at swing clubs around the Hollywood area and in San Francisco — one of the houses that Bob Chinn used to book for a lot of films was a swing house in San Francisco. It was in Pacific Heights. Just to go to a swing party was around $100; that was a lot of money in those days.

John Holmes[i]: I was first smitten by an actress, then a well-known pop singer. When those pairings failed, I began seeing a real knockout lady with a sensational body. A dancer, she had starred in films and was headlining in Las Vegas. She was also unhappily married. For that reason, we agreed never to have intimacies at her house, only at the apartment she leased for me.

Six months into our relationship, she invited me to her home. It was safe, she told me. Her husband was away on business. Besides, we'd been drinking and everything was fine with the world. My leggy friend and I were in bed when we heard a sound at the front door. Jumping from her arms, stone naked, I ran to the sliding glass door that led to the terrace. Outside in the darkness, I began to step into my pants.

I heard gunfire. Then I felt a searing pain in my leg. The force of the blow hurdled me over the rail and down the ivy-covered hillside. Still bloodied and in pain, I managed to climb back up the slope to my car and drive to the nearest hospital — where I passed out on the steering-wheel horn. When I woke up, I was facing two policemen. I told them I was a stuntman in a movie and my gun went off. One of the cops said, "Stupid. Be careful next time," and with that, they were gone.

In 2006, Laurie Holmes revealed to the *National Enquirer* that "Legs," the dancer with whom Holmes had a year-long affair with, was none other than the beautiful, nearly six-foot tall Juliet Prowse. At the time, Prowse was married to her first husband, John McCook, who died shortly after their divorce, but not before denying his wife's involvement with Holmes. Holmes and Prowse allegedly ended the relationship when she married her second husband.

Don Fernando: I remember him being afraid that he would hurt a girl. He would start stroking them. He would watch their eyes and if he thought the girl had any kind of discomfort, he would always ask them, "Is it okay? Do you want to stop?" He was a sweetheart.

We used to stay at the Voyageur Inn and I remember one time, I walked into the bar downstairs and I saw John with a girl at the bar. She was short with dark hair, a Mexican American girl and I thought, "Oh, maybe that's his girlfriend."

The next morning, she was on the set and she's only about four-foot-ten, but it's the only girl I ever saw take John to the hilt when he was fully hard. I'll never forget this. Bob was covering his mouth so he wouldn't laugh because he'd never seen that before. Remember, Bob knew him from the beginning.

We're all thinking, "Where did it go?" She had multiple orgasms; orgasm, after orgasm. That's the hardest I'd ever seen him.

He always said he was 14-and-a-half inches, but I think he was 13 inches. That's a lot; take out a ruler and add an inch.

Bob Chinn: I remember once, after Freeway Films had moved its office to Highland Avenue in Hollywood, Jeff Neal [who wrote *Blonde Fire*] and I were busy editing a film one afternoon when a young woman from Minnesota walked in, asking to meet John Holmes.

I gave John a call and the first thing he asked was, "What does she look like?"

I replied, "She's not unattractive."

He said, "Would you do her?" to which I replied, "I probably would," and then he said, "Well, I'm on my way."

She had come all the way from Minnesota just to meet John Holmes, who she had seen playing Johnny Wadd in my films. She had done her research to find Freeway Films, thinking, I guess, that John must surely be there. Jeff and I were just blown away.

John showed up and I let them use my office for their meeting, while Jeff and I continued on with our work. About an hour or so later, she exited the office with a big smile on her face, and John sheepishly followed. She turned, kissed him goodbye, and left.

"What was that all about?" I asked John.

He replied, "She just wanted to fuck me."

Busted

Some time after John had finished his probation for pimping and pandering, in which he had offered up information to Detective Tom Blake to avoid a jail sentence, John and some of his associates were arrested during the making of *Honey Throat*. The 1980 release about a "full service" salon for women starred Holmes with Eric Edwards and Serena.

Eric Edwards [h]: Once upon a time, a group of us were filming in a small town, in a beauty shop at night. We took all the precautions; we put up Dubitine — a black material — over the windows. John was on the set along with the talent and also five or six crew members.

Serena: I lived in New York and was in Connecticut to make a film. Most of the movie was shot in a beauty salon and we were shooting at night after the beauty salon had closed. We had put up blackout curtains. They taped it to the windows so you couldn't see in.

They turned on these big, huge movie lights. I don't know if they even have them anymore, but they make you sweat. They were really, really bright and extraordinarily hot. They turned those on and I lay back in the chair to get my hair washed, and John came over and was going to have intercourse with me.

All of a sudden, there's a rap on the door. It's right in the middle of our scene and there's knocking. We're going, "Oh shit."

So we open the door, and there are the cops.

Eric Edwards [h]: Come to find out, a couple of policeman wondered why all these cars were parked in the parking lot that is normally empty at that time. Later on, we found a small hole in the Dubitine that they peeked through for nearly two hours before they called in the paddy wagon.

Serena: Whoever taped up the windows didn't go to the very bottom, and there was half an inch of light pouring out. The cops were making their rounds, checking on businesses and they saw the lights coming from the beauty salon. They knew that wasn't right.

Eric Edwards [h]: The next thing we know, we're being arrested. This poor town had some of the largest stars in porndom under their jurisdiction. They packed us all into this bus, John and I included.

On the bus trip over to the jail cell, I remember, specifically, one of the guards saying, "Hey, you're John Holmes, aren't you? And you're Eric Edwards. I got all you guys' tapes. You're cool."

Serena: I get to the jail, and we're all talking about not saying anything, and I was crying. I was really upset, hanging out of the bars of the holding cell, along with the girls that I was with.

Down the hall, there are more cells and then there's the reception area where you get your fingerprints and all that, and the cops are all laughing. It's like they're laughing at us. This really stunk.

Then I'm kind of listening to them and they're all going, "Oh yeah, John Holmes, man! He's the best!"

John was out, strutting around the hall. Everybody was locked up, including the men, who were in another cell. John's cracking up, talking with the cops, and all the cops — including the women cops who take the fingerprints and work in the station — were all asking John for his autograph.

Eric Edwards[h]: Come to find out, they were breaking every rule in the book: they put five people in one-man cells; putting all the girls together; putting all the guys together. They weren't equipped to bust a large set of people. We were pacing back and forth in a cell built for one and the night guard was another fan, getting John's autograph through the bars. It's kind of weird — here these guards are the biggest fans of this man next to me, and yet we're on this side of the bars. There's something wrong here.

Serena: We did get released and I didn't even have to go to court. That was the real John; that was real stardom. The rest of us could just sit in the cells, they didn't care, but he was something different.

International Appeal

Nineteen-seventy-nine established a milestone in John Holmes' film career when he was hired to travel to Europe to star in three vehicles, along with "The Grand Dame" of adult cinema, Gloria Leonard. Leonard began performing in X-rated movies in her late-30s, but her maturity was not a deterrent. She epitomized feminism and served to debunk the theory that all women who work in adult films are coerced into the field by an oppressive male. Leonard was a former Wall Street stock broker and copywriter for Electra records prior to her initiation into the adult film genre, where she proved to have better-than-average acting abilities, in films such as *The Opening of Misty Beethoven*.

She met John while filming *Johnny Does Paris*, the first of a trio of films the pair made while in France.

Gloria Leonard[h]: I didn't meet John Holmes until very far along in my career, because I was East Coast and he was West Coast. Somebody decided to make a movie in Europe with John and me. I didn't meet him until Paris. I was somewhat apprehensive, here was this legend, "The King," and of course, some of my girlfriends at the time, such as Lesllie Bovee, Samantha Fox, and the other women who had worked with him said, "Just be prepared. He's really big, and a little crazy."

When we first met, we hit it off immediately. Actually, the first day we met was on the set of the film. It was palpable — the sexual tension — because this was the first time for both of us. That's how we met, and later on, he demonstrated his ability to be a prima donna, at which time I told him this set wasn't big enough for two, so he backed off a little.

While in Paris, Holmes and Leonard completed the filming of *Johnny Does Paris* and *Extreme Close-up*. In *Extreme Close-Up*, a rather interesting but slow-paced feature, John and Gloria portray an artistically talented couple playing a sexual-psychological game with a beautiful brunette writer, played by Delania Raffino.

> *Gloria Leonard*[h]: We shot in Paris probably for a week or 10 days, and we caravanned out to this chateau many, many miles away on the coast of Brittany, and we were living in this chateau, which was quite grand. Everyone was French, with the exception of a handful of American actors and actresses.

In Brittany, they filmed *La Belle et le bête*, which concluded their trip to France. While filming at a chateau in Brittany, the director abruptly cut her sex scene with John, just as Leonard was getting into it. Unfazed, Holmes took Leonard by the hand and led her to an empty room, where they completed the action off-camera. When they were finished, Leonard opened the door and discovered that several crew members had been eavesdropping on their private lovemaking session.

> *Gloria Leonard*[h]: After about five days of shooting in Brittany, somebody came down with the clap. On a porno shoot, this is tantamount to the bubonic plague. The Americans blamed it on the French; the French blamed it on the Americans, and so we sat down and tried to figure it out — who had slept with whom and who had possibly been exposed. We came up with, I think, 21 people who could be at risk. Well, we dug up an old country doctor who, I don't think, saw 21 people all year, let alone all of a sudden, for something like this! In order not to embarrass ourselves and the doctor, we arrived in groups of twos and threes.
>
> However, in France, they don't administer a shot of penicillin; they issue a prescription for it, along with a hypodermic needle, and you're sort of left to your own devices to find a nurse, or somebody to give it to you.
>
> We'd gotten all our medicines, and John, being the ever-boastful character and the ever-rich imagination, proceeded [to say] that he had once worked as an ambulance attendant and that he was quite proficient in administering hypodermics.
>
> I allowed him to administer my injection. We were in this opulent 16th century chateau, looking up at the chandeliers, my ass is up in the air, and he plunges the hypodermic into my tush. I'm lying there, thinking, "This may be the only case on record where the person who

has, perhaps, given me the disease has given me the cure!" That's my most memorable moment with John.

Evidently, John had fond memories of his sojourn in France with Leonard. Several months after they had arrived home, Gloria Leonard received a huge box of photographs from John that documented their time together, and he also sent her a sterling silver straw from Tiffany & Co.

Gloria Leonard[h]: John was very self-conscious, very insecure. He would bite his fingernails and cuticles down to the quick. Regardless of what time he had to be on the set, he would always find something to procrastinate. It was much more difficult to get him on the set than the women, very often.

Overexposed

Unfortunately, in the years he was energized by cocaine and made his best films, John had begun to show his prima donna tendencies and seemed to have sensed that the changes in his life would take him to a new, darker place. But John never asked for help. The fall was so remarkably fast that friends did not realize he needed their support until it was much too late.

Bob Chinn: In the beginning, he was a lot of fun. The porn industry itself was young and he was young, and we were having a lot of fun making these things. Success can lead to corruption. He had a degree of success, but boy, the downhill slide was sudden and fast.

Don Fernando: John seemed to never have money. On the set, he would always hit Bob up for money. He'd ask if he could borrow some cash. He would just roll his eyes and say, "Later," because Bob knew what he was going to do. He was going to do a disappearing act, where he'd go to The Tenderloin. The Tenderloin is a drug area in San Francisco.

He would do it in the bathroom, until he was freakin' high, but he didn't want anyone to see him. Bob Chinn would cover for him and say, "He has [an] anxiety disorder." Bob would say things like, "Oh, he's not feeling himself today." John would be stoned and trying to cope.

Bob Chinn: I first became aware that he had discovered cocaine around the time we were shooting *California Gigolo*, but then again, just about everyone else had discovered cocaine by that time, so it was really no big thing.

Or was it? John became obsessed with cocaine. Whereas most of us realize we will never recapture the initial high that we first felt with the drug and eventually get to the point where we can either take it or leave it, John could not leave it. He wanted more and more. It became a very expensive habit. He had always smoked, but with cocaine, he chain-smoked.

Alan Colberg: Coke was always forbidden, and I know that people, including John and others who I will not mention, were doing it behind my back. It was always problematic.

I remember seeing a movie that he made. I forgot who showed it to me, whether John showed it to me, or the producer or the director showed it to me. There were two gals and two guys — John and another guy. They were so pumped up, so obviously high and they're just screwing and screwing and screwing and screwing. This one's screwing that one, and that one is screwing this one. It was more like an Olympic event than anything else. It certainly didn't have anything to do with lovemaking. I saw these, and I said, "My God, they're all so high, it's surprising anybody can do anything." I could just see the cocaine floating in the air above them. It was sad, because it wasn't sexy.

Jamie Gillis: Everybody was in one way or another involved in drugs. I had some early pre-porn drug experience that kind of scared me, so I swore off drugs. Sex was my drug. I loved the sex part of it so that was enough for me, but I saw people, beautiful people, totally destroy themselves. It was a terrible time for drugs. People weren't themselves anymore. They were changed into some sort of drug monster. Nothing else mattered but the drugs.

Alan Colberg: I don't care if you were John Holmes or some executive producer of a TV show — cocaine to Hollywood was the death. The best thing that ever happened to Hollywood was [that] cocaine eventually fell out of popularity; it was no longer cool. If you were using coke, everybody waved goodbye to that person because in a little while, [he'll] be gone.

The last time we saw John, he came to our house, and said "I'm on a set, and I need to borrow some props." He took a few things from our house that we never saw again. That was kind of the last time we saw John. Things had just fallen apart. I was no longer as active in the business, I was having some physical problems because of drug use, and we just kind of passed in the night. There was nothing left to talk about. The people that John was hanging with then were very undesirable.

Co-workers and friends could no longer dismiss John's disintegration into a drug haze, which happened swiftly. It seemed that John's extraordinary fame, pitted against his insecurities, had suddenly caught up with him and he grew weary of being John Holmes.

Bill Amerson: Every time we'd get on the elevator, girls would say, "You're John Holmes! Can I see your dick?" Never a, "How are you?" That really upset him. The adoration changed him. John wasn't really a likeable kid. He had grown up and he didn't have a lot of friends, but all of a sudden, everybody wanted to be his friend. The fact that he was a star — that changed his personality. He was tall, gangly, not good-looking, and he couldn't act worth a shit. But nobody cared; he had a big dick.

Bill Margold[h]: I think basically, what Johnny was, was a victim of his own fame. I think that he was a person that had no understanding of what fame is. Fame is omnipresent; you have to answer to the bell every day when you're famous and sometimes you don't want to get up. And in order to get you up, you use things to get you up to avoid the reality of being up. Johnny had to deal with that. He was preyed upon by an awful lot of people who just wanted to be around The King. That was very, very sad, and I think he was overwhelmed by it. He was overwhelmed by the fact that he was as famous as he was, and it destroyed him in the long run.

John Holmes[c]: On a one-to-one basis, 99 times out of 100, they don't accept me for who I am. They see me as a fantasy. They see me as someone on a screen. It's really hard to achieve what I want sexually and mentally from a relationship with someone who's trying to fuck a Walt Disney character, which I'm not. I'm just a human being.

Jim Holliday[h]: I once asked him if he felt abused and taken advantage of, and his answer was that he thought he had lost millions on contracts, getting screwed here and there from the companies who were marketing his product. Just his very nature, he was such an unassuming guy. I don't think he was caught up in the legend — he was not the kind of guy that would go downtown to a place — like the Original Pantry, that's open 24-hours a day for 70-odd years, never without a customer — and walk in and say, "Hi, I'm John Holmes, the Porn Star." That was not what he was all about.

Julia St. Vincent: He hated the industry. Well, I don't know if he did at first. When I first met him, he was just there, in a stupor. As time went on, he was bitter, jealous and upset because they never recognized him. We didn't even want to hire him. The reason we did was because I could control him to an extent, but not really. If he really wanted to be an asshole, I couldn't control him.

He aspired to be a director. He actually begged me, one time, to make him a director and I wouldn't. He was so upset. I was going to have this guy, Jeffrey, be a director for me, for a project I was trying to find funding for. John got wind of that and wanted me to put him in it. I couldn't though. He'd have blown the money and been an idiot. I remember thinking for hours, "How can I get John some job? He needs a new identity." What would you do with a guy who's been a well-known porn star? I could reinvent myself 100 times, because who knows Julia St. Vincent? But when you're a porn star, everybody in the world knows you. I couldn't figure out what to make him.

Sharon Holmes[h]: [Our lives moved in] much more separate directions, especially when he got deeply involved with the drugs. I was continuing my life and he was coming in and out of it, like a visitor, like a brother or like a family member. I was John's safe house and the only person he could be himself with — could show his vulnerability. His low self-esteem was there.

I don't think anyone else was aware of it, but John had developed a different persona. "This is John Holmes, who I have created." This is the side people saw; they didn't know about the other side and I don't think they knew his capabilities, as far as what he could do artistically, other than artistically pornographic.

If he was on a shoot that was nearby, he came home and he went out that next morning. Because this was safe, he could be John. We were a happy family. We were still very, very close. The relationship became that of a best friend, a confessor, a support. I was his crutch. I was his window to "normal home life."

Bill Amerson[h]: He had no friends except me. That was how he wanted it. He didn't like people because people didn't like him. He felt all they wanted to do was see him as a piece of meat. He didn't like it. He wanted to be a real person, but that was impossible. After all the hype, the movies and everything else, that was it. People would get a hold of him, wanting him to come to their parties as a novelty item, to watch him fuck. He didn't like it. Would you? He didn't want to be known as "Johnny Wadd." After a while, he just wanted to be a person. That never happened.

Joel Sussman: He's a shooting star, isn't he? The ultimate "young boy comes to Hollywood," is successful, but burns out because he couldn't handle it. Emotionally, he was a child; he was never a man. Everywhere I look, that's the John I like. That's what he and I shared together; we shared the good little boy. He was a real bad little boy, too.

The court finds that the correct record of the birth of the applicant is as follows:

1. PLACE OF BIRTH:	2. USUAL RESIDENCE OF MOTHER: (At time of delivery)
(a) County.... Pickaway	(a) State.... Ohio
(b) .... Ashville (City, Village, Township)	(b) County.... Pickaway
(c) Name of hospital or institution:	(c) .... Ashville (City, Village Township)
(d) Mother's stay before delivery: In hospital or institution.... In this community....	(d) Street No....

3. Full Name of child. Holmes Surname	John First	Curtis Middle	4. Date of birth: Aug. 8, 1944 (Month) (Day) (Year)
5. Sex: Male	6. Twin or triplet	If so—born 1st, 2nd, or 3d	7. Number months of pregnancy 9	8. Mother married? NO

FATHER OF CHILD

9. Full name.... Surname First Middle
10. Color or race .... 11. Age at time of this birth.... yrs.
12. Birthplace.... (City, town or county) (State or foreign country)
13. Usual occupation....
14. Industry or business....

MOTHER OF CHILD

15. Full maiden name.... Holmes Mary June Surname First Middle
16. Color or race .. W. 17. Age at time of this birth 25 yrs.
18. Birthplace.... Washington C.H. Ohio (City, town or county) (State or foreign country)
19. Usual occupation.... Railway Clerk
20. Industry or business....
22. Attending Physician or Midwife:
Name .... Dr. Hostler
Address .... Ashville, Ohio
M. D. midwife, or other....

21. Children born to this mother:
(a) How many other children of this mother are now living? 3
(b) How many other children were born alive but are now dead? 0
(c) How many children were born dead? 0

John's mother, Mary, was separated from her husband at the time of John's conception. In 1986, before his final trip to Italy, John was given the original, handwritten copy of his birth certificate — which lists his biological father's name, Carl Estes — instead of this corrected version. It was then John learned that he and his older siblings did not share a biological father.

John's family in rural Ohio called him "Johnny Buck."

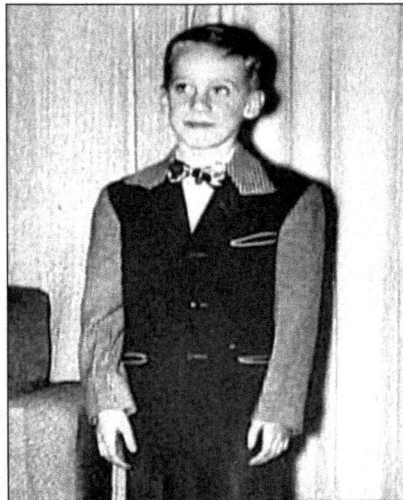

Mary Holmes saw to it that John and his siblings had perfect attendance at their Baptist Sunday School.

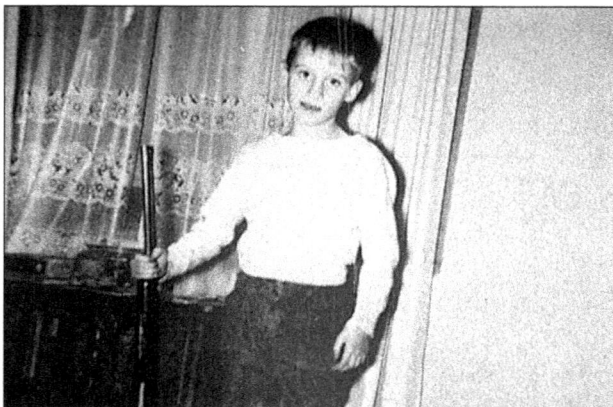

John at age seven.

John (age nine) caring for his brother, David, on the porch of the family home in Pataskala, Ohio.

Ten year old John with his puppy.

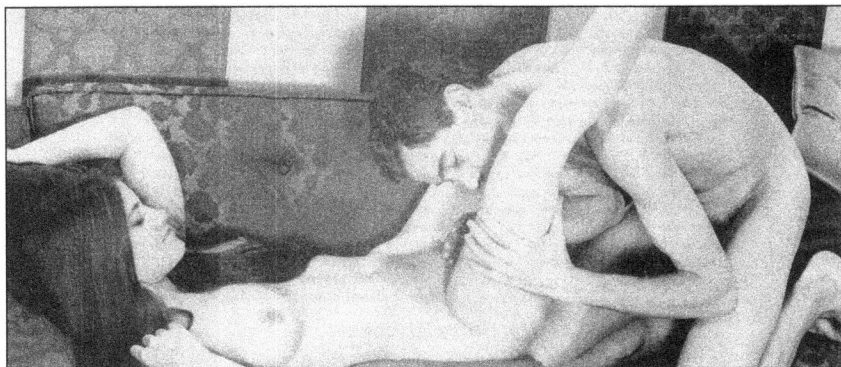

In the early days of John's career, photographers were careful not to show any pubic hair — and took great care to conceal John's penis, as this 1965 still illustrates.

Artist's rendering of an incident in 1968 when John's wife, Sharon came home from work and found John measuring himself in the bathroom. He announced that he had found his life's calling — adult magazines and movies. He had already begun to appear in hardcore films.

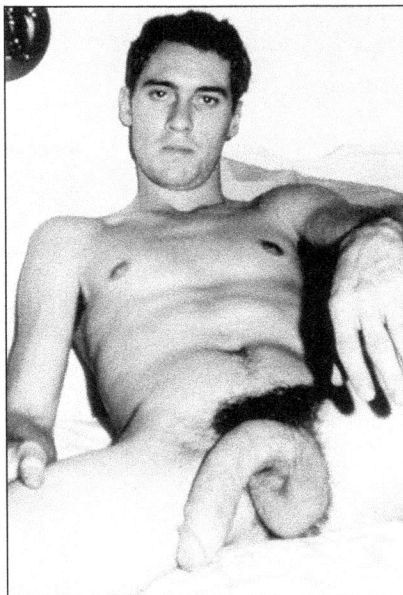

This photo from the early days of John's career showcases his amazing size and physical fitness.

John plants a tender kiss on the lips of his frequent costar and girlfriend during the early days of his career, Miss Sandy Dempsey.

Private Dick, Johnny Wadd, demonstrates his persuasive powers toward Andy Bellamy in the 1970 film, *Johnny Wadd,* the first of the nine-part series directed by Bob Chinn.

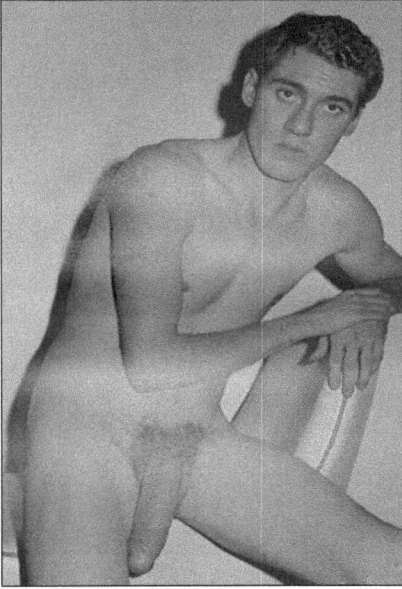

Before the days of Photoshop, John shows off what he's got.

This early '70s promotional photo evokes his most famous character, Johnny Wadd.

A still from the 1975 film, *Confessions of a Teenage Peanut Butter Freak.*

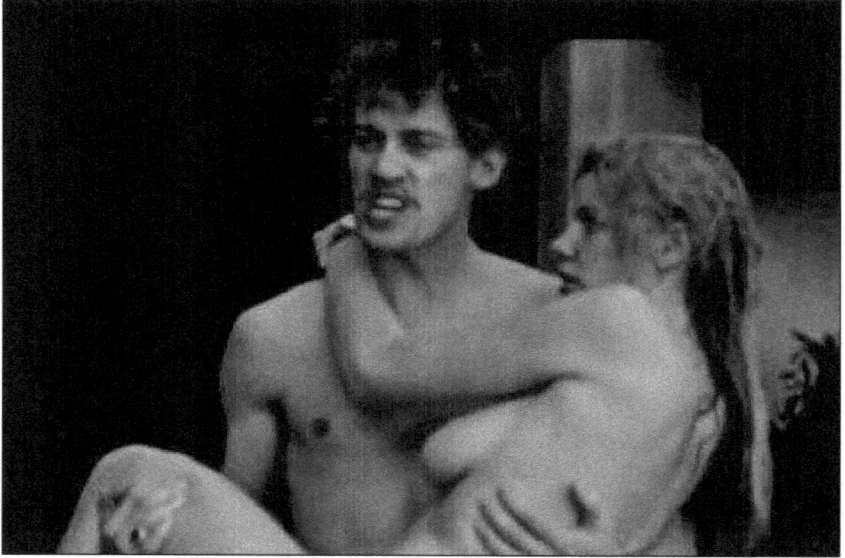

As the "Zodiac Rapist" John carries a damsel in distress in the 1972 film, *Zodiac Rapist*, a parody of the Zodiac killings that took place in Northern California from the late 1960s through the early 1970s.

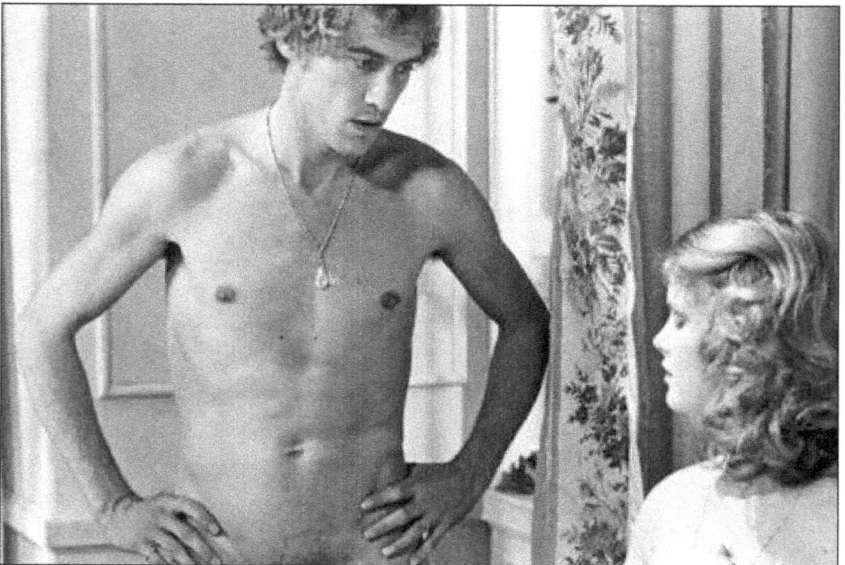

"Father Clement" surprises virginal Jean Jennings in the Mitchell Brothers film, *Autobiography of a Flea*.

Johnny Wadd seeks revenge for the death of his best friend, Sam Kelly (played by Dick Aldrich), and blows away the bad guys in *Tell Them Johnny Wadd is Here*.

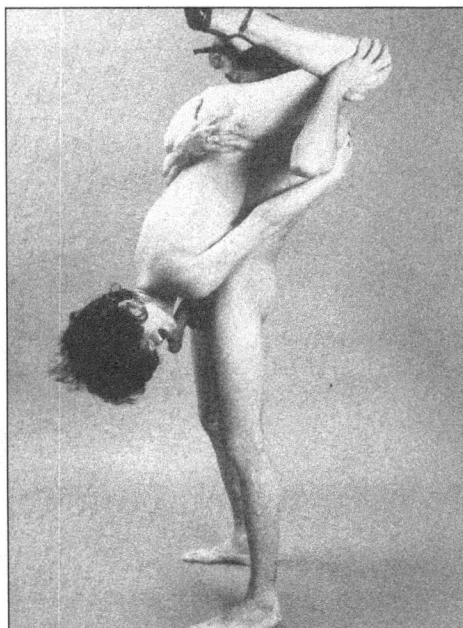

John and Rene Bond team up to perform a neat trick.

On his business card, John provided his prospective employers with the number to his answering service. No one had his home phone number.

John always said that Rene Bond was his type.

John and Linda Wong pose for a publicity photo for the 1977 film, *The Jade Pussycat*.

Johnny Wadd in action, in *The Jade Pussycat*.

In 1997, mainstream director, P.T. Anderson effectively exposed a new generation of people to the Johnny Wadd series, after *Boogie Nights* mimicked several scenes from Bob Chinn's series — such as this bar scene form the 1978 film, *China Cat*.

In *China Cat,* Johnny Wadd chats up Shari (Jennifer Richards).

Looking pleased after completing a Swedish Erotica shoot.

This photo from the book, *Sex Star's Favorite Positions* shows John sampling from his lactating partner's breast.

This is one image from a pictorial shot by the talented photographer and camera man, Joel Sussman. John could trust his friend Joel to take only the best photos of him.

In parallel with his legend and sense of humor, John answered the publicity questions for the 1977 film, *Fantasm Comes Again*.

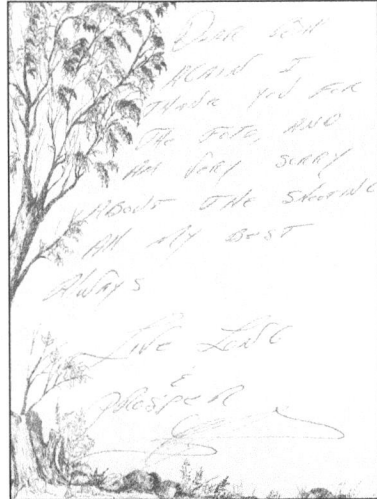

After John refused to appear in the pool scene for *Fantasm Comes Again*, he returned his pay to Bill Margold with a personal note. In it, John thanks Bill for giving him a "foto" of Warren Oates with a machine gun from the 1969 film, *The Wild Bunch*.

John and former pin-up model, Candy Samples, manage
to do some impressive posturing.

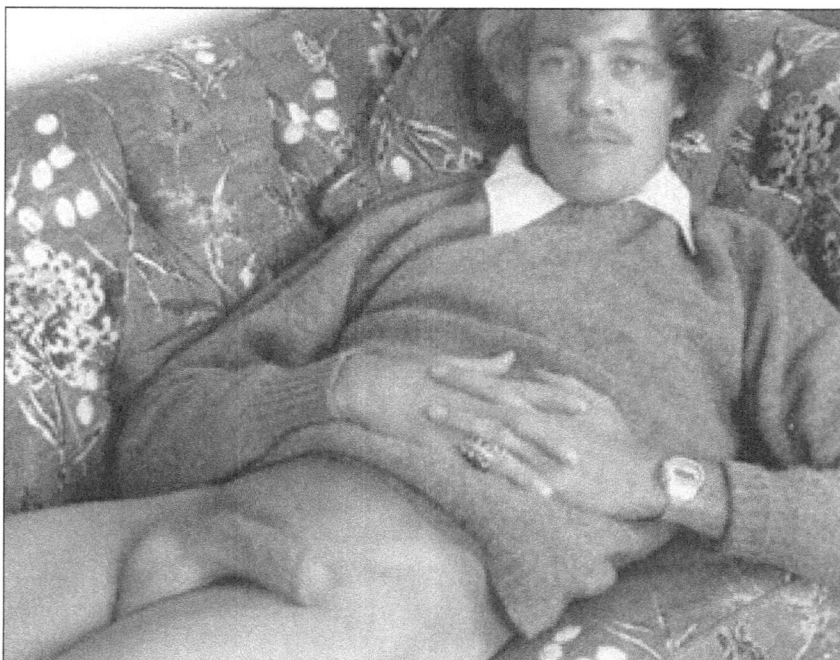

John catching up on rest after a hard day at work.

John and an unknown, yet jovial bride.

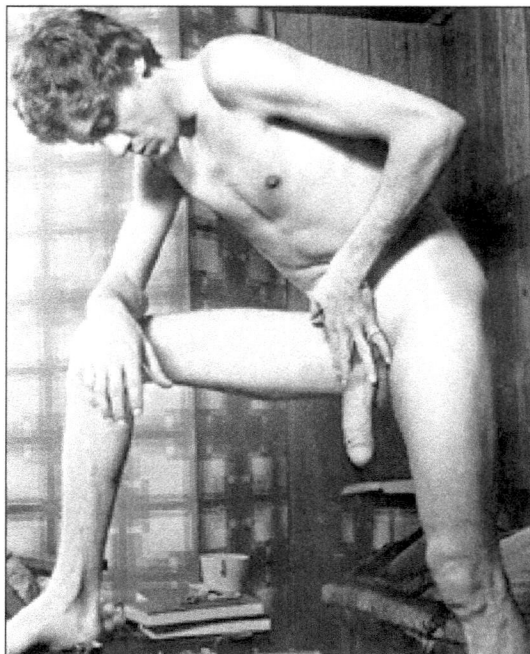
Lengthy Credentials.

John and Linda Wong (as John's housekeeper) engage in a little hanky-panky in *Stormy*. Note John's famous, dragonfly ring on his left ring finger.

JOHN HOLMES: A LIFE MEASURED IN INCHES

John reaches into his pocket for his Marlboro cigarettes while standing on stage at an Adult Film Association of America show in the summer of 1978.

John and producer for *Lust at First Bite*.

Porn's royalty, The Platinum Princess of Porn and The King. The two worked together numerous times during the Golden Age of pornography.

"She said, 'Some friends of mine have the best coke in the world.' I said, 'No, I've got the best coke in the world.'"

JOHN HOLMES

6.

Prisoner of Paradise

Chemical Dependence

Waikiki Wadd

Bob Chinn: John and I had just finished a shoot. We were tired — we'd just finished two films back to back and so we were sitting in the hotel room with this film man, Joel Sussman, and I said, "Why don't we take a vacation and go to Hawaii?"

When Chinn, Sussman and Holmes went on a working vacation to Hawaii to film scenes used in *Prisoner of Paradise* (1980), Chinn also shot footage for *Waikiki Wadd*, a title which Holmes had mistakenly used when referring to *Tropic of Passion* (1973) in his autobiography.

Bob Chinn: When we went to Hawaii to shoot *Prisoner of Paradise*, we were in Honolulu for a few days before going on to Kauai, so I decided to shoot some background footage with John for a new *Wadd* project there. If we had completed this film, it probably would have been the best *Johnny Wadd* film of the whole series.

There is a long story as to why this film was never completed. I believe this project is mentioned briefly in Julia St. Vincent's film, *Exhausted*, and the footage that we staged of me directing John in her film was supposedly for this project — we put *Waikiki Wadd* as the title on the clapper-board.

Waikiki Wadd — the film that should have been, but never was — would indeed be my personal favorite. I remember shooting an extended chase scene around and through stalls of the old open-air Chinese market with John (because I happened to be there, of course, I was cast as the villain). We both thought at that time this was the best we had ever done.

We shot around the canal area and the old shantytown wooden buildings that are no longer there, as well as the Swing Club (where John had done his live act a couple of years before) and other seedy servicemen haunts. We also filmed around the old Chinese herb- and medicine shops and I introduced John to the somewhat-illegal Kwan Loong Medicinal Oil, which he became almost addicted to sniffing. The version now available in Chinese shops is not the same one that John and I enjoyed, as it lacks a couple of the banned ingredients that promoted a "light-headed" feeling.

We also did some filming at the old Wo Fat Restaurant on Hotel Street, which was a favorite eating place for John and me. It was there that I introduced him to a Chinese dish that is unique to Hawaii — steamed kumuu fish, which is made with a rare, colorful fish found around the coral reefs. What he loved about the delicious dish was the hallucinogenic feeling you got after eating it.

When John and I were there, Hotel Street was still pretty much the same way it had been back during World War II, with the seedy bars and nightclubs, and the ramshackle wooden buildings facing Maunakea Street of Honolulu's Chinatown. I knew at the time that urban development would eventually change the area and I wanted to document the old Honolulu that the servicemen knew and remembered in *Waikiki Wadd*. That's why we shot so much footage there.

I really didn't have any specific story in mind at that time. Whenever I saw a location I wanted to use, I would improvise something on the spot. For example, if I saw a building that looked interesting, I would set up a shot and have John walk up to it, pretend like he was checking an address on a piece of paper, then walk in. Then I would shoot him exiting the building and going down the street.

The same thing with the open-air market in Chinatown, which was interesting because of all the exotic cooked food and fresh meat, fish and produce stalls. I had him tailing me as I went through the market, talking to various stall owners, then when I would see him and try to get away — the chase begins.

I would have built a story around all of this later. We would shoot the interior for the building that John had entered on a soundstage and we would continue the chase and confrontation under more controlled circumstances. We also shot a lot of footage of John driving, which not only provided running time, but was an excuse to show more scenery and street scenes. In all, we shot about an hour of really good background footage in Honolulu, mostly in the Chinatown district called "Hell's Half-Acre," and around the Hotel Street honkytonks. This would have probably edited down to 30 or 40 minutes.

Next, we moved on to the much more rural island of Kauai for the *Prisoner of Paradise* location footage shoot. The Hawaii working vacation which produced the location footage for *Prisoner of Paradise* and the footage for the unfinished *Waikiki Wadd* was one of the best times in both of our lives. For once we were at peace with each other and the world, it seemed, in the tropical location where I had spent my childhood. We were on the rural Hawaiian island of Kauai and immediately went to work on the project; first, by having him keep track of props and costumes, scheduling, transportation, and constructing whatever sets were needed. By making these things his responsibility, it ensured that things would go smoothly with him because any problems that might possibly arise would generally be his fault. I knew that if he had too much spare time on his hands, he could become bored and difficult, so I prevented this. Everything ran rather smoothly.

Some of the locations were in remote areas — we would have to go through jungle undergrowth to get to the beaches, in some places, and I left it to John to either find or make a trail. He loved doing this. I spent much of my early childhood on Kauai, which is where my mother was originally from. This was the first time John had ever been there and he fell in love with the island. We were walking along the beach, not far from our hotel — just the two of us, enjoying the sunset — and John said, "Bob, someday when you don't know where I am, if you can't find me, look here. This is where I'll be."

What Laurie Holmes said about John wanting to make $1,000,000 and just disappear was enlightening. I believe that was truly what was on his mind when we were standing on the beach on Kauai that day. He had finally discovered his paradise — the place where he could truly disappear and be reborn. If only he could have convinced himself to forget about those million dollars he wanted to earn. If only he had just stayed, he would probably still be alive today. Instead, he went in the pursuit of an unattainable dream that quickly turned into a tragic and fatal nightmare.

Light-fingered

Bob Chinn: After the Hawaii shoot, we returned to Los Angeles and I set about working on projects that I had promised to do. In the meantime, we assembled the location footage we had shot for *Prisoner of Paradise* in the editing room at Freeway Films, but I would take the project to Caribbean Films, who financed a buy-out with us and agreed to put up the larger-than-normal budget required for completion.

Seka: *Prisoner of Paradise* was fun because I got to be blown up. I played a German Nazi bitch, so it was more fun, in that way, but I always loved working with John.

According to Laurie Holmes, *Prisoner of Paradise* was also one of John's favorite films to make, in part because he believed the sex scene between himself and Mai Lin (billed as Miko Moto) was first rate. The scene is immensely erotic and the affection between he and Lin is believably realistic, as was the set, which Chinn meticulously crafted.

Bob Chinn: The way we set it up — it was just beautiful. I worked hard on that movie. It's just a little warehouse in Oakland and there's an alley adjacent to the warehouse, in the back, and I set up the whole Asian street scene. I got all the extras and all that stuff. It was a lot of fun. I really liked that scene. John, when he came to the set, was so impressed by the outside and of the stalls and everything, he said, "I've got to do well in this scene."

John Holmes [i]: Things got worse for me. With money growing increasingly short, I began looking for things to steal.

Bob Chinn: Things started disappearing from the set. He was stealing things to pay for his habit.

Bob Vosse[h]: Bob Chinn had taken John over to Hawaii and they had taken some shots on the beach — they had this big wooden box floating in on shore. They did all the interiors on my stage in San Francisco a few weeks later. John was sort of nervous after this little incident with Gail and I was getting concerned with him. One of the things you try to do is keep people busy.

John mentioned, "Boy, I wish we had kept that box. We should have that box to put on the set."

So I said, "John, why don't you go in the back, we have a carpenter's shop, all the lumber you need, you can build that. Do you remember what it looked like?"

"Yeah," [he replied]. He went back there, spent all day, just about, hammering and cutting. He built a similar box.

I think they shot a scene or two, but I noticed that night [that] John was leaving — he had that big box on his shoulder. John was pretty strong. He was going down the steps and he was really straining. That thing was heavy.

I went over and I said, "John what do you have in that box? That box is not that heavy."

"Oh...," he started.

I said, "Set it down." I pulled it down, opened it up and looked in it. He had taken all of my tools, all the drills. He had taken all the food out of the refrigerator, all the leftovers—the milk, orange juice — everything. This again, was John. He did have a little problem. If you left anything out, he might take it home with him, but never quite this conspicuously.

I would tell the people, "Put away your money, put away any jewelry, antique jewelry, even any drugs, don't leave them out. Hide them." I didn't tell them particularly why; I just didn't want to be responsible. The problem is those were John's three favorite things — he loved little antique jewelry and this kind of thing. He was such a charmer; he would give it to the other girls.

A number of times, I had to pay the people for this, quite often it was $200 or $300 for things that were missing, and sometimes there would only be John and one other girl there. He was the only one that left the room, so you know — and time after time, the same things. It was pretty obvious John was taking things. Never anything real serious, but it was quite an irritation — and costly.

Bob Chinn: "Aunt Peg," or Juliet, is one person that didn't like John at all. Although I never worked with her — she was never in any of my films — I know for a fact that she hated John.

Bob Vosse had directed Holmes and Juliet Anderson together, who became known for her character, "Aunt Peg," a character that debuted in an early *Swedish Erotica*, during the height of John's difficulties with drugs, when his light-fingered hands were well known on sets. Unfortunately for Anderson, who at age 39 quit her job as a teacher to act in pornography, she was one of very few women who claimed to have a negative experience with John Holmes.

Juliet Anderson [h]: The first time I met John was on the set of a film, one of those short loops, about 12 minutes long when it was finished. It was being done with John Holmes, Sharon Kane and me.

During the filming we ad-libbed a lot. There really was no script. Sharon was down on her knees, John whipped out his cock, and she looks at his large member — she looks at me and says, "Aunt Peg, it's so big!" That's how I got the name, Aunt Peg, and it stuck. It became one of *Swedish Erotica*'s best sellers. Without John's being there, I probably wouldn't have gotten the name, Aunt Peg.

Working with John was definitely unpleasant. He was rude, insensitive — I could say a lot of things. He just didn't want to be there. He didn't like what he was doing. I put up with it for a couple of times. After that, I let it be known I would not work with him again. I wasn't used to being treated that way. He didn't just treat *me* that way. I could see he was that way with everyone. I didn't know he was on drugs.

There was another reason I didn't enjoy working with John — and that was his very large cock. I have never been into size, and to me that was a dangerous weapon and it hurt. I had to make it known that he'd better not try to force himself too much or I would cut it off. He was good about that because I think he believed me.

After I let it be known that I would not work with John any more, a couple of years passed and I didn't socialize with "the crowd," so I hadn't realized that he was having a lot of problems. I heard a few things here and there. I did know that there was a special person assigned to him on sets to follow him around, to be sure that he didn't pocket valuables because we'd shoot in people's homes. He would take them and sell them to support his drug habit.

Bill Amerson: There was never anyone assigned to watch him so he didn't steal — he always did steal. John would open his briefcase and it'd be full of all this shit that he had and we'd make him return it. He didn't steal it because he wanted it; he stole it because he loved the action. He was a lot like a kleptomaniac.

He did mule drugs to pay for his habit. John would steal things from people. He would break into offices at night and steal computers and sell them for drugs. John would go to the airport and steal bags and sell whatever he found.

Alan Colberg: The last time we saw John, he came to our house and said, "I'm on a set and I need to borrow some props." He took a few things from our house that we never saw again. Things had just fallen apart.

Paradise Lost

Bob Chinn: The catch [with Caribbean Films] was that I would have to "ghost direct" the project for Gail Palmer and they would put her name on it. Gail was a nice girl, though I haven't seen her for years and years. She didn't have a clue. It doesn't really matter to me whether people think she directed.

Seka: I never saw any confrontations, but if somebody started arguing with one another, I just went somewhere else. I didn't want to be around it because if arguments started and you were close, you were going to be right in the middle of it, so it's like anything else — you leave. I never saw John when he didn't act like a gentleman.

Once while filming a rip-off of the television show, *One Day at a Time*, called *One Way at a Time*, director Alan Colberg witnessed John's growing problems controlling his temper. John actually got into a fistfight with the producer after John had showed up a day late for filming for the 1979 feature. It would not be the last time that John was involved in a physical alteration on a film set.

Bob Chinn: The producer had arranged for a TV crew to come shoot Gail directing, so we lost one day setting up something with her supposedly directing. I had to tell her how to say, "Action!" and "Cut." That was really interesting. John got really mad because we were losing a day and they had a big fight. He wanted to get the thing finished. The crew was not happy; this was wasting time. I think it came to blows, actually.

Bob Vosse: John was working for another production company; they were shooting *Prisoner of Paradise* and the producer had arranged to have a CBS news team that was going to come in and interview John. Their angle was on this film, they had a female director, Gail Palmer.

This was quite a test for John's mood. The producer and I were standing close by. John was in the makeup chair and Gail was talking to him. They were briefing him a little bit about what they were going to say on CBS when they interviewed him. Gail was trying to get him to go with the script a little bit, since they had extra time. John didn't like scripts and didn't want to have any part of the script. The producer and I walked away and in a minute, we heard smash! bam! boom!

We looked over at the makeup table. John and Gail were fist-fighting, into the face as hard as they could. The makeup girl was screaming all over the place. In two steps, Harry, the producer, was there and pulled them apart. They were killing each other. About this time, there was a knock on the door. The CBS crew was there. They came in; they were ready to go. They were throwing the cameras over their shoulders. Ann says, "Ready to go?"

I said, "Yeah."

And the first question was, "John, how is it working with a female director, Gail Palmer? What are your feelings about her?"

This is the hypocrisy. He said, "Oh, she's the greatest director, the most sensitive I've ever worked with." This is less than two minutes after he had his fist right in her eye.

Bob Chinn: The very professional San Francisco crew soon grew weary of this nonsense, deplored the deception, and they made the way they felt known to the producer. Somehow the film was completed, but it was not the film that I had envisioned, nor was it the film that I had originally wanted to make.

John is the abject lesson of how to handle success, I guess. He was always a very addictive personality. He chain-smoked. He would get addicted to just about anything. First, he loved the ritual of cocaine; of having to go into the bathroom and sneak little "toots."

Cocaine, which tends to excite and energize can also instill a false sense of power and addiction to the drug comes with some very intrusive side effects. The expression, "coke dick," is used to describe the condition of a male's sexual arousal being impeded by excessive cocaine ingestion, causing a delayed orgasm. In many cases, large quantities of cocaine can prevent a man from climaxing altogether.

Bob Chinn: One thing I had noticed was that the sex scenes were more difficult for him on this film and they took much longer than usual to shoot. I attributed it to his drug use. I have always had a hard and fast rule, never to have drugs on the set and although John promised me that he had left his at the hotel, I knew he was lying. I knew that I could not work in the future with someone who would break this rule, which would endanger the project in case of a bust.

The last film I made with him was *Prisoner of Paradise* and by the time we got the studio and were shooting that stuff, the cocaine was getting to a point where he couldn't get a good erection. This had never happened before and I didn't like it. At that point, he couldn't do anything because he just liked going in the bathroom, tooting on some coke and coming out.

John had always been a reliable sex performer in my films. The only time I ever had a major problem with him was when we were finishing up the soundstage shoot on *Prisoner*, doing the scene between him and the girl who played the Japanese guard. It was not her fault. John had just done too much cocaine that day. It took hours to shoot that scene to make it look half-way acceptable and by the time we were finished, the crew and I were exhausted.

Bill Amerson: The cocaine would shoot him up and the marijuana or the alcohol would bring him down to where he could sleep. This went on for three or four years and then John got introduced to freebase and then he started smoking cocaine, smoking freebase. John discovered something in his life that made him feel like somebody else.

John had got to a point where he didn't like what he was doing. Freebase distorts your thinking a lot. He still tried to work and he got a reputation. People didn't want to hire him anymore because he was known as either not showing up or spending most of the time in the bathroom.

David Clark[h]: He would say, "I need to talk to somebody." He would say that and then one day I realized, there went that famous ring, there went the watch and the weight was coming off.

I remember one day, I was looking all over for him. He had to be on the set. John was cuddled in a fetal position, hiding in one of the wardrobes. I found him and said, "John you need to go on."

Joel Sussman: The bad little boy is the one who sits and does coke in the bathroom and would not come out for three hours.

Bill Amerson: There were times when he was on a set and I'd get a call from a producer saying that John had locked himself in the bathroom and asked me for help. I would talk to him on the phone and tell him to get his head out of his ass and do what he was getting paid to do, or I would go to the set and talk to John.

Bob Chinn: My schedule hadn't allowed me to even think of completing *Waikiki Wadd*. Armand at Freeway was upset that I was doing so many projects for other companies, so he brought in Lee Frost to direct two quick films for Freeway, in which John appeared. Unfortunately, they had a very difficult time with John, who by now had discovered freebasing cocaine and was totally unreliable, both on the set and as a performer. As a result of this, any possibility of Armand approving a Freeway-*Wadd* project was at that point negated.

John would come to the editing room on Hollywood Boulevard and hang out with Jeff [Fairbanks] and me while we were cutting *Prisoner*. He was repentant about the way he had acted on the set of the shoot and while I forgave him, I was still reluctant about working with him again. Occasionally, all three of us would take time off and head for Las Vegas for a day or two.

A couple of years earlier, John had met Chris Cox, the owner of a gay night-club where John hung around and sold drugs. He was constantly looking for new opportunities to turn tricks. Not long after that, Cox introduced John to Ed Nash. Nash was another nightclub owner with whom John quickly became a friend and an associate.

Bob Chinn: One thing that was apparent was that John had become much more heavily involved with cocaine. In the past, he had come around while we were editing or working on scripts, and would give us some coke or share what he had with us, before we went to dinner at Musso and Frank's. But now he was trying to sell it to us. One night, he even treated us to drinks at Eddie Nash's Seven Seas, on Hollywood Boulevard.

Actually the fact is, I had decided to abandon [*Waikiki Wadd*] after John had become increasingly difficult to work with and had become very heavily involved with drugs. It all happened in what, in retro-spect, was a relatively short period of time, but the changes in John were drastic. That's the reason I stopped working with John. Also, the crew people can't work that efficiently. I don't care if they go out and smoke grass or do some coke after the shoot—do whatever they want, but not during the shoot.

Insatiable

Bill Amerson: Even though he had problems [with] drugs and alco-hol, John still remained a star. There were times when he was heavy into freebase and couldn't perform. As far as popularity goes, people still loved John.

Although so much of his money was going to support his habit, John Holmes had achieved meteoric heights as a male pornographic performer. He was often asked to guest star in cameo roles for motion picture productions, including *Insatiable*, starring Marilyn Chambers. John was hired to appear as Chambers' ultimate "fantasy lover" in the film's final scene.

Marilyn Chambers: In *Insatiable*, I did the last scene in the movie with him and I remember Stu Segal (well actually, he called himself "Godfrey Daniels" at the time) the director, we were shooting this in San Francisco. Stu said, "We're going to go pick John up at the airport in San Francisco." I was totally nervous. I'd heard so much about him. I was not afraid but just totally shy.

We picked John up and he and I were sitting in the back seat, and we were talking and I was just kind of looking at him in awe, going, "God, this guy is really smart. He really is fairly articulate."

When you look at some of the interviews with John Holmes it made him seem like such a dope and he wasn't. He was very kind. He was very gentle. He was so not the John Holmes I thought he was going to be. He didn't come marching up going, "Hey! Move over, bitch!" He was a really meek gentleman.

I don't know now if he told me he was married, but I know he told me that he had a sheep farm. He said that he was just kind of a country boy and he was doing all this so that he could live a normal life. John never let on who he really was. He was "John Holmes," the façade forever. I have to really applaud him for that because he didn't ever really let anybody know who he really was and I think that's the true meaning of a star.

Ernie Roebuck, who was a lighting technician and gaffer before doing cinematography for television and more recent adult videos, had witnessed John's dramatic use of cocaine during the filming of the 1980 film, *Insatiable*. Before filming one day, Holmes purchased an ounce of cocaine in San Francisco. Later that afternoon, having used up all his supply, he told Roebuck that he was looking for another ounce.

Ernie Roebuck [h]: The first time I actually noticed John really using a lot of drugs, when I knew about it, was when we did *Insatiable*. He had already cranked through an ounce in the morning, and he had a "fuck scene" to do. I never saw him have a problem with a "cum shot," but I think he would just get somewhere in the middle of hard and soft, and after he started doing drugs, that was good enough. I remember when I first met him and he wasn't doing drugs. His dick was huge and I never saw it get hard again, probably not even on *Insatiable*.

[Marilyn Chambers] was supposed to meet him in *Insatiable*. They're in this gym and she's supposed to deep throat him and she can't. She tried for hours, she tried so many ways. She tried every fucking position. She tried forever, until Chuck [Traynor] kind of pulled her outside. What was going on was his dick was bending in her throat, so she couldn't deep throat him.

Marilyn Chambers: John was doing a lot of cocaine. We all were. What can I say? I never did it when I actually had to do a scene in a movie or be on stage. I saved it for later because I always wanted to be the real me. I might have had a couple of drinks, occasionally to loosen up, but it wasn't like I was out of my mind.

When John and I actually were getting ready to do the scene, it took forever. He was in the bathroom. He was doing coke — like, a gram up each nostril. I remember it was hot and it was a black room, where we had to have this black stuff all around and all the other guys were ready and John comes out and he can't get it up. It was like a big, floppy, old worm. What he would do is hold it at the base and try to squeeze some of the blood into the head. So we really had a difficult time with that. He never really got totally hard, but I think we faked it enough to make it look pretty real. Apparently people liked it because they bought the movie.

John's obsession with cocaine put his livelihood in jeopardy. He opted to work sporadically in a few softcore movies when the pressure to provide the "money shot" became too much for him. Candy Samples and Uschi Digard were two busty babes initiated into the business by one of the original directors of erotic films, Russ Meyers. The women teamed up with John to capitalize on the popularity of the disco era in a film called *Disco Sex Party*, in 1980. A similar softcore feature was made around the same time, *John Holmes and the All-Star Sex Queens*. Again, it starred John Holmes with Candy Samples, Uschi Digard, Serena and Kitten Natividad, another one of Russ Meyers' protégés.

> *Kitten Natividad*[h]: I was hoping I would get to feel his cock and put my lips around it. Of course, when we did softcore, you'd have to cover the head. He was very nice, and right away, I got a big crush and a big hard-on for him. We worked real well because I would follow his directions. He liked to be a director. He always liked to pick one woman he was going to go down on, and it was me. He was really good at it.
>
> At that time, coke gave him that euphoric feeling. On our break, we went to the bathroom, and he had a bottle of scotch and some coke. It was recreational, but he always had some, and he was very generous with it. We did it off the toilet seat.

Julia's Diary

> *Julia St. Vincent*: My uncle got cancer and he died in May of 1980. In the meantime, John and I had secretly become friends. We'd been having a secret thing, because I really didn't want my uncle to know. He would have been mad at me — and lots of other people because even back then, it was kind of like, "You're dating John Holmes? What are you thinking!?" So it was a fine line. Sort of like drug friends, you know?
>
> I never talked about him for a number of years. He may have been the King of Porn, but he was no wonderful person. I don't have a lot of good, nice things to say anymore. You grow up and you kind of realize you were had by this guy. This guy dragged you through the coals and

you forgave him, and forgave him, and forgave him. Now look at your life because of your inability to love or trust anyone afterward.

Julia kept a diary to help keep her emotions in check throughout Armand's death and the events with John. In a box, she has saved the diary along with tattered pieces of love notes, drawings, poems, and photographs. Her collection of mementos from the relationship was larger until an incident where the two impulsive lovers had an argument over her collection of letters and files. John had been concerned that she may have been saving the letters and files with the intention to write a book about him and he was not happy about that prospect.

> *Julia St. Vincent*: I've written like 1000 files and letters. I'm a pack rat and he didn't want my stuff. He was pissed off. He didn't want a record being kept of things. So one day, we got into this big, fucking argument — this was before we did base, but we were coked out. We ripped my house apart. He went through all my shit and was like, "I'm just a file in your file box. You keep files on people," and blah blah blah… Which I do. I still do it and I still have some stuff that was left, that he didn't realize was on him.
>
> I had a root canal and he came over to my house to take care of me. He was so sweet to me. When he left, he said, "Go back to bed." When I did, there were two little monkeys in bed that he'd left for me. He did sweet little things. He was always a very nice guy, but he had a schizophrenic personality.
>
> So he took the monkeys and the bracelet he'd given me — a bunch of little stuff. So we put it in a bag and we got into his car, that step van that he had for a while, and we drove down the freeway and threw it out the fucking window. At the time, I was pretty fucked up because I'd been doping up with him. When it flew, I was like trying [to catch it] and I thought I'll come back later. Later I got in my car, drove there, but couldn't find a damn thing.

Julia had memorized part of a poem that John had written for her, which boldly paints the image of how much John loved her:

> *Julia St. Vincent*: "Were it mine in words to give, then listen for a sigh.
> "Not loud enough to split the darkness, not fashioned from a lie,
> "But a whisper from my heart, love.
> "It comes from deep inside."

John also presented Julia with a stylized line-drawing in which he enhanced his favorite feature of hers — he would tell her that she had luscious lips. The drawing encompasses the disco-y, glam hippie vibe that she explored during the time she was with John. His representation of Julia's full, wavy hair is reminiscent of a photo of her directing *Exhausted*, when it was dyed blonde. The most captivatingly accurate aspects of this drawing are her sensuous-yet-skeptical eyes and high cheekbones. The drawing is in charcoal, which lends to its sensual-but-simple appearance, but John's use of the negative space behind her portrait illustrate his precise attention to detail and his gift of artistic talent.

As much as John demonstrated his love for Julia and the other women he had loved, John's drug addiction began to override his ability to make good choices.

> *Julia St. Vincent*: [Reading from her 1980 diary,] "March 16. We are in the coffee lounge. I'm very tired. I've been here too long. I will have to go home tomorrow to rest. Maybe I should see Yvonne," who was my shrink, "Armand is just quiet."
>
> He had been just screaming and screaming, really in pain. The cancer — one minute to the next, went to his brain, and he didn't know anyone. He was like a two-year-old. That night, I told my uncle, "I gotta go to a shrink."
>
> He says, "Really?" He got upset because he knew I was going to leave. I was mad, so I told him I had a shrink appointment, even though I didn't. I said, "I'll be gone for a couple hours."
>
> I went home and my aunt said, "Come right now, something's happened."

Julia sped over to her aunt's house to find Armand crawling on the floor like a baby and screaming in agony. An ambulance was called to transport him to the hospital.

> *Julia St. Vincent*: My uncle was writhing in pain and I tried to tell them to just turn that siren off because you're driving him insane, and they said, "We can't." When we got to the hospital and they finally shot him up with whatever, he became quiet, so that's why I said he became quiet.
>
> When we got to the hospital, John came over there and Armand was in there, dying. John was pulling out filthy, fucking pornography that was from the guy's house. So here he is and you're hoping that he'll pass and go to Heaven or something, but you're constantly being reminded by The Asshole that he's a filthy, sick predator. Back then, I really didn't have any issues about it because no one ever said, "Oh, my God, he's a sicko."

Occasionally, John would write something in Julia's diary, either as himself or to try to impersonate his girlfriend. Julia still has the diary with excerpts of John's handwriting. Thirty-five-year-old John would write things in her diary, for instance, on March 16, the same day as the cancer entry, John had added, "Because John was going to bang the fucking shit out of Mom." Today, St. Vincent finds the behavior inexcusable.

> *Julia St. Vincent*: I mean, can you fucking believe it? The funny thing about it is: I never got mad at him. At the time, I didn't say, "You heartless sicko." I just went, "Oh my God!" I never got mad and said, "Get out of here." It didn't occur to me that you could do that. He was being an asshole.
>
> He said to me, "Julia, the day you ever get mad about anything, I don't want to be anywhere around you." 'Cause he knew that if I ever finally realized what a fucking piece of shit he was, how horrible he'd been to me, and how angry I was, that I would probably kill somebody, which, it never happened.

Julia is confident that John did not have sex with her mother or her sisters, so this was likely a fantasy of John's, which he boasted about in her diary and perhaps, in *Porn King*. Along with the physical remains that evidenced their chaotic relationship, Julia also has a copy of John's book, *Porn King*, which she has scoured for evidence of their relationship, seemingly in an attempt to pin down what she meant to John.

> *Julia St. Vincent*: [Reading from *Porn King*,] "Sex has taken over my life. Films, however, were no longer my primary outlet. Over the next several years, I became involved in numerous personal relationships. A girl from San Diego — a fiery redhead."
>
> Okay, I'm from San Diego. I'm the only one that I know of that he knows from San Diego. I do believe that the connotation of the fiery redhead refers, in my opinion, to me because he used to call me "fiery," because I was an Armenian.
>
> Anyway, it says, "Within a few weeks, I was not only seeing her, but her two red-headed sisters." I have two sisters, no brothers. "Then I found myself with her red-headed mother. It worked out well; at least until they started talking and discovered I was doing all of them. Red-heads, talk about tempers." He knew I had a temper, but I never got mad. "It didn't really matter because there were other ladies." He may have written part of this book and put in shit like this — that was kind of true, but not really.
>
> My mom was in the hospital, John was in the hospital and I was in the hospital when my uncle died. When he died, we were downstairs. I knew that when he died, I had to leave. I couldn't handle a couple of things. One thing that I couldn't handle was John running

around and I couldn't handle seeing another human being dying that I'd known.

In total shock over the death of my uncle, they argued in the hall over whether to let him go. They let him go. John and I went into insane hysterics — laughter. We burst into laughter.

We were sitting on these stairs that go down and my mother was on the telephone, and I said to John, "What is she doing?"

He said, "She's calling people to tell them that he died."

I said, "What do you mean — just calling 'em and saying, 'Hi, Armand died. Goodbye.'" John and I were sitting on the floor, literally rolling in laughter, when I turned around and my entire family came walking through the fucking lobby toward us, in a row.

I was embarrassed. We weren't laughing that he died. I think we were just laughing because we spent so many days there.

When my uncle died, there was no restriction anymore. Not only that, but from John's perspective, I believe he realized I was pretty vulnerable. I had a lot of money because — I didn't inherit the company, but I was in charge of running it. My family knew that if he had a will — and I believe he had one written, but it wasn't finished — that I would have inherited the company, because he would buy me clothes, hair, makeup, nails — stuff to make me, to redefine me for this role. He died within six months of knowing that he had cancer. I mean, one day he was fine and the next day, he was dying, and then they kept telling me to ask him to do his will. I couldn't ask a dying guy — now I probably could — but at the time, it just seemed so insensitive. "Oh, you're dying? Can you write a fucking will?" Now I would say, "You don't write a will, your kids aren't getting shit, so write one."

Alone in L.A., Julia shared an apartment with her friend, Rhonda Jo Petty for about six months following Armand's passing. Petty noticed a change in John that corresponded with his cocaine use. During the making of *Little Orphan Dusty*, they did not use cocaine together, but by 1980, Petty admitted to using so much cocaine with John that she had to be "wheeled out" onto the set. The actors' use of cocaine became apparent in the films as well; in later films such as *California Girls*, Petty and Holmes appear to be overacting, having lost the seamless flow they had achieved in *Little Orphan Dusty*.

Worse yet, Petty felt that John influenced and dragged her friend, Julia, along his downward spiral.

Julia St. Vincent: Rhonda's perception was, as mine was, that John lived there, but John didn't really live there. Her perception was that he lived there because he was there every fricking day. We had Thanksgiving dinner together. He didn't have his own bedroom or anything, and he didn't have his clothes and shit there. He had some things there, so yeah — for those six months that Rhonda lived with me, he was there a lot.

Sharon Holmes [h]: I don't know how many people were fed by me, like Christmas or Thanksgiving, he would say, "I have friends who don't have anything to eat," and would pack up eight pounds of turkey, stuffing, the whole bit. Gee, they may have thought he was a great cook — I was the one cooking it; it was coming out of my house. John could have not have cooked anything. S'mores were his specialty, and that was it. He couldn't boil water and he couldn't make coffee.

Exhausted

Older, but still gullible and naïve, Julia spent a lot of time with John at her apartment. She did not know that he was married or that he also had another girlfriend, although she spent hours of time trying to find out more about him through adventurous solo visits to Bill Amerson's home and her film, *Exhausted*.

Bob Chinn: After Armand's unexpected death, his niece, Julia, took the reins of the company. She and John were very close and she came up with an idea for making the pseudo-documentary *Exhausted*, using footage from the Freeway John Holmes films that I had directed. By this time, drugs had made John totally undependable on a professional level. About a week after we shot the footage of John and I on the supposed set of *Waikiki Wadd* [for *Exhausted*], the Wonderland murders happened.

Julia St. Vincent: That's the thing about my credentials: I didn't have any. I was abandoned; essentially, there was nobody in L.A. but me. For a period of time, my mom did live there. She came up to run another business. I was pretty much left alone, like, I had nothing. My whole world had been the business with my uncle.

Well, that's how it all came to be — instead of inheriting, I was appointed. I was supposed to get a share of the business, which I ended up getting screwed out of and I ended up leaving because they would not cut me in after I finished those two [Lee Frost] films and started making *Exhausted* on the side. They found out about *Exhausted* and then they sued me.

Exhausted is perhaps the most important contribution to keeping Holmes' legend alive today. This cleverly-edited pseudo-documentary inspired Paul Thomas Anderson to make *Boogie Nights* in 1997, which brought Holmes back into public thought, nearly ten years after his death. St. Vincent admitted that some of her motivation while filming the interview clips was to document this stage in John's life, when she could see that he was teetering on the edge and about to hit rock bottom. At that time, *intervention* was a relatively new term, particularly when related to drug addiction.

> *Bob Chinn*: When his primary goal in life became scoring drugs, I realized that we could not work together again. By the time we appeared together in Julia's *Exhausted*, I had not seen John for a while and was surprised to see what a real mess he had become. I remember saying to him, "John you look like hell! When are you going to get it together, and straighten your act out?"
>
> He answered by saying something about not having had much sleep lately.
>
> This was the extent of my intervention. I wish I had done more, but I really did not realize how serious the problem had become with him. I don't know if I could have done anything to help him. I doubt it. He was the kind of guy that was going to control his own life even if it was rapidly spiraling out of control.

Two Girls and a Guy

> *Dawn Schiller*[h]: I was in love with him. There were wonderful times at the very beginning, when there was happiness, when there was content. When he was good, he was very, very good — and then when he was bad, he was evil. There was no in between.
>
> Things went downhill when cocaine got involved, to be honest. That was the drug that he could never kick. That was the one that he liked the best. That was the one that I liked the best. It's a very addictive drug. Pot, could take or leave it — drinking, the same way. Acid — if he brought it home, we did that — or mushrooms, or hash oil; all kinds of things.
>
> We did this every night after Sharon went to bed. He got a little scale, and then I was doing the weighing and he had me doing the cutting and folding the little packages. I never did any of the selling. I just did the packaging. And we were doing lines. I became addicted with him and he kept me fed. He made sure that I had that bit to keep me along with him because he didn't want to be alone. Sharon didn't touch it, it wasn't her thing.

> *Sharon Holmes*[h]: We got along. I was much more tolerant at that point. At this point, I literally said, "You go your own way. This isn't what I want to do. From now on, it's my rules, or don't stay here."

Dawn Schiller[h]: It got to the point that if he needed to do something that he didn't want Sharon to see, he would do it in the bathroom. The bathroom became his office. The phone went in. The cord would go in the bathroom. I would go in, the briefcase would open. Eventually, it started getting done in there.

I was getting high, from school, before I even met him. That was life. The impact of selling, in my mind, wasn't taboo. It was his business and I never interfered with anything other than what he told me to do. I never had to go deliver or anything. I never knew who got what. I would hear little things, "Oh you see that person on TV? I just sold him three grams." When I first realized that this was bad, little things would be gone. Pieces that I had, things that he had given me — rings eventually went.

Sharon Holmes[h]: From the 1980 to the first part of 1981, in one month's time, John took our credit cards and charged $48,000. Jewelry, furniture, televisions, etcetera. What he was doing was selling them.

Dawn Schiller[h]: He was stealing from Sharon at this point now and he needed to cover his bases there. He needed to blame me, which I suspect is the reason for my name being crossed out of the pictures and things like that.

Sharon Holmes[h]: We're talking about mister and missus accounts, so I literally called these people up and I said, "You change them to missus accounts, you drop his name and you do not issue him a credit card. I will not be responsible. I will not pay you any of that money unless you do so."

He escalated with stripping the house. It just didn't bother me at that point because he was out of control and the less I saw of him, the happier I was. He could fake it over the telephone; we still talked. I basically asked him how he was and so on. He'd always say, "Fine," and he wanted to know what I was doing, if I was going out and who I was seeing, and still wanting to have that contact and know if I was okay.

I'd let him ramble on as long as he wanted to and then say, "I have to go to bed, I have to get up for work in the morning," and end the conversations.

He was getting so bad at that point. I asked him, if he couldn't clean up his act because of the drugs to find someplace else to stay. I think he was staying with friends, periodically, for maybe four or five weeks and then he'd come home and say, "I'm clean," for maybe three or four hours.

I just finally said, "No, you can't do this. You can't do this."

Dawn Schiller[h]: There were messages from a [Julia] that came almost all of the time, and they were love messages. They were different from any other message. Sharon didn't know about them, because this wasn't one of her things that she did for John.

I believe I asked John about that, and he did some denying. "Just to say I love you," I mean it was pretty blatant, the kinds of messages that she left with the service. They were in a relationship, and they were in love, I came to find out. John was supposed to come home and he didn't, then those messages would be there right after he came home. If he did have this other love relationship, why was he letting me pick up the messages? I think I was old enough to understand. I had enough balls to realize that I didn't like that.

His outbursts had become rough already. This was one of the things, other than the items being missing from the house — these messages were on top of the more violent attitude, on top of shoving and pushing, on top of cruelty. Emotional cruelty was coming out of him that was not there before. Probably there all along, but the drug brought it out.

Julia St. Vincent: I lived in the top loft, where you could see everything around, and I didn't have any curtains on during the day. I was young and I was kind of fearless. [John's] friend came over, and the guy was wearing these white pants and a different kind of shirt. We were kind of screwing around, but not really.

A couple hours later, John came over, wearing the same shit the guy was wearing, that was completely not stuff that John would ever [wear] — like John would never wear white pants; he would always wear jeans.

During the day, from the street you could see up — I believe that John was at the end of the road, spying on me or something. I'm not sure how that went down. I thought to myself, are you sure you aren't delusional? Then I thought it could be that he told the guy, let me borrow your stuff. Something like that — or they planned it ahead of time. This guy was a paramedic that John knew. At that time, I was on freebase, so it could be I was just insane, but I found it extremely suspicious that he would be wearing something that he never wore before, right after that guy was there, and he's asking me, "What were you doing?"

This was when the two worlds kind of — not purposely, but accidentally — collided. Around that time was when Dawn called me. I was like, "Who are you?"

Dawn Schiller[h]: My relationship with Sharon at that point was drifting away. I was losing that stability. In one way he was taking it away from me, in punishment. The whole family aspect of the relationship just fell apart.

He developed a love relationship with another woman, and two was good — three was a crowd. I became jealous and I had her phone number. I felt betrayed by him, so that's why I justified going to see [Julia].

Julia St. Vincent: When my uncle died, John spent three straight days with me and that is when I think she went, "What the fuck is going on?" because he wasn't at home, so she called about three or four weeks after my uncle died and said, "Is Armand there?"

My secretary picked the phone up and said, "Somebody is asking for Armand."

I said, "Shit, I'll take it." I would have informed someone that Armand had died. I got on the phone and said, "Are you a friend of Armand's?" I forget what she told me, but one thing led to another and she said she was a friend of John's.

She waited a day and then called again, acting like a different person.

Dawn Schiller [h]: I was devastated. I was depressed. My world was falling apart. I took the initiative one day when he wasn't there for a few days and I went out to a pay phone. I called and said, "You don't know who I am, but are you seeing my boyfriend?"

Julia St. Vincent: She said, "Are you John's girlfriend?"

And I thought, first of all, I'm not going to tell you if I'm his girlfriend — I don't do that, I'm in the business and have producers and people that I associate with and I certainly don't want them all to know that I'm screwing people and most of all, that I'm in love with this guy. So I said, "I'm his friend; why?"

Dawn Schiller [h]: I said, "Did you know that I'm his girlfriend?" I did a very childish thing. But I had no choice. Nothing was changing and I couldn't stand it.

Julia St. Vincent: She said, "Well, can I meet you? I want to talk."

I'm like, "Who are you?" (At this point, I was filming *Exhausted*.)

"Well, I'm his friend and I'm really worried about him." It gave me enough to realize that he was with someone who was looking for him for a good reason, so I agreed to meet her.

When I met Dawn, we sat at Denny's. I saw her and she said, "It's me," so I sat there.

I went, "What's up?"

She's like, "Well, I'm worried about him, because he didn't come back."

"How do you know him?"

And she's like, "Well, he lives right there and all his friends--." And then she told me everything — about his marriage, about her, about everything.

Anyway, so we start comparing notes and it turns out he told her — and I'm not kidding you, *verbatim* — the same catch lines, like "The honeymoon's over, baby," and stuff like that. Exact words. "You're breeding stock, I want to marry you." "I should run away to Vegas with you right now." He told her virtually the exact same things, "I picked you for my mate." He told me this and said the exact same words to her.

Laurie Holmes: At the time, he was really heavy into drugs and it was the '60s and '70s — there were orgies all around and he was a porn star — he probably had several thousand mistresses!

Julia St. Vincent: I'm not sure how Dawn rectified the situation. I had to say, "Wait a minute. This is one confused puppy, who has told two women…," so obviously, he either loved us both the same or doesn't know who he loved. That's the conclusion I came to.

I took her to Bill's house and Bill had no idea [about Dawn], so who knew him, really? I believe Dawn did know him the best out of anybody, in the "homebody" life. I don't think she has any idea how he acted with me or on the set. Bill may have known John to have a good orgy and a good party, but he certainly didn't know anything, because believe me, I spent days trying to get something to figure the guy out, and I never could.

At the time he was with me, I believed that he was living [with me] — he was there most of the time and doing tricks. Our hobbies were listening to music and getting fucked up, and hoping that one of my friends would come over. Partying. He didn't sit around like Dawn talks about, how he did crafts and shit like that. He wrote, supposedly, poetry. He wrote me a poem he said was for me, but I don't know if that was for me, really. He drew a picture also, that he said was me, but I question everything now.

But no, he didn't sit around my house doing arts and crafts. We were making movies, thinking of schemes, and running around town. We weren't homebodies. I never saw John reading; John had A.D.H.D. I don't recall him ever reading a fucking book. We were running around town, partying with people, going somewhere, having sex, or working. Nobody was sitting around knitting. Dawn may have a different perspective, I guess, because it was like a homebody deal. I saw more the jetsetter side of him.

Dawn's experience is a little different. First of all, John never hit me. Not once. I think the reason that he didn't was because he knew that even though my uncle was gone, I was not unprotected by people, like the "fathers" that adopted me. So he knew that it couldn't be acceptable. The other reason is because I just couldn't accept it. I've never been hit by a man and no one's going to ever fucking hit me. That's where I draw the line.

After Dawn informed Julia about her and Sharon's relationships with John, the reality of their situation hit home and they began to worry how John would react when he learned that Dawn had contacted Julia.

> *Dawn Schiller*[h]: Then I became very fearful of going home because I had crossed that line. I knew he'd be mad. It was a very desperate move. It wasn't something to be taken lightly. It was something that I don't know ever could be repaired with him because it was something he'd never, never allow. I said, "I don't know what I'm going to do. I'm not supposed to tell you this, but something has to happen."
> She said, "Why don't we meet at this Holiday Inn?"

John had also confided in Julia about how he had been abused as a child, at the hands of his stepfather, Harold Bowman, "He had told me that he would swing John around by the legs and arms when he was angry." It seemed to her that the abuse John suffered as a child contributed to his instability when drugs were involved.

> *Julia St. Vincent*: I took her to a motel because I knew John was going to flip. He was going to get mad. We had to figure out what to do.

> *Dawn Schiller*[h]: She said, "Why don't you come home with me tonight? Don't worry, you're safe." She took a big sister attitude with me. We went to her apartment and I think at this point, there was cocaine involved.

> *Julia St. Vincent*: The next day, I took her to my house and we came up with this plan that I would call him and say, "Hey, John. What's up? Come on over."
> He said, "What are you wearing?"
> "I'm not wearing anything. Come on over." I had called his answering service and within 20 minutes, he returned my call.

> *Dawn Schiller*[h]: That night, John called. She said, "It's him." I just froze. She said, "I'm alone, why don't you come over?" She got off

the phone and said, "Don't worry, It's all right. There are two of us; he can't do anything."

Julia St. Vincent: Dawn and I looked at one another and said, "Oh no, what the fuck did we do?" I told her she was going to have to hide in the bathroom or something. I had a studio apartment and we were in the shower behind the curtain and we came up with this plan that when John comes in, I'm going to tell him, "The honeymoon's over and I've picked Dawn to be my mate."

Dawn Schiller[h]: A half hour later, as promised, he knocked at the door. [Julia] answered the door and I stood behind it. He walked in all happy, his gregarious self. "Hi, how have you been?" He gives her a big hug and a kiss, went to [set] down his briefcase and open it up. Identical to what he does in our home situation — so he cared for her as well. It became factual then.

Julia St. Vincent: She was hiding in the shower and he came to the door and I let him in and I said, "Hi," and we hug and kiss and I said, "John, I've got to tell you something." He sat down in the chair and I'm dancing around because I'm flipping out.

I kept dancing around, getting really stressed and then all of a sudden, he slammed his hand down on the table. Slapped the table as hard as he could and said, "What the fuck is going on with you?"

I walked back into the other room. He came into the room and sat in the chair. The guy was as white as a ghost. I said, "John, please don't be upset! Please don't be mad at me!" I was going through this whole diatribe, "I'm sorry. I don't mean it." Dawn came out of the bathroom.

Dawn Schiller[h]: He saw me standing there and his face dropped. I'd never seen that expression. He was caught so unaware. I mean he was usually three, four, five — as many steps ahead of every angle.

When somebody is cold cocked, there is a look on their face. I will always remember that look. I'd never seen it since, or before.

He looked at me and said, "You, in the truck." I obeyed. He just turned his back on her. "How dare you both betray me?" We were both crushed, devastated. We thought we had the strength in numbers and we were going to stand up. But that look was precious. It didn't last.

Julia St. Vincent: John stood up and said, "Dawn, get in the fucking car."

I said, "Dawn, don't do it." They both start walking out the door and I'm following them and I'm screaming at her and he's screaming at her. We're yelling and screaming and Dawn was sitting in the van and

John and I are talking and laughing now because I said, "John, you've got to promise me you're not going to do anything stupid."

He said, "I'm not going to do anything."

"You've got to sign a note that says you won't touch her."

He said, "Okay." So I wrote the note and he signed it.

I made John sign a piece of paper that said, "I promise not to touch her or to hurt her." If he signed the paper, she could get into the car. Not like I really had any power, but we were all pretending that I did. She got into the car and they ended up leaving. A few days later, they came back. They needed a place to stay, or they came back to get toasted or whatever — they came back.

I had a loft, and I paid about $1200 rent. She was from a blue-collar family, and I was more like a white-collar family. So she comes in and looks around. I really didn't have many things because I was young, and I could live with nothing. I had a futon, umbrellas with plants, a wicker table — nice stuff, but there wasn't much of it. On my balcony, I had garter belts, kind of alternative, hippie-girl.

She said, "How much is this?"

And I said, "Oh, it is $3000 a month."

John looked at me, and he said, "Don't do that to her." He was pissed because I was fucking with her head. I'm not a hurtful person, but you know, I was fucking around and he was mad, so he was protecting her.

They came back and she looks around, he gets mad at me, and then we started getting stoned, then they ended up staying there.

We became friends — we had a little thing. She initiated it, but I think he might have made her initiate it; I don't know. She knew more about it than I did, which was really surprising. Frankly at the time, I remember thinking, wow, she fucking did that like she had no problems with it at all. She took my hand and took me to the bathroom. She started it. Took me in the bathroom, washed me up, did all this nice stuff, then she said, "Now, let's fuck."

She's the one who seduced me. Made a bubble bath up and I was the giggly little "Oh-my-God" one. She went from being a little girl to this other woman who could do that. John stayed in the other room. He didn't do anything. After that, we both had a bath, we went back to bed and then we ended up having that threesome. That went on for days and days and days and days.

I know that it happened afterward, but I don't remember her being happy. I think I initiated it and she was like, "Leave me alone." So, it didn't really go on. We might have discussed it, about us all living together and stuff, into perpetuity.

You have to understand at the time, I was really in love with him. So, with him bringing in someone new, you know, what were we going to do? Plus, me and her bonded, I think. The reason we bonded was because we both were abused women. There is no doubt in my mind that I'm an abused woman, even though I've never been hit.

Dawn Schiller[h]: [Julia] invited me up to Seattle to go to a wedding. There was a wedding up there and we went roller skating around the park and we came back.

Julia St. Vincent: I asked her at one point — because people around me had this theory that John was using me as a trick, like I was one of his clients, and that he had told somebody that I was just a trick. Well, first of all, people don't get this emotionally involved with tricks and beg them not to leave. Things that happened between us, but you never know, because I was — maybe he was looking for a meal ticket. I did pay for some things — I bought a helluva lot of dope, but somebody told me that wasn't true. Dawn could claim it, that I was a trick and that she was told to do it, or that she was out of her mind, doped up, which was the case. Who can argue with that?

Anyhow, so they ended up staying for a while. Then one day, I came back from work and they had completely destroyed my place — completely fucked it up. They had given me little things, like pictures. Those were on the kitchen floor, broken. They were gone and I didn't see them for months, or days — or however long.

I don't know why they demolished my place. Maybe they got into a fight. Maybe he was trying to prove to her that I didn't mean a fucking thing and they ripped stuff up. I don't know. She could have said, "She's a fucking bitch, why are you with her?"

I can't really say I was jealous. She was more of a curiosity to me. I really looked at her more as a kid — like a lost bird — than someone to be jealous of. Although there were moments I'm sure I got jealous, and I was pissed about the way they did things. It was kind of a presumption that we were together, and then they fucked me over. Eventually, I got over that. I had another boyfriend, around that time, a guy that was a producer in the industry, but he was a 50-year-old. So we had several relationships going on; there were like several roads being taken at one time, so I wasn't really jealous. It seemed to have, mostly, kind of dwindled by the time I found out about her. So when she came in, it wasn't like, "You bitch!" It was more like, "You're kidding!" No wonder I've been tortured all this time. 'Cause I used to see him go down the road when I went to work, and he would take off the other way, toward Glendale, but I didn't put two and two together.

I was pretty much out of the picture. I did not want much to do with him, or her, or anything. That's one of the reasons I made *Exhausted*. I knew he was going to be downhill from that point on and I thought, if anything ever happened to him, I'll have this movie. Plus, you know if you watch it, I bait him constantly — I'm trying to figure out what was going on. Like, "How do you treat women in your personal life?" — What the hell were you doing, you sick pervert? Did you love me or not? I spent hours trying to figure out.

Laurel Canyon

Joel Sussman: He came to me — I was living in Laurel Canyon at the time my daughter was born, actually in 1977 or 1978. He said, "I'm not going to be in touch with you for a while because I'm involved with some stuff I don't want you to be involved with, since you have a really nice life with your family."

I found out after that why he went. You have to know when you're going a different direction than the people around you. He was saying, "I'm going down this road now." I knew he was going into a bad, bad place in his life, going into Laurel Canyon. I didn't cut off with him because I wanted to; our lives just kind of flowed apart. He became more involved with his scene, and I became more involved with my house and raising my child.

Julia St. Vincent: At one point, we were up for like four days straight. I was seeing a shrink, and he didn't like my shrink because he was pissed that I was getting fixed. I said, "I gotta go to my shrink."

He said, "What are you talking about?" and it escalated. He said, "You can't go there all fucked up! Let me give you some of these to get you back to normal," which were Quaaludes. So I took the two Quaaludes and I was getting ready to go to the shrink, and he said, "Are you sure you can drive?"

I was coming onto them, and I said, "Fuck yeah, I can drive." Little did I know, I got in my car and was almost killed. I hit a guardrail at 60 miles an hour and John came out from behind me. He was following me. I was beyond the exit where I was supposed to be, by two exits. I hit the guardrail, he came behind me and he pulled me out of the car. I was unconscious. I remember thinking, "Wow, this car is driving itself." After that, I don't remember anything, except John picking me up and carrying me into his car.

I ended up in the hospital. I was in a concussion. I wasn't supposed to do anything. I was supposed to stay in the hospital for observation, but because of John's temper and everybody's fucking bullshit, I ended up with my mom, John and my shrink running through the hospital, insanely, screaming, "Who did this to my daughter?" I stayed with my shrink, and the next day, John came and got me.

He took me to these peoples' house that lived in the foothills of the canyon. They were kind of like hippie people, and not of the same league of people that John and I knew. People we knew were grips and camera people and porn producers. These people were from some-where else. They were just druggies.

Anyway, we went to their house and we were smoking this dope — with a concussion and I was literally shaking 'cause I couldn't even function. The guy laid out a pile of dope that I swear was just huge. Then he went to the bathroom, and John took a leather pouch and scooped a substantial amount of the dope into the bag.

Paul Thomas: I think the best Holmes story that I have was on the set, during a *Swedish Erotica*. He asked me to take care of this satchel that he had every night when we went to bed in Los Angeles, and I took it home with me. When I got it home, I looked inside. There was like $350,000 — cash — in there.

I brought it on the set with me the next day, but he wasn't there. He showed up about two hours late and said, "Where's my satchel?" I went out to get it, and it wasn't there. I had to tell him the money was gone.

He split. He wasn't angry, he didn't get mad and he just split. About two hours later, the money showed up. He didn't show up for about three days. When he heard that I had it again, he came by and got it from me. He never yelled, he just very quietly [said], "Thank you."

Julia St. Vincent: It turned from a huge pile into a little, tiny thing. Then he turned to me to "shush." Well, I had a concussion; I was totally fucked up. I was petrified because these are kind of low-life people; the guy looked like a biker dude — like he could kill us.

The guy comes up, and he's like "What happened to the dope?" instantly.

John said, "Nothing, it's there."

"Uh-huh. Where's the rest of it?"

John said, "That's all there was."

I'm sinking into the wall, getting nauseous. Does he really believe he's going to fucking pull this shit off? They dropped the subject, but I was so shaky from the concussion and scared to death, so I said, "I'm really sick, can I lie down?"

The girl came in and took me into the baby's room, to a bunk-bed. I'm on the bottom bunk, which was next to the wall. I'm laying there, shaking and shivering, and flipping and vomiting, and I hear through the wall, where he goes, "Well, I think if she did, I'll find out." In other words, he set me up. John knew damn well I didn't touch that dope, but he set [up] his fucking best friend — who has done nothing but forgive him, give him money, love him — and he pretended to this guy that I might have stolen this dope and he would get it back for the guy. I'm listening, horrified.

When we left, and I said goodbye to the girl I had bonded with, who now didn't even want to look at me.

We got in his car and he took me to my house, which wasn't far around the corner after you get out of the canyon. We went to my house and I immediately flip, because I'm thinking, "They're going to come kill me!" So, I get into my car — I'm barely able to fucking move — I go to a phone booth to call up a friend and I'm telling him, "I've got to come over. I'm scared."

He's like, "What the fuck are you doing?" He's Dick Aldrich. He's my "uncle." And he's like, "You gotta quit doing the dope."

As I'm in the phone booth, I see John driving by me, like on the way to my house. I'm ducking in the thing, trying to keep out of sight and thinking, "What the fuck's going to happen?" I never found out who those people were, and what the hell went on. All I know is that I was just fucking floored, watching him.

Julia's description of the inhabitants and location where she witnessed John stealing some dope and Paul Thomas' perfectly illustrates just how deeply John was involved with his addiction. He had become associated with characters far shadier than those he had ever encountered in Ohio or on a porn set in California, all in his pursuit of the next high.

In the audiotapes used to make *Porn King*, John claimed that an unidentified girl he picked up on the freeway ramp introduced him to an unrivaled group of outlaws who lived and dealt drugs out of a rented house at 8763 Wonderland Avenue in the Laurel Canyon neighborhood of Los Angeles.

> *John Holmes* [q]: She was very heavy into drugs, and I picked her up on an on-ramp. She was going the same way I was; if it's a girl and she's fairly attractive, I'll give her a ride. We got to talking and she recognized me. She said, "You're really John Holmes?"
>
> I said, "Yes."
>
> "You do any coke?"
>
> I said, "Yes."
>
> And she said, "So do I, but I'm out." So I gave her a hit of coke and she said, "What are you going to do?"
>
> I said, "I'm going to go and I'm going to pick up some coke."
>
> She said, "Some friends of mine have the best coke in the world."
>
> I said, "No, I have the best coke in the world."
>
> Anyway, I took her up to the Wonderland house, dropped her off and waited downstairs. They said, "Bring your friend up."
>
> She said, "Come up please, please, they want to meet you."
>
> I said "Oh, okay," so I went upstairs with her. Everybody was, "John Holmes…" and I wound up hanging around the place, which is — I spent a couple of months there.

All the other people who were at the Wonderland house were heroin addicts, armed robbers and burglars. They loved to pull burglaries; they loved to pull armed robberies. If they could have done it an easier way, they would have, but that was their main thing. They would start getting sick on withdrawal and they'd whip out some guns, jump in the car and go through the streets, trying to find a house that looked deserted.

They grabbed everything they could. Plenty of the time, I sat at the Wonderland House and watch[ed] them come back from an armed robbery and with canvas bags of money and garbage baggies full of jewelry and uh, they'd just knocked somebody's house up. And if they ring the door bell and a maid is there and nobody else is home, they'd slam the door and tie her up and take whatever they could find.

Today, Joy Audrey Gold Miller, William R. Deverell and their formidable leader, Ronald Launius are remembered collectively as the Wonderland Gang.

Once married to a Beverly Hills attorney, 46-year-old Joy Miller had become estranged from her husband and two daughters after she became addicted to heroin. The lease to the house on Wonderland Avenue was in her name and she shared it with her boyfriend, 37-year-old "Billy" Deverell. Deverell was fond of tattoos and, like Miller, was addicted to shooting heroin. His complexion was pocked by acne scars.

Deverell's arrest record was child's play in comparison to that of Ron Launius — with 27 homicide cases connected to him. A heroin addict who had also completed a tour in Vietnam, Launius did not put up with John's charms and his affinity for bullshit. Allegedly, John feared Ron and avoided him as much as possible, although John frequently visited the house to score drugs from the gang.

High in the Hollywood Hills, Volkswagens and Rolls Royces maneuvered the curves, up to the Laurel Canyon neighborhood to score drugs from 8763 Wonderland. From the balconies above the garage, the gang would throw sacks out to their customers. That summer, there were contracts on their lives because they had sold a pound of baking soda for $250,000. They were going to die.

Ed Nash

Dawn Schiller[h]: He started taking me with him when he went on runs. I never went into anybody's home. He'd always make me wait in cars, hidden. Nobody could see me, waiting with a coke can to pee in and a freebase pipe. He'd come by every 12, sometimes 24 hours, drop a freebase rock, just enough for me to keep high enough to not make a move. John had sold just about everything. From what I gather now, every place that he went when he left me in the motel rooms, he was stealing from people. I knew what the people looked like who lived there but I was never introduced to them, except for Eddie Nash.

John Holmes [q]: I knew Ed Nash for about a year and a half before I met anybody at Wonderland. He did heroin himself; he was a heroin addict. He would smoke it. It seems funny, but it was his favorite thing in life to do. He did the thing that'd killed John Belushi: speedballs. He'd take heroin, cocaine freebase, mix it up and smoke it in a pipe.

During Holmes' most frenetic months, Ed Nash figured prominently into the equation. Born Adel Gharib Nasrallah in Palestine to Lebanese parents, Nash had immigrated to the United States in the 1950s, when he was in his twenties. One of the most fascinating things about Ed Nash is the fact that he whole-heartedly embraced the concept of "The American Dream." Nash had humble beginnings at Beef's Chuck, a Hollywood Boulevard hot dog stand. While waiting on tables himself at Beef's Chuck, in a chef's hat, Nash romanced an elementary school teacher from Santa Barbara. She lived in Hollywood with her autistic son and would often take him for hot dogs. Ed loved her son and offered to "fix it up for you to take him to a top brain surgeon. ... No strings attached."

By the mid-'70s, Nash was worth over $30,000,000. He owned 36 liquor licenses and several well-known nightclubs. There was the Odyssey Disco in Beverly Hills, the Paradise Ballroom, Ali Baba's, and the Kit Kat strip club. The Seven Seas had a tropical motif and belly dancers. Soul'd Out was a recreation of Harlem in Hollywood. The Starwood featured sex, drugs and Rock and Roll; when John met Nash, the Starwood averaged 25 drug busts per month. One search of the club yielded a box of 4,000 counterfeit Quaaludes marked, "FOR DISTRIBUTION AT BOX OFFICE."

Nash had been involved in several underhanded deals that helped to manifest his empire. By the time Holmes met him, Nash was a drug addict who preferred to remain at home, clad in his maroon silk robe or sometimes just in his bikini briefs. Drugs had not helped Nash to age well. At just 52 years old, he was missing part of his sinus cavity, a lung had been removed, and he had a steel plate in his head.

He owned a beautiful home at the end of a cul-de-sac, with a pool, a sunken living room, a white stone façade, a painting by Rembrandt — in addition to literal piles of jewelry, money, drugs and stashes of weapons. Nash's 300-pound bodyguard, Greg Diles, slept with a sawed-off shotgun in his bed. John became a semi-permanent fixture at Nash's, where he called John, "Brother." Nash enjoyed showing John off to his visitors, "Let me introduce you to Mr. John Holmes."

Bill Amerson [h]: He went to running drugs for the Mob, if you will. He did mule drugs to pay for his habit—[but] credit card fraud?

Absolutely not. John was a thief. John would break into offices at night and steal computers and sell them for his drugs.

L.A.P.D. Detective Tom Lange knew of Ed Nash, who had been indicted in 1979 for charges of burning down his own buildings for insurance money. His lawyer for the case was also the President of the Los Angeles Fire Commission, which was responsible for investigating the fires.

> *Tom Lange*: Well, when you're dependent upon cocaine, you get it where you can get it. He got it there [at Wonderland Avenue] and he got it with Ed Nash and he was an intermediary between the two. Stealing things, and then they were fencing the things that he was stealing for them. He was setting up people to get robbed such as he did to Ed Nash. That's what led to the murders.

Sometimes, John treated Ed Nash to sexual favors from young women. An attorney and long time acquaintance of Nash's had told Sager, "You'd walk into the house, there were various girls walking around in various states of undress. Some were quite attractive. Others looked like they'd been sucking on the pipe a little too long."

> *Julia St. Vincent*: My friend, Jackie, who was my uncle Armand's girlfriend, was a hooker. John and I were at [my] house and she called me. John said, "Let me talk to her." He told her that there was this Israeli guy that wants girls, but he's kind of kinky and weird, but he said he pays really well.
> I'm like, "How much?" He ignored me, but then he spilled it out that it was like $500 or more. I figured, "I'll do it for that." I never was a hooker, but I figured, "Well, that's a lot of money, fuck it. I'll do whatever."
> That girl was found dead, outside of one of Nash's clubs, in a car. It was an overdose and I never got over that. I just see those dominoes, going down. Jackie died the first of September, 1980. That's when he took her to Nasrallah and that's when she died outside the Kit Kat Club — she died in the hospital. She was an orphan who was adopted and she had a brother. Her brother called me and said, "Please help me, because I think someone killed her."
> I said, "How do you know she didn't overdose?"
> He said, "'Cause she never shot needles." Which I never knew her to, either.
> I went there, she was in a coma and she died within hours. They found her in a car at that thing, and they never investigated it as a murder. That was shortly after John told her about the Israeli guy, that she happened to end up at his club, dead in the parking lot? Jackie was the type of person who would blow it, do stupid things.

Dawn Schiller[h]: I got to meet Eddie Nash, after sitting outside of his house (probably more days than he knows) and learning how to lower my body temperature and my breathing so that I didn't steam the windows. People would guard his house and they would walk around the car.

John basically sold me for dope. He needed to get high and he gave me, the teenager, in trade. One time it was on my birthday and it was an experience. I was drilled with the story that I was supposed to be his niece from Oregon, in town, looking into nursing schools. My name was something else — I can't even remember what it was supposed to be. I knew that it was for the drugs because I wanted the drugs, too, at this point. We didn't have any.

I was told, pretty much, how I was going to be treated the moment that I would go in. That I would probably be left sitting in the living room, with drugs in front of me, with money, and jewelry. If I touched a thing, my body would disappear in the desert somewhere because I was being watched with a two-way mirror somewhere.

I was left in the living room for hours with all these things in front of me. At that time, I was so addicted to coke, that it was intentional on Eddie Nash's part because I wasn't the drug-free niece — he tested you to see if you were on dope. It wasn't hard to figure out. I broke out in a cold sweat, waiting to be called into the bedroom.

He paid me in coke and then I was to go out. John would be waiting to pick me up. I turned it all over to him and I told John, word for word, everything that happened. He back-handed me so hard, my tooth went through my lip because there wasn't as much cocaine as they'd originally bargained on.

Loss of a Friend

John Holmes[i]: Just like sex, no matter where I turned, someone was offering me a silver spoonful. It took a few years, but I was on my way to losing everything to finance my addiction. Because my attitude had changed, I even lost friends and associates.

John often spent time with Amerson and continued to maintain a connection with his godchildren. By all accounts, John's relationships with the Amerson children were mutually caring.

Sean Amerson[h]: At the time, John was really fucked up. He was a nutcase even more so than normal. You take a hyper kid and you put him on crack — he bounces off the walls. Essentially that's what John was at the time. He looked really bad. He looked like shit.

I remember seeing his car; he had a Galaxy 500 convertible, an old red one. And when he'd got it, it was brand new. It was completely pristine and rebuilt. It was really a nice car. To show how far he'd gone back, he'd ripped the back seat out of the car and had been using it for storage, like it was a truck. And it had dents and dings all over it. Top was torn; it had been raining inside the car. Anyway, it sort of shows you how he'd really declined. He was just scummy.

Denise Amerson[h]: I was really kept away from a lot of that. Of course, I knew that he was high a lot, [but] I didn't know to the extent. In my family, when I was growing up, we were kept away from a lot of what was going on, although we were in the middle of what was going on. I never saw John doing drugs, but I definitely saw John high. I definitely saw that he lost a lot of money to drugs and that he lost a lot of his soul to drugs, but I think that was inevitable in the business.

I think, feel and know about John. Yeah, I know how high he was; I know about all the drugs, my father was a drug addict, too. I was there, that's how I was raised, but yet I was the goddaughter and I was treated differently. I'm sure that what I was told a lot of times was different than what the adults at the time or people at the time would have known.

Julia St. Vincent: The same time frame, my $20 gold piece, a money clip that was given to me when my uncle was in the hospital, dying, was stolen out of my jewel box. John knew about it because he was there. It was a liberty eagle [$20 Liberty Double Eagle gold coins were made from 1850 to 1907]. It's very rare and it's supposed to be worth a grand, or some huge amount of money.

When I said, "Oh my God, I can't find my money clip," John told me, "I bet you your apartment manager stole it."

Now mind you, my locks were re-keyed by John's brother, David. They put in [what] are supposed to be the most fool-proof locks. That was the lock that was in place when this happened.

Gloria Leonard[h]: I had gotten married, moved out to California from New York and had run into him quite by accident. I'd just moved into this house in Los Angeles and he showed up on my doorstep. I don't know how he found out where I lived. I was with [adult film-maker] Bobby Hollander at the time.

Bobby Hollander[h]: I came home from work one day, early, at about three o'clock. I opened up the front door and the house smelled like fried grapes. I said, "What the hell is this?" I didn't notice any other cars or anything strange, except the odor in the house. Sure enough, the first person I saw facing me was John Holmes.

John was standing in front of a coffee table. He was very nice; it was almost like it was his house. I noticed he had a suitcase — it wasn't a briefcase or an attaché; it was like a plaid, little-kid-runs-away-from-home suitcase and it was on the coffee table with the lid up. He was holding something in his hand and the smell was coming from this area. I walked in and Gloria said, "Oh, Bobby, I want you to meet John Holmes."

I took a look in the suitcase, and he said, "Well, do you want to get a little buzz?" There were six freebase pipes in this suitcase and a blowtorch. The thing was out there with glass, with the dippers in it and 151 Bacardi Rum to make the torch. There he was, taking one of those blasts on the thing. This was my first meeting with John. It was an enjoyable afternoon and he was a complete gentleman.

Gloria Leonard[h]: We told John that we had some chores the next morning and we'd be back at the house at a certain time. By the time we got home my house was totally robbed. Everything that I had ever owned was just wiped out. I'm quite convinced that it was John.

Bobby Hollander[h]: I absolutely remember bragging about getting new cars the next day. We had an 11 o'clock appointment to pick up the cars. The only people that knew we were getting the cars that day were John and Gloria's friend, Peggy.

We got the cars the following day and drove home. We got home, walked in the front door and the house was a-shambles. The television was gone, the VCR was gone, cameras were gone, jewelry was gone, and the bedroom was completely ransacked. I had a couple of guns at the time — they were gone. The police brought it back a year later. The only one that knew that we were going to be gone at that particular time that day was John. Checking with the neighbors after calling the cops, they saw a van being driven away with a description of John, who I believe burglarized the house. In those days, in 1981, he was using drugs pretty good. Coke was nothing new to him. It wasn't new to me, or to a lot of people that we associated with. Whether it was in the industry or that time of season, it seemed to be the "in" thing to do.

Julia St. Vincent: One time I came home and my staircase was filled with a kitchen table and furniture. It was really old and clunky, like dungeon stuff. It was stacked up to my door. I used to call him, only through the answering service, so, I called him and he called me back. I said, "What is this stuff?"

He said, "Oh I thought you would want that. It's furniture for your house."

I said, "No, I don't want it; come and take it."

I told John, "You're going down and I'm not going with you." That's why John lost me. He didn't lose me because he gave up his desire for me. He was going to fucking hell and I wasn't doing it.

He cried and said, "I'm not that bad. I'm a good guy."

And I said, "I know you're a good guy, but this isn't where I'm going. When you get it together, let me know." He just kept going on with his addiction.

We were filming *Exhausted*, however, it was only a few weeks before that I had told John, "It's over. You're out of here. I'm not doing this anymore."

Sharon Holmes [h]: In 1980, he couldn't get work or he couldn't get enough money to support his habit; he began robberies. He began pilfering out of our house. I'd come home and I hadn't seen him in months and realize half the china cabinet was gone.

When I would ask if he knew where Dawn was he would say, "No, she's gone back to her mother's in Oregon."

After John and Dawn left Julia St. Vincent's home in shambles and had worn out their welcome at Sharon's, the couple stayed with people John knew. In parallel with his problems with freebase cocaine, John had grown more controlling and abusive toward Dawn.

Dawn Schiller [h]: A lady that he worked with in a movie was turning tricks in her home. She had a little condo unit in a massive apartment complex alongside the freeway in the Valley somewhere. Her name was Michelle, and that's all I remember. He walked me in and announced to me that I was going to be — you know — um, she had a list of clients that I was to see.

He sold me to her to take care of her clientele because he got whatever money was my cut, and she got the cut for providing the business. He eventually stole from her and blamed it on me in his level of drugs. And while he was out, she became very abusive. If I was hungry, she wouldn't give me anything to eat. In my eyes, he was the only one that had authority over me and he just passed it on to her.

On January 14, John stole a computer out of a car's trunk while Dawn and Michelle visited an apartment in Marina Del Ray. When John and Dawn were later arrested in a parking lot, Ed Nash bailed them out.

Dawn Schiller [h]: I had an issue and I complained while we were out driving one day. The fucker, he just pulled off the freeway and threw me in the trunk and wouldn't let me out until I agreed to go back in there. But this was another point where it was intolerable for me because I didn't love anybody else but him.

One night, he asked me to draw his bath and asked me to get a cup of coffee. He hadn't taken his eyes off of me. He gave me the moment to take make my break. I went out and I mixed the coffee. A sliding glass door was behind me and I ran down to the nearest Denny's.

I did call my mother collect and she said that she would send a ticket to the bus station in Glendale. I didn't really know where I was. I had no driver's license, since I wasn't allowed to drive. The freeway system was a mystery to me. The bus wasn't leaving until the next day and she'd have a ticket there.

There was a little old man in the Denny's and he saw that I must have been crying. He thought that I was hungry, so he bought me a bowl of chili and he started to talk to me. I told him what was happening. He lived in a semi-retirement home with other people of his age group. He said he would let me sleep on his floor if he could touch my butt and I said, "Is that all?" It was kind of a cute thing because I slept on his floor that night. They had a community dining room where they had their meals served. Everybody was in on it because I had to be smuggled in. The people that were running the place couldn't allow me to be there. It was against the rules. It was toast-under-the-table kind of thing.

I was able to make a phone call there to the guy at the Glendale Bus Station. I didn't have a ride and he offered to come pick me up. I asked him, "Has there been anybody asking about me?"

He said, "Somebody like that just left." So the guy believed that I was desperate and apparently that I was in trouble. He drove out, picked me up and then brought me back so that I would get right on the bus. He loaned me five dollars to have sandwiches on the way. I made it; I got away and I think I was up there a couple of months.

Sharon Holmes[h]: The last time I saw him before the murders was in March of 1981, when our dog died. Buttons was a black miniature daschund, probably the greatest dog I've ever owned, and she died of old age. He happened to call about an hour after she died in my arms. She was being treated for liver failure and she just came in one morning after breakfast, begged to be picked up and howled this ungodly howl in my arms.

He called me about an hour after this had happened. He came home and he built a coffin for her, which was fine; I didn't say anything. He felt he had to do this because he adored the dog, also. If he could have taken her with him he would have, but I wouldn't have allowed any of my dogs or the cats to go with him because I couldn't count on him. Of course, I had her cremated, but I let him build a coffin because he felt he had to do this.

This was the last time I saw him. I did not talk to him again until probably the first part of June. He had called and said he had run into Dawn and she was going back up north to her mother's, but that she was fine, everything was A-OK.

Countdown

Dawn Schiller[h]: John called every day. He called before I even arrived and begged me to come back. He told me how much he loved me, that he was sorry and that he'd never hit me again, it was the drugs, "If we just go away from the drugs, everything would be all right."

I cringed. I believed that to be true, and I didn't. It was just hard. I didn't believe he had the strength to do it. There were too many days where he'd taken my hand, walked out to the middle of the street and taken the freebase pipe, smashed it into the street and said, "That was the last one that I'll ever have."

Early in the summer of 1981, the Wonderland Gang had a visitor staying with them named David Lind, an acquaintance of Ron Launius. In keeping with the other Wonderland residents, Lind was a needle junkie. He had brought along his girlfriend, Barbara "Butterfly" Richardson.

Tracy Raymond McCourt was another associate of the Wonderland Gang. Although he, Lind and Launius were friendly enough with Holmes, it is widely believed that John resented Launius for using him as a court jester at parties. Purportedly, Launius would demand that John "show it" to guests. In the same vein, there was absolutely no love lost between John Holmes and David Lind.

John Holmes[q]: Two guys that were living at the Wonderland house had gotten into some kind of trouble in Sacramento and they were flying to Sacramento once every other week for some court case. They hadn't solved their court case in Sacramento the last time they were there. When they were there the last time, somebody had tried to set up a big narcotics scheme with someone and at that point in time, they met David Lind, who had nicknamed himself "The Bounty Hunter." He hunts down people who owe on drug debts and he cooperates with the police.

David Lind is a sadist and he works with the police department. So, if David Lind is picked up for an armed robbery or a burglary, which he does, he turns in evidence. He says, "I'll tell you what I'll do, I'll turn over three of the biggest coke dealers in town." Lind is associated with all the scum I would associate with. Everybody hates his guts, everybody wants him dead. He's a crook. He's the guy that likes to, if you're not home — but your old lady is — and you owe a drug debt, he'll tie her down, naked, spread-eagled, put an iron on her stomach, plug it in and leave.

There may be some truth to John's accusations about Lind being a police informant, as Lind had served time for charges that included burglary, forgery, assault with intent to commit rape. Lind was also a member of the Aryan Brotherhood. A motorcyclist, he had tattoos and needle tracks covering his entire body.

John Holmes [q]: I was a go-between. Nobody knew anyone else. The cocaine they got from somebody else and the banana crates full of Colombian marijuana they got from somebody else. When I told Ed Nash that the people at the Wonderland house were interested in buying heroin, I knew Ed had a connection with heroin people.

Eddie said, "I'll tell you what I'll do. I'll supply you with the heroin, but you have to understand something: Heroin people are not like cocaine people. Cocaine people run out of cocaine and they run out of money. They won't go grab a gun and try to kill somebody to get enough money to supply their habit. Heroin is a totally different animal and it's a totally different type of people." He said, "We'll deal through you, but understand that if they start giving you a bad time and start giving you trouble, you come to me and you tell me, and I'll handle it."

Well, they turned over the antique gun collection. They'd sell some antique guns, very Davy Crockett-like. These were very valuable museum pieces, and these two hookers at the Wonderland house handed me a solid gold chain and they would trade heroin for it.

I would take the jewelry to Nash. Nash would say, "Well, it's worth about this much."

I'd take the heroin back to the Wonderland house.

But they wanted it back and said, "We want all the jewelry."

I said, "You're going to have to pay the value of the heroin to get the things back." Well, they couldn't ever reach a point where they had enough money to get it back. They were under the impression that they could sell the antique guns, which they'd sold for a few grams of pure heroin for a lot more money.

So Nash said, "I'll hold the guns and jewelry for a week."

Dawn Schiller had been home in Oregon with her mother, but that did not stop John from contacting her and using his charms and some lofty promises to lure her back into his arms.

Dawn Schiller [h]: He wheedled his way back in and I started to believe him — wanting to get away and just be with Sharon and I, and just live our lives, which I assumed to be in Glendale — away from the industry and away from everything that just messed up his head, messed up his emotions; away from the drugs. I thought that he really felt safe in Glendale and I did too, from what I remember.

We had good times and what I didn't know was his plan was going to be robbing Eddie Nash, and that was going to be his big bank that he was going to run with. Anyway, a week before the murders, he had talked me into going back and I flew down. He met me at Burbank Airport from Oregon. Immediately — first thing that he did was pick up someone else's baggage off the lift and walked away with it. I pretended I didn't [see it].

Ron Jeremy: He would steal luggage off people. I'd heard from people that he'd done that, in [*WADD*]. That's heinous, man. Imagine some poor schmuck who has their life, phone books and photographs — suitcases are so personal — and what did he get out of it all? When he needed money for drugs, he would steal. Even today, with terrorism, it's still the honor system. If you get off a plane really early and you grab some luggage, you can run with it. They don't check the little slip that attaches to it.

Dawn Schiller[h]: I didn't get to see Sharon. It was motel after motel, until one day. I realize now, [this] was the time when the robbery of Eddie Nash's was taking place. [He] left me in a motel nearby, down the street, actually, Laurel Canyon [Boulevard]. I think that I've been in every motel on that road, if they even exist anymore. He left me there, the rent expired and he said that he'd be back.

Dawn came back to John on June 27, 1981. John and Dawn had a sweet reunion at a motel, but then the next morning when she awoke alone, she found out that John had not paid for the room. Unable to pay the bill, the motel's management put her out onto the street.

Dawn Schiller[h]: Here I was, just back from Oregon — and all these promises — and I was standing on an extremely active street, not knowing what to do, not knowing where he was and what was going on with my bags.
A few pimps approached me and then this van pulled up with what looked like some guys. They looked like they were working construction, just done with work, and this lady was driving it. She came up and said, "Are you OK?"
"No," I said. "My boyfriend was supposed to be back. They kicked me out. I don't have any money and I'm not supposed to go anywhere. He only knows that I'm here."
She said, "Is there any way you can contact him?"
I said, "Well, his answering service."
She turned out to be a Christian support organizer for a group of others that belonged to the church that was painting someone else's

house for them. She said, "You can call him and leave a message, and you can stay with me until he picks you up."

I was crying on the street, so it was the safest thing that approached me and I said OK. We got to her place and I left a message. She seemed really nice. She wasn't a pusher of the religion, but she was a Christian.

June 29, 1981

Little did Dawn know that while she was staying overnight with the Good Samaritan, John was helping to orchestrate a robbery at Ed Nash's house. It was early in the morning on June 29, 1981.

John Holmes [q]: Everybody at Wonderland — they didn't want to go out for an armed robbery. They wanted the guns back and they wanted the jewelry back so they could sell it to buy heroin. They said, "You go and tell Nash that we want the guns back and we want the jewelry back or there's going to be trouble. You can tell him that yourself and you give him the money we owe him." So they gave me a handful of money. They owed about $1,000 worth of credit for the guns and then another $1,000 for the jewelry.

The Wonderland gang scrounged together $400 to send John to Nash's. It was a less than two-mile drive from Wonderland Avenue to Dona Lola Place.

John Holmes [q]: They were really frantic and everybody was getting sick from withdrawal, so they wanted to make the big plan to rob Eddie Nash's house. They said, "We're gonna put a gun to your head and you're gonna go to the front door of Eddie Nash's house. We're gonna hide in the bushes and when Eddie Nash opens the front door for you, we're gonna rush the door."

Well, you don't do that at Eddie Nash's because Greg Diles and one of the other bodyguards would open the door. No one opens that door without a gun in their hand, so there was going to be a shootout. I said, "That's not gonna work, you're gonna have a bloody shoot-out on a cul-de-sac in the Hollywood Hills and the cops [will be] there in 30 seconds. The only way to get into that place is to sneak into it."

They said, "You figure a way to sneak us into that goddamn house or we're gonna blow your head off."

So I said, "I'll go see what I can do."

I went down to Eddie Nash's house and for the last three days, I'd been going to Eddie Nash's house and saying, "These guys are getting crazy, Ed. These guys want to come here and hold you up. They are serious, and they have guns, and they're pissed off."

Well, Eddie's on a ten-day freebase jag; hadn't slept for ten days and he was half out of his fucking mind. He'd say, "Fuck you; get out of here. I told you, these guns are mine now and the jewelry's mine. Fuck you."

It was a matter of finding a way to get them into that house, because Ed Nash wouldn't do anything about it and these people wanted the guns back. They considered them their guns and Nash considered them his guns. I just wanted out. If I could raise the money, buy the guns and jewelry back from Ed Nash, I could take the goddamn guns and jewelry back to the Wonderland house, give them the guns, give 'em the jewelry, and keep the cash, that would be the end of it.

Nash jacked the price up and he wouldn't back down. We had these two armed camps; I was the only one in between. So I had a choice: open warfare or somebody was going to get killed and I was going to be implicated in the murder, heroin and drugs.

I'd been there all night long, two or three times, trying to figure out a way to get those guys into the house without a shootout. I was locked into a real bad position. Finally just about dawn, Ed Nash said, "I'm gonna go to bed."

While trying to convince Nash to give back the goods for a cheaper price, John had inadvertently smoked up $400 worth of freebase with Nash. It was dawn by the time John left Dona Lola for the Wonderland house.

John Holmes [q]: I went down the hallway and I unlocked the back bedroom sliding glass door, which no one ever used that back bedroom anyway, so I unlocked the sliding-glass door. I went back and I said, "This is the gate you have to jump over; this is the door I left unlocked."

For me it was the only way out. I was gonna be in the middle of a goddamn gun battle and there was gonna be people killed. Ed Nash was not backing my actions, so I left with the goddamn back door unlocked.

With hopeful optimism, John believed that Nash would understand his predicament. Back at the Wonderland house, John found Lind, the only one not in a heroin-induced slumber, and said that the coast was clear. Three hours later, the rest of the gang was ready, so Lind asked John to make the short trip back to Nash's to verify that the door was still ajar and that Nash was still in bed.

On John's way back from Nash's, he saw McCourt driving the opposite way on Dona Pegita. "It's time," Holmes said and then he smiled and raised his fist, "Get 'em, boys!"

John Holmes [9]: They told this other guy (they called him Cherokee), "You can pay off your debt and make a few bucks if you drive the car." He was the fourth.

They pulled up in front of the house, went over the gate and went through the open sliding-glass door, got the drop on Ed Nash and Greg Diles, tied them up and humiliated the shit out of him. David Lind and the two guys who went in the house [Launius and Deverell] — those were the ones who committed the robbery. Kid [McCourt] sat in the car for 45 minutes, waiting for them to come out.

They went really overboard; they called him names, they said, "You're dead. I'm gonna kill you." David Lind fired once and burned Greg Diles' back and finally, Ed Nash just gave them everything and told them where the stashes were at, gave them the code — everything.

I went back to the Wonderland house while the robbery was going on and pretty soon, the car pulled into the garage, screeching tires, and they ran upstairs, bags full of stolen jewelry and money and cocaine and heroin. Everybody was happy as hell. They pulled out scales and they weighed out the cocaine, gave me my share and my share of the money. Because they had to have a driver, instead of me getting a fourth, I had to split my fourth with this driver guy. I went back and gave it to Ed Nash.

At ten in the morning, Lind, McCourt, Launius and Deverell returned. Holmes jumped up and asked, "So what happened? How did it go down?"

Against Lind's orders, Ron Launius had told John some details about the robbery. However, the Wonderland guys hid about $100,000 of cash before the loot was divvied up with John, who was forced to split his share with McCourt. After smoking rocks of cocaine in the bathroom, John came out to the living room, where the Wonderland gang alternated between heroin and cocaine. John complained about only getting $3,000 because he knew Nash had much more than that.

Dawn Schiller [h]: [John] called back the next day. He said, "Stay there. I'll be right there."

He came in, and not really knowing this girl — she lived with her sister and her sister was not Christian — when he arrived, he asked if anybody wanted a line. The girl that picked me up didn't say anything, but her sister did. She said, "Sure."

He pulled out his briefcase — the largest pile of cocaine that I've ever seen in my life.

He had a couple of Tarot cards in his briefcase and he used them for drawing out lines. Anyway, we all got high. I didn't question the pile, but he told me, "This is how we are getting out of here." I was under the impression that we needed to sell it and it was our bank.

Then again, I was under the impression that Sharon was involved and it was going to be his retirement.

He and I went to the store. We got back and we tried to buzz ourselves in. The girl's sister wouldn't let us in — she was standing on her balcony, waving a Christian flag, swearing that he was the Devil because he had used a Tarot card, that was the Devil, to cut his coke. I'm pretty sure he didn't even remember where he got it — it was the least on his mind. So we were forced to go and rent a motel, again. I think that he wanted to keep her home as a cover, which would have been much safer.

"I realized it was John, so I just left the latch on the door, and I said, 'Why are you here?' He asked if he could come in, and I realized from the night light in the entryway that he was covered in blood."

SHARON HOLMES

7.

Revenge on Wonderland

The Wonderland Murders: July 1, 1981 - July 12, 1981

Retribution

John Holmes[9]: I didn't want to see anybody ever again. I had set up the whole fucking thing. They were so stoned out of their fucking minds on heroin that I scored, trying to set the whole goddamn robbery up so nobody got shot. And the fuckers were in there shooting heroin; Nash told me they'd take his heroin into the bathroom and were shooting up — during the fucking robbery!

To keep me out of trouble with Ed Nash, the agreement was that after the robbery they would take a blanket, smash the back glass and cut the screen to make it look like they broke in, but they left it wide open. They didn't give a shit. And then, they got on the phone and told everybody — every junkie in the world that they're gonna pay off all their debts. They're getting on the phone and they're calling up Mr. Howard [one of their other drug suppliers] and saying, "We just robbed Eddie Nash." They're calling all their friends; everybody!

I had allowed David Lind and his group to sneak in the house, get the drop on the robbery and leave. Instead, when they got there, they didn't smash the glass. They told Ed Nash that I'd set the fucking thing up because they didn't care — they're leaving the fucking country. They're going to Hawaii. They're going to disappear into thin air. They're getting what they want, so everything is left on me. It was like they wanted me to get so criminally involved in it that they would put everything off on me. It was insane.

They think Ed Nash is going to be satisfied with killing me and he's not going to come after them, but they humiliated him. They don't understand, they humiliated him — they took his money, but a lot of the anger in Nash wasn't that they took his money; it was that they humiliated him and they shot his bodyguard.

I wasn't going to run from anybody. I called Nash. He said, "Oh everything's fine, everything's great, come on up," but I knew something wasn't right, after he'd gotten tied up, beat up and robbed of everything he had in his house. He had to have known it was me. I was the last one in that house.

I called up Nash, who lived right down at the bottom of the street, so he wouldn't have time to plan anything, and he said, "The police have been here looking for you." I called three or four other people and they said, "The police have been here looking for you. They've been here looking for you — they think you're dead."

I went out to tell Nash about the robbery, explain to him why the robbery went down and how I saved his fucking life. They had wanted to blow the place up, all because Nash didn't keep his word to me. He didn't cover me like he said. He allowed me to get in there on trafficking.

Tom Blake[h]: [John said,] "I called up Nash and said, 'Hey what's happening?'"

Nash advised him, "Hey, everything is cool. Why don't you come on up?"

John Holmes[q]: When I went to Nash's house it was to say, "You didn't back my actions like you said you would." He met me at the front door with a gun. He split my lip wide open with a pistol .357 and held me for 18 hours. During that 18-hour period, people came up to buy cocaine. He had two guys with guns sitting there; there was blood all over the place. He had told everybody there that he was going to kill me. Now, the more people he told, the safer I felt because in the narcotics world, everybody's a goddamn rat. You want to stay out of jail; you rat everybody else off.

Ed Nash disappeared into his bedroom and I was left totally alone while everybody was in the back bedroom for four hours. I was just left alone with one of the bodyguards in the living room.

Tom Blake[h]: John said, "I went up to Nash's house that evening and Nash said, 'Hey, I know what happened and you are going to do what you did for those guys on Wonderland Lane what you did to me.'"

John Holmes[q]: [When Nash came out of the bedroom], he said he was going to kill me if I didn't kill them. Ed Nash is pissed off at me. When Ed Nash told me to go up there and collect a baggie full of eyeballs, I didn't know how I was going to do it. Every gun, every room, every table had pistols, guns, knives, everything. I was to go in there, open-handed, no weapon, and off these guys. Five people, it was insane.

Tom Blake[h]: Nash is a very powerful individual and his bodyguards are a couple of black males, about 300 pounds, big boys. John feared for his life. Nash said "If you don't do it, I'm going to kill your wife, your friends." I believe Nash had an address book of John's with all the names and addresses of his relatives.

July 1, 1981

Tom Lange: He was intimidated and threatened by Nash. [He said,] "You're gonna tell me what happened," and when he found out, [he said,] "This is what you're gonna do. You're gonna let 'em in, they're going to do a number and then you're gonna leave."

The message to Holmes would have been, "Don't send them in when they're having a party; we want them all out." That's why [the murders occurred] at four a.m. "We want to hit these people and send them a message and beat their heads in. We're not going to do it when they're still up and about." You might get shot coming through the door. You let them in when it's safe to let them in.

I'm thinking that Nash sent some people over there knowing that he had, perhaps, a house full of bad guys — McCourt might have been there, Lind was supposed to be there and they knew they were armed and dangerous. You're not going to send one or two people over with pipes into a den of six or seven, cold-blooded, robbing, thieving killers who are dealing dope. Launius, Lind and Deverell certainly had that reputation. Launius was a suspect in the Vic Weiss murders in 1978 — a big sports promoter out here. So these weren't people that you'd play with. You're not going to send one or two people, so common sense would tell you that he probably sent several people.

John Holmes [9]: I went up to the [Wonderland] house and Nash's bodyguards followed me into the house. They parked down the street near a school and I parked in the driveway near the house. It was really quiet and I figured everybody was asleep, but what the hell would they be asleep for? They'd just scored an immense amount of money and drugs, so there should have been a hell of a goddamn party going on.

Ed Nash must have known to send me into an armed camp to kill all these people with my bare hands. I think he was hoping that they would kill me and that would be the end of it. I think that was it, but anyway, when I got there, the gate was open. They always kept the gate closed, well, it didn't matter about the gate because the gate was broken; if you pulled on one of the bars on the gate, the gate would just pop open. It looked like you needed a security key to get in, but just pull on this bar and the gate popped open. The gate was already open, so I went up the flight of stairs into the house, knocked on the door. There was no answer.

I went around to the back. The backdoor was slightly open. [There usually was a] really big goddamn pit bull in the back, and he wasn't there. I thought, "Fuck, they left." That was my first impression — that the house was empty. The doors were open and the dogs were gone. I thought, "Well, they left early." That was it. I looked in the crack of the door and I saw red, splash of red, and thought "Oh, God." That's when I started to count the bodies.

Funny thing is that I counted more bodies than the police did. That could have been a shock; walking in and finding what I thought was six dead people. But there were two people upstairs, another person in another room, and two people downstairs. And I thought there was another person. After I'd gotten through the initial shock, there was nothing worth saving. Whoever killed all these people took everything they could get their fucking hands on.

According to John's tape-recorded accounts, he remembered a story of a man who had attacked Nash about a year before. That man had mysteriously disappeared. Having believed that it was a matter of life or death, John admitted that he began to search frantically among the bodies and blood spatter for valuables to bring back to Nash.

John Holmes[q]: I went around the house and I took every fucking thing I could find of any value whatsoever, threw it all in the back of my car and took off. That was just as the sun was coming up the following day. I pulled into Ed Nash's garage and they closed the door and I started unloading stuff and they started going through it.

Ed said, "Where's all the money, where's all the guns?"

I said, "This is everything that was there." I dumped everything out of my car at Ed Nash's house. Ed Nash always thought that I'd loaded it into other cars and took it and dumped it somewhere; I mean, I'd gotten a wallet, clothes and jewelry boxes. I didn't know what was in the jewelry boxes, but nothing valuable — nothing like handfuls and boxes full of chains and gold.

He said, "You did it, you really did it." He acted surprised that I came back. There's blood all over everything now because there's blood all over in the house. I have blood on my shirt from picking up the things that I'd put into the car. Ed took everything I'd dumped. He was very smart about it.

A lot of the bodyguards he had were black and he loaded all the stuff into their cars and had them drive to East L.A. We drove down alleys and through closeouts with the chest of drawers. I had pulled out a couple of chests of drawers and threw stuff in it and he threw those in a trash can. I said, "Aren't you afraid somebody will find all this?"

He said, "Nah, cops don't come down here. This is East L.A. All this stuff will get picked up by black people and black people don't turn shit in." Not one piece from the house has ever been turned up. He was right, he was absolutely right.

The Crime Scene

John Holmes[q]: You gotta realize — these people I knew for months and they were all dead, splattered all over the house. You couldn't have made a bigger mess of those people if they'd gone through a garbage disposal. I mean these people were massacred. It wasn't a bullet to the head. These people were purposely tortured to death. That's why I don't think Ed Nash was pissed off enough to do it, you know, I believe that his bodyguards were capable of doing it.

The first officer arrived at the residence of 8763 Wonderland Avenue between 4:10 and 4:20 p.m. on July 1, 1981, twelve hours after police believe the murders took place. Detective Tom Lange was assigned to investigate the multiple homicides and arrived on the scene at 6:20 p.m., after paramedics and police had been there.

> *Tom Lange*: This is a multi-level home, it's a two-story, but with three different levels. The entrance from the east, there's a walk-up step on the east side and the steps go up to the door, and when we were there, there was a gate that someone would have to man. The gate was generally kept locked.
>
> Of course, we found out that it was a dope pad. People were dealing dope out of there for some time. The L.A. County Sheriff actually had the place under surveillance. As we entered, we were told initially that there were four bodies inside and that the fifth victim had been removed was in bad shape and it was a female, not expected to make it.
>
> We were talking about the crime scene and how extensive it was and we were going to be there for a while. We were there for about 24 hours, at least initially, and we didn't move the bodies. It was very warm and all the windows were shut up, so we wanted to expedite without ruining any evidence. So, we had a couple of photographers go through, but then one of the guys from the lab said, "I have a big 16-millimeter shoulder-mounted camera and if you want to use that, you could probably do this."
>
> I thought, well, why not? I'll narrate it and start out the front and just do like we do our normal walkthroughs.
>
> It got kind of cumbersome though because we had the cables and you had to hook those up to a generator. It wasn't the portable videocams like you have now. It was kind of clumsy to do that, but as it turned out it probably was the right thing to do because it was introduced into evidence. It was the first crime scene video for a murder scene that was ever introduced in the state of California. We felt that it would show a relationship between, not just the victims and the evidence, but the brutality of it. Wouldn't the jury like to look at this? Which they did.

In our age of celebrity gossip and true-crime-inspired dramas, it is not surprising that the scene of the Wonderland Murders has taken on a life of its own. James Cox was motivated to make the 2003 Lions Gate film *Wonderland* after he saw the crime scene tape, which he had rented from an underground video store in Los Angeles. The crime scene video was available as a special feature on the *Wonderland* disk and briefly sold as a DVD version with higher-quality resolution.

Tom Lange: As we entered, to the left there was a living room area on the first level. That was where the first victim, Barbara Richardson, was found lying on ground on her side by a sofa. It appeared that she'd been attacked while lying on the sofa and was knocked off of it. She'd been bludgeoned, there was quite a bit of blood.

Blood splatters everywhere — there was cast-off from the weapons that we later determined were pipes. There was cast-off as high as the ceiling. The [murderer's] hand was coming back before it would come down and strike somebody. So it's blood that's flown off of the pipe with the hand coming back before swinging down and hitting again. They were beaten several times with that. There was evidence of narcotics paraphernalia in there.

In his narration during the crime scene video, Lange notes the patterns of blood spatter in the room. A large soaking of blood on the back corner of the couch cushion provided evidence that Barbara Richardson's killers struck her on the head while she slept on the couch in a pink-and-white sleeping bag. Her lifeless body was found in the space between the couch and the coffee table. Large drops of blood that ran down the wall behind the speakers indicated that Richardson had continued to receive traumatic blows to her head after falling from the couch. She had no injuries that suggested any attempt to defend herself.

Blood striped the walls so thoroughly that it looked as if the walls were deeply textured cement. Throughout the residence, there were transfers of blood: footprints on the carpeting, smears on the pillar, the walls of the stairwell by the front entrance and the light switch plates. The steps and hallway were littered with empty drawers and socks that evidenced ransacking, which could have occurred during the 12 hours between the murders and police arrival.

The Launius' bedroom showed evidence of looting as well. The closet and bathroom lights were left on and cold water was left running in the bathroom sink. In the closet there was an overturned, white cast-iron chair with blood on several of its legs. Blood also covered a pair of brown leather cowboy boots and the phone, which lay on the floor by the bed. The nightstand drawer by Ron was open to reveal one hypodermic needle. One more lay on top of the nightstand. Lange also noted that there was a pellet gun, hanging barrel-up on the wall of the Launius' bedroom, with another gun in the closet.

Tom Lange: Towards the back of the house, there are three steps up to the back bedroom where Ron Launius was. Ron Launius was in bed. He'd also been attacked by a pipe because his skull was basically pulverized. His wife had been removed and was the one survivor, Susan Launius. There was quite a bit of blood. She was beaten on the bed and found on the floor. There was a tremendous amount of blood on the floor, and of course throughout, with the same cast off and spatter.

The bloodstains on the wall of the Launius' bedroom included a large, oval-shaped one where Susan's head had rested while she moaned in the hours before emergency medical technicians arrived on the scene and transported her to the hospital. Pieces of her skull were wedged against her head injuries in such a way that prevented her from bleeding to death and her finger was amputated. Apparently, she had attempted to defend herself from the blows.

> *Tom Lange*: On the upper level, we had Billy Deverell and Joy [Miller] was lying across the bed. Their skulls were pulverized. That was a mess.

Billy Deverell was slumped against the wall in a sitting position with his left arm resting on the television stand. The television was left on to Channel Three. At the corner of the bed, police noted a hammer. Consistent with the blood spatters throughout, a curtain that covered the doors to the outside patio was covered in blood that extended onto the ceiling. Joy Miller was found lying on her back on the bed with her legs dangling off the edge at her knees and her arms at her sides. Grey brain matter oozed from her nose as a result of the vicious beating.

It was determined that the murder weapon was a threaded steel pipe.

> *Tom Lange*: Other than the bodies and all the blood and the gore, what struck us was that it was a "message killing." If you just want these people to go away, you're going to come in and shoot them in their beds; you're going to kill them. This was a message — they were beaten savagely.

The Investigation

Lange and his partner, Detective Robert Souza, were tipped off to Holmes as a possible suspect by Lind, who reported the details of the Nash robbery to the police.

> *Tom Lange*: [John] was afraid of Lind. His girlfriend, Barbara Richardson, was killed and she was a nice girl. She had no record. She was from around Sacramento. She was a really nice girl and he really cared for her. He thought that the one girl who had lived was Barbara and it was Susan. When we told him that Susan lived and Barbara didn't, he went berserk on us. We had him in the interview room and he's just screaming, jumping up and down and throwing things around.
>
> This was pay back; this was a message-killing. Greg Diles, one of the suspects — he'd been arrested with pipes with bicycle handles on them. The county Sheriff arrested Greg Diles with a pipe in the back

seat of his car before the murders and he had a bike handle on one of them. It was a weapon he used when he was a bouncer in one of Ed Nash's nightclubs. He had a history with pipes.

Our contention in filing murder charges on Holmes was the fact that he let the killers into the house at a very early hour, like four a.m., with the knowledge of what they were going to do. If you're going to do that and you let me in, and my buddies are going to beat five people's heads in, you have now become a part of this. I'm really going to make you a part of this by making you take a couple of swings with a pipe.

Tom Blake[h]: Something else that John said about Greg Diles — I think that Greg has a fetish: the shotgun and a lead pipe. He always had a lead pipe in his house for defense and I believe those guys up in the Wonderland Lane were killed with a pipe or some type of instrument like that.

Julia St. Vincent: John came home one time with a nunchuk type of thing and he told me it was made out of platinum, the hardest metal on earth — some fucking bullshit.

One night he took that bar and he said, "Do you realize what could happen if this bar hit you?" I had a futon couch. [I was] lying in the thing, thinking to myself, if he hit me with that fucking bar, I'd be dead.

When he swung that thing, the look in his fucking eyes when he did it, it was like when that murder happened. I could completely see him. Not only do I believe that he was capable of doing it, but I believe that he could have done it single-handedly. The amount of rage in him and the way that he swung that thing that night, just as a kind of threat to me, was fucked up.

I just saw this fire and I went, "Whoa."

Bill Margold[k]: It was the summer of 1981. I was managing Reb's Sunset International, located at 6912 Hollywood Boulevard (on the third floor) — the biggest nude theatrical modeling agency in the world — and we handled most of the major adult entertainment/hardcore/XXX industry talent of that era, including a legendary fellow named John C. Holmes. And we were breaking assorted laws (albeit highly specious ones involving pandering and prostitution) every day of the year.

The two detectives brazenly entered my office, and without even giving me a chance to welcome them (which I wouldn't have) sat down in front of my cluttered desk. "So what do you know about what happened up in the Hills?" one of them snapped, his query bristling with haughty condescension. And the other one, with equal disdain for me and my surroundings, virtually parroted his partner with, "Yeah, what do you know?"

Julia St. Vincent: They were terrible. A normal person would have said, "Did you have an affair with him or something, because you were with him how long?" They didn't ask me, "Did you ever see him get violent?" They didn't try to be my friend. They said "Did you know him? How well did you know him? Did you know any of these [people]?"
"No, no, no."
"Bye."— And they were gone. I mean of course, what do you want me to say? "Yeah, I knew him, and plus…" I wasn't in the mood to be a snitch back then. Now, I probably would jump to the plate and say, "Yeah, I knew him and I think he did it," but back then, that wasn't in my consciousness.

I lied to them and they left. It wasn't hard. They didn't pry — there was no sitting in a chair, strapped down and being beaten. They asked me a couple of questions and I answered them in the way that they would want me to answer them if I didn't know a thing. They took it at face value and left.

The Handprint

Bill Amerson[h]: The morning of the murders, John came home. John was living with me at the time. He was bloody and he had told me what happened. He kept looking out the window. He was afraid that someone was following him. He had extreme paranoia. Part of that was the cocaine; the cocaine had pretty much fried his brain. John was delusional; John was frightened at the time. John was afraid that someone was going to kill him.

The fact is that John was there at Wonderland. The fact is that John did leave a bloody handprint on the wall. The fact is that the way that happened is that John was trying to save Susan's life. John had picked her up, she was the only one left alive. John picked her up and was carrying her to another room to see what he could do. That's how John got bloody.

Actually, the fact was that John's handprint was found at the crime scene, but Amerson was remiss in making the claim that it was a bloody handprint on the wall at the Wonderland. The handprint was on the bedrail, not on the wall, and it was not bloody, although many people did believe that it was a bloody palm print, due to false reports in a 1988 *Los Angeles Times* article. Even so, Holmes' handprint on the bedrail was a crucial piece of evidence for the prosecution, as it suggested that he may have gripped the bedrail with one hand while using a pipe to hit Launius with the other.

Tom Lange: It was important to our case when he went on trial that Ron Launius was lying in a bed that has an old-fashioned railing. Just above where his head would be lying was a partial left palm print from John Holmes. The significance of the dynamics of it, [would be] to steady himself if he's striking down.

Tom Blake[h]: It was a hand print on the bed where the murders were committed, but I believe that they were able to explain that in court because John was up there all the time. It was not unusual to have John's hand prints all over the house because he visited these people on a daily basis. He went up there to do his crack, and his coke, and drinking, and probably having sex, or whatever. It would be like you coming to my house now. You got your hand prints wherever you touch, right?

John Holmes[q]: They started checking phone numbers and finger-prints and, of course, my fingerprints were in every goddamn room in the house, but I'd stayed there, slept there, and I'd used the phone [to] call several people I know.

John's *Real Wonderland* Story

Laurie Holmes: John made many audio tapes about his life during the last five years he was alive. Part of the tapes included his side and theory of the Wonderland murders and the robbery at Eddie Nash's that occurred not long before.

In 1999, I took the Wonderland portions of the audio files down to the homicide division of the L.A.P.D. John told the whole story and named whom he believed to be at least one of the killers. I did not want to be withholding evidence to a still-unsolved multiple-murder case. The detective listened to maybe two minutes out of approximately 180 minutes of audio files, turned the recorder off and stated that the tapes were not important. I asked if he at least wanted a copy of the tapes. He told me no.

I then asked if David Lind was still alive, as John was deathly afraid of David Lind 'til the day he died and I needed to know if David Lind was still a threat to me. The detective got on the computer, and ran David Lind: a violent criminal, with a record at least ten feet long, never did much time and had dropped off the face of the earth some-time in 1988.

One year later, in 2000, Eddie Nash was served a 42-page federal indictment, in which, once again, John was named in conjunction with the Wonderland murders. I leaked a few blurbs of the audio files to the media, so that a gag order could not be put in place on the audio files. The F.B.I. found out about the tapes, and sent an agent all the way from Texas, to retrieve the tapes from me. I cooperated and turned over the audio files to the agent. It always struck me as a little odd that the L.A.P.D. didn't bother to mention the tapes to the F.B.I., but they didn't. The F.B.I. analyzed the audio files and once again, cleared John and his name of any and all connection to the Wonderland murders. They deemed the audio files as a death-bed confession as well. The agent was nice enough to return the audio tapes to me for further use.

Large portions of these audio tapes are available on a DVD called, *The Real John Holmes — The Wonderland Murders Exposed*, which is sold at Laurie's website, *www.johnholmes.com*.

Laurie Holmes: In early 2003, I heard on the news that Lionsgate was making a Wonderland Murder movie. My P.R. man and I contacted the producer of the film and told them about the audio tapes. We were told they, "already had their story"—they were not interested in the tapes.

On the very day of the premiere on Hollywood Boulevard, I got a phone call from Ron Jeremy, telling me he had been given two last-minute tickets to the premiere and thought it would be a gas if we went together. I told him I had a birthday party to go to, but that I could probably catch at least part of it. While waiting for the movie to begin, I spoke with the same guy that had told us before that he wasn't interested in the audio tapes. [But at the premiere,] he told me that he had never heard of the tapes, which couldn't have been less true.

We sat down at our seats and the movie began. I didn't like even the first minute of the movie and began to feel ill just for being there, so I left and I went to my friend's birthday party instead. Thank God! If I had stayed for that movie premiere, I would have made the front page the next morning, and it wouldn't have been good. I would have probably went off on everybody and been arrested in the process. As for my ex-coworker, Ron Jeremy? I can only wonder if he had a clue what might have happened and sought the publicity.

Val Kilmer plays John Holmes in *Wonderland*. The 2003 film depicts John at his worst, from pimping out Dawn to Nash for freebase, to planning the robbery of Nash's estate with the Wonderland Gang, and includes a controversial re-enactment of the murders in which its director, James Cox, took a rather bold step of artistic license.

Ron Jeremy: I brought Laurie Holmes, John Holmes' wife to the premiere and Val Kilmer got annoyed at me. He said that she bad-mouthed the movie. That's the honest-to-God truth, Val Kilmer was actually mad at me because he thought that my date, Laurie

Holmes — who is not depicted in *Wonderland* because she was a part of his life after Wonderland, so the filmmaker did not include her character anywhere in the movie — bad-mouthed the film.

I said, "No she didn't." He didn't want to hear it. He was really, seriously mad and wouldn't sign autographs for any of my friends. I said to him, "She liked the movie, but she was upset because it showed John swinging the baton."

The second-to-last scene in the film shows Cox's rendition of what could have happened the night of the blood-soaked killings. After being buzzed into the apartment, a group of large men burst inside, wielding pipes. As heads split open, Greg Diles points a gun at John and says, "Get to work," handing John a pipe. John put his hand on the bedrail above Launius' head and swings, tentatively at first, but his face transforms to a primal grimace as he stops shuddering and crying, and he swings with increased intensity and fervor.

With this scene, the film appears to stamp Holmes with a guilty verdict by showing him swinging the pipe. In part because the filmmakers were not interested in Holmes' accounts of the murders, Laurie believes that *Wonderland* was an organized attempt to defame The King of Porn.

> *Laurie Holmes*: I was so depressed [about *Wonderland*] because I've spent my whole adult life trying to commemorate him and I felt like everything that I'd ever done was lost; that it was a waste of time. But it isn't because people will get over *Wonderland*. They'll get tired of hearing all the bad.
>
> I would have to say that's what hurts everybody that loved him the most. He was such a unique, compassionate, wonderful guy and to have him portrayed the way Hollywood portrayed him — and continues to portray him for their own greedy ambitions. I'm not saying that everything John did during [his] relationship [with Dawn] was right. Certainly, he made mistakes, but it's very hurtful for those that loved him — that goes for me and for anybody that loved John.
>
> About a year after *Wonderland* premiered, I got a call from the same F.B.I. agent that had flown out from Texas years before to retrieve the tapes. He was very nice. He said that a couple of his buddies had rented the movie and wanted to know what I thought of the movie. I stated, "I don't think the murders were ever solved or ever will be because the L.A.P.D. never wanted them to be."

"Wonderlanded"

Beneath the story of murder, some say that *Wonderland* glamorized drugs with its parallel love story of John and Dawn. The movie begins when John picks up Dawn at the apartment of the Good Samaritan (played by Carrie Fisher). It is a sexy reunion in the bathroom when John opens his briefcase to show Dawn the cocaine that was his portion of the score from the robbery.

Despite the high, sexy feeling achieved during the beginning of the film, by the end of the film, as Cox described, viewers' skin will crawl. Many people, including Bill Margold, perceived in the film as a powerful anti-drug message, with the Wonderland Gang paying the ultimate price and John living a life riddled with guilt.

> *Bill Margold*[k]: By the summer of 1981, fate caught up with almost all of them. And that's where director James Cox and his band of writers including Captain Mauzner, Todd Samovitz and D. Loriston Scott come in. Feeling that what happened on Wonderland in the early hours of July 1, 1981 deserved unearthing, the filmmakers have presented the most disturbing motion picture I've ever endured. By the time that it was over, my gut wrenched, my nerve-endings felt like they had been sandpapered, my eyes were filled with tears. I called Mr. Cox and thanked him. Thanked him, not so much for making the most painfully powerful anti-drug statement film since *The Man with the Golden Arm* — but more importantly, for wisely not making a film about the adult entertainment industry's involvement (because there wasn't any) in what happened on Wonderland Avenue. And finally, I thanked him for showing how drugs destroyed the life of an over-age, juvenile delinquent, who indelibly proved that all men are not created equal.

Cocaine is a major character in the film. During filming, the actors and crew would snort dried milk, to create the look and ambiance of coke parties — and coke withdrawal. Cox described freebasing cocaine to be "an atom bomb that explodes in your chest and flies out to your capillaries," but when the supply runs out, desperation sets in. Cocaine addicts frequently exhibit violent behavior that may not be congruent with that of their sober personalities.

> *Bill Margold*[k]: The Wonderlanders — Dylan McDermott, Josh Lucas, Tim Blake Nelson, etcetera — are appropriately shallow and essentially soulless examples of drug-dealing, double-crossing weasels (the only animal besides man who kills just for the sake of killing), most of whom were viciously bludgeoned to death, and dispatched to Hell in the early morning hours of July 1, 1981, by a group of revenge seekers purportedly sent by Nash, and led by Holmes. This brings us back to how I responded to the detectives the morning after the Wonderland Massacre.
>
> "Were those people who died, drug dealers?" feigning ignorance in my reply.
>
> "Yeah, of course they were, you know that," the detectives chimed in duty-bound unison.
>
> "Good," I hissed back, "then they deserve to be dead." The detectives looked at me as if my words had ignited the right fuses in their

tiny brains, and then sardonic grins started to crease their round faces. They both nodded and left immediately.

It has taken 22 years for a filmmaker named James Cox to searingly validate my sentiments. And I think that the spirit of John C. Holmes (dead since 1988) would agree as well.

Lisa Kudrow, as Sharon Holmes, the wife of John, a character who came to light only after the events on Wonderland went down, brings a snide, somewhat smug sense of superiority to her performance of a woman who is in over her head, but nevertheless seemingly sort of likes the sense of danger…and perverse celebrity of being associated with a perverse celebrity known as "The King." Sometimes love can be measured in inches.

The real Sharon Holmes appears to be a woman with integrity in *WADD;* she hardly seems to be a woman who enjoyed sharing in John's "perverse celebrity." Although Margold seems to have missed the boat in describing her in this way, he has drawn attention to the fact that *Wonderland* does not explain why Sharon, an otherwise strong, proud woman with a moral compass, would welcome a mother-daughter type of relationship with her husband's under-age lover or endure almost 19 years of marriage to John.

The Bathtub Confession

> *Bill Margold*[k]: Val Kilmer does his best to portray John C. Holmes, but Val is simply too damn healthy-looking to make it work. However, for a couple of seconds in a bathtub, just as he starts telling his version of what happened on Wonderland, damn if I didn't see The King come alive. And for those chilling moments of making the hairs on the back of my neck stand up in petrified horror, Kilmer and Cox are to be applauded.

In fact, Dawn and Sharon were often present on the set of the movie to provide inspiration for the actors of the film, including for the bathtub confession scene, which shows Sharon's memory of Holmes in their home at the Glendale apartment complex on Wednesday, July 1st. (In Mike Sager's 1989 piece, "The Devil in Mr. Holmes," it is said that John was at Sharon's home at 3:30 a.m. on July 2nd.)

> *Sharon Holmes*[h]: He was probably in the house between two and six o'clock. It could have been earlier, it could have been later, but nothing was moving in the streets. He came knocking at the door and this is the first time I had literally seen him since March. I see very well in the dark and I realized it was John, so I just left the latch on the door and I said, "Why are you here?"

He asked if he could come in and I realized from the nightlight in the entryway that he was covered in blood. It was in his hair, around his ears, his clothes — he wasn't dripping, but you could tell something had happened. He asked if he could come in and I said, "Yes, what happened?"

He mumbled about he'd had a car accident and so on. He said, "Could you help clean me up?" Dope that I am, I let him in the house and he said, "I have to get into the shower."

When we got into the bathroom, I figured he had a cut over his head; this was where all the blood on the upper torso was coming from and he kind of ducked away from it. I realized he wasn't bleeding — the blood was coming from somewhere else.

He said, "I need to get in the tub." This is classic John, from 1973 on — anything unpalatable or difficult for him to get through, he got into the bathtub. It was like Macbeth washing his hands of the responsibility, besides which, it's probably not comfortable being covered with other people's blood. Part of it was his own; there were small scrapes and things like that on the upper torso and near the hairline over one eye. He got into the tub — it was a shower and tub combined — ran the water as hot as he could stand it and kept dunking himself.

I attended to the cuts on his face and that sort of thing. He looked worse than I had ever seen him. I said, "There wasn't an accident. What happened?"

He looked me straight in the eye and he said, "I was involved," or "I witnessed," — I honestly don't remember — "with murders." And of course, nothing would have been out by then, so I had no idea what he was talking about. I think he probably felt I'd pick something up, but we weren't in tune at that point.

He said, "I was at a murder and four people got killed. Somebody is after me." He said, "Four people were killed in front of me." He proceeded to tell me about the robbery that had occurred the day before. The setup was carried out in a demeaning manner to Eddie Nash and that these people, who had cut him in for drugs and money stolen from Eddie Nash, were killed.

I said, "What do you mean they were killed?"

He said, "Well, I had to take them to the house because Eddie had my book and he told me he'd go back to Ohio and take care of my family if I didn't square it away with him."

So he took the people to Wonderland, got them through the security door and he was, according to him, he was thrown up against the wall and held there while two of the three people he took there carried out the murders.

I don't think there's anything anyone can tell you more appalling than they participated in a murder or were responsible for it. I asked, "You stood there and watched this?"

"Yes."

And I said, "These people were your friends."

He said, "They were dirt. They were filth. It was them or me." I don't think I said a whole lot. He said, "I want to go ahead and get cleaned and I need a couple hours of sleep. Is that okay?"

I said, "That's fine," thinking, Jesus, how can I get him out of my house? I'm figuring they're going to be right behind his heels soon. I'm going to have to defend my dogs. I don't think I was concerned about that because I knew John would have been very careful about how he got back to our house — he had always been. Nobody did ever find us, other than Tom Lange.

He slept for a couple of hours, left probably between six and six-thirty and he said, "I'll call you in a couple of days."

I said, "Take care of yourself."

Then I called up and said, "I can't come to work." I was devastated. I just couldn't believe, no matter what he had become, that he could be involved in that. I had to learn to find a way to live with this. He sold his soul that night. To stand there and watch a slaughtering like that and do nothing ended his life. It literally ended his life; he had nothing to live for after that.

Originally, when Sharon was questioned by Detective Lange after the murders, she did not divulge anything. In fact, in her first newspaper interview in late July of 1981, wherein she announced to the public for the first time that she was Holmes' estranged wife, she reiterated what she had told the police, "He never intimated [to me] that he knew anything about [the murders]. The only thing he really said was, 'Yes, I knew the people and yes, I had been in the house shortly before they were killed.'"

> *Tom Lange:* There was enough to certainly file a case on him. If we'd had Sharon, it would have been a much stronger case, but she wasn't cooperating initially. She didn't want anything to do with it. She may have been in fear; she may have still empathized about John and not wanted to hurt him. I don't know what her reasoning was at the time, but she wasn't cooperating.

Only one month after John's death, in the April 14, 1988 *Los Angeles Times* article, "Holmes' Confession in Bathtub: Told Wife of Role in 4 Murders," Sharon described yet another account of how and when she first learned of her husband's role in the murders. According to the April 1988 article, John crawled into their bedroom early on the morning of the murders in his bloody clothes. He offered no explanation to her about the state of his clothing, other than having been "in an accident." Then, Sharon said, he slept fitfully, while moaning about blood and pain.

In 1988, Sharon also told the newspaper that John was forced at gunpoint to drive to Nash's house the day after the robbery because he had been spotted wearing some of the stolen jewelry. There, as John described, he was evidently beaten severely and held prisoner for hours.

Scott Thorson, an ex-lover of pianist Liberace, confessed that he was doing hits of coke in Nash's bedroom while John was kept by the bodyguards. According to Thorson, Nash was incensed about the robbery and railed, "I'll have them on their knees! I'll teach them a lesson! They'll never steal from anyone again!" During a 1990 trial, Thorson reported having seen Nash and Diles "beating Mr. Holmes up," and threatening that if Holmes would not "take him to where those people were who robbed him, he would have every member of his family killed."

In the years that have passed, a few people have questioned the existence of the address book, but Julia St. Vincent possesses a few pages that she photocopied from John's black book. The photocopied pages are full of names and numbers for several of John's work acquaintances, including Bob Chinn and Bob Vosse (for whom Dawn had misspelled the name, Bob *Fosse*, as in the famous dance choreographer), plus a few mainstream celebrity connections, including Ringo Starr (although no phone number is listed for Ringo, his name is written in John's flourishing cursive).

Explaining to her that he had no other choice with his family in danger, Holmes told Sharon that he rode with three armed men to the Wonderland house and buzzed the outdoor intercom. Recognizing Holmes' voice, the person inside unlocked the security gate, allowing Holmes to be followed upstairs with three armed men behind him. Inside the house, Sharon said that John was held against a wall. While in the comforts of his bath several days after John allegedly climbed into bed with his bloody clothes on, he told Sharon, "There was a whole lot of screaming going on."

> *Tom Lange*: Sharon was married to him. I think she empathized with him a great deal, maybe more empathy than sympathy. She cared about him to a certain extent. When we first went to Sharon, if she'd said, "He was here and covered in blood," he took a bath or got into bed — whatever he did.
>
> We got so many different stories from [John] and Sharon. If we had Sharon's story initially, we probably would have convicted him. Sharon didn't want anything to do with it.
>
> She just didn't give us anything, initially. She didn't say, "Hey, he was covered in blood and I still have the clothes." That would have been great. The blood on John's clothes would have implicated Sharon in an indirect way, because she would have been a percipient witness.
>
> That is the problem with any witness. You have to take everything as discoverable and false statements come in and the jury throws it out. It's always a problem. If she'd given us that in the beginning, that statement, we probably would have had what we needed.

Back at the Motel

Dawn Schiller[h]: I was watching the news in the motel room. John wasn't back yet and they were pulling bodies out of the Wonderland Avenue house. I knew that house. I'd sat in the car in front of that house many times. I'd seen those people go in and out. And my heart just went into my gut because I just knew.

When John finally got back — he was gone overnight and he came back about midday — I didn't say anything about the murders, of course. He looked tore up. I mean he looked like he had been in a fight, but I can't remember anything specific. It was a mental beating. Emotionally, he had been completely drained. The eyes were definitely just bloodshot red.

He took a couple of Valium and lay down and went to sleep. I was still up and I watched him toss and turn. He screamed, "Blood! Blood! There is so much blood!" That was the final gut stabber for me. The day before, things had been hopeful. We had money and a big pile of coke — there was hope. And then he comes back a day later, the money's gone, the big pile of coke is gone, and he's screaming about blood. No, this isn't good.

John woke up after having the dream of blood. I asked him in the morning, "What was that dream about?" And he went white, like he didn't realize what he had said during his sleep.

He told me, "I lifted the trunk and it gave me a bloody nose yesterday. I opened it up and hit myself in the nose and got a bloody nose," which was a lie. He could have just said, "I don't remember." You know, it would have been good enough. That was another bad sign.

In the same article from April 14, 1988, in which Sharon shared the story of John's bathtub confession for the very first time, Dawn was also quoted, but she used the pseudonym, Jeanna Sellers.

As Sellers, who was reported to be a neighbor of the Holmes' at the apartment complex, Dawn stated that, "[John] said, 'They stuck a gun to my head and made me go back in [to the Wonderland Avenue house] and open the door.' That's what he told me; [that they] made him watch." Like Sharon, Dawn never revealed this to the police ever during their investigation.

Tom Lange: Sharon still cared for John. Sharon's game was that she didn't know anything and Dawn's game was doing what she was told, being the good little girl who didn't say anything. [Dawn] was fairly forthright initially, but she didn't convey to us what John had really told her around the time of the murders, even the hearsay type stuff. She just wasn't forthright to that extent. I think that she was in a great deal of fear, certainly, around the time that that happened. She was a young kid; she didn't know any better.

I have no quarrel with either one of them. I'm not saying I'm so sure that any one of us wouldn't have done the same thing under the circumstances. It's just that we came to them initially and they were not forthright with us for whatever reason. But you don't take those things personally. When Sharon said one thing, one time and another thing another time, which one do we believe? That's the problem with all of that.

The Initial Arrest

Dawn Schiller[h]: I was doing his nails and he was lying on the bed facing the door. They broke the doors down with guns and put guns to our heads. They took us both in and they separated us. They even took my little dog, Thor, in a little doggie jail thing. It was kind of cute.

John and Dawn were taken into custody on July 12, 1981, when John was arrested on the grounds of a bench warrant for receiving a stolen computer. Incidentally, the computer had been stolen from Julia St. Vincent's apartment manager. Nevertheless, the police already had suspicion of John's role in the Wonderland murders, because David Lind had painted a picture of John's motive for the investigators. In the days following the murders, Lange said, John had bounced around between several different homes and motels. When police caught up with John, he and Dawn were staying at a motel in Sherman Oaks.

Dawn Schiller[h]: They took us into separate rooms and they grilled us about the Wonderland Avenue home. They threw names at me. I didn't know any names. They didn't show any pictures to me. That was something that John did, I think, not to entrust me with names — not have me know who anybody was, so all I could tell the police was "No, I don't know, I don't know." And I didn't.

It was an all-nighter. One would leave and another one would come in and ask me the questions again. There wasn't any hot light or anything. I wasn't beat up.

They let me go, basically, and they kept John. I said, "Well I don't have anywhere to go." I was in my pajamas still. They gave me my dog back (they liked him cause he pissed on somebody they didn't like's locker). I said "Sharon is the only one I know." I was really scared at this time, I mean, this was serious stuff. Whereas before, I wouldn't go to Sharon because I was ashamed of her disappointment in me, I had nobody else to turn to at that point.

They drove me over to Sharon's and she just opened the door. I told her, "John's been arrested."

She said, "I know. Come in, well, you better come in."

I sat on the couch. We didn't say anything. It was pretty silent. I didn't know what to say and I found later that she already knew. I guess that she had been talking to Tom Lange. We talked about John — caring for him and worrying about him. At that point, I said, "Well, they kept him."

"I know," and then she went into kitchen, brought me something to eat, and we watched TV in our regular positions in the living room for a little while — in silence, pretty much. The animals just lay with us, pretty tentatively. She went to bed and I fell asleep — probably both did a Valium.

That was the relationship with Sharon — she already knew something. She didn't have to ask a lot of questions to drain you emotionally. She was very understanding and compassionate at that time with me, which I was very surprised and happy for. Regardless of the situation that was going on, it was like home; a safe place again.

We slept and we got up, and I think we got a call from John. She kept it very short, hung up and said, "If we don't get him out of jail now, he's going to be killed." He called, I guess, and he told her that he had received a death threat from Eddie Nash.

I don't know what Sharon was thinking, but I thought, "How are we going to do that?"

She said, "I don't know." I mean, he had already robbed the house of anything of value and I had no bank.

Murderer or Victim?

By that point, reports of Holmes' connection to the Laurel Canyon murders had spread all over the news. Many people who knew John watched the developing case against Holmes with a high level of personal interest.

Sean Amerson[h]: The John that I knew — that I understood and had a connection with my heart, that I felt inside me — wasn't capable of doing something like that. I just couldn't think he could ever do that. I just couldn't see him do that. Now, my dad, I could see doing it on a Thursday, but John, never. Never.

I could hear John telling the story about it. I could see where he would be there — he'd be fucked up, shit would go down and he would jump out a window, take off running down the street to a bar and tell five people. And when he told the five people the story was larger then it ever really happened. I could see that happening in a heartbeat, but actually John, himself, killing anybody? — John stepped over ants.

It just wasn't part of what I thought his personality was. I feel I'm a pretty decent judge of character and so I didn't buy it.

Joel Sussman: I was in Laurel Canyon when that was all happening — I knew the house, where it was. I was really surprised because I thought he was much more together than that. It just amazed me that he got involved in that drama, but he was Johnny Wadd; to him, it was always an adventure. I'm sure that when it was happening, it wasn't the real thing to him; it was just another adventure he was doing because I think that he became his character. You take off your clothes in a telephone booth enough times and you think you're Superman.

Denise Amerson [h]: I was young, but I certainly knew then and I certainly know now — I don't care who John confessed what to — John did not kill anybody. There is just no way. No way. I don't care how bad he was into his disease of addiction; there is nothing that would ever make John do that. I know that.

Seka: It was kind of hard not to hear about it and then when I found out that John was involved, I was horrified. I didn't think he had that capability at all. That's what was so surprising about it. I didn't know what to think. I still don't believe he had anything to do with it. I think he was caught between a rock and a hard place with the situations he had put himself in; he got himself pretty well screwed up.

Bob Chinn: My initial reaction was disbelief — somehow I just could not bring myself to believe that John was involved in the murders. It seemed to me that the John that I had known wouldn't be involved in such a thing. After thinking about it awhile, however, knowing how obsessed he had become with drugs, I began to wonder. Like everyone else I could not help but follow the case in the newspapers and after reading about the facts as they came out about the crime, it became pretty apparent that he had been involved. I was truly saddened by this realization.

Don Fernando: He was a lamb. People can say whatever they want about John, but to this day, I'll never believe that he did what some people say he had done in the Hollywood Hills. I just can't see him doing that. That's not the John I knew. According to the coroner, the force needed to crush those people's skulls would require very powerful, big men. I believe to this day that John had nothing to do with it, not with the physical act.

Jamie Gillis: I don't think anybody ever felt that John killed anyone. There was talk about that, but we just could not even imagine [him] — even on his worst day — being guilty of that. On the other hand, he certainly was involved in one way or another in what happened. I guess people felt a little bit like once he started playing in that league, when you're talking about people who will kill in that kind of fashion, I guess maybe people were afraid to talk and deal with John.

Tom Lange: I don't think he wanted to kill anybody. I don't think he had the cashews to kill anybody. I really don't. He was a thief. He got tied up with a bunch of bad people.

Tom Blake[h]: I don't believe that John was in there when the murders went down, but he knew and they set him up. He was probably as guilty as Greg Diles and the rest of them because he was directly involved with the murders by setting it up.

Candida Royalle: I was completely shocked and just so blown away, I mean, I had no idea. I knew he had a life that was secret, that most of us didn't know about, but that was just over the top. That was just a big shock—a big, big shock. It wasn't like he was someone who [was] staggering around drunk or stoned all the time when I knew him.

John wasn't a completely bad person. I've known people who were just mean, nasty, bad, ugly people. John wasn't that and that's why I think it was so incredibly shocking. Because he was a nice guy! He was a gentle soul. It wasn't that he was a psychotic or an evil person. I really think that his emotional problems were compounded by the fact that, rather than get help, he medicated himself and that was the wrong thing to do. It doesn't help.

The Biltmore

Tom Blake[h]: Everybody heard about the murders and heard about John being involved with Nash. I knew that he was running around with Nash and those people before the murders went down. I heard that he was using dope because the people who were working the porno section of administrative Vice at that time kept telling me, "Hey, we got word from other snitches that John is really strung out."

I said, "You got to be kidding me! When I worked with John, he didn't use that stuff."

He said, "The guy is strung out, he's using it. He's a mule; he's trafficking for a guy named Nash up there in North Hollywood."

"Boy, he really changed since I met him."

Tom Lange: We had to be careful for many reasons in this situation, one of them being that this was a high-profile case, with John because he was a so-called porn star, along with the involvement of an organized crime figure, Ed Nash.

Nash was a suspect and certainly the motive was very strong. We'd done a background on all these people. We were finding out that Nash had been very insulated in the city for all these years. Nobody could ever nail him and there was a reason for that; you had political corruption and you had police corruption. He was a very insulated individual. This was rampant. That's why he walked for so many years and basically, he got away with anything he wanted. So he was a hard nut to crack.

We found out that the feds were investigating him and there were dirty feds involved — corrupt feds. They had come to our department, behind our backs and said that we were dirty and we were in bed with Ed Nash, [which] forced our department to investigate us — when they were the ones that were involved, thereby derailing the investigation [of Nash's role in the murders] for a number of years.

Sharon Holmes [h]: I'd seen the name [Ed Nash] in John's book, in his black book. It meant nothing to me. I don't know the sleaze. I don't look for this kind of information. At the time of the murders and at the time of the trial, this is when I learned who he was — what he was. He was a mystery to me. He wasn't a part of my life. I honestly knew that I was safe; John had protected me. I never really feared for my life for any reason, because he would have upheld what he had done and protected me, like he had always done. So I had no reason to worry about that.

He truly made sure I was protected. No one knew he had a wife until I put the information out in the paper, seven years after the murder, when John was dead. I mean, there must have been some astounded faces — 19 years of marriage. It must have been very eye opening for a lot of people.

Tom Blake [h]: After these murders went down and John said, "Hey, you don't know Eddie Nash that well."

I knew he owned a lot of adult nightclubs, [and was] involved in the adult nightclub business. Nude bars and things like that. I knew he was involved with Israelis, but according to John, he was one of the big people involved in the Israeli Mafia.

In a 1990 trial in which Nash and Greg Diles were charged with the 1981 murders, Scott Thorson appeared as a witness. He nervously chewed his lower lip while he repeated condemning statements Nash had made about a year after the Wonderland murders. He alleged that Nash said, "Things have gone too far, that it had turned into a bloody mess." Not only that, but he also claimed that Nash followed that up with a threat: "He said that people have a habit of disappearing in the canyon. 'By the time they find you, Scott, I'll have every tooth in your head pulled so they can't identify you.'" Although Nash's attorney, Jeff Brodey, accused Thorson of having fabricated the account by drawing from newspaper clippings, he was put into the federal witness protection program.

Indeed, John may have feared Nash for good reasons, so in an attempt to get him talking, Lange and Souza treated John with a degree of deference and allowed him to confer with his former L.A.P.D. contact, Tom Blake.

> *Tom Lange*: It was our lieutenant who wanted another team to deal with Holmes and he wanted to bring more people in when he realized it was going to be a high-profile case. There was going to be a lot more to it. I think they'd found out that he'd been dealing with Tom Blake in the position of an informant: "Maybe he will continue on that way and give some information." There were other reasons to give him the carrot before the stick. Let's see if we can get something by giving him what he wants."
>
> At this point the problem was, of course, that John was a sociopath. He wanted what he wanted. It was all about John. He was going to tell us what was convenient for him to tell us. He was going to give us just enough without implicating himself. He's not going to say, "They had me stand over him, I grabbed the bed frame and I took a couple of whacks." He's not going to say that; you're sure as hell not going to implicate yourself in any way in the murders [and say] that you let the killers in, knowing what they were going to do. This was the basis for the filing on Holmes.

> *Tom Blake*[h]: Tom Lange or Bob Souza called me because John told them that he wanted to talk to [me]. I said, "No problem. I'll be glad to help you in any way possible."
>
> "Well, maybe you can help us solve this crime. Maybe he will tell you who was involved in this crime." They knew that they didn't have the evidence or corroboration of evidence to say Nash and these people are involved in this crime, so they wanted me to come in, talk to John, at which time I got involved in the murder investigation.

> *Tom Lange*: It started at the Biltmore, without Sharon and Dawn, initially. John said he'd like both of them there; he wanted some Johnny Walker Red and he wanted room service. And this was in the Vice-Presidential Suite. We happened to know the guy in charge of security there, who was an L.A. cop, so he gave us a suite that wasn't in use. What the new people — who our lieutenant brought in — wanted to do, they wanted to handle Holmes away from us, thinking we would work the suspect angle and Nash angle.
>
> John Helvin [who passed away in 2007] was the person interviewing Holmes with his partner. John Helvin has a very soothing, calm way about him and very straight-laced. The thinking was maybe he

could deal with Holmes and Holmes would respond. The mistake was that Holmes spoke out of both sides of his mouth — he wanted to do what was good for John, but he could care less about our case. So that was the wrong way to deal with him because he took everything we would give him and just gave us what he wanted to give us. That was right up until his dying day.

We had to move away from the Biltmore for some reason. Up at the Bonaventure, it was much of the same. He was demanding — he wanted this and he wanted that. He loved the attention. We remarked that it was like he was playing one of his roles, with all the cops around like Johnny Wadd, all the security and the bet was maybe he'll give us something like Nash.

"I'm Going to Tell You a Story."

Tom Blake [h]: This was a deal that John, Tom Lange and Bob Souza agreed to, that John requested to have Dawn and Sharon spend a couple of nights with him some place that would be secluded — some place that would be secure to talk about his problems and he wanted me to be there.

Sharon Holmes [h]: [John] called and said, "Will you come? Because I'll need you."

I said, "What's involved?"

He said, "We're going to a hotel in downtown L.A. and the police will be talking with me, but I need you because there may be something I need to ask you. What should I respond? Do you think this is okay?"

Dawn Schiller [h]: Tom Lange called her and she spoke to him. She kept it short again. Tom Lange showed up and he said that he needed to talk to both of us. We both needed to sit down and he said, "This is the deal. John is worried about his life in jail. He's been talking to us. We're willing to protect him if he tells us why we need to protect him, but he won't do it unless he speaks to you two first. So are you willing to go, see him and go talk to him?"

I said, "Yes," and Sharon agreed. I asked him, "How was he now?"

He said, "We have him in a safe place now. We have moved him from jail." He told us to just take some things overnight. He said, "You are basically going to be in a room with him. I don't know what he has to discuss with you, I don't know how long it's going to take, but then we are going to need to talk to him."

We made arrangements for the animals. We took a deck of cards because there was going to be some time on our hands.

We packed up with him and took off. He drove us down to the Bonaventure Hotel in downtown Los Angeles, where we were met by other officers, I suppose, they were plainclothes. They searched our bags and this may have been Blake.

We had a two-room annex thing. We went into one hotel room. John was not there where the cops were organized.

Tom Blake [h]: I believe I spent about three nights, three days out there talking to John, Sharon and Dawn, hoping that maybe John would soften up and say, "Hey, I'll tell you all." During this period of time John said, "I'm going to tell you a story. I will never ever testify. I never told you this story, but I'll tell you this story."

That's when he told me the story about him being involved with the people up in Wonderland Lane the night before the murders [June 29]. Drinking, smoking, using crack — whatever — getting loaded. That's when they made the plan that he would go to Nash's house, spend some time up there and about two or three o'clock in the morning would leave with the back door slider open. And these guys from Wonderland Lane would come up there and all they were supposed to do is take the dope, the money, some jewelry, and split.

He said, "Yep, I did that. That thing went down."

Tom Lange: We were off the record; I think that's when I told him, "You know we're interested in Nash. We think Nash had something to do with this." This was still when we were trying to have Holmes in our court. We didn't know for sure if he'd been involved. We kind of suspected that he may have been intimidated into doing it. I said, "We want to know who did this."

And he said, "It was Nash," just like that—"It was Nash." It was one thing to mention that under those circumstances, but it's another to testify to that in court and he never would.

Tom Blake [h]: He said, "Hey, if I testify against these people or say anything, Sharon's going to be dead. The rest of my friends and family are going to be dead, what do I accomplish?" So he said, "I'm going to take my chances. You can put me in jail, you can do whatever and I'm going to take my chances. Tom, I'll deny whatever I told you. Hey, I'll die in jail," but he's not going to testify against Nash and his group.

Tom Lange: He needed to make a bold confession, not little admissions where he ended up playing a game. If he did that, then he would have been a witness and given immunity. But instead, he played the game. Therefore we had to put this so-called domino theory into effect to pressure him. We offered him the moon, the sun and the sky. We needed him because he was the pivotal figure for the initial motive of the robbery that set up the murder scene. We needed that testimony.

John's Proposal at the Bonaventure

Sharon Holmes[h]: She and I were left in the room while John was talking with police and the district attorney in the other side of the suite.

Dawn Schiller[h]: I guess they talked to him, [then] opened the annex door and we went in — John was in another bedroom suite and we all hugged. But it was very tense, extremely tense; Sharon and I not knowing what it was that he had to say to anybody, suspecting the worst.

We asked how he had been and he said, "Better, now that I'm with you," and we really didn't talk. I think that the first night we ordered food. He said, "You can order whatever you want." We watched TV and we kind of relaxed in our comfortable state of just being at home. It was like the familiar feeling, it was a real comforting feeling after all the stress. It was something that was healing at the moment.

There was one California King-sized bed. He laid in the middle and Sharon and I lay on either side, which was one of the first times that we ever did that, other than crashing out for a nap after, you know, in the hot afternoon or something. We all just went to bed and we slept. He had arm around me and I'm pretty sure with Sharon as well. It was something that we all needed.

Sharon Holmes[h]: I often have wondered what they thought of this, these two women and John in this bedroom. It's true, there was no place else to sleep so there were three of us in a king-sized bed — John in the middle and Dawn on the other side.

Tom Lange: Sleeping in the same bed was strange to us. The women could have been in another room, it was a suite. I didn't eyeball it, but that's what was heard. That's what was said — I was told they'd slept together, I'm not saying they took their clothes off.

Dawn Schiller[h]: I remember Sharon staring out of the window at the Bonaventure. We chain-smoked and cried and ordered meals served with guns. Back and forth, they would speak with John, and John went out into the other room, [which] I assumed was to inform them that it was a "go." Everything was all right and we'll do this exchange because these two will be with me now.

He said that he needed to talk to us both and he went into the bathroom with Sharon first.

Tom Lange: The pressure was on John. We would have rather not filed a murder charge against John. We wanted him as a witness, but he would have to have been completely forthcoming.

John had worked out a tentative deal in which he, Sharon and Dawn would be protected as witnesses in exchange for his cooperation in revealing the identities of the murderers. He asked to have a private meeting with each of the women to discuss joining the witness protection program. Detective Lange recalled that he was granted time alone with each of the women, alone in the bathroom and out of the listening range of the officers, which also enabled John time to strategize.

Tom Lange: On top of that, John visited Sharon at home shortly after the murders. The two of them would have had ample time to talk alone then.

Sharon Holmes[h]: This is when I found out more about what he had really been doing involved with Eddie Nash. Bits and pieces came out. Dawn and I were comparing notes about our experiences, but not talking about them in great detail.

I told him that he couldn't stay in the house and he said, "I don't want to because I know this makes it easier for someone to try to find me." Of course, in the hotel John didn't have any drugs so he was pretty straight, but he was awfully shaky. I guess the gist of the matter was they would see about making arrangements as long as he testified against Eddie Nash. Whether he was just completely terrified for himself and his family or just for his family — I don't know, but he said "No." There was no way he would do that.

He asked me if I would go with them and I had told him the last night before we left the Bonaventure, "Even if this works out, I won't go with you. I've lived with enough upheaval and there'll never be a life for us because you can't change."

He cried and he begged and he pleaded. For him to have been able to stand there and watch these people slaughtered — I couldn't live with that. When you've done something like that, you'll never be the same again and I didn't want to put up with screaming and nightmares. I didn't want to have to relive through that kind of experience all of this. It was just the complete opposite to what my life was about. My life was about life, not about death and drugs and porno and that sort of thing. I didn't want to do this. I couldn't provide any kind of a support for him any more.

Dawn Schiller[h]: They were in there a while and he came out and said, "I need to talk to you, too, Dawn."

Sharon said, "Yeah, he's going to need to talk to you."

We went into the bathroom and he said, "This is it. I've just talked to Sharon and I need to talk to you, too, but you two are my life and I don't want to do anything without you ever again. I know a lot of things that make a lot of people scared and the police want to know what that is, and I'm not going to give it to them because I don't want to endanger the two of you any more than I already have unless I know that you are safe and that we are together.

"They'll protect all three of us if I tell them what they want, but that means that we are going to have to change our names, change our identities and basically, our old selves are going to have to be dead. You are not going to be able to contact your mom or your dad. It's called a police protection program. They'll give us different names and they'll give us a different place to live in a different state. We can bring the dogs, but the three of us can be together. I need to know if you'll go with me."

I said, "Did you do it?"

"No." But [he explained that] when he went to go pick up his messages at his answering service in Santa Monica, he got in the car and there was a gun put to the back of his head. He was forced to let the murderers into the Wonderland house because he had the security entrance pass, or they recognized his voice and they opened the door for him. He said that he had to watch it happen.

He said that Sharon had already said, "Yes." He told me that she had already agreed and I said, "Well, me too. Yes, I'll do it." Then we told each other that we loved each other. I think [we] cried. We were sitting on the edge of the bathtub.

Sharon didn't offer any information about what they had spoken about when they were in the bathroom alone and I didn't offer any either 'cause from what John had told me, it was the same thing. So I didn't know that she had said, "No, I won't." Had I known that at that point in time, he would have had no leverage.

ASSOCIATED PRESS. PHOTO BY WALLY FONG.

8.

On The Lam

John & Dawn Across America

"Take Care of Him."

Because Sharon would not agree to join the witness protection program with John and Dawn, he refused to go on the record with any information about the Wonderland murders. The police had had enough of John's games and without a concrete reason to detain him further, they turned him loose with specific instructions to remain in Los Angeles.

Dawn Schiller[h]: After about three days of this between the Bonaventure and the Biltmore, John came in and he said, "Well, that's it."

I said, "What do you mean?" And he said that they were letting us go, and I said, "What do you mean? What happened to the protective custody?"

He said, "Well, they don't want that anymore."

Well, it didn't make sense to me, but the police were packing it up, everybody was leaving and they drove us back to Glendale — all three of us — and let us go.

John Holmes[q]: After they turned me loose, the cops put me in a car and drove back out to the valley to a car impound. My whole car, inside and out, was covered with silver powder. They fingerprinted the entire car. The cops went one way and I went the other way.

Sharon Holmes[h]: We were brought back to my house. Basically, when we got back, he and Dawn left together. I think they were going back to find a place and he said, "I need to get my stuff together. I need to run because the police are going to be after me and worse than that, Eddie Nash is going to be after me, so I have to go."

Dawn Schiller[h]: I assumed that Sharon was going to go also. He told me that Sharon was going to stay here and make sure that everything is okay with the animals and that she's going to meet us later.

We bought a bottle of black hair dye and I dyed his hair black. Sharon's Chevy Malibu, which was blue with a black hood, turned out with a gray primer hood and red body, spray-painted; with big spray-paint drips all over it. It was a rush job. We packed our [things] in paper bags and packed them in the back. Sharon was running some other errands for us.

To get the money together was another issue.

Sharon Holmes[h]: When I got back, I talked to my [boss]. I didn't talk about why, [but] I said, "I need a couple of days off. I need to move and I need to move quickly."

[John] asked if he could borrow money from me and I said, "I know you're not borrowing it; you need it. I have $1200 dollars. You can have it. Meet me in the Safeway."

So we met there and he had no place to stay that night. Dawn was not with him that night. He said, "I need a place to stay and I need to bring Dawn."

I said, "No, but I have the keys to another place where I'll be moving and you can stay there," so he stayed at the place where I was going to live. He and Dawn stayed there, in the attic that night.

Tom Lange: I think he was fearful. He had a difficult decision, that's why he took off to Florida. The cops were going to nail him or Nash was going to nail him, but then what does he do, in the middle of it, before he leaves? He goes to Nash and tries to get money from Nash! So he's not thinking straight, perhaps. I don't know, but he sure as hell didn't want anything to do with us. He's telling us just enough to keep us interested and to protect himself. He's not about to give himself up.

Dawn Schiller[h]: He went up to ask Eddie for $1,000 or something like that. He said, "Eddie's one of the ones that wants to kill me."

I said, "How are you going to do this?"

Well, he played a poker hand. He said, "I'm going to tell him that I didn't tell the police anything, but I did tell a few people in writing and if I don't return with the money — if I don't return and [he] decides to kill me..." he told them that the letters would be distributed and that everybody would know everything.

The person that was supposed to do that was me. But there were no letters. There was nothing. It was a bluff and it worked, but he only got half the money.

John Holmes[q]: So I headed down to the bottom of Laurel Canyon, in Ventura and I called [Ed Nash] with a payphone. I said, "I'm down at the bottom of Laurel Canyon."

He said, "Come on up," and I said that I need some money to get out of town quick. So he said he had $500 — cash. "I want you to come back in a couple of hours. I'll give you some more so you can get out of town."

So I split, with the $500 and I hid out. I stayed in Eagle Rock for three days. [Dawn] stayed with me all the time. I got a hold of my brother and a couple of other people and I told them I needed some money to get out of town for a while. I finally came up with, after paying for the hotel and everything, $150. That's what I left town with: $150 and a beat-up car.

Sharon Holmes[h]: He, again, asked me if I would go with him and I said, "No, I won't go."

I went over to Dawn when I had told him that because I thought he was going to beg and plead again. I turned my back on him. I looked over at Dawn, I hugged her and said, "Take care of yourself, and take care of him the best you can."

Dawn Schiller[h]: Within 24 hours release from the [Bonaventure Hotel], John and I took off from the Lucky Parking lot — I think that it was the Lucky Parking lot in Glendale. We left Los Angeles — myself with him — for the final time and said, "Goodbye," to Sharon.

My understanding was that she was going to meet up with us later. The last thing she said to me was, "Take care of him."

And I said, "Okay."

There were no drugs from the point of the arrest up to this point. He was getting more of his old self back, more of his old personality. The mood swing thing was not there, so that took the violent edge off of him. He was more of the needy, loving person that I remember him [being] in the beginning.

John and I took off, and that was the last time I saw Sharon, until seven years later. She's not a very huggy-kind of person, anyway. I mean, she's not one of those touchy-feely people with John; it was rare if I ever saw a lot of that with [she and] him, anyway. That's not her personality.

Sharon Holmes[h]: I walked over to my car and then went home. That was the last I saw of him until he ended up in jail — or the last I even talked to him because he didn't want us to be in contact, for fear the police might be tapping my phone and find out where he was.

Meanwhile, Julia St. Vincent had just completed making the John Holmes "documentary," *Exhausted* just before John and Dawn ran away. *Exhausted* enjoyed an extensive run at adult movie theaters across the country. In fact, it knocked *Deep Throat* out of the Pussycat Theater on Hollywood Boulevard after a 12-year run.

At the time of the movie's release, John's newfound notoriety incited extensive media coverage and wide-spread publicity. The timing of the film's release could not have been better if it had been strategically arranged. Police invaded an advanced screening of *Exhausted* in July of 1981, thinking the film's subject might be in attendance.

The Suspects

Annette Haven [h]: I got this panicked phone call from John and this never happened — John didn't call me up on the phone to visit. We worked together, we were personal associates, but we didn't hang out. It was unusual to have John call and want to lean on me. He was terrified. Somebody, he said, was chasing him; he was being chased by people who were trying to kill him. It was kind of a garbled conversation. I really didn't know that he was having the problems he was having, but the standing policy at my house is, if anybody is bothering you, you can come up to my house and hide because if anybody comes through my door without my permission, I'll blow a big hole in them with a .44 Magnum.

I offered and assured him that he would be safe there and I would protect him.

Then he never came up. I don't know what happened. All of the stuff hit the press and it was just horrible. I didn't know where to contact him. I kept hoping he'd call.

Many of John's associates have said that John called and asked for a place to hide or actually stayed at their home during the days after the murders and after his release from police custody. Amerson had told the police that John had also visited him, covered in blood.

Bill Amerson: It was six o'clock in the morning. I got a phone call from a friend of mine. He said, "I saw your boy come out of the house and there are five people dead." He was a hit man. He took a contract to kill all these people.

They were going to die that day, no matter what; there were three different people that were going to kill them. There was a guy named Cowboy and his partner's name was Whitey. They had got ripped off and they were going to kill them.

My friend, D. Samuel, who was a notorious hit man, was paid $20,000 to go and kill them. He was sitting outside of the house, waiting to go in and kill them when he saw John come out. He called me and he was worried and said, "Your boy came out of an apartment and everybody's dead."

Tom Lange: It is my recollection that Amerson was indeed interviewed. What he had to say was certainly of little value. Due to the circumstances of this case, any statements by anyone on the periphery were either self-serving or led nowhere.

John Holmes [9]: It all comes down to whether Ed Nash did it, David Lind did it or Mr. Howard did it. There are only three people who could've done it. I slid out from underneath because Ed Nash believed that I did it. At the same time, David Lind thought I did it, so that's why he wants to kill me.

I don't think Ed Nash had anything to do with it. I think it was David Lind or it was Mr. Howard and his mafia in Los Angeles.

Three years after Holmes' death, evidence was introduced by the defense during Ed Nash's trial for conspiring to commit the Laurel Canyon murders that a man named Howard "Fat Howard" Cook of Los Angeles, had been owed money for drugs by the Wonderland gang. Allegedly, he had sent a hit man named Paul Kelly, along with others over to the Wonderland house.

Kelly's girlfriend, Maggie Coffman, provided evidence for Nash's trial on a tape recording where he says to her, allegedly before the murders, "You know I love you and I want to marry you but I have to eliminate a few, a few people that you care about, right?"

One, as Coffman told police, was Ron Launius. The prosecutor informed the jury that Kelly may have been one of the murderers that night, but Nash had ordered the hit. At the time of Nash's trial, Paul Kelly was serving time in state prison for an unrelated conviction.

Tom Lange: The Wonderland bunch did rip off several people — some legitimate business people and some dope dealers. I'm sure many wanted them taken out, but there was only talk and no action. There was no credible evidence that other hits had been ordered. The evidence at the Nash trial was not evidence, but the ranting of a local psychopath by the name of Paul Kelly. The defense used this, somewhat successfully, to take the onus off of their client. There was never any substantive evidence linking Kelly to these murders.

"Fat Howard" was the guy who brought Lind to us in the first place. He was a petty criminal who did not possess the cashews for a hit. He only wanted favoritism and insulation from the cops. He was known more as a thief and receiver of stolen property, with a knack for speaking out of both sides of his mouth at the same time.

The Getaway

Sean Amerson: No matter how screwed up his life was, he always checked in with me to make sure I was OK. He even called me once right after the murders while on the run with Dawn, just to tell me not to worry, he was fine.

Dawn Schiller [h]: After we left L.A., he was the caring boyfriend that didn't want me hurt and he protected me again. He turned back into his old self. You could talk to him again. The old personality was coming back. The situation was still fucked up, but his personality was back, and we had my little dog, Thor, with us. He was that loving guy again who could crack jokes, make you laugh and just make the room glow, you know?

He would sing with the radio, with that baritone voice (that you couldn't tell him was off-key). You didn't dare tell him that he couldn't sing! I sang along with him and [he] was back to a child-like nature, pretty much. It was fun.

We drove through Vegas. I waited in the parking lot there, because he wanted to go and play roulette. He just wanted to go put one down on double-ought, his favorite spot.

Bob Chinn explained the importance of double-ought — it had been lucky for John in the past. Just a few years before on one of his trips to Vegas with Bob Chinn, John had won $12,000 on the spot playing double zeros. Julia also observed John's luck at roulette while they had been in Las Vegas together.

Dawn Schiller [h]: He came out very quickly and I said, "What happened?"

He said, "I went to sit down at the roulette table, and I saw some-body that wasn't good. We are getting out of here." That was the only tense moment, until after we were in Montana.

John did not know that the police had arrested Ed Nash within a month after the murders following a seizure of more than $1,000,000 worth of cocaine, money and weapons. Unbelievably, Ed Nash made bail, but there were two more drug raids at Nash's property on Dona Lola Drive.

Tom Lange: We interviewed John's step-brother a couple of times out here and he was not that close to John. John never talked to him. I can't remember what [David] said exactly, but my recollection of John and his half-brother is that they were not close; "John is doing his thing, and I'm doing mine. I really don't get involved in that stuff. We don't see each other that often."

He told us they spoke seldom and rarely saw each other. All we can do is go on the evidence. He was not cooperative to a great extent. Sharon certainly wasn't, and the girlfriend wasn't. Nobody was. It's not like on television, where we can beat it out of him or we can leave a secret bug in there when we leave. We can only go on what people told us in 1981; that was a long time ago. Sharon said different things, as did John's brother.

Sharon Holmes[h]: I remember, I guess, he'd been gone about five weeks. Tom Lange and his partner came to my house, wanting to know where John was. I assumed he might go back to Ohio for a short period of time, but I had no idea how he would go, or whatever. I didn't want to know. I told him straight out, "I have no idea. Yes, he did leave. Yes, I did give him money because I wanted him gone." I never saw them after that. I never heard back from John until the day after he was jailed in L.A.

When she first made it public in 1981 that she and "John Holmes — Porn Star" had been married for 16 years, Sharon also illuminated a few more aspects of John's private life. "John started out with pot, but then coke began to be the thing...household debts now approach $30,000." Sharon indicated later that this debt was one of the reasons behind her seeking divorce from her infamous husband.

Sharon also spoke of John as a "divided man" and said that he confided in her his personal desire to lead a more conventional life, "[John said,] 'I would love to sit back and be able to drive a truck and be a 9-5 guy, like everybody else and forget everything that's ever happened.'"

Sharon added, "That's his dream." She claimed that John had attempted to reconcile his work in pornography, by using a line that became one of his personal mantras, "That's my body, not my soul."

She concluded, "John paints, he writes, he sculpts. There isn't anything in wood he couldn't build. There isn't anything he can't repair. There's a lot of energy there. Where he directed it is where his problems began."

John Holmes[q]: [We] wound up in Montana and then I was broke. The weather was turning cold and I had to get out of cold weather. There were no jobs in Montana because of the winter, and we were starving to death.

Dawn Schiller[h]: We got to his sister's house in Montana and she let us stay for a couple of days. We were the boyfriend-girlfriend team with the little dog. She let us stay on her couch. We fried up chicken and did the back-home Ohio-kind of meals.

A couple of days later, we got a phone call from his mother in Ohio, telling us the F.B.I. was just there, they were looking for him, and they were probably on their way to his sister's, in Montana. That was our cue to pack up our bags and get the hell out of there. Except this time, when we left, it was a little tenser because now we were wanted by the F.B.I as well. His mother told us that they had informed her that we were armed and drug-crazed, which was completely untrue. We were drug-free, had no weapons and were not on a spree of any kind other than getting away from being endangered.

John Holmes[q]: So I headed back to — this was the first snow falling — Los Angeles and picked up some goddamn payphone, about four months later. I called Ed and I said, "This is John Holmes, down at the bottom of the hill. I'm about to see you."

And he said, "Come on up," so I went up, again. He gave me $550 and I told him I wanted to get a new I.D. and start some place else, in a new state. He said, "Well, you come back tomorrow morning and I'll give you enough money to do that."

Now the next thing Eddie Nash should have done was what? — Turned himself in and called the police or he could have called a couple hit men and had me offed at the house. Figure, if I'm not there, there's nobody to testify. He ordered those killings. That never came up, even though I didn't do it. He'd still ordered them.

With all the rats in the goddamn narcotics business [and] the counterfeiting business, I don't think he thought I could keep my mouth shut, not being criminally inclined. So I took the $550 and I split. I left for Florida; I drove all the way across the United States.

Close Call

Dawn Schiller[h]: From Montana, we packed up quickly and took off. John's foot was a little heavy on the pedal and I'll be goddamned if we didn't get pulled over for speeding. We were sweating bullets. We thought this was it: he's going to run John's license, he's going to find out that we were wanted. It wasn't on the board yet — we got stopped just outside of Billings, within moments of getting this phone call from his mother, pretty much.

John Holmes[q]: This whole time, the F.B.I. had a nationwide alert out for my car. They had the California license plate and I drove all over the United States for six months. One cop who pulled me over — the old man was getting ready to retire in a month. He lived in Montana — he let me go! I couldn't believe it. He must have taken a real razzing for that. Before he retired, he let the number-one, most-wanted criminal in America go. We got back in that goddamn car. We shot back up on the freeway as soon as the cop was out of sight and I drove 85 miles per hour all the way across that goddamn state.

Dawn Schiller[h]: I was raised in Florida. That seemed far enough away. I said I was raised there. I kind of knew the area. He didn't want to go to Ohio.

We traveled down through Arizona and we stopped. We went to the Grand Canyon and we went to the Big Meteor. We went to the Petrified Forest and we stole pieces of petrified wood in our shoes. We did all the tourist junk and we had some money because he did have money from Ed Nash.

Unfortunately, the pictures that Dawn had which documented their days as tourists have been lost.

Dawn Schiller[h]: I don't remember any other good stops. I know Oklahoma was way boring. It doesn't have any hills. Mississippi and all those kinds of places were pretty nice because they were different and swampy. We went through at night, with the fog, and we talked about Mardi Gras. He tried to come up with a Creole accent and it wasn't working! But there were still no drugs and he still wasn't violent at me again.

John Holmes[q]: They were looking for a blue car. We stopped at a little, dinky town, just before Salt Lake City. I bought a quart of this black enamel and two paintbrushes. I painted one side of the car and she painted the other off this dirt road. Tractors and horses went by and threw dirt on the wet paint. We finally got it painted and we shot out of there.

So we're driving down the freeway in a wet, painted car, dirt stuck on it. At the checkpoint, they didn't stop us because they were looking for a blue car and I had a black one.

We painted our car five times across the United States — five different colors. It wasn't funny at the time, it was like "man on the run" and it was very terrifying.

But doesn't it sound like a lot of fun to you, like a big adventure?

It was not fun at the time!

During her interview for *WADD*, Dawn remembered that she had not asked John, "Did you do it?" in the bathroom of the Bonaventure hotel in Los Angeles. Instead, she said, the conversation actually had come up at the Fountainhead motel on Collins Avenue in Miami.

Dawn Schiller[h]: I don't think that he told me that in the bathroom. I don't even think that I would ask that. I think that came up, like in Florida, after we were wanted by the F.B.I. In talking about "why's" and things like that — he was more of his old self and we would communicate. It wasn't, "You do as I say and don't speak." That personality was going away.

It was always inferred that it was between Eddie Nash and the people that were killed and John. There were no other people considered in the situation.

In Louisiana and Mississippi, we were running out of money, so he started thieving cars that were parked at the motel for anything he could again. One of the first nights that he did this, he came back with a gun. It was a .38. So we did end up armed with a little .38 handgun and we made it down to Florida.

We [stopped] at the Fountainhead Hotel — a transition-type of hotel. We rented a room and got talking to the manager. The manager's name was Rosie and he called her "Big Rosie," and she was. She was a sweetheart.

Her boyfriend worked, doing a remodel on another hotel down the road, and hooked John up with some construction work under a fake name. I got working as a maid — cleaning in exchange for rent — as they knew we couldn't afford it and they were very understanding about it and helpful. They've seen a lot of people in our financial situation.

There was old Joe, who ran the snack shop in the back, who made his own sausages; we all got to know each other.

John started doing some drawings. One of them was my dog, which he had signed, not with his regular scribble-signature. He actually wrote his name out.

Dark Clouds and Desperate Measures

Dawn Schiller[h]: Pretty soon, he started to get introverted and he got arguments started. Money was the issue. It came to the point where he was being dominating again and insisted that I just walk out on the beach and turn a trick for some extra cash.

"Don't tell anybody and keep it very secret," so that we could start earning some money to get out of there and get a home somewhere. Nobody recognized him there. Here we were established and trying to be regular, and then it turned into having a sideline — having to lie and hide certain things from the people that were helping.

He started to get violent again at that point, because he didn't like me going out and being with other people. It's his possessive nature. When I came back and I turned over the money, he timed me — waited at the door, watched across the street. It started back into the old arguments, that I was dirty, I was corrupt, I wasn't any good, and he wouldn't touch me until I stripped down and had been in the tub with hot water to purge myself of all sins. It got very twisted. He wasn't hitting, but he was pushing.

I cried, "This doesn't make sense! This hurts, stop!" My world crashed again around me. Now there was no hope, because I couldn't blame the drugs. I didn't know what to do.

He was out of energy and he was tired. Looking at the big picture, it was a pretty hopeless scene. He started to hit, he started to slap and push. I got scared. I stopped all arguments; I withdrew.

One night, he wanted me to go out on the beach and I said, "No, we've got to stop it here. We've got to stop it, because it's tearing you up and this is not how we need to do this." I was older now. I had a little bit more sense. I knew that I could pose an argument to his plans.

He just backhanded me. I was shocked. He threw a few more punches and I was down on the floor. I stayed quiet. I was laying there, waiting for more blows and nothing happened. He turned, but I was on the ground near the door.

It was hot in Florida and the door was open a little. I made a run for it. It was daylight, but it was after dinner time and everybody was down at the pool at Joe's Snack Shop, having Italian Sausage Night. I ran towards the pool, towards people to protect me.

He was running after me and he caught up to me right by the snack shop, by hair that was flying behind me. He yanked me down, jumped on top and pummeled the hell out of me in front of everyone. The nice, kind, generous, you know, big-hearted guy that everybody thought was living there had just turned Dr. Jekyll and Mr. Hyde, publicly. He beat me and dragged me back to the room, where he shut the door and stayed quiet the whole night.

The next day, he got up and went to work in the morning, as usual. A few minutes after he left, there was a knock on the door. It was Big Rosie and a few others that had lived there, Joe from the Snack Shop and another lady, Louise, who was a stripper. They just took over. They said, "Grab your things, get your dog, you are out of here."

I said, "I can't," and they said, "Oh, bullshit!" There was no fighting Big Rosie. She's one tough bitch. The stripper had a little girl, and was staying at the hotel because she was going through a divorce and needed somebody to watch her five-year-old daughter while she worked at night. Her divorce had just settled. She received a house and was moving that day.

She said, "You got a place with me." I had an entourage of support, which I never had before. It was incredibly powerful and it gave me a voice. He wasn't bigger than me anymore. He couldn't beat me up if I said, "No."

He got the phone number, I guess, from Big Rosie or her boyfriend. I guess he begged it out of them. After a couple of days, there was a call and this was the last time that I ever spoke to him. I cried when I heard his voice and I knew he was crying.

He said, "I know what I did was wrong, and I'm sorry." I had heard this before, the old story. He said he was sorry and could he please just see my face one more time? "That's all I need. That's all I'll ever ask of you again."

I said, "No." It was one of the hardest things to tell him, "No," and know that I would never see him again. "I'll never see you again where you can touch me or you can hurt me."

A Lead

Frank Tomlinson, another L.A.P.D homicide detective, became inclined to pursue Holmes during the same time that John and Dawn were breaking up at the Fountainhead.

Frank Tomlinson: I had a very unique assignment. I was taken to robbery-homicide division and given the freedom to never come to the office. The captain said he knew the work that I did. He said, "Just go solve murders. I don't ever expect to see you, except on payday." So it did create some conflict in the office because nobody else had that kind of freedom.

After I was at the crime scene — I didn't know who John Holmes was, but I had seen and heard enough that I knew that he would be instrumental in solving the case. I was just there to help the other guy and I left to work on some of my [other] cases, which took me out of town. When I came back to town, I got together with some of the guys to find out what had happened, and this is the part that's sensitive for me because — in any kind of work, you don't always agree with the way other people do it and it doesn't mean somebody's right and somebody's wrong. You just approach it differently.

I felt that Holmes had actually out-foxed some of the guys that had been handling him. He was able to con them into believing that if they did certain things that he would give them information. I always got the information first before I helped anybody and so, when I found out that it happened, I wondered what they had done with him. Well, they got upset when they realized that he'd taken advantage of them and had just thrown him out.

They just let him walk and so I assumed he would be dead by then, because he was instrumental — or whoever was behind these murders wouldn't let him walk around. I had a break between my cases so I approached these guys, and said, "Look, I've got free time, if he's still alive, I'd like to find him, and see what he's got to say."

So they said, "Well, go ahead." My whole focus was to see if he was alive and if I could find him. I started looking for anyone who knew him — any family members and then I would go out and do research to connect the dots.

I went to see [relatives] in Oregon, and they lived on a ranch — really rural. They were friendly, but I didn't actually believe they were giving me all the information. One of the resources I had was a person who could pull phone records for me and so after I left, I had phone records pulled and found out they had been calling Florida. That led me to do a little bit of research in Florida and I figured the area that he was most likely in. Once I had that figured out, then I went back to the detectives handling the case to see if they wanted to go with me when I went to see him. Lange went with me. We located a girl-friend of his down there.

I believed he would be dead. I was actually surprised that the people responsible were dumb enough to let him get away. Why would they do that after they killed four people? Why would they let the one guy go?

Dawn Schiller [h]: I was away from John and I felt that I could call my mother. I needed to make some connection with my family because John was no longer my family, so I called my mother and said, "This is where I'm at. I'm not with John anymore."

"We heard a lot about it on the news."

I said, "Have the police been there?"

"Oh, no, no, just what we saw on the news."

I said, "Okay, this is where I am. I'm in Florida and I've left him, so don't worry about me any more. I'm alive; I've done nothing, so there is no reason for anybody to go after me. I just want to let you know."

Tom Lange: Initially, we found her in Florida. She was working at a strip club in Miami. Frank had already talked to the brother. I didn't go on that Oregon trip. It was Frank and that's maybe how it happened — the brother found her. The brother lead somehow led us to that strip joint. She was working there. Frank went in there, and Frank didn't drink at all. He went in and had a Coke or something just to I.D. her, while we were outside waiting for them to leave.

Dawn Schiller [h]: The next day, or a couple days later, I got a phone call. It's my brother, who lives in Oregon, near my mother. He said, "Hey, what's going on? Mom just gave me your number, said you were in Florida. I'm down here, back in our old town where we grew up in Carol City, visiting."

He showed within a half an hour and he had this nice, white, generic-looking car. I said, "Whoa, where did you get this?" This was like a Lexus to me. He gave me a great big hug and he had a six pack in the back seat. We drove just a few blocks away.

He said, "The park's right here."

Tom Lange: We were following them through Miami and we went to a park. He told her what was going on and that we wanted her to cooperate. Then he said something like, "They're here now and they're watching us." We saw her jump up.

Dawn Schiller [h]: He knew the area very well and just as we're pulling in, he put his hand on my knee and said, "I have to tell you something."

I said, "What?"

"Well, the cops are here."

I said, "What? Get the hell out of here! Turn around!"

"No, they need to talk to you."

I was slapped with the reality that he didn't have a license, we had beers opened up and I'm set up. I said, "What do you mean?"

He said, "They need to know where John is." I tried to get out of the car, I remember. He just kept his hand on my knee and I said, "I'm not going to do this. You son of a bitch! You fucking son of a bitch. How could you do this to me?" I felt betrayed, completely.

He said, "Dawn, they don't want you, they just want to know where John is."

"I know that, but what makes you think that I'm going to tell them? Just because I'm not with him doesn't mean that I want to arrest him." We were pulling up as this was going on, parking and there were officers standing by. One of them was Lange. There was a local officer. They stood at the door; they didn't jump on me, like an arrest. They were respectful and very considerate.

I was crying hysterically. My brother went to get out of the car and came around to my side. I wasn't going to get out. I said, "I'm not telling them shit. I am not telling them anything. You can tell them to forget it."

Frank Tomlinson: She was naturally very hesitant to help us. It took us a while, seems like a couple of days. We couldn't have found him without her. We finally convinced her that it was in his welfare for us to find him, rather than to have somebody else. We convinced her that his life was in danger from the guys that were involved with that murder.

Dawn Schiller [h]: I just remember sobbing, letting loose and [my brother] put his arm around me. He told the officers, "Just give me a minute," and he walked me down to the water, and he started to cry. He said, "Look, there are a lot of contracts out on you and John, and the police want him. John's going to be dead within a week if something doesn't happen."

Frank Tomlinson: That's how we found Holmes. I traced him to Florida; the girlfriend helped us to set up the location where he was on the beach, at a motel.

John's Arrest for Murder

Dawn Schiller [h]: I found a business card from the Fountainhead and I pulled it out. I said, "He's here," in room such-and-such. "He's probably working as a painter. Here are his hours. He's probably going to invite you in for coffee. He's tired. We are both tired and there's no need to go banging doors down.

"Don't hurt him. Don't hurt him because he's not going to fight you. You have to do me one favor."

They said, "What?"

"After you have arrested him, call me and let me know that everything is okay; that he's safe."

Frank Tomlinson: Once we knew where he was, we just set up surveillance across the street and waited for him to come out of his room. He walked out and we walked up and we grabbed him.

With the assistance of the Dade County Public Safety Department, Detectives Lange and Tomlinson set up surveillance outside of the Fountainhead Hotel. At approximately 8:00 p.m. on December 4th, 1981, Lange and Tomlinson observed John going into room number 43. By 8:45, they had arrested him.

John Holmes [q]: I was apprehended by two Los Angeles policemen, taken to jail, then court. As it turned out, [Dawn's] brother had been arrested. With her information about my whereabouts, they released her brother.

I did not fight extradition. Screw it. I hadn't done anything! I just wanted to go home and get it over with. I was tired of running!

Holmes said that he lived in the room alone and he allowed officers to search his room. He was transported to await booking at the Dade County Jail in Miami. According to police records, John had said that he thought that something was going to happen because he knew about the murders, but he would need some time to think of what to do next.

Help From Above

Frank Tomlinson: The one thing that I made clear when we got him, I took him aside and I told him that things were entirely different than they had been before. I warned him not to try to do what he had done in Los Angeles, or else it just wouldn't be good for him to do that. He seemed frightened of me, which is what I tried to accomplish — I was the bad guy. He was pretty careful around me.

Dawn Schiller[h]: It was the next day, or that evening when Tom Lange called and told me, "Well, we got him and we're about to get on a plane and go to California. Just like you said, he offered us coffee." This was something that he did when anybody came to the door because he was a coffee nut. "We sat around and he was kind of expecting us. He kind of looked relieved. He's okay."

I said, "Thank you," and that was the end.

Holmes appeared before Judge Wright in Florida's Dade County Circuit Court on Saturday morning at 10:30, December 5th, 1981.

Frank Tomlinson: We caught him on a Friday and I had to get back to Los Angeles on Saturday. Saturday morning, they had a court hearing because he had the right not to waive extradition, which meant we couldn't have brought him back with us and so, we went to court that morning. He got the public defender.

They were giving him all his rights that he can fight extradition and we can't take him back. He's going along with the whole thing and then, toward the end of his conversation with his attorneys, the judge is waiting for his answer. He turned around and looked at me. I was in the first row. Nobody was in the court because it was a Saturday morning and I just gave him a look, like, "Be careful with what you do."

And he turned around, and he said, "I'll waive extradition."

We grabbed him and took him out of there. Then we had to find a flight to get back. The one flight that was going to L.A. was booked and there was no way for us to get three people on the flight at the last minute.

So we're walking out of the airport, and we walked past a guy coming in. He's obviously a pilot and we stopped him and said, "Hey man, we're in a bind here. We need to get to L.A. Do you have any ideas?"

He said, "Well, they just called me because the flight was booked up and they want to take another flight to L.A."

It was like, "Sign me up, we're going with you." We got on his plane, flew back here. L.A.P.D. was waiting on the tarmac.

At the same time that Tomlinson had been a part of Holmes' arrest, he began investigating the Bible for answers to his own spiritual questions. His research eventually led Tomlinson to retiring from the L.A.P.D.

Frank Tomlinson: The reason my time was up at L.A.P.D. was because — working around death all the time, I had begun to get curious about how all of this plays out if there's a God. I always believed there was a God, but I realized I don't know anything about Him. Being in a morgue everyday, you think, "One of these days, I'm going to be out there and some dumb detective's going to watch them doing an autopsy on me." And so I ended up becoming a Biblicist.

On the way back, John sat next to me and he acted like he was sleeping. I found out later that he wasn't. I was reading my Bible because I was always reading the Bible; I was really curious about it and a stewardess saw me doing that. She knew I was a policeman, so she came down, sat on the other side of me and just talked to me. She had questions about life and what I was studying. I had a conversation with her about that.

We got in on Saturday. When we got him off the airplane, he took me aside and he said, "Could I talk to you tomorrow?"

I said, "Okay, I'll come downtown." I turned him over to the detectives who handled the case. They booked him for murder.

Big John.

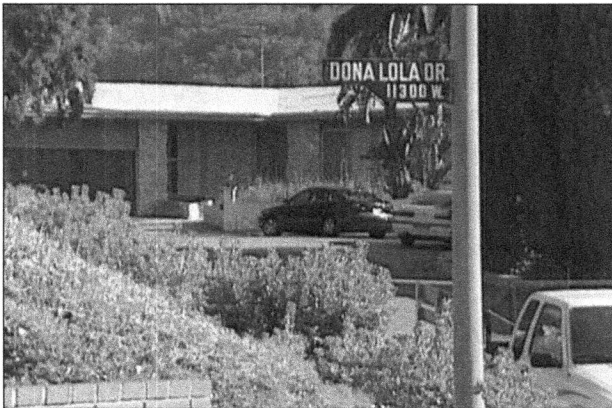

A recent photograph of Ed Nash's former home on Dona Lola Drive in the Laurel Canyon neighborhood. John met Ed Nash, a notorious L.A. nightclub owner, in 1978.

Image courtesy of VCX.com. For this scene in the 1980 film, *Prisoner of Paradise,* Bob Chinn told John to think about the saddest thing that he could, in order to convey his character's emotion.

8763 Wonderland Avenue in the summer of 2006. The white, three story building has been nicely renovated; in 1981, it was dilapidated and the balcony was rusty. According to John, he met its residents — the so-called Wonderland Gang — in 1979 or 1980.

Julia St. Vincent directs the 1981 documentary, *Exhausted: John Holmes the Real Story*.

With bloodshot eyes in December 1980, "Mr. Wonderful" answers St. Vincent's interview questions for *Exhausted*.

In this clip from *Exhausted,* which was shot in June of 1981, John says, "He allows me to block my own sex scenes, so that's good."

When Julia St. Vincent asked John if most directors allow him to do that, John said that only two or three directors trusted him to do this. Bob refuted his statements with a chuckle, "Block his own sex scenes? I don't allow you to block your own sex scenes!"

To which John replied, "See, I don't tell him how to edit and he doesn't tell me how to fuck!"

Wearing a custom-made, orange leather suit from North Beach Leather, John rifles through Julia St. Vincent's purse. She had convinced him to attend an awards show that night because she thought he would win an award, but he did not.

Early on July 1, 1981, John was forced to lead a group of murderers to the Wonderland house. According to John, its security gate was broken at the time.

Ron Launius

Billy Deverell

Joy Miller

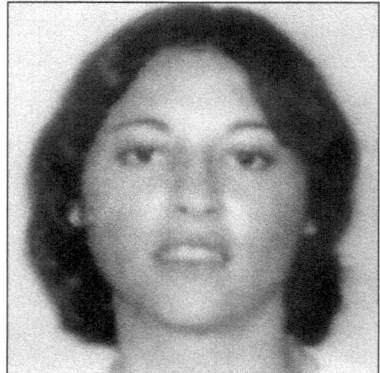

Barbara Richardson

Barbara Richardson lies dead between the couch and coffee table at the Wonderland crime scene.

On December 9, 1981, John was escorted to a police van after appearing before the Los Angeles country municipal court. ASSOCIATED PRESS. PHOTO BY WALLY FONG.

FRANK TOMLINSON

ASSOCIATED PRESS. PHOTO BY WALLY FONG. APRIL 28, 1982.

9.

Atonement

The State of California vs. John C. Holmes

The Confession

Frank Tomlinson: He asked if I would come out and see him the next day. On the Sunday after we brought Holmes back from Florida, I pulled him out of jail and sat down with him in the office at the robbery homicide division.

On Sunday, December 6, Tomlinson contacted Holmes, who stated that he wanted to tell the officers the truth about the murders. He asked to speak to his brother Dave, and arrangements were made.

Frank Tomlinson: I placed Holmes in a chair at one end of the table and I sat at the other. There was no one else present in the room. We sort of began to negotiate the way this was going to happen. I warned him again that it'd be way safer for him, if he was going to lie to me, not to say anything at all because if he said something I found out was a lie, I would intentionally hurt him. Somehow, I would find a way to hurt him. He said he understood that, but then he turned the subject to the Bible. That's when I realized he was awake [on the airplane] when I thought he was sleeping and he was listening. He said he was very interested in that and he wanted to know if I'd get him a Bible. I told him the next time I saw him, I'd bring him a Bible.

The next time I saw him, it was early the next week. When I went back to see Holmes, it was to finalize an agreement with him. I asked him if he'd thought about what I proposed and he said, "Yes."

I asked him if he did it and he said, "No." The obvious thing, then, is you know what happened there, so what sort of an agreement would we make for you to tell me that and then trust me to keep you safe?

Tom Lange: Frank runs investigations a little bit differently than most. We call it a little bit unconventional. He took Holmes on as one of his private, little projects. Frank is a devout man of God and he went on the Bible route. They ended up on the floor, on their knees, praying over the Bible. Frank got kind of a missionary confession.

Frank Tomlinson: I brought him a Bible. When he asked me to pray, we did so at the conference table and I was looking at him the whole time. We did not pray over the Bible, look at the Bible or talk about the Bible. I simply delivered it to him as he requested.

I prayed with him, but even in my prayer, it would be that God knows the truth, so I was praying that, "God, you better emphasize this to him. He can fake me out, he can't fake you out." I trust God to reveal the truth to me and if I find out and it's clear, then I will hurt this guy. He believed that part of it, too.

I don't do spiritual discussions; I just talk. I don't think he had many questions about it. He was just interested that I was interested in it and the only thing that most people would consider spiritual is that he said, "Will you pray for me?" and I said, "Sure," so I did.

Tom Lange: They were praying. The entire conversation between Frank and John Holmes is discoverable. He's not going to lie. He's going to say, "Yes, we did have a discussion about the Bible and my beliefs and his desires." How's the prosecution going to use that? I mean, that's going to be challenged. If John would have been forthright and said, "This is what happened," fine, but he didn't want to do that.

Because you're using religion — you're on your knees, praying with the Bible and this is called a police penitent. The situation was an exception here. It can be barred, as far as bringing it as evidence. Frank didn't do it to get a confession so that he could nail Holmes. He did it to save his soul. A prosecutor cannot put that on [in court]. The problem with putting it on is how it was elicited with the Bible, praying on your knees with the Bible in the Captain's Office.

Despite the accusations from his peers, former Detective Tomlinson maintained that he did nothing out of line by fulfilling John's desire to pray together and was emphatic that his growing interest in the Bible did not compromise his work as a policeman. In fact, Holmes apparently had given Tomlinson enough information to pursue an arrest of Ed Nash.

Frank Tomlinson: I would never get on the floor and close my eyes with any suspect. Lange and [Prosecuting Attorney Ron] Coen make it sound as if I used religion on people and that I didn't know how to successfully prosecute murders.

I told him that his rights were so important that I wanted to go over them point by point with him so that he understood exactly what they were. And I told him once again that he had the right to remain silent. He stated that he understood his rights.

I asked him if he wanted to give up his rights so that we could talk — the right to remain silent and to an attorney. He nodded in the affirmative, so I told him that I wanted him to understand that if a case was filed on him and we subsequently ended up in court, that I would be sitting in a witness box and he would be at the counsel table, and everything that he told me, I would testify in court. He stated that he understood that.

At that point, I told him I would just like for him to tell me everything that happened in regard to the murders. He stated that after Nash was robbed, Nash made him tell who had robbed him. He said that Nash held him at the Nash house, took his address book and wrote down names of his family. He said that he did that in front of him and that Nash told him that if he ever talked to the police he would kill someone in his family. That was why he was afraid to tell me what happened.

On December 7, John told Tomlinson, "I knew what was going to happen, but I had no choice. I had to set things up and let them in. I was there when the murders happened, but I did not see anyone. I was just there."

Tomlinson said to him, "Dawn told me that you said Nash's niggers made you let them in."

Holmes replied, "I can't be specific and give you the race."

Frank Tomlinson: At that time, I told him that one of his palm prints had been found in a location and in a position above one of the victims. He stated that he had not hit anyone. I told him that I had just realized that perhaps Nash had made him strike one of the victims, thinking that if he were involved in the murders he would be afraid to talk. I assured him that he was just as guilty of first-degree murder for what he had told me in regard to going to the house to allow killers inside so that the people could die, as he would be if he had struck one of the victims. He, again, repeated that he did not hit anyone. He said that he did not know how his palm print would have been near one of the victims.

He was very nice to me, but I didn't know anything about him. He was pretty safe with me in that respect. It wasn't like I had a lot of questions about his fame. I just wanted to keep it on the one thing — these are the steps to you telling me who did those murders. He seemed genuinely afraid of telling me. It was like he knew that his life was at risk because he was there.

Good Guys, Bad Guys

Frank Tomlinson: This was not my case. It belonged to Lange and Souza and I respected their authority to handle their case however they wished. My partner and I had successfully prosecuted a number of cases with prosecutors from Coen's office and they all respected our work.

My partner and I solved more murder cases than anyone else at R.H.D. [robbery homicide division] and we handled major cases that resulted in contracts being placed on our lives. My partner and I always developed informants. That's how we solved so many murder cases.

I developed information from a woman in Bakersfield when I was looking for Holmes. She knew Eddie Nash and she said, "The reason nobody's ever going to talk to you is because he tells everybody that he pays off the police. So, they'll never, ever touch him on these murder cases." Holmes told me the same thing that Nash would say that nobody will ever mess with him for murder.

I made an agreement with him. I said, "I will go book him for murder first and then you better trust me and give me the information. If I can't book him for murder and something does happen where I can't accomplish that, then you're not on the hook for telling me anything at all."

This was towards the end of my time as a homicide detective. All the freedom that I had to solve murder cases, which was the freedom to go anywhere and do anything — my partner and I went to South America, Canada, everywhere — had changed. The guys who had brought us into that division to solve murders retired and new guys came in to manage the office. They had the authority to decide what we were going to do, so I sat down with the captain and said, "This was the deal. I've got all the evidence that I need to go grab Nash and I'm going to get him for murder." And I was ordered not to do that; first time in my career I was ordered not to arrest somebody.

Tom Lange: The political climate was such that they didn't want us making precipitous arrests. It pissed us off.

Frank Tomlinson: Politics. It happened at election time, must have been around the fall of the year and the police chief was running for mayor, the mayor was running for governor, somebody else was running for attorney general. It's like, let's not mess with this thing. Those things were adding up for me to realize the clock's ticking for my career.

So I went back to Holmes and told him that I was ordered not to do this and I'm keeping the agreement; he didn't have to tell me anything and then, I was out of the whole thing.

Understandably, Prosecutor Coen wanted to have someone charged with the multiple murders in Laurel Canyon and maybe he had ulterior motives for desiring to pin Holmes for the murders. Perhaps at that time, he thought a guilty verdict implicating the most famous adult performer would help his career; he later became judge in the Los Angeles Superior Court.

Ron Coen[h]: I was in the organized crime division of the district attorney's office. I was not the head — I became the head later. I heard that Holmes was arrested. My boss had the case at first. I've always wanted as many big cases as I could. I asked for it and took it over from the very beginning. It was unlike other cases, wherein this particular case, the district attorney's office got involved in the defendant's arrest. We were actually able to help in the investigation — put our point of view out, what we would like the investigators to ask, things of that nature.

Tom Lange: What we had were knowing his intentions to the killer by letting him in and not alerting the victims. We had the palm print. We went with these things and tried to convict him. If we had convicted John Holmes, he would have become a witness, real quick.

Frank Tomlinson: The D.A. went ahead and filed the murder charges against Holmes. I was not privy to any of that. I was called in to Coen and he told me what he wanted me to testify, too. I told him that I didn't believe that Holmes had committed these murders, but that I could not go any further with my investigation. But he said he was going to put me on the stand to testify. In my cases, my partner and I never took a case to a D.A. unless we knew it was the right guy. We had cases where the D.A.'s we worked with would have filed murder cases and we said, "No," until we're convinced. This was one of those cases where I was not convinced that he killed anybody, so I would have never filed that case.

Incarceration

Sharon Holmes[h]: I never heard from John until the day after he was jailed in L.A., when he was brought back from Florida and then he called me and said, "I need you to come and see me."
I said, "For what reason?"
He said, "You're the only person I know who doesn't want something from me. I need you so I can come down; I need to get my head straight." This wasn't an emotional involvement for me at this point, not as husband and wife. I would do this for anybody if they asked me for my support.
I went down to the jail crowd twice a week. He needed support from somebody who didn't want something from him. Everybody — I guess God and everyone else — wanted to go in and visit him. Every reporter, everyone in the porn business — I guess there was a problem because I don't think felons can visit jail mates. There are a lot of people who would not have been able to visit him.

Bill Amerson: He wouldn't talk to me. He sent a message to me through a guy who got out of jail that he didn't want me to come to jail because he didn't want to associate, which was really stupid because we were associated anyway. But to be on the list to see people in jail, the prisoner has to write down the name and John wouldn't, so I couldn't go in.

Sharon Holmes[h]: My first question when I saw him, other than looking at him and saying, "God, I've never seen you look so bad," was, "Where is Dawn?"

And he said, "She ran off with a lesbian. I don't know and I don't care where the hell she is."

Julia St. Vincent: Dawn's story is great because she happened to be the one who [ran] away with him, but if you listen to the two stories, they were pretty fucking similar. He had used exact words to her that he had used to me. I guess I was always in love with him. I don't really know.

You'll see the picture of him when he was first arraigned, where he looks at someone — he's looking at me. That's the first time I had seen him in months. He looked over immediately when he walked into the courtroom and went, like [she hung her head low], "Yup, I'm fucked."

I'm sure that my visits are completely documented. The guy that was the detainee/holder was actually the husband of my lawyer's secretary. They let me in whenever I came there. I brought him the clothes he wore. I went out because I knew his sizes and all that because I had that *Exhausted* suit. I bought him a suit for court, the shoes, and I was allowed to go in with the lawyers.

We talked about, like, nothing — which is about what I talked with John about everyday. Our relationship was all about whatever came up at that second. I knew he wasn't going to tell me if he killed people. I'm not an authoritative figure in his life where he's going to admit, "Yeah, I killed them." I mean, even if he did, what would I do with that information? He had a persona that he had to keep, which was the one in charge.

He was like stone, but he did tell me, "Don't talk to Dawn because she turned state's evidence." I didn't believe him. In essence, it was true.

Sharon Holmes[h]: I'm a KFWB [980 AM] listener; I cannot drive my car without KFWB being on and every once in a while, I would get a blip and I would turn the radio off and then I would drive erratically — no, that's a joke, but that was all I had, bits and snatches. John would never talk about the trial itself, other than to say, "So-and-so testified and what a bunch of bullshit." Nothing in depth. He didn't ask anything of me, other than to be there and to be me, so he got that.

With no one willing to bail him out while he awaited his preliminary court hearing, John stayed at the Los Angeles County Men's Central Jail. Dr. Vonda Pelto was the resident psychologist at the jail during the time of John's incarceration. Dr. Pelto was hired to assess and consult with all of the high profile cases. John's frame of mind fluctuated between optimism and fear.

Dr. Vonda Pelto [h]: I went into the module known as 1750, which is a keep-away area in the jail on the main floor. I went in and introduced myself as Dr. Pelto, the psychologist and said I was down to see Mr. Holmes. The deputies pulled him out of his cell. The deputies were very cooperative by the way and introduced me to John, then told me that I could use a little room, which was across a hallway from the deputy booth.

In this small room were a desk and a barber chair, so when I saw John, he was brought in and his right wrist was handcuffed to the barber chair. So he sat opposite me; I at the desk and he in the barber chair. I had actually seen films of John before — some of his porn stuff, but I was struck with how tall he was and how very thin he was. He was somewhat pale, kind of a little scraggly beard, not as much hair as I expected on the top of his head. Just a scraggly looking, kind of soulful, sad-looking dude, I thought.

I explained first of all, that I was a psychologist in the jail and that I was there for him, and if he had any problems he could always see me. I did a regular intake interview, asking different questions about his background. He said that he was in jail and he was still in the process of the court hearing at that time.

I said to him, "It's probably like being held between a rock and a hard place. If you say who did it, you're in bad trouble and if you don't say who did it, you're going to be held by the grand jury."

He laughed and said, "You're right."

Tom Blake [h]: I was probably out there five or six times talking to him and see if he would come across but he told me, Hey, he'll die in jail, but he's not going to testify against Nash and his group.

John Holmes [f]: Newspapers and magazines rolled up tightly make a weapon like a wooden club and several times I was swung at, but I was lucky enough to stay out of range. Once, I had my arm wrapped around a cell bar and somebody tried to take my eye out with a pencil.

Dr. Vonda Pelto [h]: There were many threats on his life. On one incident, another inmate tried to poke his eye out with a pencil and on several occasions, they tried to shank him with a homemade tool that the inmates made. If you kill a celebrity, that kind of makes you a celebrity also; that's what [John] felt. [Prison officials] moved him after [inmates] tried to kill him, I think the last attempt, they put him in a solitary cell in 6000 and then he was really restless there. He had a very difficult time being there.

John Holmes [f]: I was in what was called the high-power section, where they stick newsworthy people who, if they are injured in jail could be an embarrassment to the county. Bad things happen to people in jail all the time. They're raped, killed, stabbed, and robbed — and you never hear about it. But if somebody is in the newspapers two or three times a week and he comes into court with his arm in a sling or his neck in a brace, there are going to be questions from the press, so people like that are put into a protective situation.

Most inmates are incarcerated in what is called the main line — six prisoners to a cell. Everyone in high power has his own cell so nothing can happen to him that might prove embarrassing. Just about everybody in high power was accused of mass murder. Everybody had been in and out of jail for years, except me. I was the one with a contract out on my life, so when we had to go to court, none of them would ride in the same van with me. In high power you go everywhere in handcuffs, accompanied by a deputy.

I never put a deputy in a position where he could get angry with me. I was always friendly, always had a kind word. In fact, most of the deputies brought in their porno video tapes, eight millimeter box collections or porno playing cards and I signed thousands of autographs for them.

Dr. Vonda Pelto [h]: John said that he really didn't like dating beautiful women because often times they had nothing between their ears and if you tried to have a conversation and say, "What do you think about Kipling?" they'd say, "Gee, what group does he play with?"

That was John's idea about women, but he told me that I was very attractive. — Very manipulative, very clever. He abided by all the rules in the jail and that was smart. He was a clever kind of man that way and he knew his best bet was to abide by the rules. He was very friendly with the deputies, and the deputies all liked John. I have his autograph.

Sharon Holmes [h]: We didn't really talk about the trial, the preparation for it, any of that. We talked about old times. He wanted to know what I was doing. One of our cats and two of our dogs were still alive. He begged me to send pictures of what had happened at the house and pictures of the dogs. He wanted to know what my family life was like, and of course [my] Grandma was living with me, full time, at that time.

He would occasionally try to impress me with the people in the cell block with him and, "Gee, the cops are really good to me. The sheriffs here are really nice."

John Holmes [f]: The Skid Row Slasher murdered 11 winos as they slept on downtown Los Angeles streets; Kenneth Bianchi, the Hillside Strangler, had murdered 11 women; and Angelo Buono, his cousin [were all held in high power]. There was one guy who had sexually molested his own two little boys, killed them and then burned his house down. The head of the Black Mafia in Los Angeles was there. So was the guy from the Israeli Mafia who was convicted of dismembering two people at the Bonaventure Hotel. He was as nice a guy as you'd want to meet. I also played gin rummy through the bars of my cell with a kid awaiting trial after turning evidence against the Freeway Killer, Kenneth Bonin, who had tortured and murdered 21 boys in Orange County and Los Angeles.

Sharon Holmes[h]: His attorneys never contacted me. The public defender was the only one I got a subpoena from and thank God he was replaced! Before the private attorneys, when he still had a public defender, I got a subpoena that I was going to have to appear for the public defender because they needed character references. I looked at that and I thought, "Oh, my God." Then I'm thinking, "Nothing to worry about." Everything I knew was hearsay. Nothing was going to do anything. I think if it had ever come down to it for a character reference, if they needed that sort of thing, I couldn't have done it and I wouldn't have hidden behind "a spouse can't testify." I just couldn't have done it. I was through with lies, so it's probably just as well that he got private attorneys.

He got his attorneys the next time I visited him, so I told him that I had gotten one and he said, "You don't have to worry about that. They've assigned me private attorneys. You won't have to be worried about being involved in any way." Of course, I didn't say I wouldn't be involved in any way; I just left it at that.

Mitchell Egers[h]: Originally there was a private attorney. I don't recall for what reason he couldn't proceed on the case, but the judge asked my partner, Earl Hanson, to represent John Holmes because it was obviously a case that required two attorneys. He asked me to be co-counsel with him, and both Earl Hansen and I were the attorneys for Holmes because of the judge asking my partner.

I can't recall how much of the time he was in his own cell and how much he was with the others. He was with other prisoners; he told us about them. As a matter of fact, he was quite popular in jail, I think, with the guards and with the inmates. At that time, everybody knew who John Holmes was. He was famous. Many people had seen his movies, probably many more than admitted seeing his movies, but he was undoubtedly The King of all the actors in the porno movies. I don't think anybody to this date has equaled his stature in the movies.

Either my partner or I saw John in jail almost every night. Of course, every night in jail, we couldn't talk about the case, so we talked about the case as much as necessary and we talked about other matters.

He became fully absorbed in whatever it was we were talking about. That, I think, is part of John's charm. He could talk about cooking, he could talk about the women he took out, about the movies that he was in, the places he had visited, the countries that the films were made in — I think at all times he could focus on what was under discussion. I found him to be a charming man, an interesting man. He had knowledge about a variety of subjects that surprised me. For instance, who would think that he would know a lot about cooking? He certainly made me believe that he was knowledgeable about it — about his plans for writing a cookbook. It was going to be a book combining sex and cooking. He expected it to be a bestseller when –. Maybe it would have been.

Dr. Vonda Pelto [h]: He talked easily to me. He was very verbal. I wouldn't say he was very bright, but he was very street smart. He knew about people and how to handle people. Very manipulative and very charming — that was John.

I thought, my God, had I met this guy in a bar — I was single at the time — and he said, "Hey Vonda, want to dance?" I would have said, "Sure."

Mitchell Egers [h]: As far as his demeanor was concerned, he was always worried and concerned, of course, but there were times when we just enjoyed talking to each other. That was the observation of my partner as well.

Al Goldstein also met with John several times during his jail term and trial. Goldstein decided to follow John's trial and write a story about Holmes that would debunk many of John's embellishments and fables. "The Harder They Fall," was published in the April 1983 issue of *Playboy* magazine.

Stunned by the appearance of John's eyes that bulged with fright on the other side of the Prison Plexiglas, John complained to Goldstein about the lousy prison food and having no bail money. "I resisted the impulse to ask him whether or not the famous Holmes' cock was being used in jail," Goldstein said in the *Playboy* article.

John Holmes [f]: In high power, there was no sex since everybody had an individual cell and it was one man out at a time. If you got close enough to one of these prisoner's bars, they'd kill you — they wouldn't try to kiss you. But on the main line, where they had six men in a cell, there was quite a lot of forced sexuality. Sexual molestations and stabbings increased when the air conditioning went out for nine days while I was there. In jail, they find that the higher degree of temperature, the higher degree of violence, so they keep you very cold in a constant, controlled environment. Male prostitutes were also available in the main line. Put somebody who is bisexual in prison and if he wants a cigarette bad enough, he'll become sexually involved with someone.

Despite John's incarceration, Goldstein discovered that he and Holmes were comfortable together during the first meeting. John inquired about Goldstein's son, by his name. The moment was touching and made more so because it had been seven years since Goldstein and Holmes had last talked. "I could not possibly imagine committing murder: a man who remembered the name of my child, casually mentioned years earlier. It put our meeting on a basis of friendship."

John told him, "I grew a big, ugly beard and hung out," about the months spent on the lam. For the first time in nearly 20 years, John had some privacy and anonymity as they ran from the police.

Dr. Vonda Pelto [h]: He talked some about his career. He told me that he was no longer actually acting in the porn flicks, but now was writing and directing and told me of the movie *Exhausted*, which was coming out just about the time I was seeing him. He explained that even though the movie purported he had sex with 14,000 women, in reality, it was only 13,870.

I tried to figure out how on Earth he could do that. The thing he told me, in reality he'd only made love with five women, but he didn't name them.

Often after a shoot, he would take one of the women and they would go in the shower and actually have sex; the other was just for the camera. I asked him how it was to have sex with a woman and keep an erection with all these women for such an extended period of time and he said what he would do with the women was to focus on one part of the body because oftentimes they were not terribly attractive to him, but he could focus on the eyes, or the hair, or the hands, or the breasts, or some other part and that would keep him erect to do the films. Overall, he enjoyed the profession — it was something he did well and was very successful at.

John Holmes [f]: I'm satisfied with my role in adult films. I was doing a lot of cocaine. Under cocaine, you become mentally bored with whatever you're doing. A lot of the ups and downs I was going through were narcotic ups and downs. It was a side-effect of the drug.

[In prison,] you can get just about anything you want; it's just tough to do it. Many people hide hypodermic needle kits in their cells. There's cocaine, heroin, acid, Quaaludes, speed. I so resent the inactivity in jail that I wouldn't do anything to harm the recreational drug trade that goes on there. There's plenty of grass. What you do is smoke it at night, so the deputies won't smell it. The lights go out at ten. They do a 10:30 bed check, and they don't come back again until two o'clock in the morning. When you smoke it, it disperses into the air conditioning filter. People start to scream at night, too. It turns into a jungle, an after-hours zoo.

Breakfast was at 5:30. It was either pancakes with no syrup, French toast with no syrup, five different kinds of prepared eggs, or "shit on a shingle" — chipped beef and gravy on toast. I hated prison food so much that I cut pictures of casseroles from the food sections of magazines.

I had a pet cockroach that I used as a food taster. When he wouldn't eat, I wouldn't eat. He wouldn't touch about half the food in there.

Dr. Vonda Pelto [h]: I don't know if he gave me the name of the cockroach, but he had a pet cockroach. He fed it, took good care of it and kept it in one of those little, cardboard matchboxes.

John Holmes [f]: The three things I missed most in jail were food, freedom and sex. I hadn't had a wet dream since I was 16, but I returned to them in prison. You build up so much sexual pressure and tension that your subconscious releases it in your sleep, all over your jumpsuit. You don't have wet dreams thinking about Chevrolets.

[My cell] was nine feet by 12 feet long. In that space, there was a bunk, a small desk with a stool and a toilet. All I could do was pace around four feet and then turn around and pace four feet back. There was no television, no newspapers, no magazines. I wrote quite a bit — poetry and short stories. I also did yoga and calisthenics. And once a day for 45 minutes, I did transcendental meditation.

There was a one-way mirror that runs the entire length of the tier. You could look through the mirror and catch the reflection of the guy next to you. The mirror was about ten feet away, so it's always like you're talking to someone ten feet away. When I first got out of jail, it was difficult talking to someone up close.

Other than the times I met with one visitor a day they allow or with my attorneys, I worked as a trustee for three hours a day, pouring coffee for the other inmates or sweeping down the tier. They called me The Porno Janitor.

Dr. Vonda Pelto [h]: John was very hyper and his cell was located parallel to about eight other cells. On the opposite side of the cell was a long runway. On the other side of this cement runway was a long hallway, which paralleled the runway and it was all one-way mirrored. The deputies could go back in this hallway and see all the inmates along this cell row, without them seeing the deputies. I went back one day, actually, to see a different inmate, Arthur Jackson, who was right beside John and John was madly pushing a push broom up and down the runway. I said, "What's going on here with John?"

He was moving very fast up and down, up and down, up and down. Obviously it was clean. They said that John was so hyper that they gave him this trustee position and gave him this push broom because he was too hyper to stay in the cell. When he was a kid, he was probably A.D.D., attention deficit disorder, because he was extremely hyper.

He was a voracious reader. He could read almost a book a day. He did a lot of reading. He swept the thing out in front, he played with his pet cockroach, he chatted with the deputies, he made friends with the inmates in his row. When he saw me, he talked about jewelry making, which he said he did. A bit about films; light conversation.

He was kind of mischievous, I think. One of the freeway killers was also in the block, and he told the freeway killer that he had a crush on me. The freeway killer said he did, too. It was one of the young boys, not one of the principals. John said, "If you really want Dr. Pelto, you can have her."

The young boy said, "No, you can have her." The young boy wrote me a poem and I saw John. Immediately after seeing John, I saw this young boy. John walked by as the young boy and I were about to go into the interview room. John looked at me, smiled and winked.

Mitchell Egers [h]: I feel that he had a charisma about him that was so noticeable. The charisma was such that I could see other attorneys in the attorney room at night when my partner and I would go there, come over just to be introduced, perhaps, but after they were introduced, they couldn't stop talking to him. He showed everybody a real interest in them, and I guess that's the secret to being a very dynamic and successful person, regardless of what field you're in.

Dr. Vonda Pelto [h]: He was an interesting man. Very sociopathic — this simply means that he could use anybody in any way to his advantage, without feeling any guilt. I was never privy to any of the information about the Laurel Canyon murders, except what I read in the paper. I was very careful about never asking that type of question. I didn't want to be subpoenaed by the attorneys, which would have put Mental Health and the sheriff's department in an awkward position, as well as me. I didn't think he probably bludgeoned them, but I would not have been surprised had he been there. But he didn't tell me that. That was just a guess.

Preliminary Hearing

John Holmes' preliminary hearing was held in the municipal court on Tuesday, February 2, 1982. Mysteriously, the transcripts from John's actual trial have come up missing from the county clerk's office in recent years, but the transcript from the preliminary hearing is still available.

During the preliminary hearings, John remained silent and uncomfortable in the tan Sears-Roebuck suit that Julia had bought for him. Goldstein had his mind on John's penis: "While the reporters from the *Los Angeles Times*, the *Herald Examiner* and the *Daily News* attentively took notes, I felt curiously dazed by the proceedings, as if the courtroom atmosphere had lobotomized me. All I could think about was cocks."

John's capable attorneys were former L.A. prosecutors and both were U.S.C. Law Graduates. According to Goldstein, Hanson was "the articulate, dapper, gray-haired senior partner, the eloquent debater and consummate strategist," and Egers, "the Jewish intellectual in glasses, the law mechanic."

Of Prosecutor Coen, Goldstein said, "a stocky, square-shouldered man who wore the sleeves of his shirts too long, reminded me of a white James Brown. His strategy was straightforward enough: scare the fuck out of Holmes and force him to finger the real killers. Until he does, keep the pressure up to the point of trying to prove that Holmes actually killed someone that morning at Wonderland."

Twenty-five-year-old Susan Launius, the only survivor of the murders at the Wonderland house, took the stand during the preliminary hearing. After undergoing a double radical mastectomy, she had not been living with Ron when the robbery at Nash's occurred, but unfortunately, she had spent the night after arriving around seven or eight o'clock in the morning on June 30th, 1981. Her estranged husband had driven her to the house, where she stayed through the day and met Joy Miller and the other frequent visitors to the Wonderland house. That evening, they lay in bed and watched TV for the last time together.

> *Susan Launius*[d]: Ron was with me. I was lying down on the bed and I believe I was watching T.V. It seemed like there was a bunch of people coming in and out. Then at one point, it seemed like some people were moving faster. I'm not sure if there were three or more [people] or —
>
> I recall making a statement that I'd seen shadows, but — they seemed like they were brown, dark eyes, kind of looked right through me. I was in the living room. I remember that. I was standing there and that person came up to me and just kind of looked straight at me. He looked to me like he was colored. He seemed around 30. He was kind of young looking and very well dressed. He was slender, but that is all I can remember. He seemed to me like he was not — he was light-complected, sort of like high-yellow.

Coen pointed to John, who was sitting at the end of a table, and asked "Do you know that man?"

Susan Launius replied, "No, I don't."

Mitchell and Egers asked John to stand so that Launius could get a better look at him and note the color of his eyes and hair. She confirmed that she had never seen John Holmes before in her life. Due to her brain injuries, the only survivor of the attacks remembered nothing more about the assailants.

> *Susan Launius*[d]: [I had] massive head injuries and my left leg partly paralyzed because of my head injuries. And [I lost] a finger. They operated on my head [and removed a portion of skull].

> *Mitchell Egers*[h]: It was a very difficult time in the trial. If she would have stood up and pointed to John Holmes, the case might have turned out differently, but she said, I can only recall the figure that I saw. There was sort of a shadowy figure and I couldn't tell anything about him and I cannot identify that man there at the counsel table. There was no identification and the case could then be tried on circumstantial evidence and lack of intent.

Of course, one key (albeit circumstantial) piece of evidence against John was the print of his left palm on the bedrail above Ron Launius' pulverized head. The palm print was found 23 inches to the right of the left corner of the headboard.

> *Frank Tomlinson*: Those types of things helped Coen believe that he really did the murders himself, but once you saw him physically, you realized this guy couldn't kill four people. I mean, he's not that strong. He just doesn't have that kind of power.

> *Ron Coen*[h]: It was just a palm print. It was on a bed frame. The indications were [that] Holmes was holding the bed frame with the victim on the bed and he was beating the victim with his right hand.

Robert Sexton was a Fingerprint Specialist with the Los Angeles Police Department during the murder investigation. During his testimony, he reported that his findings showed fingerprints belonging to several people and identified four different areas of the Wonderland house in which Holmes' prints had been found. Sexton, however, could not help the prosecution's case any more than that; he could only identify that John's palm print was found, in addition to other incidental prints (on a cassette tape case in the kitchen, the underside of the glass table in the nook, and on the back of the chair in the dining room that was closest to the front door). Asked if he could speculate about how the prints were made during the cross-examination, he simply replied, "I cannot date fingerprints, sir."

Despite the lack of any concrete evidence to support the prosecution's view that John swung a pipe, they remained determined that they could prove this suspicion to the jury.

Ron Coen[h]: He let the killers in with the intent that everybody would die. The view of the Los Angeles Police Department and myself at that time, and still today, is that the actual killers would not have let Holmes live unless he participated, himself, in the murders. So I have absolutely no doubt.

Tom Lange: John Holmes was not allowed into Ron Launius' bedroom. John Holmes was terrified of Ron Launius. [Ron] considered himself to be a killer; he was a killer for hire. Ron Launius hated Holmes. He constantly intimidated him, possibly threatened him. It wasn't a matter of Ron Launius walking up to him and saying, "I forbid you to walk into my bedroom," [but] he didn't want anything to do with him.

[John] would never go into his bedroom. We heard that from associates of Launius, we heard that from associates of Billy Deverell, who was also killed. We heard that from Holmes himself. He said he was terrified of Launius. We heard that from Tracy McCourt. We heard that from David Lind.

Launius was a bad-ass and he would intimidate and threaten Holmes, he'd make fun of him. Holmes was visibly upset when he was around Launius. He wouldn't want anything to do with him, so what the hell was his palm print doing over his body? That's the real significance. What the positioning of that palm print tells me is that he was forced to take a couple of whacks, "and if you don't, John, you're going to be victim number six."

Tracy McCourt[d]: We were all like brothers. We all went to one room to the next room. It was no big thing.

Unlike what Lange had suggested about the level of hatred between John and Launius, John's attorney, Earl Hanson, confirmed with Lind during the preliminary hearing that John was "free to roam the house if he so desired." Lind also said that he had observed that Holmes and Launius were friends, although Launius had a volatile personality. Holmes was friendly with everyone at the house with only one exception, according to Lind.

David Lind[d]: To a certain extent, Mr. Deverell really didn't care for Mr. Holmes that much — didn't trust Mr. Holmes.

[Launius] made mention of the fact that Mr. Holmes owed he and Mr. Deverell a considerable sum of money and that he better do something about it. As a matter of fact, [Ron Launius] threatened John Holmes on more than one occasion. Ronnie was had a Jekyll-Hyde personality. He was on-again, off-again.

Lind and McCourt

David Lind[d]: [I first went to 8763 Wonderland] the first week of June, 1981. I was in residence there continuously throughout the incidents. Joy Miller, William Deverell, Ronald Launius, Barbara Richardson, and I [slept there]. Quite a number of people [spent the night during that period of time]. We were engaged in drug trafficking and [the number of visitors] varied. John was welcome at that house, any time.

John Holmes[q]: There are three or four guys in jail who want to kill David Lind. Every time the police arrest him, he has to go in protective custody because David Lind rats them out. He doesn't go to jail; he rats people off. He is supposed to be serving time for an armed robbery that he committed, during this whole time I was involved with him, but he didn't serve any time or parole. They held him in protective custody at an L.A. county jail and he served some time on another case in Sacramento for an armed robbery or a burglary and drug sales he was involved in.

Tom Lange: Lind would consider being an informant if it suited his position, not unlike most persons of his ilk, but not in the true sense. Lind was a Sacto-area biker — a rough character — record of dope, some weapons violations, if I recall, some theft. Did hard time and knew the system and how to work it. I don't know about a protection program per se, but again, he knew how to work the system and when and how to inform.

David Lind[d]: I'm serving a seven-month sentence in Sacramento. [My prior felony convictions were for] receiving stolen property, forgery and assault with intent to commit rape. That was in 1970. I was sentenced for possession of a controlled substance.

John Holmes[q]: The police kind of turn their backs and look the other way because he's the grade-A police informant. He is associated with all the scum I would associate with. Everybody hates his guts; everybody wants him dead.

Tom Lange: Lind was an excellent witness and he testified throughout. He's a bad ass, but he was very credible — very bright guy. Bob Souza, my partner, was a biker-type around the same time that Lind was and they both grew up in the Sacramento area. They struck a chord. He got along with Lind because he treated him as an equal. Although it wasn't the way things should normally be done, many of the people we interviewed were under the influence and taking drugs during the interview. We would sometimes take a six-pack of beer and sip on a beer, they'd be doing drugs, and we'd just get a little more down to their level.

David Lind[d]: Approximately one week prior to the incidents, Mr. Holmes [initiated the conversation about the robbery]. Mr. Holmes was acquainted with a gentleman by the name of Edward Nash. At that time, I didn't know what is who it was and he suggested that Mr. Launius, Mr. Deverell and myself should rob Mr. Nash, as Mr. Nash was in possession of a considerable amount of narcotics, cash and jewelry. The defendant was a frequent visitor of Mr. Nash's house.

Tracy McCourt[d]: [The regulars at the Wonderland house included] John, me, Ronnie, Billy, and Joy and the girls, but they didn't get involved really. They were just there. It was just us fellows, but then, all of a sudden, David Lind pops up from nowhere. I don't know where he came from — most of the time, he was not present.

When I walked in the house after I had been there a little while, John was rattling off about long time money and lots of cocaine. He was talking about it, but lots of people talk that way — say there is a lot of money when there isn't that much money. I just thought it was one of those conversations. I don't think I remember him saying the word *Nash*.

On two occasions, we went over there and traded a gun and some gold and stuff, so someone could get in the house and leave the back door open. We traded for China White, so I believe all of us did some of it at one point or another. I don't think John did, because John didn't do China White. It is actually [fentanyl], but yes, it is supposed to be heroin.

David Lind[d]: In our association that was drug related, John used to purchase heroin from Mr. Nash for Mr. Launius and Mr. Deverell, and there were times when there wasn't any cash exchanged. There were articles such as weapons and jewelry for collateral. John would take them from the house at Wonderland Avenue and proceeded to take it to Mr. Nash and then come back with the drugs.

The plan was that John was to go in the house and leave an exit or entrance open for us to enter and commit the robbery. Mr. Holmes drew an entire diagram on a piece of paper, about 24 inches square, as to how the inside layout of the house was.

Tracy McCourt[d]: There were some plans drawn [of Nash's house at 3315 Dona Lola Place]. They were made out by John and Ronnie was drawing on them to find out where the bodyguard slept, where the guns were, how many windows were in the back of the house, and you know, the whole thing.

Ronnie was always taking over everything, so I guess he probably was [in charge], but we all pretty much had our say in the thing. At one point, Billy and I were going to do it ourselves because everybody didn't want to do it.

We planned it. We made a couple of dry runs. We had to call it off a couple of times. One time, everybody was going to forget it and me and Billy were going to do it and John kept going in [Nash's] house and doing so much cocaine that he wouldn't come out for 45 minutes — three or four hours later, sometimes.

David Lind[d]: Approximately one week prior to the robbery, Mr. Launius, Mr. Deverell and I took a look at it. I didn't like it and they deferred to my opinion. Then we went back to the house. It was a couple of days after that, that Barbara Richardson and I left for a few days and we arrived back at the house on Wonderland Avenue — Sunday the 28th, I believe, and that is the date preceding the robbery. In the afternoon, late, around noon.

Joy Miller was there at that time. Joy Miller indicated to Barbara Richardson and I that Mr. Deverell, Mr. Launius and Tracy McCourt were at that time, somewhere near Mr. Nash's house — what is it they say in the business? — casing the house for the robbery. I was in the residence, at the house. I was living there and about that time, Ronnie called and asked me to stay there, that he was coming back.

Tracy McCourt[d]: All of a sudden, the gun I had lent to me was taken back. It was a bunch of things going on. All of a sudden, David was going in the house with a gun. I was originally supposed to — before this other party took his gun back — I was supposed to go in there with a gun. Somebody came and picked it up while I was — I fell asleep on the front couch.

David Lind[d]: Mr. Holmes arrived there sometime about mid-afternoon. Mr. Launius provided Mr. Holmes with some money in order to purchase some narcotics from Mr. Nash, to enter the house and leave a door open for us to enter. Mr. Launius, Mr. Deverell, Mr. McCourt, and I were to then proceed to Mr. Nash's house and enter through the entrance that was left open and proceed to rob Mr. Nash.

Between approximately three o'clock Sunday afternoon and about three or four a.m. the next morning, Mr. Holmes had made two or three trips to Mr. Nash's house in order to make sure that it was a sliding-glass door. A rear guest bedroom was left open as an entrance-way to the house, that would be to the right of the house and the bedroom was located in the front, but as from inside the house, it would be a rear bedroom.

Mr. Holmes returned to the residence on Wonderland Avenue approximately three to four a.m., as I stated before, and informed Mr. Deverell and Mr. Launius and myself that everything was fine and Mr. Nash was in bed, Mr. Diles was going to bed; that they were all there and he proceeded to tell us that we should do it as quick as possible, as something might change in the interim.

Mr. Launius and Mr. Deverell had a drug habit. We had a hard time getting together. I didn't [use heroin] at that time, no; [I used] cocaine. We did not get out of the house until eight o'clock in the morning. We proceeded to Mr. Nash's residence — I am referring to Mr. Tracy McCourt, Mr. Billy Deverell, Mr. Ronald Launius, and myself. [The robbery took place] on a Monday morning, at nine o'clock.

We were all armed. [I was carrying] a Smith and Wesson .357 Magnum Model 94 stainless steel revolver. I was carrying a knife. It was a rigid model knife, a razor back. It was a hunting knife. Approximately, the blade was at least eight inches long, total length approximately 12 inches; about half the size of a bayonet. Mr. Deverell had a Model 59 Smith and Wesson, 14-shot, nine-millimeter pistol. Mr. Launius had a 7.5 millimeter Beretta automatic pistol and Mr. McCourt had a Colt, National Match Gold Cup 45 automatic pistol.

The only conversation that was pertaining to the people in the house was that Mr. Diles would be the one that we would be most seriously concerned with. There was no reason [to discuss the fact that no one was to be hurt]; the way it was laid out, we were just going to go in and out. Nobody had, at the Nash residence, any familiarity whatsoever with Mr. Launius or Mr. Deverell or myself to my knowledge, at that time, other than John Holmes. There was no need for [wearing masks]. There was a product on the market called Liquid Band-Aid. We put that on our fingertips, all of us, [at] the Wonderland residence [to conceal fingerprints].

Tracy McCourt[d]: We received a call from John and he said it was cool, so we left the house and on the way, we saw John. We stopped and he told us to, "Get him." He went like this, "Get him!" So, we went to the house.

Coen asked McCourt if it was a pre-arranged signal for John to call and say it was cool, meaning to go ahead with their planned robbery of Nash's ranch.

Tracy McCourt[d]: I don't know. I don't think he was supposed to call. I think he was supposed to come back to the house. There were so many of us involved in the planning of the thing, I don't know who actually took the call, even. Some of us were asleep.

David Lind[d]: Mr. Holmes stayed at the residence on Wonderland Avenue along with Joy Miller and Barbara Richardson. We instructed Mr. McCourt to park the vehicle in such a way as he could observe the street in front of Mr. Nash's house. Dona Lola ended in a cul-de-sac and he backed in such a way and parked on the right-hand side, facing out, where he could see traffic coming in and where he could also have a good view of the house.

Then, Mr. Deverell, Mr. Launius and myself proceeded to the right front area of Mr. Nash's residence. There was a chain-link fence there and as it was not connected to the side of the house, we just pushed it forward and it gave us access to the sliding-glass doors, which were left open by Mr. Holmes and entered the guest bedroom.

There was a doorway leading into the hallway there, which leads into the middle of the house. I really can't describe it, other than the fact that it has a recreation room leading off it, the kitchen—everything goes off that area of the house. Mr. Launius opened the door and was listening there for about a minute or so, and then the three of us proceeded down the hallway to that area.

I was the first one in that area. I observed Mr. Diles coming out of the kitchen with a serving tray in his hands. I had in my possession, at the time, a leather case containing a San Francisco police officer badge — number 1820 — along with false identification, identifying me as a police officer. I shouted the words, "Freeze! Freeze! Police! You are under arrest!"

At that time, Mr. Launius and Mr. Deverell also threw down on Mr. Nash. All three of us were armed. We had weapons and we displayed weapons.

Mr. Diles was directly in front of me and Mr. Nash was to our right. We identified ourselves as police officers, we — all of us — had handcuffs, and we proceeded to handcuff Mr. Diles and to lay him on his stomach next to a wall — between the pool table and a wall, which is just in front of the kitchen. Mr. Launius and Mr. Deverell had Mr. Nash on his knees.

While he waited inside the car reading the newspaper, the crack of gunfire disrupted McCourt. During the cross examination, he said that after the robbers hopped into the getaway car, Launius admonished Lind for firing the gun.

Tracy McCourt[d]: [Lind] accidentally fired some shot and he just missed the bodyguard's leg or something like that. I know, in the house, anything could have happened. He could have shot him in the head, for all I know.

David Lind[d]: There was an accidental gunshot discharge while I was handcuffing Mr. Diles. Ron Launius bumped my arm and the weapon went off. Mr. Nash immediately fell to his knees and asked Mr. Launius to say a prayer. Mr. Diles was the person that I was handcuffing and the weapon was in back of him, and subsequently when the shot went off, he suffered from powder burns which caused him to bleed very minutely over an area approximately six to eight inches in diameter from the muzzle flash of the weapon.

I proceeded to finish handcuffing Mr. Diles and laid him on the floor and put a throw rug over his head so he couldn't observe what we were doing.

Mr. Nash was on his knees with his hands behind his head and Mr. Launius and Mr. Deverell proceeded to take Mr. Nash into his bedroom and I followed shortly thereafter. He was not struck physically. I recall Mr. Nash on his knees, asking if he could say a prayer.

Mr. Nash was asked to lay face down on the carpet of his bedroom and Mr. Launius proceeded to a wardrobe closet where there was a floor safe, as we had been informed by Mr. Holmes. We asked Mr. Nash for the key and/or combination. Mr. Nash told Mr. Launius that. He gave him the correct answer, I guess you would say, and Mr. Launius proceeded to open the safe and withdraw what would be a half-pound storage Ziploc bag, polyethylene, which was approximately three-quarters full of what looked to me at that time to be cocaine.

Mr. Holmes had informed us earlier at the residence that there was also a laboratory vial — approximately eight to ten inches in length, half-an-inch in diameter — full of heroin, which he called China White, in the area of Mr. Nash's dresser. We proceeded to pick that up. Also, there was an attaché case full of money and jewelry. We found everything. Inside the attaché case was a considerable sum of money in twenties, fifties and hundred dollar bills and considerable amount of jewelry — gold jewelry, diamonds. I know it was found in Mr. Nash's bedroom because I made several trips in and out of the bedroom as Mr. Launius and Mr. Deverell had control of the situation in there. I was going back and forth from the living room to the bedroom and looking out the front door to make sure that we weren't disturbed because of the gunshot earlier.

At that time, we couldn't really ascertain how much was there, but it was not as much as Mr. Holmes indicated should have been there. Mr. Launius continued to question Mr. Nash as to where the rest was. In regards to the drugs, Mr. Nash told him that they were at the Starwood, but there was also a sum of money in an attic off a hallway, right outside his bedroom where there was a wooden ladder. At that point, Mr. Deverell proceeded to climb up the ladder and entered the attic, and the money was in a brown paper bag. Exactly $10,000.

While Mr. Deverell and Mr. Launius were dealing with Mr. Nash, I was in the process of going through the house for weapons and in Mr. Diles' bedroom, I found a sawed-off 12-gauge shotgun in his bedroom closet, which I proceeded to unload and set on the pool table, and in Mr. Diles' closets, there were two antique long guns. One was a flint-lock rifle and the other was a Colt revolving shotgun. On Mr. Diles' bedroom dresser, there were two cap and ball percussion, black powder pistols. One was a model 1856 Colt revolver with an engraved cylinder. This was the smaller of the two. Another one was approximately the same type. They were both antique guns. Of those four particular weapons, the only thing familiar about them to me was the fact that those weapons had been taken to Mr. Nash's home by Mr. Holmes prior to the incident to be held as collateral for the purchase of narcotics and that they had been obtained in a prior burglary, and were given to Mr. Holmes to take to Mr. Nash. I recognized them by description. Other than that, I had never seen them before.

I proceeded to look under Mr. Nash's bed, as Mr. Holmes said Mr. Nash kept quite a number of guns in his house and I didn't particularly care to get shot. I pulled out a Browning nine millimeter automatic pistol, which appeared to be a commemorative issue. It was nickel-plated with a gold trigger and a gold hammer, in a brown vinyl case. There was a grayish-green metal box, approximately ten inches long, four inches in height, which would describe the petty cash box. Inside that, there were Quaaludes and cocaine.

As we were getting ready to leave, Mr. Launius again started to question Mr. Diles about the whereabouts of the rest of it and he proceeded to pull out a knife and started to cut Mr. Diles. At that point, I interfered and I told him, "We have got everything we need here. Let's go."

After that, I opened the front door, signaled to Mr. McCourt. He started to back the vehicle up. Subsequently, I told him to stop and then Mr. Deverell, Mr. Launius and myself, in that order, proceeded out the front door. Mr. Launius was carrying the attaché case, which he had put the bag of cocaine in and the gray-green metal box and I think he had the heroin vial in his pocket. I came out last, carrying the two antique rifles, which were wrapped in a white plastic, like a shower curtain. They were concealed. Mr. Deverell got into the front passenger side. Mr. McCourt was driving the vehicle and Mr. Launius and I were in back. We drove to the Wonderland Avenue address.

Mr. Holmes was waiting inside the door when we arrived. On the living room side of that area, which is a small foyer there, the right hand side leads to the kitchenette and the rest is living room. It is on a split-level. The first thing that Mr. Holmes wanted to know was just exactly what happened. He seemed to be very excited about it. He was happy that we were able to accomplish what we set out to do. I instructed Mr. Launius not to tell him anything. Mr. Launius proceeded to talk to him.

Immediately upon entering the house, we went to the rear bedroom on the first level there, which was Mr. Launius' bedroom. We put everything on the bed and everybody was in the bedroom. There was quite a bit of excitement because of the situation and then I said, "Well, let's get this over with," and we proceeded to the nook area, a glass-top table. We had a scale in the residence. We proceeded to weigh out the drugs and to count the money at that time. [Holmes] was sitting in the chair [Lind indicates a chair to the left of the glass-top table, closest to the bathroom]. Mr. Launius was sitting here [the chair to the south of the table, closest to the kitchen]. Mr. McCourt was sitting here [the chair to the east of the table, closest to the stairs]. Mr. Holmes was alternating between these two chairs [the chair closest to the stairs and the chair that is closest to the kitchen].

There were five of us involved in the robbery: Mr. Launius, Mr. Deverell and myself were to receive 25 percent of what we took, and Mr. Holmes and Mr. McCourt were to split the remaining 25 percent, which is 12 and a half percent.

Immediately after everything was divided up, Mr. McCourt left the residence and Mr. Launius, Mr. Holmes and myself were seated in the living room. At that time, Mr. Holmes made a statement to the effect that it still wasn't enough money; he didn't have enough to pay his film editors and as there was still a considerable amount of jewelry to be peddled to a fence, that he was going to wait around for that money. Mr. Deverell took the jewelry to the fence and came back a few hours later with the money, which was early evening.

Tracy McCourt[d]: John and I got half of a split and everybody else got full splits. That is how it was divided. Plus, by way of a scale. I was around the table, Billy was around the table, Ron was around the table and John, I think. [John was sitting] to my right. As soon as the money was divided up, I left about five minutes later.

Tom Lange: The Wonderland bunch had no plans to go or do anything, other than to split up the booty and the dope and once again get blasted. They were all stoned when they were attacked at about 4:00 a.m. This group was blown out of their minds on dope most of the time and retaliation would be something that only a sober person would have considered.

Tracy McCourt[d]: Billy and Ronnie and I promised each other we were all going to move the next day and it didn't happen.

Most of the narcotics were done prior to that robbery. There wasn't that much sales going on there that I saw. We all did speed occasionally so, you know, we were up all night 'til daytime. Speed freaks coming here all the time. The people that did come and go were all of certain, shall we say, niche, you know? I mean, if you weren't in that little clique, you didn't just walk in that house or you were not even around none of those people. I can't believe that anybody could just walk in that house, especially after what just went on, especially with five or six guns in the house. Those dogs bark and that was one of the reasons they was there. It was a lock. Ron told me several times, "Man," he said, "You know, I bet nobody could get in the house without somebody hearing it."

David Lind[d]: Number one, there was an electric gate that could be only entered with a key or by pressing a buzzer inside the residence and then identify yourself to open the electric gate. Number two, after we exited the robbery, we had all agreed that nobody was to come into the house, at all *period*, even drug-related business. That was to be conducted away from the house, directed to the Laurel Canyon Country Store, which is on Laurel Canyon [Boulevard].

Jim Morrison of The Doors lived in the Laurel Canyon neighborhood during the late 1960s. In his song, "Love Street," he described the Laurel Canyon Country Store as, "the store where all the creatures meet." Although under new ownership, it is still open today and is covered in colorful murals. Inside, towering shelves crowd the narrow aisles and outside, Laurel Canyon Boulevard twists up the mountain toward Wonderland.

After the robbery, Launius used the phone at 8763 Wonderland to arrange for his customers to deal with him at the Laurel Canyon Country Store.

David Lind[d]: That was an everyday occurrence. The use of the telephone for that particular — that is what he did. He dealt in narcotics.

I was making preparations to leave. I was there until Tuesday morning, approximately nine or ten o'clock.

Tom Lange: Lind was scheduled to be back in L.A. right after his court appearance the following day. He felt Barbara would be safe there with his badass buddies. My recollection was that Lind was in Sacramento taking care of some traffic warrants at the time. Whatever it was, rest assured his alibi was checked and rechecked.

Actually, Lind had not gone back to Sacramento, according to statements that he made during the preliminary hearing. He said that he stayed at a Mr. James Fuller's house in Monrovia, which is about 30 miles east of Laurel Canyon. And in an earlier police statement, Lind explained his absence from the Wonderland house during the murders, allegedly by saying that he had been in the company of two women, named Terry and Cindy.

Laurie Holmes: David Lind's alibi for the murders was that he was in a motel room getting high with two females. David Lind was in on the robbery at Nash's — set up the whole scenario from the beginning, as a matter of fact. He knew Nash would retaliate.

Why would he leave someone he cared about there in the first place when he went off with two other females? Not to mention the fact that besides being a violent criminal who was known for having the reputation that he loved to kill and torture, he also did very little jail time throughout his criminal career. John often cautioned me about being followed and answering the door, even if it appeared to be a cop, as David Lind — John told me — had access to every kind of uniform there was.

David Lind[d]: I received a phone call from a Mr. Jimmy Arias [a.k.a. Jimmy Vegas]. He called me and told me that everybody on Wonderland Avenue, in the house, was dead. This was shortly before noon Wednesday.

We had stayed up all night. [Mr. Arias] had been in the residence at eight o'clock that morning, and [saw the bodies]. He told me he walked in. The doors were open. He was there with a fellow by the name of Paul [Kelly]. That is who drove him over. They were supposed to put Mr. Launius on a plane that morning to appear in a case in Sacramento.

Time of Reckoning

Frank Tomlinson was last to speak during the preliminary hearing. He took the stand to share what he could about John's confession, but was careful to uphold his promise to John since Nash had not been arrested for murder.

Frank Tomlinson: He stated that he had no choice in going there and that he had to set things up and let them in.

Ron Coen[h]: This is where the mind of a police officer and the mind of a lawyer or prosecuting attorney differ. I remember asking the lead investigator at the time, "When you talk to Holmes, I need to find out if he let the killers into the house with the intent that everyone should die. That's felony murder." I stressed to the investigator, "When you talk to Holmes, did he let the people in the house with the intent that the people should die?" Very simple.

He came back and said, "I've got your confession."

I said, "Really? That's great. What did he say?"

"He said he let everybody in the house."

I said, "What about with the intent that everybody should die?"

He said, "Well, that's what he meant."

I think I blew it right there. I just exploded.

Frank Tomlinson [d]: I told John that I had gotten a statement from Dawn Schiller regarding the fact that she claimed he had told her that "Nash's niggers" were the ones that made him go there and let them in. Those were her words. He stated that he could not be specific and give me a race.

I asked him, "If I arrested Nash and Diles for the murders, would I be making a mistake?"

And he stated, "No. Ed Nash is the most evil man I have ever met. He has people around him that would kill for him, even if he was dead," and that he knows this to be a fact and therefore, cannot tell me anything specific in regard to the murders or testify against Nash because he would be jeopardizing his own family. He said that he knew he would probably be killed in jail, but that so far, Nash had left his family alone and he could only assume that had occurred because he had not talked.

At the conclusion of the preliminary hearing, Judge Nancy Brown determined that there was sufficient evidence to proceed in Holmes' murder case with a trial by jury.

The Trial

Mitchell Egers [h]: He took an active role, but he made it quite clear to us that he wasn't going to take the stand. His active role continued right through the selection of the jury. Somehow, he had the ability to feel who was going to be a good juror and who was not. He disagreed with my partner and me on some of the potential jurors, but he had such strong feelings about it and I had learned to have confidence in his intuition. My partner and I listened to him on the picking of the jury to some extent, and he was right. He just knew people. He could focus on them and understand something about their personalities based on a short questioning of the jurors.

The district attorney left on two women, as I recall, that had seen his movies. I thought that he shouldn't have left them on. Certainly, they would have been good for us, after all, if they would admit publicly that they saw John Holmes movies they didn't feel there was anything to be embarrassed about. I think they related to John Holmes and to the movies and liked him. I felt much more comfortable after I knew they were going to be left on the jury.

[The prosecution] had hoped, I believe, to force an admission or confession from Holmes by charging him with the murders and they thought that after he was charged with the murders that he would tell everything he knows. They realized he was under duress. They introduced evidence that Holmes had been beaten up before the time of the murders. My conclusion was that they were charging him with murder, knowing there was duress and hoping that because he was charged with the murders he would be forthright with them and he felt, of course, because of the duress, that he could not be.

Ron Coen[h]: Duress — when a person is forced under threat of death to commit a crime — is a defense to most crimes. It is not a defense to capital murder. It was briefed on both sides and I prevailed. The judge ruled that the defense of duress does not apply in this case and cannot be used. Consequently, there would be no evidence put on from the defense that the defendant was acting under duress of bodily injury, or any other kind of duress.

Mitchell Egers[h]: We lost the issue of duress. We thought at that time we were on solid legal ground. We said that John Holmes did not commit murder, and if he was forced by duress to open a door or to show where the victims live, that defense of duress should be available to us. The judge ruled that out. Whether the duress was sufficient to excuse him from the murders is something else. Obviously, they thought it was not sufficient. They got the judge to accept the fact that duress in a murder case is not a good defense and they proceeded.

The official murder trial commenced at 8:30 a.m. on February 17, 1982. The same witnesses for the prosecution who were present at the preliminary hearing were called to testify. There were no witnesses on John's behalf.

Al Goldstein ("The Harder They Fall"): It was difficult to tell just who was on trial during the opening arguments. Egers said that "fingers of guilt" pointed to Nash; Hanson was quoted as saying that Nash was a "spectator" in the proceedings; even the prosecution claimed the murders were Nash's revenge. "It's not a question of 'Who done it?'" wailed Egers, "but of 'Why aren't the perpetrators here?'"

Tom Lange: Ed Nash sat in the back of the courtroom watching the proceedings. He sat there and stared at [John]. He had two of them — excellent defense attorneys, Mitchell Egers and Earl Hanson. Excellent prosecutors, very credible. That certainly helped his case, but they put him up as a victim and in many ways, he was a victim. He was on trial and maybe he shouldn't have been. Maybe he should have been a witness, but the only way we would have gotten him as a witness is if he would have been convicted of those murders.

Mitchell Egers[h]: We wanted to have him on the stand. In all of our tough cases, our murder cases, we prefer to put the client on the stand. Not every attorney shares that opinion as to how to proceed in a criminal trial, but that's the way we think. We wanted John on the stand. We knew that we were going to have to show something to get a not guilty verdict.

Ron Coen[h]: It's always nice, especially in a case like this that is circumstantial, to have the defendant take the stand. I would have loved to cross examine him — loved to! He was an actor. He would act by sitting in the chair, crying at the appropriate times — poor, poor pitiful me attitude. I wanted him on the stand so bad, I could taste it.

Mitchell Egers[h]: How are we going to show lack of intent if he couldn't take the stand? We had to show it through the police officers. One of the key pieces of evidence was the fact that there was a meeting at the Biltmore Hotel downtown, where the police surrounded the hotel, protecting the hotel, protecting the room, up on the roof, and there was even a helicopter flying around the hotel. Well, if the police would take such extraordinary measures to make sure that nobody was going to get to Holmes when he was going to talk about what had happened, surely the police were fearful something was going to happen to him. If all those police were necessary, Holmes had a right to be fearful and wonder about what was going to happen to him if he talked. That was how we showed a lack of intent.

There was a videotape that showed the interior of the house where the murders took place. I don't recall exactly what a voiceover said during the course of the videotape, but I have seen the videotape and heard the voices before the trial, of course, as had my partner. While it was possible to object to whatever may have been said as a conclusion by the police officer who was speaking, obviously, my partner and I didn't feel there was anything damaging about the voices and we didn't object.

I think that the jury certainly paid close attention to the videotape. I could see they were concentrating on it, but there was nothing in the videotape that connected John to the murders. It was a videotape showing the interior of the premises. It was interesting. It was certainly absorbing, but that didn't connect John to the murders. I didn't feel, nor did my partner, that this was going to further the prosecution's case, but I think that was probably the first instance of videotape being used in a major case in the United States.

Again, Tomlinson had difficulty in taking the witness stand during the trial because of his promise to John.

Frank Tomlinson: I got caught in between. I can still remember sitting there, looking at the jurors, thinking, these people are really confused by my testimony because I would not say anything that indicated that Holmes had confessed to me. I only told them that he was there and that he knew what happened. What I left out was I had been ordered not to follow through on my investigation. I was caught in the middle. I would never do that if I could go back and do it again.

We had a pretty strong military influence; in those years, L.A.P.D. was the best. Every guy that got on this job was screened to be the best at doing this. You really stuck to that chain of command and you didn't betray people. I didn't want to expose the inner workings, so I just left it hanging right there, but Coen kept pushing me to get more and I wouldn't say it.

I had known [John's] attorney from some other cases. Not well, but we had passed and so he could come up and trust me. Everybody knew they could trust us. If we said we were going to do something, good or bad, we did it. We never bluffed anyone. When it came time for cross-examination, his attorney didn't know what to ask me.

He came up and he said, "Man, what's going on between you and Holmes? I wanted to cross-examine you, but he said no. Holmes respects you so much that he wouldn't let me ask you any questions."

So I knew there was something really working inside of Holmes, that he had this sense of God — probably the same way I did — and he knew the life he had chosen was really dangerous, so I only saw him one time after that. The other guys, especially Coen, didn't understand that part of it and so they sort of made it afterwards, as if I'd taken Holmes' side for some reason. They made it look like Christianity — which I was just investigating, like all of my other investigations — was behind me not coming forward with the truth. It was actually just the opposite. I told them the truth and they didn't want to believe that.

Mitchell Egers[h]: I remember very clearly that the prosecutor (now Judge Ron Coen) stated in his closing argument that there was a bloody fingerprint on the headboard near one of the victims and that wasn't correct. It had to be corrected there, before the jury. There were fingerprints, there was blood and it was on the headboard near one of the victims, but there were no bloody fingerprints. I remember quite clearly. That was the impression that some had in the courtroom before it was clarified by the defense.

The judge limited the closing arguments to one day because Earl Hanson had made that request. It was a legal maneuver on his part. That day, Coen kept his closing argument short, but Earl Hanson delivered a compelling, half-day summation. Afterwards, there was little time for Coen's rebuttal.

Mitchell Egers[h]: And my partner, very cleverly and very ably, in closing argument, argued there was no intent to commit murder and he did not know the people were going to be murdered. Lack of intent of defense is always allowable in a murder case. So the judge's prohibition about duress and the defense of lack of intent was substituted for that.

Ron Coen[h]: It must have been amazing. I was always a TV-type lawyer. I was a fist-pounder; I was a finger-pointer. I would strut around. I would be dramatic. I know I did that in this case. Not well enough.

The Verdict

The jury deliberated for four days, giving the defense hope that a murder conviction was unlikely. Ballots were eight to four and then nine to three in favor of acquittal, but when a juror named Kathy Wood noticed and read aloud the instruction from Judge Sheldon, "No person may be convicted unless there is some proof of each element of the crime independent of any confession or admission made by him outside of his trial," the next vote was unanimous. John Holmes was acquitted of four charges of first degree murder on June 25, 1982.

Tom Lange: I had believed that he was going to be convicted. I think that there was enough of a case against him and the jury knew full well that the police and the prosecutor's motives was a conviction.

Ron Coen[h]: The case to me was strong. The whole theory was to get a guilty verdict with special circumstances to be found true and then to negotiate with the people that were more involved. I went up to my office, when I heard there was a verdict, I knew — I knew it was guilty. At least — in the very least — murder in the second degree. I walked into that courtroom very cocky. I said to all of my friends on the press, "Come on in, you're going to see something really good."

Coen was dumbfounded as he and Detective Tom Lange believed that the jurors had misunderstood the instructions and were misled about the weight of Holmes' confession to Frank Tomlinson.

Ron Coen[h]: I remember the feeling that I had as the clerk read the not-guilty verdicts. The feeling of heat that went through my body, the feeling of — I was hoping for a hole to open up in the floor so I could fall through. I remember having to go to the bathroom very badly. It was not a happy experience. I was totally shocked and humbled, very much so. Where I strutted into court, I slinked out.

Tom Lange: I think there was a great deal of sympathy. Certainly empathy, initially, but it all changed to sympathy. The two outstanding attorneys, they had mostly an all-woman jury. There were only two or three males. It was the sympathy factor and John Holmes was a victim. All that was true, even if he was a lot of other things, too. The irony of this all is, if he'd have been convicted and gone to prison, he probably wouldn't have died of AIDS and at least he'd be alive today.

Al Goldstein ("The Harder They Fall"): Had the jury been influenced by Holmes' work in porn? I found it odd that although none of the jurors had, in the selection process, evinced any prior knowledge of Holmes, *Johnny Wadd*, or any of the Holmes' personae, several had known my name — that according to a clerk who said the jury was impressed that I was in the courtroom.

Mitchell Egers[h]: I think that the jury, in the end, believed that John knew a lot more than was revealed in the course of the trial. After all, he didn't take the stand. I thought my partner made that final argument brilliantly and we showed lack of intent. The jury felt that they could not show that Holmes, who was involved in some way, was guilty of the murders; they felt he didn't intend to have anybody murdered.

Ron Coen[h]: They didn't, in my view, listen to the complete instructions. The corroborating only need be slight. We have a palm print, so much motive that it was blatant — the corroboration was there or the judge would have taken the case away from the jury after I rested, so there was sufficient corroboration.

Funny story, a juror called after and said, "I should have voted guilty."

I said, "You son of a bitch. Too late, thanks."

Mitchell Egers[h]: Well, the prosecution thought that the jury misunderstood the instruction. I felt that the jury did what was right and justice was done in the case. It wasn't a question of did Holmes know something about what happened; knowing something and being guilty are certainly not synonymous. The jury felt there was no proof that he was involved, that he had an intention to have them killed, and that's why he was found not guilty. I don't care if the prosecution thinks the jury misunderstood the instruction. I think that the jury knew very well what they were doing and they were looking for a reason to find him not guilty. They were not going to convict him.

Dr. Vonda Pelto[h]: I went down one day to see Arthur Jackson, the one that tried to kill Theresa Saldana. I came around the corner, and Angelo Buono and John had just come back from court. They were being strip-searched. When I rounded the corner, I thought, Vonda, a nice girl wouldn't go down there because they're both nude.

But I thought, what the hell? And so I went down. John was really funny. Angelo, right away put his jump suit back on. — Not John. John stood right there in the buff, hanging down to his knee, chatting with me. The deputies got very nervous about this. The deputies were kind of whirling around, finally they said, "John, you can put on your clothes now."

When we went into the little room and he was manacled down to the barber chair, he laughed about the deputies' reaction. He said, "Dr. Pelto, any time you want it, you can have it."

I said, "Thank you, John." He was cute.

This is [from journal:] 6/25/82 at 3:20 p.m. in his cell block. I said, "Just saw *all* of John Holmes. He had just returned from court and was being searched. He really is 13 inches long, even when he's hanging. He was delighted he was acquitted. He was leaving."

He said, "Now people are treating me like I'm human again. Some people wondered why I looked so relaxed. It was because I knew I was innocent and that everything would be okay."

Mitchell Egers [h]: He was thrilled, of course. I went to the jail when he got released that night. I took him out of the jail. My partner lent him a Volkswagen bus to go wherever he was going to go. He didn't have any cars at that time.

Sharon Holmes [h]: I had seen him the 23rd [of June] and was supposed to go in on the 25th, but of course, he was acquitted. My mother called me. She had heard it on the radio. Because I was working, [she called] to let me know that he had been acquitted. I was visibly shaken. I think I must have turned white. Nancy rushed me into Dr. Neticom's office, slammed the door, and I said, "I can't work. I can't stay here. I have to make a final decision in my life at this point, where my life is going to go, and I can't do it here." Doctor came in and I explained, and they sent me home.

He was released to his attorney. He went to their office and called me from there. He wanted to see me and I said, "No, I don't think that's safe, and I don't think I'm interested."

He said, "Well, let me call you. I need to go out to dinner."

I said, "Okay." He called me up, must have been close to 11:30 that night, and again asked me if he could come back or if I would go with him — that he would try to make another life somewhere else and get out of the business.

The first time in my life that I ever used the word *fuck* — I said, "Get the fuck out of my life," probably just that coldly because I couldn't handle any more. I still couldn't deal with the fact that he had been involved in this and that no matter what he was denying; he was involved in it. It didn't matter what the reason, he was still involved. That basically was the last time we ever spoke. I did not see him at all after that period of time. He specifically asked me not to.

Contempt

Mitchell Egers[h]: I think [John] took a little vacation and my partner and I went on a short vacation, only to find out he was back in jail when we came back with a contempt charge. I came back and he was still in jail for that contempt of court and failing to tell the court or answer questions the prosecutor wanted to know.

Although John was acquitted of all charges pertaining to the murders, he was subpoenaed to appear before the grand jury to answer questions regarding the identities of the killers. John believed that if he told the grand jury all that he knew, he would be putting his own life and those of his family and friends at risk, so he refused to talk. After the acquittal, which freed him from jail for 32 days, Holmes was put back into custody on July 27, 1982 for his refusal to cooperate.

Denise Amerson[h]: He was in jail from a long time. I knew what was happening, but I just didn't understand why he was in jail for a long time if he didn't do anything. In my family, I didn't really ask a lot of questions because I just wanted to go to school and be normal. I always knew that everything was going to be okay no matter what. I always felt safe and protected in that they could handle everything and for the most part, they did.

John Holmes[f]: If you're serving 90 days or five years, each day that goes by is one day closer to the time when you can walk away. With me, the judge said I held the key to my own freedom. He told me that I could walk out anytime I wanted. All I had to do was agree to participate in my own murder and the murders of my family, friends and business associates. That was like purgatory. That was punishment worse than a sentence.

I'd been pushed around for so long that I felt I had to do something. I regretted that the only bullet I had left in my arsenal was my health, but I had to show in some way that I resented having my Constitutional rights dismissed.

I was miserable. I didn't enjoy it at all. For the first few days, I thought of nothing but mounds and mounds of caviar. I dreamed about being chased by a strawberry cheesecake. All I could think about was how hungry I was and whether or not they would ever let me out.

Hundreds of signatures were collected in a petition that cited Holmes as a political prisoner, including those of some jurors who had acquitted him and Barbara Wilkins, who subsequently wrote a piece about John's case for *Hustler* magazine in 1983. Wilkins was among those who signed a poignant letter on John's behalf to Judge Julius Leetham of the Superior Court of Los Angeles:

> *Letter to Judge Leetham, September 24, 1982: John Holmes was offered immunity last year by the District Attorney of the city of Los Angeles if he would testify about what he knew about the Laurel Canyon murders.*
>
> *When he refused because to do so would put his own life and the lives of his family, friends and business associates in danger, he was accused of the crimes himself. He risked life imprisonment rather than compromise his principles.*
>
> *Last June, he was acquitted of all charges.*
>
> *In America, if a person is accused of a crime, tried and acquitted, he is freed.*
>
> *But not John Holmes.*
>
> *On July 27, 1982, John Holmes was subpoenaed before the Grand Jury of the County of Los Angeles to answer the same questions he had just faced life imprisonment rather than answer. He had two choices:*
>
> *He could answer the questions put to him, and commit suicide.*
>
> *He could refuse to answer, and be held in contempt of court.*
>
> *He refused to answer.*
>
> *Theoretically, a person who won't answer questions put to him by the Grand Jury can be held in contempt of court, and therefore, in jail, indefinitely. In actuality, a person held in contempt of court has always been released when coercion, which is permissible under the law, becomes punishment, which is not permissible.*
>
> *Bill Farr, the reporter who wouldn't surrender his notebooks in the Manson Murders, was held in contempt of court for 42 days. At that point, the longest anybody had every been held in contempt of court in California history, the court decided the attempt to coerce had crossed the line to punishment. Bill Farr was freed.*
>
> *But not John Holmes.*
>
> *In Russia, a person is routinely held in custody, accused of no crime, never brought to trial, given no chance to post bail, and released when the state decides to release him, if ever.*
>
> *That's Russia.*
>
> *John Holmes has now been in contempt of court for 60 days. He is accused of no crime; he has been offered no bail. He is serving no sentence. He is just there, in jail. Forever.*
>
> *That's America.*
>
> *John Holmes makes pornographic movies. He has admitted that he used cocaine. But, while that may offend the public morality, to make por-*

nographic movies is a First Amendment right, and no charges have been brought against him because he used cocaine.

John Holmes has been on a hunger strike in the infirmary at the Los Angeles County Jail for the last 30 days. He has vowed to starve to death rather than to testify about what he knows.

Surely, to try to coerce John Holmes to testify has crossed the line to punishment.

Or is this America for everybody but John Holmes?

John Holmes is a political prisoner.

This isn't right. This isn't decent and this isn't the way we do things here. Free John Holmes.

Twice in August and once in October, Holmes faced the grand jury's questions with tightly sealed lips. On October 6, Judge Leetham ruled to continue to keep Holmes under contempt of court.

Superior Court of the State of California[e]: *The witness Holmes made some gestures in custody toward a hunger strike, but it appeared that he obtained food from various sources and finally abandoned the hunger strike effort altogether on or about September 29, 1982. Witness Holmes' weight is presently within five pounds of the weight he had on August 26, 1982.*

The witness Holmes has contacts within the community who not only furnish food at conferences with the witness Holmes in the county jail, but who have written the court with respect to his release. Such contact of the court may be compared with contact of the court by victims' relatives.

Letter to Judge Leetham, August 6, 1982: *We are the parents of Joy Miller who was a victim in the Laurel Canyon Murders. We would like to thank you and the grand jury for remanding John Holmes back to prison for contempt of court. Again, please accept our personal thanks for your decision.*

Mitchell Egers[h]: When I came back from vacation and found him in jail, I asked the judge to release John Holmes based upon danger to him — a very real danger to him if he talked before the grand jury. My partner and I argued that there was justification for not talking at times if it looks like there is going to be great danger to the person who talked — loss of his life, perhaps. We established during these arguments with the judge that there was a real danger. Even though the defense of duress was not allowed during the actual trial, certainly we could show that he was in danger from others. Judge Leetham didn't accept what we had to say and didn't release him, the court of appeal didn't, and the Supreme Court didn't.

Superior Court of the State of California [e]: *The charging or prosecution of the persons involved in the Laurel Canyon homicides is dependant upon identification established by the witness Holmes. A lawful order was given by this court to the witness Holmes to answer questions put to him by the District attorney in a proceeding before the grand jury and similar questions were asked of him before this court. The witness Holmes is able to answer the questions posed, but has willfully and unlawfully refused. Further, witness Holmes was present and understood the order to answer questions concerning the participants in the Laurel Canyon homicides and injury.*

The efforts of the witness Holmes to avoid testifying appear to be motivated by an effort to protect the identity of the real malefactors rather than an honest, articulated concern for safety of himself or family. The failure of the witness John C. Holmes to answer questions lawfully posed to him with respect to the Laurel Canyon homicides and injury is a willful and contemptuous act toward the grand jury, the court and the system of justice, which can only be destructive to the public order. The failure and neglect of the witness Holmes to testify and answer questions as required of him is motivated in part by his desire to protect persons involved and in part by a belief that this court will not persist in its effort to coerce the testimony required.

The witness Holmes has had no consistent and articulated theory in declining to answer the questions posed and has willfully and opportunistically presented whatever reasons occurred to him at any particular moment. Further, the episode of the hunger strike demonstrates an insincerity of purpose and how quickly the witness Holmes may abandon one course of action for another.

The court now orders that the witness, John C. Holmes, be retained in custody by the sheriff, the sheriff being directed and instructed that any day the petitioner requests permission to testify, he be brought before this court forthwith and that the sheriff in any event bring the witness John C. Holmes before this court on November 8, 1982 for further hearings.

Holmes spent a total of 119 days in jail for contempt, which set the record at that time in California history. Most adult industry insiders felt that his time in pornography was over, Goldstein explained, "Those he hadn't alienated with his drug-induced craziness now shied away because of his association with the murders."

Freedom

Ron Coen [h]: Eddie Nash was a target suspect in the organized crime division. It was known and felt that he was involved in these murders. Nash's house was raided three different times by three different agencies and I was there for each and every one of them. First by the sheriffs, and twice by the Los Angeles Police Department. The first time the sheriff raided, Greg Diles fired at the S.W.A.T. deputies and the deputies fired back. Everybody missed. Certain items were found; certain sexual items, a lot of dope. I had that case.

While that case was pending, there was another raid by the Los Angeles Police Department. This time again, S.W.A.T. was there. Every window on the house, again, was broken. On entry, more items were found.

The third raid — someone had overdosed and died in Nash's house. That was good enough probable cause that there was dope there, so a third warrant was drafted. I remember talking about which day to have the raid. Nobody could agree. This was on Thanksgiving week. Finally, it was on a Wednesday before Thanksgiving. On the third raid, every window was broken and the squad entered. This time, the media was there. We have no idea who called the media, but they filmed the squad entry. Nash had just received a two-pound shipment of cocaine — pure cocaine. It was just by fortune that was discovered. Nash blamed one of his associates for snitching him off to the police. All three cases got consolidated — tried together as one — and that's the case in which Nash was convicted and went to the state prison.

Nash was unable to meet his $5,000,000 bail. Behind bars, he composed two notes to John: "Jhon [sic] I swear man I will forgive you for what you did to me if you snapp [sic] out of it and tell them the truth and come and save me out of my miseries," and, "Jhon [sic] you know as God is your witness that I am innocent and that I never sent anybody with you to kill anybody anywhere or anyplace. So don't you think it's about time to tell the truth?"

John Holmes [f]: I received a communication from the people who had previously threatened my life if I testified. They told me to go ahead. If I hadn't done so, the court would have kept me in jail forever.

Probably not coincidentally, John broke his vow of silence on the day of Nash's arrest. Even that day, John had two requirements of the grand jury before he would testify: (1) he would not be prosecuted for perjury for anything he would say (2) probation restraints against him would be dropped.

John Holmes [f]: Eventually, I answered every question asked of me for two and a half hours more. They obviously believed me on every count or I would still be in jail.

Ron Coen [h]: In fact, Holmes got in front of the grand jury and made some innocuous, "There were killers there, but I didn't know who they were," but he talked. The fact that a person is in custody, in this case, Eddie Nash, doesn't change the power of that person.

Mitchell Egers [h]: Finally, when others talked in the case, Judge Leetham lifted the finding of contempt and John was released the same day.

Al Goldstein ("The Harder They Fall"): Later that night, November 22, 1982, John Holmes walked out of prison a free man, as free as a man can be when he's constantly looking over his shoulder.

In his drug case, Nash's lawyer argued that the $1,000,000 cocaine supply seized at Nash's home was for personal use. Nash was sentenced to eight years in prison and a $120,350 fine. Incidentally, Nash was released after serving only two years of his eight-year sentence. It was later revealed by one of Nash's associates that he had bribed the judge with a substantial amount of money in exchange for his early release.

Scott Thorson came forward to police in 1989 with his statements about Nash and Diles beating John up after the robbery. This information gave police the opportunity to file charges against Nash and Diles, who were then tried in 1990. The trial was observed by two juries, one for Nash and one for Diles, but both juries were hung; the Nash jury came back with an 11-1 guilty vote, but the Diles jury came back with an 11-1 decision to acquit. As it had turned out, Nash had bribed the holdout juror in the 1990 case, but when the trial was done over in 1991 with new dual juries, both Nash and Diles were found innocent. Greg Diles passed away in 1995 of liver failure and his brother, Samuel, who was also suspected, but was never charged for his involvement in the murders, died in 2002.

In the year 2000, Nash was arrested again. The 2000 indictment stated that from 1975 to '92, Nash and his associates dealt heroin, cocaine and marijuana out of the Seven Seas, the Starwood, the Odyssey, Ali Baba's, and the Kit Kat Club; and engaged in murder, violence, intimidation, bribery and money laundering. Five of Nash's associates were named in the indictment as co-conspirators:

Hovsep Mikaelian (a.k.a. Joe McLean) was accused of storing and distributing drugs for Nash. Mikaelian was already serving a 14-year federal prison term for a 1997 conviction for narcotics trafficking, wire fraud and tax evasion. His brother, Hrant, was also accused and pleaded guilty in 1999 for an unrelated international money wire fraud and laundering case.

Harry Diramarian, an accountant who worked for Nash and the Mikaelians awaited sentencing for money laundering and bribery activities.

Greg Diles was described in the indictment as a participant in the Laurel Canyon murders, but was later cleared of all charges. Holmes was also accused in the indictment of trafficking drugs and taking part in the killings, despite his 1982 acquittal for the murder charges.

Laurie Holmes: It's a known fact that many wanted the Wonderland gang dead, as they had stepped on many toes and were out of control. The Hollywood hills were then and probably still are prime drug territory. While it's true, according to John that Eddie Nash ordered the hits, it's one thing to order a hit and another for the hit you ordered to be carried out by your people.

John arrived at the Wonderland house after the fact. He wandered through the house, grasping and scrambling through one of the most gruesome, bloody messes that anyone could even imagine. He was ordered to kill people — or be killed — and was forced to enter the house, only to find the people he had spent many days and nights partying with bludgeoned to death. John was never a killer; John Holmes was a lover. John was never a murderer; he was a drug addict!

> *"John Holmes was a very private man. He was good to me and my son. He taught us, a lot like a mentor does."*
>
> LAURIE HOLMES

10.
Lady Blue
Reclaiming Life and Rebuilding the Legend

Life with the Amersons

Although Ed Nash was temporarily put away when John was released from prison in November of 1982, John continued to be on guard for others like David Lind, whom he believed was still a threat.

Bill Amerson: He got out of jail and came right to my house from jail. That's how I started protecting him. He was the godfather of my children. He loved them and he loved me. He taught my daughter to drive. He needed someplace private to go — that was me.

Denise Amerson[h]: John moved back to our house with us and weird things started to happen. My sister and I weren't allowed to stay in our house by ourselves and then, the car blows up in the driveway. So I started asking questions, "Who is doing this? Why? What's going on?"

[John] told me that he didn't do it, and whatever I needed to know, he would answer the best that he could.

He didn't really know anything except to be John Holmes and he wasn't real happy with that person or that title. The rest of the world couldn't separate what he did for a living and who he really was inside. He wasn't such a strong person and in the industry, there were a lot of drugs; there's a lot of chaos, there's a lot of bullshit. He got lost in that.

Bill Amerson: John said something to me one time that has carried — I've never forgotten this. I had two motorcycles and I would go for a motorcycle ride and I would let him use my other motorcycle. We were in West L.A. one night at the corner of Southdale and Bundy, and I said to John, "We're going to turn left here. We're going up to the mountains. Follow me."

He looked at me, and there were tears in his eyes. He said, "I would follow you anywhere." I've never forgotten that. He later bought the motorcycle from me. I gave it to him and he said that he would give me the money. Then, he wrecked it.

We went to movies, we put a new roof on my house, we'd watch football games, hockey games. We went to Vegas a lot. He had no friends except me, and that's how he wanted it.

Ron Jeremy: I know that Bill and John were very, very close. He was his closest friend, bodyguard and advisor. He lived with him, he took care of him.

Sean Amerson[h]: As far as their friendship was concerned, it was sort of like a love-hate/marriage thing. On one hand, John would do something that was absolutely nuts and my dad would just wig out about it. Then he would look down, shake his head and go, "Fucking John." He would realize it was John that was doing it and that sort of made it OK.

Bill Amerson: I took my three children in the motor home and we left him home. We were gone about seven days. I had a tree in my front yard — pine tree, it was beautiful. It was worth five or ten thousand dollars, I was told.

Sean Amerson [h]: I remember coming home one day in the car, pulling up in the driveway. We had a long driveway that went up to the house at the top of the hill, and there was this huge tree behind the house. The tree wasn't there anymore. It was such a landmark; you were used to pulling up the driveway and seeing this huge tree that spread out along the top of the roof. We went through [the] house, through the back and there was John with a saw.

He'd been in the tree all day, cutting down the tree. John said, "I'm pruning. It was about time somebody pruned the tree." He had on grubby clothes and was climbing up the damn tree with this saw, to saw the rest of the tree down. It was amazing. This tree was almost the length of one side of the house. It had been there since I was a kid. He chopped it down. There were no leaves left; there was nothing, just a big pile of stuff down at the foot of it.

Bill Amerson: As soon as I pulled into the driveway, the tree looked like a toothbrush. He'd decided to trim it. It was the ugliest damn thing I'd ever seen, but he thought he was a gardener. He didn't know what he was doing, but he was never afraid to try.

Sean Amerson [h]: If it had been anybody else, they'd have been dead. My father's typical reaction was violence and ranting and raving. It was almost comical how he looked down, shook his head and said, "John," and he walked away. That's typically how it went.

The King's *Marathon* Comeback

In spite of John's acquittal, there were few associates in the adult business willing to help to jumpstart his career. Bill Margold was instrumental in securing John his first job after being released from jail, for a December 1982 production called *Marathon*.

On the set of that film, John met 19-year-old Laurie Rose (a.k.a. Misty Dawn). Laurie was a part of a group living together above Nash's Seven Seas nightclub, known as "The Hole in the Wall Gang" because of their tendency to knock down walls to expand their residence for new tenants.

Laurie Holmes [h]: When I first met John, I was a San Fernando Valley girl. I did porn in the Valley; I wasn't a San Francisco person. [*Marathon*] was the first film that I'd gotten that was up in San Francisco. I drove all the way up the coast, checked into the hotel and that morning, I was with another actor and he goes, "Oh, that's John Holmes."

And I really freaked out. I go, "Should I take my gun on the set?" He's like, "No, no, don't do that."

I remember walking up going, "Hi, I'm Misty Dawn."

Bill Margold: Laurie asked me to introduce her to John.

He grinned and said, "Okay." That was it. He liked tiny people. There was a sense of protection there, as I think a lot of men want to protect women. You want to hug them and pull them toward you.

Laurie Holmes: [John] was mesmerizing. I knew him for 1000 years at least. He had a very hypnotic way about him. That's one of the things that made him a star. He was very charming. He'd charm the pants off your own mom — literally. He was very classy, very worldly.

Some of the girls got jealous and it kind of got into a bad scene, and he took me under his wing and protected me. I'd driven up to San Francisco to do this movie and I was really out of my realm.

After rumors spread that Laurie had stolen from the dressing room, an actress threatened to cut her face. In a caring gesture, John took Laurie into his dressing room, where they enjoyed each other's company for the duration of the shoot.

Ron Jeremy: John would take some of the beautiful girls from the set out into the backyard and take snapshots of them. He was sort of like an amateur photographer. He would talk to some of the photographers and they would say to me, "He really kind of knows what he's doing," and he could discuss things like history and world politics, so he seemed to be well-traveled.

He would never talk much about his personal life. We talked about current events, food, massaging, sex techniques — we both liked to give head to women. He really took pride at being good at that and so do I. He'd give a girl a back massage, and he would know the parts of the body and muscles used in the massage. I have my master's degree, so when he mentioned body parts, he was right on target. He discussed certain things about the penis, so he knew some things. I wouldn't call him overly intelligent — I'd say he had about average intelligence, but he seemed well-traveled and he knew enough about certain fields so he could come across as intelligent.

Laurie Holmes: He was very sophisticated, considering where he came from. He'd been around the world and he had a few clues — let's just put it that way.

There were the women with the big boobs, like Uschi Digard and Candy Samples, and they had real, terrible backaches. He would rub their backs. He was a wonderful, wonderful guy and he was very gentle. He wasn't often rough with anyone.

Ron Jeremy[h]: He'd leave with girls and give them the massaging technique. I'd watch John massage girls and take them into the woods. It was really funny. Or he would take them into the corner. That would kill me because he'd do the exact thing I'd do; one of my favorite techniques in foreplay is giving backrubs, and this was what John was doing, too. I said, "Who took this from whom?" The little bastard.

In the film *Marathon*, Margold and Drea were invited to the ultimate swingers' orgy hosted by Jamie Gillis. Several big-name players are invited: The King, Jamie Gillis, Ron Jeremy, Herschel Savage, Misty Dawn, Mai Lin, and Sharon Mitchell. But after an accident lands Bill Margold and Drea in hospital beds, the party continues atop the bandaged pair.

Bill Margold[h]: I shared a sequence with John, Jamie and Ron Jeremy. It was called "40 Inches of Meat." In December of 1982, my hateful ex-wife Drea demanded to be involved in what amounted to be a small gang-bang in *Marathon*. I'm dressed as a bear in that part of the movie. She said, "I want The King, I want the Hedgehog, I want The Assassin," which was Jamie Gillis, and she said, "I'll take you, too." The King did her first.

Drea told me after she'd worked with The King; that he was very good at what he did. I could see it, in that he prepared the women. He would knead them and he liked playing with their orifices and making sure that they were ready to be penetrated. It wasn't just a thrust in blindly and do whatever he needed to do.

Laurie Holmes: John was the master of his domain and he had his degree. He knew from an early age that he had to be gentle because of his size. It's something he definitely learned to do at an early age. He wasn't out to hurt anybody.

There's something that they call in the industry, when a guy works with a woman that he really, really doesn't like and she's an absolute bitch, it's called a "grudge fuck." I don't know exactly who with, but there were times when he had to work with somebody that he didn't like. John used to say he would take the best part about that person, whether it [be] their toes, boobs — or whatever was their best asset — and focus on that. When you see his eyes shut, that's what he's doing.

He's focusing in on whatever was the best part of that person. If he couldn't find anything good about them, I guess, if the heart was so ugly and he couldn't focus on anything, then I'm sure he got a little rough, but that was only one out of 1000 times.

According to both Margold and Laurie, John and Laurie did work together in *Marathon*, although the scene was cut from the DVD version of the feature. The two also engaged in sex off camera.

> *Laurie Holmes*: [Sex on the set] wasn't really that great because we were on set and there was a lot of pressure. There's work and there is play. When you're on a set, all you can think about is that you want the scene to be good. You're working and it's not the same as one-on-one with somebody. You've got lights and they're hot, and you've got the crew. You've got downtime and people in the background. It's lights, camera, action, and all you can think abut is, "Do I look good? Did you like my scene? Are you going to hire me again?"

After the *Marathon* session was completed, John gave Laurie a phone number where he could be reached back in Los Angeles.

> *Laurie Holmes*[h]: He gave me his number, back at Bill Amerson's house. I waited a couple of days before I called. Still being very nervous from the Laurel Canyon thing, I'd go up to the house. At first, I'd do a few lines, a couple of times. I didn't really do drugs; then I thought: I really liked him. I bought coke from him. I didn't even do it; I was giving it away to my friends, just to go up and see him.
>
> He had a big thing about bathtubs, Vitabath and all that. It was like his religion. We'd just hang out the whole night, have sex and take a bath. We had so much fun. We went everywhere, laughing, making spectacles out of ourselves. We were real entertaining to ourselves, I guess — I don't know about others.

California Valley Girls & Dreams of Misty

In January of 1983, not too long after their first on-camera encounter, Laurie and John met in front of the camera again for *California Valley Girls*. Prior to the shoot, Margold picked John up in his brown 1978 VW van, the Bear Mobile.

> *Bill Margold*: [John] parked his car and I picked him up in a parking lot down at Ventura and Van Nuys. I walked up to him and said, "Come on, King, we're going to make a movie." I don't think I ever called him John. I think he accepted that pretty easily after I told him he was The King in '73, when he walked in my office.

I think he would have preferred a limo or to have traveled in a car rather than a van, but the van was not ugly at that time. It wasn't as old and battered as it is now, but I think Johnny would have preferred something more regal. He said, "Okay." He locked up his car at Ralph's and off we went.

I think John was content since he knew he wasn't going to have to fuck on-camera. It takes a lot of pressure off your mind. When I designed that character for them to practice on, I told [director, Hal] Freeman, "I want The King in this scene," and I remember sitting there, blocking it out before The King even showed up.

Freeman said, "How much is he going to cost?"

I said, "Whatever he costs, he's going to be the star of your damn movie." He was paid $1500 for the scene. I don't know who set his price; it might have been Amerson.

Bill Amerson: I got him a movie called *California Valley Girls* by promising the producer that I'd guarantee any money he might lose if John fucked up.

Bill Margold: John was only hired for the one scene in the film. I think [John] was having a lot more fun by the time he got to *Valley Girls* because he was the center of attention.

California Valley Girls was written by Mark Weiss and myself. I created the concept and then Mark wrote it. *California Valley Girls* was the story of four Valley girls, obviously, hired to work in a down-and-out escort service. It's sort of cute.

John's scene in *California Valley Girls* is definitely one for the record books. Robert (played by John Holmes) is surrounded by a group of Valley Girls, including Misty Dawn, who take turns practicing fellatio on his extraordinary appendage in preparation for their prospective clients. Once they have the technique down, Robert exclaims, "Now I know how a mother dog feels," a line written by Bill Margold.

Bill Margold: There's a beautiful line in that movie that Mark wrote, where Becky Savage and Shaun Michelle are in bed, talking about their bills. Shaun says, "I open up the drawer and the bills are screaming at me."

So Becky says, "Well, close the drawer!" That's Mark. I couldn't hold a candle to his ability to write. Mark didn't write sex, he wrote to the point of sex.

Cindy Shepard probably did the best job of acting, but Laurie has the best line in the movie, where they're sitting in a car before they go to school and Laurie, being the dumbest of the four Valley Girls, says, "I wish there was something like learning dots, so you could eat them and then know your homework." It's an inspired line. It's brilliant because that was Mark.

It also features an all-star cast: Hershel Savage, Eric Edwards, Paul Thomas, and Ron Jeremy. Each of them being, of course, tricks. There are many unique situations in the movie, and the music is brilliant because Kenji wrote the entire score for the film. It has a hilarious score.

Kenji, a multi-talented still photographer who worked with Holmes during his comeback, took the photo of John standing naked with the length of his penis covered by a group of women's hands. The famous photo was used for the cover of *WADD*.

> *Bill Margold*: Hal stole the music from him and never paid him for it.
>
> I expected to see my name as director and I got assistant director. I never got credit because that's when Hal Freeman and I fought. I thought that was really stupid because Freeman spent more time chasing the women around than he did do anything else. I directed the sex scenes.
>
> In the hot tub scene with Eric Edwards and Kimberly Carson, you can hear the fireworks at the Super Bowl going off. It was shot in South Pasadena. In fact, if Eric Edwards had not shown up on Super Bowl Sunday, I would have had to climb into the hot tub. Drea would have killed me if she'd come home and found out I'd done the sex scene. Luckily, Eric showed up two hours late and did the scene, which was perfectly timed to fireworks going off in the background. We couldn't have thought up a better soundtrack.

Not long after John started seeing Laurie, he sat her down and asked her why, at 19 years old, she had chosen to work as a pornographic actress. Laurie confided in him that she wanted to be able to afford to send her young son to a private school, so John told her that he would continue to work and pay for her son's tuition if she would quit her job as an adult performer.

> *Laurie Holmes*: John was a very romantic person. I don't think I'll ever meet a man who is even a quarter as romantic as he was. I'll never forget the time that I went back to work for this one film because I wanted to work — this was before Penguin. I got this job that was really too much for me, but I was trying hard because I was bored. He had a dozen red roses delivered to my job with a diamond bracelet.

Apart from a handful of films including *Nasty Nurses* and her starring role in the 1984 VCX feature, *Dreams of Misty*, where she plays a sexologist (and John does double duty with a cameo and a production manager credit), Laurie did very little in adult movies while she and John were together.

Laurie Holmes: I hated *Dreams of Misty*. The part was not me; I was too young to play a sexual psychologist. I remember the scene with that girl that he ended up working with and she and I ended up not getting along. I don't know [her name]; she came and went real fast. She was shoving pizza down her throat and I didn't like her. I thought she had horse's hair.

A Full House

A couple of months after meeting one another, Laurie moved into the Amerson home to be closer to John. At the Amersons', Laurie slept in John's bed, although she had a separate bedroom so that she and John could both maintain privacy and "alone time." John was pleased with his role as godfather to the Amerson children, and he took pride in becoming a mentor to Laurie and a step-father to her young son.

Laurie Holmes: How many men would do that for a stupid porn girl and her son, to take them in? I think that John saw some things in me that were much like him. He wanted to help me and guide me and my son. He was very good to me and my son. He taught us, a lot like a mentor does. I've always kept my son out of it, as far as naming names or anything. My son wouldn't want that, but yes, John loved him very much.

Bill Amerson[h]: John became a surrogate father for this little boy and they went everywhere. They went to Disneyland, they went to Magic Mountain. John did everything with this little boy. He loved him — totally loved him.

John sought to protect and be a good father figure, as he had with the Amerson children and several of his young girlfriends, so it is no surprise that he established a close relationship with Laurie's son and his young, petite, brunette mother.

Laurie Holmes: We were always honest with him. We said to him that we did things that society didn't agree with, that was our personal business. We never lied to him. We told just what he needed to know and nothing more. We didn't elaborate because he was a child.

In spite of what people think about pornographers, we're family people. Your work is your work and you don't mix your family up in that. We were a very private family. You would think, "Oh, John Holmes! — Parties and so on," but that was the John Holmes before me. The John Holmes that was with me was a very private man.

John Holmes[f]: When I'm away from a movie set, the last thing I want to do is go to a pornographic film or think about one. A baker doesn't go home and eat cookies all night, either.

Someone once asked me to rate the sexual performances of porn actresses I've worked with. There's no way I could do that — simply because that's not real sex to me. The way I touch a person I love to be with, smell that person, make love to her, is a fact. It's different when I go back to my tricks or my movies. I know what is real and what is fake. Good sex is like fine wine. It isn't something to be guzzled. I roll it out. I taste it. I smell it. It can't be done in a dark room.

John loved Laurie as much as he had loved any of the other women he had been with, but it was sometimes difficult for Laurie, who was not much older than the Amerson children, to cope with John's responsibilities as the kids' godfather.

Laurie Holmes: They were his godchildren, yes. There were other people who claim to be their godfather, too, but John really was their godfather. John did care for them.

He had to do the Amerson thing. He had to play the game. I would hate it because we would be having a family evening, and all of a sudden, one of the kids would need to be rescued because they were screwed up somewhere. So much for that; he'd have to go right over there. He was just doing the right thing. He was always there for those kids. I will say that.

Kicking the Habit

Laurie Holmes: When I first met him, he was still smoking a lot of coke. He'd just gotten out of jail and he went right back to it. I was mesmerized and hypnotized by him, and I wanted to be with him so bad that I started doing his drugs.

Al Goldstein ("The Harder They Fall"): It was late afternoon on the second day of the 1983 International Winter Consumer Electronics Show, a huge annual technological orgasm spread across acres of convention floor. All the X-rated companies were ghettoized in the Hilton, across a parking lot from the mainstream, where Toshiba and Sony reigned.

John Holmes strode up to me out of nowhere. He was signing autographs for Caballero Control, a distributor of X-rated films, many featuring his famous anatomy. He gave me a nudge in my anatomy. "You're gaining weight, Goldstein," he rasped. "You should be on the same diet I'm on, the Cocaine Diet." He was thin, almost emaciated, reminding me of the haggard specter he was when he entered jail.

Bill Margold: I told him, "You're going to kill yourself."
And he said, "I don't care." That was my counseling at that point in time.

Laurie Holmes[h]: I think he had an addictive personality. Whatever it was he was into, he was addicted, immediately. When he got into drugs, immediately he was addicted to drugs. He was addicted to scotch — that's for sure. I'm not sure if that was to wash down the drugs or if he liked the taste or whatever. Definitely addicted to sex, there's no denying that! So at the same time, I guess he was addicted to the business. Whatever he did, he did it wholeheartedly.

Bill Amerson: He went along with anything I wanted, except giving up the drugs. I tried to get him to quit, but he couldn't do it. I did do drugs, but I stopped. We were standing in my driveway. He had tears running down the side of his face. I said, "John, let me help you."
He said, "You did this, why can't I?"
"John, because I'm stronger than you are."
"I know. I've done a lot of stuff, and I'm all messed up."
"John, you can't. Let me help you, let me show you how to stop."

John Holmes[f]: It was a matter of willpower. I just stopped. Quitting cocaine is like quitting cigarettes, only it's ten times harder. The craving is there, but after the first three days, it gets a lot easier. My mind cleared up immediately. I wondered why I hadn't done it years ago.
I'll never do it again because I realize it's disgusting. It's expensive, it's decadent, and it's habit-forming. At the time I was doing cocaine, my career was at a low point. Now that I'm through with cocaine, I'm starting to come back to another plateau. I've got a good energy flow.

Laurie Holmes: Of course, [sex] off the set was better, when I started to really get to know him and after quitting the drugs.

Many people noticed a positive change in John, who in fact began working out at the gym and was able to (mostly) give up cocaine for long periods of time, although he would always smoke pot.

Laurie Holmes: The end of John Holmes fortunately wasn't the Wonderland murders. John recovered from his addiction and rebuilt his fame, career and life. He became a spokesperson against drugs and an inspiration to many. John never blamed anyone but himself for the trouble he got himself into. He put his marriage to Sharon, his relationship with Dawn and the murders behind him. He was a wonderful husband, a great father and the best mentor I could have ever had. He was and always will be my very best friend.

It wasn't that there was John Holmes and there was Wonderland, and then it was no more. He did build himself back up. I went through cold turkey with him and he actually did speeches at Venice Beach against drugs. It was heartfelt; it was stuff he believed in. What really made John remarkable is that I've known a lot of people on drugs, and not many people could be into drugs to the extent that John was into them and then pull themselves out. He pulled himself out of it, recaptured his fame again and rebuilt his life.

I'm not saying that he probably didn't slip once in a while. Once on drugs or alcohol, many people do slip and he probably didn't even want me to know about it. I'm not saying that he was perfect, but for the most part, from day to day, he was not on drugs. He wanted [sobriety] and not only did he want it, but he tried to teach others that drugs are bad. He got off drugs and he was just a totally different person. He was a kid again, a wonderful guy. He was my life.

Back in the Saddle

John Holmes[f]: As long as there's a demand, I'll work in pornography: acting, producing, directing, distributing, and the photography end of it. Pornography is still a developing art. Major cinema has hit a peak; it has reached technical perfection and has no place left to go. In pornography, we are still finding more sensitive ways to portray what people are going to see in the sexual film. It gets better each year, more visually complicated. It grows in strength. There is plenty of room left for anybody who has artistic knowledge or value to work.

Marilyn Chambers: When VHS came out, that was a huge turning point. Then, people started shooting on video. It was like you could be the straightest, staunchest person in the world and this is a person's human nature — they are curious about sex. Everybody has sexual fantasies. That's a private thing that you do in your own home, or behind closed doors, unless you're a swinger. Everybody doesn't have to know what your sexual fantasies are.

Slowly, John revitalized his career with guest-starring roles, often performing a single scene. In some ways, John's infamy in association with the murders assisted in refurbishing the Holmes' dynasty. Industry mainstays, like Marilyn Chambers, who had previously teamed up with John for *Insatiable*, would be one of the first household names to work with him after his release from jail in the 1983 film, *Up 'n' Coming*. John's appearance at the conclusion of the film in a ten-minute orgy scene epitomized the fact that his name still attracted attention and guaranteed dividends, no matter the quality of the movie.

Marilyn Chambers: He came out and we did the *Up 'n' Coming* thing. I remember sitting in a room with John, and he was kind of waiting for his scene. He'd become way more introverted. He was always introverted, but he became more so. His intellectual side had sprung out. He obviously had time to think about stuff, read, and find out who he was. He really became almost a Zen-like person. He showed me what he could do; it was unbelievable. It was like a push-up on one hand.

He was really controlled. He learned how to control his spiritual side and his physical side, where he had really looked inside of himself when he was in prison. He had become a different person and, obviously, the drugs weren't as important. He wasn't loaded out of his mind — just really, really quiet.

Richard Pacheco [h]: That day on the set, we were all there in the morning, except for John. This was right after he got out of jail from protective custody. When he came on the set, it was about mid-afternoon and we said hello.

John pretty much kept to himself. We would all sort of sit over here and he would sit over there, and we'd wonder what his life had been like. I remember it got cold and we were all bundling up. John was sitting around naked, seeming quite comfortable. The jokes were, "That's what prison will do for you."

Marilyn Chambers: We had some little heart-to-heart talks. I can't remember anything we talked about. It wasn't seriously personal, but I remember it being deep. He would talk about books that he had read and philosophies that he was interested in, like Tai Chi. He had become more disciplined because he didn't have anything more to do. He was a different person. He had put on a little weight; he was in great shape.

Richard Pacheco [h]: There was a balcony overlooking where the set was, and I was up in the balcony. That's where the food was and I was having some lunch. All of a sudden, I start hearing these screams. I glanced over and John Holmes had his Little League baseball bat in Marilyn Chambers' bottom. Marilyn was on fire.

It was the greatest sex scene I ever saw. The look on Marilyn Chambers' face — you know how a baby gets when they're out of control crying? Just unrestrained life. Her face was just mesmerizing.

Well, when the movie came out and I saw this scene, they kept the camera in tight on the genitalia, the whole scene. You never see Marilyn's face — they missed it completely. You can't tell this scene is anything; all you hear is this faint noise in the background. It was a complete, total waste.

Juliet Anderson never did work with John again, but like Marilyn Chambers, Anderson recognized a positive change in John's personality after his time in jail. Two years after her bad experience working with him when she played Aunt Peg, she bumped into him in 1983 while they were working on separate films being made at the same studio.

> *Juliet Anderson*[h]: We were on the same set together and he was working with someone else. I noticed immediately how much he'd changed, both on- and off-camera. He was actually a pretty nice guy. At one point, our paths crossed and I said, "Hello, John."
>
> He said, "Oh, hi, Juliet."
>
> I started to pass. He said, "No, wait a minute." He stopped me, and he said, "I want to apologize for having been such an asshole." I was astounded. He said, "I know I wasn't easy to work with. Well, I was really strung out on drugs and I want to apologize."
>
> I said, "Well, thank you, very much."
>
> I stuck out my hand to shake his hand and he said, "How about a hug?" And so, we gave each other a hug. It was a heartfelt hug and that was the last time I ever saw John.

With each successive movie appearance, John proved himself and regained the trust of his employers. His mere presence re-established his foothold on the world of adult entertainment and reminded XXX audiences that John C. Holmes was porn royalty. In addition to his guest star roles, John worked on writing his memoirs, which he had commenced while incarcerated. It seemed as if John was engaged by the prospects of the future.

> *John Holmes*[f]: I've got seven films lined up now, some of them things I've written. There is talk of cable television, a movie of the week and there is the autobiography to finish.

John's Only Gay Feature Film

> *Bill Margold*: Titus was doing a film called *The Private Pleasures of John Holmes* with Manny [Gonzales]. I'd written *Caught From Behind*. They didn't have a location for it and I was looking around fairly early in '83 after I'd done *Valley Girls*. All of a sudden, I'm in my office on Hollywood Boulevard and in came this respectable looking middle-class lady. Titus said, "This is Nancy Conjure and she has a location in Palos Verdes."
>
> I said, "What do you want for your location?"

She said, "Can you get John Holmes to fuck me?"
I looked at Titus and I said, "I guess."

Laurie Holmes: He got ripped off on [*Private Pleasures*]. He was supposed to make $1,000,000 and he never saw anything like that. I have all of the original paperwork. It was horrible.

Bill Amerson: Manny Gonzales came to me with John, and said, "I want to make a gay film and I want John to be in it."
I said, "No."
John said, "No." Manny Gonzales made an offer that John couldn't refuse: $200,000.
So we talked about it and I said, "I want you to use condoms."
Manny said, "No condoms."
To John, a great deal of this was really about the money and it was great that Manny's whole plan was that he would fuck little girls who looked like little boys, and put mustaches on them. All the guys that he supposedly had sex with were women. We put mustaches on them. In one scene, he's having sex and a mustache falls off.

Bill Margold: I think a lot of people fantasized about having sex with John Holmes. I think that was part of the mystique in the nature of things. People would pay for that opportunity. So I said, "I'm sure that Titus could arrange it," not realizing that he would arrange it by having her substitute for one of the men in the upcoming gay movie.
She was one of the orifices. Titus put that together. If you study the bottoms that are being entered, there is one that's a little more cupcake-y than the other ones. That's Nancy Conjure.

As part of the arrangement to film *Caught from Behind* at Nancy Conjure's home, her fantasy to have sex with John Holmes was fulfilled in *Private Pleasures* as one of the so-called "stunt butts." A behind-the-scenes photo documents a woman wearing a fake mustache over her smile while John has his hand down the front of her pants. On the other hand, John, with his penis simultaneously in Joey Yale's mouth, looks bored throughout the film.

Bill Amerson: However, John did have sex with Joey Yale, who was a gay porn star. John actually did anal sex with him and I believe that's where John got AIDS. The biggest thing with Joey Yale was that it shouldn't have happened on the set.
I don't even recall how it happened. John was not to touch another man. That was the plan, but for it to be more realistic, I guess — I wasn't there.

Laurie Holmes: It wasn't him. John was not gay, he didn't have anything against it, but it wasn't his cup of tea. He was having such trouble doing that movie. Yeah, the money was appealing, but it was hard for him. He was having such trouble with it that they dressed this old lady up like a guy, and cheated the shot!

He really had a rough time with that movie and he was adamant that I never watch that movie. He said, "I don't want you to watch that movie."

According to John in *Porn King*, he returned to substance abuse to drown out his feelings about making the film. Perhaps the arrival of AIDS in America had weighed on John's mind while filming *Private Pleasures;* in contrast, he had no problems entertaining the fantasies of several gay and bisexual lovers in the past, both on and off camera.

Bill Amerson: He felt guilty that he'd fucked Joey Yale in the ass. I was upset. I told him it was really stupid. I don't care how much money a man can get. The risk of AIDS with a known homosexual who fucks everybody in town is not a good risk.

Shortly after making the film, John became ill and attributed it to a reaction from the illegal narcotics. He was briefly hospitalized.

John Holmes[i]: While the doctors never told me what was happening, it was the drugs I'd taken to get through the gay film. I'd been clean for eight months before then; now my body was rejecting them. I was going through post-freebase blackout. My lungs, my brain, even my sense of existing were fried to hell because of my stupidity. One would have thought I would have more sense, considering the mess drugs got me into before.

I was doing drugs again, but not as heavily and not all the time, as before. If there was anything to be learned from my earlier experience, it was that there was a time and a place for me to get high, and one definite wrong place and time was during the production of a film.

Most of the time I just smoked marijuana and Misty joined me in that.

At this crossroad during John's comeback, Holmes and Amerson were hired in 1984 by VCX to fulfill different capacities. Amerson produced movies and apart from performing, John also worked as a line producer for VCX, where he first met the writer, Raven Touchstone.

Raven Touchstone: I wrote for [porn director,] Scotty [Fox]. John Holmes was line producer. It was the first movie I ever wrote; it was called *Intimate Couples*. Scotty brought John over to my house to go over the script just before they were going to shoot it, and that was my very first introduction to John Holmes. His wrist and hand were in a cast; he had fallen off a motorcycle. He was very sweet; he was very gentlemanly; he was very courtly.

My roommate was in her bedroom, jumping up and down, screaming, "John Holmes is in our house! John Holmes, the biggest cock in the world, is in my living room!" She was very excited. She went out, met him, shook his un-bandaged hand and cried, "Oh, I love you so much!"

Everybody had heard of him. I had never seen anything he had done — I had never seen a porn movie. The first movie I saw of his was *Insatiable* with Marilyn Chambers, and I was impressed with a couple of things. One was the scene where he — very manly — picks her up and moves her. He's so masculine in that scene. The other thing that impressed me was the size of his dick. In one scene in that movie, it was bent down and I thought, "That looks just like the pipe under the sink. Wow, that's really impressive."

[John was] very attractive. He looked healthy. This was in '84. He looked healthy; he looked strong. He didn't look wasted. He was very diligent about going over every line, making sure he understood everything I wrote, making sure he knew how they were going to shoot it. It was VCX. That's why he was connected to it.

After that show, he contacted me about writing a straight movie for an actress named Terry Moore, who was working in mainstream films. She was kind of a B player, not a big star. I said, "Sure, fine, just let me know."

I'd lived in this town all my life and whenever anybody says, "Would you like to do blah, blah, blah?" 99 percent of it never happens, but just in case, I always say, "Sure." He knew people who were producing the movie.

Terry Moore was a second-string Hollywood star who was 55 when she posed for *Playboy* in 1984. And that same year, she claimed that she had never divorced her first husband, Howard Hughes. Although she had three other marriages before Hughes' death, she did receive a settlement from the late billionaire's estate.

Meanwhile, in Porno Land, newcomers like Kimberly Carson, Bunny Bleu, Amber Lynn and Ginger Lynn — each of them almost 20 years younger than Holmes — were eager to work with the legend.

Ginger Lynn first met John at the airport before flying together to film in San Francisco. At the time, Ginger was fond of smoking marijuana and recalled that when she walked through the metal detector, she forgot to put in her pipe. At that moment, John took on a big brotherly role and snatched it away.

Ginger Lynn[j]: John had a boyish charm. He had that naughty smile. You know he's been up to something, but you don't know quite what, and I always felt like he was going to catch me doing something.

Immediately, she and John connected on a sexual level, both on- and off-screen. On location, she would often visit him in his hotel room for private passions. "Not that I was ever in love with John, but sex off-camera with John was that same passion that you have when you're with a partner you've been with for a long time."

Years later, Ginger was flattered when Laurie Holmes told her that John had said she was one of his two favorite costars. "It made me feel special because I always really, really liked John."

All compliments aside, when Ginger and John united on the set, they demonstrated their potent sexual chemistry. Like the women before her, Ginger was astounded by the size of John's penis, "My best estimate as to how big his cock was is from the film *Those Young Girls*. John plays my agent in this scene and his cock literally, when I'm sucking it, was from my wrist to my elbow. That's a big cock. That's 12, 14 inches?"

Those Young Girls was a script conceived by Ginger Lynn, featuring Harry Reems and Traci Lords. Lords was only 16 when it was shot, so all copies of the feature were destroyed once the movie became part of a federal case. The producers were charged with child pornography, but were later acquitted when it was proven that Lords had provided them with a falsified driver's license when she was hired.

Passing the Torch

Under the umbrella of VCX Productions, John met Buck Adams, a novice to the adult industry, in 1984. At that time, no one knew that he was the kid brother of Amber Lynn, a popular adult actress. The truth came out when they were scripted to have a sex scene together in *Body Shop*, a film which details the conversion of an auto-repair garage to a "full service" center where customers receive carnal perks from female mechanics. Buck Adams and Amber Lynn revealed that they were brother and sister, so the scene was nixed — prior to any incestuous actions taking place — and Adams' role within the film was reassigned. The set of *Body Shop* was also the location of Adams' first meeting with Holmes.

> *Buck Adams*[h]: He was a big guy. I don't know exactly how tall he was, and he always wore cowboy boots, so it made him look even taller. I was telling one of my big, fabulous boxing stories and he came walking out, so it just froze me. There he was.
>
> He really did have this presence — everybody would freeze to listen to John Holmes talk. He [said to me], "You, buddy, you're much too ugly to do these kinds of movies." I was about ready to take a crack at him, and he goes, "but so am I. I'm the most famous son of a bitch there is. You're going to play my brother in this movie and I'm going to direct you."

It was my first time on a set, of any type. "Wow, OK, what do I do?"

He goes, "Here's what you do. You've got to lie on top of this car engine." They pulled this car in and nobody let the car cool down. He goes, "Lay up there, on top of the hood and this girl's going to go down on you. When it's time, so we can see it all happen, you reach around and quietly pat her on the butt, and she'll raise up her head and the magic will occur."

I looked at him and said, "Why don't I just tell her, 'Lift your head up?'"

He goes, "Because you're not supposed to talk on camera, dummy!" The car was sitting there, idling. [Cinematographer] Jack Remy was shooting this thing using a video camera, which to him, was like the kiss of death, so he's disgusted by everything.

John goes, "Shut the car off, so the fan doesn't cut off his feet," and the last thing he tells me is, "Remember, don't say a word."

I'm so keen to impress — you know, first movie — I slid my legs down the side, tape rolling. She said, "Could you lean over here?" and when I did, my leg laid up against the hot exhaust pipe. It's burning.

Then John goes, "Wow, you're doing really good here, I'm getting another girl," so he ran in this blonde and they're both going at me. My leg was sizzling and pretty soon, with all this excitement going on, it's time, but she had no idea why I'm tapping on her. She thought I'm telling her to go faster, which she started to do. My leg's burning and I was slapping away, but she doesn't know what's going on.

Jack Remy dropped the camera. I was just sitting there, having a leg fried. [John] came over, looked down and he goes, "You moron! What the hell are you burning your leg for?" There's a big hole burnt in my leg. He looks at it and goes, "You deserve a second chance. Not today, but on the very next movie." From that time on, I worked in almost everything John Holmes and Bill did together. Bill and John were quite a pair to work for. They always took care of me, so I kind of let the bad stories go in one ear and out the other.

John & Laurie's Happy Family

In late 1983 John, Laurie and her son moved out of Amerson's home into their own apartment in Encino, California.

"Nobody ever came over," said Laurie, "Nobody knew where we lived. His words to me were, 'Friends can get you killed.'"

Many people who knew Laurie and John confirmed that they were a loving and happy couple. In 1984, while at the Sherman Oaks Galleria to see a movie with Mark Weiss, Margold saw John and Laurie with her son in tow.

Bill Margold: I went, "Oh, there's The King. Hi, King and Laurie," and this google-eyed-looking kid. To me, it was significant that they were all holding hands. The little kid was hanging on and John looked absolutely "middle America."

Paul Thomas: I know [Laurie]. She's very sweet, caring, loving, and giving — very free with sex, very open, never a cross word for anybody, sexually adventurous, mischievous. Probably, she was a pretty good mate to him.

Certainly one factor that helped in John and Laurie's relationship was that they could relate to one another's experiences as adult performers. Laurie always understood that John's public persona belonged to his fans.

Laurie Holmes: People would come up all the time. I would fall back with my son and let him have his time with fans. One time, we were at the movies and a whole group of little midgets came up and said, "Can we get your autograph?"

John Holmes[q]: Never give a fan a bad time. If they come up in the middle of a business dinner, my investor's there, and ask me for my autograph, I think it's only polite that I take them back to their table and sign the autograph, which makes them feel good and then I get to meet the whole group. If I'm just dining by myself or with two or three friends, and somebody comes up and asks for an autograph, then I give them an autograph. I always date it — might be worth something to them some day.

Never give a fan a bad time, and never be shocked by anything anyone says — ever. Because some people walk up and say things that have never even crossed my mind to think of: "Will you touch my nipple?" "Will you sign my wife's titties?" "Will you sign my panties?" I think there are a lot of people who recognize me and have the good taste, because of the people they're with, not to come over and say, "Hi, I know who you are and I enjoy your work. Keep it up." That's a heavy regular, "Keep it up." "Keep a stiff upper lip." Never be shocked by anything anybody says.

Although Sharon and John remained married throughout circumstances that would have been deal breakers in most marriages, Sharon finally filed for divorce after a tax lien against her estranged husband threatened her own finances.

Sharon Holmes[h]: I didn't realize that [John] was back in L.A. and doing porn because again, this is not a part of my life. I had no idea what he was doing. He could have been a shoemaker for all I knew, but I didn't want to know. Then it came out that he had come back to L.A. after he was acquitted and went right back into the business.

Laurie Holmes: They were married for many years, but it wasn't actually until 1984 that they got their real divorce and at that time, he and I were already together. I remember him coming home and saying, "I have something to tell you, honey."

I said, "What?"

He said, "I've never told you before, but now that it's final, I can tell you that my divorce is final."

I'm like, "Okay, I didn't even know you were married!"

He goes, "Well, really, I haven't been."

Laurie said that John proposed marriage to her on two occasions. Once while dining at a favorite restaurant, he revealed his dream to her, "to make $1,000,000 and disappear," to a location that he never revealed. Although that dream never came true, the small family lived together quite peacefully in California.

Laurie Holmes: He loved to read. He used to say that books were so much better than movies. And I didn't like to read, so he would sit there and read to me and my son for hours. *Sybil* and all kinds of different things.

John was a movie buff. He would watch four or five videos a night that he would rent — well, at least three. *Dr. Zhivago* — he loved that and all sorts of movies — mystery movies, Humphrey Bogart — just all kinds of movies. He loved and really appreciated them because he wanted to be a real film producer. He really appreciated good acting and the art of putting a movie together. He loved the movie, *Terms of Endearment*. John also liked the theme from *Casablanca*, as well as the movie, of course.

John liked all kinds of music. He loved [the composer, Antonio] Vivaldi, "Four Seasons," but he also liked the Eagles, Led Zeppelin, Bread, Barry Manilow, Fleetwood Mac, etcetera. When John was on his death bed, I played and dedicated to him the song, "Everything I Own," by Bread. He loved "Landslide," by Fleetwood Mac and "Free Bird" by Lynyrd Skynyrd.

"Landslide," one of John's favorite songs, was written by Stevie Nicks the night before her father died in 1974. The song is about the fragile nature of life and relationships. Perhaps the song had a special, personal meaning for John, who had been abused as a child; Laurie speculated that he wanted to provide for children in all the ways in which he should have been cared for and loved.

Laurie Holmes: He loved to build things, he loved to work with tools, with wood, and he gardened. You name it. He didn't really draw. He was more of a builder, but he did love poetry and he loved to write really abstract poetry.

"Lady Blue" by John Holmes, dedicated to Laurie
'Tho it seems ten lifetimes, it has only been ten months.
And each day I spend less hours thinking about the things we've lost
It is only in the night when my thoughts are not my own.
When I can't control my feelings, when my heart begins to roam.
It's these hours that I'm sleeping, that my love returns to you.
Can't let go of these feelings.
Oh, how I love thee, Lady Blue.

Laurie Holmes: Fishing, camping, garage sale-ing, going to the movies, going to the beach, going to museums — loved fire crackers, amusement parks, as well as the great outdoors. John was fond of all God's creatures. We had cats, dogs and birds. He had a great respect for animal life and believed you shouldn't kill what you didn't eat.

He was a wonderful man and, gosh, he took me and my kid in and he taught us so much, but his laughter — I would have to say [I miss] his laughter [the most]. He could just make you laugh — anyone! And he was very compassionate. I used to get the cramps and he'd get hot, wet towels, lay them on my tummy, and run back and forth from the bathroom when they got cold. How many men would do that for you?

Coming to Terms

Laurie Holmes: In the very beginning, John seemed fearful of Eddie Nash. Then, one day, I received a phone call from an old friend, a photographer, who rented the entire second floor in Eddie Nash's building across the street from the Chinese Theater. My friend was calling me to give a message to John to call Eddie Nash. I was wary, but gave John the message. John and Eddie talked on the phone and came to some sort of understanding. After that, John no longer feared Eddie Nash.

In 1984, after Nash's release from prison, he had told friends that jail saved his life. He moved to a small condo in Tarzana and began taking college business courses at night.

Laurie Holmes: John never stopped fearing David Lind. Nobody knew where we lived, not even Amerson. Bill Amerson never knew where we lived after we moved out of his house. We were always very cautious, looking in the rearview mirror — always, because [John] always had that David Lind thing going; he was deathly afraid of

David Lind and other people. He didn't want them to get a hold of me and use me as a way to get him.

As Al Goldstein had suggested, John was as free as a man could be while constantly checking over his shoulder. Kenji said that he and Holmes would talk about fishing and Holmes would relate stories about his (non-existent) daughter. During their talks, John showed Kenji a belt buckle, which concealed a small knife blade that Holmes may have kept for personal protection.

David Lind notwithstanding, John's life was relatively stable and he kept a low profile, however, his reputation as a womanizer remained. In a 1985 interview, John responded to the question about his current girlfriend with the quip, "Which one?" It was a subtle indication that at 40, he still did not live monogamously. Never having been content to be a one-woman man, it was something that Laurie learned to accept as a consequence of loving John. She understood that his flings were relatively harmless because he always came back to her, and she also knew that he would have accepted it if she had wanted to be with other men, although she did not.

> *John Holmes*[q]: I like sexually oriented people — swingers and people who go to orgies because they want to go to orgies, not just because they're forced to go. I think they have the best of every part of the world. They do what everybody else does; they have occupations, families, homes, but also they have sexual freedom, so they're really kind of special.

> *Laurie Holmes*: I was alright with it; it didn't bother me. I didn't want to be with anybody else, so I wasn't. I'm not saying that he was an angel! He was a man, after all. I'm sure there were times that he wasn't faithful.

John was a stud for hire, which included servicing men on occasion, although Laurie never witnessed these incidents first-hand. When asked if John was still a dick for hire in the mid-'80s, she said that John didn't hire himself out in the same capacity then as he might have done in the old days; however, he had been servicing a wealthy, older woman in Beverly Hills for money.

> *Laurie Holmes*: That man absolutely loved women. John was a whore and that meant money for love. He didn't do that when he was with me, although he did have one woman on the side that he was playing games with. I never answered his phone, but I would sit there when he was on the phone with her. "Yes, Darling, I love you."
> I'd be sitting there, rolling my eyes back and he'd be smoking a joint, thinking, Is it over now?

John Holmes [i]: I liked to fool around with other women. For me to tell Misty one thing while I practiced another, would have been looking and feeling like a fool. I didn't believe in double standards. While I knew that Misty would never want to be with another man, she was the type to go after what she wasn't supposed to have, so had I told her she could be with only me, she probably would have found herself with someone else. It didn't bother me for her to be with other girls. In fact, I encouraged her because to me, that was different.

Although she was probably ignorant of the exact who's and where's, Laurie knew he never fooled around with Sharon or Dawn after they were an item. Unbeknownst to John, Dawn was in Thailand with her father, where she kept busy with work and furthered her education. And Sharon never spoke with him after they had parted ways following his 1982 prison release; however, she believed he did strange things to show her that he was still around.

Sharon Holmes [h]: John used to watch me. I didn't want contact with him and he never initiated contact. I think if I'd been startled, he would have tried to make things back to the way they were. I just pretended I didn't see it. He used to play this trick and drop paint splatters on freeway exits, places I shopped — this kind of thing — to let me know he was there.

Julia St. Vincent said that she was one of John's sexual conquests in 1983, but only for a couple of fleeting occasions.

Julia St. Vincent: I was married in 1982, and in 1983, I'd had an affair with him even though I was married. I guess you would say I was lost in my marriage and it wasn't working for personal reasons. I went back and saw him. I went to Bill's house and we did it in his room there. I slept with him and I slept with someone else in the same month or two.

I was trying to figure out what was wrong with my life and I was looking for comfort. I was looking to find something that I was not getting in my marriage. I thought, "What the hell?" I was depressed and I was fucked up, so I went back to familiar territory.

John was like, "Okay." I think I might have done it a couple of times, but it wasn't a long-lasting thing. I wasn't back with him.

In 1985, that's the last time I saw John. I was seven months pregnant with my son. It was December of that year or January — I had seen John. Seven months pregnant, and well, he came to my office. The girl comes up to my office because I was one of the honchos there at Image (who made the *Insatiable II* movie). She says, "[Julia] there's a guy here — John Holmes."

Everyone's heads were raised off the desk and they all looked. I said, "Tell him I'll be out in a minute." She left and I got my shit together and walked out there. I just looked at him and walked toward the door, and he followed me out the door. I'm like, "What the fuck are you doing?" I'm in a legitimate business office — we're not in a porn company anymore. It was in Hollywood.

We took a walk around the corner and John put his hand on my stomach, looked at me and goes, "Ohhhh," and he said to me, "I'd like to bang the shit out of you right here." He pointed into the bushes, like I'm going to get in there! This is 1985 and he's still trying to fuck me.

By some stretch of the imagination, maybe he could have construed the long implications, like a woman being pregnant for 14 months or something. He did know I was pregnant, the way he put his hand on me like he'd owned a part of it or something, almost like he was suggesting it's our thing to share, but it wasn't.

John was sterile, but he may have been excited for Julia because he always wanted to have children.

Laurie Holmes: John was sterile because he was ill as a young boy. He wasn't sensitive about his fertility. He didn't have a problem getting hard; he just didn't have any fish in the sea. He never had a problem with it.

> *"For Penguin Productions, if I don't have a lead role in it, then I try to always have a cameo. We've found that we'll push 2,000-5,000 more pieces of video tape if I happen to have a scene."*

JOHN HOLMES

11.

The Climax

King Penguin

A Lasting Impression

Bill Amerson: I wouldn't exploit him for a long time. He worked with other people and I was his best friend, and I would not put him in a movie. I didn't want to make any money off his dick. He never understood that. He would say, "Look, I'll star in a movie, I'll work for free, it'll make a lot of money."

I said, "No, I don't want to exploit you."

Sean Amerson [h]: I've lost count of how many sets I've been on with John. From the time I was really young, up until the time he finally passed away, I was on a lot of sets. It's just a blur. My memories of him have absolutely nothing to do with him in the adult business. I don't think of him that way. I can tell you the story about John in a dress in *Girls on Fire* and how funny he was trying to walk in those heels. I'm sure five people can sit here and tell the exact damn story. I was there, big deal. It wasn't really who he was, though. That was the John Holmes character that he was playing. He probably could have walked okay in those heels, but it was funnier if he tripped.

Ginger Lynn worked with John again for *Girls on Fire*, which was released in 1985. The big-budget feature was produced by Bill Amerson, under his alias, Bill Williams, for VCX and sported a well-balanced blend of young talent and veterans. In *Girls on Fire*, Charity (Kimberly Carson) is married to a mob man who is being investigated for fraud by two insurance agents (Jamie Gillis and Bobby Bullock). When Charity's husband, Tony Cardoza (Frank Holowell) catches the investigators with their pants down in the presence of his wife, he enlists his blundering sidekicks (Bill Amerson and John Holmes) to pursue them. Hilarity ensues when Holmes, Gillis and Bullock find themselves amongst lingerie models preparing for a fashion show. For the role, John Holmes (along with Gillis and Bullock) dons a dress, a long, curly-haired wig and stilettos, but he still manages to have a hot sex scene with Ginger Lynn, who is a featured model in the fashion show.

John Holmes [q]: I think it was about the biggest production we've ever done on film. We had well over $100,000, and we had almost everybody in the business who was worth having in it. A few people we wanted in it were in New York, so we couldn't have them, but we've got most of the biggies in it. The dialogue was good. Everybody who reviews it says, "Oh good, a story with sex instead of sex with a story!" Isn't that wonderful? Maybe I should be an actor even! I think it's good for the business.

Girls on Fire was one of the most aggressively promoted movies of that year, with billboards all over Los Angeles and New York City. Ron Jeremy was invited to interview the stars on the red carpet at its premiere on February 7, 1985, on Santa Monica Boulevard in Los Angeles. However, Vince Miranda, co-owner of the Pussycat theater chain, did not have the proper equipment for recording the interview, so Miranda improvised by tying the plug end of the microphone around a door knob, while the reporters with working microphones and equipment recorded the interview on tape.

Ron Jeremy [h]: A great experience with John is when they had the big opening of the Ginger Lynn/John Holmes movie called *Girls on Fire*. They had me as the guy doing interviews because I'd been doing interviews at the AFAA shows. Months after that AFAA show, I did such a good job of interviewing, they said take the mike, go out to John and interview him. Then all the other cameras, whatever news stations were there, doing this big promotion of the Pussycat Cinema — having a man put his footprints in their concrete like they do at Grauman's Chinese just a few blocks over there for the straight actors. Rumor had it he was going to dip his dick in the cement, but that was just a rumor.

So I interviewed him with a microphone. He had just come out of jail. I patted him on the back. All of a sudden I felt — he goes, "Yeah Ron, it's a gun."

"Okay, I'm sorry."

"I'm nervous. I don't trust anybody." He had an ordeal. He was afraid, he carried a gun, and so did Bill Amerson, who was looking after him. John goes, "Don't pick up my jacket to expose it."

"I'm not going to do that, you idiot!" So, I asked him, "What's it like being back at work again, being in this great movie with Ginger Lynn?"

Raven Touchstone: What happened at the premiere was funny because they made the announcement, "Come see what John's going to put in the cement." There were a ton of photographers and everybody, the whole gaggle of them, moved over to him.

Ron Jeremy [n]: "Is there anything else you want to put in there?" I teased him. "Come on! Dip it in! We all know you want to." He laughed and declined the penis dip, and we actually managed to have a good interview.

Raven Touchstone: They were all standing around and he got down, put his hands in the cement, and they were all going, "Boo!" What did they expect him to do? Whip it out and slap it into the cement? There were 40 photographers, booing him.

At the end of the interview, when all the other reporters with working microphones had left, Ron Jeremy told John the truth about his own microphone.

Ron Jeremy [h]: We're talking in the mike and John goes, "Ronnie, please man, are you getting all this in the microphone?"

I said, "John, let me tell you a secret. You're talking to a door right now. This microphone is attached to a door. They told me this would look good. Vince Miranda gave me a microphone and he attached the other end to a doorknob." I said, "This isn't going anywhere." So I interviewed John Holmes for a doorknob.

Penguin Productions

John Holmes [q]: We did work for VCX, but they let the production team off. I was the producer, line producer, production editor, and writer, so we started our own production company — my partner and I. He did *Girls on Fire*. He's been in the business for 20 years and he's really good to get along with. He's the best partner in the world, so we're starting our own production company called Penguin Productions and Brand X video will distribute [our films]. We're really involved in doing this. Personally, I've been writing scripts, directing and producing films.

The latter part of 1984 brought about a major change in John's life, when he and Amerson formulated Penguin Productions. As a partner in his own operation, John's dream was still to achieve financial stability and retire to a secret location, while his personal relationship with Laurie remained strong. She was also employed by Penguin and worked in the office as a full-time office manager.

Laurie Holmes: He was a partner. We had a company, Penguin. It was a 50-50 partnership and that's how the company began. We were making some really good films with John at the helm. Companies were giving us terms, not because of Bill Amerson, but because of John; not because he was the star, but because of his word, they would give us terms.

John Holmes [q]: After you make 2,200 films of anywhere from eight-millimeter to super-16 to 35 and all forms of video, you learn what people want and what they don't want. Just to get my name on the box is worth that much more money. If it's starring, we'll sell that many more. There are certain people in the business that if you know they're in the film, they'll sell enough product to get your money back and make a profit. Because we've started Penguin, I'm in every one of them.

It is evident from the films that Holmes enjoyed his new responsibilities as co-owner of Penguin Productions and (unlike during the late-'70s) John generally did not allow his recreational drug use to override his professionalism on the sets. His employees and costars respected his work ethic and appreciated that John respected them, too.

Sean Amerson [h]: The office was dark a lot. There was a desk off in the corner — a big desk with a couch underneath it. My dad's kind of a large man to begin with, so there's a big desk, a big guy at a big chair and you're sitting on a lower couch, in the dark, with a little light on.

Off to the side was another desk that was equally as high and that was John's desk. I would come in and out continually throughout the day, regardless if he was in a meeting. He'd just say, "I want you to come in and observe what's going to happen in this meeting. Just go sit in the corner somewhere." I'd just observe what was going on, and later, he'd ask me what it was I thought had happened.

John was never excluded from a conversation, whereas there were plenty of times when I had to get up and excuse myself, because the conversation was something I didn't need to be a part of or I wasn't needed to be in the room. I can't ever remember a time when Dad asked John to leave the room, regardless of what the conversation was about. I think that's because of the trust level the two of them had, so that speaks of what their working situation was.

Michael Glaser: I was one of the first people in the VHS video business. I put the first duplication systems in a lot of adult and mainstream companies. Eventually, I became a broker doing that and then on with adult companies doing what they call dubs — duplicating VHS.

I first met John at Penguin and then I saw him over at his partner's house in Sherman Oaks. To be honest, I don't remember if it was for business or fun. I was there with my editor friend when I was involved with mainstream and the adult business.

I was at his operation called Penguin Productions which was run by John and his partner. John was very friendly and he seemed like a nice — just a nice gentleman. He was always smiling and in a good mood, at least when I was around him. I found him to be pleasant even though he was in this particular type of business. I never really worked with him, but I never heard anything bad. John's partner was more the business-man and I believe, the director, and John was basically the talent.

Sean Amerson [h]: It was interesting — the dynamics — in terms of how the two of them, together, dealt with people. Dad would carry on the conversation, but John almost acted like a lieutenant. He would interject things. They had this sync going on and it was not good cop, bad cop, but it allowed my dad to be more of an asshole than he needed to be. John was able to bring levity into the situation and sort of lighten up the individual, at which point my dad had the ability to go for the jugular in a situation or make a better deal. The timing that the two of them had, from my perspective, was one you only get when you hang out with somebody all the time.

You always knew that they had some sort of private joke going on between the two of them when it came to people. For two really strong people to be that close, they each had their different ways about them. John was always bouncing around and telling a story, and my dad was more reserved and quiet, but he was a lot more intimidating of a figure. John was the opposite of the intimidation factor. The two of them worked really well because they were always in sync. They had the same goal — whatever it was they were going to do, they attacked it as a team. As far as their work ethic was concerned, I don't think I've ever seen my dad interact with anybody before or since in the same way, male or female.

Richard Olson: My relationship with John Holmes started when I was hired as a sales manager of Penguin Productions. When I was hired, John was working the phones, trying to push our product to distributors, as well as collect delinquent debts, which are quite common in this business. Needless to say, John was not a very good salesman. He was, however, a damn good bullshitter. He had the kind of personality that you just couldn't help liking.

John Holmes [q]: We've been relying on one thing. Most of the major studios will shoot ten times the films. They'll shoot Cowboys and Indians, they'll shoot monster movies, and they'll shoot detective films. We're kind of limited in this part of the industry because we shoot sex films. So now, we're putting storylines into them, action, and quality — we're hiring better writers and better technicians. We're getting up there with the majors.

There are a lot of union people out there who are really top notch photographers, sound technicians, recording technicians, still photographers, editors. Right now, we have a guy who does a lot of album covers for major rock groups, and he's our art-design-layout person. He isn't getting enough work to sustain his type of lifestyle by strictly making album covers or doing paperback book covers, so he also does our boxes, our one-sheets, our fliers, and our posters. He's strictly top notch and when the major studios hire him, he makes $3,000 a day. When we hire him, we get him for $300 a day.

A major motion picture, 70-millimeter, Technicolor cameraman can make up to $800 a day. We pay $350 a day. That's because they're unionized and when we list our cast and credits, we don't give their actual names. We'll make up names for them, because if the union found out that we were using unemployed cameramen who are in the union, they would get into a lot of trouble. It's part of the business. Everybody knows we're doing it. If you have 2,000 cameramen in Los Angeles County, only 90 of them are going to be working at any given time. The unions are actually a very good thing and they are a necessary function of making major motion pictures, but there's always this overflow. They get the bits and pieces and the scraps of meat that the studios throw out the backdoor, because their regular men are too busy to handle it. These guys can't make house and car payments and feed their families, so [Penguin] will give them work.

> *Buck Adams* [h]: I worked in everything they did there. I did so many movies for them. [John] was never cross with me. He never treated me bad and I never saw him treat anybody else bad. Sometimes, people would be really obnoxious with him. He'd just blow them off and go along his merry way. I adored the guy.

There was an ongoing mathematical joke between the two adult actors. John would say that since he was 14 and ½ inches and could appear in up to three scenes per day that translated to 43 and ½ inches of dick; and Buck would say that although he was nine inches, he could appear in six scenes per day and that translated into 54 inches of dick. According to Buck, John would laugh and then say that there was "no need to share that with other people."

John would joke when he was hanging out with the guys, but in truth, ever since the 1970s, when people began to recognize him and would ask to see it, he wanted to be respected as a human being. Buck Adams said that once, when someone had announced at an event, "The finest pieces of meat are with us tonight!" John was angry and shouted out.

On the other hand, if John felt that an appropriate situation presented itself, one of his lines was, "That's right, baby, I'm bisexual — you buy me, I'm sexual."

> *Buck Adams* [h]: Somebody always asks me, "What about the bad things?" To be honest with you, I can't remember a bad story. John and Bill — they're the guys who made Buck Adams a porno star.

Indeed, Buck Adam's services were requested several times by Penguin, including for the 1985 film, *Marina Vice*, Penguin's spin on the hit television show, "Miami Vice," which starred Don Johnson and Phillip Michael Thomas. Shot on location at Marina Del Rey, Patti Rhodes-Lincoln directed the film, in which Buck Adams and Billy Dee star as the renegade detectives staking out a drug lord named Johnny Costa. In his role as Costa, Holmes appeared to emulate a notorious person from his past.

Lottery Lust also stars Adams, as an accountant who watches his life take a turn for the worse when he wins $1,000,000 in the lottery. Women suddenly flock around him and he becomes suspicious as to whether or not the attention he receives from females and old friends is genuine. Adams shoulders the lion's share of the sex scenes, which are quick-paced, sweaty displays with some rather acrobatic moves. In *Lottery Lust*, John Holmes and Bunny Bleu hook up together when she requests John's assistance regarding a power outage in her home. With his signature slow-hand style, John is tender with teensy Bunny before the film concludes on a happy note.

> *Bunny Bleu*[h]: We first met on the movie I did called *Lottery Lust*. I found him to be a really nice gentleman. He was very intelligent, which really shocked me — he didn't look the type, but he was very intelligent. He knew a lot. He enjoyed cooking quite a bit and always wanted to be a gourmet chef. He used to tell me which wines to mix with which types of food.
>
> I was very nervous because I thought he was somebody. I didn't know what to think and especially, when I saw his thing. I was nervous the whole day. He was trying to relax me; he told me he'd be real nice and easy, which he was. He was one of the easiest guys I've ever worked with, especially being that size. After we started the scene, I got more relaxed. I really did enjoy working with him. He was very thoughtful of other people. He always had that gentle way about him, which is hard to find in a man.

> *Sheri St. Claire*[h]: I did a film called *Lust in America* with John Holmes, and if I can remember correctly, John Holmes showed up late. I was a nobody and he was a celebrity, so we're standing there waiting for him to show up. That was the first time that I'd ever met him. I was in awe; I was just amazed. I was finally looking at John Holmes.
>
> He was a really nice guy, and treated me right. He tried to make me feel secure and that I was a valued person. He tried to make things go easy on anybody he ever worked for. He was an awfully nice person to work with. As far as John personally, I never really got to talk to him in depth about his lifestyle and what he was into at that time. He was a very professional businessman and he expected you to be the same. I appreciated his being easy to work with. After all, he could have made it very difficult if he wanted to.

> *John Holmes*[q]: For every legitimate businessman who would have concern about his own business and financial reputation in this community, there are 20 that are not quite so honorable. They will stiff you if they can get away with it, which is why they started calling me John C. Holmes. The C stands for cash. Not really, but it's kind of a joke. I always request cash. If you insist on paying me by check, I'll take it and then when the check cashes and I have the money in my hand, you

get back a $70,000 camera or rolls of film stock that you can't put the film together without. When I get my money, you get your film.

Once, at Penguin, Kenji had noticed that some videos had come up missing from Penguin's warehouse and when he mentioned it to Amerson, he simply explained, "That's just John. John steals," which was interesting because if it were true in this case, John was literally taking from himself since he co-owned Penguin.

John Holmes[q]: Out of 2,270-something projects that I've been involved in, I've been ripped off 30 times before [I took] matters into [my] own hands and said, "Okay, this is bullshit. I get cash, or you won't get your product," but that was mostly in the beginning.

You really have to find a place where fans can mail letters with complaints or with compliments, or requests for autographed pictures. I have an address.

The Penguin office did provide fans with an address to which they could send letters, which was important to John, but he was often unable to personally reply to the resulting piles of fan mail.

Sean Amerson[h]: The bald poodle story is kind of a funny one. In high school, I had a full-time job doing odds and ends in the office. We would get fan letters from all over the world — different, stupid things. John had this stock reply: he'd take *Johnny Wadd* tear sheets and he'd sign them. Then it got the point where I'd sign all of John's tear sheets. Then, I would snip some hair from this poodle, and there was a little note that I'd write, something along the lines of "This was my pubic hair." Eventually, the whole backside of this poodle got to be blank. There just wasn't any fucking hair left, because John had so many fan letters I was snipping the dog all the time to get these little black hairs and I would sprinkle them inside the envelope, lick it and send it off. That's the bald poodle story.

There was actually a time when I opened up this letter and it looked like this X-ray. It was a circle. I didn't know exactly what it was. It was from this woman who had an X-ray of her uterus and sent a letter to John saying that she could fit everything inside of her. God, there were some nutty people out there!

Accolades

Bill Margold: Without the presence of John Holmes — without the personality, without the enigma of John Holmes — this industry would not have gained the sociological prominence that it did in the 1970s.

Jim Holliday [h]: The reason he became an icon, first and foremost, is the obvious anatomical factor. I'll never forget doing a lecture at the Institute for the Advanced Study of Human Sexuality in San Francisco, with a whole room of sexologists whose work I'd read in *Playboy* throughout the years and never figured I'd even meet them. After the lecture, I was in the little green room. Several of them came up and this world-famous guy, who shall go nameless said, "I enjoyed your talk. By the way, just how long do you think John Holmes really is?"

I was a little devastated. Here's this world famous sexologist and what he wants to know is the size of John Holmes' dick.

After two decades in the business, Holmes was inducted into the X-Rated Critic's Organization Hall of Fame in 1985, the year after it was founded by Bill Margold and Jim Holliday. The XRCO Hall of Fame was unique because it enabled writers and editors from the adult entertainment industry to partake in the annual voting process. Holmes' recognition for his unrivaled contribution to the adult industry was long overdue.

Jared Rutter: I was the first chairman of the XRCO and remained so until 2003. John Holmes was the first actor inducted into the XRCO Hall of Fame on February 14th, 1985 at Gazzari's on Sunset Strip, now the site of the Key Club.

Tony Lovett [h]: The very first XRCO awards — I just went up and introduced myself to John. He was a very nice person. I had seen him on some sets, but that was the only time I ever spoke with him.

Jared Rutter: That first night was a long one. The show was interrupted by a power blackout and delayed about two hours. Most of the guests, including Holmes, stuck around until the lights came back on. It was the video coverage of the event that caused the blackout. The big lights blew out the circuits in the ramshackle club. They were still shooting videos like films in the mid-'80s, a long time before small, handheld cameras. Fortunately, we were in the midst of a February heat wave and the warm weather allowed guests to mingle in the parking lot and street during those two long hours.

The late porn actress, Shauna Grant, who committed suicide at 20 years old in 1984, was also commemorated on the same evening of Holmes' induction into the XRCO Hall of Fame.

Bill Margold: On this particular night, we were also playing homage to Shauna Grant. Ron Jeremy was the emcee and all of a sudden, the transformers started blowing out. The power completely went out, with lightning shooting out of the transformer. Outside in the parking lot, all our enemies were saying, "Ha, ha. You're never going to do this," but Shauna was on our shoulder and it was going to happen. Within two hours, everything was fixed. We went back in and did the show.

When everyone went back inside Gazzari's club, Jim Holliday announced Holmes' induction with a short-but-passionate speech from his heart.

Jim Holliday[g]: Our first inductee into the Hall of Fame began in 1964. The man was the first to carry a continuing character into several films. The character was Johnny Wadd. In 1976, he showed the world — and something I'm tired of hearing, "He can't act." I'm tired of that! Look at *Eruption*, 1976! He's still at it, ladies and gentlemen. Our first inductee is The King, John Curtis Holmes!

Applause and cheers permeated the room when Holliday announced John's name. Holmes was dressed casually in cowboy boots, jeans, a short-sleeved white shirt and a brown vest. From the small, round table where he sat, John flashed a broad grin and butted out his cigarette in the ashtray in front of him. Slowly, he rose from his chair and began to stride toward the podium.

Along his path, he touched the hands of those reaching out to him. John's comrades were genuinely proud of their industry's hero and continued to clap and shout after he and his long legs took the stage. John kissed the blonde who handed him his award on the cheek, and for a few moments, The King stood before the crowd of his peers, obviously bashful, with flushed cheeks. Truly humbled, he offered a few words of thanks.

John Holmes[g]: I'd like to thank the people who stood by me when I was down and the people who helped me to get back on my feet.

Jared Rutter: The video [of the event] is no longer available. The company, AVC, is long gone and the title was pulled from circulation in 1986, during the Traci Lords underage scare. Traci was a presenter that night and even though she had no sex scenes on the tape, it was pulled anyway.

Historian Jim Holliday made the induction and Holmes seemed to be deeply moved by the honor. There's a photo of him on stage, holding the award with tears in his eyes. He seemed to be even more moved when John Leslie, who was the fifth actor inducted, paid tribute to him. Leslie, at the time, was the hottest male performer in the industry and when he praised Holmes as a role model who opened doors for all the actors who followed him, John leaped on stage and embraced him. I believe it was the most memorable moment of the evening.

John Leslie[h]: I always thought he was a real good person. I approached him as just a person. Everybody wants to be known as a human being, and he was a very dynamic person with a great sense of humor. I thought he was very bright, very sharp.

Bill Margold: Holliday did all the inductions, but saved John Leslie, who was the last of the five men to be inducted. John [Holmes] was the first. Leslie said, "I'm not going to accept this unless the man who is the most important of all of us comes back up here." Holmes, like the little boy he always was, sort of shrugged shyly, came across the stage and they hugged. I turned to Holliday and I said, "Now, we are history." John was ecstatic.

Sex, Lies & Videotape

In 1984, in connection with the Child Protection Act, President Ronald Reagan set up a commission to study pornography and stated that its goal would be to gather more accurate and acceptable results than those found during Lyndon B. Johnson's 1968 Presidential Commission on Pornography. Ultimately, the 1968 study had recommended sex education and advocated restriction of children's access to pornography, but recommended against restrictions for adults.

With renewed efforts to produce different conclusions, Reagan appointed far-right wing Edwin Meese to Attorney General. Meese fronted the Attorney General's Commission on Pornography, also known as The Meese Commission. Wasting a $2,000,000 budget to research the effects of sexually explicit materials, each successive round showed that pornography is not as damaging as congress wanted to prove it was — just like the 1968 studies had shown. Throughout their research, the commission pressured convenience stores to remove adult magazines from their store shelves and threatened freedom of speech. Finally, the results were published in July of 1986, with comments from the Surgeon General, C. Everett Koop, who truthfully reported that no evidence of harm from pornography could be found.

Bill Margold[m]: In fact, the Meese Commission proved very little. It did, however, provide me with my first great international platform where I had a chance to speak to the people for 45 minutes, where I gave my famous quote, "No one ever died from an overdose of pornography."

Throughout the revival of the anti-pornography commission, sales of VCRs and adult video tapes rose dramatically. In 1986, 13,000,000 VCRs were sold and 20 to 25 percent of video sales and rentals were X-rated. Clearly, people enjoyed the ability to watch dirty movies within the privacy of their own homes, but unfortunately, a lot of adult theaters closed down with the advent of video.

During this period of rapid growth and consumption of the adult video market, even John Holmes faced the debate about pornography.

John Holmes [q]: People denounce us publicly, but then they go home and look at nude magazines and watch their home movies. We are constantly denounced because of the social position we are in, but because we make billions of dollars a year, the U.S. Government is not about to abolish us.

God bless the A.C.L.U. [American Civil Liberties Union] because they're the only ones who really seem to give a damn. Hell, the A.C.L.U. has defended me at times and because of that, I approve. The mere fact that they are fighting for a government principle that was written by our ancestors — even if it's something people don't agree with — is a very honorable thing.

No one wants to step out of the boundary. No one wants to be the one who says, "Okay, I'll do it." But imagine if you came up with $1,000,000 cash, up front, and you hired a major film star to do an X-rated film. Do you know what it would gross? Do you know how many people would want to own that videotape — how many people would go to theaters to see it? If you gave her $1,000,000 upfront and then you gave her $5 a take, you'd sell 4,000,000 tickets, and from theatrical alone in the United States, she could make $20,000,000.

Let's pick up Jane Fonda or somebody that's one of the "Charlie's Angels" and get them to do an X-rated. It would be the last film she would make, but of course, with $40,000,000, who gives a shit?

Although not exactly a Charlie's Angel, Amber Lynn was one of porn's most admired stars during the start of the video age. She and Holmes appeared together in three major films, including a torrid Jacuzzi encounter in the 1985 film *Rubdown*. The bubbly scene is memorable due to their terrific on-screen chemistry and because of the way that John casually guides her through the process.

Amber Lynn also appeared with Holmes in *Dickman and Throbbin*, a humorous, tongue-in-cheek adaptation of the television series *Batman*, with dead-panned dialogue that would even make Adam West and Burt Ward proud. Sexorcists Dickman (Holmes) and Throbbin (Tom Byron) work into the night to extract the inner nymph from virginal maidens, like the pop-tart played by Amber Lynn.

She was also in a feature in which John and Ginger Lynn appeared together again — another 1985 high-budget project, *The Grafenberg Spot*. Its producers, The Mitchell Brothers, had success with the Golden Age film, *Behind the Green Door*. In *The Grafenberg Spot*, Leslie (Ginger Lynn) is dumped by her boyfriend (Harry Reems) because he is alarmed by her streaming ejaculations into his face during cunnilingus. In Ginger Lynn's scene with John Holmes, he plays a welder who becomes the focus of her sexual fantasy.

The scene was unique as Ginger recalls. Hanging from a bar, she was lowered onto John's penis. His face was covered by a welding mask. The petite actress had to align herself until he fit snugly inside of her, and she is still amazed that they were able to make it work, "I had a child, years later, 20 hours in labor and a C-section, and it was easier to go through that than it was to get that dick inside of me!"

Technical Difficulties

Occasionally as a middle-aged adult actor, Holmes was afflicted by an inability to achieve an erection, especially if he had a late night before having to film a sex scene.

> *Raven Touchstone*: I worked with him on *I Dream of Ginger*. That was the most interesting time with John because he could not get an erection. We were in this little house in the middle of summer under intense lighting, suffocating and he was trying so hard. He was pumping that thing — he's pumping it and he's pumping it, and his veins were sticking out. His hair was curling in the back from perspiration. Sweat was pouring down his face and he was trying and trying for hours! People were tiptoeing around. The cook was cooking in the kitchen, a little dog was running around and everybody was whispering — everybody was mouthing behind his back, "Don't disturb The King! He's trying to get it up!"
>
> He took two girls in the bathroom to fluff him — two beautiful girls, Bunny Bleu and Christy Canyon. He had these two girls in there, busting their jaws for an hour trying to get him hard. [He] came out, he apologized. He said, "I'm sorry guys, if I'd have known I was shooting today, I wouldn't have partied so hard last night."
>
> Well, why wouldn't he have known he was shooting? Of course he knew he was shooting! His big role in the movie was to get hard and enter Christy Canyon for one second. Of course those were the days before Viagra, so it was really a scene.

Most of the time, however, John was able to achieve an erection, occasionally to the astonishment of his female counterparts!

> *Ernie Roebuck*[h]: When video first started to come around, Sheri St. Claire was supposed to do a scene with John Holmes. She was giving him head and I was over by the video camera. Bill Amerson was directing.
>
> I was looking at the monitor. I could hear her voice over the headphones. She was in awe working with him in general. She wasn't sure if it would work at all. Over the headphones I heard, "I can't believe this! I keep sucking on it and he keeps getting bigger and bigger, and I have to move farther back and farther back!" We all busted up.

Sheri St. Claire [h]: He might have had a little bit of trouble at one point in the scene, but he was the kind of person that had that very professional attitude and if he had problems, he wouldn't just throw up his hands, walk away and say, "Forget it." He would put us all in it, and if it took a little longer, it took a bit longer. After all, we're working with John Holmes. You have to have a little bit of patience.

It did eventually work and we were able to get things done. The whole time he was a very professional person. He was a very good actor and he had that professional attitude that he carried through. He was all business; he didn't mess around. He knew his lines; he knew what he was doing, but I guess that comes with experience and years of being in the business. He knew what was expected of him and he came, ready to give his all, which he did.

Ernie Roebuck [h]: [Sheri St. Claire] wanted to do anal [with John in *Backdoor Romance*]. We were doing day exterior, out in somebody's backyard. I was in front of her, giving her moral support or something and she had a hold of my fingers when it started. All I know, is she had a hold of my fingers so hard, I thought she was going to break them! I was screaming louder than she was.

W-Pink TV

Ron Jeremy: On the set of *W-Pink TV Part One*, it was me, Harry Reems and John Holmes. He had a jacket that had his name on it, a robe. I met him before that scene, but *W-Pink* is where we shake hands. It shows where he had climax on his hand. He shakes my hand and I say, "I'm not paid enough for this." It's a very funny little bit, where he shakes my hand and I got Wadd's wad.

Miles Kidder directed the three legends in *W-Pink TV*, which was released in 1985. Holmes appears as himself on the scene of a television news set where the disgruntled newscasters have taken over the channel with displays that are as funny as they are sexy. In a game called "Beat the Cock," three blind-folded female contestants join the mystery guest (Holmes) in sexual shenanigans. Ali Moore was paired with John during the Beat the Cock segment, but she was actually underage at the time of filming, unbeknownst to Paradise Visuals when the feature was in production. Surprisingly, when the 20th Anniversary Edition of the film was released on DVD in 2005, this scene of hers with Holmes was left intact while others were cut.

Ron Jeremy: John would call me "Little Penis."

I'd say, "Good lord, John. I hit the damn cervix, for God's sake. Where are you gonna go? You and I both end up putting the whole thing in anyway, except you end up leaving more outside. What are you going to do, enter the cervix? For you, sex is a pap smear." He would call me "Little Dick," and I would call him, "Mr. Pap Smear."

The Legend Continued

Sheri St. Claire [h]: I think that with the way that he was built, he couldn't help but be put on a pedestal and there was this shrouded-in-mystery thing about John. People can't quite believe that he was so endowed. I think they were rather amazed about the whole thing and because of that, being put on a pedestal and being made a so-called celebrity, he really lived and breathed that.

Sean Amerson [h]: The John that was your friend would try his damnedest to convince you that Fords were actually made by Chevy. He would have a really good idea that they were made by Chevy and go into detail about it, "No, no, seriously, they started off in this little garage in Detroit," and go on and on about the intricacies of these two brothers who started building cars together, and they were in the same family and stole each other's blueprints. You knew he was full of shit, but it was a harmless story that he fabricated, obviously. At the same time, everybody in the room was immersed in the conversation and enjoying the hell out of it. It didn't hurt anybody.

Richard Olson: When it came to stories, he was hard to beat. With 20,000 women under his belt, I'm sure you can imagine what most of his stories were about. He used to show up at the office, a couple of times a week, just to hang out and bullshit. He didn't look any different than he did in any of the many loops and movies I had seen over the years. He was always laughing and having a good time.

Sean Amerson [h]: The first argument over wine I can ever remember was at the dinner table between my dad and John. I was amazed that either one of them even had a clue about wine, whatsoever. I didn't even think my dad drank and the next thing you know, they're screaming at each other across the table about this, that and the other thing.

I looked at my dad and said, "You don't drink wine."

Dad said, "But there was a point when I used to."

John, being one of the best storytellers I've ever seen in my entire life, could tell you exactly where the grapes were grown and what the name of the old woman who owned the property was. He had to go there — had it in the conversation, "This was made in the Valley. There are only four grapes that looked this color because it's actually not purple, but it's sort of a pale blue," and make you believe it.

I would sit there and watch them go back and forth. My dad knew he was full of shit, but it was the sheer enjoyment my dad got, goading John into coming up with these sort of stories.

Buck Adams[h]: The only other person that I ever heard that could spin a yarn as good as John was Bill Amerson and that's funny that they were sort of cronies. They'd get something between them. It was like watching popcorn pop; they'd be jumping around. They could tell the best stories.

Sean Amerson[h]: There was John Holmes, the King of Porn, and then there was the John that you got to see when you were with him as a friend, as I think Buck did, because I know they spent a lot of time together.

Before Christmas one year, Buck Adams and John Holmes worked together in San Francisco. With animated detail, Adams shared the story of an occasion when he and John came upon a guy in a ratty, old Santa Claus suit, ringing a bell beside a bucket to collect donations. Buck threw in $20 without a word, but John asked him, "Are you on drugs?"

The guy explained that he had lost his job a week and a half ago and was trying to collect enough money to buy Christmas presents for his children. John appeared dubious as he asked him questions about his kids and what gifts he would buy for them, but according to Buck, the father was able to keep his story straight enough to convince John of its validity. To the beggar's surprise, John reached in his bucket and gave Buck his $20 back before taking out his wad of cash and handing over $500 on the stipulation that he get off the street, out of his ridiculous costume immediately, and spend the cash on gifts for his two children.

With a huge smile on his face, the guy walked away, leaving his bell behind. Although Buck did not understand what his friend did next, John looked around before pocketing another bell for his collection.

Bill Amerson[h]: John did a lot of things that made him feel good. He would give money to poor people. I mean, we were in downtown Los Angeles and a derelict asked him for a cigarette. John went to the liquor store and bought a carton and gave it to him. That was just John. John had a heart as big as the world. John would do anything for anybody, except himself.

Buck Adams[h]: [While in San Francisco], we stopped at some bar in the gay section, and I was like, "Are you really sure you want to stop in here?"

He goes, "Oh sure, I love thrilling these guys." We walked in there and there were people, literally, falling off bar stools. They couldn't believe John Holmes was in this bar. We sat there and had a couple of drinks until we missed the flight. Every time I went somewhere with the guy, it was always some absolutely beyond-belief story. I tell people these stories. They just look at me, "Aw, bullshit," but it really was the truth.

In addition to contributing to his legend, John continued to enjoy interacting with his fans during his time off-screen and at conventions such as the Consumers Electronics Show held in Las Vegas. From 1978 and until 1994, the C.E.S. was held bi-annually, with a winter show in Las Vegas and a summer show in New York City.

Ron Jeremy: He was very, very personable. I didn't see any ego. He and I were both flown out to Las Vegas. It was then called the Consumer Electronics Show, then AVN separated it into its own show. He was being sent first by Caballero, known then as VCA, and I was being sent by Collector's Video and by Hal Freeman for Hollywood Video.

It was an honor to be among the first two guys flown in there. He was first, then me. It was always girls — I mean, who wants to see men? Back in those days, it was just me and John Holmes, then along came John Leslie and Jamie [Gillis] would go, and then Harry Reems when he did his comeback.

Richard Olson [P]: In 1985-6, the adult section of the C.E.S. was held at the Sahara Hotel. The night before the show was to start, I have to say I couldn't believe it when two of the stewardesses came up and started pampering John. They said they had seen some of his movies and if they only would have had more time, would have liked to go out on the town with him in Vegas. Talk about your fantasies!

Ron Jeremy: We had a lot of fun in those days. [I was] in *Playgirl* magazine. It said, "Here's Ron Jeremy, who is the star of the '80s." John Holmes saw this. I don't know if I showed it to him, but he came over to me and said, "What the hell's this?" It was very funny. "What the heck is this, 'Ron Jeremy, the star of the '80s?' Why am I even working? I'll just be your bitch. You'll support us both." So we did this pose where he was my bitch. He's playing like he's my girlfriend. That's a great photo.

We would write notes back and forth. Some of them were really cute, like when I'd sign someone's autograph, I'd say, "Are you going to go to John Holmes?"

"Yeah."

I'd write a note and say, "Hang this photo above John Holmes'," or "Tell John that the lab tests are in. You're diseased."

He'd say, "Tell Jeremy it's not just a cold sore," or "Your check is not in the mail." We'd end up writing notes, back and forth, on actual photographs we were giving people.

I'd say, "Let me see what he wrote."

He had done, "I want to make you sore," or something like that, then it was, "Loved last night, still sore?" I used to do a thing about "breast wishes," and drew a pair of boobs. I think he had even copied that a few times, that little bastard.

While John and Ron Jeremy enjoyed sharing the limelight, Ginger Lynn related to the fans because she had experienced similar feelings in his presence. One time, she asked John for his autograph. Happy to oblige, John wrote, "Warm wet kisses, wherever you want." Ginger still has the autographed picture.

Michael Glaser: [The AVN Award Shows] were held at the Tropicana Hotel, where I used to go a couple of times and was in the presence of John Holmes. Those couple of years, I would see him at various parties and things. At the VSDA [Video Software Dealers Association] show, which was connected to the Consumers Electronics Show in Las Vegas, they would have the adult area partitioned off and, being in the mainstream business, I had mainstream clients.

All of a sudden I heard John yell, "Michael Glaser! How are you doing?!" He'd pulled the curtain across and there was John Holmes. He was pretty tall, so you could see him from far away. I sort of pushed him away a little bit so there was no conflict or anything like that [with the mainstream client]. I think he knew that I was in both businesses at the time. That was when I was doing duplication for various companies.

John invited me to a party at the Tropicana hotel and I remember going up the elevator, and we went into this suite and opened the door. There were probably eight to ten hot tubs there, with girls filling up the inside of the hot tubs. It was like a buffet of whatever you wanted. That's the kind of thing that went on.

Bunny Bleu[h]: We went on tour in Texas, signing autographs in adult book stores. After we'd finish our signing, we'd go out to dinner, kick back in our room and talk. On this tour, there were women that would line up outside the bookstore, around the block, practically. Some women would actually piss their pants. I would go, "My God, what do you think about that?"

He said, "I don't know what to think. It's just amazing how women take me."

One lady actually came back for more autographs. She went home, changed, cleaned up and came back. That takes a lot of balls. After peeing my pants, I don't think I would come back and see him again.

He was one of the few that were really terrific in this industry and he made it a lot of fun. He was just an enjoyable person. I'm sure his fans miss the hell out of him, especially women.

Sharon Mitchell: The women loved him. Guys revered him. Guys always wanted to rub shoulders with him and have that kind of crony thing. He was very sweet to everyone and he would never have that star attitude. He loved the fans. He loved to talk to people; he was extremely personable. He called everyone Darling. He never would seem uncomfortable. He would always stay until [he greeted] the last person in line. He was very good with the fans.

In his free time at home with Laurie and her son, John continued to document his life in audiotapes that would later be used to create his autobiography, *Porn King*. At the time, he had hoped to title his autobiography, *The Monkey Tree* and include a poem that would explain the meaning of the title.

John Holmes [q]: The Tree of Life represents the roots of man. It's who we are, it's where we're from. The branches are the different directions a man can take, live, or exist. You can live in the lower branches, or you can live in the upper branches. The branch that I've decided to live on is neither high nor low, but it's the one branch that everybody looks at. When you're dead, those that you leave behind will put you in a part of that tree. Subconsciously, we place them somewhere in that tree. It represents what was, what is and what will be. It's eternal.

> *"One year after my first AIDS test, when I had tested negative, I decided to have another test. This time, the results were not as good."*

JOHN HOLMES

12.

Rehearsal for Retirement

End of an Era

Arrival of AIDS

Richard Pacheco[h]: Herpes was a disease, which in the wrong context could have serious consequences. For me, in 1979, with my wife
trying to get pregnant with our first child, we learned a birth with a
herpes-infected woman could be brain damaging to the baby. At that
point, I started saying to producers and directors alike, "I won't work
with anybody who has herpes." That was not greeted well by most
producers and directors, who didn't want to hear anything about what
you wanted.

Contracts with health-oriented demands would soon become more common,
as new sexual-health risks emerged. Although it is likely that AIDS was introduced to the United States in the 1970s, everyone was ignorant of its existence
for over a decade. Beginning in 1981, doctors noted an unexplained outbreak
of opportunistic infections among gay men on both coasts of the United States.
Americans became concerned about the risks of contagion, so the Centers for
Disease Control (CDC) began investigating the staggering amount of new cases
of Karposi's sarcoma and other opportunistic infections.

In July of that year, a doctor from the CDC assured the public that there
was no apparent risk to the non-homosexual population because at that time, no
one outside the gay male community showed signs of the mysterious virus, so
experts wondered if the use of drugs called Poppers had put the gay population
at risk. But by December of 1981, it became clear that intravenous drug users
were also at risk, after several were diagnosed with the rare pneumonia that had
been documented among the gay men.

By the middle of 1982, 452 cases had been reported among 23 states, but
there was still no name for the virus that many people were referring to as "gay
cancer." In July, the CDC introduced the acronym AIDS, which stands for
Acquired Immune Deficiency Syndrome and identified four risk factors: homosexuality, intravenous drug abuse, Haitian origin and hemophilia A. But even
the CDC still did not precisely understand the methods of transmission or the
cause of AIDS.

Some Americans were apathetic about AIDS because they believed that it
only affected gay men and drug users, but late that year, a 20-month-old baby
died from AIDS-related infections after receiving a blood transfusion. By 1983,
doctors were puzzled and panic set in among the public after non-drug using
women and children in America were diagnosed with AIDS and contributed to
the 3,000 known cases (and 1,000 AIDS-related deaths). As a result, the CDC
added a fifth risk group: female sexual partners of men with AIDS.

Richard Pacheco[h]: In 1984, on November 4th, I believe, there was a
headline in the *San Francisco Chronicle*: "Two men get AIDS by having
sex with women." It was the first announcement of the heterosexual

transmission of AIDS, and it was the end of the sexual revolution, because now, we were back to that notion that some serious bad could happen here. For the first of the AIDS epidemic, there was no talk of "safe sex." Nobody knew what was causing it. In Florida, they thought mosquitoes spread the disease, which was logical. There was panic.

Doctors recognized that HIV (human immunodeficiency virus) caused AIDS in 1984 and developed methods to test blood for HIV antibodies in 1985. By that time, the virus had been documented in all parts of the world. The actor, Rock Hudson, died from AIDS-related infections on October 3rd, 1985. Everyone worried about their risk of contracting HIV.

> *John Holmes*[i]: [Penguin] was producing some pretty good flicks; the company was definitely in full swing. There was only one real concern on everyone's mind: AIDS. The AIDS epidemic was starting to hit hard and although no one in the business had been reported as having it yet, we were all starting to get worried.

The CDC had done its best to educate people about the risk behaviors associated with HIV and stress that it was not meant to be interpreted as a means of discrimination, but the public's level of fear was illustrated when 13-year-old Ryan White, a hemophiliac boy who had gotten AIDS from an infected blood transfusion, was banned from his classes by school officials. The American President did little to assuage the fears of the public. Asked whether he would send his own children to public schools if there were a student with AIDS at the school, President Ronald Reagan answered, "It is true that some medical sources had said that this cannot be communicated in any way, other than the ones we already know and which would not involve a child being in the school. And yet, medicine has not come forth unequivocally and said, 'This we know for a fact, that it is safe.' And until they do, I think we just have to do the best we can with this problem. I can understand both sides of it."

> *Richard Pacheco*[h]: I thought the AIDS epidemic would last about six months or a year and I'd come back. I'm still waiting. I don't think I want to take off my clothes any more — and I don't think you'd want to see it if I did! In growing up through the '60s and '70s, the rose opened and I don't think anyone of us ever dreamed that rose would close again, but it did. Now, the thoughts are for the children. The cautionary flags we give to them are real and meaningful. We all pray they come up with a vaccine and a cure soon.

Pacheco was not alone in praying for a cure. Rhonda Jo Petty explained that she left the adult industry in 1986 because of growing concerns over AIDS. Two of her friends, including porn actress Lisa DeLeeuw, had died from AIDS complications and according to Petty, some people even intentionally overdosed to avoid contracting it. Many other adult performers joined Petty in retiring from their work or amending their sex practices.

Annette Haven[h]: I went to safe sex exclusively in January of '86. I had been asked by a girlfriend from my go-go days — she wasn't in the X-rated business, but she was hanging out with a male who was a needle freak. He hung out in shooting galleries and he had open, running sores on him. Problem! He was also bisexual, and so she asked me to do some research on AIDS and I did. Because of who I was within the context of the industry, I got through to all the main researchers at UCLA and UCSF. All I did was tell people who I was and *boom*, I got a red carpet because they wanted access to our industry through me. We were a good study group and so they gave me all kinds of information.

Negative

John Holmes[i]: Bill and I tried to organize an AIDS testing program within the business, along with some other people, including some screenwriters and still photographers. Our goal was to form an organization that would require AIDS test results on every actor — male or female — we hired for a film. Everyone at our company, including me, got tested that year and our results all came back negative.

Laurie Holmes: At that time, the test wasn't very good and it was expensive. Penguin was willing to pay for the cost of the test, but the actors felt it was an invasion of their privacy.

John Holmes[i]: There was the matter of expense. An AIDS test was very costly at that time. For a disease that posed such a threat to our society, you would think the cost could have been a little more reasonable early on. To be brutally honest, I believe the way they handled it then was rather primitive. For example, it wasn't necessary to give the lab your real name, so as to protect your identity in case your test came out HIV positive. I used the name "Karl Marx." Misty was "Betsy Ross," and Bill was "Jack Daniels." There was even talk about putting people with AIDS in the old Japanese internment camps to isolate them, much as lepers were at one time.

Bill Amerson: My ex-wife was an HIV nurse. I was with her and saw the patients. It became appalling to me, what was going on. I knew I was in an industry that could contribute to that and I didn't want to, so I talked to John and told him, "We're going to start doing the test," and he said, "Okay."

So we went and took the test, and we both came back negative. We got other people started on the crusade. *Rocky X* was a movie that I made. In there, we do a thing at the beginning of the movie, where Buck Adams and Jerry Butler both talk to people about being tested. We did a big promotion on that. Little by little, people started thinking it was okay.

In 1985, John Holmes and Bill Amerson were truly pioneers regarding their proactive attitudes towards AIDS tests, which were new that year. The ELISA (Enzyme-Linked Immunosorbent Assay) became available that year, when its use for blood donors became mandatory. The test works by detecting antibodies associated with HIV infections that can be detected within three weeks to six months after the initial exposure. The early tests probably required closer to six months to show antibodies, so a negative test result did not necessarily equate to negative HIV status, but today, negative results from an ELISA are very reliable.

> *John Holmes*[1]: Misty wasn't making films anymore, but I was. Since we were unsuccessful in organizing AIDS testing within the business, I was still at risk, which meant Misty was at risk as well. Every time I made love to her, we were taking a chance, but that was more on my mind than hers. As time went on, I found myself pulling away from her. We began to have stress all around us, within our private lives and within the company, brought on by our daily head games. All my life I had made money for other people and companies. Now it was time to capitalize on my own name within my own company. I felt it would be my last chance of getting a large sum of money and breaking away from the business, which would make things easier at home.

That winter, John requested permission to revisit his most famous character.

> *Bob Chinn*: I did see him once, after he got out of jail. He'd changed. He'd put on some weight. I said, "I hope things are working out for you, John."
> And then I moved to Hawaii with my family. I'd been there maybe for three years when I got a call from John. He told me he was dying — that he had colon cancer — but before he died, he wanted to make one last *Johnny Wadd* movie. I said I wasn't interested in making more *Johnny Wadd* movies. He said, "No," he wanted to make it himself; he would have someone else produce it.
> He asked my permission, so I said, "Sure, go ahead."

John reprised his role as the lady-killer detective for the final time in *The Return of Johnny Wadd*.

Raven Touchstone: I was cranking out maybe three scripts a month and [*The Return of Johnny Wadd*] was just another script. I watched a number of *Johnny Wadd* movies, in order to get a hit on his character. I just sat there and I wrote it. They told me how many sex scenes — they always do — what combinations they want and sometimes, they told me who they're going to use in different roles and I can write for those people because I know who they are. But it never seemed to me to be a big deal. It only became a big deal after he died, when it was the last *Johnny Wadd* movie ever made. As far as I was concerned at that time, there'd be ten more.

John Holmes[i]: Since the AIDS threat was hanging over my head, I somehow found it easier to play around. As terrible as it sounds, I really didn't care what happened to anyone else, but it would have killed me if I were to infect Misty with the virus. The Surgeon General was reporting that it takes four to 16 weeks for the HIV antibody to show up in the blood system, so even if we had been successful in our efforts to organize AIDS testing among all the actors, the reports would not have been up-to-the-minute accurate. As it turned out, it was a good thing that I wasn't giving all my attention to Misty.

Positive

John Holmes[i]: It was around February 1986, not that many months following my first AIDS test that I felt my health slipping away. The earliest sign was an infection in my ears. Although I had seen my doctor about the bleeding, he passed it off as having been in the artillery while in the Army. That made sense to me. But as the days passed, I started getting a rash, not just any rash, but one that would break out on the most visible, valuable part of my body. Every time I had sex. If I had sex long enough after breaking out with the rash, I would bleed. Maybe it was that opening to my blood system that caused me to catch the virus so easily. I guess I'll never know for sure.

In as little as two to four weeks after HIV infection occurs, some people may have symptoms, although many people are asymptomatic for as many as eight to ten years, or even more. Symptoms are flu-like: fever, swollen lymph nodes, as well as joint and muscle pain. These symptoms of acute HIV infection tend to last about two weeks and then the feeling subsides. Sometimes a pink or deep red, splotchy rash spreads over the body two to three days after the fever develops. The rash can also manifest as lesions with clear borders in the esophagus, around the anus and on the penis, as John had described the rash that he had thought could have caused him to be susceptible. A small red rash is visible on John's left thigh in the 1986 film, *Coming Holmes*, during the conclusion of the scene in which John engages in sex acts with Ami Rogers and Cheri Janvier. Its filming was between his first and second HIV tests.

Bob Vosse[h]: *Naughty Girls Like it Big* by Essex — that was the last one he did in this country. And he worked with Angel Kelly in that. He did a good job. His health — he looked good at the time, I must say. In fact, I complimented him when he was taking a shower. I said he had a suntan, which he usually didn't and he actually looked good. Although it's questionable at what point he knew he had AIDS, I don't think he did then, but it wasn't too long after that he discovered, and of course, he went down real fast.

Laurie Holmes: During that year, John was basically working exclusively for Penguin Productions. He made about six heterosexual films during that year — no gay films — and it was after that, he tested positive.

In the summer of 1986, John learned that he had been infected with HIV and made two movies in Italy after the diagnosis.

Bill Amerson: John and I took the second test, and the doctor called and said, "I need to see you in my office."
I said, "What's the matter?"
He said, "Well, there's good news and bad news." So, I took John up there. I was terrified.
We got to the doctor's office, we sat down and he said, "Okay, I don't know how to tell you this. There's a problem. Bill, you are okay."
I stared at John and I thought, "Thank God, I'm okay," being selfish. John turned white. The doctor told him he'd been exposed to HIV — that he was HIV positive.
John kept on walking around the room saying, "I'm gonna die, I'm gonna die."
The doctor said, "John, listen to me. You've got another 25 years to live. Stop drinking, stop doing drugs and start exercising. They're going to put you on some vitamins and you'll live 25 years. This doesn't mean you're going to die."
John still kept saying, "I'm gonna die."
We went home and my wife, who was an HIV nurse, explained to him also. John immediately smoked twice as much — he was smoking five packs a day, he doubled his drinking of JB Scotch and he started doing more drugs. He was convinced he was dying. The only thing that pisses me off, still to this day — he didn't have to die. He didn't have to! He pretty much killed himself.

John Holmes[i]: When I first got the devastating news, all I wanted to do was run away — from myself, from Misty and from the whole world. But I knew I would be able to keep the news hidden for only so long. So I stayed and waited for the other shoe to drop, and while I waited, I began doing more and more drugs. What did I care? If I was going to die and that was simply a matter of time, according to my doctor, then I wanted to do everything I could to make it as quick as possible. I smoked eight packs of Marlboros a day and drank a lot more scotch, too. Drinking helped to clear the phlegm from my throat, which made it easier to breathe and alcohol helped to take the edge off the drugs. Misty and Bill kept trying to give me vitamins, but I never took them. A wasted motion, I convinced myself. At that point, I certainly wasn't interested in prolonging the inevitable.

Laurie Holmes[o]: He didn't want anyone to know and he honestly was never going to work again. Not only that, he was never going to have sex again. I never had sex with him again after that. That was him. Of course, back then, they didn't have condoms that big, like they do now. Ignorance was so abundant about HIV and we were no different. I slept with him, I cuddled with him, I took care of him. I came home during my lunch breaks and gave him an enema, if that's what he needed. I loved him and supported him at the end as best as I could.

John Holmes[i]: Misty had to be tested again, too. While we weren't having a lot of sex during this period, we did get together just two weeks earlier. Her test came out negative, but we both knew it wouldn't be until after the second test, months later, that we would know for sure. That was a long couple of months for both of us. Thank God, her second test was negative. Thank God, I haven't infected the love of my life.

Working While HIV Positive

John Holmes[i]: It has been said that everyone has his or her time and destiny, and I can only believe that this was mine. "Why me?" Why was it, I wondered, that the most famous and successful porn star had to be the first person in the industry reported to have AIDS? There were many more actors and actresses doing much nastier things than I had been doing. It didn't make a whole lot of sense to me.

I probably shouldn't have admitted to anything because I soon started to feel better, well enough to even consider working again. During the fall of 1986, I was invited to Italy to star in three adult films. The deal was for three weeks at top dollar, first class all the way, all expenses paid. Ordinarily, I'd have been packed within the hour, but several tempting opportunities to work at home had also come along. I had one week to make up my mind.

It didn't take more than a few days to sort out the work offers. Whichever I chose, I knew that I would be taking the chance of giving AIDS to someone, either at home or in Italy. I thought long and hard about my decision. But I realized whichever I chose, I would be working mostly with my same circle of people from the San Fernando Valley. Maybe I wasn't thinking clearly, but I figured if they didn't get AIDS from me, it was likely they would get AIDS from someone else in the business. At that time, I had believed it was a local actress who had infected me. I wasn't out for revenge or to hurt anyone, I only wanted to work. Desperately.

Laurie Holmes: He was offered [to do the Italian films] more than once and he kept saying, "No." This is a man who was dying. Medical bills, prescriptions — all adding up. He finally said, "Yes," only because he found out that a lot of the stars that they were going to be used in Italy were being flown from the San Fernando Valley. What goes in front of the camera goes behind the camera and we thought everybody was going to die, so when he found out they were flying out of San Fernando — we were ignorant, definitely — we thought if they didn't get it from him, they would get it from somebody else.

Meanwhile, it was a lot of money. We had a lot of bills by that time and I was working, but he didn't want me to work at the office anymore. He said to me, "I don't want you going back there any more." He was really looking out for me, but none of that money that he made from Italy ever made it past his desk. I had to borrow money just to get him cremated. John got the money; it's just that it was not $1,000,000. The price offered to a porn star isn't the same as a real movie actor.

Bill Margold°: He was offered a deal he couldn't resist. If they could get John Holmes over there to make two movies, they would get worldwide distribution rights to have John appear in the movies.

Bill Amerson: He and I had a lot of words about [his working after he tested HIV-positive], but he did anyway. He was fucked up and dying. He was smoking a lot of cocaine and would take 50-100 Valium a day. His mind was so fucked up; he didn't know what he was doing.

John flew to Italy and made a pair of films with the San Fernando Valley actresses, Tracey Adams and Amber Lynn, in addition to the Italian actress, Cicciolina. Also known as Ilona Staller, she was a member of the Italian Parliament. Not surprisingly, Staller holds a liberal stance on many political issues, including famously offering her sexual services to the late Saddam Hussein and Osama bin Laden in exchange for peace in the Middle East.

> *Laurie Holmes*[o]: The only ones that knew [about John's positive HIV status] were myself, the partner, the partner's wife, and the doctor. The doctor didn't know John was going to work.

The production team of the Italian films, Paradise Visuals, were among those unaware of John's condition.

> *Ron Jeremy*[h]: He went to Europe to work with Cicciolina, Tracey Adams and Amber Lynn. I knew he fucked Cicciolina because she told me about it when I was in Italy years and years later, and that's kind of mean, that he knew he had it and went to work anyway.
> I asked Bill Amerson, and he said that they did know. I asked Bill, "Why didn't you stop him from going?"
> And he said, "I couldn't stop him."
> I said to Bill, "Why didn't you call Italy and warn them what's coming across the ocean?" That would have stopped them.

> *Dr. Sharon Mitchell*: I didn't have a problem with it, so long as he told everybody, but I don't think he did that. I remember him first telling people and then, it was like everybody forgot or something. I remember when the word was out that he was positive. I think it was well after he had worked with that second set of people, after he went to Italy and worked with Amber. I don't think he was forthcoming when he first got HIV.
> A lot of us knew that he was positive, so when I heard these people were working with him, I thought, "Well, they must know he's positive and they must have made their choice, and they must be doing an all-condom movie." That's what I thought. Now, whether he just buried that whole thing — these are actresses that have been around for a while. Cicciolina's no idiot. She had been around for a long time.

Today it is easy to criticize Holmes' decision to work while HIV positive and not to protect his sex partners by informing them of his status or using condoms. However, in an August 16, 1987, *Los Angeles Times* article Bill Amerson said, "I don't think anyone would tell anybody," if any performer had tested positive for AIDS. "It's not a good thing for the country that people are getting AIDS, but as far as the pornography[o] thing goes, maybe it is a good thing. To me, porno is getting worse. It's getting sleazier, more disgusting. I haven't shot a picture for six, eight months."

Prior to appearing with John in the Italian films, Amber Lynn had shared a jovial relationship with The King. She would tease him that he was a "freak of nature," but on the other hand, she was a star. Always one to have a quick retort, John said to her, "Yeah, you might be a star, but I'm a superstar."

Needless to say, she was hurt after John's death when she learned that he had exposed her and their costars to his virus, but after celebrating a decade of sobriety in 2008, she was able to forgive John. Amber Lynn came to the realization that "John wasn't evil; he was an addict," and because of her experiences with addiction, she understood that his rational thinking had been compromised by years of drug abuse. After conquering her own demons, she bears a message that drug addiction is a serious problem that can involve a good, decent person in activities in which he or she would normally not participate. Indeed, John is an illustration of just how harmful chemical abuse can be.

John Holmes[1]: The trip to Italy won out. Money certainly was a factor, but there was also the opportunity to see the hillsides of Italy one more time — a place I had always thought was so beautiful, had great food and wonderful people. The clincher, however, was the opportunity of working with someone new. Her name was Ilona Staller, but she was better known as "La Cicciolina," an Italian film star, she was also a member of the Italian Parliament. The movie was to be called *The Rise and Fall of the Roman Empress*.

Ron Jeremy: Cicciolina's fine. I worked with her since. She's been tested since then many times. She was annoyed that happened. He worked with a couple of girls overseas and every girl is fine.

It was pure luck that no one contracted HIV from John Holmes, but surprisingly, the risk for a woman to become infected from having sex with an HIV-positive man is one in 1,000. Blood transfusions and sharing needles rank as first and second highest threats of passing the virus, but it is important to note with risk-related statistics that infection can occur the first time in 1,000.

Whereas it appeared that John may not have had luck to his advantage with statistics, his costars in Italy did. Although he kept it secret that his partners took a roulette spin with their lives by having unprotected sex with him, John remained professional on the set and expected the same of the production crew.

John Holmes[1]: Filming in Europe can have its drawbacks. Some years earlier, while working in France, we had to shoot the entire production twice, once in English and again in French. As soon as a scene was finished in one language, we went back and did it again in another, line by line until we got it perfect. Then we went on to the next line. It was a bore and I hadn't the foggiest idea what I was saying in French.

The Italians were 50 times more professional. They had us work straight through in English only, and then dubbed the finished product. They also stayed sober on the set. The French crew was drunk by midmorning and literally dropped the cameras while film was rolling.

The pair of Italian films, *Carne bollente* (which translates to "*Hot Meat*") and *The Devil in Mr. Holmes*, were made approximately 20 years after Holmes' first appearance in hardcore movies and concluded one of the most extensive careers in the life of any adult film actor. Although both were filmed in 1986, the production company waited to release *The Devil in Mr. Holmes* until 1987. The decision to sit on the film proved to be a bankable one — Holmes' final release was a top rental for 1988, certainly due in part to the fact that Holmes passed away shortly after the film's release.

John Holmes[1]: It wasn't until the shoot was about over and I was about to leave Italy that I began to really fall apart. I knew that something was wrong almost immediately, but the signals kept growing stronger. It was then that I decided to stop in Ohio on the way back to California to see my mother, perhaps for the last time. It had been years since we had seen each other. We hadn't even talked since she called while I was locked up during the murder trial.

My mother is such a special lady. Through the years she even earned the name, "Mother Moses," because she knew things and felt things before they happened. I had hoped to surprise her by showing up as I did. I hadn't called, written, or anything to let her know I was coming. So, when I rang the doorbell and she asked, "Who is it?" I replied, "Jesse James." The joke was on me, when she opened the door, held out her arms and said, "I knew you were coming, Johnny Buck."

John's Declining Health

John Holmes[1]: The stopover in Ohio to see Mom was like an injection of miracle medicine for me, but the high of being in her company amid familiar old surroundings faded as the miles stretched between us on the return flight to L.A. It was difficult for me to get into the routine of office work and my time there became very limited. Gone were the 10-12 hour days, the old dawn-to-dark work schedule. At first, I would cut out just after lunch and make for home. Within about three months, I wasn't showing up for work at all. Screw it, I told myself. Why bother going in? I certainly wasn't accomplishing anything.

John never made another film and never had sex with anyone again, including his wife, Laurie.

Laurie Holmes: He really went downhill after that. It was a mental thing, too. He knew that he could never do that again. He just couldn't.

As HIV infection advances, people often experience nausea, vomiting, diarrhea, loss of appetite, and associated weight loss. Sometimes, there is also inflammation of the liver (hepatitis) or of the pancreas (pancreatitis). John, who was always a lean man, became noticeably gaunter.

Buck Adams[h]: I knew he was sick and I knew there was something more wrong with him. John was always a thin guy — he verged on emaciated, he was so thin — but you could tell there was something really wrong with John. I guess I had got a really wild look and Bill came over. Bill told me, "I'll let you know what's going on when we get out of here."

He called me into the office and he had John sitting there. John went through this story with me. He said, "I have ARC," or "They think I have ARC."

"What is that, like a super cold, or you have cancer? What is it?"

And he goes, "I don't know what it is. I don't pay any attention to that stuff." Then we started hearing about [the] AIDS virus.

John Holmes[i]: It was nearly two months after my life-changing talk with my doctor that I was reminded it was time for me to make my annual appearance at the VSDA [Video Software Dealers Association] show in Las Vegas. I felt absolutely horrible and I looked even worse. The banner above me read, "JOHN HOLMES, IN PERSON," but the letters should have spelled out, "JOHN HOLMES, THE WALKING CORPSE WHOSE HEART STILL BEATS!"

I sure didn't want to show up in that condition, but I had to be there, not only for the company, but to keep up appearances, such as they were. I was so self-conscious that I found myself repeatedly asking Misty if my makeup was all right. "You look fine," she'd say, adding a confident smile. Only then was I able to face the world and act as if everything was hunky dory.

In the past, I had looked forward to attending the four-day event. Now just the thought of being among all those people terrorized me. There were so many to greet, everyone I knew plus the thousands of fans who wanted autographs and pictures taken with me, some suggesting really wild, suggestive poses. I loved my fans, but they could be demanding. More than a few even groped me as we coupled together for "the shot of a lifetime." I smiled and laughed and made it seem like great fun, but it took its toll on me.

Dr. Sharon Mitchell[h]: I had known John was sick. You couldn't *not* know John was sick; you had to be in a state of complete denial. I remember the last time I had seen him was at a Consumer Electronics Show in Las Vegas and we talked. I had just started producing and directing a line for VidCo, and he was wishing me luck with that.

I saw him being present, signing autographs and I saw something very interesting at that time, which changed my view of fans ever since — when a fan looks at you, no matter how you look, you're still as big as life to them. I knew that he was sick because I could see his gaunt look, his skin, his weight, and his appearance. I believe that when the fans looked at him, they saw John Holmes, larger than life. I remember that impressed me because I saw he brought joy to these people.

Bill Margold: At the convention in '86 when I had Viper at my booth, all of a sudden, Amerson and The King show up. From a distance, The King was already looking a little bit haggard, but then, I shook his hand and it was the eeriest thing I'd ever gone through. I just sensed that there was something horribly wrong and I couldn't figure out what it was. I turned to Viper and said, "I've shaken the hand of a dead man." That's something that I'll never forget. I close my eyes now and see it. It's not fun.

Al Goldstein [h]: The last time I saw John, he was signing autographs at the Consumer Electronics Show, the porno division. I was really surprised the lines for his autograph were not as big as for Ronnie. I mean, it's amazing. Ron Jeremy had more fans. I guess, inch for inch, and pound for pound, Ronnie of course, is 350 pounds, but if you were to measure dick size and cock weight, Johnny Holmes should have had the larger amount of people cueing up for him.

But there was a sadness. Here was a man who had walked away from a murder trial and who was in the diminishing stages of his life. He knew about AIDS. He was dying.

Sasha Gabor [h]: I had met John Holmes, probably '85 or '86 — either the CES or the VSDA in Las Vegas. I was into drugs, too. I had coke in a little brown vial and I said, "Mine is better than yours. Mine is Pink Peruvian Flake." He said his is better than mine. I went to the bathroom, tried out his — it was a bomb. He tried out mine and said it was excellent, so basically, we both had good drugs. Sad story, but we were all into it in those days.

John Holmes [i]: Somehow, I made it through the convention only to fall into bed, back in Los Angeles for a long rest. My days of getting out of bed and going to work became fewer and fewer. I began having hemorrhoid problems, which resulted in my going to the hospital for surgery. The procedure, which was simple, didn't concern me. What did was keeping my identity secret. That wasn't always easy, since I was recognized almost every place I went. The confidentiality of medical records meant little if a nurse or an orderly, or someone in the hospital were to find out John Holmes was a patient.

Having everyone know that I'd had a hemorrhoids operation was no problem, only we decided instead to tell everyone that I had colon cancer and that I had to have six feet of my intestines cut out, but we knew that if someone started digging into my recent medical history, it wouldn't be too long before the real truth would be out all over Hollyworld.

As John's physical appearance worsened and he disappeared from films and videos, rumors circulated. John dealt with this the way he had done throughout his life: he told stories to hide the painful truth. He told people that he had colon cancer, which was believable because of his hemorrhoid surgery in October 1986.

John Holmes [i]: The surgery itself was successful, but by this time my immune system was so raped, I didn't know if I would ever heal. Sure, the hemorrhoids were gone, but the pain was worse than before. I probably should have left the bastards alone because word did get out about me. Now the press was banging at my door, wanting to know if it was true that I had cancer — or did I really have AIDS?

"AIDS?" I said, with a tone of disbelief that they were even asking me this question. "No way," was my reply. "I have cancer," I tried my best to convince them.

Laurie Holmes [h]: It was very hard. He was in a lot of pain. When he first found out that he had AIDS, his first thought was, "Well, better do something to protect the industry." He didn't want to bring anything down on the industry, so he came up with he had cancer. I'd sit there and I'd listen to him spin his tales: "They took out six feet of my intestine."

The minute he found out, his whole theory was, "I can't have sex any more." That was his life, whether it was on film or off film. He didn't want to live; he didn't have the desire. He started smoking more. He'd always taken a lot of Valiums because he was an insomniac, ever since the Laurel Canyon thing. So he started doing those more.

Then he had some problems with hemorrhoids and he had some surgery. The hospital still didn't know — at this time, they were not doing AIDS testing before surgeries. He didn't heal from that, so he was in pain constantly. Doctor kept prescribing more Halcion and Valiums. He took them several times a day. He really didn't know what was going on, at that point. He was losing it more and more.

Bill Amerson: No one knew because I came up with a story. I wouldn't let anyone know he had AIDS because I didn't want to tear apart the industry. I wanted him to have some dignity. I said that he had anal cancer or something like that. A lot of people, to this day believe it. Bill Margold believes that John didn't have AIDS.

Sean Amerson[h]: The first thing I can remember hearing about was Dad telling me John had colon cancer. They thought he had cancer. They weren't exactly sure what he had. They were really concerned about telling my sisters because they were concerned they would react poorly to the whole thing, so he didn't want to say anything.

Dr. Sharon Mitchell: I thought that everybody knew that the colon cancer was a result of HIV.

Ron Jeremy[h]: I didn't know he had the virus. I had suspected it. I understand Bill [Amerson] had known all along. My friend, Sasha Gabor, had an inkling as well. We knew he had intestinal cancer. Now, I know that's one of the opportunistic viruses that you get if you are HIV positive.

Sean Amerson[h]: When it came out he had AIDS, I was around him all the time because he was always around the office. AIDS was still that mystery disease epidemic that was only a step shy of Ebola. We didn't know! I remember John would drink out of a cup and put the cup down, and I would not want to go anywhere near the cup for fear that I might catch it. I think that I saw a lot of people pull back, in a lot of respects, because nobody knew what was going on about it and we didn't want to die.

He was just getting more and more out to lunch. You could see he was losing grasp of a lot of things. His stories got a lot wilder. There was a phase where it seemed like he was going to come back and he was going to be okay, before he found AIDS. After the trial and after he got out of jail, it seemed like he cleaned himself up and he had shaved, was dressing up again. He seemed okay. Then, when the AIDS thing happened, he went significantly downhill, quickly. He just really didn't care about a lot of things.

At the same time, this is when my dad started to really go downhill. I think he had met a young girl and the two of them started seeing each other. He started going down a path that took him a long time to get back from. I don't know if they were doing it together or not, but I know that both of them were doing a lot of drugs. His life really started to fall apart also. The two of them, all of a sudden, weren't together any more. I think he knew that he was losing his friend and he was really having a problem dealing with that. I could be completely wrong and this could be completely out of left field. In retrospect, I think part of the decline of my dad really was when John started to get sick and go downhill.

Denise Amerson[h]: For about nine months, John kept telling me he had the flu. He didn't want me to know he had AIDS or cancer of the colon. I didn't know what was going on. Every time I saw him, he was sicker and sicker, and he would just joke around, and say he had a bad virus — that he had the flu. I remember one time, he came over to visit at my dad's and he came over with a ski mask over his head. I said, "What are you going to do? Rob a bank or something?"

He said, "No, my head's cold," and it was in the middle of summer. I took that thing off of him and he had these spots all over his head, and all his hair was gone.

I said, "What the hell is wrong with you?" and he said that he just had the flu and that he'd be okay.

Then I was working at the company, Penguin Productions, and he wasn't coming to work anymore. I would call him and ask him when he would be in because I needed to go over some things with him and he'd just say, "I'm calling in sick. I've got the flu. I've got a cold."

Whatever. I went to his apartment; I was pissed off. I hadn't seen him in a couple of weeks and I wanted to know what was going on. I realized that he was really, really sick. He got really angry with me for coming over because he didn't want me to see him like that. He was getting very, very skinny and very distorted, but making jokes and trying to protect me and my feelings. "Everything's fine." But obviously, I knew that things weren't fine.

The Wedding

On the 24th of January in 1987, John and Laurie were married at the Little Chapel of Flowers in Las Vegas, Nevada. According to Laurie, John had proposed to her on more than one occasion at The Marmalade, a restaurant they frequented in the San Fernando Valley.

Denise Amerson[h]: He called me on the phone and he said, "Do you know anything about any wedding that I've had? Recently? Did I get married?"

I said, "What do you mean?"

He said, "I just found this picture on my coffee table. I'm in it and Laurie's in it, and she said it was our wedding picture. I need you to help me out with that — I don't remember."

He was joking and I said, "Yeah, you had a big, huge wedding. Don't you remember?" I was laughing.

I'm sure he loved her in a lot of ways. But did he want to marry her? I don't think so. From my point of view it's what kind of relationship she had with him, but not if you asked him. He would get angry if I said, "your girlfriend," "your wife," — anything. She was definitely in his life, but I don't think as a life partner.

He was just joking about it and I said, "I don't know."

She got on the phone and told me they were married now and that at the office (because she worked at Penguin, also), I can refer to her now as John's wife, instead of the bookkeeper or the secretary.

I thought it was all a joke, then I asked my dad, and he said, "Yeah." He said that he'd gotten the same phone call that John was confused about whether he'd gotten married. I don't think that there was a wedding there. I certainly never attended any wedding and if John had a wedding, I think that we would have been in it. There is a wedding picture, though. He was pretty sick at the time.

Sean Amerson: She latched onto him and he never seemed affectionate to her ever, that I remember. She was more of a pet than a significant other, and I was there everyday from the beginning. It wasn't until the end when he was very sick did their relationship seem to take a turn where she was more a mother hen and he was too mentally deteriorated to care.

Because of John's anguish, he was consistently under the influence of sedatives and pain medication. John overused his medication, but because of its potency, even the prescribed dosage could have caused him to forget their marriage in Las Vegas.

Bill Amerson: He and I talked about it before. I said, "Look, what you might do," because Laurie had a baby, I said, "if you want to leave him with something, marry her, get an insurance policy for $100,000, and that will take care of the baby."

He called me and said, "I think I got married."

John didn't know he was married. He called me from Vegas and he said, "I think I got married." If you ever see a wedding picture of him, look at it. He took about 50 Valium. Were he sober, he wouldn't have gotten married.

Despite the Amerson family's doubts about John's intent to marry Laurie, the couple seemed to have shared a loving relationship and evidently, she did not profit from the marriage as he had no assets. Considering the illustrations that Laurie has shared about John, in which he obviously cared for her and her young son, it is plausible that John would have wanted to continue to provide for his wife and stepson after his death.

Ron Jeremy: I worked with her before he did and she was all excited to work with him. She worked with John Holmes, and then they had a relationship. I'm not going to say he was madly in love with her, but there were some feelings there. When people have a war with each other, they say things like, "Oh, he didn't care about her, he didn't care about them." We all want to speak for the dead man, but only he can do that.

Slipping Away

Someone had told Don Fernando that John was dying and he wanted a chance to say goodbye to John, who had touched his heart while working together in films such as *The Erotic Adventures of Candy* and *California Gigolo*. Fernando talked to him while John laid in bed, dying, feeling lonely and discarded by the industry he had played such an influential role in making successful.

Don Fernando: He always put up a smokescreen. He absolutely denied that he had HIV. He made up a very elaborate story that he had colon cancer. It was typical John because he probably did have cancer of the colon. That's one of the ramifications of HIV, which many people get just before the end is near. People who die of HIV have a whole score of problems and I'm sure that carcinoma is one of them.

He said, "The L.A.P.D. has it out for me. They've always had it out for me." He was in denial that he had HIV, so he was saying that people were spreading around that he had HIV and the L.A.P.D. was behind spreading the rumor that he had HIV. Maybe he was embarrassed. He said, "Everyone has abandoned me." He said that everybody had abandoned him except for Bill and Laurie.

Bob Vosse[h]: He was in L.A., and he called me in San Francisco. I think we both started crying. I guess in spite of all the bad things I've said — because he's had good and bad — I really loved the guy.

Jamie Gillis: When he was dying, I tried to make some gesture. I called Bill Amerson to see how he was. I remember him, specifically, telling me that John believed in some kind of reincarnation or an after-life and that he was okay. He was dying, but he was okay with that.

Another time, I think we were sitting around at Bill Margold's place with a bunch of guys and saying, "You know, John's dying. We should go say hello."

I couldn't get anybody interested in doing that.

Don Fernando[h]: He said, "I have to be optimistic in spite of my cancer."

I said, "Are you in a lot of pain?"

He said, "Yeah, I'm in a lot of pain, but the worst pain is that nobody cares about me anymore." That really made me sad. That hurt me because I always saw him as The King. He died four weeks later.

Sasha Gabor[h]: He was rumored to be HIV-positive. My company asked me, could I get a hold of him, get an interview and take pictures, preferably with him and me in the picture? I didn't know where John Holmes was, so I talked to Bill Amerson at VCX. He put me in touch with Misty Dawn.

Misty Dawn, that little sweetheart. I had no idea that she was married to John Holmes. I could never believe that little, 80-pound girl could ever take John Holmes, but she did!

I talked to Misty Dawn. I said, "Misty, help me out. I'd really like to do this interview. Whatever he says, that's going to be it. I'm not distorting it, I'm not doing anything with it against John. It's going to be a pro-John interview."

She gave me his phone number and I called up. "John, can I bring some goodies over to you?"

"No, no, no, Sasha, no more. I'm down."

"John, let me come up and see you."

"No, no."

"We're old buddies, let me do this interview." He gave me the address. I went up to his apartment. I was absolutely not prepared for the sight that met me. John Holmes looked ghastly. He looked, maybe, worse than Rock Hudson.

After initially learning he had HIV, John did relapse into using cocaine again, but he found that narcotics worsened his condition and at this point, John claimed to have limited himself to those prescribed by his doctor. That is why he had refused Gabor's offer to bring over some goodies. One of John's prescribed drugs was Halcion, a sedative that is generally used for insomnia. Once while under its influence, John was physically abusive to Laurie. This isolated incident, according to Laurie, could be blamed on the chemicals in his brain. She forgave him because she recognized that this was not the same John with whom she had fallen in love.

Laurie Holmes: It's very, very strong; stronger than morphine. He was in a lot of pain those last couple of years and it became a never-ending supply of Halcion. I took a half of one of these little pills once, when I had the cramps, and it knocked me out cold for 38 hours.

He would take these handfuls at a time, several times a day and during that period, yes, he was abusive, but it wasn't him. This is the medication that you can go and kill your own lover and not even remember it. That's why they stopped giving it to people, because it was stronger than Oxycontin. That was the only incident. I can't blame it on him. It was Bill Amerson's doctor, who was prescribing [Halcion] to him. He was in a lot of pain. He had a hemorrhoid surgery that didn't heal because of his HIV. Can you imagine having a hemorrhoid surgery that didn't heal?!

John Holmes[i]: Misty and I have had to move again. Without any notice, the rent on our apartment was raised to nearly $1,000 a month. Impossible. Now the landlord in our new place is giving us hell about our animals. To make matters worse, my salary has been cut off at the company. My partner has told Misty that I am out; the company is his alone. What is he doing with all the incoming revenue? He is not paying me and people are calling me at home because he has not been paying our account-payables, some of whom had given us credit based only on my word.

One drug, Halcion, keeps me out of it most of the time. When it doesn't seem to be taking effect or working quickly enough, I increase the dosage without the doctor's knowledge or approval. My temper flares too much at times, so I tend to take an extra dose before Misty comes home. I want to be asleep when she arrives that way I don't have to hear about Bill and his backstabbing. That way, I won't lose my temper. Now, I feel my life is all but over. I lie in bed. I watch television. I wait for Misty to come home from work. I am in and out of sleep. I am getting more confused with each passing day. The days go by, and yet, time has no meaning for me. Lying in bed, I worry about money and mounting doctor's bills, about the very real possibility of having to find a less expensive place to live. I worry about Misty. She comes home every night with a migraine headache. She tries to tell me the scoop for the day, but there are times when I can't keep up with her in my mind. I feel I am losing it.

In advanced stages of HIV/AIDS, symptoms worsen from headaches behind the eyes, to pain from normal eye movements due to swelling of the neurological tissues, including the protective layer around the brain (meningitis). Peripheral nerves in the appendages can become inflamed to the extent of paralysis. A person can also have swelling of their brain (encephalitis), which John experienced.

Sasha Gabor[h]: He blanked out, several times. He went away in memories several times, but he would come back and talk coherently. Towards the end of the interview, I said, "John, I really need a picture of you."

At that point, he became very vehement about it. He said, "No, I don't want the world to remember me like this. I want the world to remember John Holmes. I don't want them to see me like Rock Hudson."

"John, I really need to document it. I need a picture with you and me, just one quick snapshot."

"Absolutely not."

I had to respect his wishes. The man was dying. I couldn't just grab the camera and do a quick shot of him. That wouldn't have been fair to my buddy. He was my buddy, not very extensively, but we were on good terms.

Laurie Holmes: It was hard for [my son and me] because he was just a little boy and John was in a lot of pain, but John was a very good father, a very good family man and a real homebody for the last five years of his life.

The Veteran's Hospital on Sepulveda Boulevard

Sean Amerson[h]: When John started getting really sick, they put him in the hospital and the next thing I heard, there were problems with finances in the company. I don't know what happened with that. I don't necessarily know if it was important to my dad, either. I just know, all of a sudden, everybody was broke and John was dying, and my dad was wasted. Everything in that world was just completely blown up. It was gone.

Laurie Holmes[o]: When John got sick, Bill Amerson incorporated the company and incorporated him right out of it.

Bill Amerson: I had a deal with John, if he would work and do what he was supposed to do and get off drugs, I would give him 40 percent of Penguin. That never happened; he never got off drugs. He would come in at noon and go home at one. Shit like that.

John was in really poor shape. His legs and feet would swell, his ears would bleed, and he had lung infections.

Laurie Holmes[i]: John was in the V.A. Hospital for the last five months of his life. His basement room had only one window, up toward the ceiling, so it provided no view and little outside light. It was a large room, painted a dull, powder blue, almost a Wedgewood color. Nice for dishes, but not a hospital room! His bed was pushed against the far wall, giving the room a stark, empty feeling. I never knew what state of mind John would be in when I visited. Just being in the "Blue Room" was enough to depress anyone.

One thing I could always say about John, even in his darkest days, was that he had class and charisma. As poorly as he felt and looked, he treated the nurses like ladies, even the ones who were not always on time with his painkilling morphine. Despite his dreadful condition, he had those women wrapped around his fingers. It appeared they liked John a lot. He might have been half-dead, but he never lacked charm, right up to his dying day.

John Holmes[1]: Mother arrived yesterday. She is with me now and it is wonderful to have her here. I checked myself into the Veteran's hospital a couple of days ago. At least now, my pain is lessened from the morphine shots. The Veteran's Administration has offered to pay for AZT medication, but I have declined. Why delay the inevitable? Mother and Misty are getting along great together. There was a time when I wondered if she would like Misty. Not anymore. How could she not like her?

Although Laurie and John's mother, Mary Bowman, had not met before, Laurie had already been in contact with members of John's family. John wanted everyone he loved to have a token to remember the happy times. "We sent off a lot of the stuff I liked, but I understood. He sent our dog, Charlie, to his sister," Laurie explained.

Laurie Holmes: We had a very good relationship. She stayed with me for a couple of months, but it was very hard raising a little child, going to work 40 hours a week and going to the hospital every night. She spent a lot of time with him in the end. He said she was wonderful and I have nothing ill to speak against her. She's angry, just like I am, just like a lot of people who cared about John are angry at this point, and she's not going to open up because she just wants to remember her little boy.

At that time, Mary was concerned for John and David to make amends for undisclosed things in their past, according to Laurie. "John's family did love him. They come from a religious background in the Midwest — a rural background — so you can imagine how his family might have felt and still do feel."

John Holmes[1]: Misty has been asking Mother about my childhood and Mother is full of stories, some I have never heard before. Maybe I have, but very little makes sense now. Everything seems so long ago and so far away, almost as if she's speaking about someone else. I was a special child, Mother says. I had a gift of making everyone laugh, even in the worst of times. Her voice is soft, warm, and loving.

"I have never regretted bringing John into this world," Mother confesses, "even though the circumstances in which John was born were difficult. That's why I could never blame him for the way he lived his life. I could never do that."

Hearing Mother say those words has brought me a calmness I haven't felt for many years. It's wonderful to know that she has come to accept things that before, she couldn't even understand. She may have never approved and that's fine. Her acceptance is all I need.

At the Veteran's Hospital, John did not have many visitors. John wished to be remembered for his happier, healthier days — as Sasha Gabor recalled, he did not want people to see him "like Rock Hudson," so Laurie supported John's decision to prohibit visitors.

> *Laurie Holmes*: At John's request, I made it so he could receive no other visitors, other than the cops, which I could not stop. John was done with it all, in his mind, and didn't wish to express anything at that time.

> *Denise Amerson*[h]: Before he died, it had probably been about two or three months since the last time I had seen him. I wasn't allowed to see him. [Laurie] apparently decided that John wasn't allowed visitors and that our family wasn't to be involved in his life. Since she had his last name, she had the right to do that. I didn't understand what was going on. I just knew that my godfather was really sick. I missed him and I wanted to see him, and for some reason, I couldn't.
> I stayed at the hospital every day for about two weeks outside, trying to get in to see him. He would call the office and ask why we weren't there to see him. He was sick and he didn't feel good, and he was lonely. He wanted us to bring him some things to cheer him up and make him feel better. He'd call and ask if I would bring him Jack-in-the-Box or a teddy bear. Who knows what was going on in his head, but he kept waiting for us to come and see him, and I guess he didn't know that we couldn't.

> *Sean Amerson*: I can hear John's voice, how scared he was, how abandoned he felt because we weren't there with him. His phone call, begging us to come see him has haunted both Denise and I, and is an unresolved issue. It's truly one of my life's regrets that I could not be there for him when he needed me.

> *Bill Amerson*: I don't remember [John's hospital stay]. That's kind of a blur to me. I didn't really want to know about it. Before he died, he called me. He said, "Bring me two packs of cigarettes and some candy bars."

> *John Holmes*[i]: Worry seems to occupy most of my time these days. Worry, television and sleep. But even as I stare at the television screen in a half-stupor, my mind turns to dark thoughts. Misty tells me a

"John Holmes Relief Fund" has been started to help with the medical bills and some money has come in from long-time friends and business associates.

If my story ever gets published, I want these people to know how truly grateful I am to them. You know who you are. The funds have helped a great deal; my medication is over $80 a week. That amount sounds really piddly now compared to what I used to spend on illegal drugs, but with me not working, it's a real concern.

Laurie Holmes[h]: Not many [donated] though. He was very hurt. He felt like people had turned their backs on him. His whole attitude was, "God, I've made all this money and they won't return my phone calls." He was really hurt by it.

John Holmes[i]: Bill won't talk to me, but I have heard from people close to me, that he has told them I really don't need the money. The cash from the "Relief Fund," he is saying, is going to support my drug habit. He's right in a way. The money is buying drugs, but not the drugs of old. To take those would only intensify my pain. The drugs I take now are received legally, from my doctor.

The John Holmes Relief Fund received donations from about ten people in the industry, according to Laurie Holmes. Donors included Gloria Leonard, Annie Sprinkle, Suze Randall, Ron Vogel, Caballero, and Jon Martin.

Jon Martin[h]: I knew that he was not doing very well. A couple of people called and asked if I could send down a few bucks to John. Right there, I think it was pretty close to the end. A group of people and I sent him about $200 or so to see him along. At that point, he might have been homeless. I don't know what he had; it doesn't make a damn bit of difference. The point is, he's not here and the thing is, that from everything I have heard, the last few months of his life were not quality years. Maybe he's a little happier now.

Alan Colberg: John did have AIDS at the end. I think he called me about two weeks before he died. He wanted to talk to [my wife] and me to say goodbye and to let me know that he didn't want us to cry for him, which we weren't going to anyway. He said that he had colon cancer, and I accepted that as being what his malady was at that time.

John Holmes[j]: The thought of suicide has crossed my faltering mind more than once. Suicide is tempting — not to be free of agony, but for money. I've done just about everything else for pay, why not suicide? If I decide to end it all, my life insurance will still be honored and Misty will collect $100,000, enough to set her up for a few years, at least. How I would love to make her life easier and how easy it would be for me to do just that. Only one thing stops me: my mother. I know it would kill her for me to take the cowardly way out, despite the absence of all hope. She wouldn't see it that way, but that is how I look at it.

Laurie Holmes [h]: I had tried to keep John's whereabouts secret. That was possible for a while, but once word got out, the phone began ringing. John wasn't up to talking with anyone about anything and I really didn't want people to see him in such poor condition. There were a few exceptions, of course, his family and a few close friends, but I had to refuse anyone else and instructed the hospital to admit no one without my approval. One day, however, I got a call from a nurse at the V.A. to tip me off that the cops were on their way. The nurse didn't say, but it was obvious what they wanted: a deathbed confession from John regarding the Laurel Canyon Murders.

I raced to the car and headed for the freeway, breaking every traffic law possible to make it to the hospital before Detective Tom Lange and his team got there. Even if John had wanted to say what he thought might have happened on Wonderland Drive, I knew his mind was such that he could very well say what never happened, and for John to say something stupid, might put me in danger or even sign my own death warrant.

I'd been tipped off that they were on the way. I drove very fast, cut out of work. I got there. You never knew what state of mind he was going to be in from one day to the next. Some days, he was all there and some days he thought Reagan had a bomb outside.

So, I got there. I didn't want them to trick him into saying anything. He could have spun a whole tale that would have come down on someone else that wasn't true. I told him they were coming here. "Do what you have to do. Don't say anything. Just act like you're out of it and I'll cover for you." I remember peeking out the door and they were coming. I go, "John, they're coming."

He moaned and groaned the whole time. About five or ten minutes into him moaning and groaning, and not saying anything, Detective Lange turned to me and said, "What about you, do you know anything?"

I go, "I don't know anything."

Tom Lange: We had to make an appointment at the Veteran's Hospital because John was in an isolation ward. When we arrived, John wanted to sneak out and have a cigarette in the hallway by the stairwell — a designated smoking stairwell away from his room.

Laurie Holmes [h]: During the last month, it was touch and go. He had been starving himself, too, for all that time. At first, as long as he had his Super Sugar Crisps, his scotch — which they didn't know he had — and his cigarettes, he was fine.

John was 90 pounds and his fingernails were two inches long.

Tom Lange: He was so emaciated. He said his fingernails even hurt. He was in so much pain. He couldn't stand to be touched. He could hardly move around. He couldn't walk and had to be in a wheelchair. He was very emaciated, but he still had his game on, as far as stroking us along. Later, I read where Laurie reiterated what we'd thought: that he was playing us. He was still running a mental game.

Tom Lange had told Mike Sager in 1989, "There's no mystery. John Holmes didn't go to his grave with anything but a very bad case of AIDS. He told us everything initially, right after it happened. But it's one thing to tell someone something and it's another thing to testify to it in court."

Tom Blake [h]: I was told he was dying of AIDS. Like I said, I was told by my superiors not to get involved, not to talk to him, which I did not do. I washed my hands completely, after my involvement in the investigation.

Frank Tomlinson: Had I known that he had AIDS and was dying, I would have tried to get him aside and find out what was going on for him, but I didn't even know that. I didn't know he was sick until he had already died. I would have wanted to know what was going on for him.

Mitchell Egers [h]: There was no formal dismissal of the attorneys. We got to be very friendly with him. My partner and I saw him shortly before his death, we went there, but it was to talk to him to find out certain things about what we, ourselves, didn't know. I think it was probably a few days before he died. But we weren't there when the police were there. I didn't know that the police had interviewed him there in the hospital.

Meanwhile...

Sharon Holmes [h]: I found out about the AIDS in a rather strange way. Tom Lange's partner was going out with a friend of [my friend] Nancy's. Nancy is the one who told me. I knew when he had it that he was not long for this world. I did not know how close to death he was at the time I found out about it.

Dawn Schiller[h]: [I] came back to the states in '87, but I stayed up north pretty much because I really felt a need to finalize things with John and I had a friend of mine that lived there. I wanted to find Sharon again. It was really important for me to heal all the old questions. I loved her and I cared about her. I just wanted to know, a lot of times, why didn't she stop him from hitting me? And I knew that she knew what was going on. I needed to apologize for what I felt — that it wasn't my intent to cause any upheaval in her life. I never meant to hurt her.

Sharon Holmes[h]: I think it's rather interesting that when he was admitted to Sepulveda, I missed running into him and probably his mother by about three weeks. My father had been in that hospital for three months, having an aortic aneurysm repaired and my dad and my mom stayed with me for an additional three months while he was recovering. So, they had left just shortly before John had died. I never said anything to them about the AIDS when I found out about it because he was going to die, and I figured they would find out about it at that point and I could reassure them.

I didn't have any reason to be concerned about myself because I hadn't been in contact with him. I mean at that point, it was seven years and that was the longest anyone had contracted HIV, so I had nothing to worry about.

Dawn learned that John had AIDS from a newspaper article. Rumors that Holmes was dying of AIDS received attention as early as June of 1987, but eventually more journals printed the story.

Dawn Schiller[h]: The *L.A. Times* article came out [with the headline]: "John Holmes, Dying of AIDS." He was at the V.A. Hospital.

Laurie wondered if perhaps a former business associate of John's could have leaked his condition to the press prior to his death.

Laurie Holmes: Nobody knew that John had HIV until someone broke the news to the newspaper about two months before John died, while he was in the V.A. dying and had no contact with anyone.

In about January 1988, while John was in the V.A. dying, someone leaked the news to the *L.A. Times* that John was dying of AIDS. At this time, John was in pretty bad shape and wished to talk to nobody but his mother, myself and my son.

But interestingly enough, in the early months of 1988, reporter Tony Lovett had been preparing to write a piece about John Holmes for *Hustler* magazine. In his attempt to confirm the mounting rumors that the porn icon was indeed suffering from AIDS, Lovett did some digging around. It is quite possible that Lovett's persistence contributed to the *L.A. Times* finally breaking the story of John's illness and impending death.

Tony Lovett[h]: I did manage to get the information out of the nurse at the V.A. Hospital, which was my one accomplishment in terms of breaking the story and verifying that in fact he had AIDS. That's what started the whole ball rolling, in terms of putting the information out there.

This was at the very beginning of my career as an investigative reporter and I got a tip that he was in the V.A. Hospital and the tip inferred that he might have AIDS, but none of it was verified. This was some chance through some trickery to — *(A)* verify that he was in the hospital and *(B)* to find out and verify that he did, in fact, have AIDS. Once I had that out of the horse's mouth from the nurse, I called Larry Flynt because they had given me some of my first gigs in writing the piece. They said they were very interested.

Dawn Schiller[h]: I wanted to see him, mostly with a "Fuck you, asshole," and "I'm better than you ever thought I was and I'm standing here to prove it." I was worth everything and more than he ever let me believe I was. I just needed to see his face one more time and then there was a part of me that still cared about him. It's the sick part that needed to see him again, because of the way that we had seen each other last and the words that I remember from him, "Can I just see your face one more time?" And I had said, "No."

I tried the pediatrician that [Sharon] used to work for and there was nobody there by that name. There was a new staff.

There was a quote in [the *L.A. Times*], from Sharon. It said, "ex-wife," and I went, "Oh, are they divorced?" I was always under the impression that Sharon would never leave him, no matter what. I called the guy who wrote the article from the *L.A. Times* and I told him who I was, and I said, "Here is my number, and I don't know if she wants to talk to me. Can you just let her know my number and leave it up to her what she does with it?"

A couple of days later, I got a call and it was her. She was in town and we arranged to meet at Clancy's, that old fish bar in Glendale. I think that we were both nervous. We sat, talked and we drank wine, and I asked her all those questions. I found out mostly that John was lying to both of us at the same time. I was made aware of a lot of the control that John had over Sharon. Although it wasn't physical — mental torture he inflicted on her, as well.

She told me that they'd divorced. She said that he had tried to find her. She said she was pretty sure that he tried to find me. I said that I wasn't aware of it, that I was completely in another land, on the other side of the world. We left each other's company and we promised to get together.

I told her that I wanted to see John. I told her I needed to go see him and she understood completely. He needed to know that I wasn't the dumb, ignorant, hillbilly, piece of shit that he treated me like. Sharon said, "This was always why I was by your side. You were worth more than he ever treated you, and I knew that, but I don't think it's a good idea for you to go there."

She said that she understood that he was already in a comatose state. His mother was praying next to him, and his mother and I didn't have a good relationship. (She referred to me as "the Devil" and that I was the cause of everybody's woes — that's what I always heard at Christmases.) I told [Sharon] that I still cared about him and I couldn't deny that. She said, "It wouldn't do you any good."

"People just don't think that they're going to get it, because they see so little of it, and they don't realize just how much of it we do see."

DR. SHARON MITCHELL

13.

The Death of The King

Poster Boy

Saying Goodbye

After his mother's reassuring words of acceptance, John relaxed for his final moments. Laurie was depressed and exhausted from the emotional toll of caring for her dying husband, and found herself reconsidering John's advice to enjoy her life and meet other people. She wore a new black dress to go out with some friends, but went to visit John first. It was the last time she spoke to him. John was in bed, with his mother and his brother David by his side. He complimented her on her dress and John stayed awake to have one final conversation with Laurie. "I love you, Daddy," she said to him as he left.

> *Laurie Holmes*[1]: I remember his words and the way he said them, just like it was yesterday. "I know," he replied softly, "and I love you, Baby."

John slipped into a deep coma that night and did not awake the next day. On her way to see him again, Laurie bought a cassette with Bread's song, "Everything I Own." Laurie found that its lyrics spoke to her feelings for John, who had cared so much for her and she would have given or done anything she could to have saved him. That night John's mom, Mary Bowman, slept at Laurie's apartment and the phone rang. It was the hospital, calling to say that John had passed away. John died with his eyes open.

> *Laurie Holmes*: I've never seen a more peaceful look in anybody's eyes in my life because I had to close his eyes. I tried to and I couldn't do it; they wouldn't shut. I was young and that's what you would see in the movies — you close their eyes, but I found out that it doesn't happen that way. Not in real life, no.
>
> He believed in reincarnation. He really believed in cremation and when he was gone off this earth, he just wanted to go as easily as he could. It was all written into this master plan, long before we were ever born. He really believed that. There was a reason that he met me at the time that he did, and that we became close. I was there with him for the last five years. There's a reason for everything.

It was John's final wish that Laurie view his naked body before he was cremated to be sure that no part of him would end up on a shelf in a jar as a conversation piece. After seeing to it that his body was intact, Laurie watched as John was put into the oven and returned to pick up his ashes that night. John had requested that his ashes be dispersed from the commercial fishing barge from which he and Laurie had taken fishing trips together in his healthier years, so David drilled holes in John's urn and then covered them with tape. During their final night together, Laurie hugged John's urn while she, Mary and David waited until morning on the boat. When the sun peeked over the horizon, Laurie peeled the tape from the urn and released John's ashes into the Pacific Ocean, off the coast of San Clemente Island.

Laurie Holmes: [John was] the best man that I ever had! I was 24 years old when he died. For the last couple of years I had nursed him and gone through a lot of hell because I loved him. You're 24 years old and you've already had the best — nothing sexual, I'm talking, just the best man. I've spent my whole life trying to find a man who would be just half as good to me as he was. Of course, I've failed miserably most of the time. He was my life. Like my son said to me, "You never will, Mom."

John's Memorial Service

Dawn Schiller[h]: It wasn't more than a couple of days later, even before I could make my final decision about going to see him, the article in the *L.A. Times* came out, "John Holmes Dies of AIDS." March 13, 1988. I wanted to go to the funeral, but according to the *Times*, it was a private thing, and he had a new wife. I found out about all this stuff and they were all the people that I didn't want to be around. Sharon agreed that they would only want to promote the fantasy image of who he was and who I never knew him as. It would be nothing good for me, so she basically talked me out of that idea.

Sharon Holmes[h]: [Dawn] came back, probably about six months before John had died, but stayed with her mother in Oregon. She was in L.A. before John died. The first thing out of her mouth was, "I want to go to the funeral."

I said, "Dawn, you and I have got to talk." We basically met in a restaurant in Glendale that afternoon. I told her what was going on. I said, "The last thing in the world you need — Eddie Nash — is still out there. John was acquitted and they're still looking for someone to blame. You don't want to be involved with that. Besides, you've made a life for yourself, so why be involved?"

Denise Amerson[h]: It was the only thing that we could do. It was something that shouldn't have happened the way that it did. A memorial service instead of a funeral service because John's body had already been taken care of; Laurie had him cremated. But we needed some type of closure. We wanted to have something for him, so my father planned a memorial.

[Laurie Holmes] took away the chance to say "Goodbye," to some-body who I had in my life everyday for 18 years. That's not fair, so that was the reason we had the memorial service, because we weren't even able to have a burial, because she cremated his body, without anybody even knowing.

It was only going to be for family and close friends, but somehow the media got hold of the information and although the service was nice inside, it was very painful. He was going to be missed, and not because he was Pornoking, John Holmes. It was a small ceremony and it was very heartwarming. It was beautiful and we got to say goodbye the best we could.

Jim Holliday[h]: I can tell you in all honesty, the single toughest thing I've ever had to do in this industry. First — it's two-fold, when we knew John was in the V.A. Hospital, I remember Jamie Gillis and I were discussing: do we want to go out and see him, knowing that he was not going to be the same John? We both decided to see him in a ravaged condition would not be good. We'd rather choose to remem-ber the healthy, robust John.

When he died, Bill Amerson asked me to do the eulogy at the memorial service. I immediately turned to a couple of other critics, and they left me high and dry. So, going out to Forest Lawn, I don't think I've put as much concentrated thought into anything. I didn't want to do it, but I thought I owed it to Bill and to the memory of John.

Bill Margold: Holliday went there and delivered the eulogy. He spoke from the heart. Holliday was a spontaneous person. I heard that it was very dramatic.

Ginger Lynn was one of the few, if not the only female sex performer that was invited to and attended the small memorial service the Amerson family had organized for John. Denise Amerson said that her father had given out the wrong address of the memorial service, but perhaps he had intentionally done so to avoid what surely would have been an even bigger media circus. John's memorial service was held at the Old North Church in Hollywood Hills' Forest Lawn, in Los Angeles.

Ginger Lynn[j]: The anger that I did feel was not about the fact that John died of AIDS. I was angry at the way the public dealt with it — the accusations, and the Meese Commission, and the whole "por-nography is evil and ugly and bad."

When John Holmes died, the innocence of pornography died along with him. I think it was a time that changed everything. I remember being at John's funeral and I was one of the few if not the only one of the women that worked with him that went to the funeral. It was actually quite disgusting. The press showed up and I couldn't get out. They actually had to take me downstairs and out through the back of the church because the press was everywhere. It was so intrusive and ugly, and the media turned it into something dirty.

Jim Holliday[h]: That whole day is to me, a sample of how the adult industry is perceived by the mainstream world — they just don't get it. I remember leaving — there were people running around because apparently they'd sandbagged the service and piped the stuff to the reporters outside, and they wanted to know, "Where's this Jim Holliday guy?"

I remember telling one of them from Channel 4, "He's around the other side of the building." I made it real quick to my car and split.

The notion when they did their report was, "Only 50 people bothered to show up." That's an example of how this industry is completely and utterly misunderstood. Only 52 people were invited and I challenge anyone from the real world to have 50 out of 52 people showing up. It's a pretty high batting average and a perfect example of how the real world can't get anything right about [the] adult [industry].

Bill Margold and Jamie Gillis were the two people who chose not to go to John's funeral.

Jamie Gillis: I can't remember if I was living in L.A. at the time. I think I might have been living in New York. It's nothing personal about John, but I just don't travel easy for anything. I hate flying and I'm the kind of guy who didn't come back for a very close family member's funeral.

Bill Margold: I don't regret not being there. I just wasn't ready to do that.

Denise Amerson[h]: When we got outside, we were bombarded by news and television. They were attacking my brother and my sister and they tried to shelter us, but it was just too much. I was 18, confused and didn't like being in the public eye. I don't like that part of the family life. I just wanted to say, "Goodbye," to my Godfather.

Sean Amerson[h]: I didn't go through all the emotions at the time because I was trying to be there for my sister who was really upset.

Hearing the News

Tom Blake[h]: I felt bad. I enjoyed working with the man. He was very productive. To me, he was one of the biggest assets I had in my involvement in investigating the production and distribution of porno here in southern California. Without his help and assistance, I would not have been able to do all the cases. I was probably one of the busiest investigators in L.A.P.D. My crew were kept hopping doing investigations because of the information that John fed us. It was real enjoyable working for him.

Bob Chinn[h]: When I found out that John had died, I was very surprised. He told me had had cancer, but I was surprised to find out that he died of AIDS. I just hadn't been around the business and I didn't know. It was a total surprise.

Kitten Natividad[h]: I heard he had been with men and I couldn't believe it, but I guess when you're hard up from drugs, you'll do anything. I found that really sad because he never did anything to hurt me, he never insulted me. I never wished that on anyone anyway, and since I liked him, I was very sad.

Paul Thomas: When I found out he had AIDS, I was in denial because then I was scared that I had it. I wouldn't test. It seemed the proper ending for Holmes, or anyone else in this business. It seemed not surprising at all, in fact, it was surprising that we all didn't have it. That was amazing: not that he had it, but that we all didn't have it. I'd crossed swords with him many times. He was with a girl and three seconds later, I was with her, so it was surprising that we all didn't get it. The fact that he got it and died from it was perfect. Tragic, but perfect.

Ron Jeremy[h]: I was sad because it was such a frighteningly scary, horrible way to die and the fear of knowing you're going to die. What really broke my heart — actually made me shed a tear — was reading the [Mike Sager] *Rolling Stone* article ["Devil and John Holmes,"] it said how his ears were bleeding. He went through a slow, painful process and I imagined what was going through the guy's mind.

Juliet Anderson[h]: I was living up in the mountains in a small town and I hadn't kept track of what was going on in Pornoville. I got out of making films in '84. I said, "Goodbye, I quit," and then I moved to a small town. It was sometime later, while I was living up there I heard that John had died. The scuttlebutt was that he had died of AIDS. It wasn't in the paper that he had died of AIDS. I wasn't surprised, but I was sorry to hear that he had to die that way. Other than that, I didn't know the details. I was just glad [my] last experience with John was very heartfelt and very touching.

Ron Jeremy: The things I disrespect are the things he did to others: stealing suitcases, traveling across the world with HIV. These are things that are really, really bad. Again, it didn't affect me directly. You can often like somebody, but know they've done some bad things outside of your realm. Outside of my world, he did some very, very bad things, but to me, he was always very, very nice.

Buck Adams[h]: When it's somebody like that, that's bigger than life, you almost don't believe stories about their demise. I guess I avoided the issue. Then one day — I'm trying to remember where I was sitting — I was in somebody's office about a job, and somebody walked in and said, "Did you hear John Holmes just died?" I don't think it really registered to me when I was sitting in the room.

I was living in an apartment by myself and I started drinking. About eight hours after I heard it, [I went] through all those stories — the good times, the bad, the ups, the downs, the movies, the parties, and all that kind of stuff. I think it finally hit me there; just sat down and had a good cry about it.

Julia St. Vincent: My husband called and told me about John, that John was dying in the hospital. I couldn't bring myself to call him because it had been years and I knew if I heard his voice — if I'd called to talk to him — that I'd hear it again for the rest of my life. I just couldn't do it and then, he died. I felt terrible and I called Bill, because I knew he lived at Bill's.

I said, "Do you think John knew?"

I was all teary and he said, "Yeah, I think he did." I was trying to say I was sorry.

Sharon Holmes[h]: I felt bad that he allowed himself to die in this way. I had always hoped that he would find there was something else he could do with his life.

Bill Margold[h]: I felt that a chapter of the industry had come to an end, but I was very, very emotionally moved by the moment.

Ironically, the production of hardcore pornography became legal in the state of California in August of 1988, less than six months after John Holmes died of AIDS. The California Supreme Court's decision in the *California vs. Hal Freeman* case effectively legalized pornography. John played an indirect role in bringing about the Freeman decision because Freeman had been arrested for hiring talent for *Caught From Behind 2: The Sequel*. As fate would have it, John died before he could ever work legally in the pornographic movie industry.

The Need for AIDS Education

When HIV/AIDS first became a problem in the United States, there also was no database to track outbreaks of the virus within the industry. Today there is a database, thanks to a former adult actress who earned her doctorate and founded the Adult Industry Medical Healthcare Foundation. Dr. Sharon Mitchell is responsible for most of the HIV testing among performers in the Los Angeles area. Her expertise in HIV testing and tracking more recent outbreaks within the adult industry qualifies her to speak about Holmes' case.

> *Dr. Sharon Mitchell*: Usually when people contract HIV, they contract it outside of the industry. That's been my experience running this place, but I've only been doing testimony on the industry from the last ten years. It seems like a lifetime, but before that, very few people were getting tested. I mean, even when John came out and said, "I'm positive," I started to get tested on a regular basis and I started to ask people for tests, but not everybody did. There's a complete possibility that he could have worked with somebody who was positive, and it could have come from the industry at that time, but I don't know.

No one is known to have gotten the virus from John, however, testing was not yet frequently used and many performers were transient, as they still are today.

> *Laurie Holmes*°: We tried to track the girls he worked with that year. So many people die of AIDS and you don't hear about it because you might have known them by a different name. Many times in this industry, people come and they go.

> *Dr. Sharon Mitchell*: Certain people have dropped out, and you knew that they had HIV. Some people have said, "I've got HIV, and I've got to go," and some didn't, they just dropped out. It's very easy to fall off the face of the earth in this business, and we'll never find you again.

> *Ron Jeremy*: Every girl is fine. HIV isn't easy to catch because you have to do it in the rear end. Magic Johnson's wife is okay. You have to do it in the rear end, where you tear blood vessels and the capillaries. He climaxed outside of them. John Holmes fucked a girl in the ass, but he did not cum in the ass, so it's perfectly safe. The affected sperm must go into the rear end. Of course, that's why they're fine. If there's infected sperm there, even with the slightest tear, which you

often will, it can go right to the blood. Whereas the vagina, it was built by Mother Nature for that type of work. It lubricates itself. The ass — although there isn't anything wrong with it — was not built for that, which is why gay people get it and straights don't.

Hopefully, Ron Jeremy's above statement jumps out as blatantly wrong to all readers; this is an illustration of the need for better HIV and sexual health education in the United States. Of course, the method of John's ejaculation does not play a significant role in the fact that none of these actresses were infected with HIV. According to a 2005 survey, 55 percent of HIV-positive women had acquired HIV from having unprotected sex with an infected male lover.

Ever since John's death was reportedly AIDS-related, people have been very interested in discovering how and from whom John contracted HIV. It is all speculative, however. Modern HIV knowledge lends credibility to some ideas, while canceling out others and exposing common misconceptions.

Bob Vosse[h]: It's a shock to hear any friend comes down with HIV. That's the first thing you hear, and you never know quite when that's going to develop into AIDS.

I have no way of confirming any of this, but John was in jail for contempt of court for a year and very shortly after he got out of jail— seemed it was the next day after he got out of jail—he was up at the stage in San Francisco, shooting and so forth.

I said, "How was it, John? How'd you do?"

He said, "Well, it was rough, but I made a lot of money." I never questioned or asked. I don't like rumor and running into these, but I don't know.

Bob Chinn[h]: We asked him about that a few times. He insisted that he was straight. I do know that there were some gay loops that he was in. I didn't really socialize with him, so I don't know his private life that well.

Mike Sager[h]: The main explanation was — he wasn't gay, but he did at a time, make money for sex — there were wealthy men that would pay to be with him. The speculation always was — why would somebody want to have John Holmes as the receiver? It was the common thought that if John Holmes was the top, then his gay sex was at least not something he would have gotten AIDS from. I don't know whether that was medically sound. I think that John Holmes probably serviced men and women alike, for money — there wasn't ever any indication that he loved men.

There are HIV risks involved with every sexual activity and therefore, condoms and frequent HIV tests are a necessary precaution to protect oneself from unnecessarily dying from AIDS complications, as John did.

> *Jon Martin* [h]: You hear right away that he died of AIDS. I don't like that. I live in San Francisco. I have a lot of friends that have passed away from the disease. We know that he did do a few boy-boy films after he had some problems. So what? As we know, this disease certainly is not totally dependant on whether you're gay or straight. A straight person can die from this thing, the same as a homosexual.

The risk of being infected with HIV is five in 1,000 for being the receptive (bottom) during unprotected anal sex, but the risk for insertive (top) during anal sex is much less. In fact, the risk associated for a man engaging in unprotected insertive anal sex is very close to that of a man or woman having "bareback" vaginal intercourse. Even fellatio (both insertive and receptive) carries a small risk that condoms prevent.

The highest risk is associated with a blood transfusion — a staggering 90 percent infection rate for those filled with HIV-positive blood. Mandatory blood testing has made transfusions very safe, however, so today there is virtually no risk. But John had never had a blood transfusion.

The second-highest risk is associated with needle-using narcotics users, which prompted a short debate about John's history with drugs. According to a *Chicago Sun-Times* article from March 21, 1988, Margold was misquoted as saying that John had used intravenous drugs. Some people who did not know John well wondered if he may have used needles, but most people vehemently agree that John did not, including Bill Margold and other directors and associates who witnessed John's drug use. No one in John's professional or private history — not even Lind and McCourt — reported ever having seen John Holmes injecting himself with a needle. Sharon and Laurie Holmes have both attested that John was terrified of needles.

> *Bill Amerson*: I don't know 100 percent that he wouldn't do it, [but] I don't believe it.

> *Bob Chinn*: I don't think he was an intravenous drug user. He was scared of needles.

> *Bill Amerson* [h]: I spent a good portion of time with John when he was loaded and he never ever wanted to use a needle.

> *Alan Colberg*: John never used drugs intravenously, that I knew. It's decades later, and we know a lot about how one can get AIDS. Sure, you can get AIDS from any kind of sexual relationship. We know

that now. What can I say? Gee, I wonder how John got AIDS. He didn't shoot drugs.

John's *Private Pleasures?*

There are only two scenarios that are the most plausible suggestions for how John Holmes may have been infected with HIV. John had about equal chances (in terms of the probability of becoming infected) by Joey Yale in *Private Pleasures* as he would have from having sex with an infected partner (female or male) within the year prior to his second positive HIV test. There is also some evidence that uncircumcised men, such as John, may be at an increased danger of getting HIV from all unprotected sexual activities.

John experienced flu-like symptoms two weeks after filming the gay feature in which he is shown as the recipient of fellatio from Joey Yale and anally penetrating the bottoms of Nancy Conjure and Yale, a gay adult actor who died from AIDS in 1986.

One contradiction remains to the *Private Pleasures* scenario: John's first HIV test results were negative. John began testing a full two years after his on-screen sexual encounter with Joey Yale and, by today's HIV-testing standards, six months is the maximum amount of time it could possibly take for antibody-testing methods. But the testing method was new when John first tested in 1985, and there was a high but inexplicable rate for both false negatives and positives, with some regularity. The quality of all modern HIV testing methods is much better.

> *Dr. Sharon Mitchell:* They were dealing with the ELISA methodology, which is the antibody. The antibody can take any healthy, young person [an average of] six weeks now. ELISA antibodies weren't as accurate as they are now.
>
> Sometimes today, people can go up to six months and it would go undetected. I'm sure he was testing every six months. So someone could have had it and not even come up on a test. He could have had it a week after the first [test], which was negative. You never know.

Given the possibility that Holmes could have had a false negative for his first test, the question of how John got HIV will never be answered with certainty. But Occam's Razor is the principle that can be paraphrased: "All things being equal, the simplest solution tends to be correct." Bearing that in mind, the false negative for his first test may tilt the scales in favor for John to have contracted HIV through his sexual exploits in the year prior to his second test.

> *Bill Amerson:* John was really the nicest guy in the world. He'd do anything for anybody. John worked all day long: 12-13 hours. He'd get paid and he'd find a hooker, have sex with her, then give her all

the money he'd made in the day. That's who he was. He would find someone who was on the street and down and out. Not a high-class call-girl, but someone who needed the money. He would give her the money. He didn't know who she was. He didn't care about money.

The other possibility is John got AIDS from a girl that we shot a movie in the Marina who had AIDS. She told everybody after the movie that she had AIDS and she needed 80 bucks.

Conspiracy Theories

Modern medical knowledge rules them out, but there are many creative ideas about how John could have been exposed to HIV.

Although she has since been in support of the more plausible scenarios, in the epilogue that Laurie Holmes wrote for *Porn King*, she pondered a statement that John made, "Run for cover! The government is trying to bomb me," and recalled that John and Bill Amerson had gone to Washington, D.C. to fight the Meese Commission. By a stretch of imagination, Laurie wondered if John may have been intentionally infected to make a case out of the industry the government had been trying to sabotage.

Behind the scenes, two members on the Meese Commission were guilty of crimes worse than putting sex on film. No charges were filed, but Father Bruce Ritter, who had been on the Meese Commission, was accused of having sex with young men at the Covenant House, a homeless shelter that he ran for teenagers. Charles H. Keating was convicted in 1989 in connection to the savings and loans scandal. This does not mean that anyone from the Reagan administration would be capable of injecting John to harm the reputation of the industry. Laurie's idea seemed ridiculous to many people, but to this day, she does not rule this out completely. She is also not the only one with an alternative suggestion for how John could have contracted HIV.

> *Bill Margold*: What he showed me on that set was somewhat interesting. He was sitting there, basically naked and his legs had little black marks all over them.
>
> I said, "What are those?"
>
> He said, "People would walk up to me [in jail] and jam pencils into me and break them off."

As his psychologist Dr. Vonda Pelto had noted during her interviews with John while he was in prison, inmates strategized and even tried to kill John. It was the reason he was kept in solitary confinement. Even so, Margold believes that John would have craved privacy and may have avoided using the bathroom, resulting in a buildup of toxins within his colon, an idea which he has called "institutionalized constipation."

Modern research, however, implies that there is no need to worry about poisoning from toxins while constipated. There is no evidence that toxins can leak from the rectum into the body, or that constipation leads to colon cancer. Margold recently admitted that he has been in denial about the infiltration of AIDS into the adult community — a disease that symbolized the end of innocence and defiance for Hollywood's subculture.

Bill Margold: I was one of the last to ever reconcile myself to the fact that this man was going to die. When I was told he was sick, I had built up the story about the concept of institutionalized constipation, bowel cancer, rectal bleeding — between Holliday and I, we created an incredible mythology of lots of internal problems. This industry was not ready to deal with HIV and I just wasn't going to have any of it. Institutionalized constipation sounded good.

But then, of course, along comes March [1988], and I get the phone call from Holliday. I'm watching *The Guns of Navarone*, ironically, and Viper's sitting in her chair and I think Pogo [one of the cats] was on her lap. Holliday said, "The King is Dead," and I hung up the phone.

I felt that a chapter of the industry had come to an end.

AIDS Testing Today

Laurie Holmes: They finally organized AIDS testing after he was gone.

As far as the industry is concerned, it's gone through a lot of changes and there are not stars like there used to be. They used to make stars out of you, and they wanted stars to keep the audience captivated, to keep them coming back to that same star. They don't give a crap about that now; they just want new faces.

Dr. Sharon Mitchell: John made me aware that there was HIV in the industry and that's clearly something that everybody didn't want to look at. I thought, this is a reality now, and I'm just going to have to suck it up, and go get my test.

I was getting mine every three months because I was a heroin addict. I was going to a methadone clinic, of course, and getting my HIV test. I was asking people at the methadone clinic, "Would you test my friends from the porn business for free, on the county, being that they'll be my partner?" They said sure, so I would send people to the methadone clinic to get tested.

If John hadn't been positive, I don't think I would have gotten that awareness to really look at that. That's something that's been, even to this day, indestructible — the amount of denial that's in the adult entertainment industry, when it comes to HIV and STDs.

Marilyn Chambers: I was freaking out, like, "Oh, my God, *Shit!* What am I going to do?" I was tested every six months, for ten years after that.

Jamie Gillis: From what I understand, I think AIDS can be in your system for a very long time before it shows up. I don't know if it's still accurate information, but I think I've heard you can have it for up to ten years before it shows up.

Candida Royalle: I would say finding out that he had AIDS was very shocking because, of course, it had implications for the entire industry. Everyone was dying to know how he could have gotten it and where he might have gotten it. Did he get it from the industry? Did he get it from a woman on the set? Did he get it from a man? It really had an effect on all of us.

I was just starting to get known for my own projects then, and I would go on these talk shows, and they just loved hitting me with, "Well, how do you know you don't have AIDS?" It was so insulting. My God, I worked with the guy in 1979!

In the late-'80s, some people were unaware of the window for HIV testing. With the exception of slightly less reliable ELISA tests in 1985, most false negatives were caused by a low number of detectable HIV antibodies in the blood, so a test 12 weeks to six months after the incident was, more often than not, accurate.

Many people misunderstood and thought they should get tested for ten years after their first unprotected sex with an infected partner because many worried about some sort of "AIDS dormancy." It has been a source of confusion, because a person can go eight to ten years without noticing symptoms of HIV infection, however, even without symptoms, a person with the virus would test positive for HIV within the window period of the testing method.

Don Fernando: I think the industry was affected because he had HIV and he was so recognized. Remember those were the days before e-mail, before computers, before a surge in media. If it had been someone else during that era, who wasn't so recognized, it wouldn't have been a big deal. His dying was a real wakeup call: this is a risky business.

Bob Chinn: I'm glad it's there, but I don't know if it's enough because after you've had the test, you could still have a relationship with somebody and pass it on. I don't like the thought of people putting themselves at risk for something that's really unimportant.

Dr. Sharon Mitchell: [In 2008 at AIM] we use PCR-DNA, an early detection method that can tell just 10 days after exposure. We can't guarantee that no one's going to get it, but we can guarantee that we're going to catch it very quickly. But we can't keep HIV out of the industry. It's just an impossibility.

PCR-DNA tests, which can be used to estimate the viral load of HIV present in the body, have not been approved by the Food & Drug Administration (FDA) because these tests are mostly accurate for people who already know their status and simply want to track the progress of treatment. One reason why the tests may not work is because the virus can go below detectable levels during modern prescription treatments, but the patient is not cured and can still infect someone else because the virus is protected by macrophage cells, a reservoir for HIV.

Because of this, a person undergoing treatment for HIV with undetectable viral loads can still have and transmit the virus, thus putting the entire adult industry at risk, which is using an unapproved method for HIV testing. It is a sacrifice that many are willing to make unnecessarily. Tests that rely on HIV antibodies, such as ELISA, have shown to be the most reliable testing methods. In addition to frequent testing, "condom-only" movies are the safest for today's adult performers.

> *Dr. Sharon Mitchell*: I think we should be paying for an entire battery of tests, including pap smears. Everything that we recommend in our newcomer packet should be paid for by the company. I think that since they're not going to use condoms, that they should choose this test every two weeks or every ten days. They should really tighten all the window periods, so that there is less of a chance of anyone getting anything.
>
> The way it is now, one person works for 40 companies and one company doesn't want to take the responsibility of paying for it, and they want to put all that responsibility on the actor, so they're doing the minimum with what they can afford. We're looked at as a necessary evil.
>
> And then, they could always use condoms, God forbid! What the fuck is that about? For Christ's sake, we [AIM] offer condoms. You can't even see these things! My theory is the public's going to watch porno, one way or the other — you make it, they're going to buy it. If there's a condom, they're going to buy it.
>
> They say, "We'll sell more without a condom." Why? There's still that theory that people want to see what they can't do. No one lives without a condom in real life, so they want to view people at risk, or whatever. It would probably take a survey to find out.
>
> I used condoms most of the time from when I started testing. I would work with people that I knew continuously and if I worked with someone that I didn't know that well, I would always use condoms. Even I was "condom optional" and I was wrong because I worked with Marc Wallice once without a condom while he was positive.

As a living illustration of the advances in HIV-specific treatments in the years since John's death, Marc Wallice is still alive. Fortunately, Dr. Mitchell escaped infection from this exposure. Many former adult actresses share her support for condom use in today's pornography, especially in the age of amateur pornography that has grown popular on the Internet, in which testing is unlikely to occur often, if at all.

> *Seka*: They don't require people to wear condoms. You don't see a whole lot of films that portray safe sex.

> *Serena*: I wouldn't fuck anybody without a rubber, except the man I live with. I wouldn't be in movies now anyway, but even if I was in movies, I wouldn't go unprotected. I don't care what it looks like. I've seen a lot of gay movies with condoms and it never bothered me.

> *Bob Chinn*: Awareness is very important and the one segment of American society that is very aware, are people in this industry. They do what they should for the most part. For a lot of people now, it's become a business. Before, it was just people making a few bucks doing something that they didn't think was wrong. They do it right because their livelihood depends on it.

As Bill Margold had suggested in our foreword, AIDS gave John Holmes a Jesus-like status in the industry, full of legend and legacy. His death illustrates the danger of narcotics use and the importance of consistent HIV testing and condom use for people in and out of the industry. Perhaps, as Margold seems to suggest in the foreword of this book, John died as a hardcore martyr — so that people would learn from his life.

"I kind of hope I'm on the Late, Late Show. Seriously, like Bogart. Bogart never hit prime 'til he was way past dead. I would like to be on the Late, Late Show."

JOHN HOLMES

14.

Remembering John

The King's Legacy

Laurie Holmes: John was unique because of his appendage and because he was a forefather, which is very important. I'm sure if he were around today and if he was in any physical condition to do so, they would probably still want to make John Holmes movies. Because he died when he did and the way that he did, it almost made his movies more valuable. When anybody like that dies young, it makes their legacy more unique.

Sharon Mitchell: He has the biggest dick and he was the King of Porn. That's all you really need to know. I really think that was John. From *Johnny Wadd* — anything he did, he did the best he could. And he loved what he did.

Julia St. Vincent: You can compare him to that Long Dong guy, whose member wasn't that attractive; it was just long, like a pool cue. John's was more like this major fantasy. It looked good.

Don Fernando: I refer to him as The King. I know there will never be another John Holmes. He's just like Elvis Presley. There will never be another Elvis Presley, just like there will never be another John Holmes.

Ron Jeremy: I don't mind them calling him The King because he was the biggest draw. His name on a marquee would guarantee box office. It never happened before — it hasn't happened during, and it hasn't happened since: no man's name could outsell a girl.

John Holmes — this skinny, white guy with a huge penis going into some beautiful girl was enough excitement that people just wanted to see it. To hell with the story line, to hell with the fancy backdrops, to hell with traveling around the world — they just wanted to see that gigantic penis and that beautiful girl!

Marilyn Chambers: I don't want John to be portrayed as an asshole or a stupid guy with a big dick. He was, in his later years, very articulate. He never lied to me, as far as I know. He was a gentleman and he was true to his word with me always. He always delivered when he had to, in all aspects. He was not a mean person. I don't think he had a mean bone in his body.

Ron Jeremy: It was almost like he fell from the sky. We had heard he was half-Jewish: "We want to claim the bottom half." That was one of my jokes. We had heard everything under the sun, from a Mid-Eastern birth to that he was born to a sheik, to a countess, to a priest. The thing about John was that he wasn't 100 percent truthful. In a way, though, I think this added to his legend. He had this gigantic penis. No one knew where it came from or how.

Marilyn Chambers: He did some stupid interviews, but the real John Holmes was a lot different than anybody knew and I think it was a shame that nobody ever got to know the real John Holmes.

Kenneth Turan [h]: Given how his energy was, whatever else about him may or may not have been made up. His energy and his excitement seemed genuine. It's very hard to fake that. You can make up stories; you can't become a different person.

Dawn Schiller [h]: What's the story about the Phoenix and the flame, where it burns itself up? He was a Leo, so also I thought about him being a fire sign. A triple Leo, according to him.

Al Goldstein [h]: I think that John Holmes was the man that flew to the sun. The sun melted his wings and he died at the altar of his fantasy. There will never be another John Holmes.

Kenneth Turan [h]: It was so sad to think that he had to come to this; that someone who was so alive and just so excited by his life ended up that way. It was very sad to hear about that. It's a real American story, what happened to John.

Serena: I think he had this sadness more than a lot of people. Maybe it's because he was put in the spotlight because of this thing that he had.

Bob Chinn: People are always going to be curious about somebody that is endowed like he. So there's that curiosity factor that got a shot in the arm with *Boogie Nights*. And with *Boogie Nights*, they reached a whole new mass audience that had never been aware of it before.

Bill Amerson: I hear people talk about John. I hear some of the people where I work say, "You guys remember a guy named John Holmes?" I just listen to them. I don't say anything. I don't even get involved in the conversation. It used to be that people would all know who he was. If it wasn't for John, they wouldn't have a job.

Candida Royalle: It's amazing because he's unlike anyone else. Who's like him? There's no one like him. No one! There's not another poor, sort of hapless, skinny, not-very-good-looking guy who turns out to have a huge, overly endowed penis, and ends up going into the movies, becomes famous because of that piece of his anatomy — who then deals with his personal issues by getting involved with all kinds of bizarre drugs — who then gets lost and out of control and ends up helping to create one of the ghastliest multiple murders in history — and then to go get a brand new, horrific, sexually transmitted disease, and then goes and does a couple of more movies which could potentially infect these other young, innocent women. It's just one thing after another.

Bob Chinn: I think *Wonderland* is one view of John — the total disintegration of somebody that was moderately successful, but couldn't control himself. That's pretty sad. I wish I had seen him reading books. Maybe he wouldn't have ended up that way. When you don't have a life other than an overriding obsession with something stupid, you end up that way. Many people like that just wreck themselves eventually, but something like what John was doing, freebasing and all that, it's extremely addictive. Once you're hooked to that, that's it. It takes a really strong personality to overcome it and he just didn't have that personality.

Joel Sussman: He taught me not to overdo my drug habit and he taught me that maybe what you have is enough. I learned that partly through him. The price isn't worth it. Sometimes what happens in the society we live in is they never teach you, "Stop." They never teach you that you don't have to continue conquering.

Laurie Holmes: The way he's been portrayed has been wrong and people have this perception already in their mind. There's nothing you can ever do that's going to change it. It's better sometimes that they just don't know.

Marilyn Chambers: I think he was misunderstood, not only by the public, but I think he was also misunderstood by himself. I don't think he really ever had a home life. I don't think he ever had a real personal life. He was always living on the edge, and that was his life. It's difficult to be that person 24 hours a day, seven days a week, and come down off of that and be somebody else.

Sharon Holmes[h]: I still think of him. I think it's terribly sad that he wasted all the talents he had. John may have been famous for pornography, but that's not who John was. It's not how I remember him. I remember John as being an insecure, unhappy person. Our life together was totally divorced of what he did in most respects. I think of him as being the person who was probably the unhappiest husband in the world.

Bill Margold: The last time I saw John, we were up at a place in Beverly Hills making some kind of movie. I remember he was off in the garden, a beautiful place. Nobody was even around him. I just looked at him, didn't even go over and say anything. I don't know why, but that was the last time that I ever saw him. He was all by himself and now that adds another layer of sadness to the whole thing. I don't know why I didn't go over and say anything to him. I guess I sensed he wanted to be alone.

Gloria Leonard[h]: I wasn't terribly surprised that he met the demise that he did. I sort of am a believer that you are as strong as the support system that you create for yourself and John was essentially a loner who didn't let a lot of people close and get into him. That was kind of sad because I really was fond of him. I had a great affection for him. He really was, underneath all that bluster, really kind of a cool, nerdy dude.

Jim Holliday[h]: There are basically two kinds of people that walk the planet: ants and grasshoppers. Like the fable, ants will work industriously all summer, saving up for winter; grasshoppers will fiddle and take their chances when the cold comes. I've accepted the fact that I'm a grasshopper. John was also a grasshopper — he just sort of lived life by his terms. I will always remember the positives. When you are a grasshopper and you are on the edge, you can get involved with negative aspects that tend to harm you, but you cut through it.

Buck Adams[h]: Everybody has their pluses and minuses. If you spend too much of your life worrying about peoples' minuses, you get caught up in it. It all kind of caught up to me after that. When I say there was the good and bad, the best and the worst of everything in John, I guess that's true about all of us. There's the best and the worst in each and every one of us.

Ron Jeremy: I actually liked John Holmes. We never had a problem; he was always nice to me. We used to goof around at different events. He was a good guy! What's wrong with anyone who wants to make love and not war? He wasn't a fighter, he had no great physique, no muscles whatsoever. He had a big penis, what was there to dislike?

Joel Sussman: If there was a moment where you needed somebody, he was there. I got divorced, and whatever I needed, he was there for me. He was the guy who was there when you needed him, and he was also there when you didn't need him! But I think he was a genuinely beautiful soul.

Laurie Holmes: His laughter was better than any medicine, any drug or any therapy. He was a practical joker, too.

Dawn Schiller[h]: When he walked into a room, he didn't have to take his clothes off. He didn't have to. He had a smile; he had eyes that just drew you [in].

Mitchell Egers[h]: I remember one instance where I introduced a female attorney and she couldn't get over the impression that he made. She called me up the next day to tell me how impressed she was with him. I think most people were impressed with him. He had that type of personality, he had that charisma. He was able to look at a person and make that person feel important because, he — John Holmes — was interested in the person. If you knew him for a few minutes, you liked him. I think that was part of the charm of John Holmes. You could like him and he would certainly be interested in whoever it was he was talking to.

Ernie Roebuck[h]: John was really a sweet guy. I never knew him to be a bad guy. He was never mean to me, never uncool to me, never had a harsh word to me. It was always a pleasure to work with him. He was always funny and a pretty good guy and, so, I miss him.

Seka: He really, really was a nice person, just a down-to-earth nice man.

Sean Amerson[h]: [In 1997], when [the X-Rated Critic's Organization] asked me to take the award for him for Lifetime Achievement, I was really proud and surprised they asked me to do that. Until I had to sit down and think about what it was I wanted to say. I didn't really get upset about it until that day in August, when it was, "I'm going to go stand up in front of 2,000 people on television, and tell them why I'm taking this award for John." That's when it hit me that John had gone.

I think up until that point, I had fallen conveniently into a little denial about the fact he was gone because I just didn't want to deal with it. When he finally went, even at the funeral, it was such a media bullshit event, that I had so much aggression and anger about the whole thing, I smacked around a camera guy. I didn't deal with any of those emotions, any of those feelings up until that point.

I started remembering John, digging in the garden, just silly little things like that — all the real, fond memories that I have of him — seeing John on his hands and knees in the backyard, coming in the sliding-glass door into the living room, going, "Next year, we're going to have grapes."

My dad looking up at him, saying, "What?"

"Well, I took some grape seeds and I planted them." John had planted grape seeds in the ground, in the backyard, and had spent a lot of time on these little furrows.

Denise Amerson [h]: To me, there is one conversation to sum up who he was, in a nutshell. John had always been — as well as my dad — there for us. I was raised in a crazy, crazy world and they tried to keep some normalcy. John was always behind me, no matter what I wanted to do, what I did, or how much trouble I got myself into. He was right there and he never asked me for anything in return. Except there was one time, when he did say that he needed to talk to me about something serious and I guess it was when he started to get really sick. He knew that he was really sick and I didn't know that he was, but he sat me down and told me that he needed something from me and that it was really, really important that I had to promise him.

I said, "Anything that you need."

He said, no matter what happens in life — no matter how old I am, or if I'm married or not married, or if he's dead or he's alive — he asked me to promise him that I would never ever watch a movie with him in it. That was the only thing that he's ever asked of me and it was so extremely important to him.

I said, "Of course." I've kept that promise. I've never seen anything with him in it and I realized after he died why. When I really thought about John and about all the times he shared with our family, everything started to fit together about who he really was inside. I know it was important to him because he was ashamed of that part of who he was.

If I had a date or something, he would feel that it was necessary for him to tell me that it's not good for girls to be promiscuous. He had nothing to worry about and I just thought that was odd, and would come back with comments like, "Oh yeah, look who's talking. You slept with probably the entire nation and listen to your own advice."

He would always say, "That's my body, not my soul. That's the difference." That was his favorite saying to me, "That's just my body, not my soul. You have to know the difference."

I'm not saying that he didn't reap the benefits. [He] milked it for everything he could and he could have gotten out of the business at any time before he got involved as he did, but it was great for him in a lot of ways. But I think that inside, he just didn't want to be John Holmes anymore.

Bob Chinn: I did manage to go to that beach [in 2007], where John and I stood those many years ago. It was twilight and against the beautiful Kauai sunset, I recalled those past times and I thought, Well, John, I'm here — so where are you?

As I turned to leave, a gust of wind blew unexpectedly, sending a sudden chill up my spine, but the breeze slowly died down and everything was quiet again, except the sound of the waves breaking in the distance before they rolled in and washed up onto the shore.

Laurie Holmes: He's always there, but the effect is that I've made it my life to protect him and I realize that sometimes I need to let go, but then he will come back and he will remind me or something will happen out of the blue. He's always there.

Bill Amerson[j]: I love him. I'll always love him. There are times when I get really emotional, and I'll go to a place where he and I have been, and it hurts still. He's one of the best friends I've ever had and I miss him. There will never be another John Holmes.

Sean Amerson[h]: His passing away was like my dad dying because at the time when he was in my life, he was the person who took care of me. He was the person who made sure I had something to eat. He was the person who let me know when I had done something wrong. He was the person who I respected the opinion of.

Denise Amerson[h]: If his name is continually in the press, written about, or heard about, I think it should be as a whole person as well as a celebrity, or as a drug addict, or as an adult film star — or any of that. I just think that it should be rounded out and that's because I love him. I did and I always will.

Dawn Schiller[h]: I loved you, [John].

Sean Amerson: In short, I don't really care about his drug abuse, the adult industry or the mass murders. None of that affected my relationship with him. That's not who I knew. I miss him, and the kindness and bond between a scared, abused little boy and a man no one understood was a human being.

Laurie Holmes[i]: John may have made mistakes in his life, but as anyone who really knew him can't deny — his best asset wasn't his penis. It was his heart.

After being released from contempt of court on November 22, 1982, John spoke with the press outside the Los Angeles County Jail. Asked what he was going to do next, John said that he was going to keep a low profile, but had to get back to work. ASSOCIATED PRESS. PHOTO BY DOUG PIZAC.

This photo accompanied *Hustler* magazine's June 1983 interview with John. PHOTO BY LADI VON JANSKY.

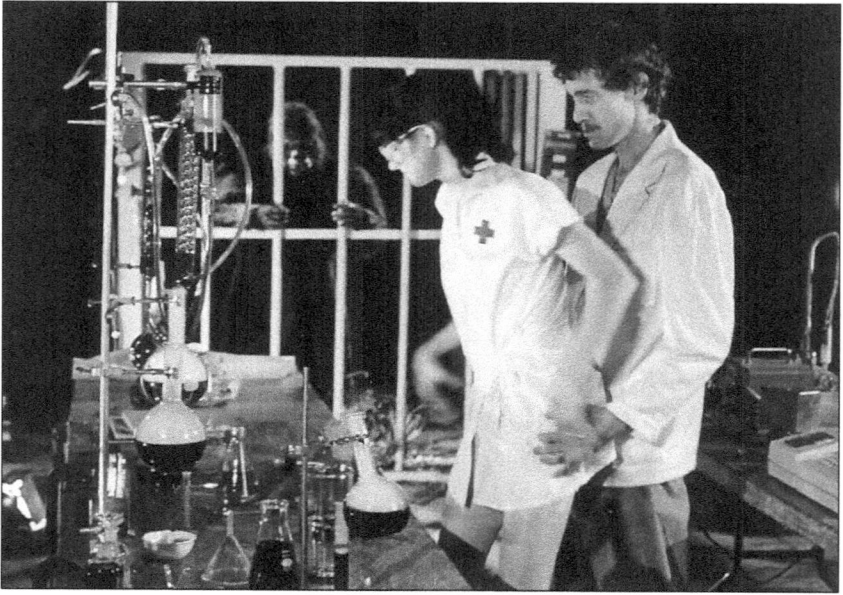

John with Drea.

A glamour photo of Misty Dawn (Laurie Holmes) that Kenji took during the early 1980s.

A 1983 VCA promo shot.

Bill Amerson and John with a happy, young lady.

With the Amersons — left to right: Bill, Denise, Sean and John. John took an active, fatherly-type of role in the kids' lives.

Denise Amerson with her godfather.

John loved to fish.

Here, he is fishing off the Channel Islands during the summer of 1983.

Relaxing on set between takes.

John and Laurie share a passionate embrace at a 1983 convention.

A kid at heart, John enjoyed going to theme parks. In 1984, he and Laurie model western attire at Knott's Berry Farm.

Palm Springs, California.

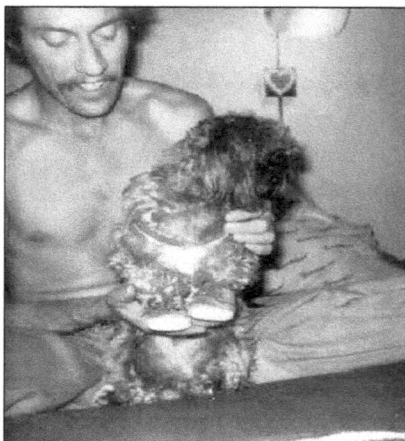

John and Laurie's good friend, Charlie.

Throughout John's life, he loved his pets.

John spent Christmas (1984) with Laurie and her son.

From the palm trees in Hawaii to the pine tree in Amerson's backyard, John loved to climb.

A pensive moment in the great outdoors.

John and his stepson share a quiet moment along with their dog, Lady. John had rescued Lady from the pound and nursed her back to health before finding homes for her six pups.

John applied his stepson's Halloween makeup in October 1985.

This never-before-seen photo reveals John and Laurie as a happy couple.

Building was a life-long Hobby of John's.

Having fun on the set of the 1985 film, *Girls on Fire* with Murray Perlstein and Bill Amerson.

Ron Jeremy pinches the guest of honor's cheek at the premiere of *Girls on Fire*. The premiere was held on February 7, 1985 at the Pussycat Theater. John's costar, Ginger Lynn, laughs while John's best friend and business partner, Bill Amerson, smiles proudly.

On February 7, 1985, John left a lasting impression in West Hollywood.

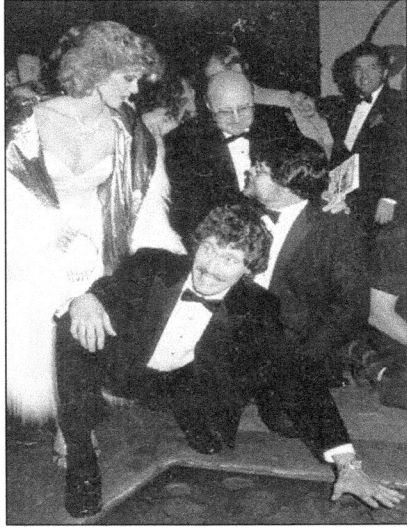

John's costar, Ginger Lynn, Bill Amerson and Murray Perlstein were among the attendees of the evening.

"An Evening Together with John Holmes and Seka," for a 1985 pictorial.

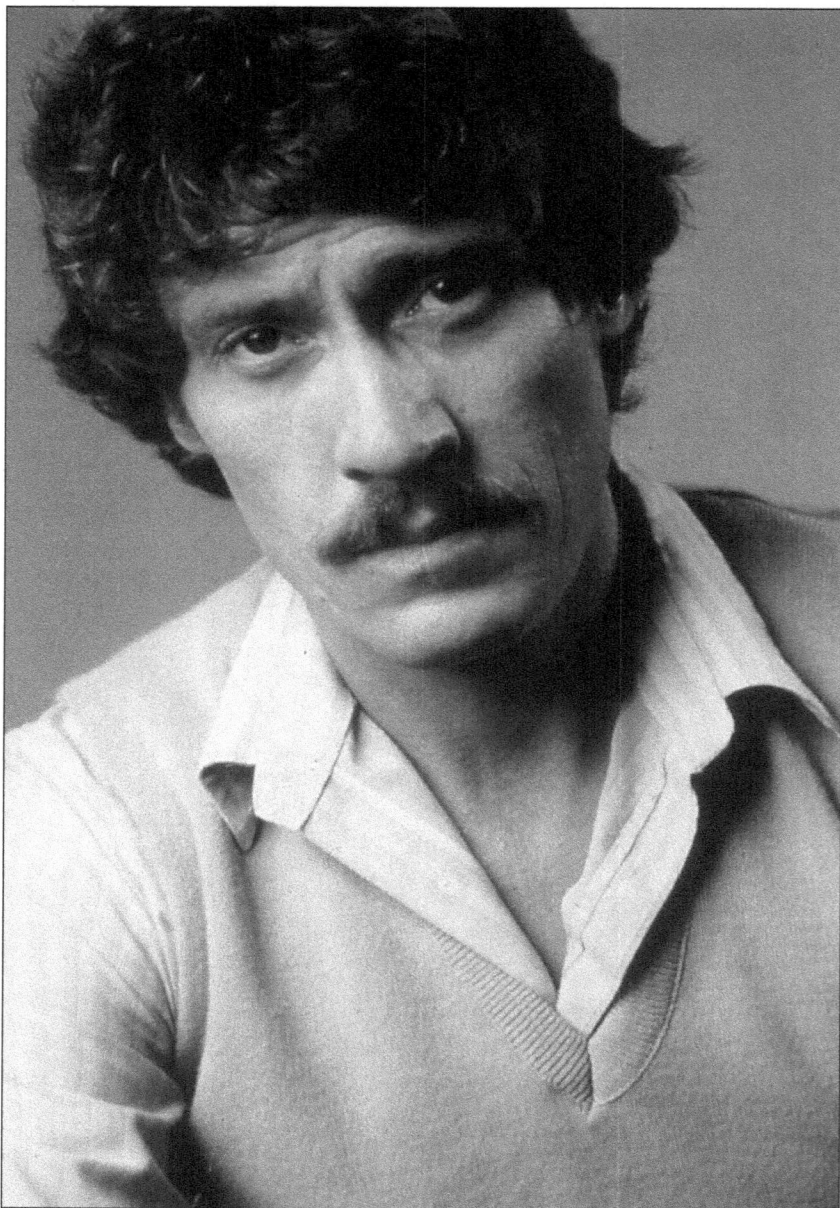

In 1985, John Holmes and Bill Amerson began their own adult video production company, Penguin.

The King's Court.

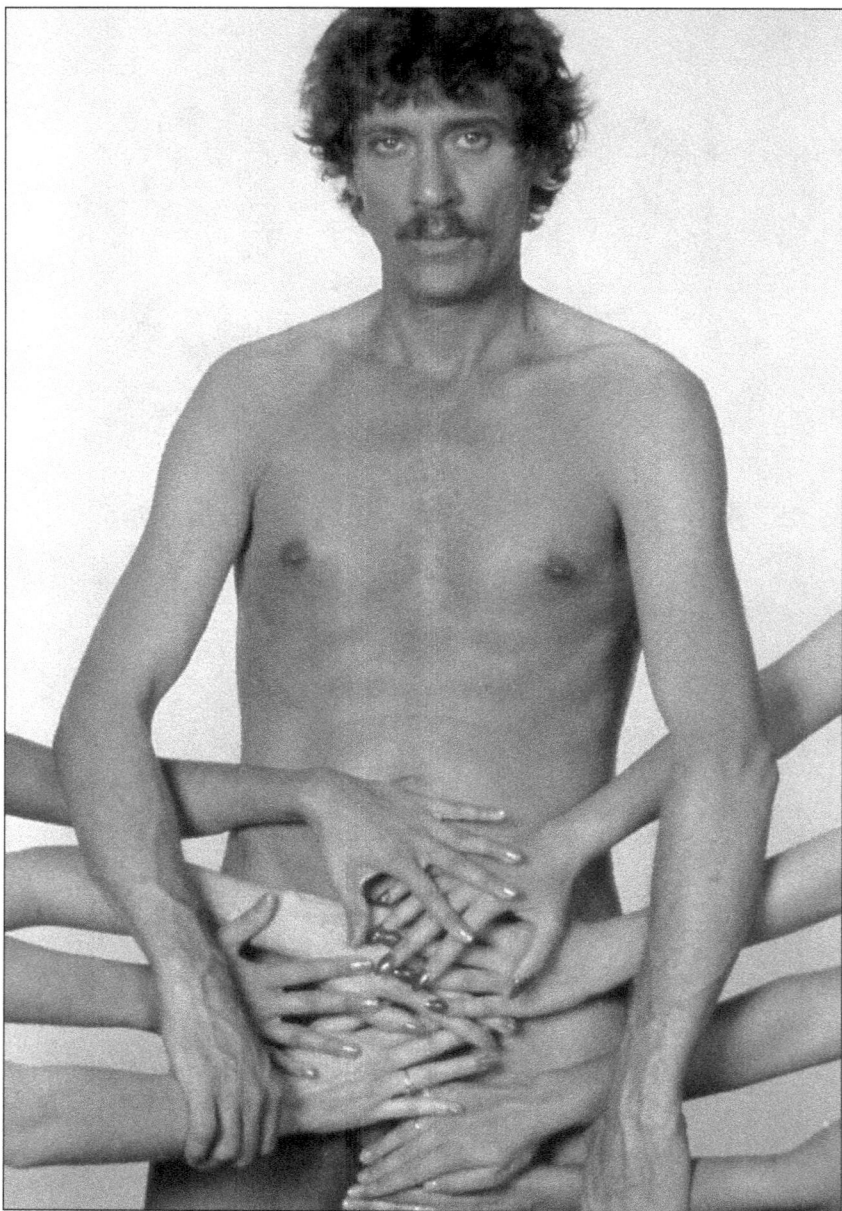

"Hands." Kenji got the idea to shoot this — which has become one of the most famous images of John Holmes — while shooting John with the women in the photo we've captioned, "The King's Court" on the previous page.

JOHN HOLMES: A LIFE MEASURED IN INCHES

This photo was taken by Kenji during the same session as "The King's Court," and "Hands." John would say that he could tell if he was working with a woman who wasn't into the scene. During this shoot, Kenji recalled having to remind the woman to stay close to John and she quipped that she was just trying to avoid "the anaconda crawling up" her leg!

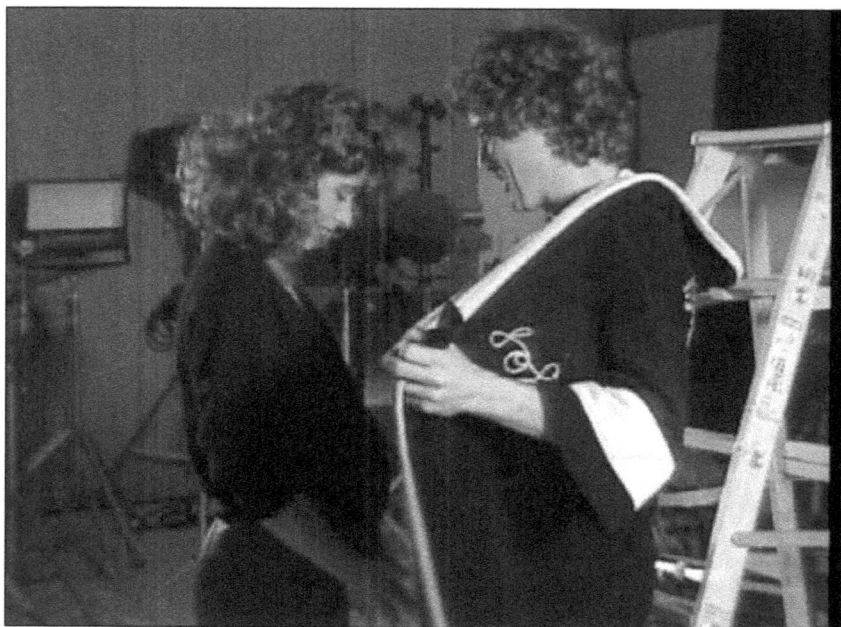

Image Courtesy of Paradise Visuals. Christy Canyon is wowed backstage on the set of *W-Pink TV.*

At age 41, John charms two lovely actresses in this 1985 still.

JOHN HOLMES: A LIFE MEASURED IN INCHES

John and one of the girls pictured in the "King's Court" ensemble, pose together in this mid-1980s photo.

The famous diamond-encrusted "JH" pinky ring is visible on John's left hand. This photo, with *Saturday Night Beaver* costar Bambi Allen, was taken in the garage of Bill Amerson's home. The Sherman Oaks residence was frequently used for Penguin Productions movie sets.

John and co-star, Sheri St. Clair cozy up in this publicity photo for *The Return of Johnny Wadd*.

Kimberly Carson, who played the good cop shadowing Johnny Wadd in *The Return of Johnny Wadd* assumes a subservient position.

John with a small dog and Cicciolina in *The Rise and Fall of the Roman Empress,* shot in Italy in the fall of 1986.

Candid.

Holmes' fans would stand in long lines to get his autograph and he was sure to accommodate each of them. John's motto was to always show a fan a good time.

Laurie and John were wed on January 24, 1987 at the Little Chapel of Flowers in Las Vegas, Nevada. Laurie was 23 and John was 42.

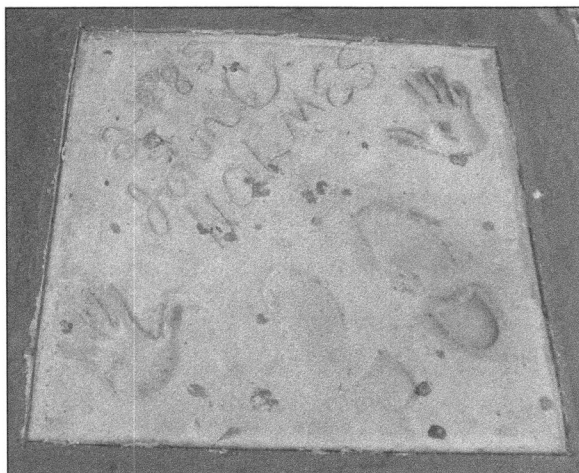

As seen in the summer of 2006 — John's impressions outside 7734 Santa Monica Boulevard in West Hollywood, California – the former location of the Pussycat Theater.

FILM (AND LOOP) OGRAPHY

Combining the total of his loops and features, John appeared in well over 1,000 erotic scenes from 1964 to 1986. In his first three years in adult entertainment, he mostly worked as a nude model for magazines. But at that time, John also appeared in numerous mail-order, softcore, black & white loops. The early loops were softcore and nudists films until 1967, when many people pushed the boundaries of stag and peepshow loop-making into hardcore, which became increasingly popular during the last three years of the '60s. One of John's first hardcore loops was made that year by director Kirdy Stevens. The loop can be seen in Stevens' 1979 hardcore film, *Little Me and Marla Strangelove.*

The entire time John was appearing in films, most producers and directors did not keep records. To boot, several of the early loops and features have not been transferred from the masters and are not widely available outside private collections. Some films have disintegrated or been discarded — some have even been lost in natural disasters. Some loops on compilations are given new titles, which makes compiling a John Holmes filmography a difficult task.

The following is the most complete Holmes filmography to date. It includes 150 loops, 306 features (everything available on DVD plus many titles that are not) and 27 compilations (limited to those made during John's lifetime, plus *The Angel in Mr. Holmes*). There may be hundreds of forgotten Holmes loops among those that have yet to be transferred and those that have been lost or damaged forever, although there are probably far less than 100 undiscovered or forgotten feature films. Titles, directors and original release date are listed (if known).

1960s Loops

Holmes and Friends
PEEPSHOW SERIES: UNKNOWN
Softcore. John Holmes with Nora
Weiternik and Rene Bond.

Title Unknown
PEEPSHOW SERIES: UNKNOWN
Hardcore, circa 1967 loop by Kirdy
Stevens and Helene Terrie.

Just Good Friends
D: UNKNOWN
Release Date: May 7, 1969
See synopsis, page 572

1960s Features

The Ball is in Your Court
D: UNKNOWN
*Release Date: August 4 and 5, 1968
(Production Date)*
One of John's earliest hardcore features,
at 50 minutes, with four softcore scenes
and one hardcore scene. Features Ann
Perry. Producer made a similar feature
(unknown title) at the same time.

Behind Locked Doors a.k.a. Any Body ... Any Way (original title), Behind Closed Doors, Then Came Ecstasy
D: CHARLES ROMINE
Release Date: 1968
Holmes in hardcore scenes throughout,
uncredited. (1970 R version, Box Office
International Pictures.)

The Ice House a.k.a. Cold Blood, Crime on the Rocks (Spain), Love in Cold Blood, The Passion Pit
D: STUART E. MCGOWAN
Release Date: July 9, 1969
John Holmes as nude dancer, uncredited.

Body Lust
D: UNKNOWN
Release Date: 1969
John Holmes and Harry Moran with
Angela O'Day and Sue Johnson.

1970s Loops

The Joys of Sex
PEEPSHOW SERIES: 13 1/2"
See synopsis, page 567

Big Bad John
PEEPSHOW SERIES: 13 1/2"
With one woman.

The Photographer
PEEPSHOW SERIES: B #105
See synopsis, page 567

John Holmes Collection
PEEPSHOW SERIES: BLUE VANITIES CLASSIC
STAGS #10 (1992 COMPILATION).
Holmes' cum shots with seven women.

Hot Cream & Cherries
PEEPSHOW SERIES: BLUE VANITIES #291 (1998
COMPILATION).
See synopsis, page 569

Untitled Peepshow Loop
PEEPSHOW SERIES: BLUE VANITIES.
With two women.

Terrible Aunt Candy
PEEPSHOW SERIES: DIVERSE
See synopsis, page 568

Artists & Models Ball
PEEPSHOW SERIES: DIVERSE
See synopsis, page 568

Big Boob Casting Call
PEEPSHOW SERIES: ERO/PHASE
PRODUCTIONS
See synopsis, page 568

Big Tit Hookers
PEEPSHOW SERIES: ERO/PHASE
PRODUCTIONS
See synopsis, page 569

Big John + 3
PEEPSHOW SERIES: HOLLYWOOD CLASSICS
John Holmes and Jamie Gillis with
Helen Madigan and another woman.

14 Inches Deep
PEEPSHOW SERIES: FANNY FILMS #7
See synopsis, page 569

Big Surprise
PEEPSHOW SERIES: FANNY FILMS #9
John Holmes with ladies, Pat Manning and Tina Russell. Anal.

California Girl
PEEPSHOW SERIES: JH #2
See synopsis, page 571

Barbershop Trio
PEEPSHOW SERIES: JH #3
See synopsis, page 571

Prime Cunt
PEEPSHOW SERIES: JH #5
With one woman.

Scheming Photographer
PEEPSHOW SERIES: JH #5
With one woman.

Deep Thrust
PEEPSHOW SERIES: JH #12
See synopsis, page 571

Help thy Neighbor
PEEPSHOW SERIES: JOHN'S GIRLS #2
With one woman.

Mind Blowers
PEEPSHOW SERIES: JOHN'S GIRLS #5
See synopsis, page 570

Fanny Up
PEEPSHOW SERIES: JOHN'S GIRLS #6
With one woman.

Campers Pickup Mountain Girls
PEEPSHOW SERIES: JOHN'S GIRLS #8
See synopsis, page 570

Jamie's Willing Student a.k.a. Young Girl's Desire, Georgina's Wine Orgy, Virgin Cock
PEEPSHOW SERIES: LIMITED EDITION #2
1980.

Title Unknown
PEEPSHOW SERIES: LIMITED EDITION #9
With Connie Peterson and Lisa DeLeeuw.

Title Unknown
PEEPSHOW SERIES: LIMITED EDITION #10
John Holmes with Phaedra Grant and a scene with John Holmes, another man, and Lisa DeLeeuw.

Bitches in Heat
a.k.a. Sink It, Sweet Music, Try Me
PEEPSHOW SERIES: LIMITED EDITION #17
John Holmes with Seka.

Hot Pink Holes a.k.a. Sex Games, Winner Takes All, Stretch Me
PEEPSHOW SERIES: LIMITED EDITION #18
John Holmes with Hillary Summers and Seka.

Hot Trick
PEEPSHOW SERIES: LIMITED EDITION #77
John Holmes with Phaedra Grant.

Water Nymph
PEEPSHOW SERIES: SWEDISH EROTICA #80
See synopsis, page 573

Can't Get Enough
PEEPSHOW SERIES: NYC #14
With three women.

Japanese Massage
PEEPSHOW SERIES: PH #1
See synopsis, page 573

Fool Around
PEEPSHOW SERIES: PLAYHOUSE #4
With one woman.

Morning After
PEEPSHOW SERIES: PLAYHOUSE #5
With one woman. Maybe '70s or '80s.

It Takes a Thief
PEEPSHOW SERIES: PLAYMATE #1
See synopsis, page 574

Deepest Throat
PEEPSHOW SERIES: PLAYMATE #6
See synopsis, page 574

Super Cock
PEEPSHOW SERIES: PLAYMATE #7
See synopsis, page 574

Wild Beauty
PEEPSHOW SERIES: PLAYMATE #11
See synopsis, page 575

Girl Scout Cookies a.k.a. Big John Holmes and the Girl Scouts
PEEPSHOW SERIES: PLAYMATE #17
With Gilda Grant and another woman. Shot in 1973.

Bondage Beauty
PEEPSHOW SERIES: PLAYMATE #27
See synopsis, page 575

Modeling
PEEPSHOW SERIES: PLAYMATE #27
See synopsis, page 576

Lovely Rita
PEEPSHOW SERIES: PRETTY GIRLS #2
With one woman.

Big Dick I
PEEPSHOW SERIES: PRETTY GIRLS #7
With one woman.

Big Dick II
PEEPSHOW SERIES: PRETTY GIRLS #8
With one woman.

Big Dick III
PEEPSHOW SERIES: PRETTY GIRLS #9
With one woman.

Playmate of the Year
PEEPSHOW SERIES: PRETTY GIRLS #11
See synopsis, page 576

Bick Dick V
PEEPSHOW SERIES: PRETTY GIRLS #16
See synopsis, page 577

Pretty Girl of the Year
PEEPSHOW SERIES: PRETTY GIRLS #29
John Holmes and "Charming" Billie.

Susan & Becky
PEEPSHOW SERIES: PRETTY GIRLS #40
With two women.

Morning Coffee
PEEPSHOW SERIES: SEX AND THE MOVIES #1
See synopsis, page 577

Wet Dreams — A Fantasy
PEEPSHOW SERIES: SUNSET STRIP #1
See synopsis, page 577

The Virgin Next Door Part 1
PEEPSHOW SERIES: SWEDISH EROTICA #1
See synopsis, page 578

The Virgin Next Door Part 2
PEEPSHOW SERIES: SWEDISH EROTICA #2
See synopsis, page 578

Park Lovers
PEEPSHOW SERIES: SWEDISH EROTICA #7
See synopsis, page 578

Hollywood Starlet
PEEPSHOW SERIES: SWEDISH EROTICA #10
Sequel to Park Lovers.

Big John Part I
PEEPSHOW SERIES: SWEDISH EROTICA #12
See synopsis, page 579

Big John Part II
PEEPSHOW SERIES: SWEDISH EROTICA #13
See synopsis, page 579

Behind the Ate Ball Part I
PEEPSHOW SERIES: SWEDISH EROTICA #15
With one woman.

Behind the Ate Ball Part II
PEEPSHOW SERIES: SWEDISH EROTICA #16
Sequel to *Behind the Ate Ball Part I*.

15" Commercial
PEEPSHOW SERIES: SWEDISH EROTICA #17
See synopsis, page 579

Pier Passion Part 1
PEEPSHOW SERIES: SWEDISH EROTICA #20
With one woman.

Pier Passion Part 2
PEEPSHOW SERIES: SWEDISH EROTICA #21
With one woman.

Lustful Shower
PEEPSHOW SERIES: SWEDISH EROTICA #28
With one woman.

Marilyn's Portfolio
PEEPSHOW SERIES: SWEDISH EROTICA #34
Featuring Marilyn Chambers.

Title Unknown
PEEPSHOW SERIES: SWEDISH EROTICA #44

Title Unknown
PEEPSHOW SERIES: SWEDISH EROTICA #47

Polynesian Princess
PEEPSHOW SERIES: SWEDISH EROTICA #51
With one woman

Cockcycle
PEEPSHOW SERIES: SWEDISH EROTICA #52
With two women.

The Mountain Cabin
PEEPSHOW SERIES: SWEDISH EROTICA #55
John Holmes and Sharon Thorpe.

Black is Bigger
PEEPSHOW SERIES: SWEDISH EROTICA #56
See synopsis, page 580

The Invitation
PEEPSHOW SERIES: SWEDISH EROTICA #59
John Holmes and Victoria Winter.

Three-Way Split
PEEPSHOW SERIES: SWEDISH EROTICA #60
With two women.

Lost Weekend
PEEPSHOW SERIES: SWEDISH EROTICA #64
With one woman.

Away Too Long
PEEPSHOW SERIES: SWEDISH EROTICA #67
With one woman.

Seaplane Sex
PEEPSHOW SERIES: SWEDISH EROTICA #68
See synopsis, page 580

Anatomy Lesson
PEEPSHOW SERIES: SWEDISH EROTICA #72
With four women.

Rock Hard
PEEPSHOW SERIES: SWEDISH EROTICA #75
John Holmes and another man with
Connie Peterson.

The Swap Meet
PEEPSHOW SERIES: SWEDISH EROTICA #76
See synopsis, page 580

The Reluctant Seducer
PEEPSHOW SERIES: SWEDISH EROTICA #81
John and another man With one woman.

Passionate Pilot
PEEPSHOW SERIES: SWEDISH EROTICA #84
John with two women.

Stuffed Rears
PEEPSHOW SERIES: SWEDISH EROTICA #87
With two women.

Sorority Stud
PEEPSHOW SERIES: SWEDISH EROTICA #91
With two women.

Bubble Bath
PEEPSHOW SERIES: SWEDISH EROTICA #92
See synopsis, page 581

The Steam Room
PEEPSHOW SERIES: SWEDISH EROTICA #96
John Holmes with Paula Wain and
another woman.

A Sexy Afternoon
PEEPSHOW SERIES: SWEDISH EROTICA #100
With one woman.

Around the World
PEEPSHOW SERIES: SWEDISH EROTICA #103
See synopsis, page 581

Sexually Yours
PEEPSHOW SERIES: SWEDISH EROTICA #107
John Holmes, Cris Cassidy and another
woman.

Morning Interlude
PEEPSHOW SERIES: SWEDISH EROTICA #108
John Holmes with Linda Wong.

Title Unknown
PEEPSHOW SERIES: SWEDISH EROTICA #110
John Holmes with Seka and Desiree
Cousteau.

Double Header
PEEPSHOW SERIES: SWEDISH EROTICA #112
John Holmes and Joey Silvera with Phae
Burd.

Fire and Spice
PEEPSHOW SERIES: SWEDISH EROTICA #115
With one woman

Hot Tub — Hot Lips
PEEPSHOW SERIES: SWEDISH EROTICA #116
With two women.

Super Pimp
PEEPSHOW SERIES: SWEDISH EROTICA #119
John Holmes and Chris Cassidy With one woman.

The Swizzle Stick
PEEPSHOW SERIES: SWEDISH EROTICA #121
With one woman.

Rear Attitude
PEEPSHOW SERIES: SWEDISH EROTICA #123
With one woman.

Hot House Honey
PEEPSHOW SERIES: SWEDISH EROTICA #124
See synopsis, page 581

Virgin in Heat
PEEPSHOW SERIES: SWEDISH EROTICA #127
With one woman.

Rectum Hell
PEEPSHOW SERIES: SWEDISH EROTICA #132
See synopsis, page 582

Moving Parts
PEEPSHOW SERIES: SWEDISH EROTICA #136
With one woman.

Triple Pleasure
PEEPSHOW SERIES: SWEDISH EROTICA #140
With one woman and Jonathan Younger.

Nature's Delight
PEEPSHOW SERIES: SWEDISH EROTICA #142
With two women.

Balcony Pick-Up
PEEPSHOW SERIES: SWEDISH EROTICA #147
With two women.

Hot Trio
PEEPSHOW SERIES: SWEDISH EROTICA #150
With two women.

The Secretary
PEEPSHOW SERIES: SWEDISH EROTICA #155
With one woman.

Treasure Chest
PEEPSHOW SERIES: SWEDISH EROTICA #156
John Holmes and Connie Peterson.

A Fantasy Come True
PEEPSHOW SERIES: SWEDISH EROTICA #165
With one woman.

Private Lessons
PEEPSHOW SERIES: SWEDISH EROTICA #166
John Holmes and another man with Sharon Kane and Juliet Anderson.

The Warlord
PEEPSHOW SERIES: SWEDISH EROTICA #172
See synopsis, page 582

The Mystic
PEEPSHOW SERIES: SWEDISH EROTICA #175
See synopsis, page 582

Asian Beauty
PEEPSHOW SERIES: SWEDISH EROTICA #177
See synopsis, page 583

The Bridesmaid
PEEPSHOW SERIES: SWEDISH EROTICA #180
John Holmes and Chrissy Peterson.

Through the Looking Glass
PEEPSHOW SERIES: SWEDISH EROTICA #182
John Holmes and Mike Ranger with Candida Royalle.

Classy Saleslady
PEEPSHOW SERIES: SWEDISH EROTICA #191
John Holmes with Annette Haven.

Shower Beauty
PEEPSHOW SERIES: SWEDISH EROTICA #206
See synopsis, page 583

Outside Activity
PEEPSHOW SERIES: SWEDISH EROTICA #209
John Holmes with Liza Dwyer and another woman.

Wild Co-Eds
PEEPSHOW SERIES: SWEDISH EROTICA #214
John Holmes and one man with three women.

Laces and Spice
PEEPSHOW SERIES: SWEDISH EROTICA #216
See synopsis, page 583

Very Happy Reunion
PEEPSHOW SERIES: SWEDISH EROTICA #221
With two women.

Stud Ranch
PEEPSHOW SERIES: SWEDISH EROTICA #222
John Holmes With one woman.

Wild Co-Ed Party
PEEPSHOW SERIES: SWEDISH EROTICA #227
John Holmes with a blonde and a
brunette.

Climactic Ending
PEEPSHOW SERIES: SWEDISH EROTICA #230
With one woman.

Games Room
PEEPSHOW SERIES: SWEDISH EROTICA #234
See synopsis, page 584

Sweet Alice
PEEPSHOW SERIES: SWEDISH EROTICA #240
See synopsis, page 584

Fixer-Up Her
PEEPSHOW SERIES: SWEDISH EROTICA #264
John Holmes and Misty Regan.

Refreshing Break
PEEPSHOW SERIES: SWEDISH EROTICA #270

Dr. Feelgood
PEEPSHOW SERIES: SWEDISH EROTICA #276
With two women.

Ski Bunnies Pt. 2
PEEPSHOW SERIES: SWEDISH EROTICA #295
John Holmes and another man with
Desiree Cousteau and Seka.

Improper Stranger
PEEPSHOW SERIES: SWEDISH EROTICA #296
John Holmes and Seka.

Body Reunion
PEEPSHOW SERIES: SWEDISH EROTICA
#1118
With Serena and Johnny Keyes.

Surprise Package
PEEPSHOW SERIES: WATERGATE GIRLS #2
With a busty brunette.

Pleasure Pole
PEEPSHOW SERIES: WATERGATE GIRLS #3
See synopsis, page 592

Big Load a.k.a. Large Economy Size
PEEPSHOW SERIES: WATERGATE GIRLS #5
See synopsis, page 592

Watergate Girls
PEEPSHOW SERIES: WATERGATE GIRLS #6
11 minutes and 32 seconds. Eight
millimeter. With one woman.

Bare Harbor
PEEPSHOW SERIES: VIP #2
See synopsis, page 592

Pool Party
PEEPSHOW SERIES: UNKNOWN
See synopsis, page 576

1970s Features

Gang Bang
D: UNKNOWN
September 1970
As Stud #1.

Carnal Knowledge
D: UNKNOWN
October 1970
Softcore sex. As Big John.

Anomalies: A World of Dreams
D: UNKNOWN
1970
Hardcore with Lynn Harris.

Doctor I'm Coming
D: ROD KILLY
1970
Billed as "John Helms."

Door to Door Salesman
D: UNKNOWN
1970
Hardcore with Sandy Dempsey.

I Want You
D: UNKNOWN
1970
John Holmes and Uschi Digard, both
uncredited.

Johnny Wadd
D: BOB CHINN
1970
First installment of series. See review, page 514

Sex and the Single Vampire
D: MODUNK PHREEZER
1970
See review, page 540

Sex Psycho a.k.a. Widow Blue
D: WALT DAVIS
1970 or 1971
John Holmes with Rick Cassidy, Walt Davis (non-sex) and Sandy Dempsey.

Flesh of the Lotus
D: BOB CHINN
December 1971
Second of the *Johnny Wadd* series. See review, page 502

Aphrodisiac
a.k.a. Sexual Secrets of Marijuana
D: DENNIS VAN ZAK
1971
With Sandy Dempsey, Eve Orlon and Lynn Holmes.

Blonde in Black Lace
D: BOB CHINN
1971
Third of nine in the *Johnny Wadd* series. See review, page 479

The Girl Next Door
D: VERONICA STONE
1971

Hunter
D: E. NICKOLS
1971
With Sandy Dempsey.

Kama Sutra
PRODUCED BY PHIL TODARO.
1971
John with Uschi Digard and Ann Myers.

Love Boccaccio Style
D: SAM PHILLIPS
1971
See review, page 521

My Tongue is Quick
D: UNKNOWN
1971
See review, page 526

New Girl in Town
D: DAVID STEFANS
1971
See review, page 528

Olé
D: UNKNOWN
1971
With Ramone Narone. Performers are hypnotized at a party.

S.M.A.S.H. or How to Get Hung
D: IVAN STEPHENS
1971
See review, page 543

Superstud
D: UNKNOWN
1971
John Holmes and Gerard Broulard with Judy Angel and Lynn Holmes.

Teenage Fantasies a.k.a. Rene Bond's Sex Fantasies
D: FRANK SPOKEMAN
1971
Compilation.

Turn-on Orgy
D: UNKNOWN
1971
See review, page 562

The Zodiac Killer
D: UNKNOWN
1971
Notable underwater sex scene.

Benny's Bungles
D: UNKNOWN
1971 or 1972
See review, page 476

The Baby Sister
D: UNKNOWN
1972
With Sandy Dempsey and Rene Bond.

Big Beaver Splits the Scene
D: UNKNOWN
1972

Cabin Fever
D: UNKNOWN
1972

The Coming of Angie
D: UNKNOWN
1972

Double Exposure
D: UNKNOWN
1972
With Sandy Dempsey.

Evil Come, Evil Go
D: WALT DAVIS
1972
See review, page 499

Four Women in Trouble
D: UNKNOWN
1972
See review, page 503

Hot Summer Night
D: UNKNOWN
1972
With Rick Cassidy.

The Liberated Woman
D: PAT ALLEN
1972
See review, page 516

The Orgy Machine *a.k.a. The Incredible Sex-Ray Machine*
D: UNKNOWN
1972
With Uschi Digard.

Pornography in Hollywood
D: CARLOS TOBALINA
1972
Documentary. Holmes appears on a magazine cover, uncredited.

Sex As You Like It *a.k.a. The As You Like It Sex Service*
D: UNKNOWN
1972
See review, page 540

Stolen Girls
D: UNKNOWN
1972
With Judy Angel.

Tropic of Passion
D: BOB CHINN
1972
Fourth in the *Johnny Wadd* series. See review, page 561

Wet & Wild
D: MICHAEL FINDLAY
1972

Deviate Doctor
D: UNKNOWN
1973

Erotic Intrusion
D: UNKNOWN
1973

Exotic French Fantasies
D: MIKE MCDERMOT
1973
With Andrea True and Eric Edwards.

French Schoolgirls
D: UNKNOWN
1973

The Group
D: UNKNOWN
1973

Helen Bedd
a.k.a. Helen Bed
D: GARBIS TORIAN
1973

Lollipop Palace *a.k.a. Frenchie's Lollipop Palace (working title), Lust Goddess*
D: KIRDY STEVENS
1973
John plays a patron at a brothel.

Panama Red *a.k.a. Acapulco Gold, Panama Red: A Perfect Smoke*
D: BOB CHINN
1973
John has a cameo as Bobo.

Ride a Cocked Horse
D: UNKNOWN
1973

Rings of Passion
D: WILLIE CREPS
1973
See review, page 533

Strangers When We Mate
D: DAVID STEFANS
1973
See review, page 545

The Swinging Playboy
D: UNKNOWN
1973

Teenage Cowgirls
D: TED DENVER
1973
See review, page 553

The Winning Stroke
D: UNKNOWN
1973
See review, page 565

Zolotia
D: UNKNOWN
1973

Black Velvet: The Big Deal
D: UNKNOWN
1973 or 1974
See review, page 477

Panorama Blue
D: ALAN ROBERTS
February, 1974
Compilation. Tagline, "The World's Mightiest Adult Film."

The Danish Connection
D: WALT DAVIS
March 1974
See review, page 489

Fulfillment
D: BILLY THORNBERG
October 25, 1974
John pleases different actresses. Auburn-haired beauty, Brigitte Maier is in this film.

Beyond Fulfillment
D: BILLY THORNBERG
1974
With Barbara Barton and Linda McDowell footage from early Holmes' loops.

Cheri
a.k.a. Cherri
D: SIMON L. EGREE
1974
See review, page 484

I Want You
D: M. BAUDICROT
1974
Billed as John "Johnny Wadd" Holmes.

Le Journal érotique d'un bucheron
a.k.a. The Erotic Diary of a Lumberjack
D: JEAN-MARIE PALLARDY
1974
John is uncredited. Filmed in France.

The Life and Times of the Happy Hooker *a.k.a. Life and Times of Xaviera Hollander*
D: LARRY G. SPANGLER
1974

Oriental Ecstasy Girls
D: PIERRE HARDY
1974
With Sandy Dempsey, Sandi Carey and Candy Samples. Tagline, "Let me be NAUGHTY with you TONIGHT."

Oversexposure
D: UNKNOWN
1974
The first of four films with Andrea True — who had a hit with the disco song, "More, More, More."

Sex Freaks
D: M. C. VON HELLEN
1974
Taglines: "Filmed in the capital cities of the world, an erotic odyssey, three years in the making."

The Swing Thing
D: UNKNOWN
1974
See review, page 551

Teenage Fantasies #2 a.k.a. Young Woman's Fantasies, Young Girl's Fantasies
D: PAUL LYONS
1974
John Holmes appears in a fairytale sequence with Rene Bond.

Teenager a.k.a. The Real Thing
D: GERALD SETH SINDELL
1974

Three Came Running
D: UNKNOWN
1974
See review, page 559

Teenage Lovers a.k.a. Hot Teenage Lovers, War and Piece
D: UNKNOWN
March 1975
See review, page 556

The Kowloon Connection
D: HARRY WHO
September 1975
See review, page 515

Around the World with John "the Wadd" Holmes
D: D.C. CANARD
1975
See review, page 474

Confessions of a Teenage Peanut Butter Freak
D: ZACHARY STRONG
1975
See review, page 487

Country Girls
D: UNKNOWN
1975

Executive Secretary
D: UNKNOWN
1975

In Memory of Connie
D: UNKNOWN
1975

Love Explosions
D: UNKNOWN
1975

Masked Ball
D: DAVID STEFANS
1975
John is the host of the ball.

Oriental Sex Kitten
D: HARRY WHO
1975
See review, page 530

Personal Services a.k.a. Queen of Sex
D: MICHAEL MINGHIA
1975
John Holmes plays a sailor, B. C. Buzzard, and is featured in two scenes. Costars Cyndee Summers and Peter Boll. Tagline, "She'll make you an offer you can't refuse!"

Puss*O*Rama
D: MULTIPLE.
1975
Compilation. Includes scenes with Brigitte Maier.

Sex Station
D: UNKNOWN
1975

Sunset Strip Girls
D: UNKNOWN
1975

Sweet Julie
D: UNKNOWN
1975
Costars Rick Cassidy.

Young and Wet
D: UNKNOWN
1975

All Night Long
D: ALAN COLBERG
April 1976
With Ric Lutze in a contest to see who can sleep with the most women in one night.

Softie
D: UNKNOWN
May 5, 1976

Liquid Lips
D: BOB CHINN
July 1976
Sixth in the *Johnny Wadd* series. See review, page 519

Fantasm
D: RICHARD FRANKLIN
July 16, 1976
See review, page 499

Big Abner
D: LEONARD KIRTMAN
August 1976

The Autobiography of a Flea
D: SHARON MCKNIGHT
September 1976
See review, page 475

Cream Rinse
D: R.J. DOYLE
September 10, 1976
See review, page 498

Hard Candy *a.k.a. Lollipop Girls in Hard Candy*
D: STEPHEN GIBSON
October 1976

Love in Strange Places
D: ROBERTA FINDLAY
November 1976

The Spirit of Seventy-Sex
D: STU SEGALL
November 1976
See review, page 543

Tapestry of Passion *a.k.a. Black Magic*
D: ALAN COLBERG
November 1976
See review, page 552

Black Widow's Nest
D: UNKNOWN
1976

Candy's Candy
D: UNKNOWN
1976

Dear Pam
D: ROBERTA FINDLAY
1976
See review, page 489

Fuzz
D: UNKNOWN
1976

The Girls in the Band
D: UNKNOWN
1976

Starlets
a.k.a. X-Rated Starlets
D: DAVID SUMMER
1976

Sweet Punkin', I Love You
D: ROBERTA FINDLAY
1976
See review, page 550

Sweet, Sweet Freedom
D: ROBERTA FINDLAY
1976
See review, page 551

Tell Them Johnny Wadd is Here
D: BOB CHINN
1976
Fifth in the *Johnny Wadd* series. See review, page 557

The Touch
D: UNKNOWN
1976
See review, page 559

Her Last Fling
D: BRUCE VAN DEBUREN
January 1977

Blonde Emmanuelle
a.k.a. Disco Dolls, Hot Skin
D: STEPHEN GIBSON
February 1977
See review, page 478

Ecstasy *a.k.a. Extasis (Venezuela)*
D: BILLY THORNBERG
April 1977

Young, Hot 'N' Nasty Teenage Cruisers
D: TOM DENUCCI & JOHNNY LEGEND
April 1977
See review, page 554

Black Silk Stockings
D: BILLY THORNBERG
May 1977

Ultimate Pleasures
D: CARLOS TOBALINA
May 1977

The Jade Pussycat
D: BOB CHINN
July 1977
Seventh installment in the *Johnny Wadd* series. See review, page 512

Fantastic Orgy
a.k.a. La Orgía fantástica (Venezuela)
D: UNKNOWN
September 9, 1977
With Annette Haven and Lesllie Bovee.

Fantasm Comes Again
D: COLIN EGGLESTON
December 26, 1977
See review, page 501

Fantastic Orgy
D: UNKNOWN
1977
With Annette Haven, Sharon Thorpe and Desiree West.

Candi Girl
a.k.a. Jet Sex
D: JOHN CHRISTOPER
1977

Casanova II *a.k.a. The New Erotic Adventures of Casanova*
D: JOHN HOLMES & CARLOS TOBALINA
1977
See review, page 483

China Cat
D: BOB CHINN
1977
Eighth installment in the *Johnny Wadd* series. See review, page 485

Female Athletes
D: LEONARD KIRTMAN
1977
With Annette Haven. Billed as "Johnny Wadd (as Johnny Wadd)."

The Fire in Francesca
D: UNKNOWN
1977

Dr. Gonad's Sex Tails *a.k.a. Teenage Madam, Madam Lust*
D: RICK TAZINER
1977
See review, page 492

Hard Soap, Hard Soap
D: BOB CHINN
1977
See review, page 507

The Passion Seekers
D: WALT DAVIS
1977

Ultimate Pleasure
D: CARLOS TOBALINA
1977

Bottoms Up Series 02
D: UNKNOWN
1978

Carnal Encounters of the Barest Kind
D: DONALD BRYCE
1978

The Erotic Adventures of Candy
D: GAIL PALMER & BOB CHINN
1978
See review, page 495

Eruption
D: STANLEY KURLAN
1978
See review, page 496

Homecoming
D: UNKNOWN
1978

John Holmes Exposed
D: MULTIPLE.
1978
Compilation with Sandy Dempsey,
Serena and Maria Tortuga.

Jungle Blue
D: CARLOS TOBALINA
1978

Ladies Bed Companion
D: UNKNOWN
1978

Lusty Princess
D: CARLOS TOBALINA
1978

Remember Connie
D: W.P. EMERSON
1978

Scriptease
D: UNKNOWN
1978

Sex Pageant
D: UNKNOWN
1978

Tough Cookies
D: UNKNOWN
1978
With Muffin MacIntosh and Ashley
Welles.

Summertime Blue
D: JOHN CHRISTOPHER
March 1979
See review, page 546

Honeysuckle Rose
D: ROBERTA FINDLAY
October 1979
With Serena, Hershel Savage and
Samantha Fox. John plays a pig farmer.

Extreme Close-up
D: CHARLES DESANTOS
December 1979
See review, page 498

Johnny Does Paris
D: CARLOS DESANTOS
December 1979
See review, page 514

Blonde Fire
a.k.a. Fuego ardiente (Venezuela)
D: BOB CHINN
1979
The final (ninth) installment of the
Johnny Wadd film series. See review, page
478

California Gigolo
D: BOB CHINN
1979
See review, page 480

Candi Girl a.k.a. Candy Girl, Jet Sex
D: JOHN CHRISTOPHER
1979
With Herschel Savage and Samantha
Fox.

Deep Rub
D: LEONARD KIRTMAN
1979

Dracula Sucks a.k.a. Lust at First Bite
D: PHILLIP MARSHAK
1979
See review, page 522

French Kiss
D: UNKNOWN
1979

*Hot Child in the City a.k.a. Hot Stuff
in the City*
D: JOHN CHRISTOPHER
1979
Tagline, "At Home in a tenement, or a
penthouse!" John Holmes is billed as
Johnny Wadd.

Hot 'n' Spicy Pizza Girls, We Deliver
D: BOB CHINN
1979
See review, page 509

I Am Always Ready
D: CARLOS TOBALINA
1979
See review, page 510

Inside Desiree Cousteau
D: LEON GUCCI
1979

Johnny's Sex Stories
D: UNKNOWN
1979

Little Me & Marla Strangelove
D: KIRDY STEVENS
1979
Includes late 1960s hardcore insert loop featuring John Holmes and Sandy Dempsey.

Little Orphan Dusty
D: JAACOV JAACOVI & BOB CHINN
1979
See review, page 517

New York City Woman
D: ROBERTA FINDLAY
1979
See review, page 529

One Way At a Time
D: ALAN COLBERG
1979
Spoof of the television show, "One Day at a Time."

The Senator's Daughter
D: DON FLOWERS
1979
See review, page 539

Sex Machine
D: JOHN TRAYNOR
1979

Sheer Panties
D: CHRIS WARFIELD
1979
A Sweet Alice Poster is seen at the theater.

Sissy's Hot Summer
D: ALAN COLBERG
1979
See review, page 542

Superstar John Holmes
D: ALAN COLBERG
1979
See review, page 548

Sweet Captive
D: LEE FROST & LEONI VALENTINO
1979

Taxi Girls
D: JAACOV JAACOVI & BOB CHINN
1979
See review, page 552

That's Erotic
D: JOSEPH F. ROBERTSON
1979
Compilation.

John Holmes: Master Cocksman
D: UNKNOWN
Release Date Unknown
See review, page 513

Supercock
D: UNKNOWN
Release Date Unknown
See review, page 547

1970s/1980s Loops

Marilyn on Deck, Parts 1 & 2
PEEPSHOW SERIES: CONTINENTAL CLASSICS
John Holmes and Luther Worth with Marilyn Chambers.

Lustful Reader
PEEPSHOW SERIES: CONTINENTAL CLASSICS
John Holmes and another man With one woman.

John Holmes & Rene Bond
PEEPSHOW SERIES: PETER BENT #8
With Rene Bond and Victoria Winter.

Little Miss Jersey Maid
PEEPSHOW SERIES: SWEDISH EROTICA #303
John Holmes with Michelle Weiner.

John's New Girlfriend
PEEPSHOW SERIES: SWEDISH EROTICA #314
With one woman.

Personal Invitation
PEEPSHOW SERIES: SWEDISH EROTICA #317
With one woman.

Fly Girl
PEEPSHOW SERIES: SWEDISH EROTICA #321
With one woman.

Tender Loving Care
PEEPSHOW SERIES: SWEDISH EROTICA #528
John Holmes and Paul Thomas with two women.

Sexing It Up
PEEPSHOW SERIES: SWEDISH EROTICA #1101
With two women.

John's Bedroom Caper
PEEPSHOW SERIES: SWEDISH EROTICA #1104
John Holmes and Paul Thomas with Connie Peterson.

Up My Hill
PEEPSHOW SERIES: SWEDISH EROTICA #1108
With one woman.

Steaming Sauna Party
PEEPSHOW SERIES: SWEDISH EROTICA #1113
John Holmes with Connie Peterson and Paula Smith.

Different Strokes
PEEPSHOW SERIES: SWEDISH EROTICA #1120
With one woman.

1980s Features

Body Candy
D: DALE J. MARTIN
January 10, 1980
With Juliet Anderson. Tagline, "This one melts in your hand and your mouth!"

Rockin' With Seka a.k.a. Seka's Cruise, Fallen Angel
D: ZIGGY ZIGOWITZ JR.
February 5, 1980
See review, page 535

Aunt Peg
D: ANTHONY SPINELLI
September 24, 1980

Insatiable
D: STU SEGALL
September 24, 1980
See review, page 511

Balling For Dollars
D: UNKNOWN
1980
With Ashley Welles and Mike Ranger.

California Girls a.k.a. The Champ
D: UNKNOWN
1980
See review, page 481

Disco Sex Party
D: UNKNOWN
1980
See review, page 492

Ecstasy
D: BILLY THORNBERG
1980

Garters and Lace
D: BILLY THORNBERG
1980
See review, page 503

Honey Throat
D: JOHN CHRISTOPHER
1980
See review, page 508

John Holmes and the All-Star Sex Queens
D: UNKNOWN
1980
See review, page 513

Let Me Count the Lays
D: DAVID STEPHANS
1980
See review, page 516

Over Easy
D: J.T.
1980

Prisoner of Paradise
D: GAIL PALMER & BOB CHINN
1980
See review, page 530

The Seduction of Cindy
D: LEON GUCCI
1980
John Holmes appears in a clip.

Sexual Heights
D: CARLOS TOBALINA
1980
See review, page 541

Stormy
D: JOSEPH BLANSKI
1980
See review, page 544

Sweet Cheeks
D: JOSEPH F. ROBERTSON
1980
See review, page 549

That's Porno a.k.a. The Raincoat Crowd
D: JOSEPH F. ROBERTSON
1980
Compilation with Jessie St. James and
John Seeman as hosts.

Undulations
D: CARLOS TOBALINA
1980
See review, page 562

Aunt Peg's Fulfillment
D: ANTHONY SPINELLI
April 3, 1981
See review, page 475

La Belle et Le Bete
D: CARLOS DESANTOS
1981
With Gloria Leonard. Filmed in Brittany,
France. Based upon "The Beauty and The
Beast."

Best of Gail Palmer
D: UNKNOWN
1981
See review, page 477

Classic Erotica #1
D: UNKNOWN
1981

*Dallas School Girls a.k.a. Dallas
Schoolgirls*
D: JOHN CHRISTOPHER
1981

*Exhausted: John C. Holmes, The Real
Story*
D: JULIA ST. VINCENT & BOB CHINN
1981
See review, page 496

Extremes
D: UNKNOWN
1981

Homecoming
D: UNKNOW
1981
Costarring Lisa DeLeeuw and Connie
Peterson.

The Little French Maid
D: JOSEPH F. ROBERTSON
1981
See review, page 517

Love Goddesses
D: JOSEPH F. ROBERTSON
1981

Electric Blue #005
D: UNKNOWN
1982

Up 'n' Coming
D: STU SEGALL
January 7, 1983
See review, page 563

Flesh & Laces II
D: CARLOS TOBALINA
September 1983
See review, page 501

Bottoms Up Series 4
D: UNKNOWN
1983

California Valley Girls
D: HAL FREEMAN & WILLIAM MARGOLD
1983
See review, page 482

Cum Shot Revue #1
D: MULTIPLE
1983
Compilation with John Leslie and Jessie St. James.

Erotic Fantasies #1
D: MULTIPLE
1983
Compilation.

Erotic Fantasies #5
D: MULTIPLE
1983
Compilation.

Flight Sensations
D: JOSEPH F. ROBERTSON
1983
Compilation.

Heat of the Moment
D: UNKNOWN
1983
See review, page 507

Lingerie
D: JEROME BRONSON
1983

Marathon
D: CARLOS TOBALINA
1983
See review, page 524

Marilyn Chambers' Private Fantasies #1
D: JACK REMY
1983
Footage with Holmes in gym was shot in 1980 at the same time Insatiable was produced.

Moments of Love
D: H. HERSHEY & JOE SHERMAN
1983
John has a cameo.

Nasty Nurses
D: PAUL VATELLI
1983
See review, page 527

The Newcomers
D: WESLEY EMERSON
1983

The Private Pleasures of John C. Holmes
D: J.J. ENGLISH
1983
See review, page 531

Snow Honeys a.k.a. Turbo Sex (U.S.A: Video Title)
D: JOSEPH F. ROBERTSON
1983
Tagline, "They'll melt your inhibitions!" Includes archive footage of Rene Bond, Serena and Georgina Spelvin.

Swedish Erotica Superstars #1
D: MULTIPLE
1983
Compilation. Featuring Seka.

Swedish Erotica Superstar #2
D: MULTIPLE
1983
Compilation. Featuring Brigitte Monet.

Sweet Alice
D: JOSEPH F. ROBERTSON
1983
With Seka and Desiree Cousteau. John plays a medic at a ski lodge. Filmed in late-'70s.

Those Young Girls
D: MILES KIDDER
November 1984
See review, page 558

Backdoor Romance
D: JAMES SPHINCTER
1984

Bedtime Video 1
D: MULTIPLE
1984
Compilation.

Bedtime Video 3
D: MULTIPLE
1984
Compilation.

Bedtime Video 4
D: MULTIPLE
1984
Compilation.

Best of John Holmes
D: MULTIPLE
1984
Compilation.

Body Shop
BILL AMERSON
1984
See review, page 480

Candy Samples Video Review a.k.a.
Candy's Bedtime Story
D: UNKNOWN
1984
The hottest of Candy's hardcore features, in which she takes on John Holmes and Patty Douglas in one of three torrid scenes.

Critic's Choice #1
D: MULTIPLE
1984
Compilation with Jamie Gillis and Annette Haven.

Critic's Choice #2
D: UNKNOWN
1984

Dreams of Misty
D: MAX STRAND
1984
See review, page 494

Ebony Lust
D: UNKNOWN
1984

Lingerie
D: JEROME BRONSON
1984
With Misty Dawn and Ron Jeremy.

Open For Business
D: MULTIPLE
1984
Compilation.

Passion Play
D: UNKNOWN
1984

Singlehanded
D: UNKNOWN
1984
See review, page 542

Studio of Lust
D: PAUL CRANE
1984
With Candida Royalle, Don Fernando and Laurie Rose (Misty Dawn).

Suburban Satanist
D: UNKNOWN
1984 or 1985
See review, page 545

Girls on Fire
D: JACK REMY
February 7, 1985
See review, page 504

First Annual XRCO Awards a.k.a.
Nights for Legends
D: SCOTTY FOX
February 14, 1985
John C. Holmes was the very first erotic performer to be inducted into XRCO's Hall of Fame.

Connections Live
D: UNKNOWN
1985
With Ginger Lynn.

Cumshot Revue #2
D: MULTIPLE
1985
Compilation.

Down & Dirty
D: CHARLES DESANTOS
1985
See review, page 493

Frankenstein
D: PHILIP MARSHAK
1985

Free and Foxy
D: JOSEPH F. ROBERTSON
1985

The Good, The Bad and The Horny
D: JOHN HOLMES
1985
See review, page 505

The Grafenberg Spot
D: ARTIE MITCHELL
1985
See review, page 506

Idol a.k.a. The Idol
D: JEROME TANNER
1985
With Helga Sven, Mark Wallice, Jaqueline Lorians and Jessica Wylde. John Holmes plays himself and is wearing a cast on right hand, partway to his elbow.

Jawbreakers
D: ALBERT BERRY
1985
Compilation.

Looking for Mr. Goodsex
D: JACK REMY
1985
See review, page 520

Love Champions
D: CARLOS TOBALINA
1985

Lust in America
D: S. WILLIAMS
1985
With Sheri St. Claire. John plays a gardener.

Marina Vice
D: PATTI RHODES-LINCOLN
1985
See review, page 525

Night on the Wild Side a.k.a. Beyond the Wild Side, Café Erotica, Wild Nights
D: CHARLES DESANTOS
1985
With Janey Robbins and Kay Parker. John plays a bartender and has a finger cast on his right hand.

Passion Pit
D: CHARLES DE SANTOS & DUCK DUMONT
1985
With Little Oral Annie in a daydream sequence.

Rubdown
D: UNKNOWN
1985
See review, page 536

Scandal in the Mansion
D: JIM REYNOLDS
1985
With Helga Sven, Marc Wallice, Bunny Bleu, and Lisa DeLeeuw.

Superstars of Porn #2
D: MULTIPLE
1985
Compilation.

Treasure Box
D: PATTY RHODES-LINCOLN
1985
See review, page 560

Tribute to the King
D: MULTIPLE
1985
Compilation.

Whore of the Worlds a.k.a. Lust in Space 2
D: MILES KIDDER
1985

W-Pink TV #1
D: MILES KIDDER
1985
See review, page 564

The Return of Johnny Wadd
D: PATTI RHODES- LINCOLN
January 1986
See review, page 532

Rocky X
D: PATTI RHODES-LINCOLN
February 1986
See review, page 536

*The Adventures of Dickman &
Throbbin*
D: JEROME TANNER
1986
See review, page 473

The Bigger The Better
D: UNKNOWN
1986

Chastity and the Starlets
D: DAVID SUMMERS
1986

Chastity Johnson
D: SCOTTY FOX
1986
Script written by Raven Touchstone.

Coming Holmes
D: TONY VALENTINO
1986
See review, page 486

Diamond Collection 75
D: UNKNOWN
1986

Double Penetration #3
D: UNKNOWN
1986

Good to the Last Drop
D: MULTIPLE
1986
Compilation.

Great Sex Scenes #1
D: UNKNOWN
1986

I Love L.A. Part 1
D: JACK REMY & LEE COOPER
1986
See review, page 510

Lottery Lust
D: PATTY RHODES-LINCOLN
1986
See review, page 521

Lucky Charm
D: UNKNOWN
1986

Lust Vegas Joyride
D: UNKNOWN
1986?

Naughty Girls Like It Big
D: BOB VOSSE
1986
See review, page 528

Only The Best #1
D: MULTIPLE
1986
Compilation.

Oral Majority #3
D: UNKNOWN
1986

Salt & Pepper
D: UNKNOWN
1986

Saturday Night Beaver
D: PATTY RHODES-LINCOLN
1986
See review, page 537

This Stud's For You
D: UNKNOWN
1986

*The Rise and Fall of the Roman
Empress*
D: RICARDO SCHICCHI
January 27, 1987
See review, page 534

The Devil in Mr. Holmes
D: GEORGIO GRANDE
March 1987
See review, page 490

Honey Buns
D: JEROME TANNER
1987

Lifestyles of the Blonde & Dirty
D: ROBERTA FINDLAY
1987

Nudes at Eleven #2
D: DAMON CHRISTIAN
1987

Orgies
D: UNKNOWN
1987

Princess Charming
D: CHRIS MONTE
1987
Compilation.

Private Thighs
D: DAMON CHRISTIAN
1987
Compilation.

Seka Story
a.k.a. Seka
D: MULTIPLE
1988
Compilation. See review, page 538

The Angel in Mr. Holmes
D: BILL MARGOLD
1988
Compilation. See review, page 473

SELECTED FEATURE FILM REVIEWS

John Holmes was effectively immortalized through over 20 years of service as an adult film actor. In the words of Sharon Mitchell, "I know where to find him, I can always press play."

The Adventures of Dickman and Throbbin ★ 1986

Also known as *Dickman and Throbbin*. Tagline: *"They're here and sex will never be the same..."*

This film could have been much more interesting if it used Dickman (Holmes) and Throbbin (Tom Byron) more frequently. Instead, the film drags on, sex scene after sex scene, and the heroes don't show up until much later. Holmes wears a mask for all his scenes, which is funny since this is an attempted parody of the characters *Batman and Robin*, but also a bit creepy. John also appears to be weary and spent, which is sad considering all of the tribulations he had been through.

There are a few interesting sex scenes with Byron and Holmes double-teaming a lady in guy-guy-girl action. There are only two sex scenes with John Holmes, which can also be viewed on Bill Margold's *The Angel in Mr. Holmes*. These are by far the best scenarios of the entire film. In one, Holmes and Byron double dick Kitty (Keli Richards). In this scene, you can clearly see John's initials monogrammed in diamonds on his famous pinky ring — it makes one wonder what happened to that!

In the second scene, Dickman and Throbbin are hired to sex up Amber Lynn, who plays a teenage star. This scene is worth watching for Holmes' funny, dead-pan monologue to Amber about her pussy. However, Amber Lynn's believability as a naïve virgin is far less than that of Desiree Cousteau in *Pizza Girls*.

Skip this one, unless you really will feel satisfied by Throbbin's lines, which are very funny (including, "Holy Hemorrhoids, Dickman!" and "Holy douche bag, Dickman, I think I'm going to throw up."), but too seldom.

87 min/color. Unavailable. Amber Lynn, Jessica Wylde, Joanna Storm, Kari Foxx, Keli Richards, Pat Manning, Regine Bardot, John Holmes, Marc Wallice, Peter North, Steve Drake, Tom Byron. *Director:* Jerome Tanner. *Producer:* Western Visuals.

The Angel in Mr. Holmes ★★★ 1988

Constructed after John's death, this movie contains film clips with narration by Bill Margold. The first clip showcases the late Jim Holliday inducting John Holmes into the XRCO Hall of Fame in 1985, while the end of the clip shows

John Leslie expressing his awe at Holmes during his own induction. After being summoned by Leslie, Holmes returns to the stage as he and Leslie embrace during a classic moment.

This film is a great addition for a collector, as well as an ingenious way to showcase snippets from Holmes' career. The film clips include a scene from Holmes' early career with Seka from *Swedish Erotica*; a highly erotic scene from *Taxi Girls* with Nancy Suiter; a threesome from *Tough Cookie* that includes an arrangement of four or five *Star Wars* songs; a scene from *Scriptease* with an interracial threesome to a Burt Bacharach tune; a scene from *The Champ* featuring Rhonda Jo Petty and The King having sex to disco music on a waterbed and roller skating in knee-high sport socks; a foursome scene from 1984 with John, Jennifer Turley, Misty Anderson, and Jessica Wylde that includes a rip-off of Michael Jackson's "Thriller," in addition to John's favorite trick — coming onto multiple women's faces at once. The final two sex scenes in the film are from *Dickman and Throbbin*, where you can see John's diamond "JH" pinky ring.

Bill Margold's narrations are, as he admits, pretentious at times. While watching the film with Margold in his apartment on August 7, 2004, he disclosed that he couldn't even read his notes because he was wearing glasses from an old prescription. The following day (8/8/2004), Bill emceed the "Fit for a King" event to recognize John's 60th birthday, at the Erotic Museum on Hollywood Boulevard. There, he showed the 1984 Rhonda Jo Petty scene, to which the crowd erupted in cheers and applause at seeing her deep throat John Holmes.

In his narration for some of the clips on *Angel in Mr. Holmes*, Margold made up the actresses' names — Spikette, for example. However, the film clips he chose for the compilation are among the best of Holmes' career, and Margold's heartfelt intention to honor The King (as he nicknamed Holmes in 1973) is evident.

88 min/color. Unavailable. Amber Lynn, Ashley Welles, Jennifer Sands, Jennifer Turley, Jessica Wylde, Keli Richards, Misty Anderson, Muffin MacIntosh, Nancy Suiter, Rhonda Jo Petty, Seka, Spikette, Bill Margold, John Holmes, Tom Byron. *Director:* None credited. *Producer:* Western Visuals.

Around the World with John "The Wadd" Holmes ★★ November 1975

Also known as *Around the World with Johnny Wadd*. Tagline: *"Johnny Wadd is back from his escapades in 10 countries!!! Now...You can meet his girls from across the sea!"* (Not a *Johnny Wadd* film, but John is credited as John "The Wadd" Holmes.)

The opening credits of the video are shown in widescreen, promising a classy and interesting beginning — but what follows is not. The film uses stock footage with a John Holmes voiceover that regales his listeners about his sexual escapades between homes in San Francisco, Las Vegas, New York, London, Paris and Rome.

In what would make for the quintessential reality show, John is in pursuit of the ultimate woman who can handle his 13 inches of love. In each city, he encounters one girl and embarks upon passionate sex scenarios. Every scene includes John Holmes, but the constant voiceovers that link sex scenes may only be of interest to the extremist fan of dirty talk.

The finest aspect of this movie is John's appearance — this is 31-year old John Holmes — handsome, with his slicked back hair and a healthful physique.

79 min/color. DVD. Becky Sharpe, Cyndee Summers, Patti Lee, Suzanne Fields, John Holmes. *Director:* Donald U. Canard (Donald Duck — get it?), *Writer:* Donald U. Canard. *Producer:* Donald U. Canard.

Aunt Peg's Fulfillment ★★½ 1981

Tagline: *"Every man's dream."*

Hollywood producer, Peg Norton (Juliet Anderson), personally auditions prospective actors for an upcoming film project. Peg is anything but bashful when she invites well-built Tyrone Tips (Johnny Keyes) to drop his pants so that she can check out the goods during an audition at her home. She handles his organ aggressively while giving the startled actor head. Before he has an opportunity to object, Peg engages him in doggie-style. All the while, Peg is mindful to not wake her niece, Sheila (Sharon Kane).

Soon, Peg leaves a still-aroused Tyrone alone in the living room, but he sees Sheila naked in the hot tub. Within minutes, it's *deja vu* all over again for Tyrone.

Back at the office, Peggy chats with director (Richard Pacheco) who has grown weary of working with what he considers to be "no-talents."

Peg's illicit adventures continue when she meets up with her niece and informs her, "I'd like you to meet a friend who knows a few things about anatomy." Sheila has been studying the subject in school and Aunt Peg's friend is none other than John Holmes, in a scene borrowed from a *Swedish Erotica* loop. The three of them plant together on a bed. Sheila and Peg take turns doing 69 with John before the scene concludes with a double facial. The scene is trademark Holmes: the girls lie side by side with their mouths open and there is enough to go around for everyone. Despite beginning work in erotic films at 40, Anderson quickly crowned herself as the incomparable Aunt Peg, in the sex scene between herself, Kane and Holmes.

In a clever skit, Peggy entertains two men in her home that evening, played by Mike Ranger and John Leslie. She runs between the bedroom and living room to entertain the two men, who are unaware that the other is present. Anderson commands the screen with confidence and a diabolical flair.

78 min/color. DVD. Anna Ventura, Erica Boyer (as Joanne McRay), Juliet Anderson, Sharon Kane (as Sharon Maiberg), Suzanne French (as Suzy Reynolds), Aaron Stuart (as Arthur Bark), Eric Stein, Herschel Savage, John Holmes, John Leslie, Johnny Keyes, Mike Ranger, Richard Pacheco. *Director:* Anthony Spinelli. *Writer:* Anthony Spinelli. *Producer:* Arthur Cutter.

The Autobiography of a Flea ★★★★ September 1976

This film was based upon an anonymous piece of French erotica from the 19th century. In this Mitchell Brothers feature film, a flea living in the pubic hair of Belle (Jean Jennings) narrates sexual encounters between people. John Holmes (as Father Clement), Paul Thomas (as Father Ambrose), John Leslie, and Annette Haven all have large roles in the film. While there is no doubt that Paul Thomas is a better actor, the scenes with John Holmes highlight John's size with some humorous lines at his expense.

Music for the film is entirely instrumental: church organ pieces whenever the ribaldry is occurring within the church walls and elaborate 19th century harpsichord pieces when the action is at Belle's family home. Although unusual for erotic films, the music seems appropriate and unobtrusive.

John appears with a clean shaven face in this film and at 32 looks young and healthy. His scene with Annette Haven is probably the steamiest sex in the film, as he scales an exterior wall and climbs into bed with the unsuspecting maiden. The excellent costumes and hairstyles are consistent with the 19th century. The dialogue and cinematography of this Golden Era masterpiece are superior, and the film showcases a variety of camera angles and sexual positions. It includes the taboo subjects of the original book — incest and satirical looks at the inequities in life.

93 min/color. DVD. Annette Haven, Jean Jennings, Joanna Hilden, Artie Mitchell (non-sex), Dale Meador (non-sex), John Holmes, John Leslie, John Rolling (non-sex), Ken Scudder, Michael Dolan (non-sex), Mitch Mandell (non-sex), Paul Thomas. *Director:* Sharon McNight; *Writer:* Adaptation by Sharon McNight. *Producers:* The Mitchell Brothers.

Balls in Action (This film has not been ranked.) 1968

Trailer for film has a comical voiceover. John plays a guy named Mammoth and stars with "Rubbery Teenybopper." Although this film was probably made, its existence is unconfirmed.

Benny's Bungles ★★½ 1971 or 1972

Benny (John Holmes) hosts a soiree in his home along with his live-in girlfriend, Sondra. Apart from entertaining his guests with some of the contraptions he acquired from various prison torture chambers, Benny engages the gang in a game of strip dice. (If you roll a seven or an eleven, you must remove an article of clothing.) Benny and Sondra set their sexual sights on two of their guests, Tony and Jane.

When Tony insults Jane after he loses a roll of the dice, Benny comes to her rescue, whisking her away from the group to have sex together in the nearby bedroom. Holmes and his dainty, auburn-haired costar gently fuse their bodies together. Jane inhales Benny's sword as Benny seductively laps her earlobe prior to climaxing upon her buttocks.

During their post-coital cuddling, Sondra and Tony burst in on Benny and Jane and an exchange of expletives colors the air. Benny escorts Jane home and when he returns, he discovers Sondra and Tony making out in his swimming pool. Jealous and temporarily maniacal, Benny retrieves one of his bungles; a homemade electrocution device guaranteed to teach them a lesson.

John's darkly comical character, Benny, makes this film intriguing because shades of Holmes' off-screen personality and his propensity to spin wild tales are on display as Benny has the group transfixed while reveling in a concocted explanation about how he'd obtained the items in his homemade collection. John is captivating in his incarnation of this oddball character in retro attire: white pants, white socks and black sandals (commonly worn during the early-'70s). The soundtrack alternates between Spanish guitar and lively jazz arrangements featuring a bass clarinet.

Approximately 45 min/color. DVD.

Best of Gail Palmer ★★★ 1981

A greatest hits compilation of porn films, the first of its kind. Gail Palmer does narration to tie the clips together from *California Gigolo, Prisoner of Paradise, Hot Legs, Gail Palmer's Candy Goes to Hollywood* and many more. The film has a feel to it that is similar to a video promoting a tourist destination, if the tourist destination were vintage erotic films. There are some great sex scenes and even one from *Prisoner of Paradise* featuring John Holmes and Mai Lin, in which Palmer points out "actual tenderness and love." This best-of collection leaves the viewer turned on and interested in seeing the other films.

105 min/color. DVD. Delania Raffino (as Barbara Bill), Carol Connors, Desiree Cousteau, Dorothy Le May, Georgina Spelvin, Jade Wong, Jessie St. James, Kandi Barbour, Kitty Shayne, Laurien Dominique, Lisa Eldridge, Lisa Sue Corey, Liza Dwyer, Mai Lin (as Miko Moto), Nikki Anderson, Penelope Jones, Rhonda Jo Petty, Seka, Sharon Kane, Susan Nero, Vanessa Tibbs, Veri Knotty, Blair Harris, Don Fernando, Jesse Adams, John Holmes, John Leslie, Jon Martin, Ken Scudder, Paul Thomas, Richard Pacheco, R.J. Reynolds, Turk Lyon. *Director:* Gail Palmer. *Writer:* Gail Palmer.

Black Velvet: The Big Deal ★★★ 1973 or '74

Also known as *Black Velvet: Falcon Pac 21.*

Black Velvet — The Big Deal showcases Holmes in a silent 13-minute masturbation scene that begins as he straddles a shiny, black motorcycle. His curly hair is longer, but brushed off of his forehead, revealing his brilliant blue eyes and attractive, clean-shaven face. This was shot during his pre-drug years when Holmes was in great shape.

With love, Holmes wipes the chrome of the bike with a white cloth, moving forward and then backward to ensure that the entire body of the machine is clean. As he moves about, he rubs his crotch through his dark jeans and removes his denim jacket and long-sleeved shirt before unzipping his pants to reveal his swollen member.

Carefully at first, he thrusts toward the front of the bike, before caressing himself with both hands. John's hands move fluidly up and down the shaft of his expanding penis — pausing every so often to squeeze the bike's handlebar. John uses two hands, one on his cock and one on his testicles, with his back on the seat of the motorcycle and his eyes closed. With increased velocity, John eventually erupts all over the glistening black surface of the engine.

50 min/color. DVD. Bill Eld, Doug, John Coletti, John Holmes (masturbation only).

Blonde Emmanuelle ★★★ 1977

Also known as *Disco Dolls in Hot Skin; Disco Dolls; Hot Skin.*

With two of the most attractive adult performers of the Golden Age, Serena and Mike Ranger, heading up the all-star cast, this campy film manages to weave a believable plot within the fabric of this 3-D feature. The 3-D glasses (two sets are provided in the recent DVD release with special features) are not that effective in the end, but they do add some psychedelia to the lively flick.

Chick (Ranger) sets his eyes upon Emmanuelle (Serena) after she steps out of a helicopter. The two are immediately smitten and although the starry-eyed pair tries to communicate their passion, Chick can't sustain an erection long enough. His lover's lust is left smoldering.

Chick is the manager of a nightclub where beautiful dames tend to congregate, making his problem below the belt an increasing concern, so he decides to talk to a shrink.

Meanwhile, Harry Balls (Bill Margold) is wanted by the police for reasons that are not clearly defined. Balls and Chick team up and convert the club into a brothel while Balls tries to keep away from the policeman (Con Covert).

There are some entertaining bits including Pat Manning's portrayal of a dominatrix and an erotically heightened girl-on-girl segment featuring Serena and Lesllie Bovee. Bill Margold said that he had promised John several women to "play with," and so, John Holmes (in an uncredited appearance) simultaneously entertains three women as the grind-fest ensues around him.

The film's shocking ending foreshadows a page right out of John Wayne Bobbit's book.

Color. DVD. Christine deShaffer, Ingrid Irvin (uncredited), Irene Best (uncredited), Lesllie Bovee, Maria Tortuga, Monique Faberge, Pat Manning, Sandra Rogan, Sherry Windom, Serena, Susan Wong, Uschi Digard, Bill Margold, Con Covert, David Penny (uncredited) Elmer Pasta, John Holmes, Lee O'Donnell, Mike Ranger, Robert Bullock. *Director:* Stephen Gibson. *Writers:* Ann Onymous, Mark Thunderbuns. *Producer:* Stephen Gibson.

Blonde Fire ★★★★ 1979

Tagline: *"So hot you'll melt in your seat!"* Final (ninth) *Johnny Wadd* film.

Johnny Wadd arrives in South Africa in pursuit of the Blonde Fire diamond, a priceless piece in the possession of some shady individuals.

Shortly after checking into the hotel, Wadd showers, but senses someone prowling in his room. He takes his would-be assailant, Tarine (Phae Burd) by surprise when he commands her to drop her weapon. She and Johnny trade snide remarks before he fights her to the bed and cuffs her hands to its post.

With her vulnerable, Wadd proceeds to try and interrogate her. When she refuses to comply, he strips her down and performs cunnilingus. According to the expression of gratification on her face, it would seem that she isn't opposed to his interrogation methods.

Afterwards, Johnny is off to meet a friend at the Honduras Club. There at the bar, a bad dude secretly tampers with Johnny's drink and he slumps over. When he regains consciousness, he finds himself naked outside and the sky darkens.

Fatima Hamoud, a beautiful dancer from the club, whom Wadd had ogled hours earlier, rescues Johnny and initiates sex with the dazed detective, who rises to the challenge. The next morning, Wadd is presented with the Blonde Fire diamond by two business associates (Jessie St. James and Jon Martin), but he quickly realizes it's a fake and has an idea about where he might locate the genuine article. Johnny confesses that the "real" Blonde Fire is waiting for him back in San Francisco, where he will arrive shortly.

John Holmes and Seka, arguably the top two stars of their day, do not disappoint when they finally unite at the conclusion of the film. Much of this sequence was shot with the late cameraman, Kenneth Gibb, standing on a ladder above John and Seka to achieve the desired effect. Seka's platinum-blonde hair and pale satin skin against the deep turquoise background is striking as she and John make tender love.

A secondary hot scene features John Holmes with sexy Jessie St. James; in the only time the two stars worked together. *Blonde Fire* is a satisfying and climactic conclusion to the *Johnny Wadd* movie series.

85 min/color. DVD. C. Rose (non-sex), Dorothy Le May, Fatima Hamoud, Jessie St. James, Kitty Shayne, Phae Burd, Seka, Carl Adams, Charles Scott, James Price, John Holmes, John Seeman, Jon Martin, Peter Kenyata (non-sex). *Director:* Bob Chinn. *Writer:* Jeffrey Neal. *Producers:* Freeway Films.

Blonde in Black Lace ★½ 1971

In this very rudimentary third installation to the *Johnny Wadd* series, John reflects in the opening narration, "The detective business is all about the '69' position with *My Girl, Friday*." That remark pretty well sums up this quick flick, shot in one day, in sequential order, at the Venice Beach canals in Los Angeles.

Johnny is hired by a blonde, Judy (Susan Draeger), who hopes to catch her husband engaged in extramarital sex, so that she has grounds to divorce him. Apparently, Judy's hubby forces her to participate in unpleasant erotic acts (like screwing the bodyguard) and she wants the freedom to call her own shots. Johnny's task is simple; photograph Judy's husband involved in a three-way with a blonde (Chlorine Stillwater) and a brunette. When Wadd discovers that he's lost the evidence secured on film, he returns to the scene of the crime to find Judy's husband dead. (John's white straw hat makes its final appearance in the *Johnny Wadd* series.)

Blonde in Black Lace is a predictable, ridiculously low-budget film, made for less than $1,000, but it proved to be a resounding success with adult movie audiences. It is interesting to observe the evolution of *Johnny Wadd* movies as the budget and popularity of the series rose.

82 min/color. VHS. Barbara Bosquet, Chlorine Stillwater, Eve Orlon, Mycle Brandy, Susan Wescott (a.k.a. Susan Draeger), Bob Chinn (as Bob A. Lain, non-sex), John Holmes (as John Duval), Jose Duval. *Director:* Bob Chinn (as Bob A. Lain). *Writer:* Bob Chinn. *Producer:* Chinn-Adrain Productions.

Body Shop ★★ 1984

Tagline: *"...for the ultimate lube job."*

This story details the conversion of an auto repair garage to a full-service center where customers receive carnal perks from the female mechanics. *Body Shop* marks the acting debut of Buck Adams on the hood of an overheated automobile in this feature as his real-life sister, Amber Lynn, stars. Buck Adams was slated to perform in a sex scene with Amber Lynn, but the idea was nixed when it was learned that the two are real life siblings.

John (who is fully erect and in take-charge mode) appears as a client (with a Southern twang) in a sex scene with a cute brunette on a cluttered counter in the repair shop.

Holmes' real life friend, business partner and bodyguard, Bill Amerson (nicknamed "Wild Bill") poses as a vice cop who inevitably busts up the highly profitable operation.

78 min/color. DVD. Amber Lynn, Tracy Duzit (as Christina Lake), Crystal Breeze (as Lisa Maria), Pamela Jennings, Shaun Michelle (as Sharon Michael), Buck Adams, Jay Serling, John Holmes, R. Bolla, Scott Irish. *Director:* Bill Amerson. *Production Manager:* John C. Holmes. *Producer:* VCX.

California Gigolo ★★★½ 1979

Tagline: *"Every woman's dream. Every man's fantasy."*

The film begins with an upbeat, sing-along theme, "California Gigolo," which is written and performed by Jay Phillips. California gigolo, John Loftin (John Holmes) espies a beautiful young brunette (Kandi Barbour) as she steps out of a silver Mercedes. He follows her and offers up some "fine lovin'."

Disgusted by his bold overtures, the woman turns him down and struts off across the street. Undaunted, John takes a gondola ride in Palm Springs where he espies Barbour again. By this time, she has obviously reconsidered his advances.

John lives in a nice home with a live-in assistant named Gomez (Don Fernando), whose main responsibility is to screen John's calls from women looking for love. John gives them all what they pay for — from a quickie with a regular customer to an elaborate role-play session at a high-rise office building.

The film is a spoof of the (1978-'84) television show, "Fantasy Island," with John as the boss and Gomez an adaptation of the show's character, Tattoo. Holmes takes a stab at serious acting in *California Gigolo*; he maintains an unabashed face when dealing with an unattractive nymphomaniac (Veri Knotty) at the office building, who asks him to pretend to be the window cleaner and rape her. But even real-life gigolo John Holmes could not help his expression of shock in a scene in which Chinn recycled Mrs. Hamilton's bottle scene from the original 1970 *Johnny Wadd*. In *California Gigolo*, John's beautiful client (Vanessa Tibbs) masturbates with an empty champagne bottle in a scene that is not included on all versions. Tibbs was actually a swinger who had wished to be in an X-rated film and was not disappointed when Chinn put her opposite the ultimate real-life *California Gigolo*, John Holmes. During filming of her scene,

Image courtesy of VCX.com. The *California Gigolo,* in person.

Tibbs' husband watched from the sidelines.

Left with only 30 minutes to think of some way to salvage the movie, Bob Chinn commissioned Jay Phillips to write the opening theme song, which ends up being the saving grace of the film. The addition of the song to the clip of the girls roller skating at Venice Beach is a highlight, in addition to John's countdown from ten to zero that accurately predicted his climax.

70 min/color. DVD. Delania Raffino (as Barbara Bills), Kandi Barbour, Kitty Shayne, Liza Dwyer, Vanessa Tibbs, Veri Knotty, Don Fernando, John Holmes. *Director:* Bob Chinn. *Writer:* Henry Plymouth, *Producer:* Eliot Louis.

California Girls ★½ 1980

Also known as *The Champ*.

This film lacks the kind of TLC that was generally attached to two major stars like John Holmes and Rhonda Jo Petty. Julia St. Vincent inherited this bomb and another one like it after her uncle Armand Atamian passed away from a short battle with cancer in the spring of 1980. St. Vincent was barely able to get *California Girls* into theaters because of its inferior production value and poor direction.

The opening scene features Rhonda Jo skating on the Venice Beach board-walk when John Holmes enters from a parked trailer and joins her. Petty looks like a pro on skates, while Holmes is shaky, but gains the hang of it. He appears to enjoy himself while making some fast-paced turns. Holmes and Petty wear matching knee-high athletic socks and indulge in a brief, choreographed sequence together.

Roller-girl Rhonda is a hustler on wheels and utilizes her skills in more ways than one as she swindles horny men out of money. Holmes is no exception. After inviting John to her place for lunch, they engage in a sex scene that is peppered with histrionics that reflect the amount of coke the actors had ingested prior to their scene. Rhonda compliments John's prowess in bed by saying, "No wonder they call you The King."

Smiling, John replies, "That's the way it is, baby."

Petty proceeds to challenge Holmes to compete against her in a roller relay. While he eagerly accepts her bet, he ups the ante by inviting Petty's girlfriend into the competition. The next day the three compete, but the two girls play it dirty by tripping John and leaving him in the dust, clutching onto his ankle in pain. The remainder of the film contains a girl-on-girl tub scene between Petty and Tiffany Clark, gratuitous blowjobs here and there and uninvolved sex that relegates *California Girls* to the bottom of the booming video-age heap.

56 min/color. Unavailable. Rhonda Jo Petty, Tiffany Clark, John Holmes, R. J. Reynolds.

California Valley Girls ★★★ 1983
Tagline: *"Takin' it to the max!"*

This is the story of four valley girls in the early-'80s — Michelle (Desiree Lane), Melissa (Cindy Shepard), Debbie (Misty Dawn) and Diane (Kimberly Carson). At the mall, the girls talk Val' incessantly. The dialogue is trendy for its time, with some great toss-off lines, including this one of Kimberly Carson's, "Oh my God! I'm growing a zit community on my face!" And when the valley girls aren't talking about boys, school, their parents or shopping, they're doing it (shopping, that is) at the Sherman Oaks Galleria.

The plot of the film comes into focus when two unemployed lesbians, Donna and Jessica (Shaun Michelle and Becky Sharp), devise a plan to hire the valley girls for their escort service. Jessica's brother-in-law Robert (John Holmes) offers up his 13-inch package as a teaching tool for the Valley girls on which to learn the art of giving head. Holmes appears in one scene, using a voice that is dubbed by someone else. He was allegedly paid $1,500 to receive head by five women for 20 minutes.

Ron Jeremy, Eric Edwards, Paul Thomas, and Hershel Savage make alluring appearances in the film as lonely, lusty, wealthy clientele who reveal their "totally tubular" wares to the young ladies. Jeremy even plays a little classical piano, which is a nice treat.

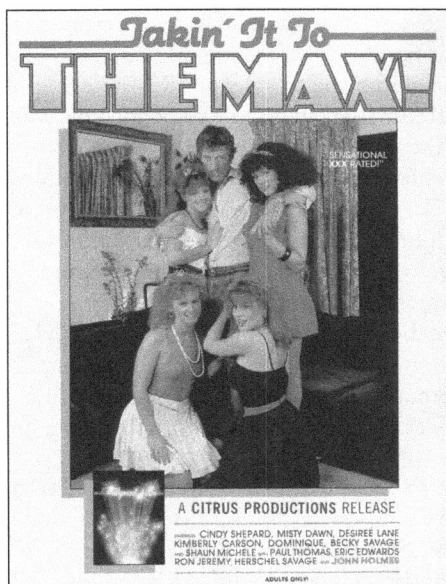

Image courtesy of VCX.com. Misty Dawn is standing to John's right (in the white blouse). The other actresses shown here are Cindy Shepard, Kimberly Carson and Desiree Lane.

There are many fun bits of trivia related to the film, which was the second time that John worked with his soon-to-be wife, Laurie. In the background of a scene, there is a familiar brown VW van that could be Bill Margold's very own "Bearmobile" (that had transported Holmes to the film's set from Ralph's parking lot). The theme song for this film was written by the still photographer, Kenji, who intended the song to be a Beach Boys rip-off, although time constraints prevented its full completion. The song is still quite memorable and funny, especially the refrain, "She's a Valley Girl. She's a Valley Girl. Takin' it to the max!"

87 min/color. DVD. Becky Savage, Cindy Shepard, Desiree Lane, Dominique, Kimberly Carson, Misty Dawn, Shaun Michelle, Eric Edwards, Herschel Savage, John Holmes, Paul Thomas, Ron Jeremy, Steve Douglas. *Directors:* Hal Freeman, William Margold (uncredited). *Writer:* Mark Weiss. *Producer:* Hal Freeman.

Casanova II (The Legend Continues) ★★★½ 1977

Also known as *The Erotic Adventures of Casanova: The New Erotic Adventures of Casanova.* Tagline: "When he made love, he made history!"

The film was originally designed as a two-part saga, according to Bill Margold. The first of the saga was to be called, *The Erotic Adventures of Casanova* and the second, *Casanova II.* Instead, the storyline was compiled into one film and released as *Casanova II.*

The film begins in the early 1700s, where Giacomo Casanova (John Holmes) and Don Juan (Bjorn Beck) conquer enemies and beautiful women. (Although Don Juan is a fictitious character, the real Casanova lived in Venice. Casanova was a famous womanizer, writer and adventurer.)

After a lengthy sword fight, Casanova carries off a young, wounded soldier to his quarters and makes the startling discovery that he is actually a she. As her dying wish, the young lady requests that Casanova make love to her. Casanova fulfills her desire, as Don Juan quenches the desires of other luscious ladies.

Fast forward to the present (1980): John, who is unaware that he is a direct descendant of Giacomo Casanova, stops at an antique shop located in the beautiful English countryside, where he purchases a small bottle of perfume to bring as a gift to his best friend and his family.

The kindly folks don't know that the perfume is actually a highly potent aphrodisiac. When his friend angrily confronts John about having bedded his wife, daughters and maid, John argues that the perfume is the culprit, not he.

He then elicits the advice of a psychiatrist (Susan Silver), but she too falls under the perfume's intoxicating spell. After conducting some extensive research, John's shrink discovers that John is the great, great grandson of Giacomo Casanova. The two devise a plan to capitalize on the perfume's seductive powers by marketing the passionate potion on a grand scale.

Adult film director, Ann Perry, plays the part of a news anchor and Bill Margold has a small role as a reporter who informs the world about the perfume's benefits. Margold also wrote the promotional ad line for this feature, which could appropriately apply to the film's star; indeed when John made love, he made history.

90 min/color. DVD. Ann Perry, Bonnie Holliday, Bridgette Felina, Cathy Linger, Paula Wain (as Christian Sarver), Maureen Spring (as Eileen Dover), Iris Medina, Justine Taylor, Mary Grant, Nancy Hoffman, Sandy Pinney, Susan Silver (non-sex), Tracy O'Neil, Blair Harris, Bill Margold, Carl Regal (as Carl Ashby), John Holmes, John Seeman (as John Toland), Frank Michaels (as Peter Johns), Rock Steadie (non-sex). *Director:* Carlos Tobalina, John Holmes. *Writer:* Edgar G. Warren. *Producer:* Miguel Merino.

Cheri ★ 1974

Also known as *Cherri; Sheri.*

The director and producer of this film are unknown — probably no one wants to own up to this bomb that could have really been something worthwhile. The strangest thing about this film is that Rene Bond is billed as having a starring role, yet she does not ever make an appearance. This movie loses its steam after the first 20 minutes.

Cheri begins promisingly enough with John and his buddies planning to go to a baseball game, while his princess girlfriend, Cheri (Susie Carlson), wants him to take her skiing on the weekend. Eventually, Cheri gives into letting John go to the game with his friends and she goes skiing alone, but only after John coerces her into having sex with him on the couch in front of the open window.

This is an example of Holmes making a solo appearance in a film for the purpose of attracting audiences. The sex scene with Carlson comprises most of John's involvement in the film, but it is humorous and spontaneous, with great adlibs. John sports a great beatnik look for the movie with long, combed-down hair and a goatee. He is stiffly aroused in this sex scene as he was obviously attracted to this pretty brunette. No skiing or baseball activities are shown in the movie, which primarily consists of randy scenes involving Cheri's weekend at the ski lodge. There, she meets two swinging couples and a man feigning injury in order to score with the chicks.

No one can complain about the lack of variety in the men used for the movie — there's skinny Holmes, a buff Rick Cassidy and the man seeking sympathy-sex with an English smile (translation: horrible teeth).

There is an orgy scene at the finale that isn't stimulating, but the film has a surprise twist when Cheri confides in the other women at the lodge that the joke was on John since he didn't partake in the weekend's sexcapades. But... Ironically, the joke is on Cheri. John was better off going to the ballgame.

57 min/color. DVD. Cindy Wilson, Flora McIntosh, Susie Carlson, John Holmes, Rick Cassidy. *Director:* Simon L. Egree.

Johnny Wadd overlooks the San Francisco Bay in the opening of *China Cat*.

China Cat ★★★★ 1977

Tagline: *"In the year of the cat, the devils bare more than their claws!"* (1977 was actually the year of the snake; there is no year of the cat in the Chinese calendar.) Eighth installment of the *Johnny Wadd* film series.

China Cat continues where *The Jade Pussycat* leaves off, as the four ladies comprising "Charlie's Devils" await instructions from their boss via conference call. With a voice similar to John Forsythe (the actor who essayed the role of Charlie in the television series), the girls' employer insists that they do their utmost to recover the jade cat from Mr. Wadd. (Watch for a brief cameo appearance by Desiree Cousteau near the beginning.)

Johnny Wadd, in one of his favorite San Francisco bars, chats up another patron and invites Shari (Jennifer Richards) to dine with him. Check out the wallpaper, the barstools, and the positioning of the waiter with Holmes and

Richards, and you'll see how P.T. Anderson borrowed this entire segment for *Boogie Nights*, right down to the dangling toothpick in Wadd's mouth.

Soon, the two are back at Johnny's apartment. As he painstakingly mixes martinis for himself and Shari, she patiently waits in his boudoir and admires his collection of rare Ming vases. When Johnny finally unzips his pants to produce his elephant's trunk, Shari remarks with alarm, "John — You're so big!"

Smiling broadly, John responds, "Well, you said you were hungry."

Shari exclaims, "Yes, but I didn't expect another feast!"

Although Chinn had been nervous about how newcomer Jennifer Richards would react to working with Holmes, she appears relaxed and at ease as they engage in light banter throughout their sex scene, resulting in a genuine, unforced flow. Not knowing that Shari is one of Charlie's Devils trying to steal the valuable china cat from him, Johnny is faced with some tough-yet-feminine opponents in this film.

Unfortunately, the picture quality in this film (and several others of its era) appears somewhat dark, as subtleties in lighting were lost when the feature was blown up to 35 millimeter. In the case of *China Cat*, the original negative had worn out, so the video masters were made from a duplicate negative, which also contributes to the gritty, dark appearance of the film on video and DVD.

Putting aside that minor issue, this film has a coherent plot, and doesn't condescend to the audience, which makes *The China Cat* an enjoyable accomplishment. Late porn guru and adult film critic Jim Holliday cited *The China Cat* as his premiere pick of the *Johnny Wadd* dynasty.

69 min/color. DVD. Paula Wain (as Christian Sarver), Desiree Cousteau, Eileen Welles, Jennifer Richards, Kyoto Sunn, Cris Cassidy, Dale Meador (non-sex), Damon Christian (non-sex), Elliot Lewis (non-sex), John Holmes, John Seeman, Mario Lewis. *Director:* Bob Chinn. *Writer:* Bob Chinn. *Producers:* Freeway Films.

Coming Holmes ★★½ 1986

Also known as *Hung Like a Horse*. Tagline: "The King is back and he's taking on all comers!"

Four young women (Misty Regan, Susan Hart, Cheri Janvier and Ami Rodgers) audition as dancers for club owner John (Holmes) and his two cohorts (Steve Powers and Tony Martino). When they've finished their routines, John encourages the women to use the amenities at the club while he and the boys confer. Ami Rodgers relaxes in the sauna when the boss approaches, hoping to engage her in physical activity.

At 41, it is fair to say that at this time in his life and career, John Holmes was an aging porn star with a weathered face and world-weary eyes; the man had witnessed far more than most people would care to see. Despite his character lines, Holmes' smile shines bright, indicating the mischievous child still living in his heart.

Holmes doesn't climax in his scene with Rodgers, nor does he in his scene with Susan Hart and Tony Martino. He saves himself for what comes later, a sex show with him, Rodgers and Janvier. Although Holmes appears weathered compared to the new comers, his talent in preparing his sex partners signifies his expertise. He gently applies lubricant to Janvier's vagina, like a gardener stroking the petals of a flower in bloom. The saxophone that weaves throughout the film accompanies this particular scene.

When John finally gets in the saddle, so to speak, a small rash is briefly evident, on the top of his left thigh. He makes an effort to conceal it from the camera. It's worth noting because in *Porn King*, Holmes claimed that he suspected something was awry with his health because of an occasional rash on his penis, which he attributed to the friction created during sex. John believed the rash may have made him susceptible to contracting HIV, but the rash is more significant because a red, patchy, bleeding rash can evidence acute HIV. John may have already been infected. This film was made in the window between his first negative test late in 1985 and the second positive HIV test in 1986.

Later in the scene, the blood is gone as the story moves toward a happy conclusion. Retrospectively, *Coming Holmes* is an appropriate title for this film as the clock counts down the weeks that led up to the final performance of The King.

78min/color. DVD. Ami Rodgers, Cheri Janvier, Misty Regan, Susan Hart, John Holmes, Steve Powers, Tony Martino. *Director:* Tony Valentino.

Confessions of a Teenage Peanut Butter Freak ★★½ 1975

Also known as *Peanut Butter Freak*. Taglines: *"Sure to make 'em spread!" "Chunky or creamy — no salt added." "Made from whole ripe nuts!" "Slides down your throat!"*

Geeky Billy (Rex Roman) isn't hip to the ways of women and his bizarre obsession with peanut butter makes him a social pariah. When the poor boy fails to score on a date, he picks up a female friend at a gas station, who invites him in for a nightcap and a few slices of bread slathered with Skippy peanut butter.

The young woman (with '70s imperfect teeth, furry eyebrows and bush) happens to be a good listener as Billy shares with her a few of his erotic misadventures. He explains that his woman troubles began when he was caught masturbating by his Aunt Opel (Constance Money) at 15 and things have teetered on edge since then. Shortly after his first incestuous experience with Opel, he was handcuffed and raped by his cousin and her best friend.

Billy recounts how his friend, Jeff (John Holmes in a comical turn; he does funny impressions of James Cagney and W.C. Fields) came to Billy's rescue and gave him a crash-course in the art of seduction — he set up a date between Billy and Gloria (Veronica Taylor), who happened to be a chess master. After warming her up with French kisses, followed by deep penetration, Jeff invited Billy to cut in, much to Gloria's chagrin. She reprimanded Jeff severely for this ungentlemanly stunt.

Undaunted, Ladies' Man Jeff was able to convince Gloria to finish what they'd started. Billy's dirty trip down memory lane has caused his girlfriend to become excited. They soon edge their way into the bedroom, accompanied by Billy's security blanket: his jar of P.B.

Peanut Butter Freak opens with a great psychedelic rock soundtrack. The plot is unusual, the film lags at times and contains overly stilted dialogue supplied by Roman who mimics Beaver Cleaver, "Gee, that's swell!"

85 min/color. VHS. Candice Harley, Claire Kimball, Claudia Stanton, Constance Money, Helen Madigan, Jo Ann McClure, Karen Reed, Kim Blaire, Mira Vane, Veronica Taylor, Barry Vane, Charles Swanson, Jacque Hanson, Joaquin Delicado, John Holmes, Malcolm Healy, Rex Roman. *Director:* Zachary Strong. *Writer:* Zachary Strong. *Producer:* Freeway Films.

Cream Rinse ★★★ September 10, 1976

In an entertaining send-up of the 1976 Hollywood smash hit, *Shampoo*, two hairstylist brothers (Peter Packer and Ceaser Ballstitch) make a bet to see which one can have sex with more women in a day. The stylists attempt salon small talk, in addition to kissing and fondling their clients before inviting them to a party that night.

Rene Bond makes an appearance in a scene with John as the saucy receptionist for the salon.

John Holmes enters the salon to drop off his wife for a hair trim. When his wife informs him that she would like to attend a cosmetics party that evening, he replies, "You already have a drawer full of cosmetics!" She is actually planning on attending a sexual rendezvous at the stylists' home.

Later, John interrupts the orgy between the two brothers, his wife and some other female clients and demands that his wife return home. John does an above-average job of showing hurt feelings by his wife's betrayal. Holmes is very healthy in his appearance, and his clean-shaven face adds to his usual boyish charm. Most remarkable about this performance is his ability to convey the emotions of his character with so few lines.

After talking with his wife, John learns that she is not being sexually fulfilled in their marriage, so he agrees to participate in the sex party with her. The orgy scene makes it more than obvious that Holmes' penis is larger than the average-sized dicks of the brothers.

The music for the film is mostly soft jazz, the kind that can be heard in some stores while grocery shopping. The most disappointing thing about this DVD is the poor quality audio and horrendous visual. However, the plot is interesting and many of the classically styled sex scenes are hot.

57 min/color. DVD. Angie Cinsalo, Ginger Peachy, Linda Licks, Rene Bond, Ceasar Balsitch, John Holmes, Peter Packer. *Director:* R.J. Doyle (as Dick Cocks) *Producer:* R.J. Doyle (as Lee Bahler).

The Danish Connection ★★★ March 1974

This was the first of only three times that Bob Chinn gave another director permission to use the Johnny Wadd character in a film.

For a softcore film, pieced together from the outtakes from *Tropic of Passion* and new footage written and directed by Walt Davis, this is a surprisingly good film. Like *Tropic of Passion*, the setting is Hawaii and John wears his curly hair slicked down, sometimes topped by the white, straw hat seen in the early (Chinn) *Johnny Wadd* movies.

During the film's opening, while Johnny climbs a 30-foot rope ladder onto a massive ship, a "Johnny Wadd" theme song is played: "Big John's got the equipment and all the ladies know / it's the biggest joint up here on earth since Adam's long ago."

Like the lyrics of the song, the plot is kooky and lighthearted. A special Danish formula used to treat impotence is sought by a wealthy boss. The boss, Herbert Steele (William Kirchner), lusts after his secretary so he hires Wadd to retrieve the coveted formula that promises four-hour erections. Steele is willing to pay handsomely for Wadd's trouble — $1,000,000.

Holmes and Rick Cassidy take turns seducing beautiful women (including Rene Bond, Sandy Carey and Sandy Dempsey) in this surreal caper and the movie showcases one of the earliest lame-o fight scenes between John and Bob Chinn, as Hercules Fong. Fong is shot by his mentor, Dr. Livingstone Presume (Walt Davis), who captures John and tethers him to a furry water bed where he is brutalized by a threesome of sexually inventive women.

The Danish Connection is recommended for its imaginative script and special effects; its good, freaky fun for an almost-hardcore flick.

86 min/color. DVD. Cyndee Summers, Rene Bond, Sandy Carey, Sandy Dempsey, Bob Chinn (as Hercules Fong, non-sex), John Holmes, Rick Cassidy, Walt Davis (non-sex). *Director:* Walt Davis. *Writer:* Walt Davis. *Producer:* Manuel S. Conde, M.D. Maury.

Dear Pam ★★★ 1976

Tagline: *"Got a problem? Ask Pam Slanders, America's sexiest Advice Columnist. But remember, do as she says, not as she does!"*

Crystal Sync stars in this comparatively highbrow adult comedy, as Pam Slanders: a woman of morality and virtue, who holds the fate of her readers within the grip of her pen.

But when Harry Phallus (Eric Edwards) writes in to Slanders about some rather peculiar sexual situations and she is appalled by his promiscuity, she breaks her vow of confidentiality. With intent, she publicly defames his character.

Mr. Phallus seduces any lovely lady who happens upon his path — including his new secretary, Gladys Migrain (C.J. Laing), his best friend's wife, and even his 14-year old stepdaughter. Phallus lost his cock ring inside of the vagina of one of his ladies.

Along with British cohorts, Richard Grandik and Barton Fartblow (John Holmes and Tony Perez, with accents that come and go) Slanders is determined to get to the bottom of Phallus' decadent sexual behavior as she plans to interview every woman mentioned in his letter to the columnist. Fartblow and Grandik quickly find themselves in compromising situations with two of Phallus' conquests and find that they can't resist their feminine charms.

When Grandik (Holmes) returns to keep his appointment with Slanders at her office, he discovers a dildo on her desk. Slanders admits that a secret admirer had sent it to her as a gift. With a smirk, Richard retorts, "It couldn't have been much of a secret admirer, if he sent you something so small."

Richard's comment precipitates a game of "Truth or Dare" before he opens his fly in a revelatory moment and shows the stunned woman just how large the real package can be. It is love at first sight for Slanders as she goes down on Grandik's grand dick with experienced vigor.

In the film's defining moment, Slanders is revealed for the phony she is during a Women of Morality event, when she is caught with Richard's prized jewel in her mouth during the evening's climactic moment.

Slim Pickins' band (music by Roberta Findlay) makes a welcome appearance, pounding out the tunes during the closing frames as an orgy ensues including the entire cast and company.

84 min/color. DVD. Roberta Findlay (as Anna Riva, non-sex), Beverly Bovy, C.J. Laing, Crystal Sync, Ginger Snap, Jennifer Jordan, Marlene Willoughby, Eric Edwards, Jeffrey Hurst, John Holmes, Tony Perez. *Director:* Roberta Findlay. *Writer:* Roberta Findlay.

The Devil in Mr. Holmes ★★ March 1987

Filmed in Italy, this was Holmes' final feature, made on the same trip that produced *The Rise of the Roman Empress*, released in the fall of 1986. Unfortunately, he didn't go out with a bang, but *The Devil in Mr. Holmes* does possess some redeeming qualities, including favorite performers of the era, Amber Lynn and Tracey Adams.

It is documented that these are the only films that John Holmes made while he knew he was HIV positive. It is disturbing to watch this film while keeping in mind that Holmes knowingly put the lives of others at risk.

The English voiceover is jarring, however, the recent DVD version is a vast improvement. One imagines the hilarity that undoubtedly arose while American actors added the voiceover for sex scenes. Do Italian noises of lust sound that different? Probably not.

The movie begins with Holmes going to his psychologist because he feels inadequate around women. After some unorthodox therapeutic treatments, John returns home and meditates while saying aloud, "Papa Satan, Papa Satan..." and POOF! Satan appears on his couch.

Satan agrees to grant John's wish of being able to seduce any woman who looks into his eyes. Sure enough, when John removes his famous fade-out aviator sunglasses, he is able to melt any woman who meets his gaze.

In an effort to demonstrate to his shrink the improvements he has made, John hosts a party in the final scene of the film. The doctor eventually partakes in the orgy sequence, which minimally includes John. He lies on the floor, out of sight until he stands up to receive fellatio, but he doesn't perform any other

Image courtesy of Paradise Visuals. The concluding scene of *The Devil in Mr. Holmes,* the second of the pair of films made in Italy in 1986.

sex acts. John is emaciated and it is disturbing to see him this way. The rest of the orgy sequence is good, with a variety of positions and artful camera work.

At the end of the orgy, John is surrounded by all of the women on the couch. He is smiling and appears happy, until the camera zooms in on his face and it falls. Holmes' eyes glaze over and he has a blank, detached stare.

In the conclusion, Satan returns to Holmes' house after the orgy to claim what is rightfully his. "I've come about that thing you owe me. You know what it is, don't you?"

On some video copies, it cuts off here — very hauntingly since some people may believe and at times John may have felt that he sold his soul and paid the ultimate price for his fame. But in the original version, The Devil forces John to give him oral sex — in a scene which was also not included on the 2007 DVD release.

This recent release by Paradise Visuals contains an excellent 90 minute interview by Bill Margold with Holmes' widow, Laurie Holmes, facilitated by Paradise

Visuals' president, Jason Green. They discuss John and his legend honestly, in addition to his decision to continue working after his positive diagnosis. This special DVD release also includes a 30-minute Ginger Lynn featurette with a clip of her and John in *Those Young Girls*.

90 min/color. DVD. Amber Lynn, Brigitte Moreau, Cicciolina, Dominique Duget, E. Farrari, Karin Shubert, Marina Hedman, Tracey Adams, Carmine Del Vechio, Christoph Clark, Ermino Casani, Jean-Pierre Armand, John Holmes. *Director:* Georgio Grande. *Producer:* Paradise Visuals.

Disco Sex Party ★ 1980

This short softcore film was obviously made to capitalize on the disco phenomenon that dominated popular music during the late-'70s. Former Russ Meyer mainstays, Uschi Digard and Candy Samples dance together under a rotating silver ball and are suddenly joined by an emaciated John Holmes. He boogies down with the bosomy starlets, who begin undressing for The King. The three sample one another's attributes and do their best to simulate oral and vaginal sex, but not too successfully.

Overall, this film is a disappointment. Holmes made a few softcore movies during a dry spell in his career, when he was at the height of his problems with substance abuse. It's not a stretch to presume that he had difficulties on set during this era since many producers and directors refused to work with him before his Wonderland nightmare.

24 min/color. DVD. Candy Samples, Uschi Digard, John Holmes.

Dr. Gonad's Sex Tails ★★ 1977

Also known as *Teenage Madam* and *Madam Lust*.

Nerdy psychologist Dr. Gonad decides to visit a cathouse in order to study the sexual habits of the ladies and their clientele. Gonad arranges to meet with Madame Rose (played by the curvaceous Desiree West). At the brothel, Dr. Gonad sees bedrooms suggesting various sexual scenarios for those with tastes ranging from vanilla to fetish-flair.

The bewildered-but-fascinated doctor (who hopes to get some action himself, all in the name of research) sits down with Madame Rose in the study and listens to her explain how she happened into her line of work. Recalling a rather indelible memory from her teenage years, Rose describes when she first took over the brothel for her mother — the former Madame. Through flashback, the scene with Madame Rose and her first customer (John Holmes) is shown. Upon setting eyes on her luscious body, John whistles low and remarks, "Your mama should have trotted you out a couple of years ago. You're a real cutie-pie." The two proceed to flirt until John produces his secret weapon.

At first, Rose is shocked because she doesn't know how to react to his massive organ, but allows him to talk her through the process of pleasing a man. Quickly, they undress and while lying in bed together, John exclaims, "Well, aren't you going to French my joint?"

Rose asks what he means and as he begins to explain fellatio to her, she fears that he'll urinate in her mouth. John patiently differentiates between urine and "love juice," and promises her that he won't do anything distasteful.

By John's climax, Rose proves to be a quick study. Holmes is fully erect while penetrating West and obviously enjoyed working with the beautiful actress (as his other two scenes with her, *The Spirit of Seventy Sex* and *Tapestry of Passion*, are equally hot).

Madame Rose smiles while contemplating her memory when a runaway named Kathie arrives at the house, looking for work. Charlene (Bonnie Holliday) listens to Kathie's tale of sexual abuse at the hands of her stepfather and assures her that she'll be treated like family while working for Madame Rose.

Charlene and Kathie share a little girl-on-girl fun before double-teaming a regular customer, a trucker named Frank (Marc MacGregor). Together, they enable his penchant for kink and watch as he dresses in women's clothing, before he expels his premature load all over the bed. Feigning disgust, the girls rub his nose in his own mess — and he likes it.

When Rusty, another one of Madame Rose's ladies, announces she's going to leave the whorehouse to cohabitate with her regular client, Patrick (Paul Thomas), the guys and gals decide to celebrate her new lease on life by orchestrating one final "going away" orgy. Patrick takes on Charlene and Madame Rose, while Frank sits solo in the middle of the action and plays with himself. Madame Rose's original customer (John Holmes) returns for the orgy.

With uncomfortable-looking Kathie on top of him in reverse cowgirl, John offers her encouraging words. This scene is somewhat difficult to watch as the actress appears distressed by John's size. She just doesn't look like she wants to be there, but offers a wan smile now and then. Generally a gentleman in all of his sex scenes, John checks in with her periodically and it seems to be no coincidence that when he moves her onto the couch, he positioned her face away from the camera. While she looks out of place and seems to await the conclusion of the scene, John talks inaudibly into her ear.

Apparently, it's all over but the crying, but the film wraps on a happy note as Rusty and Patrick exit the house holding hands while the rest of the gang bids them farewell and Dr. Gonad documents his findings. Excluding the lengthy Holmes/West flashback scene, the film is ordinary, with a repetitive theme song.

70 min/color. DVD. Bonnie Holliday, Desiree West, Kristine Heller (as Kathy March), Laurie Saint, Sheba Silas, Vicky Kaufman, John Holmes, John Seeman, Jack Wright (as Marc MacGregor), Paul Thomas. *Director:* Rik Taziner.

Down and Dirty ★ 1985

Fans of Candy Samples and John Holmes will be disappointed in this outing if they're hoping to see the two legends engaged in hardcore action.

As a swinging couple looking for a good time, John talks dirty to Candy and dotes on her large breasts, but the two well-endowed stars inevitably hook up with other partners in a fantasized orgy segment that highlights Janey Robbins. At first, John begs Candy to accompany him to the orgy (he even buys her a skimpy new blue dress) and she finally relents. Before the party, John changes his mind and decides to stay home for the weekend to play with Candy's candy instead.

The film includes great footage of the Pacific Coast highway as John and Candy envision themselves cruising along the ocean on their way to a club they call, Wild Things, where familiar adult performers come out to participate in fetish sex games.

72 min/color. DVD. Ashley Welles, Candy Samples, Janey Robbins, Lili Marlene, Don Fernando, John Holmes, Mike Horner, Morgan Grant. *Director:* Charles DeSantos.

Dreams of Misty ★★ December 1984

In this vehicle especially designed for Misty Dawn (a.k.a. Laurie Holmes), she stars as psychiatrist Dr. Misty Banks, who specializes in treating repressed sexuality.   In 2007, Laurie expressed her opinion that she was miscast in this role because she was only 20 years old. She is right (considering the average person graduates high school at 17 or 18 and then would complete six years or more to attain the proper certification), but considering the fact that this feature is not high drama, Holmes as Dr. Banks is passable.

A lithe, blonde client (Tantala Ray) describes a disturbing dream to the doctor that involves a mystery man (John Holmes) who attacks her as she sits in a wheelchair. Dr. Banks is also a part of the rendezvous, as the two women outmuscle the mystery man and force him to comply with their sexual advances, in retaliation for his aggressive tendencies.

Image courtesy of VCX.com.

When the fantasy concludes, the patient queries the doctor as to how she happened into her line of work. Her question gives way to the balance of the daydreams manifested by Dr. Banks herself, as she reflects upon some sordid fantasies dating back to her youth. It seems that she masturbated frequently while in the shower and also in her bedroom while her parents (Pat Manning and Nick Random) screwed in the adjacent bedroom. Her youthful daydreams include a photographer (Scott Irish), a fantasy lover (Marc Wallice) that she lusts after in a magazine, and her teacher. Misty imagines herself (wearing a dunce cap) with her teacher in a modest S&M scene, as she recites his revision of the

alphabet. Misty defines how each letter is to be remembered, "A is for ass, B is for boobs, C is for cunt, and so on."

Dreams of Misty manages to sustain eroticism throughout due to the evocative endeavors of Misty Dawn, Shaun Michele and Pat Manning. Nick Random is an entertaining actor and he and Manning play convincing parents.

According to Laurie Holmes, this was one of her final movie performances while she and John cohabitated since he believed that one porn star in the family was enough and didn't want her to work in more films. John Holmes was also the production manager on this project and Bill Amerson produced *Dreams of Misty* while under contract with VCX.

81 min/color. DVD. Misty Dawn, Pat Manning, Shalimar, Shaun Michelle, Tantala Ray, John Holmes, Marc Wallice, Nick Random, Scott Irish. *Director:* Max Strand. *Producer:* Bill Amerson (as Bill Williams). *Production Manager:* John C. Holmes.

The Erotic Adventures of Candy ★★★★ 1978

Also known as *Making Candy.*

Carol Connors has matured since her appearance as the nurse in *Deep Throat*! She portrays a 20-year old bimbo from Michigan State University named Candy Christian. Candy lives with her overprotective father, who believes she isn't mature enough to date, although many guys proposition her.

Don Fernando makes an appearance as a gardener named Manuel, the object of her fantasies. After lusting for him, Candy loses her virginity, but is caught by her father. Manuel doesn't speak English, so his sexually suggestive statements appear in yellow subtitles. Enraged, Candy's father tries to maim Manuel, but winds up running into a wall and being hospitalized instead. Hilarity ensues, with crazy plot twists.

John Holmes plays a used car salesman, who meets Candy in the park while jogging. He lays it on thick about his "deformity," and after inviting Candy to his home for lunch, he convinces her to go all the way. John plays his character very naturally, without any of the overacting that some of his male costars succumb to in this flick. There are some excellent uses of the camera that show off just how much bigger his penis gets when erect. During the money shot, John designs a daisy on Candy's ample breast, using his penis like a cake decorating tool, which seems to catch her off guard.

John Leslie portrays a physician who takes advantage of naïve Candy. Paul Thomas also has a speaking part, as a Hare Krishna-like devotee who tries to show Candy the benefits of his religion. The spiritual healing of his religious practice includes multiple sex positions, including a short glimpse of a male-male blowjob. At the end of Paul Thomas' counseling (and sex) with Candy, he involves her in a boy-boy-girl threesome, and the surprise is at the end.

Trivia: Carol Connors met Jack Birch on the set of this film. They are the parents of Thora and Bolt Birch.

84 min/color. DVD. Amanda Jones, Cris Cassidy (as Buffy Stevens), Carol Connors, Eileen Welles, Gail Palmer (non-sex), Georgina Spelvin, Kristine

Heller (non-sex), Lauren Black (non-sex), Lynn Ann Newton (non-sex), Pat Ray (non-sex), Stacy Evens, Bobby Bryan, Don Fernando, Ric Lutze, Eddy Cannon, Jack Birch (non-sex), John Holmes, John Leslie, John Timothy, Jon Martin (as Mickey Rivers), Joey Silvera (as Norm Buller), Paul Thomas, Robbi Robinson (non-sex), Turk Lyon. *Directors:* Gail Palmer, Bob Chinn (uncredited). *Writers:* Mason Hoffenberg (novel: *Candy*, uncredited), Gail Palmer, Terry Southern. *Producers:* Harry Mohney, Gail Palmer.

Eruption ★★★★ 1978

Tagline: *"An erotic explosion."*

A porn spoof of the 1944 film noir classic, *Double Indemnity*, *Eruption* showcases John Holmes for his second time with one of porn's premiere leading ladies, Lesllie Bovee. Shot on location in Hawaii, *Eruption* is one of Holmes' most prominent starring roles and it is a big-budget standout.

Peter Winston (Holmes) is an insurance salesman who likes to relax on Hawaiian beaches to survey single women when he's not swatting flies. Casually, he strides over to where Sandy Bevin (Lesllie Bovee) is sunning herself. Peter invades her personal space by playfully snatching the top of her suntan oil bottle, much to her chagrin. After he offers up a lame come-on line, she tells him to "Get lost."

Upon having second thoughts, she calls him back over to confide that she might be interested in an insurance policy, after all. Then they have sex on the beach. (Holmes appears to be keeping an eye out for the police because the scene was shot outside in broad daylight.)

Eruption has a smattering of everything — murder, sex, intrigue, some plot twists — and Holmes does all of his own stunt work. He shimmies down tall buildings with rope, jumps from high brick walls, scuba dives, and manages to be a convincing actor between his sex acts with Bovee and Susan Hart (who plays Sandy's stepdaughter, Angie). Watch for Holmes' funny interactions with non-sex performer, Wilt Torrance, who plays Peter's co-worker, Jackson — Torrance is either really loaded or else a terrific method actor.

82 min/color. DVD. Carrie Welton, Fifi Aldercy (non-sex), Lesllie Bovee, Susan Hart, Tracy Valdis (non-sex), Bernard Addison (non-sex), Bert Willis (non-sex), Eric Evol, Gene Clayton (non-sex), Jack Aldis, John Holmes, Joseph Lopez (non-sex), Justin Mallory (non-sex), Shell Seward (non-sex), Wilt Torrance (non-sex), Wynne Colburn. *Director:* Stanley Kurlan. *Producer:* Stanley Kurlan. *Writer:* Justin Welton.

Exhausted: John C. Holmes, The Real Story ★★★★ July 1981

Tagline: *"Over 14,000 women knew him intimately."*

As a former confidante and girlfriend of John Holmes, director Julia St. Vincent was involved in every facet of this documentary, right down to supplying her own vocals for its theme song. St. Vincent was only a teenager when she began working in the offices of Freeway Films, which was an L.A.-based adult movie company that her uncle, Armand Atamian, owned and operated. (Freeway produced the *Johnny Wadd* films made from 1975 until 1978.)

In June 1981, John answers interview questions for the film, *Exhausted*.

In 1980, when St. Vincent began her taped interviews with John, he was already on his downward spiral. Her idea was to showcase Holmes as the man behind the penis, but it became a challenging task because Holmes was alarmingly unreliable due to his quest for drugs. Despite his problems, *Exhausted* is dynamic and fascinating. In addition to street interviews with people in L.A. and Chicago, Bob Chinn and Seka were interviewed about John for the project. The interviews are melded together with classic film footage from the *Johnny Wadd* series.

St. Vincent manages to bring out the best in Holmes during some of the interview segments as he is depicted in a variety of moods ranging from mischievous, contemplative, provocative, and sincere. When asked whether or not he ever grows tired of his vocation, he wryly retorts, "I never get tired of what I do because I'm a sex fiend. I'm very lusty." To his credit, he thoughtfully answers her unusual queries, for example when St. Vincent asks which side he packs his package, Holmes jokingly replies, "I show larger on the right so if I'm going to a party and I'm in a nasty mood, I wear it right." He is also reticent about the downside of fame and explains that he is unable to live up to the expectations and sexual fantasies of the many women he encounters off-screen.

In addition to underscoring Holmes and his work, this documentary is also a platform for Seka, who speaks favorably about Holmes and his oversized appendage. She rattles off a few funny lines herself claiming a rather infamous one, "John Holmes has cum like God." Seka was indeed one of Holmes' favorite costars, but it's obvious that she was included to add a touch of porno chic and credibility to *Exhausted*, while ultimately gaining publicity.

On the set of *Exhausted* with Laurie Smith and Laura Toledo.

Unfortunately, *Exhausted* is currently out of circulation but often available for purchase on eBay. It was the inspiration for the 1997 award winning feature film *Boogie Nights* that stars Mark Walhberg as Dirk Diggler, a character loosely fashioned after John Holmes. *Boogie Nights* recreated scenes from *China Cat* and adopted Holmes/Chinn interview segments from *Exhausted*. The 2000 DVD version of *Exhausted* contains raw, never-before-seen interview footage of Holmes in December 1980, along with a director's commentary, excerpts of "Julia's Diary" and bios of the stars.

72 min/color. Not available on DVD. Annette Haven, Bonnie Holliday, Candida Royalle, Cris Cassidy, Eileen Welles, Fatima Hamoud, Felicia Sanda, Georgina Spelvin, Jennifer Richards, Jessie St. James, Julia St. Vincent (non-sex), Kitty Shayne, Kyoto Sunn, Laurie Smith, Laurien Dominique, Linda Wong, Monique Starr, Paula Wain, Phae Burd, Phaedra Grant, Seka, Bob Chinn (non-sex), John Holmes. *Director:* Julia St. Vincent. *Writer:* Morgan Lofting (adaptation). *Producers:* Julia St. Vincent, Lee Kasper.

Extreme Close-up ★★★ December 1979

Also known as *Open Invitation*. Taglines, "John Holmes gives us lessons in love, the French way!!" "An American stud in Paris."

After a voracious sexual encounter with her husband, George (Jamie Gillis), writer Laura Farr (Delania Raffino) informs him that she must leave for Europe where she will interview an erotic photographer, Margarite Heller (Gloria Leonard) for a biography.

Shortly after her arrival in France, Farr, who is an enigma throughout the story, quickly finds herself involved in an affair with Jonathan (John Holmes).

Jonathan becomes Farr's confidante and lover. When Jonathan declares his love for her, an insidious story unfolds that puts Farr as a pawn in a game of dominance between Margarite and Jonathan.

Holmes and Raffino enjoy three sex scenes in the film, but it is when he and Leonard hook up that the sparks begin to fly. Much attention is paid to foreplay and passionate kisses, however, there is no money shot for unknown reasons.

Some of the scenes have great potential, but due to dim lighting in parts of the film, they don't always come off. This is one of the three European films that put John with Gloria Leonard in Paris and Brittany, France over a period of several weeks. This is one of the first American adult features to be filmed overseas. Despite the fact that *Extreme Close Up* is slow-paced, it contains a delectable, trashy Euro flavor that keeps it interesting.

77 min/color. DVD. Delania Raffino, Denise Sloan (Denise Deneuve), Diane Sloan (as Diana Deneuve), Gloria Leonard, Daniel Trabet, Jacque Gatteau, Jamie Gillis, John Holmes. *Director:* Charles De Santos. *Producer:* Aaron Linn.

Evil Come, Evil Go ★★★ 1972

Tagline: *"No man is safe from the Preacherwoman. She's a man-hating, hymn-humming hell cat!"*

John is credited with a cameo appearance and his work as an Assistant Director in this sexy slasher. (Or could it be called a scary sex movie?) The film was directed by Walt Davis and produced by Bob Chinn and his business partner, Linda Adrain.

A self-proclaimed proponent of anti-pleasurable sex, Sister Sarah Jane seduces and kills men. She enlists the help of a lesbian to help her. The movie is fun in a campy way, although not very scary — and not terribly sexy, either. Scenes are simulated and therefore, intentionally under-lit.

John appears as a man playing pool in the bar, but it is not obvious. He has no speaking or sex scenes, although Holmes fans may find it interesting to critique John's hand at supplying gory special effects.

73 min/color. DVD. Cleo O'Hara, Doris Jung, Jacqueline Lissette, Jane Louise, Margot Devletian, Sandra Henderson, Vickie Cristal, Bob Chinn, Chesley Noone, Gerard Broulard, Jesse Dizon, John Holmes, Marc Wurzel, Norman Fields, Rick Cassidy, Roy Hankey, Walt Davis. *Director:* Walt Davis. *Writer:* Walt Davis. *Producer:* Bob Chinn.

Fantasm ★★ July 1976

Also known as *Fantale* (Australia — working title) and *World of Sexual Fantasy*.

With no clearly defined plot, *Fantasm* leaves a lot to be desired as it attempts to tie together softcore scenes with lengthy introductions by Professor Jurgen Notafrued (John Bluthal). The sex scenes present the top ten fantasies of women; of course, most of these are in fact, the fantasies that men like to think that women have!

John Holmes' "Fruit Salad" scene with Maria Welton is superb, but some of the other sequences — including a mother (Candy Samples) and son bath, and a rape scene featuring Rene Bond — may be disturbing to sensitive viewers. On the positive side, the camera work, sets and music in this film are all excellent.

"Fruit Salad" — A beautiful woman (Maria Welton) lounges in the backyard on a chaise, wearing an open silk robe. She applies baby oil onto her smooth, olive skin and smiles to herself while contemplating an imaginary visitor. Her husband is often away and he suspects that she has lovers, although it is untrue.

Seductively, she coats herself with the oil and as she reaches between her legs there is a splash in the pool next to her. As Neptune, John Holmes climbs up out of the water. He stands on the pool deck, giving the audience a full view of his impressive member before sitting down at the end of her lounge chair.

Neptune helps himself to the bowl of fruit next to the chaise, but rather than eating it, he places a blueberry inside of a nectarine and suggestively licks it. Wordlessly, his host suggestively bites a banana. Next, John covers her breasts with pineapple slices, berries and whipped cream before leaning over to consume them.

John and costar, Maria Welton, take a timeout on the set of *Fantasm* — one of the first adult-oriented films to screen at Cannes Film Festival in 1977.

Together, John and Welton enact an evocative, feminine fantasy in this scene. After a lingering kiss, the couple find themselves underwater in the pool, engaged in oral sex before intercourse. The sexy blues guitar enhances their delicate water scene and lends a classy ambiance to the sequence, which is the only hardcore scene in the movie. (This scene was reinstated when the film was re-released on DVD with director's commentary in 2004.)

Fantasm faced worldwide censorship issues as it was banned in Queensland, Australia, while Britain released a heavily cut version of the film at 69 minutes after initially rejecting it. As Ginnane explained, audiences around the world were engrossed at the sight of John's penis when he emerged out of the water as Neptune. The film grossed 13 times its budget in Australia alone and created a demand for a sequel.

90 min/color. DVD. Candy Samples, Dee Dee Levitt, Gretchen Rudolf, Helen O'Connell, Linda York (non-sex), Maria Arnold, Maria Lutra, Maria Welton, Rene Bond, Robin Spratt, Roxanne Brewer, Serena, Shayne, Uschi

Digard, Wendy Cavanaugh, Al Ward, Al Williams, Clement St. George, Con Covert, Gary Dolgin, Gene Allan Poe, John Bluthal, John Green, John Holmes, Kirby Adams, Kirby Hall, Lyman Britton, Mitch Morrill, Paul Wyman, Rick Partlow, Robert Savage, Sam Compton, Sam Wyman, Stan Straton, Thomas Blaz, William Margold, William Wutke. *Director:* Richard Franklin. *Producer:* Anthony Ginnane, Leon Gorr, Ted Mulder. *Writer:* Ross Dimsey.

Fantasm Comes Again ★ December 1977

Also known as *Fantasm 2*.

This film falls into the same trap that most sequels do — while trying to capitalize on the monetary success and the original flair of *Fantasm*, it feels contrived and falls flat. Instead of the professor providing commentary along with oddball pearls of wisdom between the scenes, *Fantasm Comes Again* employs two hosts, Libby and Harry, who are newspaper columnists attempting to address the sexual fantasies of their readers. Once again, the film contains 10 shorts, including a rape scene that features Cheryl Smith (as Rainbeaux Smith) with a greasy guy, a library bit and one at the gym. Ginnane provides interesting narrative.

John Holmes, who was scheduled to return in another "pool boy" segment, wasn't satisfied with the cold temperature of the water because he was afraid of getting sick with pneumonia, so Bill Margold stood in for him (after suffering a concussion from playing football earlier that day). Holmes appears in a brief, non-sex cameo, walking around the pool deck, and sent Margold a thank you note with his pay returned since he did not fulfill his role's obligations.

94 min/color. DVD. Amanda Smith, Andrea Murphy, Angela Menzies Wills, Brenda Fogerty, Candy Fox, Candy Samples, Cheryl Smith, Christine De Schaffer, Dee Cooper, Dee Dee Levitt, Elaine Collins, Eve Darling, Helen Madigan, Helen O'Connell, Liz Wolfe, Lois Owens, Mary Johnson, Pat Manning, Rhonda Wilcox, Rosemarie Bem, Serena, Suzanne Walsh, Suzy A. Star, Uschi Digard, Al Ward, Antony I. Ginnane, Bryant Rigby, Clive Hearn, Con Covert, Herb Layne, Jesse Adams, John Holmes, Johnny Legend, Jon Arnold, Ken Kruger, Michael Barton, Michael Karnitz, Mike Ranger, Mike Stapp, P.J. Jackson, Ray Wells, Rick Cassidy, Sam A. Menning, Tom Thumb, Urias S. Cambridge, Titus Moede, William Margold. *Director:* Colin Eggleston. *Writer:* Ross Dimsey. *Producers:* Antony I. Ginanne, Leon Gorr, Mark Josem, Robert Ward.

Flesh and Laces Part II ★★ September 1983

Director, Carlos Tobalina earned an Adult Film Association of America (AFAA) award for his work in this film as a supporting actor, which raised a bit of controversy because Tobalina has only three lines and no sex scene in the film.

The movie continues the story of *Flesh and Laces Part I*, wherein a father (Jamie Gillis) is confined to a hospital bed because of an unknown ailment. (Don't worry if you haven't seen *Part I*; the theme song will fill you in on everything you need to know plus John doesn't appear in it.) On a closed-circuit monitor in his room at the infirmary, Dad watches the sexual antics of his four adult children.

His two sons are shown in the act. The first full-length sexual encounter is between one son and an evangelist that he rapes after she comes to his door. The scene isn't particularly violent, but it isn't particularly hot, either. The second son has better luck with his partner and sets up the scene as an interview for a "personal secretary."

John Holmes enters the film after 50 minutes, as Dr. Pecker. He has few lines — the most notable of which are at the beginning of the orgy that ensues after he catches the father and his daughter making love on the hospital bed, "Reminds me of med school."

That particular line is typical for a corny-yet-smile-worthy John Holmes adlib. The ensuing orgy, however, is not as heartwarming as Holmes' boyishness. The daughter in the film has two lower-body tattoos, at a time in the pornographic industry when tattoos on women were becoming more acceptable.

Holmes looks healthy and is quite charming, although he isn't quite as appealing with shorter hair instead of his longer curls. There are some impressive shots of his appendage, though, which is considerably erect for this period in the late actor's life. He even makes his famous "monkey" expression during his climax. His cum shot is synchronized perfectly with an electric slide whistle—the payoff of this otherwise forgettable film. After the orgy is (finally) done, Harry, the father, announces that none of the adult children are biologically his and invites the whole crew to live at the mansion with him.

85 min/color. DVD. Drea, Rita Cruz, Rosa Lee Kimball, Shaun Michelle, Lynz Canon, Tamara Longley, Carlos Tobalina (non-sex), Dan T. Mann (as Dan Fisher), John Stagliano, Jamie Gillis, Joey Silvera, John Holmes. *Director:* Carlos Tobalina. *Writers:* Carter Anderson, Lester Mattson, Phyllis Wainwright.

Flesh of the Lotus ★ *December 1971*

The second *Johnny Wadd* film of the nine-part series.

Johnny Wadd and his Wadd girl, Sheila, engage in a sexually suggestive conversation before she initiates the first move. John appears amused by her efforts. Soon, they find themselves standing face-to-face, naked in Sheila's kitchen as she ponders aloud whether or not he will fit inside of her. With enthusiasm, she remarks how well endowed he is, and the home viewer is treated to a close up of John's 12 inches. They do the deed, backdoor style, with Sheila holding onto a chair before they finish on the shag carpet.

Johnny gets off and goes. Shockingly, Shelia is murdered in his absence and in this porno whodunit, he must discover who has killed her. He first solicits help from one of Sheila's lesbian friends (a frightening-looking actress) after inadvertently walking in on her while she masturbates with a ridiculously large dildo. As the case builds, Johnny learns that drugs and money are at the root of Shelia's death.

Wadd makes an important discovery that one of the suspects is a member of the Chinatown thugs known as the Lotus Gang. Soon, he finds himself confronted by Frankie (Bob Chinn) and one of their legendary fight scenes ensues. John provides a wide array of entertaining stunts, including pratfalls, flips and somersaults.

This film is considered to be the poorest of the nine *Johnny Wadd* films that make up the series because the story is disjointed and the overall effect of the sex scenes plays like an amateur porn movie rather than an erotic feature. Despite the film's lack of sophistication, *Flesh of the Lotus* served to boost Holmes' popularity as film audiences proved to be insatiable for the detective. In this film, John appears to be wearing his wedding ring on a chain about his neck.

69 min/color. VHS. *59 min/color. DVD.* Andy Bellamy, Bob Chinn (non-sex), John Holmes (as John Duval), Mike Haven. *Director:* Bob Chinn. *Writer:* Bob Chinn. *Producer:* Chinn-Adrain Productions.

Four Women in Trouble ★½ 1972

The simple tale unfolds as the title would suggest; four young women become pregnant — two by boyfriends, a one-night stand and by rape. In turn, each of the ladies visits an unethical practitioner (John Holmes) where they seek abortions. The attractive young doctor feigns interest in their problems as he asks each to disrobe and lie down for their "pap smears" — but his intent is to get into their pants. The girls aren't shy and eventually succumb to his well-oiled seduction technique. Talk about a bedside manner!

Apart from a threesome involving Holmes and two patients, there is a sensuous and slow sex scene that features John and the first (unknown) woman to enter the examining room. Holmes climaxes inside of the actress, which was uncommon during the Golden Era performances. It is rather interesting to observe John smoking cigarettes during his examinations, and he doesn't put them down while receiving head, either — dating the material back to the days when cigs were permissible in medical facilities and during porn shoots.

60 min/color. DVD. Lynn Holmes, John Holmes, Ron Darby.

Garters and Lace ★★★ 1980

This outstanding vignette was compiled from various 1970s films and loops.

It begins like a documentary on sexy lingerie — with the beautiful Barbara Peckinpaugh modeling a veil as the narrator explains its history. Peckinpaugh interrupts sex scenes throughout the video and she talks directly into the camera while the narrator comments on her lacy apparel. She has a flawless body, although she comes across a bit creepy when delivering her lines.

John Holmes appears in four of the six vignettes — along with Victoria Pink, Barbara Barton, Linda Mc Dowell, Lesllie Bovee (from the extremely rare 1976 feature film, *Tapestry of Passion*). The John Holmes scenes were filmed from 1971-75.

Ric Lutze and Jesse Adams, who later worked in a number of Penguin Productions, each have one scene, but they are inferior in comparison to Holmes' four.

The cinematography, editing and sound of this film are all professionally executed. Instrumental pieces with varied tempos accompany the scenes, and some interesting sound effects are applied in sync with the cum shots. In addition, the borrowed houses that director Thornberg chose are lush and beautiful, which gives the overall production a high-budget "feel." As an added bonus, the girls are appealing and hold up compared to today's airbrushed and siliconed starlets. This is an excellent choice for couples to enjoy together.

69 min/color. DVD. Cyndee Summers (as Anne Faulkner), Suzannah Britton (as Aubrey Turner, non-sex), Barbara Barton, Linda McDowell (as Claudia Grayson), Lesllie Bovee, Desiree West (as Patricia Lee), Veronica Pink, Jesse Adams (as Arne Larson), John Holmes, Ric Lutze. *Director:* Chris Warfield (as Billy Thornberg). *Writer:* Chris Warfield. *Producer:* Chris Warfield.

Girls on Fire ★★★★ 1985

Tagline: *"A film that sets the screen ablaze!"*

Ditzy dame, Charity (Kimberly Carson) is married to the mob. Her husband, Tony Cardoza (John Alderman), is about to trade her in for a younger model when his insurance scam comes under investigation by two randy agents, Danny and Greg (Jamie Gillis and Bobby Bullock). *Girls on Fire* is loosely based upon the classic film, *Some Like It Hot*, with Gillis and Bullock recreating the characters personified by Tony Curtis and Jack Lemmon.

When Cardoza catches the two hustlers in the aftermath of sex with his wife, he commissions his bumbling sidekicks, Rocco and Charlie (John Holmes and Bill Amerson) to pursue them. Danny and Greg make their great escape in bath towels and a comedy of errors ensues as they hide out from Rocco.

The insurance agents and Rocco find themselves across the street, where a group rehearses for a lingerie fashion show that features Suzie (Ginger Lynn) and the fashions of designer Lance Lalot (R. Bolla). Danny and Greg attempt to conceal their identities by dressing in drag, except that Rocco has the same idea.

In *Girls on Fire*, John Holmes can be seen exiting a restroom, looking hilariously conspicuous in a dress, wig, stilettos, and full makeup. Holmes seems to have great fun, slipping into a Bronx accent as he attempts to walk in the high heels.

Girls on Fire contains crisp dialogue, respectable acting turns by the entire cast and oodles of sex. Holmes and Ginger Lynn exhibit palpable sexual chemistry, proving they outmatch many porn couples of the era. Their pairing is interesting due to the almost 20-year gap in their ages. Harry Reems makes a special appearance in a billiard scene with Shaun Michelle that lacks continuity with the rest of the plot, but in porn films, anything goes!

Bill Amerson's son, Sean, can be seen briefly as a police officer at the end of the film. Having lost his dragonfly ring, John is wearing a gold pinky ring with his initials (J.H.) encrusted in diamonds. This ring can be viewed in many of his '80s films.

Although shot in 1984, *Girls on Fire* premiered on February 7, 1985, the same night John Holmes was immortalized outside the Pussycat Theater on Santa Monica Boulevard — where he dipped his hands and feet in cement. This was one of the most heavily promoted adult movies to-date, with billboards all over Los Angeles and New York City.

80 min/color. DVD. Angel, Barbara Leigh (as Blossom Leigh, non-sex), Ginger Lynn, Kimberly Carson, Misty Dawn (non-sex), Cody Nicole (Roxanne Potts), Shanna McCullough, Shaun Michelle, Raven (as Vicky Vickers), Bill Amerson (non-sex), Bobby Bullock, Frank Hollowell (non-sex), Harry Reems, Jamie Gillis, John Holmes, R. Bolla, Sean Amerson (non-sex). *Director:* Jack Remy. *Assistant Director:* John Holmes. *Writer:* D.J. Fields, Harold Lime. *Producers:* Bill Amerson, Harold Lime, M. Murray. *Production Manager:* John C. Holmes.

The Good, the Bad and the Horny
★★ 1985

This average feature takes place at a dude ranch where the dudes, led by Billy Dee, challenge some rich Beverly Hills chicks to a game of Cowboys and Indians. What results is a Sex Ed 101 weekend.

Summer Rose, dressed in native apparel, stumbles upon John Holmes playing a hung-over drifter in the woods. Her sure-fire fix for his pounding headache comes in the form of oral, cowgirl

With Summer Rose in *The Good, The Bad and the Horny*.

doggie style, and missionary fornication. At 41, John doesn't have any difficulty achieving a menacing erection and willing Summer Rose takes him in stride. The forested location is a welcome reprieve from the indoor sets, including the sound of a dog barking off in the distance.

Still photographer, Kenji took a hilarious photograph of Holmes during his sex scene with Summer Rose, where John flipped Kenji the bird.

85 min/color. DVD. Amber Lynn, Bunny Bleu, Lois Ayres, Summer Rose, Billy Dee, John Holmes. *Director:* John Holmes.

The Grafenberg Spot ★★★★ 1985

Also known as *The G Point.*

The Grafenberg Spot features a contemporary couple, Leslie and Michael (Ginger Lynn and Harry Reems), who appear to be compatible in every way — except that when aroused during oral sex, Leslie orgasms and a stream of clear liquid squirts out onto her lover's face. Michael is deeply disturbed by her orgasmic eruptions and they have a falling out. Having experienced this problem with her boyfriends in the past, Leslie seeks the advice of a sexual disorder specialist (Annette Haven), while disgruntled Michael shares the story with his buddy (Rick Savage) over a couple of beers.

Upon being reassured by the doctor that her situation is not unique, Leslie zooms off on the back of a motorcycle with a new friend while the doctor pays Michael an unexpected visit on his boat to extol the virtues of the G-spot. Leslie and her friend make a momentary pit stop at a garage, where she begins to fantasize about a welder (John Holmes). In her imagination, she is lowered onto John's erection while perched atop a bar for support. The camera contrasts John's immense size against Ginger's delicate frame before the scene culminates in mutual climaxes — with Leslie squirting onto John's face before an exchange of tender kisses.

Meanwhile, Michael checks out a special club where all of the occupants seem to be hip to the G-spot, prompting him to have an epiphany as he reconsiders his feelings for Leslie's so-called affliction. When the two are later reunited by the sexual specialist at an orgy, Michael and Leslie put aside their differences and live happily ever after — now that Michael has gained a new perspective and appreciation for Leslie's quirky habit.

The Grafenberg Spot is a seductive, good-looking film with a prestigious cast; porn's version of Hollywood's A-list. The film was written, directed and produced by the Mitchell Brothers, who were well known for the quality that they brought to erotic movies. (Traci Lords was part of the original cast, but her scenes were later deleted after it was learned that she was underage at the time of filming.) The San Francisco scenery is gorgeous and Lombard Street never looked better as Ginger cruises the paved zigzags in a sporty convertible. An added bonus on the DVD is the blooper feature.

90 min/color. DVD. Amber Lynn, Annette Haven, Fanny Fatale, Ginger Lynn, Lilly Marlene, Nina Hartley, Rita Ricardo (as Rita Erotica), Traci Lords, Harry Reems, John Holmes, Rick Savage, Thor Southern. *Director:* Artie Mitchell. *Writer:* Artie Mitchell.

Hard Soap, Hard, Soap ★★★½ 1977

Also known as *Hard Soap*. Tagline: "Lather up, guys!"

In this send-up of the '70s television soap opera, *Mary Hartman, Mary Hartman*, real-life best friends, Laurien Dominique and Candida Royalle, team up as their characters, neighbors, Penny Holmes and Linda Lou. As a porn version of Lucy Ricardo and Ethel Mertz, the pair attempts to solve the sexual hang-ups experienced by almost everyone they encounter.

Penny is married to psychiatrist/sexual therapist, Dr. John Holmes, who suffers from a deficiency of his own — the doctor is unable to launch his 12-inch rocket. In her frustration, Penny attempts to compensate for her unrequited sex drive by endeavoring to help others in her predicament, including the milkman, the paper boy, her husband's clients, and anyone else who happens to cross her path. Somewhat reluctantly, Linda Lou helps her friend to service the overflow of those in need.

After filling in as a receptionist at her husband's office, Penny is raped by the custodial engineer (Paul Thomas) and seeks redemption for enjoying it by confessing to a priest. When he turns the tables and shares some alarming secrets of his own, Penny chases him out of the house.

The next evening, Dr. Holmes arrives home after a trip to discover a sex therapy session taking place in his living room. He demands that Penny explain herself. Relieved to see her husband, Penny pleads with him to aid in her quest to cure a blind woman by revealing himself to her.

Will the blind woman see again? Will Dr. Holmes regain control of his manhood? Will the priest come out of the closet? Stay tuned! *Hard Soap* is a terrific example of an intentionally comedic Golden Age porno with a funny script (by Chinn's milkman, John Chapman), a solid cast, hot sex, and skillful acting turns (particularly by Dominique and Royalle). This hard soap is slippery and wet.

76 min/color. VHS. Anita Jenson, Barbara Ericson, Candida Royalle (as Candice Chambers), Cindy Barron (non-sex), Joan Devlon, Laurien Dominique, Mindy McGowan, Sabrina, Bekkouche Simon, Blair Harris, Charles Law, Dale Meador (non-sex), George Sampson (non-sex), Jon Martin (as Jerry Jordan), Joey Silvera (as Joe Nassivera, non-sex), John Holmes, John Seeman (non-sex), Ken Scudder, Mike Donovan, Paul Thomas (as Paul Tanner), Steve Vasari. *Director:* Bob Chinn. *Writer:* John Chapman. *Producer:* Damon Christian (as Dick Aldrich).

Heat of the Moment ★★ 1983

John Holmes demonstrates that he is back with a swagger (after his Laurel Canyon saga) in this story that depicts a day in the life of a swinger and his inner circle. Holmes and Shaun Michelle get things rolling as the film opens with the two stars beneath the covers. She begs, "Just one more time," and John tells her that he's got nothing left in the gas tank.

She persists and he tentatively agrees, on one condition: "Okay, but you have to go down to get it up." She obliges with precision and John heats her up with his big toe. After a rousing and sensuous lay that includes lots of dirty talk and warm, moist kisses, they climax quickly before John tells her that he must return home to his wife and that he must stop at the store on his way home.

While at the market, a couple of nymphettes decide to steal his yellow Jeep and drive away just as he steps outside. As they happily cruise along, the girls disrobe and happen upon a stray guy (Marc Wallice) in the desert, who is ripe for their sexual advances. After an enticing three-way, the girls literally leave him in the dust (and in the buff) before they encounter another male at the side of the road.

They attempt to seduce him with their girlish wiles, but he steals the Jeep back from them before delivering it safely to John. On the other hand, John invites a female friend, Pat (Patricia Manning), to his homestead. John, his friend and Pat go outside and see John's wife is spread-eagled before a cute New York gal-pal, Ginger (played by Misty Dawn). After observing the girls for a while, John encourages his friend to join the ladies and he whisks Pat away in his arms. Inside the den, John and Pat get down to dirty business. When it's all over, the day is still young, so they go for a dip to cool off.

According to Laurie Holmes and John's autobiography, *Porn King*, John had asked that Laurie refrain from performing with other men shortly after she and he became an item, but he didn't object if she was paired with other women. Already a couple during the making of this film, Misty is shown having anal sex, but it may have been a stunt butt — as a blemish on the behind in question intimates; Misty's tush was pimple-free when it was showcased earlier on.

59 min/color. DVD. Jennifer West, Maria Tortuga, Misty Dawn, Pat Manning, Gary Anderson, John Holmes, Marc Wallice.

Honey Throat ★★½ 1980

Tagline: *"Sweetness just drips from her juicy red lips…Spread this on your hotcakes!"*

Due to similar settings, the extra footage, the actors and director, this film was likely shot in tandem with *Summertime Blue*. Jonathan (Eric Edwards, with a cast on his right hand) operates a stud service out of a local beauty shop where female customers make frequent visits to be serviced by the owner and his star employee, Freddie (John Holmes).

"Plain Jane" Honey (Arcadia Lake), another stylist at the salon who happens to be a virgin and eats spoonfuls of honey, is hot for Jonathan, but she is unable to tell him how she feels. He can barely look past her unflatteringly large glasses and oversized wardrobe.

When the receptionist, Lori (Katie Kean), finds Honey crying as she observes Jonathan going down on Mrs. White (Serena), she invites Honey over to her apartment for a surprise makeover. The results prove to be impressive as shy, forlorn Honey is transformed into an appealing vixen. Lori schools Honey on the intricacies of sexual pleasure with a hands-on lesson.

The next day at the salon, Jonathan does a double-take and invites Honey out to breakfast. They "click" and set a date for the following evening. In the meantime, Lori asks Honey to sit in on her evening with her boyfriend, who teaches Honey to give head in preparation for her date with Jonathan.

In addition to some great sex scenes, (the Holmes/Serena sequence is footage from *Summertime Blue*), *Honey Throat* contains a sweet love story starring real life lovers Eric Edwards and Arcadia Lake, with ample disco tracks pumping throughout the film. One that stands out is during Holmes' scene with Samantha Fox; he penetrates her in the salon chair in beat with the soundtrack.

Shot on the east coast (possibly Connecticut), Serena and Eric Edwards both recall how the set was busted one night when the local police wondered why the salon's windows were covered in paper. The entire cast, including porn's multi-faceted Roberta Findlay (billed here as presenter, J. Angel Martine) were hauled off to jail. Holmes was the first to be released. According to Serena, it was because of his star power that the rest of the cast was soon set free.

75 min/color. DVD. Arcadia Lake, Patty Boyd (as Katie Kean), Samantha Fox, Serena, Eric Edwards, John Holmes, Ron Hudd. *Director:* John Christopher. *Writer:* John Christopher, Roberta Findlay (as Shemp O'Day). *Producer:* Richard Hertz, J. Angel Martine.

Hot 'n' Spicy Pizza Girls, We Deliver ★★★★ 1979

Also known as *Hot 'n' Spicy Pizza Girls; Country Pizza Girls;* and *Pizza Girls*.

The film opens with a catchy theme song and some attractive women skateboarding through the streets of San Francisco. They are on their way to work at Country Girls Pizza, where John (Holmes) interviews a prospective new Pizza Girl, Ann Chovy (played by the naturally beautiful Desiree Cousteau).

The real plot of the movie is that the Pizza Girls deliver risqué sexual requests with each pizza. This means bad business for their competition, the owners of the Country Fried Chicken (Paul Thomas and Carl Regal), who send out the San Francisco Night Chicken to protect their investment. With both the Night Chicken and a blundering detective, Blackie (John Seeman), hot on the Pizza Girls' trails, they are no longer safe to deliver the pizzas. In a strange twist of events, Ann Chovy and Blackie fall in love after a rousing sexual encounter — and the attacks of the Night Chicken also stop.

There are two sex scenes that feature John, the most provocative of which is between Holmes and Desiree Cousteau, with Cousteau mounted on a penny horse — a neat trick. John doesn't bother to undress. He merely unzips his fly to release his stiff shaft. Holmes' other scene is a three-way with Gino (Candida Royalle) and Celeste (Christine deShaffer).

Director Bob Chinn makes a non-sex cameo appearance as a co-owner of the pizzeria. Some of the more humorous moments occur when the two wise-cracking porn vets serve customers while wearing identical red-checkered shirts. John jokes with one of the patrons that he and Bob are twin brothers, "but with different fathers." *Pizza Girls* is a delightful romp with a tasty combo of sex and plot.

69 min/color. DVD. Amber Rea, Candida Royalle, Christine deShaffer, Desiree Cousteau, Donna Breaux, Laurien Dominique, Vicki Lindsay, Bob Chinn (as Danny Hussong, non-sex), Carl Regal, John Holmes, John Seeman, Richard Pacheco, Paul Thomas, Spencer Davis, Toni Damiani. *Director:* Bob Chinn; *Writer:* John Chapman; *Producer:* Toni Damiani.

I Am Always Ready ★ 1979

Tagline: "She loves it! You'll love her!"

This film begins with a unique storyline — a young woman is having sexual relations with "Porn Star, John Holmes," and gets caught in the act by her husband, who eventually decides to join in. Then it becomes a series of loops strung together with appearances by an extensive cast of well-known names of the genre. Good potential, but not worth recommending.

77 min/color. Unavailable. Barbara Wallace, Carol Lougan, Connie Peterson, Dorothy LeMay, Linda Thompson, Liza Dwyer, Marlene Monroe, Rita Mason, Ronnie Ross, Sandy Reed, Susan Madrid, Vicky Lindsay, Blair Harris, Fernando Fortes, John Holmes, Ken Scudder, Lee LeMay, Mike Horner, Paul Thomas, Ray Wells.. *Director:* Carlos Tobalina.

I Love L.A. (Part One) ★★★½ April 1986

This Penguin Production marks the final appearance of its host, John C. Holmes, who provides commentary between sequences that detail the sexual lives of Los Angeles couples, co-workers and roommates.

The first vignette involves sex therapist, Dr. Goodman (Richard Bolla), and his secretary (Shaun Michelle). The two are smitten by the scent of an intoxicating plant that causes them to spontaneously engage in animalistic sex on top of Goodman's desk. After climaxing, the blushing receptionist comes to her senses and quits. We soon learn that she is leading a double life as a phone-sex operator. She and her exotic roommate accept calls from men who pay to listen in on their make-out sessions.

We return to Dr. Goodman's office where Mary Brown (Kimberly Carson) arrives for her therapy session, only the good doctor has other business to attend to, so he leaves her in the capable hands of a blonde, male patient (Jessie Adams) and the aromatic plant. The strangers quickly find a way to combat their sexual hang-ups.

Next, Holmes introduces the viewer to a man (Shone Taylor) and woman (red-hot Sheri St. Claire) who rent apartments in the same complex. When their schedules allow, the singles relieve their pent-up sexual tensions by grinding on one another until satisfied.

The following scene introduces us to Clara (Amber Lynn), a rich, gorgeous blonde who is difficult to please. Holmes claims that her men must be "tall, handsome, smart, macho, sensitive and well hung," among other things. Amused, he confesses that once in a while "she gets lucky." During filming, Holmes was HIV-positive, so he did not appear in any new sex scenes, although footage from *Rubdown* (1985) that showcases Holmes with Amber Lynn is woven in here, including additional footage that was not included in *Rubdown.* At one point, when John has Amber on his lap, our narrator's face pops into the upper right corner of the screen and asks, "Could it be? Nah!" Then they get into the 69 position. John has more meat on his bones than usual in this flick and jokes about having love handles when Amber caresses his abs.

As narrator, Holmes appears to wrap up the video and leaves the viewers with something to think about when he intimates that the sexual situations presented in the film are representative of real people.

76 min/color. DVD. Amber Lynn, Bunny Bleu, Karen Summer, Kimberly Carson, Mindy Rae, Shaun Michelle, Sheri St. Claire, Susan Sipes, Tracy Duzit, Harry Reems, Jesse Adams, John Holmes, Richard Bolla, Ray Wells, Scott Irish, Shone Taylor. *Director:* Jack Remy, Patti Rhodes-Lincoln. *Writer:* Bill Amerson (as Bill Williams), Patti Rhodes-Lincoln, John Holmes. *Producer:* Bill Amerson (as Bill Williams).

Insatiable ★★★★ September 24, 1980

Marilyn Chambers portrays Sandra Chase, a successful model/actress. When her parents are killed in an automobile accident, Sandra vows to her Aunt Victoria (Joan Turner) during a visit to London that she will, "live life to the fullest," by exploring her sexual desires — which are plentiful.

The first of these includes an exciting Jacuzzi encounter with the pretty and uninhibited Renee (Serena). With her short-cropped copper hair, Serena is strikingly sensual as she and Marilyn bring a playful attitude to their lovemaking.

Next in a flashback, Sandra describes losing her virginity as a teenager to the family gardener, Nick (David Morris, resembling a youthful Tony Danza). After much sexual taunting, Morris takes her on top of a pool table, in one of the hottest scenes in the film.

Sandra also meets up with actor Richard Pacheco, who receives more than he bargained for when assisting Sandra with her broken-down car on a deserted road.

Later, John Leslie makes and enigmatic appearance as Roger Adams, Sandra's male costar in an upcoming venture. Leslie dines with Sandra, and Sandra's friend and assistant, Flo (Jessie St. James), prior to making out with Flo on the terrace.

As Sandra overhears Flo's cries of passion from her bedroom window, she masturbates gleefully, while conjuring up a series of fantasy lovers. They disperse suddenly, leaving Sandra alone and unsatisfied.

Moments later, a familiar long member emerges from the shadows as a surprisingly sexy John Holmes arrives in time to bring the film to a fitting crescendo. John caresses Sandra gently while planting tender kisses on her face. Every inch The King, Holmes takes charge of the fantasy, as he buries his face between her thighs before penetrating each of her chambers. When Holmes finally climaxes onto her tummy, Sandra faces the camera and pleads, "More... I want more."

Insatiable is one of the premiere films of the adult genre, with a healthy production budget, vibrant cinematography, reliable acting and enjoyable musical numbers (performed in part by Marilyn Chambers herself).

Trivia: When Marilyn opens a closet early on to retrieve a bathrobe, an Ivory Snow soap box sits on the top shelf, in a subtle reminder of her days on the front of the box before entering the taboo world of adult entertainment.

77 min/color. DVD. Jessie St. James, Joan Turner (non-sex), Marilyn Chambers, Serena, David Morris, John Holmes, John Leslie, Mike Ranger, R. Pennard (non-sex), Richard Pacheco. *Director:* Stu Segall. *Writer:* Kiki Young. *Producer:* Stu Segall.

The Jade Pussycat ★★★½ 1977

The seventh *Johnny Wadd* film.

Shortly after the story opens, a woman (Linda Wong) and Paul (Jon Martin) make love as if it's their last time. Ironically enough, it will be the last time for Paul, who is unaware of his impending fate. Unfortunately, he possesses the jade pussycat, a priceless Han dynasty artifact coveted by a crime syndicate.

When Paul fails to show up for a lunch engagement with his sister on her birthday, Jenny (Jessica Temple Smith) senses something is awry and appears unannounced at the office of her friend, Johnny Wadd, in hopes that he might help shed light upon her brother's whereabouts. A few hours later, Johnny checks into Paul's hotel suite in San Francisco and stumbles across the jade pussycat hidden in a locker. He tucks it out of sight and before too long, finds himself trading idle threats and insinuations with his old foe, Frankie (Bob Chinn).

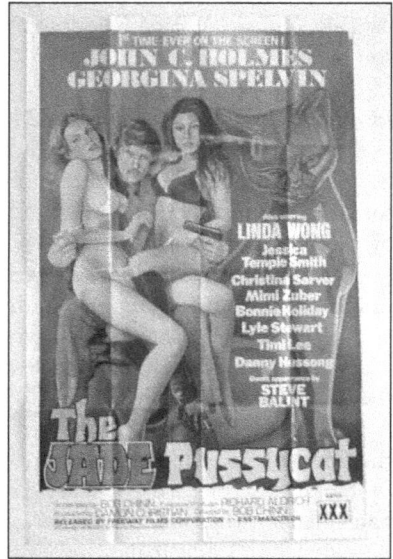

Mr. Wadd receives other unexpected visitors while away, including Alexandra (Georgina Spelvin). The two pros are cordial, but wary as they have drinks after agreeing to share the jade pussycat. Heat permeates the room when Alexandra strokes Johnny's crotch and declares, "I've heard a great deal about you."

Wickedly, Wadd responds, "Like what?"

During the sequence that follows, they share a quirky Chaplinesque interchange, where the two suddenly are in fast forward, preparing the hideaway bed for love. Johnny wouldn't be a legendary womanizer if he didn't devour and pleasure his ultra-sophisticated companion. But she outwits him. In short, she knocks him out with a lamp and makes off with a bag she believes contains $500,000 worth of jade.

For a man with no formal training, Holmes' acting in this feature is quite natural and understated as he characteristically chews a wad of gum. By this stage in Holmes' career, playing the horny detective seems as comfortable for him as slipping into an old pair of shoes. It appears as if working with Spelvin, an experienced thespian, brought the level of John's acting up a few notches although Chinn reported that the pairing of egos was challenging to work with.

80 min/color. DVD. Bonnie Holliday, Paula Waine (as Christian Sarver), Georgina Spelvin, Jessica Temple-Smith, Linda Wong, Mimi Zuber, Bob Chinn (as Daniel Hussong, non-sex), Elliot Lewis (non-sex), Jimi Lee, John Holmes, Jon Martin (as Lyle Stewart),Mark Ross, Steve Balint (non-sex). **Director:** Bob Chinn. **Assistant Director:** John C. Holmes. **Writer:** Bob Chinn. **Producer:** Damon Christian (as Dick Aldrich).

John Holmes and the All-Star Sex Queens ★½ 1980

Also known as *All-Star Sex Queens*.

This softcore feature stars John Holmes and Serena with busty starlets, Candy Samples, Uschi Digard, Kelly Stewart, and Kitten Natividad (another of Russ Meyer's protégés). Using unflattering vocal dubs, *Sex Queens* is pieced together from various film footages as it relays three distinct stories while utilizing the random loops.

The opening of this movie features John (as himself) auditioning Serena and another woman for roles in an upcoming sex film. John appears very healthy. He and Serena simulate oral sex as the camera catches flashes of his dragonfly ring, which indicates that this portion was shot during the late-'70s.

In the next loop, "Big Boob Casting Call" (1979), John auditions Candy Samples, Keli Stewart, Kitten Natividad, and Uschi Digard. He wears a white shirt, white hat and black tie. While John and Kitten engage in simulated action, the two brunettes (Digard and Stewart) enjoy some girl-on-girl fun. The camera goes back to Kitten, who is beginning to perform simulated fellatio. With her head directly in front of his crotch, two of the other actresses kiss above his package. In lieu of the money shot, John fakes his famous orgasm expressions. There are several split beaver shots, so despite not showing penetration, the loop is still racy and exciting.

The next loop used is "Terrible Aunt Candy," which also seems to be from the late-'70s. In it, John masturbates until he is caught by his Aunt Candy (Samples), who punishes him by making him take her to bed. This scene is not particularly stimulating as the actors overact with strained facial expressions. In another scene that features John and Candy from a late-'70s loop called, "Artists and Model's Ball," a painter (Samples) and her subjects (John and an attractive brunette) are shown in a three-way encounter. John is shown actually going down on the brunette, but his sex interaction with Candy is simulated.

In another loop called "Big Tit Hookers" (1979), Kitten Natividad, Keli Stewart and Uschi Digard are reunited with John, who appears gaunt in a white sailor suit. He simulates going down on Kitten, who has a big, beautiful smile, and alternately entertains Keli and Uschi, but Kitten is the main event. Natividad has claimed that Holmes would flirt incessantly with her at trade shows, by kissing her neck, in full view of her jealous husband. Another famous face in this clip is Johnny Keyes, who treats Candy and Uschi to a lusty time in a softcore three-way scene.

Unfortunately, it is possible that John may have made the 1980 softcore loops because of difficulties achieving an erection due to his excessive cocaine use. This is a far cry from Holmes' best work.

87 min/color. DVD. Bobbie Hall, Candy Samples, Keli Stewart, Kitten Natividad, Serena, Uschi Digard, Valerie Clarke, John Holmes, Johnny Keyes.

John Holmes: Master Cocksman ★½ *(Date Unknown)*

Master Cocksman feels like a compilation because there is no plot and has many cuts between sex scenes. There is an overdubbed female voice that provides information, resulting in a pseudo-sex documentary. At this point in Holmes' career, the claim is that he's made 2200 films and "has been a sexual prodigy since he was 11 years old," making this film great for a collector who feeds off of the John mythology — however, this film is also rare.

The sex scenes are hot and John is undeniably sexy in some of the shots, but the overall (lack of) quality of the sound and the lame overdubbed quotes (for example, "One may wonder how John deals with women being afraid of his giant salami…") make this one that most people can skip over without guilt.

Unavailable.

Johnny Does Paris (This film has not been ranked.) December 1979

Filmed on location in France, Johnny (John Holmes) plays an author commissioned by Gloria (Gloria Leonard) to write a novel about his exotic exploits. Surprisingly, after his arrival in the city of love, he is approached by some beautiful women who are anxious to give him a taste of French romance. These sexual conquests occur in parks, in flats and even in the underground metro. Johnny is astonished that these lusty ladies inexplicably enter his life, but happily discovers that he has his muse to craft a sizzling novel.

Gloria the patroness promises a major worldwide promotion, but Johnny soon learns that he has been deceived in the most delightful way.

Johnny Does Paris is remarkable because it is one of the first erotic movies to have been filmed overseas. According to anecdotes from the Carnal Comic Books' illustrated presentation of the movie (which contains stills from the film), the cast and crew risked arrest during the film's undertaking. In order to shoot the blowjob scene on the train, the crew manned the entrance to one of the metro cars in order to prevent other riders from entering.

During an interview with Kathy Kennedy in 1985, John explained that it was especially difficult for the American actors in France because they had to initially learn their lines in French and then the scenes were immediately re-shot in English. John claimed that the French filmmakers were not always dependable and were often intoxicated during filming.

Johnny Does Paris has become a cult classic due to its rarity. To date, it is not available in any format.

71 min/color. Unavailable. Brooke West (as Betsy Ward), Delania Raffino, Francoise Vadim, Gloria Leonard, Jeanne Rambaud, Desire Bastareaud, Jacque Gatteau, Jacque Marbeuf, John Holmes. *Director:* Charles De Santos. *Producer:* Aaron Linn.

Johnny Wadd ★½ 1970

Tagline: *"From California to the Rio Grande, He shot his wad all over the land."* First film of the *Johnny Wadd* series.

Johnny Wadd is the most significant film of the series, simply because it was the first and it ignited Holmes' fame. The series has a humble beginning — most of the movie was filmed in the Venice Beach apartment of the cameraman, Alex Elliot. The interior sex scenes feature two large paper flowers as the main backdrop, with few other props. The budget for the one-day shoot was only

$750, which was astonishingly less than any other Chinn/Holmes cinematic venture. As the star of the film, John was paid $75 and everyone else got $50. Chinn edited the film in two days and said it was in theaters by the end of the week.

At the start of the film, the private detective sits down for a smoke when the phone rings. A brunette named Wendy Bellamy (Andy Bellamy) would like to enlist Wadd's help in finding her friend, Jeannie Hamilton, who is missing. Very mysteriously, the girl's wealthy family has been uninterested in finding her.

Wadd tells Wendy that he's expensive, but she is ready and willing to pay a $1,000 retainer fee and gladly succumbs to a sexual rendezvous on the couch while Ennio Morricone's spaghetti western music accompanies the scene. The camera has a field day highlighting John's unique size as Wendy asks, "Are all detectives this big?"

John replies, "I hope not. The competition is tough enough already."

A little while later, the sister of the missing girl (played by one of John's real-life girlfriends, Sandy Dempsey) comes over and offers John double what Ms. Bellamy paid him in a bribe to the detective *not* to find her missing sister. She enters wearing a floppy black hat and blue, bug-eye sunglasses. Twice, she calls him "Mr. Wade," before he corrects her, "The name is Wadd," and follows up, "I'll take the $2,000, but that wasn't all she gave me. She gave me some incentive, too." Without hesitation, she is happy to offer some incentive.

Only a few days later, Wadd determines that Jeannie Hamilton's disappearance is somehow related to her mother's actions.

The creepy old Mrs. Hamilton comes over to Johnny's pad. Unlike his previous two sexual encounters, John can't get an erection for Mrs. Hamilton, so she demonstrates how she can get off using the longneck of an empty glass bottle!

In the end, Johnny Wadd saves the girl and discovers the shocking reason why she was kidnapped.

For the first time ever, the original *Johnny Wadd* was released on DVD in September 2008, complete with a director's commentary and interview with Bob Chinn, in addition to other extras. Although this film lacks finesse in its dialogue, acting and editing, its historical importance as the film that made Holmes famous makes it a timeless piece of the John Holmes film library.

60 min/color. DVD. Andy Bellamy, Sandy Dempsey, John Holmes, Ramone Narone. *Director:* Bob Chinn. *Writer:* Bob Chinn. *Producer:* Chinn-Adrain Productions.

Kowloon Connection ★ September 1975

The film contains the same cast as *Oriental Kitten*, so it was likely shot during the same time frame.

John, a pimp, enters toward the end of the first scene and asks a girl if she'd gotten his money yet from Jackie. Suzy Chung, in a scene very reminiscent of one in *Oriental Kitten*, devises a secret plan during the orgy to assist Jackie in getting together the money.

Suzy accompanies Jackie when she shows up to give John his money and John is rough with Jackie. He tells her to go out and earn her own money when he learns that she has borrowed the cash.

Meanwhile, Suzy is left alone with John, who discusses with her the possibility of working for him and they have sex. The high point of the film is in the concluding scene, when Suzy Chung — who remembers John's violence toward her friend — stabs John in the back.

This film is not recommended due to poor plot development and direction. The sex scenes aren't even close to scintillating and Holmes and Chung just don't exhibit any chemistry.

54 min/color. DVD. Mea Tue, Rita Cous, Suzy Chung, Toni Scott, Paul Scharf (as Dan Pole), John Holmes (as Big John Holmes), Jonathon Younger, Ray Wells. *Director:* Harry Who.

Let Me Count the Lays ★★½ 1980

According to John's boyish appearance, this movie was probably filmed in 1971 or '72.

Newlywed Holmes carries his young, thin wife (the same actress that Holmes the detective rescued in the first *Johnny Wadd* film) across the threshold and lays her down on the carpet in her wedding gown. When she reminds him that she is a virgin and he must be gentle, he downplays her disclosure but is taken aback when she inquires as to how many ladies he's known intimately.

Using stock footage, the film moves from one sexual escapade to another with various scenes plucked from other early John Holmes movies such as *My Tongue is Quick*, *New Girl in Town* and *Olé*.

John carefully prepares his blushing bride for their imminent encounter as he reflects upon the specifics of his plentiful, hot and heavy couplings. John is smart to apply lubricant to his virgin bride, but as it turns out, his new bride was not quite so virginal after all. This film isn't exceptional, but is enjoyable as an early Holmes film.

DVD. Amber Davis, Judy Lewis, Louise Netters, Missy-Ann Burns, Phyllis Wolf, Robin Ausel, Alex Elliot, John Holmes, Ramon Narone. *Director:* David Stefans. *Producer:* David Stefans.

The Liberated Woman (This film has not been ranked.) 1972

Shot in one day, this softcore movie depicts the tale of a frigid housewife who delves deeply into a world of sexual deviance and forbidden pleasures. Assistant producer, Linda Adrain, designed the outstanding poster for the feature that contains an exceptional girl-girl sex scene between Sandi Carey and Maria Arnold.

87 min/color. Unavailable. Linda York, Maria Arnold, Sandy Carey, Sandy Dempsey, Tracey Handfuss, John Holmes, Alex Elliot. *Director:* Bob Chinn. *Writer:* Bob Chinn. *Producer:* Bob Chinn and Linda Adrain.

Little French Maid ★★½ 1981

This dubbed film contains scene inserts from what appears to be *Swedish Erotica* clips.

The voluptuous Connie Peterson (with two different hair lengths) stars as a French maid named Connie, who serves under the employment of her wealthy boss, Paul Thomas.

In the opening scene, Connie walks about the premises reminiscing about her sexual conquests (and her wet pussy) while yearning for that one, true love. In addition to her regular daily duties like cooking, cleaning and mending, Connie is called upon by her boss to service him in other areas of his spacious mansion. An example of this occurs when Thomas puts in a request to his butler, John (John Holmes) to bring him a drink and asks that Connie accompany John to the master bedroom, where Thomas is waiting.

Connie becomes a willing seductress as she sheds her clothes in a salacious fashion for the hungry men and goes down on John's engorged penis at her employer's insistence. Thomas joins John and Connie, as the three engage in a multi-tiered sexual frenzy that involves double perforation and heaping amounts of oral stimulation. Connie is anything but bashful and genuinely seems to enjoy the action.

Next, Connie, John and long-haired brunette beauty Paula Smith are featured in a three-way. Then, there is a rough sequence involving Connie, Johnny Keyes and Stephen Reilly.

Holmes resurfaces a third time in yet another triangular interlude with Connie and his brother, Mike (Mike Ranger), before the insatiable Connie joins forces with pilots (Mike Horner and Bob White) who promise her a free ticket to Paris in exchange for sex. As much as Connie revels in her memories of exceptional organs and orgasms, she finds herself pining away for Mike. Connie remembers how they had professed their love for one another, in the only scene of the film that shows her with a single partner.

Peterson was well known for her unbridled sexual hijinks onscreen, and fans of this bodacious starlet in her starring vehicle won't be disappointed. However, for others who prefer a little more plot interspersed between the sex scenes, this flick won't likely be to your taste, in spite of the occasional classical musical pieces included, in an attempt to bring an air of romance to the movie. (Listen for Bill Margold who provides the vocal dubs for Holmes in the scene with Mike Ranger — truly hilarious!)

74 min/color. DVD. Connie Peterson, Paula Smith, Bob White, Don Hart, Eddie Marcus, John Holmes, Johnny Keyes, Mike Horner, Mike Ranger, Paul Thomas, Stephen Reilley. *Director:* Joseph F. Robertson (as Adele Robbins). *Producer:* Joseph F. Robertson (as Adele Robbins).

Little Orphan Dusty ★★★ 1978

Also known as *Jaws of Delight.*

Rhonda Jo Petty plays Dusty, a wayward girl who has run away from an orphanage and finds herself alone in the middle of a country road. A leather-clad motorcycle gang arrives on the scene, looking to prey upon anyone who happens along their path. They snatch Dusty from the road, and drive her off into the bush, where they rape her.

Shortly afterwards, Frank (John Holmes) ascends a hill, carrying a palette and brushes beneath his arm when he discovers Dusty, seemingly unconscious and lying naked a few feet before him on the ground. Startled, he checks her

John (as Frankie) makes love for the first time to Dusty, played by Rhonda Jo Petty.

pulse and upon discovering that she is still alive, he carries her away to the safety of his home.

When she awakes, Dusty confides to Frank that she was raped by the bikers, but because she is a runaway, she doesn't want the police involved for fear of being sent back to the orphanage. With the threat of the motorcycle gang forever at their heels, Frank does his best to protect her, but not always with success.

Holmes delivers some rather hilarious lines in this movie. The first occurs when he unexpectedly happens upon one of the bikers, immediately after the rogue has raped Dusty (again) in Frank's home. While threatening him with a knife, Frank bellows, "You might have come into this house a Gentile, but you're going to leave a Jew!"

Toward the end of the story, Frank lies at the foot of his stairs, a victim of a bullet wound. Dusty leans over to comfort him. He looks up into her pretty face and groans, "Can you take your knee off my nuts and call an ambulance?!"

Little Orphan Dusty has some high points, but the rape scenes are moderately realistic (too intense for some viewers). However, the film contains some redeeming moments: the romantic and sexual interchanges between John and Rhonda Jo are palatable and sensual. They also engage in a fisting scene together but because Holmes' hand is proportionally large to his body, he is only able to insert a few fingers inside of Rhonda Jo, rather than his entire fist — probably a good thing. The feature includes three fisting segments in all, visuals that only select audiences would appreciate. The controversial scenes have been deleted in some of the re-releases of the movie.

Little Orphan Dusty took the award for the Best Film at the Erotic Film Awards and Rhonda Jo Petty won Best Actress. *Screw* magazine voted it as one of the top ten adult films of 1978.

84 min/color. DVD. April Grant, Jo Boyc, Ming Jade, Rhonda Jo Petty, Vanessa Parker, Alan Colberg, Jakie Boyc (non-sex), John Holmes, Mike Ranger, Rick Carson (non-sex), Ric Lutze, Turk Lyon. *Director:* Bob Chinn, Jaacov Jaacovi (Jourdan Alexander). *Writer:* Jaacov Jaacovi (Jourdan Alexander), Svetlana. *Producer:* Jaacov Jaacovi (Jourdan Alexander).

Liquid Lips ★★★★ 1976

Tagline: *"John C. Holmes dares you to sit through the most erotic film he's ever made!"* This should be viewed as the sixth film in the *Johnny Wadd* series.

Johnny Wadd has safely returned home to San Francisco from his Mexican sojourn. As the opening credits roll, the music blasts and Johnny makes out with another new Wadd girl. When she exclaims, "Johnny Wadd, you're the greatest!" Wadd is already off on a caper to aid authorities in busting up another drug-smuggling operation.

The government sends agent Charlie Hammond (Monique Starr) to Wadd's apartment for a special top-secret meeting and Johnny is surprised to discover that "Charlie" is of the female persuasion. After some verbal foreplay, Holmes gets to deliver a line that rendered the supremely endowed detective famous. When asked by Charlie what sort of identification he can provide as proof that he is indeed "the" Johnny Wadd, Holmes stands up and, with a sly grin, he unzips his jeans.

Cockily, he replies, "You want identification, lady? Here, I'll show you my identification."

Charlie stares, transfixed with John's impressive appendage, with an utterly priceless expression on her face. Soon Johnny and Charlie take care of business before treating themselves to pleasure.

Partway through the adventure, the well-known 1970s performer John Seeman portrays a man held captive and tortured by the corrupt drug lords. The scene is slightly disconcerting, yet an example of the tendency of Golden Era films to intermingle sex with a dark, ominous side. Chinn intended the villains and violence in this film to be over the top in order to have more fun with the storyline following *Tell Them Johnny Wadd is Here.*

A synopsis of *Liquid Lips* would not be complete without a mention of the massage Johnny receives at the hands of Patty (Melba Bruce, who was allegedly killed a few years later when her boyfriend was involved in a drug deal gone wrong). Patty masquerades as a masseuse, in order to try to exact information out of Wadd. When she offers her services to him, Johnny wryly inquires how much more might it cost to, "Make it nice?"

With momentary hesitation, Patty agrees to give him the full treatment for $60 and soon learns she is getting more than she bargained for. With a look of orgasmic anticipation, she comments, "I don't know whether I should charge you double, or pay you!"

Johnny Wadd in *Liquid Lips*.

This movie epitomizes camp along with entertaining plot twists and turns, not the least of which is another phony fight scene between Wadd and Frankie (Bob Chinn). *Liquid Lips* is one of the best from the *Johnny Wadd* series.

73 min/color. DVD. Enjil von Bergdorfe, Melba Bruce, Monique Starr, Phaedre, Bob Chinn (as Daniel Hussong, non-sex), Jerry Mills, John Holmes, John Seeman, Mike Weldon, Vernon von Bergdorfe. *Director:* Bob Chinn. *Writer:* Bob Chinn. *Producer:* Freeway Films.

Looking for Mr. Goodsex ★★ 1985

Tagline: *"They were looking for love in all the right places!"*

An ultra-sophisticated magazine columnist (Joanna Storm) tours the country in search for Mr. Goodsex, the ideal male and literally the man of her dreams, who possesses a sexual tool of magnified proportions. While aiding her in her quest, fantasy head-hunter, Amber Lynn, allows Storm to examine her stud files. Upon settling her eyes on a picture of Jonathan York (John Holmes), Storm instantly recognizes her optimum mate. The story includes a memorable scene where Storm is seated in one of New York's local haunts.

Jerry Butler, Buck Adams, Billy Dee and John Holmes all rise to the challenge at various stages throughout the story with Holmes and Storm finally hooking up at the end for some backdoor fun. Various uncredited faces from the blue screen can be spotted within the bar crowd, including Harry Reems, R. Bolla and even Sean Amerson, while '70s star, Randy West and his partner, Tess Ferr, wiggle provocatively onstage in a choreographed dance routine.

Although it was produced after the birth of the video age, *Mr. Goodsex* was shot on film, which heightens the quality of the movie and gives it depth.

84 min/color. DVD. Amber Lynn, Joanna Storm, Lois Ayres, Taija Rae, Tess Ferr (non-sex), Billy Dee, Buck Adams, Francois, Harry Reems (cameo), Jay Serling, Jerry Butler, John Holmes, Mike Horner, Randy West (non-sex), Richard Bolla (cameo), Sean Amerson (non-sex), Steve Drake. *Director:* Jack Remy. *Writers:* Patti Rhodes-Lincoln, Valerie Kelly, *Producer:* Dino Ferrera.

Lottery Lust ★★½ 1986

Buck Adams stars as Eddie, a man who becomes disillusioned with life after winning $1,000,000 in the lottery. Work as an executive accountant might not be glamorous, but at least Eddie knew where he stood at the office. However, after winning the lottery, Eddie is uncertain if his family and friends still appreciate him now that he has the big bucks. Eddie looks at everyone through wary eyes and wonders if his luck is any luck at all. Women are easier to come by and he enjoys the benefits of his good fortune, but he is surprised that money hasn't made him happy.

John Holmes plays Mark Coyle, one of Eddie's co-workers who reap the benefits of his pal's windfall in a sex scene with Bunny Bleu.

Adams engages in a few quality sex scenes (with Gina Carrera and Nikki Charm), and although he tends to take an aggressive approach, rather than a tender one, he comes across as likeable and carries the film. In a sweet conclusion, Eddie discovers true love where he least expects it.

84 min/color. DVD. Bunny Bleu, Gina Carrera, Melissa Melendez (as Kat Harlow), Nikki Charm, Rene Summers, Tracey Adams, Buck Adams, Jason Fox, John Holmes. *Director:* Patty Rhodes-Lincoln. *Producer:* Penguin Productions.

Love Boccaccio Style ★★★ 1971

Tagline: *"Wild, ribald stories!"* *Love Boccaccio Style* includes four pieces set in medieval times, influenced by the author of *The Decameron*.

A skeptical husband secures his wife's (played by Pattie Lee) treasure box under a chastity belt and key while traveling abroad. In his absence, the woman summons the locksmith to her boudoir to relieve her from "the blockage" to her "honey pot" and invites him to unlock her pent-up passion. Suddenly, her husband returns home early and almost catches the locksmith with his tights down, but luckily he escapes in one piece.

In the second installment, an attractive woman (Marsha Jordan) seduces her husband's friend after being consumed by her curiosity as to what mysteries lie beneath the crotch of his leggings. While hidden in a trunk at the foot of the bed, her husband eavesdrops on their conversation (and nookie) before he bursts in and demands to be satiated by his friend's wife as payment for his best friend's and spouse's betrayal.

Thirdly, hard-up Masetto (John Holmes in a deep, dubbed voice) pretends he is a deaf-mute in order to sample the wares of virginal maidens living in a nearby convent. After two of the females (Sandy Dempsey and Sandy Carey) espy Masetto's "salacious salami" in his hand, the girls, along with schoolmates (Andy Bellamy and Chlorine Stillwater), begin to pay him daily visits in the woods, where he introduces them to the virtues of his stimulated manhood. Once the head mistress (Candy Samples, before silicone implants and rhinoplasty) learns what her young charges have been up to, she entraps Masetto and banishes him to her chambers to become her personal love slave.

Finally, an adulterous wife (Holly Woodstar) is brought before the courts by her husband, who wants her sentenced to burn at the stake. The oversexed magistrate (William Kirshner) has other ideas in mind. He leads her into his chambers and together, they find a way to redeem her transgressions.

This is a terrific simulated sex film, with clever dialogue, while a dedicated effort is put forth by the entire cast to make this inspired tale come to life. The acting, chamber music, exaggerated cinematic effects, snare drum solos, period costumes (and lack thereof) are great too.

68 min/color. DVD. Andy Bellamy, Angie Alexander, Candy Samples, Chlorine Stillwater, Holly Woodstar, Louis Ojena, Marsha Jordan, Miki McDonald, Mycle Brandy, Patti Lee, Sandi Carey (as Sandee Carey), Sandy Dempsey, B.M. Verdi, Billy Lane, Eastman Price, Howard Alexander, Jason Yukon, John Holmes, Lindis Guiness, Norman Fields, Richard Dean, Vincent Hill, William Kirshner. *Director:* Sam Phillips.

Lust at First Bite ★★★★ 1979

Also known as *Dracula's Bride*, *The Coming of Dracula's Bride*, and *Dracula Sucks* (softcore version). Tagline: "This time the count doesn't just go for the throat!"

Believed to have been filmed in Death Valley, this is an excellent porn adaptation of the classic 1931 horror film, *Dracula*. Jamie Gillis is featured in the Bela Lugosi role, which was inspired by the 1897 novel written by Bram Stoker. The rest of the all-star cast provides the foundation for this comical foray into the dark and depraved world of The Count.

Dr. Arthur Seward (John Leslie) along with his sister, Dr. Sybil Seward (Kay Parker), and John Holmes as Dr. John Stoker, work together in a sanitarium housed in an ancient castle. One day, a deranged patient uncovers a long-forgotten tomb. Inside, a wooden stake sticks out from the corpse's heart. Inevitably, someone removes the stake and, instantly, Dracula is reborn and begins to hunt for fresh, nubile victims. The count finds two girlfriends, virginal Mina (Annette Haven) and Lucy Webster (Serena).

B-actor Reggie Nalder (*Mark of the Devil*) portrays Dr. Van Helsing, a kindly but frightful-looking visitor to the asylum. Van Helsing suspects that the count might have been behind the mysterious and impulsive sex acts being committed by staff and patients alike. Everyone gets in on the action, with masturbatory exhibits, ghoulish lesbian encounters in the dead of night and angry anal sex doled out as a punishment for wayward visitors.

Two siblings, Doctors Arthur and Sybil Seward, satiate one another in their private quarters while Dr. Stoker takes the maid (Irene Best) on the pool table. Unbeknownst to him, she had already been Dracula's prey. She bites him and leaves the imprints of her two massive fangs on his member. Dr. Stoker is then quarantined in the dungeon with the rest of the hapless patients. Blonde Nurse Betty (Seka, in her film debut), is escorted to the basement by Henry (Bill Margold) to tend to Stoker's injury. In the first of many onscreen pairings, John and Seka's first sex scene was a staged rape that occurs after Stoker had coaxed Nurse Betty to loosen his tethers.

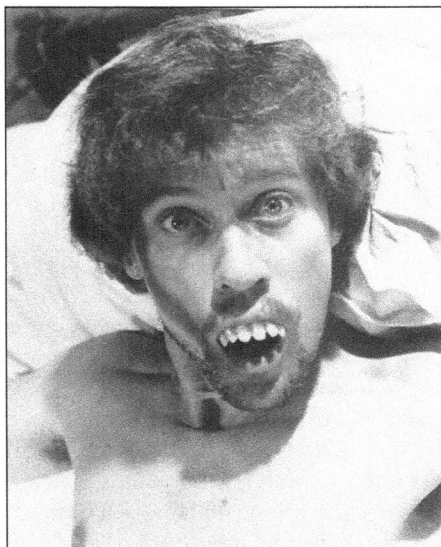

Van Helsing confronts The Count with a cross and mirror in an effort to extinguish his future lives.

A particularly unique scene features Paul Thomas and Annette Haven as they join the butler (David Lee Bynum) while he croons "Swing Low, Sweet Chariot" in a beautiful tenor. By today's standards, this semi-horror spoof would seem tame, with little gore and shoddy effects, but it's still an engaging piece with a consummate porn cast. The original musical score is lush and foreboding, with dissonant piano chords that set the tone for the gothic tale.

Bill Margold explained that he "saved" Seka's film debut for The King, even though her scene with Paul Thomas appears earlier in the movie. According to Margold, Holmes and Thomas were both smitten by the Platinum Princess and vowed to make her a star, while John Leslie also had hoped to have a scene with her in her debut film (although he did not). Margold added that after Holmes' scene with Seka was completed, John hopped on a flight to service one of his European concubines.

86 min/color, 78 min/color (softcore version). Unavailable. Annette Haven, Irene Best, Kay Parker, Nancy Hoffman, Pat Manning, Renee Andre, Seka, Serena, Slavica, Bill Margold, David Lee Bynum (non-sex), George Lee, Jamie Gillis, John Holmes, John Leslie, Ken Yontz, Kurt Sjoberg, Martin L. Dorf, Mike Ranger, Mitch Morrill, Paul Thomas, Reggie Nalder (as Detlef van Berg), Richard Bullick. *Director:* Philip Morris (as Philip Marshak). *Writers:* Daryl Marshak and Philip Marshak, William Margold, Mitch Morrill. *Producers:* David E. Emerich, Roy Karch, David Kern, William Margold, Daryl Marshak, Netie Pena.

Marathon ★½ 1983

Disguised in black, thick-rimmed glasses with an attached penis nose, the party host Jamie Gillis greets a group of friends who arrive at his abode dressed for a costume party. The sexual tricks begin immediately as people pair up. What transpires is a sexual marathon when this elite cast of adult stars (Holmes, Gillis, Ron Jeremy, Mai Lin and Sharon Mitchell) and newcomers (*Marathon* introduced Misty Dawn to John Holmes).

The idea to showcase wall-to-wall orgies, which had usually been reserved for the grand finales of adult films in the Golden Age, was original, but was not well-executed. The lack of foreplay in both script and dialogue to link together the sex scenes is hugely apparent. Excluding select viewers, the presentation of prolonged sex isn't very stimulating.

Except for Bill Margold's ten-incher, he is completely concealed inside of a bear costume at the party. Miss Sharon Mitchell manages to look both glamorous and proudly androgynous, even with two penises in her mouth (surely that was no small feat, especially with this cast of male talent!)

John Holmes held his head high in his return foray after his release from prison following his acquittal and contempt of court stays. Sporting his poor circa-1983 haircut, it appears that beneath his surgeon's mask, Holmes is chomping gum. Just like old times. He looks delighted to be back in action. First, he works in a threesome segment with a beautiful light-haired African-American actress, then he has a couch wrangle with "sultry" Drea, who is wearing black lace and a blonde wig.

The party is interrupted when Gillis receives a telephone call and announces that two expected guests, Bill Margold and Drea, are in the hospital. The party moves and continues to their hospital room at "John Holmes Memorial." At one point, Holmes sits back in a chair to enjoy the action. He looks like a king with a scepter, while holding a cane. Throughout the well-choreographed orgies, everyone is careful to maintain pointed toes, a habit of adult performers and trained dancers. There in the hospital scene, John concludes with a third woman, a cute blonde nurse. Using one of his signature moves, John gallantly gets onto one knee and swings her down onto the floor, over his thigh.

Ron Jeremy appears detached during intercourse with various actresses, but Gillis clearly enjoys the smorgasbord of women.

Marathon contains what Margold calls "40 Inches of Meat," an ongoing gangbang of his (ex) wife, Drea, who had asked to have such an experience. She is screwed first by Holmes, then Jeremy and Gillis before Margold finishes her off. Director Carlos Tobalina makes a non-sex appearance in Groucho Marx costume and Don Fernando dresses in drag.

Eventually, a doctor comes into the room, and seeing his patients engaged in sex acts with multiple partners, he yells, "If you can fuck, you can walk, so fucking walk!"

85 min/color. DVD. Cathy Coffer, Crystal Lake, Drea, Erica Greenberg, Mai Lin, Misty Dawn, Rita Cruz, Rosa Lee Kimball, Sharon Mitchell, Shaun Michelle, Sparky Vacs, Lynx Canon (as Susan Kay), Bill Margold, Carlos

Tobalina (non-sex), Dan T. Mann, David Sanders, Don Fernando, Herschel Savage, Jack Mason, Jamie Gillis, Jesse Adams, John Holmes, John Stagliano, Ron Jeremy. *Director:* Carlos Tobalina. *Writer:* Edgar G. Warren.

Using a few set props, John hams it up with Melissa Melendez (left) and Kimberly Caron (right) in the Penguin film production, *Marina Vice*, directed by Patti Rhodes.

Marina Vice ★★ 1985

The film opens with some cool shots of Marina Del Rey, as Pink Floydesque music plays in the background. The sex scenes are hot, with a good mix of old-school camera angles and new-age digitalization in the second sex scene. The worst part, if you love porno plots, is that it doesn't start for nearly an hour into the film.

Two renegade detectives (Buck Adams and Billy Dee) are assigned to stake out a drug lord named Jimmy Costa (John Holmes). They barter with two women (Kimberly Carson and Melissa Melendez) for use of the women's boat in exchange for letting them be honorary detectives.

During their pursuit, the two cops are sidetracked by an assortment of lusty women, while Costa receives a surprise visit by the sexy ladies. Acting as masseuses, they are able to get inside of Costa's private bedroom. Holmes appears healthy, although older. The resulting three-way sex scene with Holmes, Melendez and Carson is wild and imaginative, to say the least. Holding onto her white stilettos for leverage, John plunges in and out of Melendez, while French kissing Carson, who is seated on the face of Ms. Melendez.

Afterwards, Costa beckons his aid, Rocky (Sean Amerson as Sean King) to handcuff the girls, when the cops burst in to apprehend Costa and seize the white powder in his possession.

At the film's conclusion, John (in handcuffs) looks directly at the camera and musters up his best Arnold Schwarzenegger impression: "I'll be back." The outtakes on the compilation DVD, *John Holmes: The Legend Continues*, from the filming of *Marina Vice* are subtly humorous and informative. In one, John lies on his back in bed while Carson prepares to go down on him. John tells the director to let him know when the camera is going to pan from his lap to his face because he plans on taking a nap during the action.

72 min/color. DVD. Kimberly Carson, Leslie Winston, Melissa Melendez, Summer Rose, Tess Ferre, Billy Dee, Buck Adams, John Holmes, Sean Amerson (as Sean King, non-sex). *Director:* Patti Rhodes-Lincoln. *Producer:* Penguin Productions.

My Tongue is Quick ★★ 1971

Narrated by and starring Holmes, John plays Nicky Butane, the owner of a stud business. Wendy Anne Collins and Amber Davis with Susan Bosley open the feature, clad only in their panties. The women hold up placards with the film's title.

He operates from a small vessel docked at a seaside marina — likely Marina Del Rey. This film was shot on 35 millimeter, has a hilarious theme song, *"Aboard the good ship, Penis / I wish you could have seen us. Instead of pay, they let us play / upon the Captain's organ."*

Nicky employs sexy secretary Vagina Bountiful (Bosley) and two studs nicknamed Thunderballs (Mark Little) and James Blond. Nicky and the boys specialize in servicing lonely married women looking to spice up their sex lives. Because he wants to keep his operation free of the fuzz, Nicky conducts his business over a toy telephone.

Two of his clients are attractive, long-haired brunettes, Superstar (Collins) and Mae Best (Davis). After Mae arrives and quickly disrobes, Nicky compliments her on her new implants. Superstar proceeds to light a fire under Thunderballs' balls, using a cardboard cut-out of an ice cream cone.

Mae (who does a passable impression of the Hollywood siren with a similar name) hooks up with James Blond, but soon requests libidinous affections from Mr. Butane instead. She surprises Nicky in bed with a toy alligator and a strap-on dildo, both used as props during sex. Nicky allows her to have some fun before producing the real thing.

Holmes is endearing and occasionally forgets his lines, but clearly has a blast with his three female leads. They close the movie the same way it opened with the girls in their panties, along with a little self-promotion from Butane: "Nicky Butane — Private Dick. My tongue is quick. If you don't believe me... just ask your wife."

The DVD cover falsely advertises a rare interview with John Holmes, which is not included. Instead, the short interview with Kathy Kennedy is featured on *The Winning Stroke*.

60 min/color. DVD. Amber Davis, Susan Bosley, Wendy Anne Collins, John Holmes, Mark Little.

Nasty Nurses ★★★½ 1983

John Holmes and Misty Dawn (Laurie Holmes) are part of an ensemble cast of porn veterans acting as physicians and nurses in a hospital slated for imminent closure. This unique staff of medical specialists works through their daily stresses with sexual healing.

Herschel Savage and Janey Robbins star in this better-than-average feature that contains exceptional dialogue and acting on the parts of Savage and Patricia Manning. Chief resident physician, Dr. Rob Matthews (Savage), is fed up with the bureaucracy and lets his feelings be known to Dr. Warner (Manning), the new hospital administrator.

Rather than bring the hospital back into the black, Savage accuses her of incompetence and blames her unethical practices for causing the hospital to sink further into debt. He fears that patients will no longer be able to afford quality health care. Savage also has a girlfriend on the side; head nurse, Grace Simpson (Janey Robbins). Nurse Grace complicates matters by giving Dr. Matthews an ultimatum that he leave his wife (Kay Parker).

Everyone participates in this display of hardcore eroticism. A patient (Paul Thomas) and his nurse (Becky Savage) create real sexual tension in a scene with a climactic finish. She teases him mercilessly with her butt just inches from his face, as he tries to move toward it with an injured neck.

John Holmes plays Dr. Dennis A. Johnston, a horny proctologist who lusts after Cheri (Misty Dawn), a wide-eyed candystriper assigned to work under his guidance. Holmes appears ragged, but his scene with Misty is red hot. After kisses, he lays her down on the exam table and puts her feet into the stirrups. Dr. Johnston penetrates Cheri in numerous ways, including anally, while Cheri wriggles on him; the money shot is delivered on her tummy. Afterwards, she returns to the locker room, rubbing her behind in a clear indication to her coworkers that she had just "come" from Dr. Johnston's office.

Apart from the sex (and there is a lot of it), there is a funny sequence at the reception desk when a demanding actor, Jack Williams (Paul Baressi), and his sidekick make a plea for preferential and immediate treatment. As it turns out, another physician, Dr. Michelle Cole (played by Drea), remembers Williams from high school and the two make up for lost time. This film plays almost like a mainstream movie, which is a testament to the writers and to the performers. It truly makes one wonder why real sex isn't shown in contemporary cinema.

81 min/color. DVD. Becky Savage, Brooke West (non-sex), Cindy Shepard (non-sex), Drea (non-sex), Janey Robbins, Kay Parker, Kimberly Carson, Marina, Misty Dawn, Pat Manning (non-sex), Adele Robbins (non-sex), David Sanders, Herschel Savage, Jesse Jones (non-sex), John Holmes, John Ogden (non-sex), Paul Baressi, Paul Thomas, Robert Bullock (as Richard Parnes, non-sex). *Director:* Paul Vatelli. *Writers:* Ronnie Friedland, Paul Vatelli. *Producer:* Paul Vatelli.

Naughty Girls Like it Big ★★★½ 1986

Naughty Girls Like it Big has everything an adult movie should — attractive women, well-equipped men and hot sex scenes.

At first, the story is a typical get together between four girlfriends (Nina Hartley, Lilly Marlene, Angel Kelly and Porsche Lynn) who hook up for a reunion where they bring one another up to speed on the details of their past and current love lives. Their discussion quickly turns to the subject of length, and it becomes clear that the girls are size queens.

Porsche describes how she'd seduced a reserved young virgin, Lester (cutie Tom Byron) in a kitchen chair. The unassuming boy is beside himself with lust as she enthusiastically rides his rifle until he blows a gasket.

Similarly, Cindy (Angel Kelly) confesses a previous encounter with a man of unspeakably large proportions when she explains how as a teenager she'd joined forces with her teacher, Mr. Chester (John Holmes), in a flashback sequence. Holmes prepares Kelly for penetration with sweet talk and a gentle application of caresses upon her smooth, chocolate skin. As they edge closer to the money shot, John turns her around, enters her from behind and growls, "It's the back-door to paradise".

When he climaxes across her thigh, Cindy regains her composure, smiles and asks, "Will I get an 'A' for this?"

Mr. Chester grins like the Cheshire cat: "In every subject."

The girls feel the heat from Cindy's story and decide to embark in a little free-for-all as they discard what little clothing they have on and bring out obscenely large dildos.

After a brief reprieve, it is Lilly's turn to spill all and although she would rather not admit it, she soon discloses an incident where she and her physician (Ron Jeremy) got to know one another intimately during a routine visit at his office. For good measure, the doctor's nurse (Alexis Greco) joins in and the three get things rockin' on the doctor's desk.

Not to be outdone, Nina Hartley tops Lilly's story when she divulges how she'd arrived scantily clad at a construction site and proceeded to get it on with two lucky stiffs (Buddy Love and Mike Horner).

The talk inspires Cindy to call her accommodating boyfriend (Jerry Butler), who arrives just in time to entertain the four ladies in bed. It would appear that he might be in over his head but Butler isn't complaining. According to director, Bob Vosse, this film was John Holmes' last American feature. Although John learned that he had contracted HIV in 1986, Vosse doesn't believe he had AIDS during this shoot and claimed he was very healthy in his appearance.

79 min/color. DVD. Alexis Greco, Angel Kelly, Lilly Marlene, Nina Hartley, Porsche Lynn, Buddy Love, Jerry Butler, John Holmes, Mike Horner, Ron Jeremy, Tom Byron. *Director:* Bob Vosse.

The New Girl in Town ★★ 1971

Three stoner dudes are sitting around their pad, getting high, when the phone rings. A female friend, who turned a trick in exchange for cash, invites the guys to dinner. Mark (Holmes with a humongous afro and fake moustache) and Sam accept her invitation and leave Rudy alone to play with his...kaleidoscope. In their absence, a young runaway, Mimi (Julie Hayes), arrives at the door looking for her older sister. Rudy offers to help, but soon divulges that Mimi's sister has become a hooker. After they share a joint, he gives her a kiss, which escalates to full blown intercourse just prior to the housemates returning with their friend, Linda (Judy Angel), in tow.

Linda begins a seductive dance for Mark, in an enticing bit of foreplay. When he reveals his love muscle, Linda gives herself to him (with bruised thighs and all) and takes Holmes at full mast while appearing to be transfixed by his size. Soon, they are joined by Sam, who wants in on the action. Once Sam and Linda have been whipped by Mark (in a bizarre, but relatively tame S&M exhibition) and all three have climaxed, they return to the group, just in time for the two girls to get better acquainted. After some experimental girl-girl sex, Linda takes Mimi in search of her sister on Sunset Boulevard. Fortunately (or unfortunately), they arrive back at the apartment just in time for an orgy with the fellas.

Putting the reefer-induced lethargy aside, this film truly lacks vigor and the sex scenes are uninspiring. Interestingly, a billboard advertising an Oscar nomination for Bob Rafelson's *Five Easy Pieces* (1970) places the film shoot in the spring of 1971. In addition, *The History of Pornography* is on the marquee at the famous porn theatre in West Hollywood; more memorabilia from those heady times.

58 min/color. DVD. Judy Angel, Julie Hayes, John Holmes, Ramone Narone. *Director:* David Stefans. *Writer:* David Stefans.

The New York City Woman ★★★ 1979

Tagline: *"Who is The New York City Woman? Is it Georgina Spelvin? C.J. Laing? Johnny (The Wadd) Holmes is going to find out...or die trying!!"*

This film incorporates multiple scenes from 1976 films, *Sweet, Sweet Freedom* and *Sweet Punkin', I Love You* in order to build a new story centering around the former porn star, John Holmes, who has decided to leave adult movies in search of the one woman who can finally satisfy his sexual appetite.

Seated on a rooftop patio in New York City, Holmes tape records his memoirs and describes how he has been in hot pursuit to find the girl of his dreams: a woman that he hopes will turn out to be a seasoned young lady named Gloria (C.J. Laing). Gloria happens to be a friend of his pal, Tony (Jeffrey Hurst). John explains that his woman must be equipped to deep throat him and she must also be able to take it to the hilt vaginally. In the interim, he shares specifics of the carnal antics that occur between him, Tony and various other women.

By melding together footage from the previous Roberta Findlay movies, *The New York City Woman* proves to be enjoyable and John's inane-yet-entertaining narration during the outdoor wrap-around scenes brings cohesion to the story. His search eventually culminates in the four-way sexual rendezvous from *Sweet*

Punkin', I Love You, between Holmes, C. J. Laing, Jeffrey Hurst and Tony Perez, as the Slim Pickins band cranks out the tunes.

Holmes doesn't pretend to be an actor, but a showman he surely is, as he hams it up in his non-sex segments. In an impulsive move, he free-falls backwards through an open window near the film's closing.

75 min/color. Unavailable. C.J. Laing, Crystal Sync, Georgia Spelvin, Jennifer Jordan, Marlene Willoughby, Ashley Moore, Eric Edwards, Jeffrey Hurst, John Holmes, Richard Bolla, Roger Caine, Tony Perez, Turk Lyon. *Director:* Roberta Findlay. *Writer:* Roberta Findlay.

Oriental Sex Kitten ★★ 1975

Also known as *Episodes of an Oriental Sex Kitten*, *Oriental Kitten*.

The film opens with Asian actress, Suzy Chung, who portrays John's lover. The film was made in a beautifully decorated home. The sex scenes are less than stimulating, despite good music and a boyishly handsome, young John Holmes.

The movie consists mostly of orgies, including some multi-racial groupings that were ahead of their time. Admittedly, the positions used in the orgies are often artistic, even poetic, but modern viewers might not appreciate the spit-lube before penetration. The girl-girl-boy encounters tend to be predictable, although the boy-boy-girl combo is intriguingly fresh. However, the actors are much too amateurish and they don't appear to be pleasuring the woman.

John's final scene is rather humorous when he happens upon Natasha (Crystal Sync). Natasha is in a medicated trance on the couch, and when John sees her, he declares, "It's like she's stoned or something — it's wonderful. I wonder if I can get her to give me head."

The girl is completely still and corpselike while John has his way with her. It is off-putting that Natasha remains in her trancelike state, but the usual bad porn overdubs of "oohs" and "aahs" were put in there. It saves the scene somewhat that Holmes comes across as fun loving and he was reputed for taking care with foreplay and communication prior to filming any of his scenes. The best word for John is goofy, with his playful ways and offbeat sense of humor. When he leaves Natasha, after propping her up with cum dripping off her breast, he says, "No, no Natasha. Don't bother to show me out." Suzy Chung and Linda Wong, two Golden Age stars, provide a certain niche of porn fans with a little Asian flavor.

64 min/color. DVD. Mea Tue, Rita Cous, Suzy Chung, Dan Pole, John Holmes. *Director:* Harry Who.

Prisoner of Paradise ★★★★ 1980

Also known as *Nassau*, *Nazi Love Island*.

Joe Murray (John Holmes), an American soldier in World War II, is the lone survivor of a ship fire before washing up alone on the beach of a deserted island. The beach sequences were directed by Bob Chinn on the Hawaiian island of Kauai. Chinn recalled that John enjoyed climbing the palms and chopping coconuts with a machete. This film also has the somewhat-famous scene of John, larger than life, showering naked under a waterfall.

The fist sex scene is presented as a flashback and features Joe with his Japanese fiancée, Sue Lee (played by Miko Moko, also known as Mai Lin). The scene is remarkably great; in *The Best of Gail Palmer*, she mentions how it feels like actual love between the two actors, and even Laurie Holmes has shared that John felt this was one of his personal favorite scenes from his repertoire. With over ten years of acting in hardcore films under his belt, John communicates genuine sorrow in the film when Sue Lee is killed in an explosion.

Back on the deserted island, Joe happens to find a Nazi hideout, where a perverted, drunken officer, Hans von Schlemel (Heinz Mueller) and his two lesbian cohorts occupy themselves by torturing American nurses. Murray plots a way to rescue the nurses and save himself, only to be captured and fall victim to the sexual torture himself. Joe is forced to have sex with one of the Nazi bitches, Ilsa (Seka), and also with an American woman named, Carol (Nikki Anderson). Joe solemnly apologizes to Carol beforehand.

Prisoner of Paradise includes some great scenic shots of the island, has an excellent plot and believable dialogue between the actors. The film is great for the

Image courtesy of VCX.com. John and Jade Wong in *Prisoner of Paradise.*

first 40 minutes, then slows down. Unfortunately, the inside sequences were filmed in a San Francisco studio and lack the quality of the first half of the movie, in part due to difficulties with John. Despite various problems with the second half, the sex scenes are sensuous.

76 min/color. DVD. Brenda Vargo, Jade Wong, Mai Lin, Nikki Anderson, Seka, Sue Carol, Heinz Mueller, John Holmes. Directors: Bob Chinn, Gail Palmer. *Writer:* Jeffrey Fairbanks, Gail Palmer. *Producer:* Gail Palmer.

The Private Pleasures of John C. Holmes ★★ 1983

John plays a prince-like character in a kingdom of gay men in Arabian attire. For his entertainment, he forces the men to have sex with each other and pleasure him. John supplies an occasional funny remark such as when he announces the punishment for a man who touches a woman, "As a punishment to fit the crime, you must swallow the sword of death."

John receives a lot of oral sex in the movie and never reciprocates. Most of the time, he appears very bored and seldom makes the "monkey face" during his orgasms, which are shown in abundance. He appears to be in good health, although he is clearly emaciated and uncommonly aloof.

There are fresh camera angles used in the film, which really highlight John's length. He is shown penetrating Joey Yale, but all the other penetration shots appear to be with a stunt butt — a woman whose face is buried in pillows to make it appear as though John is actually having anal sex with another man. Nancy Conjure, a female swinger who wanted an anal experience with Holmes, is a known stunt butt in *Private Pleasures*. Conjure was allowed to partake in the film as payment for allowing pornographers to use her Palos Verdes home for the subsequent film, *Caught From Behind*. There are some rough cuts when the stunt butt is replaced with the actual actor, Joey Yale.

Yale died of AIDS in 1986, in addition to at least two more actors in this video; Chris Burns (1995) and Johnny Dawes (1989).

The Director's Cut DVD contains extra footage, including an early 1969 soft-core gay loop featuring John and Dave Harris.

88 min/color. DVD. Nancy Conjure, Sharon Kane, Abdul (non-sex), Chi Chi, Chris Burns, Colby Douglas, Doug Raymond, Jerry Davis, Jerry Thomas, John Holmes, Johnny Dawes, Joseph Yale, Lee Jones, Max Corral, Rocky Diangelo, Victor Young. *Director:* J. J. English.

The Return of Johnny Wadd ★★★½ January 1986

In 1986 John Holmes telephoned Bob Chinn (who had taken a 13-year hiatus in Hawaii) to ask if he could use the Johnny Wadd name in a film. It had been nearly eight years since Chinn had made a *Johnny Wadd* film and knowing that he would never make another, he granted John permission to make the film with Penguin Productions, John and Bill's company.

Johnny Wadd, the smooth-talking lothario with the baby-blue eyes, is lured out of retirement, where he returns to the criminal underworld in pursuit of those who killed his partner and friend, Warren North. To watch Holmes reprise this role is clearly a lesson in extremes. He appears older than his years and has a rough exterior to his naturally lean frame. His eyes that once glowed in electric blue, are now fatigued. At 41, he'd already shed more than a thousand skins, yet Holmes retained the subtle swagger, the charisma, the subdued voice and gentle manner that made him a star.

Johnny's initial encounter is with the daughter of an old friend, played by Sheri St. Claire (who bears a striking resemblance to Eileen Welles of *China Cat*). Like most of the women with whom Wadd becomes entangled in his attempts to crack cases and heads, she plays both sides of the fence and pretends to aid Johnny in his quest for justice while setting him up for an inevitable fall.

The standout performance in this film belongs to Kimberly Carson as a young cop shadowing Johnny Wadd. The best moments occur when Holmes and Carson share the same scenes. They play easily off one another with well-written dialogue. The hard-earned expression of world weariness on Holmes' face enhances Wadd's credibility as he cautions his young charge against the pitfalls of working in crime.

By the mid-'80s adult cinema lost some of its class and luster, and this feature is no exception, but the dialogue in this feature is sharper than some of the '70s *Johnny Wadd* films and the musical score alternates between '80s techno-pop to soothing jazz. Holmes supplies narration, just as he did in his younger days. The film includes a trademark fight scene, once again in keeping with the tradition of the original Chinn/Holmes series, with a couple of quick punches and kicks before Wadd dismantles the bad guys by the pool. It's all over in the blink of an eye.

There are a few memorable lines in this last foray, but the overall melancholy mood strikes a chord. There is something ironic and profound in the film's closing statement, while Wadd reflects upon his deceased partner's words of wisdom, "Women can kill you."

In his mind, Johnny retorts, "Yeah, but sometimes they can save you, too. It's a crap shoot."

The Return of Johnny Wadd is not necessarily the highlight of the succession of films showcasing Holmes as the lusty detective, but it succeeds in wrapping the case up neatly, while reminding the viewer that one can go home again, but ill-fated memories might lurk behind the familiarity.

Interestingly, the film showcases both Melendez sisters, Lisa and Melissa. Melissa appears in a girl-girl scene with Bunny Bleu, and Lisa performs with Buck Adams and Billy Dee. Lisa Melendez died of AIDS-related causes in 1999.

84 min/color. DVD. Bunny Bleu, Kimberly Carson, Lisa Melendez (as Denise Ford), Mai Lin, Melissa Melendez, Sheri St. Claire, Billy Dee, Buck Adams, Dick Howard (non-sex), Frankie Penn (non-sex), John Holmes, Nick Random. *Director:* Patty Rhodes-Lincoln. *Writer:* Raven Touchstone.

Rings of Passion ★★½ 1973

Shown only from the waist down, three women take long strides in high boots while an instrumental version of McCartney/Lennon's "Ob-La-Di, Ob-La-Da" plays on the film's soundtrack. Girlfriends, Claire (Nancy Dare), Monica (Monica Tite) and Julie (Julie Holmes) go out for a bit of shopping therapy and to discuss their frustration with the men in their lives.

Blonde Claire is married to a wealthy business man, Pete (Peter Hand) and although the two are in their twenties, their sex life is close to nonexistent. Claire's complaints to her husband about the lack of nookie fall on deaf ears.

In the meantime, shapely Monica has a challenge of her own. Her boyfriend John (Holmes) desperately wants to make love, but she prevents him from entering more than a few inches. In a desperate move to try to accommodate her, John uses a copper cock ring to restrict his engorgement, but Monica insists that it is still too painful.

Later, John arrives at Pete's home to drop off some important papers, only to find that Pete has already left. Still frustrated by his experience with Monica, he explains to Claire that he and Monica had a fight and broke up. Surprised, Claire comforts him by saying that he is "marriage material" and that he "has everything." In a deft reference to his manhood, John hangs his head and reluctantly admits, "I guess I have too much of everything." His candor proves fruitful and within minutes, he is wearing three copper cock rings and thrusting Claire into oblivion.

Later, vivacious Julie arrives at Claire's home for a little friendly visit and her observation of Claire's flushed cheeks precipitates a heart-to-heart talk about sex. Julie recalls a time when she had her first encounter with another woman and divulged that she, too is neglected by her husband in the bedroom. (Concurrently, Monica tries a new boyfriend on for size). Tired of obsessing about their problems, Claire and Julie decide to go to the show while their husbands plan to go to a football game. The women and their guys are in for a reality check when all good intentions are forfeited after they choose to stay home instead.

67 min/color. DVD. Nina Fause (as Clair Starlove), Sharon Thorpe (as Julie Holmes), Monica Tite, Veronica Pink, John Holmes (as Johnny Wadd), Larry Games, Peter Hand, Tyler Reynolds. *Director:* Willie Creps. *Writer:* Robert Stix. *Producer:* Willie Creps.

The Rise and Fall of the Roman Empress ★★★½ January 1987
Also known as *Carne Bollente, The Rise of the Roman Empress.*

Rise of the Roman Empress was shot in Italian and everything — including John's and Amber Lynn's lines were overdubbed later (much to John's delight). His Italian costar, Cicciolina, first ran for the Italian Parliament in 1979 and was elected in 1987.

People remember this film as one of the two movies that John made in Italy, while knowing that he had AIDS. Although it is despicable with today's knowledge about HIV transmission that John chose to expose others to his virus and not use condoms, his fragile emotional state and need for money to pay medical bills played a role in his poor decision. In August of 1987, Bill Amerson told the *Los Angeles Times* that, "I don't think anyone would tell anybody" referring to the state of the porn industry in relation to AIDS at that time.

The plot is comical; Cicciolina is the star, as a woman forced to do social work as penance for a raunchy show (including a naked, plastic baby doll and a clear, glass dildo). Upon reenacting the show for her lawyer, he says some hilarious things, including, "Lick my habeas corpus." Her punishment for her raunchy act is to help others find sexual pleasure. John is her first case. In light of the controversy involving the Italian films, John and Cicciolina click onscreen. Their connection feels effortless in many of their romantic scenes. Cicciolina has an

Image courtesy of Paradise Visuals. John and Cicciolina in *The Rise and Fall of the Roman Empress.*

exotic look, with full eyebrows and glittering, sequined fabrics. Amber Lynn, comparatively, is naturally chic, but both are uniquely beautiful.

John is very tan in some scenes, although very white in others, so he may have spent some time in the sun while in Italy for the final time. It appears that he is able to achieve a full erection at some points, except at the end, where he casually chews gum while receiving head and looks quite bored.

90 min/color. Unavailable. Amber Lynn, Brigitte Laal, Cicciolina, Judy Fatima, Maria Longo, Tracey Adams, Christoph Clark, Jean Dubay, Jean-Pierre Armand, John Holmes. *Director:* Riccardo Schicchi.

Rockin' With Seka ★★★ February 3, 1980

Also known as *Seka's Cruise; Fallen Angel.* Compilation.

Well-traveled Seka (a.k.a. Sweet Alice), a flight attendant, takes a coworker, Kim (Brooke West) under her wing to teach her how to get the best out of a man in the sack. Poor Kim is inexperienced in that department and her boyfriend is a virgin. Seka reminisces over drinks about her countless conquests with Jamie Gillis, John Holmes, John Seeman, David Morris and other hardcore heroes.

In a standout scene, John Holmes gets lost on a nature hike and happens upon Seka in an outdoor hot tub. After asking if he can use the phone to let his office know he'll be late, Holmes finds himself ensconced between Seka and her roommate, Maria, as the two ladies lap at his cock simultaneously. Holmes smiles knowingly in his acknowledgment that he'll be detained for the rest of the day as they move into the bedroom. "Who wants to go first? You?" he asks after complimenting Seka.

With a cast led by Seka and John Holmes, this compilation is worth the price of admission.

74 min/color. DVD. Brooke West, Joan Thomas, Juliet Anderson, Desiree West (as Patricia Lee), Seka, Liza Dwyer (as Tillie Sanchez), David Morris, Jamie Gillis, John Holmes, John Seeman, Mike Ranger, R.J. Reynolds. *Director:* Ziggy Zigowitz, Jr. *Producer:* Chris Warfield, Ziggy Zigowitz Jr.

Rocky X ★★½ 1986

Also known as *Rockey X.*

Boxer, Drax Spago (Buck Adams) inadvertently kills a man in the ring. A young reporter (Summer Rose), who witnessed the fatal blow approaches Drax's manager, Mr. Holmes (John with gray hair), in hopes to get the inside goods on the unexpected tragedy. Holmes invites her back to his apartment for an exclusive interview and offers to help write her story. In an explanation that could apply to his own, real-life line of work, Holmes says that the sport of boxing is a gamble and sometimes can result in death. After they reach an agreement about the proposed article, Holmes seduces her to make out with him on the couch before she mounts him reverse cowgirl.

The story flashes over to Drax's pad, where we learn that he is a hopped-up sex machine after receiving his steroid injection from the doctor (Karen Summer).

The next day at the gym, Drax encounters a young boxer named Rocky (Jerry Butler) and challenges him to a testosterone-fueled duel. Rocky accepts, but his wife (Melissa Melendez, who passed away from AIDS complications in 1999) is afraid of the sport and urges him to reconsider his decision.

Rocky X is an honorable attempt to legitimize the adult movie genre and the results are worthwhile.

83 min/color. DVD. Karen Summer, Melissa Melendez, Nikki Randall, Summer Rose, Vanessa D'Oro, Buck Adams, Jerry Butler, John Holmes, Sean Amerson (non-sex as Sean Duke). *Director:* Patti Rhodes-Lincoln. *Writers:* Patti Rhodes-Lincoln, Buck Adams. *Producer:* Penguin Productions.

Rubdown ★★½ 1985

Tagline: *"They'll rub you the right way!"*

When oversexed boss Mr. Bixby (Harry Reems) makes an unwelcome overture toward one of his attractive employees, Gail (Kimberly Carson), she quits and takes her co-workers Patty and Suzy (Amber Lynn and Bunny Bleu) with her. Back at their homestead, the girls commiserate their fate while sorting out how to pay the rent and bills. Gail suddenly has an idea to open their own massage service, and the three ladies place an ad in the paper to solicit prospective clients.

Gail helps a young married woman overcome her sexual inhibitions and inexperience as she demonstrates how to perform fellatio on her husband, while Suzy finds herself sandwiched between two males as she exceeds their wildest desires and erotic fantasies.

Meanwhile, Patty reaps the fringe benefits of her work while sharing a bubbly Jacuzzi bath with a male client (a healthy-looking John Holmes). It is an exceptional pairing of the bleach-blonde siren and the legendary swordsman. Their scene is memorable and has been incorporated into many John Holmes compilation DVDs.

At the end of the week, the girls compare notes and determine their newfound employment is lucrative. To celebrate, they invite their significant others (Jerry Butler and Shone Taylor) to sample the leftovers. Inevitably, Mr. Bixby

In a hot tub with Amber Lynn on the set of *Rubdown*.

contacts the call service for a little personal pampering and gets "sundaed" in a humorous example of payback from his former employees.

Holmes and Harry Reems are a treat in the feature, opposite the new video-age stars. Likewise, the presence of Jerry Butler, one of the sexiest men to work in hardcore, adds another layer to this lightweight flick as Amber Lynn's boyfriend.

75 min/color. DVD. Amber Lynn, Bunny Bleu, Kimberly Carson, Mindy Rae, Harry Reems, Jerry Butler, Jesse Adams, John Holmes, Shone Taylor. *Director:* Bill Amerson (as Bill Williams). *Production Manager:* John C. Holmes; *Writer:* Patty Rhodes (as Patty Pleasure).

Saturday Night Beaver ★★ 1986

The title suggests that this is a sex parody of *Saturday Night Fever*, but unfortunately, this is not a parody of *Fever*! *Saturday Night Beaver* details the saga of two brothers, played by John Holmes and Golden Age mainstay, Joey Silvera.

Tony (John Holmes) receives a telephone call from his brother, who just got dumped by his fiancée (Vanessa D'Oro). Anxious to cheer his brother up, Tony tells him he'll call back after taking care of some personal business.

Tony's personal business entails sex with the sweet, young, brunette actress, Bambi Allen. She appears uncomfortable with Holmes' size, yet she is valiant. John, looking thinner than usual, coaxes her and takes his time, until she responds to his lovemaking style with audible enthusiasm. John's "JH" pinky ring can be seen in the film.

The title is first referenced when Tony walks up to his brother and a friend (Jim Harker) in a snappy, white suit and fedora hat and suggests, "We're gonna go out and get some Saturday Night Beaver!" after one of the guys teases him for his Travoltaesque get-up. Tony insists that the guys put away their pizza and beer, and get dressed up to go out on the town. After Silvera and Harker exit the scene, Holmes picks up

John poses with Vanessa D'Oro and Angel Kelly for the one-sheet and box cover of *Saturday Night Beaver.*

the pizza box and helps himself to a piece. After one bite, he grimaces and adlibs, "God, this is horrible! No wonder these guys can't get laid!"

Tony attempts to remedy his little brother's unwelcome bachelorhood by fixing him up with a few fun-loving gals (including the cute Angel Kelly) that the guys picked up at the local club. *Saturday Night Beaver* isn't spectacular, but it's enjoyable to observe Holmes and Silvera sharing the stage, not to mention getting a load of John's *Saturday Night Fever* get-up!

81 min/color. DVD. Angel Kelly, Bambi Allen, Carolyn Connoly, Karen Summer, Mauvais DeNoir (non-sex), Tiffany Blake, Vanessa D'Oro, Gary Blue Stone, Joey Silvera, John Holmes. *Director:* Patti Rhodes-Lincoln. *Producer:* Penguin Productions.

The Seka Story ★★ 1988

Also known as *Seka*. This is a compilation film that uses archive footage from various directors.

John Holmes has the majority of scenes in this mockumentary/compilation video, but as the title implies, his role is minimal. John appears with Seka in a trio of threesomes. One is an unusual (but erotic) clip with The King, The Platinum Princess and Jamie Gillis; and the other two scenes are with John, Seka and one other woman.

An interviewer, who provides the narration, asks Seka questions, which she answers in obviously scripted drivel. When asked about her favorite people to work with, she offers her contemporaries, Mike Ranger and Paul Thomas as her two favorite leading men. A particularly hot scene with Seka and Paul Thomas follows, before the next interview question, "Does Seka like John Holmes?"

She replies, "Of course I do. I like him from the waist down."

The sex scenes in this video are particularly stimulating, partially due to the fact that all of them star Seka. However, the quality of the film editing and the shoddy Q & A makes the video only fit for fans of Seka's sex scenes — of which, there are many even today.

78 min/color. DVD. Juliet Anderson, Lisa DeLeeuw, Seka, David Morris, Jamie Gillis, John Holmes, John Leslie, Kevin James, Mike Ranger, Paul Thomas, R.J. Reynolds.

The Senator's Daughter ★★★ 1979

Tagline: *"Superspy John unlocks Lesllie's treasure with his gigantic key!"*

In an entertaining spoof of the popular TV series, *The Six Million Dollar Man*, John Galt (Holmes) loses his moneymaker in a car accident when his beautiful costar deep throats him from the passenger seat. John undergoes an experimental surgery, in which he is given a bionic eye, arms, legs, and a 12-inch penis with a poison dart!

Image courtesy of VCX. John and Lesllie Bovee live happily ever after, at the conclusion of *The Senator's Daughter* — the porn spoof of the popular 1970s TV show, *The Six Million Dollar Man.*

After a successful surgery, Galt is commissioned by the government to rescue the senator's daughter (Lesllie Bovee), who was kidnapped and taken to a cult-like commune in Tangiers. The kidnappers routinely brainwash women to convert them into seductresses. Galt's first challenge in rescuing the senator's daughter is to determine which is really her, because she's been cloned!

The sex scenes are adequate, but move too slowly in what is otherwise a fast-paced film. *The Senator's Daughter* is an elaborate production with close-ups (particularly when John goes down on Lesllie; you can see every single hair follicle) and special effects. The music is also especially well chosen, from the opening title song that mirrors the theme music from *Mission: Impossible*, to the Middle Eastern arrangements for the Tangier segments, to the raunchy guitar licks when Bovee goes down on Holmes.

72 min/color. DVD. Buff Lesbos, Gloria Throate, Lesllie Bovee, Linda West, Lori Moteurmuth, Monique Little, Nancy Crew, Sara Tulip, Alan Ball (non-sex), Alan Fink, Bruce Hopley (non-sex), Dennis Machant (non-sex), John Holmes, Manuel Stuckey (non-sex), Peter Whigam (non-sex), Rick Toole. *Director:* Don Flowers. *Writer:* Trebor Rutner. *Producer:* Weldo Gebt.

Sex and the Single Vampire ★½ 1970

John Holmes stars as Count Spatula in this absurd, campy, softcore twist on *Dracula*. Spatula (wearing gaudy green eye shadow) awakens from his slumber only to complain bitterly about his rheumatism, not to mention the lack of sustenance and sex in his life. Spatula isn't very intimidating; when a rat surprises him, he screams like a schoolgirl and jumps on the closest chair before rummaging in his refrigerator for stale blood to drink. Finding little there, he tosses the empty bottles away.

Things begin to look up for the 300-year old corpse when a carload of couples arrives at the Gothic mansion that has fallen into serious disrepair. Among the young couples is none other than Holmes' girlfriend, Sandy Dempsey. (In this film, Dempsey has a little baby fat, but she blossomed into a sultry butterfly within the year, in time for the first *Johnny Wadd*.) The kids make themselves at home and engage in an orgy while the Count lustily observes the females from behind a slightly open door.

In his state of arousal, Spatula concocts ways to retain the image of the sexy couplings. At one point, he attempts to replicate their bare bodies on canvas, until he inadvertently sits on the wet oils and has to scrap his plan. Undeterred, the Count plots to make the women his own.

55 min/color. DVD. Cathy Hilton, Lu Tomery, Robin Christian, Sandy Dempsey, Stephanie Sarver, Jesse Moreno, John Dullahan, John Holmes, L.G. Allard. *Director:* Modunk Phreezer. *Writer:* F. N. Spelling. *Producer:* Wolfgang Klutzman.

Sex As You Like It ★ 1972

Also known as *The As You Like It Sex Service*

John's screen time in this compilation is fair, but nothing extraordinary. He is introduced in the first scene as an employee of a service that fulfils sexual requests.

In the second scene, John is shown with Sandy Carey and Sandy Dempsey, in the clip "Hot Cream and Cherries," in which the two ladies make a whip cream sundae topped with nuts and a cherry atop his banana.

The opening segment shows Candy Samples in a wig and a dildo, which she uses to penetrate a willing male partner. Another scene shows a grown man dressed in a baby's diaper with his limp dick hanging out in front. While standing before a playpen, he simulates sex acts with stuffed toys in a truly unusual scene. On the upside, there are no rape scenes, so for people who want to explore their unusual fetish fantasies without crossing over into violence, this feature fits the bill.

54min/color. DVD. Candy Samples, Chlorine Stillwater, Mindy Brandt, Sandy Carey, Sandy Dempsey, George Peters, Jason Yukon, John Holmes.

Sexual Heights ★★★ 1980

This film could easily be a sequel to *Undulations*, with most of the same cast, the same director, a similar musical theme, and the same vial of coke (okay, maybe it's a different vial).

The storyline contains some good bits as it showcases the life and times of divorced bachelors during swinging 1980. John Holmes plays bachelor number one. On a leopard skin bed, he flips through a magazine when red-headed Kitty Shayne enters his room and apologizes for being late. John isn't surprised as he lays her on her back and unhooks her corset to reveal her large, ripe nipples. He tickles them with his tongue as they get down and dirty while the camera produces kaleidoscopic images of John and Kitty having sex. As was his custom, Holmes moves Shayne around for optimum camera angles until his climax.

Enter hard-up bachelors numbers two, three and four: Jamie Gillis, Herschel Savage and Jessie Adams, who ogle a porn movie depicting Serena and Maria Cruz together as the girls simulate sex. The tape inspires Herschel to take a trip down memory lane as he tells his pals about a former babysitter who teased him mercilessly and ended up being the cause of his divorce. In a flashback, we are privy to exactly how this situation came about as we observe Herschel attempting to have his way with the young girl on his couch while she begs for him to stop. His wife catches them in the act and divorces him.

This story fascinates the other men. Jamie initiates a plan that will enable them all an opportunity to screw the babysitter when he suggests that they dress up and pretend to be a family of (mostly) women. As preposterous as this might sound, they follow through with their arrangements. In the interim, John pays Jamie a visit to see how bachelorhood is treating him and Jamie discloses his idea. Without missing a beat, John asks if he can get in on the action, but Jamie is reluctant and admits that probably three men are enough for a gang bang.

Undeterred, John confesses that he has "something juicy at home waiting" anyway, to which Jamie retorts, "I didn't think you'd be suffering too much." John wishes him luck and shakes Jamie's hand just as one might do when congratulating a friend upon learning some good news.

John's lady friend happens to be Mai Lin who delivers him some cocaine and soon she becomes the recipient of his 12 inches as a partial payment. In the interim, Jamie and friends put their ridiculous plan into effect. With the help of a few joints and a porno film to help loosen her up, the gang bang goes down without a hitch. John and Mai Lin have good chemistry and are cute together, although their scene doesn't begin to compare to their legendary coupling in the opener to *Prisoner of Paradise*, shot the same year.

87 min/color. Unavailable. Holly McCall, J. Duran, Kitty Shayne, Lolita Grant, Lysa Thatcher, Mai Lin, Serena, Tawny Pearl, David Morris, Herschel Savage, Jamie Gillis, Jesse Adams, John Holmes. *Director:* Carlos Tobalina

Singlehanded ★ 1984

Singlehanded contains 74 minutes of all-male masturbation scenes. John's scene is third (beginning 15 minutes and 40 seconds in), and it appears to have been shot in the mid-'70s. Sporting his trademark frizzy 'fro and smoking a cigarette, Holmes takes a seat in a chair and begins to stroke along the length of his left thigh through his light blue pants. The camera zooms in to show the visible outline of his penis, which is certainly the longest of the seven shown in the video. Then, he unzips his pants to touch himself before unbuttoning his shirt and removing his pants, grey-blue bikini briefs and white tube socks. The viewer is treated to a fantasy — seeing just how Holmes touches himself in private, but unfortunately, the clip ends just short of three minutes and before he can climax (in some versions, John's cum shot is retained on film). The rest of the scenes in the video are much longer and the sexy, hard-bodied men are sure to excite its intended audience.

72 min/color. DVD.

Sissy's Hot Summer ★★½ 1979

Tagline: *"Her days were warm — but her nights were hot, hot, hot!"*

As the hostess, Candida Royalle brings this parody of the television series *Three's Company* a touch of class. In *Sissy's Hot Summer*, the group's valiant attempts at celibacy fail as Sissy (Jennifer Walker) and Jack (Tony Bond) get it on when Janet (Susan Nero) has her back turned. Upon catching her two roommates copulating, Janet retaliates by giving head to the landlord, Mr. Groper (Jessie Adams).

Unbeknownst to Janet, Groper is about to evict his three tenants for falling behind in their rent. The trio catches wind of his intentions and figure out a quick fix to keep their digs. The sex scenes are executed with enthusiasm and include various pairings between the three leads and their costars. Sharon Kane and John Holmes portray Jane and Tarzan in an unusual segment with Kane in a modified canvas chair. As the famous jungle dweller, Holmes improvises some amusing lines, such as, "Tarzan shouldn't have given Cheetah a fucking chainsaw. He cut up the entire forest!"

Likewise, Jack and a wealthy socialite (Laurien Dominique) enjoy a mutually satisfying sexual encounter during a hot and lively scene spiced up by Dominique's agility. Royalle's narration pokes fun at the characters' lusty appetites while she demonstrates some unique sex aids and pauses for station identification.

74 min/color. DVD. Aubrey Nichols, Candida Royalle (non-sex), Sharon Kane (as Jennifer Walker), Laurien Dominique, Lisa K. Loring, Mimi Morgan (as Michael Moore), Susan Nero, Jeff Scott, John Holmes, Jesse Adams (as Johnny Harden), Alan Colberg (as Nala Grebloc, non-sex), Tony Bond. *Director:* Alan Colberg. *Writer:* Alan Colberg, G. Lewis. *Producers:* Alan Colberg, Laurie Colberg.

S.M.A.S.H. — or How to Get Hung ★ 1971

Also known as *Smash*.

The first part of the title is an obvious reference to Robert Altman's big screen hit, *M*A*S*H* (1970) and after watching the film, it seems that the second part of the title references a sex change operation that goes awry.

Set in an unorthodox hospital, Dr. Wildare (John Holmes) and Dr. Galen Night (Judy Angel) combine efforts in an attempt to bring decorum and respectability to the medical facility. The slapstick, wild and wholly sexual antics employed by the doctors, nurses and patients, are plentiful but ordinary in this spoof that surrounds the blossoming love affair between two straight-laced physicians.

When Dr. Wildare inadvertently pats Dr. Night's fanny, she admonishes him at first, before declaring her amorous feelings. Upon stealing away from the staff, they confess their secret desires for one another and recite poetic ramblings while the soapy soundtrack soars in the background. Dr. Wildare offers up his surprise package as Dr. Knight does her best to manage his manhood with her tongue and two hands. Unexpectedly, he pops inside of her mouth and never enters her vagina.

Shortly after, the team of inept physicians discovers their gender-bending surgery is a failure and complete chaos ensues as the horny medical experts give in to their carnal yearnings.

DVD. Judy Angel, John Holmes. *Director:* Ivan Stephens.

Spirit of Seventy-Sex ★★★★ November 1976

Also known as *Seventeen Seventy-Sex*; *The Spirit of 69*.

Proprietor, Ebenezer K. Bartholomu ("as himself") is so old; he was alive in 1776 during the birth of the United States and knows all of the true stories of the founding fathers. Of course, all the stories that he narrates are sexy, with a successfully humorous attempt at relating to history. The costumes and dialogue of this film are exceptional, and the music is very good.

The first scene is between George and Martha Washington (played by the beautiful Annette Haven), followed by Paul Revere and his girlfriend, which offers a unique explanation for the famous quote, "The British are coming!" The strangest scene in the film is where Ben Franklin introduces his newest invention, a crumpet stuffer, to a woman who has difficulty climaxing.

Unfortunately, Ebenezer's narration of the oral and anal sex scene between John Smith (Holmes) and Pocahontas (Desiree West) isn't included on all versions, but the sex scene is left intact.

Otherwise, this is an uproarious and equally scintillating film with an especially hot lesbian scene interrupted by minutemen, one of which is lucky enough to take on all three women at once. Even the conclusion of the film is superb, with a note to thank the founding fathers for the First Amendment — compelling, considering the free speech amendment effectively made hardcore pornography legal in 1988.

86 min/color. DVD. Abigail Clayton, Angela Haze, Annette Haven, Desiree West, Kristine Heller, Sandy Pinney, Clay Hyde, Ebenezer K. Bartholomu (nonsex), Jeff Lyle, John Holmes, John Seeman (as John Toland), Jon Martin, Ray Wells (as Radio Ray), Tyler Reynolds. *Director:* Stu Segall (as Ms. Ricki Krelmn). *Writers:* Ebenezer Bartholomu, Stu Segall; Producer; Stu Segall.

Stormy ★★½ 1980

Tagline: *"An erotic explosion of hurricane force!"*

Eroticism is sporadic in *Stormy*, but the film has some stellar moments. John Holmes plays a pimp named "Big John" who is quite well off in San Francisco. He employs a full-time, scantily clad housekeeper, Suzie (Linda Wong), who seduces him on the living room furniture before he departs to see about business. (Wong, a favored star in her own right, is somewhat robotic in her sex scene.) After parking his car (possibly an Austin Mini) outside the whorehouse, John is told about one of the new girls, a strawberry-blonde Amazon named Lori (Lauren Black). Lori is pleased to meet John and even more pleased when he suggests that he'd like to sample the goods. John and Lori immediately get down to some hot sex that culminates in a messy facial all over her freckles, just as he'd promised. Afterwards, John informs her that she has the right technique and he anticipates that she will garner him a boatload of money.

The remainder of the movie involves additional sexual groupings between several clients and the respective ladies of the house, involving costars Connie Peterson, Don Fernando, John Seeman and Cris Cassidy. The couplings are formulaic and not stimulating, although the film does pick up near the end when John and Joey Silvera participate in a double penetration scene with blonde Christine (Phae Burd, also known as Fay Burd). *Stormy* consists of well-known names of the genre, yet it fails to take full advantage of their potential.

In the conclusion, John flies in a helicopter and reminisces about all the "fucked-up girls" he's had the pleasure to know intimately, while montages of his endless, onscreen encounters dance across the screen, accompanied by a terrific jazz flute solo. If *Stormy* had been Holmes' final movie, the narrative would suggest a far more satisfying end to his career, rather than the reality we've come to know.

80 min/color. DVD. Angel Ducharme, Chris Petersen, Connie Peterson, Eileen Welles, Phae Burd, Lauren Black, Linda Wong, Miki Star (as Moly Jack), Cris Cassidy (as Montana), Paula Wain, Suzanne French, Tracy O'Neil, Virginia Winter (non-sex), Billy Dee, Don Fernando, Joey Silvera, John Holmes, John Seeman, Ken Scudder, Ray Wells. *Director:* Joseph Blanski; *Writer:* Jack Livingston. *Producer:* Sam Norvell.

Strangers When We Mate ★★ 1973

Also known as *Love with a Proper Stranger*.

A group of strangers get together for a day of uninhibited sex, orchestrated by Dr. Freud, who slips a mild aphrodisiac into their drinks to get them started. John Holmes plays a well-hung Texan stud named Boyd who warns a loquacious bedmate, "Where I come from, the women shut up and spread their legs." Boyd knows how to please the ladies and proves it every chance he gets.

Image courtesy of VCX.com. John in *Strangers When We Mate*.

John wears his longer, blond wavy hair brushed back and does a decent job imitating a Texas drawl. He casually chomps gum throughout his numerous sex scenes as was customary in many of his films. In the final orgy segment, he pinches a cigarette between his fingers above his partner's thigh. With the dangling ash about to fall, he penetrates her from behind.

Even in an early flick that is short on plot and heavy on sex, Holmes' charisma is obvious. The entire cast uses pseudonyms.

59 min/color. DVD. B.J. Dyke, Becky Sharpe, Carla Crabbe, Connie Lingus, Mona Leasah, George Peters, Hardy Bull, Heywood Hymen, John Holmes, Kenny Dooer, Ric Lutze, Russell Blue. *Director:* David Stefans.

Suburban Satanist ★★ 1984 or '85

Although listed on sites such as *imdb.com* and *iafd.com* as a 1974 release, this is clearly an '80s effort.

Holmes looks fit at 40-something, as Jerry, with '80s starlet Shaun Michelle portraying his wife, Linda. (The opening sex scene with John and Shaun was pinched from the 1983 Holmes film, *Heat of the Moment*.) Unfortunately, Jerry and Linda find it challenging to sustain the heat they'd shared in the early part of their relationship. Linda attempts to tantalize her despondent husband by dressing provocatively, talking naughty and doing everything short of raping him, but his member won't rise to the occasion. It becomes apparent that Jerry suffers from a lack of affection and romance, and he resents being pressured to satisfy his wife every time she demands it. He confides, "Guys don't like to admit it, but we're not always able to perform every day."

When she finds out, Linda is sympathetic and has an idea to spice things up (on the recommendation of a good friend, Rosemary) that they attend a party held by their local neighborhood Satanist, Barney (Nick Random). Jerry is intrigued by the prospect of trying something new and tells his understanding wife, "I'm not afraid of looking the Devil in the eye."

The couple is welcomed at Barney's bash, and after Barney slips something into their drinks, Jerry and Linda disrobe and join the rest of the group in the darkened living room. There, Barney recites all sorts of lengthy incantations, in a scene reminiscent of *Rosemary's Baby*. Shortly afterwards, the guests pair up and begin to fornicate on the floor. Barney, in a red devil mask, motions for Linda to come to him and in a trance-like state. She doesn't resist. Soon, Barney has her right where he wants her, while Jerry comes to his senses and searches for his wife. He bursts into Barney's bedroom and discovers his wife on top of the devil.

Without hesitating, Jerry lifts Linda off of Barney's erection and proceeds to beat the crap out of Lucifer's clone. The following morning, Jerry brings breakfast to Linda in bed and the two acknowledge they've been had when Jerry reflects, "Barney hosts these cult parties just so that he can get laid."

Sure enough, but it seems that the diversion from the couple's regular routine does the trick as Jerry realizes just how turned on he is by Linda's escapades of the night before. More importantly, he doesn't have difficulty getting hard for her in the final and best scene of the film. Holmes and Michelle have a solid rapport and exhibit alluring sexual chemistry, which is partly due to their steamy dialogue. There is a funny moment at the end when Holmes spontaneously appears before Michelle, wearing the remnants of Barney's evil fest — his red devil mask.

52 min/color. DVD. Shaun Michelle, Tantala Ray, John Holmes, Nick Random.

Summertime Blue ★★ March 1979

Tagline: *"Love becomes desire and passion burns bright in the heat of the night!"*

It is impressive how a strategically chosen disco track can save a porn film from mediocrity. Barring the engaging performances by John Holmes, Serena, Eric Edwards and Samantha Fox, *Summertime Blue* isn't exceptional in any way, but it does excel in "getting down."

Two high school sophomores, Arcadia Lake (real-life girlfriend of Eric Edwards) and Jean Jennings, lament having to return to school after a long, hot summer. After warming up to some disco tunes on the turntable, they decide to share a double-sided dildo while waiting for their boyfriends, George and Joe (Edwards and Ron Hudd).

When the guys arrive on the scene, they peek in the window and are astonished to find their girlfriends sharing a 14-inch substitute for the real thing, but quietly ogle the session until the girls are finished. George is a camera buff and snaps some photos of the two girls engrossed in their delicate operation.

A few minutes later, the boys walk back into the girls' room, but don't let on about their voyeuristic antics. Instead, the foursome kick back as George expounds about the erotic adventures of his boss, John Gibb (John Holmes) down at the shipyard where he toiled over the summer months. Gibb's nickname is "Captain Tongue," and with good reason. According to George, what orifices that Gibb doesn't fill with his 13-inch penis, he explores with his tongue, causing his shipmates to shudder. Edwards explains how Gibb had requested his photographic expertise to capture some of the Captain's more exquisite sexual encounters, unbeknownst to the young women that are seduced by the horny seaman.

The first is an orgy scene, complete with raven-haired Samantha Fox, who gets whip creamed by several male admirers before being penetrated by George himself, who happened to be an invited guest of the good Captain.

Later, Edwards photographs Gibb with a bouncy blonde, Candy Johnson (Serena, who gives new meaning to the term "short-shorts") as she boards the Captain's ship, *The Chug-A-Lug*, seeking employment. Apparently, Gibb is looking for special ladies to service his men after a hard day's work — not exactly the job Candy had in mind, but she decides to give it a go anyway. Serena, who was very fond of Holmes, but claimed that she could only take "two inches," gives it her all as she works miracles with his famous member. The very catchy musical number, "Carry On, Turn Me On," by Space Feat complements the pace of their fusion. John effortlessly transports Serena around the bunk bed, moving her into preferred positions for optimum camera coverage. After they finish, Candy becomes disgruntled when Gibb pays her a measly $20 for her efforts and she quits. Gibb is left alone with his bunkmate (a stuffed koala bear) to bemoan the complexities of women: "Damn, women are just like the tide — they come in as fast as they go out. But koala bears are forever!"

When almost all is said and done, the four teenagers decide to have some fun of their own as they fuck in pairs on the living room furniture. Again, the soundtrack is energetic, with such titles as "Let Your Body Run," "Plug Me to Death," and "Get Down."

69 min/color. DVD. Arcadia Lake, Beth Anna, Clea Carson, Jean Jennings, Lynda Mantz, Samantha Fox, Serena, Eric Edwards, John Holmes, Peter Andrews, Roger Caine, Ron Hudd. *Director:* John Christopher (as Carle La Blanche). *Writer:* John Christopher (as Carle La Blanche). *Producer:* J. Angel Martine.

Supercock ★★ *(Unknown release date)*
The film opens with stills of beautiful women. Two girlfriends respond to an ad, "Models wanted." Holmes plays Mr. Henderson, who speaks with an unusual English accent, but as it turns out, he is not looking for models, but planning to sell the girls for $2,000 apiece to a shady fellow. When the girls begin to fear

that they are prisoners, they panic and try to escape, but unfortunately for them, an orgy ensues. The film is worth seeing because John plays an interesting bad guy and does a decent job of maintaining his accent throughout. There are some great cinematic angles and interesting scene changes.

Unavailable.

Superstar, John Holmes ★★★★ 1979

Superstar could be considered to be the predecessor to the Julia St. Vincent pseudo-documentary, *Exhausted: John C. Holmes, The Real Story.*

The film opens with still photos of John, including rare images of him as a young man in various sexual poses and a baby photo purported to be The King. Laurien Dominique plays a journalist who is ordered by her employer, a magazine called, *Inside You*, to interview the reclusive porn star, John Holmes. John agrees to the interview, but only under his terms: he insists that they meet in a public place, where he blindfolds her and drives her to the secret location of his mansion.

John's responses to the questions posed by Dominique perpetuate his customary semi-truths sprinkled in amongst the embellished tales. At one point, when she asks how big he is, Holmes impishly replies, "In interviews, I've reported it as being ten, 12… 14 inches long. Is that big enough for you?"

Holmes and Dominique demonstrate an effortless and flirtatious rapport while detailing sexual highs and lows shown in flashbacks. John's stories mostly entail bedding the wives of wealthy husbands, while Laurien describes an incident when she mistakenly thought she was interviewing for a porn movie with a director (Paul Thomas) before finding out he was casting for an educational video!

The hottest sex scene in the film occurs when John enlists the services of a call girl agency. A sultry raven-haired girl (Laura Bourbon) arrives, expecting to give him a massage, but John informs her that he'd rather "get nasty" instead, and offers more money for her compliance. John achieves an imposing erection, but the young woman finds it a real challenge to give him head — at first. Bourbon and Holmes appear to be having a great time in bed.

The cinematography is above average and the actors are terrific. There are some editing mistakes (typical for pornography films), but one continuity error stands out in particular. During their interview, John needs to excuse himself for a while, but informs Laurien that she is free to access anything in his house to occupy her time alone, just as long as she doesn't leave. Laurien chooses to masturbate on John's bed, as almost any woman might have decided, at least in a hardcore film. Watch closely — she wears black stockings, but when the camera cuts to a different angle, she is wearing nude stockings.

The original music, composed by Robert Somm and Steve Grossm, is mostly piano, although there is a great theme song and even a punk number with excellent porno lyrics. Sample lyrics to the *Superstar* title song are: "Babes, they wait in line / always on the road / As long as you've got time / to shoot them your load / Everybody's seen you go by, that's why you're a Superstar."

72 min/color. VHS. Amber Hunt, Laura Bourbon, Laurien Dominique, Nancy Hoffman, Sandy Pinney, John Holmes, Paul Thomas. *Director:* Alan Colberg.

Sweet Cheeks ★★★ 1980

Filmed on location in Carmel, Pismo Beach, Marina Del Rey, and Monterey.

When Regina (Becky Savage) learns that she is terminally ill with only three weeks left to live, she decides to experience all of her sexual fantasies. After donning a Wonder Woman costume, Regina enjoys a quickie in the pool with her boyfriend, Ken (John Holmes), but her mood suddenly becomes somber when she tells him he must go. Regina's risky undertakings include boating, motorcycling, skydiving, a lesbian encounter with Georgia (Rhonda Jo Petty) and screwing two guys at once. What more could a girl ever wish for?

Image courtesy of VCX.com. John in *Sweet Cheeks.*

Randy West makes a unique appearance in an outdoor bathtub scene, wearing a prissy pink apron, as he entices Regina to attend to his unusual carnal needs in a domination/submission sequence. Predictably, when Ken finally discovers exactly what — and who — Regina's been doing during her excursions, he's royally pissed, but allows her to continue to express her freedom as any sympathetic boyfriend might do. The scenery is gorgeous, with many shots of coastal sunsets and tantalizing landscapes. A rock ballad is performed live near the opening, by a band dedicating the theme song to Regina.

65 min/color. DVD. Becky Savage, Rhonda Jo Petty, Sherrie Smith, John Holmes, Randy West (as Johnny West), Kevin James (as Kevin Gibson), Mike Eyke, Mike Ranger, Steve Lacey. *Director:* Joseph F. Robertson. *Writer:* Joseph F. Robertson (as Adele Robbins). *Producer:* Joseph F. Robertson (as Adele Robbins).

Sweet Punkin', I Love You ★★★ 1976

Lowly servant, Punkin' Peel (C.J. Laing), grows weary of her lot in life and attempts to try something new. It isn't long before she is fired from a porn set for being inept in satisfying her onscreen partner (Jon Martin). Punkin' retreats to her quarters and confides to part-time cook and butler, Dixon (Jeffrey Hurst) of her despair.

In the film's subplot, two well-endowed guests, The Great Peter (Tony "The Hook" Perez) and Peter the Great (John Holmes), verbally duke it out as they boast about the beautiful women they've satisfied while showing their super-sized organs to the eager ladies in waiting.

Punkin' serves lunch to her geriatric, millionaire boss, David Crean-Smith (Marlow Ferguson). Her life takes a sudden, uplifting turn when Crean-Smith asks for her hand in marriage because he wants her to bear him an heir to his fortune. Over 200 guests are invited to their wedding, but only the millionaire's attorney, Henry Carswell (Eric Edwards), attends the nuptials as it is revealed that the blue chip crowd disapproves of Crean-Smith's new wife.

Sadly, the newlyweds will not have the opportunity to share their lives together, as David's ticker unexpectedly gives out before he has a chance to make love to his new, young bride. The lost and forlorn Punkin' has a one night stand with her late husband's attorney before once again soliciting the advice of her friend and employee, Dixon Cocks, while giving him a complimentary blowjob.

Together, they orchestrate an orgy of the century that the stuffy socialites won't soon forget. Needless to say, Peter the Great and The Great Peter's organ donations are a welcome party attraction as Punkin' takes them both on with Dixon bringing up the caboose in a salacious four-way. The band, Slim Pickins (who make appearances in four Holmes-Findlay ventures) rocks on, providing excellent musical entertainment for the naked guests.

Typical of Roberta Findlay's films, this contains some truly hilarious moments, particularly when Punkin' is verbally berated by the porn director (David Davidson) for failing to give head the way man had intended for it to be enjoyed. To the disgust of the male recipient, the director proceeds to demonstrate to the cast and crew exactly how it should be done! The comedic and clever dialogue crackles and snaps throughout the film when in the hands of some of the more seasoned thespians. John Holmes is funny as a man of Russian decent; Holmes lays it on thick whenever he opens his mouth.

80 min/color. DVD. C.J. Laing, Crystal Sync, Jennifer Jordan, Marlene Willoughby, Sarah Vache (non-sex), Beverly Bovy (as Tootsie Robysto), Marlow Ferguson (as David Dixon, non-sex), Eric Edwards, Jeffrey Hurst, John Holmes, Tony Perez. *Director:* Roberta Findlay (as Robert Norman). *Writer:* Robert Findlay (as Robert Norman). *Producer:* Robert Michael (as Robert Michaels).

Sweet, Sweet Freedom ★★★★ 1976

Also known as, *Hot Nurses.* Tagline: *"The cure that satisfies — everyone."*

John Holmes plays Dr. Mort, a doctor at the Carcinoma Hospital, who must find a way to save the hospital because patients are dying before they can pay their bills. With its *National Lampoon*-style of humor, this film manages to elicit several laughs, in what seems a parody of porno films, which means the trade-off is that the sex scenes are at times more tepid than hot. The first 15 minutes of the film set up the plot, then the boardroom meeting between hospital staff and medical bigwigs turns into an orgy under the table. When even the prudish hospital big shot, Mrs. Peckham is turned on, we're clued into the fact that the janitor has added a special aphrodisiac called "Spanish Fly" to the hospital's water supply.

Holmes inconsistently tries to use a fake voice to portray his doctor persona, which is fitting in the humorous film. He is vigorous and entertaining, and in the prime of his career. Holmes' scenes, especially with the pharmaceutical nurse (played by Crystal Sync) are the most erotic of the film. These shots use more traditional camera set-ups and feature great original music.

The end of the film is climactic, with the band Slim Pickins playing at a celebratory orgy for the hospital's successful profits and treatment of patients. The music for this film is original and excellent, credited to Harold Hindgrind (Roberta Findlay), Sweet Freedom and Slim Pickins (not the character actor Slim Pickens, but the band that makes four appearances in Holmes-Findlay ventures).

75 min/color. DVD. Crystal Sync, Jenny Baxter, Marlene Willoughby, Mousiendi, Don Peterson, Eric Edwards, Jeffrey Hurst, John Holmes, Zebedy Colt. *Director:* Roberta Findlay (as Anna Riva and Harold Hindgrind). *Writer:* Roberta Findlay (as Anna Riva).

The Swing Thing ★ 1974

John (Holmes) and his significant other, Nora (Brandy Saunders), have unappealing sex in the bathroom of their home before guests show up for a going-away bash. The couple plans to move to Europe so they throw one final sex party before their departure. Two of the invitees, Ron and Fran, arrive early, so Nora sends John to the store to pick up some libations while she entertains them in the bedroom.

When John returns, he enters the kitchen and engages Fran in a game of "hide the banana and cucumber," much to her delight. Next, he orchestrates a hide-and-go-seek adventure with the girls. Wearing blindfolds, they must guess whose member belongs to whom, using a taste test. The neighborly fun comes to a close when Nora announces that dinner is ready.

Appetizing fare, but you'll still feel hungry when it's over.

57 min/color. VHS. Brandy Saunders (as Julia Mure), May Belfort, Rita Lusty, John Holmes.

Tapestry of Passion (This film has not been ranked.) **November 1976**

Also known as *Black Magic.*

The second time that Bob Chinn allowed a friend to use the name "Johnny Wadd" with his permission was for the 1976 film, *Tapestry of Passion.* In the film, Wadd is hired to pursue a perpetrator responsible for a homicide in San Francisco.

One of the sequences from this movie is included on *Garters and Lace,* which includes a string of vignettes. John and Lesllie Bovee sizzle in a smokin' hot sex clip that includes plenty of warm, wet, libidinous kisses. (Bovee could be counted on to be vocal in her on-screen liasons with Holmes.)

In addition, another quality scene from the film features John and Desiree West in a sensual morsel that epitomizes the term "lovemaking." In the mid-'70s, the pairing of a white man and black woman was considered taboo, which made the Holmes/West scene all the more provocative.

Surprisingly, the feature was not a hit in theaters. According to director Alan Colberg, there were other factors (besides lacking the Chinn-Holmes partnership for a successful *Johnny Wadd* venture) that affected the film's box-office potential. Hopefully, this movie will find a distributor and be re-released.

77 min/color. Unavailable. Annette Haven, Desiree West, Lesllie Bovee, Sharon Thorpe, John Holmes, John Leslie. *Director:* Alan Colberg. *Writers:* Alan Colberg, Chris Warfield.

Taxi Girls ★★★ 1979

Tagline: *"Come ride with us. We'll make your meter run like never before."*

John Holmes has a small role in this film, although his presence is certainly not wasted as in some of his cameo appearances. Everything begins with a randy group of hookers in jail, where they gang-bang a receptive officer. The initial orgy sequence does not include the most scintillating camera work, but the humorous plot of the film starts right away. Ignoring all the action, the film's star, Toni (Nancy Suiter) sits against the wall, poring over the classifieds. Meanwhile, another female inmate manages to seduce the sergeant and lock all of the police into the cell — while the women escape.

Toni is the first of the hookers to find a legitimate job, driving a taxi. Jamie Gillis is her first customer and after discovering how much money she can make as a taxi driver, Toni talks her former cellmates into getting jobs as taxi girls. When the girls' plan to convince the taxi owner and manager into giving them all jobs fails, the ladies seduce a loan officer and a car dealer. This incident enables them to open their own company and put the other cab company out of business. The girls' business is very lucrative as a combo taxi-and-prostitution service.

John Holmes enters the film as Toni's caring boyfriend, who wants her to quit hooking and focus instead on her dream of becoming a stand-up comedian. John is thin and sports a goatee when he and Suiter hook up for what is considered to be one of Holmes' legendary sex scenes. They make passionate love on a black-velvet bed. The two actors are committed to their work and Suiter appears to experience genuine orgasms when John performs cunnilingus. In addition, there is a great shot of John's famous "monkey face" during his climax. (Julia St. Vincent would refer to his orgasm expression in this way.)

Toni finally agrees to quit hooking and the couple plans on meeting after her comedy gig that night. When she fails to appear, John becomes worried and suspects that Toni has been kidnapped by the competition. He calls upon the other taxi girls for backup.

Most of the music of the film is average; some of the overdubbed sex noises are below par and the scenes that don't contain Nancy Suiter are lukewarm. On some video versions, there is an error in continuity and a scene at the comedy club is repeated twice. Jaacov Jaacovi and Bob Chinn split the directorial duties, so this would account for the overall uneven presentation, although the film's plot is cohesive throughout. Jaacov Jaacovi was busted for pimping and pandering while directing one of his sex scenes, which resulted in some jail time, although interestingly enough, Chinn was not.

82 min/color. DVD. Adele Lambert, Amber Rae, Aubrey Nichols, Candida Royalle, Celeste, Hillary Summers (as Heather Gordon), Jolanda Borkhurst, Karen Marshall, Maria Tortuga, Nancy Hoffman, Nancy Suiter, Pat Manning, Penny Cash, Serena, Stacy Evans, Svetlana, Bob Arkin, George Mitchell, Jamie Gillis, John Holmes, John Seeman, Mike Ranger, Mitch Morrill, R.J. Reynolds, Ric Lutze. Directors: Jaacov Jaacovi (Jourdan Alexander), Bob Chinn (uncredited); *Writer:* Jaacov Jaacovi (billed as Jourdan Alexander), Bob Oakwood; *Producers:* Jaacov Jaacovi (Jourdan Alexander).

Teenage Cowgirls ★★★ 1973

Tagline: *"Out to the lusty west come these female wildcats who bring every man to his knees — the only way they know how!"*

This delightful porno Western is set to a great opening number, "A Cowboy's Work is Never Done," performed by Sonny and Cher. John Holmes (billed as Long John Wodd) plays Rio, a horse-thieving, womanizing cowboy — complete with chaps, a ponytail, a black hat and cowboy boots. Rio rides a white horse effortlessly as he and his partner Duke scour the parched landscape, searching for lonely women to bed and unsuspecting folks to rob. Fate soon catches up to the two randy cowpokes when they steal from the wrong customer. They are tailed by the angry hombre (but not very successfully), who wants their hides.

In the interim, Rio and Duke ride into a dusty town, where they happen upon a young, dark-haired woman (Amanda Blake) who has been left to attend to the General Store while her husband is away coal mining. After a brief confrontation, she agrees to cook the men red beans and expects they'll soon be on their way. Rio has other ideas, however, as he hoists her over his shoulder and carries her off to the barn, where he gives her something much longer and more memorable than what her husband has to offer. (Be sure to watch for the appearance of a housefly that lands on John's ejaculate after he climaxes on Amanda Blake's tummy!)

After a healthy orgasm, a good night's rest and a kiss goodbye, Rio and Duke depart for new frontiers, singing cowboy songs as they ride happily along. They soon eye a couple of attractive women, who aren't accustomed to greeting new faces. Rio's friend falls hard for the younger beauty and makes out with her while Rio returns to his insatiable cowgirl at the General Store. In round two of their sexual purging, he unfastens an infinite amount of buttons on the girl's long, floral-print dress and complains aloud, "How the hell does a woman ever get screwed in this country?" After he manages to struggle out of his own clothes, he teases her by saying he's now "too tired to fuck."

The story then edges toward an anticipated showdown when the cowboys' nemesis reappears. Holding a gun to the neck of Rio's partner's girl, he demands that the charismatic crooks return his money.

Holmes and his cohort are thoroughly enjoyable as they parlay their best *Butch Cassidy and the Sundance Kid* impressions into this wham-bam spur fest. This light-hearted fare contains a terrific line-up of country tunes, including Tammy Wynette's "Bring Him Home Safely to Me" and "The Joy of Being a Woman," in addition to Hank Snow's "Go with My Heart." The 2008 DVD re-release features a short bonus interview with the always-entertaining Ron Jeremy, reminiscing about his early days in porn.

64 min/color. DVD. Amanda Blake, Jane Wenstein, Sally Withers, John Holmes, Ted Armstrong, Wayne Johnson. *Director:* Ted Denver. *Producer:* Hal Grunquist (Roberta Findlay).

Teenage Cruisers ★★ April 1977

Also known as *Young, Hot 'n' Nasty Teenage Cruisers; Cruising for Sex*. Taglines: *"They'll strip your gears and pop your clutch!" "The '50s, '60s and '70s all come together in the first X-rated rock 'n' roll movie!"*

The best part about this film is its soundtrack, which sports a good number of rock and roll and rockabilly numbers from three decades. The story jumps all over the place, but the main event details a single night involving various people who cruise the streets while interconnecting through random experiences. Local D.J., Mambo Reaves (Johnny Legend), fills the airwaves with nonsensical ramblings.

Big-breasted Babsy Beaudine (Christine deShaffer) has escaped from an asylum and kidnaps a high school teacher, Professor Flinch (Bill Margold), who she forces to become her sex slave.

In a loop dating back to the early-'70s, Moby (John Holmes) swims the length of a pool underwater, before surprising two naked beauties, who immediately

Image courtesy of VCX.com. John as Moby in *Teenage Cruisers* — a spoof of *American Graffiti.*

attach themselves to his mouth and dick prior to being laid out on the pool deck. A kick-ass tune, "Bad Boy," performed by Willy Zoom and the Bad Boys, accompanies big boy Holmes while he does his thing. (Two other notable rockin' numbers, "Bip, Bop, Boom" by Chuck Higgins and "Wail Baby" by Kid Thomas, provide exceptional accompaniment — too good, in fact, for this film.)

More seemingly unrelated sexual scenarios pepper the film. Serena gives a first-rate performance while longing to consummate her relationship with her boyfriend Johnny, and imagines him covering her from head to toe with his load, as if from a can of silly string. Handsome Rick "The Bod" Cassidy makes an appearance in a steamy sex scene with a very willing partner. Out of the blue, two women compete in a televised, topless, bake-off contest, and another scene hints at bestiality as a beautiful woman becomes aroused while brushing her donkey. She disrobes and lies on a hay bale as the camera zooms in on the animal's big, brown eyes.

There isn't a moment to spare in this flick that makes a campy attempt at achieving the cool factor, but it lacks clarity, characterization and continuity. Still, it's jam-packed with all sorts of improbable events.

84 min/color. DVD. Anita Rangoon, Christine deShaffer, Jeanette Dilger, Lynne Margulies, Mabel Joy, Serena, Suzie Snackmeat, Tracy Handfuss, Alvis Wayne, Bernie Margulies, Bill Malin, Bill Margold, Charlie Feathers, Chuck Higgins, Glen Brady, Jerry Sokorski, Jackie Lee 'Waukeen' Cochrane, Jerry Sokorski, Joe Barr, John Galt, John Holmes, Johnny Legend, Kelly Guthrie, Kid Thomas, Kevin Bradley, Larry Conn, Lazlo Oxlips, Mac Curtis, Matt Tuttle, Paul Hajewski, Ray Campi,

Rick Cassidy, Rollin' Colin Winsky, Tony Cohn, Victor Rainbow. Directors: Tom Denucci, Johnny Legend. *Writers:* Tom Denucci, Johnny Legend. *Producers:* Pete Cicero, Tom Denucci, Johnny Legend, Steve Margulies, Victor Resnick.

Teenage Lovers ★½ **March 1975**

Also known as *Hot Teenage Lovers*, *War & Piece*. Tagline: *"A shocking glimpse into the warped morals of…teenage lovers."*

Originally shot in 1971, *Teenage Lovers* takes place during World War II and follows two days in the lives of American soldiers, Earl (John Holmes), Rick (Marlon Malone) and an army nurse named Sue (Susan Saint-Jean).

Lovers Rick and Sue flaunt their passion in front of Earl, who hasn't been laid in months. Each time they make love, Earl ogles them with ravished eyes and mutters to himself how much he wants Sue. Overwhelmed by lust, Earl covers Rick's mouth with ether and has his way with Sue, who doesn't protest too much; in fact, she appears to appreciate Earl's extra inches as she gobbles him up.

When Rick comes to, he pounces on Earl and leaves him on the ground, tending to his bloody mouth. Rick verbally reprimands his comrade for taking what doesn't belong to him until Earl spits back, "Look at the two of you! Married and everything!" The two lovers hang their heads in shame as Earl apologizes for "behaving like an animal."

The soldiers' differences are quickly put aside when they stumble across an oasis in the desert — a seemingly friendly sheik and his harem of beauties (Sandy Dempsey, Andy Bellamy and Rene Bond). The hefty and hairy sheik promises to help the soldiers return to their platoon while inviting them to imbibe with the lovely ladies. After a delicious dinner, Earl doesn't waste a moment before he's making time with Sandy Dempsey in yet another pairing of Holmes with his real-life girl. Dempsey's butterfly tattoo, vivid in most films, appears to be concealed with stage makeup as Holmes effortlessly lifts Sandy into the air while still inside of her. After turning to face the camera, he places her feet on his thighs and slides her delicate frame up and down his shaft, which appears to have the circumference of a soda can at this point. In preparation for the money shot, Earl lays his sultry harem princess on the bed and positions a satin pillow beneath her head.

Eventually, the sheik deems that the trio of guests has worn out their welcome and the next morning, after being banished from his tent, Sandy informs Earl that the sheik plans to turn them over to the Germans. Her warning is too late, however, as a single bullet blasts from the sheik's gun into Earl's back.

The film utilizes stock footage of army tanks and dusty, desert wind storms in order to create realism. Although John's outer garments are appropriate army fatigues, his striped gym socks and his navy bikini briefs do little to support the 1940s setting that the filmmakers tried to achieve. The silly vocal overdubs are yet another mild distraction — at one point, a man's voice impersonates Sue.

Interestingly, Rene Bond (billed as "Lotta Rocks"), sporting a few extra pounds, engages in softcore scenes only, as this was before her foray into XXX flicks. Because she does not yet have implants, Bond is difficult to identify until she breaks out in that undeniable, cheeky smile.

Color. *DVD.* Andy Bellamy, Rene Bond, Sandy Dempsey, Susan St. Jean (a.k.a. Susan Draeger), John Holmes (as Big John Fallus), Marlon Malone.

Tell Them Johnny Wadd is Here ★★★½ 1976

Tagline: *"When Johnny Wadd sees a woman, he takes her!"*

Shot on location in Tijuana, Ensenada and Rosarito Beach, originally this film and *Liquid Lips* were initiated as a longer project, *White Gold*, written by Bob Chinn. The script was divided into two movies for economic purposes. This should be viewed as the fifth *Johnny Wadd* film in the series.

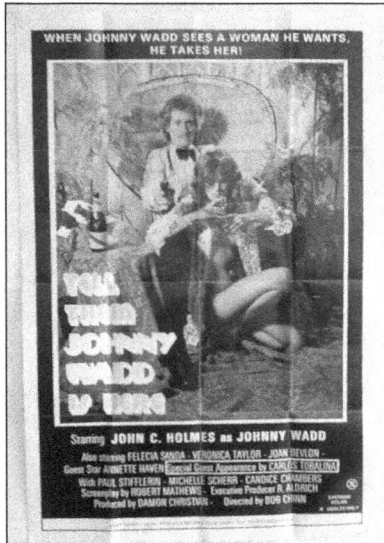

The film opens with Johnny and his latest girl (Annette Haven) about to enjoy an erotic adventure when John receives a panicked call from a friend, Sam Kelly (Paul Stifferin, a.k.a. Damon Christian/ Dick Aldrich), who is in Mexico. Sam's ex-wife, Doreen (Veronica Taylor), has married a drug lord, Tyler Elliot (Tyler Reynolds) and is addicted to heroin.

John agrees to help Sam rescue Doreen in Mexico, but he doesn't depart before pleasuring his lovely girlfriend. Haven transforms the act of oral sex into artistry while going down on John; her tongue and mouth are in syncopation with the soaring Ennio Morricone musical score that accentuates the passion exhibited between John and Annette. The fireplace snaps and crackles, creating an idyllic atmosphere of romance.

When Johnny finally arrives in Mexico, he and Sam are enlisted by Captain Torres (Carlos Tobalina), who is a part of Mexico's Special Units Vice Squad, to aid in halting the drug-smuggling operation. After spending his first night in a Mexican jail, Johnny finds time for rest and relaxation with a bevy of women, as always, while on his assignment. Johnny and Sam split up in their attempts to track down the bad dudes, and in a tragic turn of events, Wadd is left alone in the hotel room, contemplating his next move. Methodically, he pokes bullets into his gun, before spinning it around his finger and returning it to its protective sheath. The scene conjures vivid images of Clint Eastwood as *Dirty Harry*.

One of the most notable sex scenes is with Maria Louisa (Felicia Sanda who played Rod Steiger's girl in the Sergio Leone feature, *Duck You Sucker*). The lovely Mexican actress had initially signed up to do a softcore scene with John, but in the heat of the moment, the scene transformed into a hot, hardcore interlude instead.

Holmes delivers a line in this film that has since been immortalized in P.T. Anderson's *Boogie Nights* by lead actor, Mark Wahlberg. Wadd confronts a feisty blonde who refuses to give up the information he is after, so he states evenly, "I'm gonna be nice, and I'm gonna ask you one more time — Where's Ringo?" When she refuses to talk, Wadd slaps her across the face, but her lips remain sealed.

The Spanish-themed musical score, "La Resa dei conti" (also used in *Liquid Lips*) is fitting to the material, which serves to perfectly complement this soft-hearted, tough-guy, hardcore movie. *Tell Them Johnny Wadd is Here* is a pivotal arch in John Holmes' prolific career and contains a concise mystery-adventure

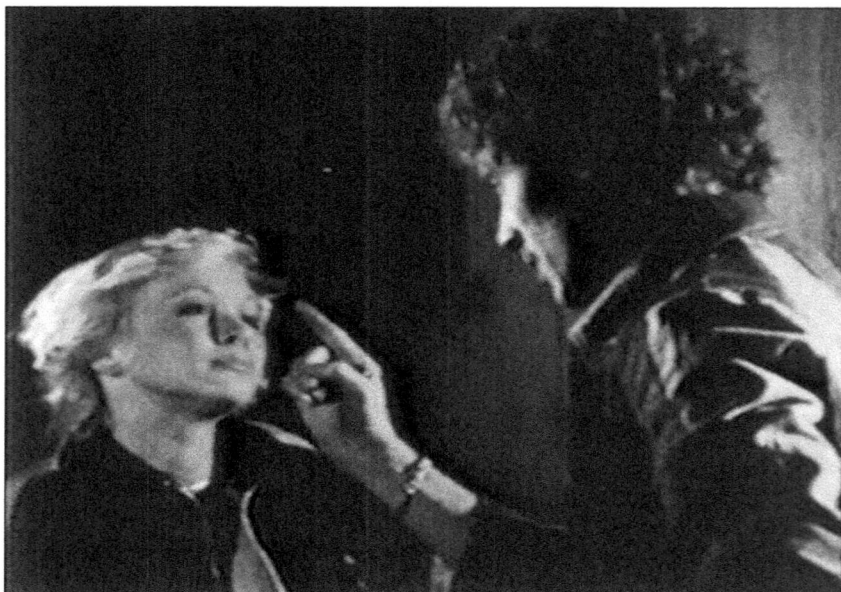

"I'm gonna be nice, and I'm gonna ask you one more time — Where's Ringo?"

story. As a high-profile and hugely profitable picture, this solidified John Holmes and Johnny Wadd as industry names. In 1976, Carlos Tobalina won best supporting actor at the Adult Film Association of America Awards for his work in a non-sex role.

74 min/color. DVD. Annette Haven, Elsa Sanchez, Felicia Sanda, Norma Posulez, Veronica Taylor, Amparo Salazar, Carl Adams, Carlos Tobalina, Daniel Hussong (Bob Chinn, non-sex), Fermin Castillo del Muro, Eddie Carrillo, Greg Anderson, Jerry Wade, John Holmes, Lazaro Valdes, Lynn Harris, Michael C. Le Duff, Michelle Scherr, Paul Stifferin (a.k.a. Damon Christian/Dick Aldrich), Rosario Carrillo, Tommy Batello, Tyler Horn. *Director:* Bob Chinn; Assistant *Director:* John C. Holmes. *Writer:* Bob Chinn. *Producers:* Freeway Films.

Those Young Girls (This film has not been ranked.) **November 1984**

Appropriately named, *Those Young Girls* is the tale of two childhood friends who reunite in the City of Angels. Adult star Traci (Lords) and her live-in costar Harry (Reems) are visited by aspiring actress Ginger (Lynn). After the two become reacquainted, Traci suggests that Ginger audition for her agent, Eric

(John Holmes). Eric quickly discovers that Ginger has no previous experience and exclaims, "You're probably perfect for this business!"

Eric excuses himself for a moment to take a phone call, while Ginger disrobes. With a ripe banana in her hand, she declares, "Lunch is served." The two begin to satiate one another on Eric's desk.

"You're one of the best girls I've ever met in this business, and I've auditioned all of them."

Feigning innocence, Ginger looks up at him with wonderment, "You mean I'm not the first?"

Eric wittily replies, "The first one this morning."

Ginger is promptly hired.

Remarkably, Traci Lords was only 16 when the feature was shot, so all copies of the feature in the United States were destroyed once the movie became part of a Federal Case. (The Lynn/Holmes' scene from this film is available as a featurette on the re-release of *The Devil and Mr. Holmes* by Paradise Visuals.) The producers were charged with child pornography, but were later acquitted when it was proven that Lords had provided them with an expertly falsified driver's license at the time she was hired. This incident resulted in a ripple effect of resentment within the adult community, toward Lords.

72 min/color. Unavailable. Ginger Lynn, Traci Lords, Harry Reems, John Holmes. *Director:* Miles Kidder. *Writers:* Ginger Lynn, Ernest Mackintosh, Frank Mackintosh. *Producers:* Ernest Mackintosh, Frank Mackintosh.

Three Came Running ★★ 1974

Holmes portrays a college professor who cons three of his female students into having coitus with him and he "borrows" their hard-earned cash. When the girls eventually get together to compare notes, they plot their revenge by dispatching him off to an attic and enslaving him for sex. Outraged by his audacity, the girls plan to fuck him to death.

Unbeknownst to the girls, the prof's pal sneaks him bananas to sustain his energy through their torture. Soon, the tables are turned and an ambulance arrives on the scene to take the women away, as the professor's stamina proves to be too much for them.

Andrea True plays the red-headed beauty, Judy. Two years later, True would record the disco hit, "More, More, More" with the Andrea True Connection.

50 min/color. VHS. Aleen May (a.k.a. Andrea True), Cheryl Britt, Nancy Dare, Sally O'Brien, Hal Buck, Jimmie Norton, John Holmes (as John Rey).

The Touch ★★ 1976

After a delayed flight, a woman named Snow arrives at the apartment of a smarmy drug lord, Mario (John Holmes). Snow perches on top of a bar stool, as Mario (clad in a royal blue dressing gown with slicked-down hair) makes a dramatic entrance. It is apparent that the two are more than slightly familiar with one another and Snow doesn't mince words when she spouts, "You motherfucker, Mario."

He smiles with smug confidence because he has a stag tape with her in it. In order for her to get the tape, he wants her to unload $100,000 worth of cocaine, which he presents to her inside of a stuffed frog. Snow reluctantly agrees to return in one week with the cash in hand.

After Snow's departure, Mario turns his attention to the slim, blonde maid, who has arrived to tidy his suite. Mario lays the maid down on his bed and undresses her slowly, savoring every moment of foreplay until he is deep inside of her.

Out on the street, Snow calls friends to help her disperse the coke. Snow considers the possibility that Mario won't fulfill his end of the bargain and give her the tape, so she cooks up a plot wherein two of her girlfriends sneak into Mario's apartment with her at the end of the week.

When the time comes, she and Mario engage in guarded banter before she announces that in addition to the money, she has a bonus for him. The two women come out of hiding and plunk down onto his lap while Snow waits patiently for the ménage-a-trois to begin. Impressed by Snow's generosity, Holmes breaks out of character for a moment and as he unzips the blonde from her gown, he quips, "This is like Fort Knox for titties!"

The girls keep Mario's hands busy and their mouths full, so that Snow can locate the tape. Armed with a tube of lipstick, she scribbles a parting shot across Mario's bedroom mirror before disappearing into the night.

Color. DVD. Jean French, Louise Barnet, Susie Carlson, John Holmes, Lincoln Regan.

Treasure Box ★★ 1985

Two fishing buddies (Shone Taylor and Jesse Adams) catch gold coins on the end of a fish hook instead of bass and believe they've made a fortune. The guys celebrate with cold beer and some impromptu sex with a delivery girl from the nearby sporting goods store, where they purchase scuba diving gear. Donning snorkels and fins, the guys search for more nuggets in the lake. Later, they solicit a financial consultant, who ascertains the full value of the coins.

Unfortunately, the two male leads are not nearly as attractive as the women, rendering the copulation scenes average, but John Holmes and Karen Summer's frantic sexcapade on the kitchen counter makes up for the underachievers.

During a break on the set of *Treasure Box* with Kimberly Carson.

This was likely shot in the home of Bill Amerson, on Crownridge Avenue in Sherman Oaks, as many of Amerson's VCX and Penguin films were.

69 min/color. DVD. Gina Carrera, Karen Summers, Kimberly Carson, Melanie Scott, Tamara Longley, Jesse Adams, John Holmes, Tyler Reynolds, Shone Taylor. *Director:* Patti Rhodes-Lincoln. *Writer:* Patti Rhodes-Lincoln. *Producer:* Penguin Productions.

Image courtesy of VCX.com. Seducing Sandy Carey in *Tropic of Passion.*

Tropic of Passion ★★½ 1972

Also known as *Fantasex Weekend.* Fourth in the *Johnny Wadd* series.

Private Dick, Johnny Wadd, makes love to his current squeeze and secretary (Chlorine Stillwater) before setting off for Hawaii to obtain the one film that stands in the way of heiress Ruth Miller (Patti Snyder) receiving her fortune.

Johnny and Ruth meet in his hotel suite, where they chat briefly and have drinks on the balcony, before he carries her inside for a quickie on the carpet. The two don't seem to "click" physically and Snyder, who made her sole appearance in this adult film, is average looking. However, two of Holmes' favorite costars, Sandy Carey and his real-life girlfriend Sandy Dempsey, both make spirited appearances during scenes with John, as well as with Mike Haven, who plays Ruth's lawyer.

Probably the most amusing part of the movie is when John asks Ruth's lawyer, Alex Royale, about a "short, stocky Chinese guy," who has been following him since he arrived in Hawaii.

Royale replies, "Who? You mean Fuk Yu?"

John begins to crack up. This short interchange epitomizes the fun, carefree mood that prevailed during the early *Johnny Wadd* days.

Tropic of Passion was shot on location in Hawaii, so many of the sex scenes feature Hawaiian music. The scenarios that Chinn creates are above average and his obligatory non-sex appearance as the bad guy, Fuk Yu, is a highlight. The club scene in *Tropic of Passion* where John appears on stage with live sex-show performer Zelda Bergesson was shot at the Risque Book Store/Esquire Theater. Holmes later worked as a performer at the same theater for a period of months after the film was completed.

77 min/color. DVD. Casandra, Chlorine Stillwater, Patti Snyder, Sandy Carey, Sandy Dempsey (as Tiffany Stewart), Zelma (as Cassandra), Bob Chinn (non-sex). John Holmes (as John Duval), John Keith, Mike Haven. *Director:* Bob Chinn (as Bob A. Lain). *Writer:* Bob Chinn (as Bob A. Lain); *Producer:* Chinn-Adrain Productions.

Turn-on Orgy ★ 1971

This film doesn't pretend to strive for anything other than what the title suggests and even at that, it's a waste of time. All of the actors are uncredited. Baby-faced John Holmes, (along with his blonde costar on the couch), is center stage among the rest of the group. It would seem that Holmes got preferential coverage even in 1971.

The participants screw and screw, and change partners like they're playing a game of musical chairs, but they appear unenthused (Too much of a good thing, no doubt). The high point of the film arrives when John orgasms after a solid 10-minute deep throat session by the young brunette, Stephanie Sarver. At the orgy, everyone applauds her diligent efforts as one woman shouts, "What are we going to do next week?" Meanwhile, John is all smiles as he reaches out for the blonde's hand to signal that he's ready for another round.

29 min/color. DVD. Debra Christian, Heather Starr, Stephanie Sarver, John Holmes, John Keith.

Undulations ★★½ 1980

Tagline: *"The ultimate trip around the world...in motion!"*

In the few times that John Holmes and Jamie Gillis appeared together, the viewer can rest assured that they are in for a unique treat. Three women (Kitty Shayne, Mai Lin and Suzanne French) host a sex talk show, which runs a brief teaser, depicting Gillis in a three-way with his real-life ex-girlfriend, Serena, and Maria Cruz. The talk show hosts have invited special guests Jamie Gillis and John C. Holmes to join them in a discussion about their preferences in the opposite sex and in the bedroom. The gentlemen allow the female hosts to dish about their intimacies first. During their descriptions, footage is shown of their experiences and fantasies.

Afterwards, the tables are turned and the ladies ask the men what they enjoy. Gillis deadpans, "I masturbate to John Holmes movies," which elicits a great round of chuckles from the group.

John confides that he prefers "petite, feminine ladies," in addition to a little pick-me-up and he produces a vial of white powder with a miniature spoon. Holmes takes a little snort before politely passing his treat around to the rest of the panel. The ladies are delighted and all three imbibe, but Jamie declines John's offer. John points out that the female talk show hosts take small, delicate toots of his cocaine and jokes that once they become better acquainted with it, they'll drop everything for another snort. The irony, of course, is that this film was likely shot during the latter part of 1980, when Holmes was knee deep in his coke addiction, which had already manifested itself in his rail-thin frame and jittery mannerisms.

When the gang finally decides to stop talking about sex and get down to it, Jamie, Kitty and Mai begin to pleasure one another, while John gives his attention to Suzanne. The camera intermittently cuts away from Holmes and French, in favor of focusing on Jamie with his nubile partners. This is rather uncommon in a John Holmes film, so perhaps it is due to John's skeletal physique and poor performance.

Although it's an unusual example of adult material, *Undulations* does manage to undulate.

76 min/color. Unavailable. Brooke West, Juliet Anderson, Kitty Shayne, Mai Lin, Maria Cruz, Serena, Suzanne French, Billy Dee, Jamie Gillis, John Holmes, Jon Martin. *Director:* Troy Benny (a.k.a. Carlos Tobalina).

Up 'n' Coming ★★★★ January 1983

Also known as *Cassie*. Tagline: *"In the history of erotic films, no one has achieved the following Marilyn has."*

Marilyn Chambers stars as Cassie Harland, a rising country songstress who sleeps her way to the top. Harland wages war against a woman she once aspired to be — now a washed-up, alcoholic country diva, Althea Anderson (Lisa DeLeeuw). Anderson is about to be put to pasture, but refuses to go down without a fight.

Chambers and DeLeeuw supply their own vocals within this big-budget production features beautiful footage of Catalina Island. DeLeeuw looks slightly heavier than she did a few years prior to this and rougher around the edges. (DeLeeuw dropped out of adult films in 1987 and passed away from AIDS complications in 1993.) Chambers demonstrates her agility in various sexual encounters that include Richard Pacheco as radio personality, Tommy Harper and Herschel Savage (who is very good in the role as Harland's hard-boiled studio executive, Jimmy King).

The film builds toward a crescendo that pairs Harland with a legendary outlaw, Charlie Strayhorn (John Holmes). Cassie is smitten when she gets a dose of Strayhorn's pleasure package, as he stands naked before her and asks, "Can I get you a drink, darlin'?" Holmes, who was freshly released from his stay for contempt of court, was reportedly brought in to save the picture by attaching his notorious name and appendage to the project. It worked.

The Special Edition DVD includes an audio commentary provided by Gloria Leonard, with a Marilyn Chambers photo section and cast bio.

86 min/color. DVD. Brandy, Cody Nicole, Lili Marlene, Lisa DeLeeuw, Loni Sanders, Marilyn Chambers, Monique Gabrielle, Tina Marie, Clay Tanning, Ferris Weel, Herschel Savage, Jay B. David (non-sex), John Holmes, John Lazar, Marc Wallice, Richard Pacheco, Steve Douglas, Steve Douglas, Tom Byron, Winston Cleet. *Director:* Stu Segall. *Writer:* Jim Holliday. *Producer:* John Harvey, Stu Segall.

Image courtesy of Paradise Visuals. John and Ron Jeremy in *W-Pink TV.*

W-Pink TV ★★★★ 1985

This commercially successful sex comedy is one of the only films featuring the legends John Holmes, Ron Jeremy and Harry Reems together.

Two television news hosts, Ron Jeremy and Christy Canyon, are in cahoots when they take over their network and turn it into a late-night sex show. The network's secret agent, Scorpio (Harry Reems), arrives incognito on the scene, determined to get to the bottom of the mutiny.

Naturally, the film showcases veterans and newbies together in various sexual acts, including a notably steamy scene between Jeremy and Canyon. Later, a refreshed Jeremy, wearing tails and sparkling bikini briefs, is the host of a special segment called, "Beat the Cock," where three blindfolded female contestants must guess the owner of the guest cock as they join him in various sexual shenanigans. Holmes is the mystery guest, although the ladies guess other adult legends who don't quite measure up, like Eric Edwards and Ron Jeremy.

All hell breaks loose when Scorpio is seduced by Christy Canyon, and soon a finale orgy ensues, with participation from much of the cast, including a young Marc Wallice. Despite her other scenes being cut because she was underage at the time of filming (a fact that the producers at Paradise Visuals were unaware of during production), Ali Moore was not deleted from the "Beat the Cock" segment with John Holmes on the Special Edition DVD, for unknown reasons. The DVD also features an interview facilitated by Bill Margold with Ron Jeremy and Christy Canyon. Laurie Holmes also joins the group for the final five minutes.

85 min/color. DVD. Ali Moore, Christy Canyon, Dallas Miko, Josephine Carrington, Laurie Holmes, Tamara Longley, Harry Reems, John Holmes, Marc Wallice, Ron Jeremy. *Director:* Myles Kidder. *Producer:* Paradise Visuals.

The Winning Stroke ★★½ 1973

Hal (John Holmes) is the friend of tennis superstar, Bart Madsen (Ric Lutze). He arrives at Bart's home, accompanied by a female fan (Amanda Blake) of Madsen and before long, Bart is busy entertaining the young admirer in the bedroom. Hal decides to have fun with a female reporter, who is impatiently waiting for an exclusive interview with Madsen.

He attempts to entice her into having sex with him by promising the interview in exchange. His intuition is right, but first he must play along with her requests. The reporter asks Hal about Bart, and he supplies some funny responses, such as saying that Bart uses "milk to shampoo his hair."

Hal and another of Bart's buds (Rick Cassidy) love using Bart's reputation to score with chicks. The best sequence in the movie is the three-way group sex between Hal and two of Bart's fans, Milly and Molly (Cyndee Summers and Jennifer West). One of the girls pets a black and white kitten while Hal focuses his attention on her friend. Holmes makes silly faces and teases the girls, while really seeming to connect with the sex. When Bart eventually joins the threesome after the money shot, he asks Hal to leave so he can enjoy the girls by himself. Hal calls him "a greedy bastard."

The re-release of this film on DVD contains an insightful, 10-minute 1985 interview with Holmes, conducted by Kathy Kennedy. John is attractive and appears to be healthy (he comments on the fact that he is still alive) as he announces the formation of his business venture, Penguin Films, with his partner, Bill Amerson. In addition, John discusses his personal preferences regarding erotic movies and provides advice for swingers.

58 min/color. DVD. April, Amanda Blake, Cyndee Summers, Jennifer West, Tawny Pearl, George Wilson, John Holmes, Rick Cassidy, Ric Lutze. *Director:* Simon Egree. *Producer:* Otto de la Croche.

SELECTED LOOPS SYNOPSES

John Holmes was in numerous loops from the 1960s through the early 1980s. The synopses of the loops are organized in alphabetical order by their production companies, if known. All of these loops were silent, unless otherwise noted.

13": *The Joys of Sex,* circa 1970.

A very young-looking John Holmes spies on a blonde girl, who is sitting on a blue velvet couch, reading a book called *The Joys of Sex.* He gets turned on watching her read and begins to lick his lips and pull at the bars on the door like he is in a jail cell. Oblivious to him, the girl also becomes excited and begins to touch her small breasts through her red dress. John moves to the window for a better view before sneaking into her place! Amazingly, she isn't startled to see him; instead, she looks pleasantly surprised. John's hair is long and slicked down, and he's wearing a brown leather jacket.

Setting the book aside, the couple moves into her bedroom for a fellatio scene in which John stands on the bed and rests his hands on the ceiling, which highlights his thin frame and impressively long and thick member. His cum drips down her neck before she lies back to have intercourse. He appears to say something to her, to which the viewer is not privy (this is a silent loop without dialogue or captions), but she smiles and looks like she enjoys him going in and out, very slowly. The camera cuts before the couple switches to doggie style and John makes his monkey face prior to having another orgasm onto her buttocks.
10 minutes.

B #105: *The Photographer,* early 1970s.

This silent loop begins with John standing above a couple making out on a bed. John plays a photographer, but he puts down his camera when they get turned on and decide to have a threesome. John helps the other guy remove the girl's panties and shows him how to hold open her vagina for cunnilingus. The other guy goes down on the girl and John French kisses her. After the two guys get naked, the girl fellates John while the other guy resumes what he was doing before. When the guy and girl do cunnilingus, John patiently waits and caresses her back with his fingers and kisses her neck and shoulders.

She mounts the guy in cowgirl-style and John stands in front of her for more oral pleasure, which inspires John to briefly pick up his camera to capture some of the action on eight millimeter film. Next, the girl lies on her stomach and enjoys a rim job from the man while she continues to please John orally, while he kneels in front of her face. The other guy gets it up again and penetrates her before climaxing onto her fur. She tastes it. John and the girl do 69 for a very brief time and then he lies back for another blowjob from her, without ever climaxing.

12 minutes.

Diverse: *Terrible Aunt Candy,* late 1970s.

In this late-'70s loop, John Holmes masturbates on a bed until Aunt Candy (Candy Samples) intrudes on his private party. Disapprovingly, she reprimands him — there is a narrator who explains this — and sends him to bed without any supper.

Naturally, she joins him in the sack and teaches him a lesson by forcing him to have (simulated) sex with her. (Interestingly enough, John and Candy acted out a similar scenario in a 1971 film called *Love Boccaccio Style,* where she played the head mistress of a convent and John pretended to be a deaf mute.) They spend a fair bit of time going through the motions of phony sex — but they aren't fooling anyone. John is far better when he has free reign to strut his stuff.

10 minutes.

Diverse: *Artists and Models Ball,* late 1970s.

This loop also is narrated. Candy Samples plays a painter whose subjects are John Holmes and a young, pretty brunette. She requests that they remove their clothes while directing them to get butt-naked on the bed. For a while, Candy acts as a spectator and they turn one another on, then she joins in.

John's oral activity on the brunette is authentic, but what follows is softcore. Candy and the brunette hold John's penis to their mouths, but it doesn't get the attention it is accustomed to, in this simulated adventure.

10 minutes.

Ero/Phase Productions: *Big Boob Casting Call,* 1979.

Wearing a white hat and smoking a cigar at the beginning of this softcore loop, John plays a casting agent who auditions three women — Uschi Digard, Kitten Natividad, and Keli Stewart. Seated at his desk, he invites the women to display their assets and remove their tops for him. After inspecting each of them carefully, he sits on top of the desk while Kitten opens his zipper. The women fondle him and simulate oral sex as John conjures his "monkey face" to suggest that he is excited and holding off his orgasm. Kitten is featured more prominently than the other two girls, and spends time handling him as the scene alternates between he and Kitten and the other two ladies.

Holmes excels as a hardcore performer, so it is unusual to see him doing anything less than the real thing, however, it is no secret that his substance abuse had impeded his stamina and ability to perform at this stage in his career.

This loop was reused in the feature film, *John Holmes and the All-Star Sex Queens,* in which the silent loop was enhanced by narration.

13 minutes. Keli Stewart, Kitten Natividad, Uschi Digard, John Holmes.

Ero/Phase Productions: Big Tit Hookers, 1979.

This loop features the same foursome as *Big Boob Casting Call.* John plays a sailor who hires the women to satisfy his sexual needs while off-duty. They roll around in bed together until John ultimately winds up with Kitten (John's history with auburn-haired women suggests that his fondness for them ran a close second to his penchant for brunettes). He lies on top of her and they engage in some tongue tangling. These two loops are designed for men with a breast fetish, but because it is simulated sex (with some beaver shots), others might be left in the cold.

This loop was reused in the feature film, *John Holmes and the All-Star Sex Queens,* in which the silent loop was enhanced by narration.

13 minutes. Keli Stewart, Kitten Natividad, Uschi Digard, John Holmes.

Fanny Films #7: 14 Inches Deep, early 1970s.

Two women walk into a living room and sit on a plaid couch before placing a call to a male-escort service. A short time later, John Holmes (with his hair combed down, wearing a light-colored suit and smoking a pipe) comes over and announces — through captions, "Here's your superstud, girls."

He takes a seat between them on the couch and they ask, "Have you got a really big prick?"

"You better believe it."

The girls insist that he show it to them, and after rubbing him through his pants, they remove it and are amazed: "That's enough for both of us," says one of the girls.

John's penis is large and firm and he appears to thoroughly enjoy both girls giving him head simultaneously. When one of the girls asks John to eat her pussy for a while, he obliges, and her friend keeps herself occupied by continuing to suck on John's manhood while lying on her back on the red, shag comforter covering the bed supporting the three of them. After having her fill of sucking his dick, the girl under John tells him to put it inside of her friend and assists him in doing so. Not too long afterward, her friend requests that John put it in her ass. John does so, just a little bit at a time, while the friend licks her clitoris.

A little while later, it's time for the friend to get some action, so John lies on his back on top of the bed and she mounts him reverse cowgirl style. John has an orgasm while both girls resume performing fellatio together on his penis. Remarkably, the money shot is filmed directly on, so that the viewer can observe John's orgasm from a seldom-used angle. The girls appear to lick some of his ejaculate, although both of them manage to spit it back out while they kiss one another. John waves goodbye to them after getting dressed.

10 minutes.

Hot Cream & Cherries, early 1970s.

John lies naked on his back and watches as Sandy Dempsey (with her cute butterfly tattoo clearly visible on the top of her thigh) and Sandy Carey make a whip cream confection atop his banana. They top it off with chocolate sauce, nuts and cherries before eating it up. John's penis is as thick as one of their fore-arms, but they manage just fine in giving him a very tasty blowjob.

10 minutes. Sandy Carey, Sandy Dempsey, John Holmes.

John's Girls #5: Mind Blowers, early 1970s.

In this installment, two girls — a blonde and a brunette (the same long-haired brunette from the loop *Bare Harbor*) — are in bed and ask to see "it" (by way of a caption). John shows it to them and the subtitle reads, "Suck it, girls." The two ladies (with big, elaborate false eyelashes) go at it together for a while before the brunette takes over so the blonde can get undressed and remove her friend's panties and taste her pussy.

He first has sex with the blonde. Next, the two girls get into the 69 position with each other and John goes behind the long-haired beauty to penetrate her vaginally. There is a rather innovative position used later in the loop, when John pumps away at her doggie-style and the blonde has her head between his legs, licking John and the other girl at the same time. At the end, he comes on the blonde's face and she laps it up.

Presumably as John earned more money with each appearance, he bought more jewelry, and in this loop, he wears a thick, gold chain bracelet, a necklace, and a ring on his left index finger.

9 minutes.

John's Girls #8: Campers Pickup Mountain Girls, early 1970s.

A truck with a camper parks on top of a hill in the wilderness. John and a fat, bald guy hop out of the truck's cab. The guys go around to the back of the truck and help two ladies — a blonde and a brunette — out of the camper. John takes the brunette's hand and the blonde is saddled with the overweight man. The couples set up their sleeping bags and begin making out with the ladies. After simultaneous acts of cunnilingus, the young women go down on the guys. John takes advantage of lying so close to the other couple and fingers the blonde. A split screen shows both blowjobs, side by side.

Both guys stand to finish undressing and then John helps his partner out of her wrap dress and the bald guy takes off the blonde's bra while they do it doggie style before switching to missionary. After enjoying more fellatio, John picks up the brunette for some vertical sex. She wriggles in his arms, clearly enjoying herself, and John has no trouble holding her. On the other hand, when the camera shows the blonde girl with the other guy, she appears to be think-ing about her weekend plans, what's for dinner — anything but the guy she's having sex with.

For a very brief switch-up, John's brown-haired girl mounts the other guy in reverse cowgirl. After she gets off of him, the couples move farther away from one another, to more private areas in the bushes. There, both guys finish the scene with facial cum shots.

13 minutes.

John Holmes #2: California Girl, early to mid 1970s.

John sits on the couch, reading a newspaper as a girl with long, silky blonde hair tries to get his attention while sitting at the bar. She pours both of them a drink and brings it over to him, but he still ignores her. With his nose buried in the paper, he pretends that he doesn't notice her as she slides out of her little black dress and panties. Beginning to get angry, she puts her hands on her hips, while John giggles behind his paper. He finally pays the poor girl some attention when she unzips his pants and begins to fellate him and he happily tosses the paper away.

He stands to take off his shirt and mouths, "Yes!" before he puts his penis into her. The girl mouths, "Oh, my God," and appears to enjoy herself while she plays with her breasts. John starts to make faces that indicate he is doing his best to hold off the inevitable orgasm for a little bit more oral action. The girl isn't able to fit more than the head of his swollen penis into her mouth. The scene concludes with a facial.

8 minutes.

JH #3: Barbershop Trio, early 1970s.

In this dubbed loop, clean-shaven John brushes the long hair of a brunette while she is seated in a barber's chair. When his redheaded assistant joins in, John instantly attends to her. John and the two women stand and disrobe. John kisses the redhead passionately while the brunette gives him head while on her knees.

Holmes spends the rest of the short with the redhead, while the brunette looks on, somewhat longingly. Finally, John orgasms onto her buttocks.

5 minutes.

John Holmes International #12: Deep Thrust, late 1970s or early 1980s.

A woman with cute, short, dark hair motions for John to come inside when she sees him out of her kitchen window. On the porch, they hug passionately before going back inside by the fireplace. He lies her down on some oversized pillows and begins gentle cunnilingus. She stands to unzip her dress, revealing a sheer, purple bra with cut-outs for her nipples and a satin, purple garter belt (beneath a prominent scar on her abdomen). John takes off his dark blue shirt and enjoys some fellatio from her while sitting in a leather chair.

Then, she lies back down on the pillows in front of the roaring fire. He carefully lies on top of her for one more kiss before entering her. She wiggles around with pleasure beneath his deep thrusts. They maneuver into a couple of other positions that demonstrate her flexibility, and clearly, the actress is into the action as her vagina is able to accommodate John to the hilt without apparent discomfort. After mounting him in cowgirl position, she gets on her back one last time for a little more fellatio prior to the cumshot. After the facial, the actress still seems to be turned on as she continues to lick and suck his member with vigor.

8 minutes.

Just Good Friends, May 7, 1969.

In this silent softcore loop that runs approximately 15 minutes, fresh-faced John Holmes and pal Dave Harris are all smiles as they enjoy a barley sandwich together at the kitchen table. Soon, they move into the bedroom where the guys get naked and embark upon a sexual odyssey of kisses and under-the-cover play.

Startling, of course, is the stark difference between Holmes' and Harris' appendages. John's is thick and resembles an elephant trunk, whereas Harris' is average-sized and unremarkable. The fellows wrap things up in the shower together. Throughout the short, John exudes an endearing effervescence that distinguishes many of his performances.

Limited Edition: Four-part, color loop with audio and dialogue, from the late 1970s.

In the first part of this loop series, John plays a basketball player and the bosomy Connie Peterson plays a sportswriter assigned to interview him. John quips, "I could tell you were a sporting woman when you came in here!" prior to their make-out in his living room. He promises to answer her questions through-out their sex session and gets her into the forward position for cunnilingus, as they chat the entire time.

When it is her turn to give him head, Connie exclaims, "You're so big!"

John responds, "You're so little … opposites attract."

After a while, it is time for the anal scene (Peterson's specialty) and John exclaims "You must have had this done before because it went right in there! Doesn't it hurt just a little bit?" He tells her how to move to accommodate him, she squeals with pleasure.

They also do it missionary style, and when Connie calls it "making love," John corrects her, "It's not making love, it's making whoopee!" The scene ends in a facial as Connie literally swoons. This loop is an example of how any mundane, repetitive sex scene can be considerably enhanced by audio.

7 minutes.

In the second part of this story, John and the voluptuous Lisa DeLeeuw are in the locker room, apparently attracted to one another. They happen to be basketball teammates, wearing matching green uniforms with green-and-white-striped socks. John initiates things by fondling DeLeeuw's large breasts, and in turn, she sits down on the bench to pull his penis out of his shorts and devours him.

They joke around throughout the scene, using basketball references, making it enjoyable to watch. When DeLeeuw asks how long the season lasts while he is penetrating her deeply from behind, John replies, "As long as it stays hard," then adds, "It goes deep into the year."

Later, she pants, "This must be what they call the Super Ball," so John corrects her that it's actually "Bowl," and that the term applies to the sport of football.

Lisa rides John in reverse cowgirl position and while she bounces up and down, he laughs, "I can feel your clit hitting my balls!" She lies on her back on the bench and squeezes her freckled breasts together, before John climaxes on them.

7 minutes.

In the third scene, John (still wearing his basketball shorts and jersey) and a girlfriend (in a black negligee) argue about his obsession with basketball. When she accuses him of thinking of nothing else but his sport, he retorts, "Well, it bought you that negligee and keeps you in tampons!"

She is also upset because she found out that one of John's teammates is a young female (Lisa DeLeeuw). John downplays Lisa's significance by explaining that she's only 19 and is the recipient of a scholarship. His girlfriend shakes her head in disbelief.

She isn't so angry that she can't supply some fellatio while the jock flips through a magazine. Next, it's her turn as she lifts her legs high into the air for John to give her his 12 inches. After turning her over, he orgasms on her buttocks.

4 minutes.

Limited Edition #80: Water Nymph, late-'70s

In the fourth and concluding scene from John's basketball storyline, John and another teammate (Biff Parker) join Lisa DeLeeuw in the shower after a game. They sandwich her and argue about who will go first, while Lisa appears to enjoy the attention provided by both men. In a boyish manner, John sweet-talks Lisa and kisses her, thereby managing to tear her away from Biff.

As a result of his efforts, she gives him head while Biff works it from behind. Biff enjoys a noisy climax, and then, in a rather creative stunt, Lisa lies across Biff's back while she and John have vaginal sex. A John Holmes facial wraps things up.

7 minutes. Lisa DeLeeuw, Biff Parker, John Holmes.

PH #1: "Japanese Massage", early 1970s.

John appears to be quite young and baby-faced in this clip, but his thick afro indicates that this was likely shot in the early-'70s. The title card misspells the word "Massage" as "Message," but we get the idea!

Naked in a waterbed with plush, velvet red covers, John and a petite girl make out. She smiles genuinely as he lays her on her back and continues the foreplay, with gentle kisses on her breasts and tummy, teasing his way down to her pussy. While he goes down on her, she runs her fingers through his long, curly locks and down his thin-but-strong arms. They sit up for more kisses and he motions for her to get up on her knees to perform fellatio. He sits back to enjoy it, while caressing her back the entire time. The camera closes in on her face before cutting to a different angle and allowing the actors time to reposition.

Again, they kiss before John moves her body to try and let the camera have a view of penetration, but his butt is in the way. After he is snugly inside of her, he moves her legs up for faster and deeper action, before cumming onto her soft belly. There is an editing mistake that results in doubling the money shot.

6 minutes.

Playmate #1: It Takes a Thief, 1973 or 1974.

John dons a black-knitted cap and black turtleneck sweater as he uses a screwdriver to cut through the screen door and break into the bedroom of a beautiful young woman (Gilda Grant). She awakens and is frightened that a stranger is in her bedroom, but he is able to seduce her with ease and Gilda relaxes. John is tender after a somewhat aggressive beginning to this silent clip.

Mark Novick, who shot this scene, recalls that it was filmed at a swingers' house in Los Angeles one evening, and that John actually had his own bedroom at the residence. Additionally, Gilda Grant wore Novick's high school ring as a pendant on her necklace during this shoot.

Gilda and John were involved in a relationship off-screen and began living together early in 1974. She was in a couple of girl-girl loops, but besides appearing with John in one other loop (Girl Scout Cookies), Gilda was never penetrated on camera by anyone else. Not coincidentally, Bill Amerson had commented that Gilda was probably the only woman who John ever truly loved.

5 minutes. Gilda Grant and John Holmes.

Playmate #6: Deepest Throat, early 1970s.

In this sizzling presentation of John Holmes with the gorgeous Brigitte Maier, the title does the brief, dubbed film justice. The plot is simple: Brigitte manages to deep throat John in a semi-erect state prior to an intense bout of intercourse. Once he is inside of her, she squirms and expresses exhilaration in response to his impressive manhood.

The camera angles are intimate, to say the least, as Maier and Holmes seem oblivious to the fact that they are shooting a film. The facial is memorable as Maier laps it up like she's eating ice cream.

According to Mark Novick, who shot this scene, Holmes fell in love with Maier as soon as they worked together. Maier, who was born in Germany, bears a resemblance to Sandy Dempsey and Juliette Prowse — two other redheads who were romantically involved with John.

5 minutes.

Playmate #7: Super Cock, 1971.

Linda McDowell, clad in a tight purple dress and cameo choker, calls a stud service. Lo and behold, John Holmes appears at her door, looking pretty cool in a comfortably worn-in, brown leather jacket. While chewing gum, he sits on the bed and they begin to smooch. There is a great close-up shot of John smiling bashfully as Linda whispers into his ear. This explosive little film contains unfortunate vocal dubs.

Reaching into his pants, she removes his organ and says aloud, "I can't believe this!"

John laughs, "You don't have to believe it!"

Linda takes him into her mouth and works on him until his penis expands to twice its size. She gets out of her dress, just in time for John to spread her knees and lick her clitoris. He stands, showcasing his erect penis, which is heavy and curves downward. Once between her legs, they start rocking and she digs a stiletto into his back before giving him head in exchange for a facial. With their attractive appearances and sexual appeal, Holmes and McDowell appear to be a porn match made in heaven.

5 minutes.

Playmate #11: Wild Beauty, 1971.

This loop features John Holmes with the delectable Linda McDowell (a.k.a. Claudia Grayson) wearing a short, silky blue dress. McDowell is beautiful, with flowing chestnut curls and she is full of spit and vinegar. John, on the other hand, is quite handsome, with a trim moustache and slicked-down hair — looking very much a gentleman. He runs his eyes over Linda's sensuous body as she removes her dress, bra and panties while bouncing on the bed.

With annoying overdubs, she asks if his "friend" can come out to play, so John removes his pants to reveal his package (which appears to be about five inches at rest).

Linda smiles, "It's looking a little wilted."

John manhandles it and gently reminds her, "It's never let us down before."

Linda performs oral like nobody's business and John's penis grows like Pinocchio's nose. Holmes climaxes into her mouth and before you know it, they're raring to go again. This time, he penetrates her sideways before he turns her over so that he can enter her anally. This is a very painstaking operation that John takes time to do correctly (he greases her up with Vaseline). Linda can't resist giggling while she lies on her tummy, hugging an accent pillow. Some versions of this scene (which has been infused into many compilation DVDs) contain the ominous soundtrack from the 1975 film, *Jaws.*

In a 1977 interview for *Eros* magazine, John named Linda McDowell as one of his "top five" favorite costars.

7 minutes.

Playmate #27: Bondage Beauty, early 1970s.

The title is written on a blue placard, which is tucked into the deep plunging, V-neck of a girl's white dress. She sits on a bed with her hands tied behind her back, but isn't in the loop, just the title portion.

John Holmes (with a goatee and moustache that curls up at its ends) surprises a blonde, sitting alone in her convertible at a hilltop lookout. He pulls out a knife and threatens her, very aggressively. He forcefully kisses her before tugging her out of her car. She tries to fight him, but he ties her up with a white rope back at his place. With her arms tied to her sides, he lifts her red dress to stick his tongue into her vagina. After cutting her free, he ties her hands and feet to the bed posts. Naked, she goes down on him, and eventually, he cuts her hands free so that she can use them. He cuts her feet free, and the girl looks happy to be there by the time she is riding on top of him.

6 minutes.

Playmate #27: Modeling, early 1970s.

After *Bondage Beauty* the curly-haired brunette in the white dress is shown again, with her hands free and a new blue placard tucked into her neckline.

The loop begins, with two long-haired beauties — a blonde and a brunette — in John's office, where he shows them a magazine foldout before asking them to undress and spin for him. Reaching over his desk, the blonde takes off his shirt before crawling underneath the desk to unzip his pants for a b.j. The brunette crawls under the desk and begins making out with the other girl. John gets out of their way. Behind them, a sign with large black letters reads, "Free Money!" Soon, John is having sex with the brunette girl while the blonde just sits and watches them. Eventually, he comes on her belly.

12 minutes.

Pool Party, 1971 or '72.

This 10-minute loop was shot during the early part of Holmes' lengthy film career. Youthful and clean cut, John and a cute guy with dark, wavy hair lay in twin beds chatting. The naked fellow gets up and approaches John in the other bed. Slowly, he rubs John's testes as John turns toward him and pets his hair. The young man does fellatio on John, while John relaxes on his back.

In the next scene, John prepares for anal penetration with lubricant and inches in slowly. The camera focuses on John's member and his veined arm. The scene cuts away and resumes, just as John climaxes between the man's legs after pulling out. Immediately following, John's friend experiences an orgasm while lying on his back.

Apart from his only hardcore gay feature, *The Private Pleasures of John Holmes,* Holmes' work in gay loops is mostly confined to the first half of his career. Throughout the '60s and '70s during his years as a gigolo, John serviced men and women alike. In a 1983 *Hustler* interview, John revealed that although he was heterosexual; he had many gay friends and was not opposed to homosexuality. He admitted that 50 percent of his target audience was gay; therefore he recognized the importance of pleasing his gay fan base.

Pretty Girls #11: Playmate of the Year, 1973 or 1974.

This loop is unique in that Linda McDowell is about seven months' pregnant. One can only surmise that she was either desperate for money or else the sheer allure of taboo enticed her.

Linda gives an unknown male a hand-job and then disappears while he gets it on with another girl. Surprisingly, she pops in on a subsequent scene with John Holmes and Rick Cassidy, where she performs oral sex and participates in an act of double penetration. Linda doesn't appear to be unhappy, but given her condition, it is difficult to fathom her sexual involvement with two males in this activity. On the other hand, when pornographic films were illegal, almost everything was acceptable.

John was rumored to have indulged a fetish with pregnant women, which adds another layer of intrigue to the shoot. Mark Novick, who shot this scene, recently mentioned that he hopes McDowell is a content grandmother today.

7 minutes.

Pretty Girls #16: Big Dick V, **early 1970s.**

John is interrupted while he peruses a porno magazine at the dining room table, when his girlfriend catches him. She surprises him by stepping on top of the foldout in her high heels. She twists her foot over the face and breasts of the centerfold as if she's stamping out a cigarette on the ground before lying on the table. John's girlfriend, a girl with wavy, auburn hair, takes his pen and draws a moustache on the girl in the magazine. John (wearing his hair combed down and a brown leather jacket) looks a little annoyed with her, but realizes that the thing to do is give his own girl a little TLC.

He stands behind her and kisses her shoulder before whispering into her ear. She grins and sits up to remove her halter dress and panties. John takes off his shirt and after making out for a bit, they get naked and have sex on the table. He winks and blows kisses to her, and looks quite excited before he climaxes all over her face.

9 minutes.

Sex and the Movies #1: Morning Coffee, **mid 1970s.**

A dark-haired brunette with somewhat of a mullet hair-do comes home in the morning and puts down her purse before pouring a cup of coffee. Through the help of captions, she wonders if John is up yet.

In the bedroom, John gets a cigarette and wraps himself in a sheet before going out to his wife in the kitchen and asking for a cup of joe. He takes one sip before standing to put his hands up her skirt. Both the actress and John wear rings on nearly every finger — and he wears his famous dragonfly ring.

A close-up of the actress's face shows some acne on her cheeks and a lazy eye. She goes down on John. After just a few pumps in and out of her while she is seated in the chair, he asks her to turn over so that they can do it doggie style. She holds onto the chair for support and makes exaggerated expressions of ecstasy mixed with a little bit of pain, which is continued with her sitting on the counter and him standing in front of her. Finally, she gets back onto the chair and he sits on the counter for her to bring him to orgasm with her mouth.

9 minutes.

Sunset Strip #1: Wet Dreams — A Fantasy, **late 1960s or early 1970s.**

This silent loop begins with a young woman (with some acne on her cheeks) driving down the freeway, but has trouble staying awake at the wheel. She becomes aroused and touches herself before arriving home.

Safe in her bed, she begins to dream about having sex with an overly endowed male (John Holmes). In her fantasy, the two quickly become acquainted as they explore one another's bodies. They do it in several positions and in a predictable conclusion, John pulls out in time for the girl to bring him to climax.

7 minutes.

Swedish Erotica #1: The Virgin Next Door — Part 1, **mid 1970s.**

John plays a Peeping Tom in this silent segment. The actress appears to be in her early 30s — older than what one might consider as virginal years — but she has an attractive face and beautiful hair. The rest of her body is questionable, with cuts on her arms and blemishes on her rear end. John waits for his neighbor to appear and then spies at her through a peephole in his apartment. He grows excited watching her change and masturbates.

Shortly afterwards, John appears in her apartment and they engage in intercourse until he climaxes in her mouth. The woman has an interesting expression on her face and is obviously unsure about the taste!

5 minutes.

Swedish Erotica #2: The Virgin Next Door — Part 2, **mid 1970s.**

In a blue room, John undresses a girl with long, curly, brown hair and a matching black bra, garter belt and sheer, thigh-high stockings. John has a little goatee and long hair, cut level with his ears. There are subtitles to help the viewer understand the film — which like most loops, is silent. The same actress from part one says, "Oh, I've got to have more of that thing," so John puts it in her. The next caption says, "You've broken my cherry."

John begins thrusting faster before moving to change their angle for the camera, with her up on top of him. After spending a short time doing it doggie style, he pats her butt to signal her to go down on him. The cinematography is beautifully artistic and innovative, including a camera roll during a close-up on the blowjob. Finally, the caption reads, "I'm going to shoot," and she waits, with her mouth open, before making a strange face, spitting his jism back out onto her fingers and rubbing it on her chest.

8 minutes.

Swedish Erotica #7: Park Lovers, **mid 1970s.**

John chews gum and wears his wavy hair greased down, a moustache and dark shades. His long blonde-haired sweetheart is cute in a short, cotton dress. The couple strolls through the park (possibly Griffith Park) to enjoy the turtle exhibit, but decides to move on as John clutches her hand while making their way home.

John removes her dress, bra and red panties, prior to entering her backside while she expresses discomfort. When they change positions, John carefully applies a gob of Vaseline and enters her vaginally. It seems to do the trick. After gliding in and out of her slowly, he climaxes fairly quickly, in a facial.

This feature contains subtitles, which are amusing, as always.

10 minutes.

Swedish Erotica #12: Big John Part I, mid 1970s.

John and Barbara Barton hook up in a poolside fling.

Barbara is the lady of the house, who takes a "skinny dip" break. The pool boy (John Holmes, in a red Speedo) arrives to do some maintenance, but Barbara can't seem to take her eyes off the big bulge in his bathing suit. In a voice that is unfortunately dubbed, John pays her a compliment while she is spread-eagled in front of him on a floating chair.

Barbara invites John to join her in the water and after dropping his suit on the deck, he sits at the top of the ladder and leans down to kiss her. Their kiss is soft and sweet, and pretty soon, one thing leads to another — and his penis is in her mouth. Just about five feet tall, petite Barton manages to get a little more than its head into her mouth, but judging by Holmes' facial expressions, he is more than delighted to have her service him.

John has his first orgasm right away and then they move to the lounge chair, where he becomes aroused again, lifting her feet over his shoulders to enter her gently. After a few minutes, he gracefully picks her up and carries her to the pool, where they finish things off on a mat. In a thoughtful gesture, John brings Barbara to climax before she returns the favor.

12 minutes.

Swedish Erotica #13: Big John Part II, mid 1970s.

John (with slicked-down hair and a goatee) and diminutive Barbara Barton really "click" on screen in this loop. He makes love to her in various positions, but the kicker is when she gives head. John is absolutely huge and Barton teases him by rolling her tongue around the head of his penis and at the top of his shaft. Eventually, she moves down his appendage, but her relentless taunting continues for quite some time, as John lies on the bed, moaning and groaning (in a dubbed voice).

When he is able to endure her teasing no more, he puts her onto her back and impales her in missionary position. She moves in rhythm to his motion. Shortly thereafter, John climaxes on her tummy. This is a very hot interaction.

5 minutes.

Swedish Erotica #17: 15" Commercial, 1970s.

John's girlfriend (Cyndee Summers) wants John to see something on the television, but when he turns it on, it's out of order. So they make out instead. He undresses her down to her garter belt and sheer, red panties before having her sit on top of the TV so that he can go down on her.

After a while, the caption says, "Turnaround is fair play," so she goes down on him for a while. After a bit of vaginal penetration, John applies a gob of lubricant and goes for the backdoor. Both her expression and the caption say, "It hurts!" John pushes in deeper, slowly. She gets onto her knees, looking uncomfortable and crying, while John continues for a bit before pulling out. The captions read, "Eat it red," and in a surprising (and unsanitary) twist, the actress does go directly from anal to oral sex and licks up his cum.

9 minutes.

Swedish Erotica #56: Black is Bigger, **early 1970s.**

Two friends, a blonde and a brunette, discuss their boyfriends — John Holmes (clean-shaven with an afro and veined arms) and a black performer who is almost as large as Holmes. The chums giggle over sodas and present photos of their guys before agreeing to engage in a foursome where they can compare their men where it counts — the bedroom. Everyone strips down abruptly as the girls produce twin measuring tapes. They are ecstatic to discover that their beaus both measure in at twelve inches.

John and the blonde begin to hug and kiss while he gently twists her nipples. The four get onto a double bed together and go to it. John employs the trusty spit-lube technique. His buddy climaxes first, followed by John, who gushes upon the blonde's face.

Interracial pairings were uncommon during the early years of hardcore, so this scene is unique. Another interesting observation is blood on John's penis as he penetrates his partner. This silent, black-and-white loop is enhanced by captions.

12 minutes.

Swedish Erotica #68: Seaplane Sex, **mid to late 1970s.**

There are production credits at the beginning of this clip, but no credits to its cast. In a slight variation from what usually happens in loops, Linda Wong begins in her garters and gets completely naked to take a shower. Outside, a seaplane lands and there is a cut to show John on the dock beside it, as if he was the pilot. The captions show him telling the plane, "See you later."

Inside, he finds Linda resting in bed, back in her black bra and panties. They start kissing and he removes her underwear for easier access. While he goes down on her, she writhes around, arching her back high as if in orgasm. John stands on the bed above her to drop his pants before she removes her bra and goes down on him. He holds her hair off her face. Then, he penetrates her. After the facial cum shot, John runs back out to the plane and says to it, "Let's go."

5 minutes.

Swedish Erotica #76: The Swap Meet, **mid to late 1970s.**

At a swap meet, Linda Wong buys a book for $5 and presents it to John, who is glad to receive her gift. With her back to him and facing the camera, she removes her white blouse and short skirt, leaving on her garter belt and stockings. Through a caption, John says, "Come here."

Lying on a bed in a blue robe, his long penis rests on his leg. After kissing him, Linda kisses and licks his belly, down to his crotch and begins to give him head before he penetrates her vaginally, in several different positions and variations. Throughout the loop, the television is on, but its picture is indiscernable. At the end, Linda lies on her back to await the facial, with her tongue hanging out of her mouth.

6 minutes.

Swedish Erotica #92: Bubble Bath, mid to late 1970s.

One of the most stunningly beautiful starlets to enjoy a brief career in adult films — curvy, Virginia Winter (also known as Victoria Winter) — and clean-shaven John Holmes, take a bath together, splashing each other between tender kisses and towel flicking. John laughs heartily after she makes a feeble attempt to get him to stop teasing her. Soon, they grow tired of foreplay as he dries her off and leads her by the hand into the bedroom.

In one of his signature moves, Holmes maneuvers Winter over his bent knee and onto the bed before joining her. She gives him head and they soon move into the 69 position. John, wearing nothing but his dragonfly ring, is very erect when he enters her. They keep it interesting by frequently changing positions, as the camera closes in, alternately on Winter's face and Johns rigid penis. The captions are not very creative, but always funny, "Ohhh … that hurts!" John has an intense orgasm on her closed lips.

10 minutes.

Swedish Erotica #103: Around the World, mid to late 1970s.

John and Paul Thomas arrive on the deck of a Connie Peterson's home and she lets them in. After closing the curtain and chatting with them for a bit (unfortunately, it's all silent and is not clear what they are talking about), John and Paul help her to fall back on the couch between them. They undress her and Paul Thomas is the first to go down on her while John takes everything off but his diamond dragonfly ring. The woman takes John's penis into her mouth and he smoothly bends down into the 69 position to give P.T. a chance to get naked, too.

With an erection pointing to the ceiling, Paul sits down on the couch. The girl stands and finishes undressing and touches her breasts to further excite her male guests. John and Paul share the task and take turns in giving and receiving oral pleasure while the other one enjoys intercourse with her in a variety of boy-boy-girl threesome positions. Finally, the actress performs double fellatio and both guys come together on her face.

After that climactic conclusion, Jerome Hellman, the producer of the 1969 film *Midnight Cowboy,* gets credited with directing and producing this hot clip.

7 minutes.

Swedish Erotica #124: Hot House Honey, mid to late 1970s.

At the beginning of this clip, there are some credits for the production crew, but not the director (Bob Vosse) or its cast. John Holmes and Jonathan Younger sit naked in an old-fashioned hot tub. Mimi Morgan (wearing a black and white printed scarf), who is there tending to the plants comes over and Jonathan tells her to take off her clothes (through captions). Mimi gets in the tub and both guys stand for her to go down on them. She alternates and before the cut, there is a long pause on a still image of her poised to take both penises into her mouth at the same time.

Outside of the tub now, the guys pick her up and lay her on a mat. There are other times when the still image is used before a cut in the loop. The guys take turns giving her head while she performs fellatio on the other one. She has sex with Jonathan first, before double penetration with John in her butt hole. She squirms between them, but appears to enjoy the full feeling of both men inside of her. When Jonathan moves out of the way to receive oral action, John penetrates her vaginally.

6 minutes.

Swedish Erotica #132: Rectum Hell, **mid to late 1970s.**

Eileen Wells (who is also in the 1977 *Johnny Wadd* film, *China Cat*) smiles as John walks up a few steps to meet her outside on a patio. She can't wait to get her lips around the head of his penis and after rubbing the crotch of his checkered pants, she finds that he's ready for her wet, hungry mouth. Shortly afterwards, however, fellatio doesn't suffice, so they take their show home and behind closed doors where Eileen removes her skirt and blouse and spreads her legs on the bed.

John buries his face between her legs as she writhes with pleasure. When she eventually rises up on her knees, he fucks her anally as the caption appears on the screen beneath her, "Screw the hell out of me!"

Another hilarious one pops up, "You've got a lot of hell!"

They keep it up, until John can't hold his load any longer and delivers the money shot in the form of a facial.

10 minutes.

Swedish Erotica #172: The Warlord, **late 1970s.**

This silent scene, accompanied by a trumpet, appears to be a continuation from a previous clip that showcased Delania Raffino and John, wearing his Eastern garb. John sits on a throne, costumed in the same satin wrap and a black head wrap, as Desiree Cousteau (another stunner and favorite Golden Age starlet, who appeared in several features with John Holmes) and a young Asian woman service his erection.

John's portrayal is serious and he gets into character, commanding the women to move the couch for some girl-on-girl action, before he joins in. Everyone gives and receives head, and the girls both have access to John's size until he is ready to burst.

10 minutes.

Swedish Erotica #175: The Mystic, **late 1970s.**

John Holmes, Eileen Wells and John Leslie come together for this entertaining short. Holding hands, John (in a white shirt and vest with grey slacks and tie) and Eileen stroll through a museum, observing the artifacts as they make their way toward a closed door.

Behind it, naked John Leslie meditates with eyes closed and his penis erect, as Eileen starts to blush like a school girl. Sensing she's turned on, John encourages her to interact with Leslie, who is more than happy to accommodate his guests.

Wells, who was known for her willingness to do anal, ravishes Leslie before participating in an anal and oral scene with the two gentlemen. She ends up with climax all over her face after a double facial.

7 minutes.

Swedish Erotica #177: Asian Beauty, **late 1970s.**

John invites a cute Asian girlfriend over to the house for a little nookie. Wearing undergarments beneath a fur coat, she calls on John, who opens the door (wearing the same, black, satin wrap described in *The Warlord*). Happy to see his lady friend, he motions for her to be seated. Standing behind her, he removes her hairpins and lets her shiny, silky mane cascade down. John kisses her sweetly and, in an erotic display, the two engage in intercourse, including cowgirl style on the living room carpet, which continues until the predicted facial. It is very rare in these loops to see anything other than a facial climax, excluding female performers who preferred to receive the money shot on their backsides or breasts.

7 minutes.

Swedish Erotica #206: Shower Beauty, **late 1970s.**

Kitty Shayne (who was also in the 1979 feature, *Blonde Fire)* takes a shower and doesn't realize that a handyman (John Holmes) is outside, trying to fix its leak from the outside. After her shower, John, in a denim jacket with patches and blue jeans, peeks at Kitty as she towels off. He sneaks into the house to surprise her. Captions convey the simple storyline.

Kitty reaches for her red scarf to cover her prominent breasts, but John takes the scarf away and ties it around her neck before they engage in gentle kisses. They move into the bedroom, where John undresses as Kitty waits for him on the bed in a seductive pose. She can't wait to take him into her mouth, and soon enough, John penetrates her from behind before thrusting between her breasts prior to his climax.

10 minutes.

Swedish Erotica #216: Laces and Spice, **late 1970s.**

Desiree Cousteau is pretty and picture perfect, wearing a light, floral dress and green scarf in a country setting, she greets John (in a three-piece suit) at the front door. Once they settle onto the leather couch, John asks her to remove her dress and discovers a lacy corset underneath, which he unfastens with ease. Desiree — with her killer figure — lies back on the couch as John kisses her breasts and explores her nipples with his tongue.

Suddenly, she gets to her feet and finishes undressing for him, as John becomes anxious for her to give him head. She swallows his inches halfway, and as she does, a faded brown spot is visible on the side of his shaft. Given Holmes' towering number of sexual partners, it is likely a genital wart and is not very appealing, to say the least. Desiree (and, undoubtedly, the director and cameraman) notices it and seems to cover the spot with her fingers during fellatio. The couple also engages in various sexual poses, including reverse cowgirl and doggie-style. Once they have exhausted themselves, Desiree lies back to accept John's facial.

Some versions of this loop include audio.

10 minutes.

Swedish Erotica #234: Games Room, late 1970s.

In an exceptional presentation coupled with audio, John is seated in a bar, smoking a cigarette and nursing a drink while a well-built brunette strips on stage. A blonde barmaid approaches him with a big smile, dainty scarf and a southern twang. John charms her by telling her that he has heard she's a primo pool hustler. With a shrug, she challenges him to a game and when they arrive at the door of the billiards room, John takes her by the shoulders and says, "Hey, are you sure you really want to play pool? Why don't we go back to my place and fool around?"

Quite certain that she wants to play pool, they enter the room and John racks up the balls. The blonde leans over to break, posing her butt in his face, which makes it difficult for him to resist asking her again if she really wants to play pool. As it turns out, she doesn't, but she does want to give him some head.

In an interesting twist, the stripper enters the room and is relieved to discover that she didn't miss out on any of the fun. John and the two ladies get undressed and climb onto the table to partake in some animal sex with lots of verbal interaction. At one point, John reminds the southern gal, "Let me know if I hurt you." When the party is almost over, John gets the girls prepped for a shared facial — a personal memento from Mr. Big.

13 minutes.

Swedish Erotica #240: Sweet Alice, late 1970s.

John and Seka are featured together as John climbs the stairs to Seka's apartment, beaming from ear to ear. He is wearing light blue pants, a track jacket, and chewing a wad of gum. Seka, with a pale scarf, appears delighted to greet her guest and after sharing a kiss (where does John's gum go during a kissing scene?), they head into the living room.

This short isn't extraordinary, but John and Seka always light up the screen together, as they had obviously established a comfort level with one another. The two veterans engage in four different sexual positions, while Seka awaits the money shot upon her quivering, scarlet mouth.

5 minutes.

Unknown Swedish Erotica loop, circa 1977.

John, wearing a plaid suit and relatively long hair, steps out with a blonde, hippie girlfriend. After parking their car on the street at night, they enter an apartment. The girl has on high, laced boots that John unfastens before they make love on a plush, red velvet couch. Throughout their amorous encounter, she makes several facial expressions in reaction to where John's penis happens to be at that moment. John holds her hair back from her face, which shows off his dragonfly ring. Eventually, he spit-lubes her and plunges in from behind while she holds onto a chair. The scene ends in a facial.

This is a silent loop, with captions.

10 minutes.

Unknown Swedish Erotica loop from the mid 1970s.

In this loop with audio and scripted dialogue, two girlfriends, Connie and Ginger (a blonde and brunette), chat away in a bedroom and wonder how they will spend the afternoon. The discussion turns to John as the brunette tells her friend in vivid detail just how big he is and how enjoyable her sexual encounter with him was. She promises her friend that she would agree, so they decide to call John and find out if he's available to stop by.

John appears shortly afterward (wearing a white, short-sleeved turtleneck and his dragonfly ring) in the backyard and waves to the girls waiting for him in the window. They don't delay getting down to business as John lies across the bed to reveal his monstrous appendage. After the brunette tells her friend, "I told you so," the blonde undresses for John while the brunette gives him head. The two girls take turns servicing John and then he services the two girls with his mouth and fully hard penis. The scene ends in a facial and everyone appears happy.

13 minutes.

Unknown Swedish Erotica loop from the mid 1970s.

In an early, silent *Swedish Erotica* segment with captions, John opens the door for two females: a busty, raven-haired girl and a small blonde. John is cute, wearing a black and white polyester shirt (that might be the same one he wore in *Liquid Lips)* and light blue denim jeans. When he closes the door behind him, the caption reads, "You girls are a beautiful sight for these sore eyes," which doesn't make a lot of sense, but John's expression, which seems to say, "Aw, shucks," is priceless!

The girls sit next to John on the bed as he unites tongues with the brunette, feels her up through her navy, polka-dot dress, and caresses her thighs. Reaching inside of her panties, he rubs her clitoris as the blonde massages his shoulders. Once the girl is wet, John stands on the bed to remove his pants, revealing grey, bikini briefs. The blonde goes down on him and from that point on, everyone takes turns. John penetrates their butts while the girls kiss and cuddle up together to await John's favorite style of money shot — the shared facial.

10 minutes.

Unknown Swedish Erotica loop from the mid 1970s.

In another early scene from the *Swedish Erotica* vaults, clean-shaven John jogs along an ocean view path wearing a black track suit, a black, knitted, skull-cap and shades. He also wears a prism necklace — one of his many pieces of jewelry.

Two young women (a blonde and an Asian) play outside on a swing set and become excited as he approaches. Affable John climbs on the swing and as he moves back and forth, the blonde pulls down his pants and white, bikini briefs. The caption reads, "I get really turned on whenever I jog!"

The girls give John head and he jumps down from the swing, places the blonde on the seat and pushes her high so that he can remove her panties and supply some oral action while she is airborne. The outside location is very windy and John doesn't remove his track jacket before taking each of their hands to lead them to a calmer spot by a rocky embankment. Surprise, surprise! A foam mat just happens to be there for the three to engage in some hanky-panky before the two ladies receive John's facial.

12 minutes.

Unknown Swedish Erotica loop from the mid to late 1970s.

John and Fatima Hamoud (who also appears in the 1979 feature, *Blonde Fire)* are great in this window steamer, with dialogue. John, wearing powder-blue, wide-leg pants and a yellow track jacket, pretends to be a photographer while his friend is away taking care of business. A beautiful brunette (dressed in burgundy-colored velvet gown) enters the store as John fidgets with various cameras. She is scheduled to do a photo shoot, so John tells her to change and suggests that she wear a man's white dress shirt instead of the baby doll attire she had in mind.

While she changes, John takes photos of her in various stages of undress before positioning her for the shoot. When she tells him that she didn't bother to keep her panties on, John seizes the opportunity to make his move. Momentarily putting the camera down, he undresses and begins to perform cunnilingus while she moans with pleasure. Hamoud is very vocal in her scene with John, who is fully hard and appears ready to pop at any time. The scene eventually culminates in a great, big facial.

10 minutes.

Unknown Swedish Erotica loop from the mid to late 1970s.

John in dress pants, shoes, shirt and tie, parks his car and dashes up the steps of a Victorian home (probably in San Francisco) to visit a female friend, who is busy fluffing pillows and putting the finishing touches on her makeup. Wearing a mauve scarf, she opens the door and invites him in.

After drawing the blinds, John's girl undresses as he watches her from the couch. The camera is positioned under her breasts as she removes her bra, which is a common trick in *Swedish Erotica* vignettes. Then she joins John on the couch for various sexual positions, including anal. John is very hard and there are some close-ups of his dragonfly ring, just prior to the facial.

10 minutes.

Unknown Swedish Erotica loop from the mid to late 1970s.

John bides his time on the couch, decked out in a pale sweater and khakis while an endowed girlfriend, wearing a red negligee and matching red scarf puts on a striptease for him. The big-boned girl (with long, dark brown hair and imperfect teeth) is enthusiastic as John gently holds onto both of her breasts (showcasing his dragonfly ring) and he tastes her ripe nipples. The couple goes at it furiously in missionary position on the couch, but in this scene, John climaxes between her breasts.

10 minutes.

Unknown Swedish Erotica loop from the mid to late 1970s.

A leggy blonde's car breaks down in front of Ali Baba's Ice Cream shop and a Good Samaritan (John Holmes) pushes it into a repair garage. Frustrated, she wonders what she'll do in the interim. John, in blue jeans and a yellow-and-blue-striped track jacket, has an idea in mind and asks (without the benefit of audio for the viewers) if she'd like to go back to his place for a drink while she waits.

Displeased by her predicament, she thinks about John's gesture for a few seconds, and then agrees. As they head off, John reaches into the back of her red convertible and hands over her purse, "You almost forgot this," reads the caption.

On their way upstairs, he fishes his keys from his pants pocket and unlocks the door. Once inside, he pours two glasses of red wine. The blonde with pouty red lips, a pink scarf, and what appears to be an engagement ring (directors, including *Swedish Erotica* director, Bob Vosse, have said that John would present some of his favorite costars with rings prior to their scenes) suddenly has eyes for John, who is already starting to undress. First, she gives him head and John reaches down to unsnap the crotch of her panties to perform cunnilingus as his famous dragonfly ring makes another appearance. They do it doggie-style until the scene concludes with a facial.

12 minutes.

Unknown Swedish Erotica loop from the mid to late 1970s.

Wearing a plush velour bathrobe, John sits at the dining room table working on his finances as his blonde wife (with a pastel pink scarf, matching panties and bra, and red stilettos) vies for his attention. This is a silent loop without captions, but the actions make the story come across just fine. She pulls every trick in the book, in an attempt to get him to notice her — even licking the king chess piece, which she lets fall out of her mouth onto the table in front of him. He stands and opens his robe, ready for her willing mouth. She kisses the head of his penis, and he seems to appreciate her efforts as he places her on her back on the dining room table.

All the cock kissing does the trick; John is really hard and she appears to thoroughly enjoy his size. When the camera closes in, John's dragonfly ring and manicured nails are noticeable. Director Bob Vosse commented that John was always well-groomed when he performed and that was one of the reasons that girls liked to work with him. She squats over his waist, taking him vaginally and from behind. Before fading to black, John's wife lies across the table with his climax glistening on her moist lips.

10 minutes.

Unknown Swedish Erotica loop from the mid to late 1970s.

Two girls (a blonde and a cherub-faced brunette) spy on John (in a yellow track suit), as he rests outside their window. After briefly discussing it, the ladies decide to invite him in. Without further delay, John gets up and appears at their sliding-glass door.

His package, hanging low and on the left, is very visible through his pants. The girls get undressed, except for their brown-and-green kerchiefs, garters and stockings, and John removes his pants and jacket. The blonde lies on top of her friend and they begin to pleasure each other. John penetrates her and in between intermittent, oral attention to the brunette, the three continue to screw. Like many of her predecessors, the blonde is treated to a facial, courtesy of The King.

In some DVD versions, this film contains dialogue.

10 minutes.

Unknown Swedish Erotica loop from the late 1970s.

John, wearing the same attire as in *The Mystic,* is seated at the kitchen table, drinking his morning coffee while studying something through a pair of binoculars. His wife, a redhead in a long, green cotton dress, entertains sexual thoughts as she stares enticingly at a large pepper grinder and steals glances at her husband. She approaches the table as John looks up and points to his coffee cup, hoping for a refresh — but she isn't interested in coffee refills.

John behaves as if it is an imposition to satiate his wife's needs, but after she pulls him from his chair, he has no choice but to oblige. After helping her out of her dress and lace bodice, he bulges in her mouth. Again, a very stiff performance by Mr. Holmes ensues. John climaxes in her mouth and she gets him hard again. He demonstrates an acrobatic move in this clip, lifting and holding her up in his arms while he fucks her rapidly. When he's ready to put her down on the carpet, he lifts her up, off of his swollen penis (an amazing stunt) and they don't lose any momentum once they are on the ground.

John wears a ring with a gold band and a black onyx, featuring a large, gold "H" on the stone.

12 minutes.

Unknown Swedish Erotica loop from the late 1970s.

John, Delania Raffino (who appears in the 1979 feature, *Extreme Close-Up)* and an unknown blonde woman star in this clip. John, playing an Eastern-inspired Svengali, is naked from the waist up and wearing a black, satin wrap with a gold sash. He and his blonde assistant, beckon a beautiful young visitor (Raffino, clad in a tiny, two-piece number, with a matching pink scarf) into his chambers. The lovely guest is tentative as John chats her up (there is no audio, only a musical soundtrack) and gets her comfortable on the couch. He plans to shag her next to the shag carpet, after warming her up with his tongue between her legs. The blonde undresses while John helps relax Raffino. Eventually, the blonde joins in. A facial follows shortly thereafter.

10 minutes.

Unknown Swedish Erotica loop from the late 1970s.

Playing a domesticated husband, John (wearing a polo shirt, dark, checkered pants and his custom-made ring) washes dishes when his horny wife (a brunette in a green slip) begins flirting with him. (It is interesting to note that in many of these scenes, the women initiate sex.) Pretending he doesn't have time for lovemaking, John resists her advances and looks down at his watch, indicating to her that his free time for sex is at a premium.

Refusing to take "No," for an answer, she begins to kiss John before getting to her knees to unzip his pants. John is already hard as she retrieves his wand from inside his pants and laps at it like a lollipop. The loving duo is uninhibited — they do it on the kitchen mat and while she holds onto a chair as John enters her from the backdoor. Toward the end, she clutches onto his length as he erupts onto her creamy, white face.

Bob Vosse claimed that part of his job description as *Swedish Erotica* director was to find petite brunettes willing to perform hardcore scenes with Holmes, as they were his preference.

10 minutes.

Unknown Swedish Erotica loop from the late 1970s.

John, wearing a white cable-knit sweater, and Kyoto Sunn (of the 1977 *Johnny Wadd* film, *The Jade Pussycat),* in an orange scarf, get together on the couch for an afternoon sex session. This is a fascinating scene because it is amazing to observe demure Kyoto take John's size. Things heat up rather quickly and fizzle out after a facial.

7 minutes.

Unknown Swedish Erotica loop from the late 1970s.

This sizzler (with dialogue) supposedly takes place on the set of a "Peggy Norton" film and features John with a petite, Italian actress (wearing a pretty red scarf), who is an equal match for Holmes' rabid sexual appetite. It opens with John (playing himself and wearing his signature dragonfly ring) and his partner, involved in the middle of their sex scene when Peggy (Juliet Anderson) calls, "Cut!"

Disgruntled, John asks Peggy if they can finish the scene before lunch, but she tells him he needs to take a break, and suggests that the cast and crew meet in one hour. After everyone leaves, John reaches for his costar's hand, asking her to stay behind so they can finish what they've started. Slightly taken aback at first, she decides it's a good idea and allows him to pull her down onto the mattress. Chuckling, he removes her black panties and says, "I've been trying to get these off you for two days!"

Not about to waste time, John invites his leading lady to sample his goods and she performs fellatio like there's no tomorrow. When he enters her doggie style, she exclaims, "God, you're big!" and switches to reverse cowgirl position.

When John eventually suggests that she needs to rest her legs, what he is really saying, is that he'd like to go anal. Fortunately for both of them, she's into it and screams, "It hurts, but I love it in the ass!" The scene finishes up with a facial — this is definitely hot stuff!

12 minutes.

Unknown Swedish Erotica loop from the late 1970s.

John Holmes, Liza Dwyer (who played "Joan the Screamer" in the 1979 feature, *California Gigolo)* and Mike Ranger star in this clip with audio. The three get acquainted and then John disappears to retrieve some beverages. When he returns, Mike's dick is inside of Lisa's mouth.

In a funny bit, John (wearing a white shirt and pants with a black star on the right, back pocket) leans down and asks Liza if she would like some wine. Liza disrobes for the men, but when they reach out for her, she says, "Wait a minute!"

John responds, "Wait a minute? What are you going to do, get dressed again?" John takes control of the positioning of Dwyer — who is humped by both guys — and even assists her as she climbs on top of Mike, prior to receiving a double facial to bring the scene to a climactic finish.

7 minutes.

Unknown Swedish Erotica loop from the late 1970s.

John, Seka and Jamie Gillis share the screen in this outstanding *Swedish Erotica* loop. John and Seka (wearing a Mexican-print dress and a red scarf) play a couple planning to go to brunch with Jamie, but they change their minds after Seka offers to put on a striptease for the two guys. Seka gives Jamie head, while John gives Seka head. The sultry blues soundtrack is great throughout the oral play, as is the dialogue between the actors.

They change things up, when Seka consumes John's penis, while Jamie (being an adventurous fellow) buries his face in Seka's bottom. There are a lot of close-ups of Seka going down on John and she is very giving as the men share her, until John decides that Jamie will wear her out. He moves her down, so that her lower half is on the couch, but her head and back are on the floor. She looks up, "Oh, do you like it this way?"

John replies, "Ah, come on, you know I do." Then he slides the head of his penis up and down her clitoris in preparation for insertion. In the meantime, Jamie seems content kissing her stocking feet, until all three agree they are ready for the double facial. This is a very hot scene, and Seka is a pro.

12 minutes.

Unknown Swedish Erotica from the late 1970s.

Wearing his patchwork denim jacket, John climbs over a high wooden fence and encounters two women; one is swimming in a pool and the other (a large, average-looking brunette) is poolside. Gesturing to both girls, with the aid of subtitles, he motions toward the hot tub, the blonde declines, leaving John and the brunette alone.

They give each other head, and what is astonishing about this pairing is Holmes' erection — as he moves a chair in preparation for sex, his appendage curves downward to the left, swinging firmly between his legs. This is another scene where a chair is used as a prop for the female to clutch onto while John does his penetration. The women's face conveys anguish, but it is only for effect. As expected, John expels his hefty load on cue.

10 minutes.

Unknown Swedish Erotica from the late 1970s.

Hands down, this is one of Holmes' most exemplary and hottest *Swedish Erotica* performances. It is also greatly enhanced by the use of genuine audio!

A large-busted redhead named Marlene arrives at John's place the morning after a soiree. After John tells her that she missed a great party, Marlene whines, "I would have come, but you didn't invite me!"

John, with devilish blue eyes and a pack of cigarettes in his breast pocket, grins as he quips, "That's because I didn't want to share you."

Marlene accepts this reason and asks what they're going to do next. John suggests a skinny dip. John quickly extinguishes Marlene's concerns about the neighbors because he says they will be shielded behind the trees. Then, he remembers they can't swim after all because he'd forgotten to fill the pool! So instead, he stands behind her and helps her out of her red dress (she keeps her yellow scarf on). John kisses each of her large breasts and then goes down on her as she exclaims, "Oh, put your tongue inside of me!"

Soon enough, she's going down on John, who is rock hard and groans, "You're going to make me cum!"

Once inside of her on the couch, he climaxes as they continue to share wet, titillating kisses. Through the magic of editing, John's ejaculate mysteriously disappears. They bump and grind as Marlene tells John what to do, "Harder! Faster! Deeper!"

He delivers as she commands, and soon he is ready for the second and final cum shot on her face and yellow scarf. The scene concludes when he asks, "Now isn't that better than a party?"

15 minutes.

Unknown Swedish Erotica circa 1981.

Scraggly-bearded John is emaciated and very rough in this performance with Seka and Lisa DeLeeuw. The women are both gorgeous, with their dainty neck scarves. John stimulates Seka and Lisa simultaneously with his fingers, while they go down on him, one at a time.

He provides Seka with some tongue action as Lisa continues to get him hard before he enters Seka. John's determined face is shown briefly throughout the scene, probably because of his ghastly appearance, as he is drawn and almost dripping with sweat. With Lisa positioned over top of Seka, he starts hammering away at her from behind, while Seka gives Lisa head. It's almost a relief when the ladies prepare for the facial, as John appears truly exhausted.

5 minutes.

Watergate Girls #3: Pleasure Pole, **early to mid 1970s.**

John lies in bed asleep on a bold, blue and white design sheet, with two young women (a brunette and a blonde with thick streaks) on either side of him. The girls are awake and start to play with John's appendage, which appears to grow larger by the second. He opens his eyes, a little alarmed at first, to discover his tool being toyed with. Soon enough, he breaks out in a broad smile.

The girls give John head until he eventually must choose the one he will screw, while the other girl, feeling passed over, keeps occupied by pleasuring herself. John tries his best to include the second girl, but ultimately climaxes before he has a chance to penetrate her.

In many of John's '70s films, the tan line from his Speedo is clearly visible; he obviously spent a lot of downtime at the beach or pool, soaking up rays. This film contains a vocal dub.

7 minutes.

Watergate Girls #5: Big Load also known as Large Economy Size, **early to mid 1970s.**

The camera shows us a brunette sitting on a bed and a man's naked torso, but that's all that needs to be shown to recognize John Holmes' uncircumcised member. The woman gets excited and starts touching herself before giving him a blowjob. He sits down next to her and unties her red halter dress to kiss her breasts. There is a close-up of their wet tongue kiss. John has a little bit of a moustache.

An interesting technique is used for smoother cuts in this and some of the other early loops. Here, the girl walks toward the camera, getting close enough to black out the view, then after the cut, she is shown with her back to the camera, walking back to the bed with John. This particular cut was a bit rough, but with more practice (or more experienced cameramen); it was perfected in other loops.

After she goes back to the bed with John, she lies down to give him another blowjob before their intercourse, which the couple pairs with lots of unbridled, passionate kisses. After a while, she goes down on him again — fast and furiously — and he holds her hair off her face until the cum shot.

10 minutes.

VIP #2: Bare Harbor, **early to mid 1970s.**

At a marina, two girls look to buy a boat. The first caption reads, "Shall we buy this one?"

The response caption is hilarious, when the other girl answers, "No, Tits, look around."

They see John, with a big afro and he invites them to his place for a drink. They sit on a gold couch and he goes to wash up after a long day's work at the harbor. When he comes back, buck naked, the caption reads, "Hey girls, look what I've got for you." Both girls go down on him and then he has intercourse with the one with dark hair flowing down to her butt first, while she performs cunnilingus on the other girl, with shorter, wavy, light-brown hair. The girls switch places after removing their bras and garter belts and John penetrates each of them again before he announces that it is his turn.

7 minutes.

Untitled/Unknown Title Loops

Silent, black and white loop from the late 1960s or early 1970s.
A small, fresh-looking young woman with thick, blonde hair gives John a blowjob before simulating sex that finishes in a facial she'll never forget. This film starts and ends abruptly.

10 minutes.

Silent, color loop from the late 1960s or early 1970s.
John makes love to two women who appear to be his roommates. The caption reads, "a few hours later," and then, John exits the shower wrapped in a towel to go into the kitchen. There, a third girl offers him a cup of coffee. John accepts and gives her the once-over before opening his towel to suggest that he'd like something else go along with his java.

John Holmes certainly seemed to be well suited for his profession, as his numerous on-screen encounters suggest that he had an insatiable sexual appetite. It has been said that he would perform multiple scenes in one day, particularly during the early part of his career when he was in his 20s.

10 minutes

Silent, black and white loop from the late 1960s or early 1970s.
John is young and hung in this loop, where he plays a photographer. A beautiful aspiring model (Veronica Pink) enlists John's services to take some snapshots of her to submit to a modeling agency. After they rendezvous at The Terrace, Victoria asks (through subtitles), "Can I see it now?"

Without further adieu, John complies and displays his package. She dives right in and provides inspiration for his organ to grow another eight inches. The subtitle that accompanies this scene is anything but subtle — "What a meat whistle!" John reciprocates, in providing Veronica with an oral treatment prior to insertion. The couple goes through the motions, which are paired with more ridiculous captions that don't do the loop justice. John climaxes at the end of the scene.

10 minutes.

Silent, black and white loop from the late 1960s or early 1970s.

In an inferior-quality loop, John and a friend with a huge afro observe as their girlfriends (with their skirts hiked up high) stand over the open hood of their car, trying to determine what might be the cause of the engine trouble. The men indicate that they'll take care of the problem as the ladies shrug and walk away.

The next segment shows the women off in a field together, enjoying some girl-on-girl fun while their boyfriends spy on them from behind the trees. Eventually, the guys decide to join them for some choreographed sex. John gets head from a girl with a slight build and blonde hair (Georgia Drugg, a.k.a. Suzanne French), while his friend accepts the services of the heavier female. Then they switch partners, all while keeping their actions — including penetration — in sync.

Suzanne French worked with John in the 1980 feature, *Undulations*.

7 minutes.

Color loop from the early 1970s.

This loop can be seen on the Blue Vanities compilation tape #380, which is comprised of material originally filmed on 16 millimeter that was unfortunately left unlabeled. John appears very young, with a clean-shaven face and short, curly hair. He lies in bed with an older woman (with a blonde beehive) and a younger brunette. The older blonde goes down on the girl and fingers her. John joins in to lick the clitoris. The blonde continues to give the young girl head while John moves up to fondle the brunette's large breasts and allow her to suck on his penis, which grows quite large and firm.

While John penetrates the brunette, the blonde looks on, notably once at the camera, looking very bored and she appears to have hurt feelings. The loop is silent, so the viewer cannot hear what she says to the couple going at it, but afterward, they move so that she can lie down on the bed. After he's out of the girl's vagina, John starts rubbing his shaft, which appears to have gone a little bit soft. The camera cuts, and then the brunette is shown using the blonde's stomach as her pillow as she starts fluffing John.

John's interactions with the older woman in this scene are reminiscent of that with Mrs. Hamilton in the 1970 feature, *Johnny Wadd*. Although there were numerous reasons why John had difficulties working with some women, it seems that he genuinely was not a fan of older women, especially in his early days as a performer. All in all, the blonde is left to come across as very needy and jealous of the other girl, like she's clueless to the fact that she's a third wheel as she plays with John's cum and tries to involve herself more in the scene — without success.

11 minutes.

Color loop from the early to mid 1970s.

John, with a moustache and long, slicked-down hair, wears a silk smoking jacket — complete with cigarette — while being pampered by three elegant women. A blonde, a brunette and Susie Carlson (who is also in the 1974 feature, *Cheri*) all wear chiffon nightgowns with nothing underneath. As they flank him,

John flashes a shit-ass grin and intimates that he'd like to be "worked over." Carrying his cigarette and ash tray, John and the three girls move toward the bed.

He gets comfortable on the mattress and continues to smoke as they massage him and rub oils onto his lean body in preparation for sex. While bantering with the girls, he makes them laugh, as they lick his penis. John kisses the brunette's nipples that are hovering over his face, and after she disappears, he makes out with Carlson as the blonde gets on her hands and knees for him to enter her from behind. Holmes and Carlson continue to kiss as he plunges in and out of the blonde before erupting onto her backside, his tongue sill in Carlson's mouth. This film contains audio.

10 minutes.

Color loop from the early 1970s.

In a terribly grainy clip, John and Rick Cassidy burst into an apartment to take on a couple of unknown damsels. The girls, who are frightened at first, soon discover that the guys are kind of cute. For inexplicable reasons (the plot is vague and lacks audio), John carries a gun, impressively wielding it around until he disposes of it in favor of the potential sexual opportunities that the women present.

Not surprisingly, two futon mattresses appear, enabling the guys and girls to do their thing. Although the visual is unclear, it is evident that John enjoys having his way with the young lady and orgasms within the allotted time frame. Rick Cassidy follows suit.

10 minutes.

Color loop from the early to mid 1970s.

In a short, narrated orgy sequence, a young, bearded John Holmes, Rick Cassidy and classy redhead, Cyndee Summers (who appears in the 1974 feature, *The Danish Connection*), share the bed with two unidentified brunettes. The mattress is no larger than a double, but the group of five manage to accomplish their work despite the space limitations.

Accompanied by a sultry, muted trumpet solo, they become a mass of mouths, penises and orifices, until John and Rick each choose a girl to cozy up with for purposes of penetration. Rick and his girl engage in a rapid screw session that causes him to orgasm before John, who is inserted deep inside of Cyndee Summers. They meld together before John pulls out to expel his load on Cyndee's stomach. Afterwards, he and Cyndee cuddle up together in a warm, post-coital embrace.

John and Rick Cassidy (who purportedly did a number of gay films under the name "Jim Cassidy") appeared together in several early 1970s loops and over ten feature films. According to adult film historian, Bill Margold, Cyndee Summers and Rick Cassidy were a couple during their foray as adult performers. Apparently, the beautiful Ms. Summers was never without a cosmetic mirror, which inspired Margold to fondly name her, "Miss Vanity."

5 minutes.

Color loop from the early to mid 1970s.

John the photographer visits buxom Veronica Pink (who sports platinum blonde hair in this loop with captions) at her home to take some nude photos. John snaps photos until she mouths the words, "eat me," indicating that she is no longer interested in posing for the pictorial. John works his mojo overtime during sex with Veronica, and especially when he enters her backside, which according to her cries of ecstasy, would appear to be her favorite mode. Holmes, who is famous for demonstrating tenderness toward his costars, doesn't hold back with Pink, who truly gets a worthwhile bang for her butt.

10 minutes.

Silent, color loop from the early to mid 1970s.

Shirtless John, wearing a pair of dark shades, observes a cute brunette dancing topless in a pair of white short-shorts. She wiggles over to him and he wiggles away — they continue to play this game until he tickles her and she chases after him into the bedroom. He leaves his shades on the entire time while they French kiss, stimulate each other orally and she rides on top of him — he finally orgasms on her abdomen. This is a really fun scene, as John and the girl laugh throughout the sex. It provides some levity and they appear to enjoy each another's company.

7 minutes.

Color loop from the early to mid 1970s.

An actress who goes by the name Vicky Perkins has a mouthful of John Holmes in this amusing clip that appears to have been shot in fast-motion — but it wasn't. Vicki's head vigorously bobs up and down on John's penis. Obviously, she is a virtuoso when it comes to performing fellatio.

When he gets her into the missionary position, John goes pretty hard and the film continues to appear accelerated. He climaxes in her mouth, but apparently she swallows it all. This film contains a terrible vocal dub.

6 minutes.

Silent, color loop from the early to mid 1970s.

A long-haired, exotic brunette lies on a couch in a white jumpsuit that has cutouts on the sides and beneath her large breasts. She becomes excited and begins to stroke herself as John makes his entrance. He lies down beside her and caresses her body through the cotton material before helping her out of the jumpsuit and unbuckling her white, platform shoes. John undresses and performs cunnilingus, lapping his tongue slowly up and down her clitoris until she squirms with erotic fervor.

The lady handles John's penis with exuberance, as she pumps it in and out of her mouth while John stands next to a plant. Once he is inside of her, she stretches her legs straight, with pointed toes, and allows him to go deep. Before his orgasm, she gives John head again, yanking on him forcefully. When he climaxes, the girl douses her lips, nose and cheeks as if it's a fireman's hose.

10 minutes.

Color loop 1975 or 1976.

Rene Bond and John Holmes share the screen in this cute loop with narration, where Rene (playing a fairy princess) kisses a toad and turns him into a dashing prince (Holmes). John literally sweeps her off her feet and carries her to her boudoir, where they disrobe and get it on. John wears his prism necklace.

Rene Bond began her career in the late 1960s sexploitation films produced by Harry Novack, who allegedly paid for her breast implants; she was reportedly one of the first women in the business to acquire them. She and fellow actor, Ric Lutze, enjoyed a lengthy romance in the early and mid-'70s, until her impulsive, brief marriage to someone else. According to Holmes' autobiography, Porn King, Bond gave the best head he had ever experienced, but the actors only appeared together in one hardcore scene after Rene divorced her controlling husband who would not allow her to work with Holmes while they were together. However, they enjoyed a softcore bath in the feature film, *The Danish Connection*.

7 minutes.

Two-part, color loop with audio 1983.

John plays a pimp, and along with a stunning black actress, he looks over the new girl (Ashley Wells). Using real audio, John pays her several compliments about her appearance:

"Wow, look at those long legs, they go all the way up to her ass."

"Mommy and daddy tired to make a boy, but they failed miserably."

The girls get undressed and John, chewing gum, discards his robe as they engage in a boy-girl-girl threesome. This scene should have been more erotic, but John has difficulty getting hard and surprisingly, it appears as if the money shot was cheated.

20 minutes.

In the second part of the story, John and his sexy, significant other converse about the possibility of hiring the new girl full time. He tells her how experienced Wells is with men and claims that she can make them a lot of money, but his girlfriend is unimpressed. She becomes jealous and reluctant to hire Wells for the house.

When John presses by trying to convince her to give Wells a chance, she relents, but with hesitation, "Okay, I'll give her a break."

John jokes, "You'll give her a break? Which arm?" Smiling, he calls Wells into the room (she is wearing skin-tight, white denims) and his girlfriend leaves in a huff. John has sex with Wells again, but the sex scene isn't stimulating and the camera cuts away before the money shot. On the other hand, the scene between John's angry girlfriend and the man she found to fulfill her needs, is hot and steamy.

20 minutes. Ashley Wells, an unknown female, John Holmes, an unknown male.

Jill C. Nelson

25 legendary women of classic erotic cinema
1968 - 1985

GOLDEN GODDESSES

*With over
300 photos,
& film highlights*

Featuring: Seka, Marilyn Chambers, Serena, Kay Parker, Ginger Lynn, Amber Lynn, Juliet Anderson, Rhonda Jo Petty, Veronica Hart, Kelly Nichols, Annie Sprinkle, Georgina Spelvin, Gloria Leonard, Candida Royalle, Sharon Mitchell, Nina Hartley, Christy Canyon, Laurie Holmes, and many many more...

Foreword by Jennifer Sugar

POSTSCRIPT
by Jill C. Nelson

When Jennifer invited me to collaborate with her on *Inches*, I eagerly accepted but had no idea what a life-changing event our partnership would entail. Working on and researching *Inches* together was an incredible experience; one that could most certainly be a chronicle unto itself full of surprising, funny and bittersweet encounters and anecdotes. I've learned that one never knows what the future will bring and I will forever appreciate Jennifer (now a beloved friend) for asking me to hop on the magic bus that brought us to our unified destination with a new perspective. About a year after completion of this book, I began interviews for my next writing project, *Golden Goddesses: 25 Legendary Women of Classic Erotic Cinema, 1968-1985,* released in 2012. The following excerpts are from the biography.

"My career has been phenomenal, but in retrospect, I'm not sure I would do it again. It's been great but it's really provided a very big stigma. It's a stinky stigma and lasts forever, unfortunately. It's something that's always going to be out there and no matter what you want to do, if you want to do mainstream or if you want to go back into the woodwork and just be a normal person, you can't. One of the most difficult things is having a relationship with a man. I'll be a spinster to the day I die. Years ago, I needed somebody. I was very needy. I was looking for Daddy. I think most of the chicks in the porn business are looking for a daddy figure. Something is definitely lacking."
Marilyn Chambers

"I think that my career has influenced my life in a positive way. I don't have any problem with my friends knowing or my neighbors knowing. Either they accept me for who I am, or we're not friends because I don't have time for that kind of narrow-mindedness. What I did does not change the kind of person I am or the kind of human being I am. Take control of your life. Don't let somebody else control your life. Own your own name. Do your own register. Do your trademark. Do your copyrights. Own your own product. Own your name so that people can't rip you off. If you have photographs done, own them. If you're thinking about getting into the business, get an education first. Go to school. Go to college and think about what you're going to do when this is all over."
Seka

"To have a long shelf life or a legacy in the world is rare. Personally, I was able to break out of the adult industry and into mainstream because my face, my image and my persona have been in many different areas. If you didn't grow above or outside of the box people will not know who you are in two years, much less twenty. We're kind of a dying breed. I'm the exception to the rule in the adult film industry. I'm not the norm and not by any means would I recommend any woman to get into this industry, or any man for that matter. Unless you are strong, extremely strong and you can deal with the judgments and the accusations and all of the bullshit that goes along with it, it's not for you. There are many more things that are wonderful if you know how to deal with it and if you have the right mind set. Most people don't."
Ginger Lynn

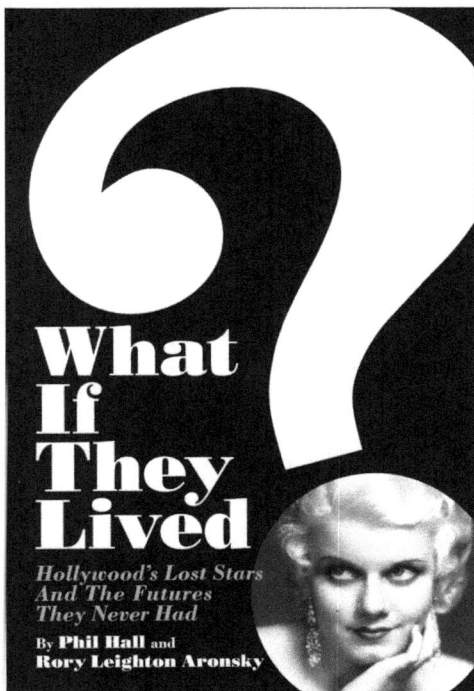

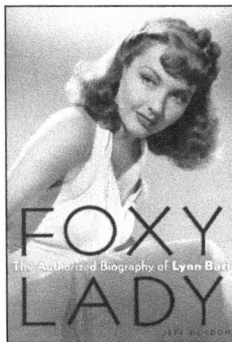

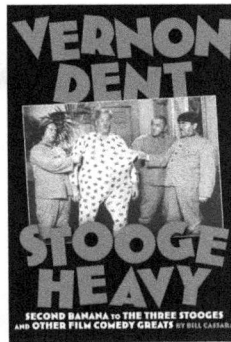